Records of the American Catholic Historical Society of Philadelphia

(Volume I) 1884-86

Unknown

Alpha Editions

This edition published in 2020

ISBN: 9789354185526 (Hardback)
ISBN: 9789354185953 (Paperback)

Design and Setting By
Alpha Editions
www.alphaedis.com
email - alphaedis@gmail.com

CONTENTS.

(3)

Officers of the Society, 1887.

----•----

PRESIDENT,
VERY REV. THOMAS C. MIDDLETON, D.D., O.S.A.,
VILLANOVA COLLEGE.

FIRST VICE-PRESIDENT,
CHARLES H. A. ESLING, 2109 LOCUST STREET.

SECOND VICE-PRESIDENT,
PHILIP S. P. CONNER, 126 S. EIGHTEENTH ST.

TREASURER,
ATLEE DOUREDOURE, 103 WALNUT ST.

RECORDING SECRETARY,
FRANCIS T. FUREY, 505 CHESTNUT ST.

CORRESPONDING SECRETARY AND LIBRARIAN,
FRANCIS X. REUSS, 3643 MARKET ST.

MANAGERS,
(Term Expires December, 1887.)

LAWRENCE F. FLICK, M.D., 736 PINE ST.
JULES JUNKER, 1233 LOCUST ST.
MISS MARGARET T. GREEN, 503 PINE ST.

(Term Expires December, 1888.)

REV. JOHN A. MORGAN, S.J., ST. JOSEPH'S RECTORY.
J. CARROLL McCAFFREY (absent from the city).
EDWARD J. ALEDO, 737 WALNUT ST.

(Term Expires December, 1889.)

B. L. DOUREDOURE, 103 WALNUT ST.
MARTIN I. J. GRIFFIN, 711 SANSOM ST.
C. CAROLL MEYER, 1802 CALLOWHILL ST.

(4)

Blessing of the Holy Father.

In December, 1885, Father Thomas Cooke Middleton, S. T. D., O. S. A., prepared the following petition, and had it presented to His Holiness Pope Leo XIII.:

Most Holy Father—The President of the American Catholic Historical Society most humbly begs leave to state : That over seventeen months ago, in Philadelphia, a Society of learned ecclesiastics and laymen was formed under the auspices of the Most Reverend Ordinary of the same city; that the aim of the Society is to search out and to gather together all kinds of records relating to the origin, spread, and progress of the Catholic Faith in the United States and other parts of North America, so as to awaken among Catholics and non-Catholics an interest in the history of the Faith.

To the end that this work flourish more and more, and the interest of his associates be strengthened, the President most humbly begs the Apostolic Blessing for himself, his associates, and their labors.

In an audience given by His Holiness, January 10th, 1886, the Apostolic Blessing was given according to request.

[L. S.]　　　　　[Signed]
　　　　　　　　　† D., ARCHBISHOP OF TYRE,
[Countersigned]　　　　　　　　　　　　　　　*Secretary.*
　　† Patrick John Ryan,
　　　　　　Archbishop of Philadelphia.

ARCHBISHOP RYAN'S APPROBATION.

The American Catholic Historical Society of Philadelphia, under the Presidency of Rev. Dr. Middleton, O.S.A., is cordially approved of and recommended by us as an institution which will do much good by preserving the records of the history of the Church in the State, and by stimulating our young men to historical studies.

　　　　　　　　　　　† PATRICK JOHN,
　　　　　　　　　　　Archbishop of Philadelphia.

Philadelphia, Sept. 6th, 1886.

CHARTER

American Catholic Historical Society of Philadelphia

IN THE COURT OF COMMON PLEAS NO. 4 FOR THE COUNTY OF
PHILADELPHIA, SEPTEMBER TERM, 1885, No. 470.

To the Honorable the Judges of said Court:

The Petition of the undersigned respectfully represents :

That they are all citizens of the Commonwealth of Pennsylvania and
have, with other persons, associated themselves for the purpose of maintaining an Historical Society as hereinafter set forth.   That for the purposes of incorporation they do hereby certify, in compliance with the
requirements of an Act of the General Assembly of the Commonwealth
of Pennsylvania, entitled "An Act to provide for the incorporation and
regulation of certain corporations," approved the twenty-ninth day of
April, A. D. 1874, and the supplements thereto, that in the proposed corporation there will be no capital stock ; that said corporation is to exist
perpetually, and that the name, style, object and conditions of membership thereof shall be as set forth in the present Constitution of said Society, as follows :—

ARTICLE I.

The name of this organization shall be "THE AMERICAN CATHOLIC
HISTORICAL SOCIETY OF PHILADELPHIA."

ARTICLE II.

The object of this Society shall be the preservation and publication of
Catholic American historical documents, the investigation of Catholic
American history, especially that of Philadelphia, and the development
of interest in Catholic historical research.

ARTICLE III.

The membership shall consist of honorary, life, active and contributing
members.   Honorary members shall be those elected by the unanimous
vote of the Society at a regular quarterly meeting, for distinguished services in American Catholic historical research or special services in the
interest of this Society.   Upon the payment of fifty dollars to the Treasurer a person may be elected a life member.

ARTICLE IV.

The officers of this Society shall consist of a President, First and Second Vice-Presidents, Recording and Corresponding Secretaries, Treasurer, and nine Managers. They shall constitute a Board of Managers. The officers and three Managers shall be elected annually at the stated meeting in December. They shall be nominated at the quarterly meeting in September. In voting for Managers each member shall vote for not more than two, and the highest three shall be declared elected. All vacancies shall be filled by the Executive Board until the next quarterly meeting of the Society, when an election for the unexpired term shall take place.

ARTICLE V.

The duties of the several officers shall be such as are usually incidental to the several offices. The officers shall be chosen for one year and the Managers for three years, three Managers to be elected yearly as set forth in said Constitution.

The names and residences of the Directors or Managers who were chosen at the first election in December, A. D. 1884, are as follows:

For one year, Bernard L. Douredoure, William Gorman, and S. Edwin Megargee.

For two years, Stephen Farrelly, Lawrence Kehoe, and George D. Wolff.

For three years, Andrew Nebinger, M. D., Rev. William Stang, and Edward Roth.

The names and residences of the subscribers are as follows:

Martin I. J. Griffin, 1935 North Eleventh Street.
Francis T. Furey, 1210 Christian Street.
Rev. John A. Morgan, S. J., St. Joseph's Church.
J. Carroll McCaffrey, Clifton, Delaware County, Pennsylvania.
Bernard L. Douredoure, 2203 Spring Garden Street.
Francis X. Reuss, 3643 Market Street.
Atlee Douredoure, 2203 Spring Garden Street.
Charles H. A. Esling, 2109 Locust Street.
Rev. Ignatius F. Horstmann, D. D., 225 North Eighteenth Street.
Jules Junker, 1233 Locust Street.
Edward Roth, 337 South Broad Street.
Rev. P. Aloysius Jordan, S. J., 317 Willings Alley.
George D. Wolff, Norristown, Pa.
J. J. Sullivan, 1705 Spring Garden Street.
Charles A. Hardy, Aldine Hotel.
William J. Campbell, 2016 Green Street.

COMMONWEALTH OF PENNSYLVANIA, } ss.
COUNTY OF PHILADELPHIA,

On the third day of December, A. D. 1885, before me, the Recorder of Deeds in and for the County aforesaid, personally appeared the above named Martin I. J. Griffin, J. Carroll McCaffrey and Jeremiah J. Sullivan, and in due form of law acknowledged the foregoing application for Charter to be their act and deed for the purposes therein specified.

Witness my hand and official seal }
the day and year aforesaid.   }

JOSEPH K. FLETCHER.
Deputy Recorder.

DECREE.

And now, to wit, December 26th, A. D. 1885, the Court having examined the above instrument, after proof of publication therewith made and filed, and having found the same to be in proper form and within the purposes and character of the first class of corporations specified in the Act of Assembly approved the twenty-ninth day of April, A. D. 1874, and the supplements thereto, and that the same is also lawful and not injurious to the community, on motion of J. Carroll McCaffrey, Attorney for the petitioners, it is ordered and decreed that said Charter be approved, and further, that upon the recording of this Charter and decree, the petitioners thereto and their associates and successors shall be and are a corporation to be known as " THE AMERICAN CATHOLIC HISTORICAL SOCIETY OF PHILADELPHIA " for the purposes and upon the terms in said petition stated.

[SEAL]   M. RUSSELL THAYER,
President Judge.

Recorded in the Office for Recording Deeds in and for the County of Philadelphia in Charter Book No. 11, page 28, etc.

Witness my hand and seal of office }
this 26th day of December, Anno   }
Domini 1885.   }   GEO. G. PIERIE,
Recorder of Deeds.

By=Laws.

ARTICLE I.

This Society shall meet on the second Wednesday of December, February, June and September. The Executive Board shall meet monthly. It shall have power to adopt rules for its own government. Seven of its members shall constitute a quorum. This number shall not be decreased without the direction of the Society.

ARTICLE II.

The Treasurer shall give bonds in such sum as the Executive Board may demand.

ARTICLE III.

The Librarian shall be elected by the Executive Board. He shall perform such services as such Executive Board may direct, be paid such compensation as it may consider just, and be subject to discharge by it.

ARTICLE IV.

The annual dues of active members shall be five dollars; contributing members, two dollars. Members whose dues remain unpaid two years shall cease to be members.

ARTICLE V.

This Constitution and By-Laws may be altered or amended at a quarterly meeting, on written notice specifying the alteration or amendment intended being given at the quarterly meeting previous.

ARTICLE VI.

In the event of the dissolution of this Society, all its property shall immediately become the property of the Historical Society of Pennsylvania.

ARTICLE VII.

1. A separate fund shall be created, which shall be called the Endowment Fund, and all contributions for the purpose of procuring a building, with fire-proof facilities, for the Society, together with such other contributions as may be set apart or received for that purpose, shall be invested, at convenient times, in good securities.

2. Such fund shall be managed by three Trustees, who shall be elected in the same manner and at the same time as the officers of the Society.

The Recording Secretary's Report.

THE preparations for the organization of our Society—which was effected two years ago to-day—were made very quietly; but those with whom the movement originated went so earnestly about it that a plan was soon formed and carried out; and the work thus begun has ever since grown steadily, but not too rapidly, in importance and usefulness. A few—very few—gentlemen met in the office of Mr. Griffin's *I. C. B. U. Journal*, and there, they having agreed that it was high time some organized effort was made to collect and preserve Catholic historical materials, one of them, John H. Campbell, Esq., drew up a form of appeal, in accordance with his own views and those of the other persons present, to which gentlemen of prominence and influence in the community were to be asked to sign their names. This having been done, the following circular letter was issued :

CATHOLIC HISTORICAL SOCIETY.

PHILADELPHIA, July 4th, 1884.

DEAR SIR :—

You are invited to be present at a meeting to be held upon Tuesday afternoon, July 22d, 1884, at 3½ o'clock, for the purpose of organizing a CATHOLIC HISTORICAL SOCIETY. The necessity of such an organization is apparent to every one. The early history of the Catholics of this section of the United States is comparatively unknown, and, as time passes, many valuable records and traditions will be lost unless gathered by the industry of Catholic students and others who may take an interest in the work.

To develop this interest and direct it towards a practical end, to extend historical research so as to cover American Catholic history, and to make plain the early work of the Church and its children in America, will be among the proposed objects of the Society.

(10)

Nothing has yet been done towards organization. The undersigned have thought it best to call a meeting, at which all could express their views and adopt some plan of organization.

Trusting that you will attend the meeting, we are

Respectfully yours,

P. A. JORDAN, S. J.,	FRANCIS T. FUREY,
IGN. F. HORSTMANN,	W. J. CAMPBELL. M. D.,
JOHN J. ELCOCK,	J. CARROLL MCCAFFREY,
THOS. MIDDLETON, O. S. A.,	F. X. REUSS,
P. BERESFORD,	JOHN H. CAMPBELL,
CHAS. H. A. ESLING,	MARTIN I. J. GRIFFIN.

By the courtesy of the Cathedral T. A. B. Society the meeting will be held at their Hall, 16th street, above Vine, at the time named.

In response to the above invitation the following gentlemen met on the day and at the place named: George D. Wolff, John H. Campbell, William J. Campbell, M.D., Thompson Westcott, Robert M. McWade, Edward J. Nolan, M.D., Michael O'Hara, M.D., Francis X. Reuss, Bernard L. Douredoure, Atlee Douredoure, William Gorman, Martin I. J. Griffin, and Rev. Thomas C. Middleton, O. S. A. Rev. Thomas McMillan, of the Paulist community in New York, who then happened to be in our city, was also present. Mr. Campbell called the meeting to order and stated its purpose. On motion of Mr. McWade the same gentleman was chosen President *pro tem.*, and Mr. Griffin Secretary *pro tem.* On behalf of the Cathedral T. A. B. Society, Mr. Campbell tendered to the proposed new organization the use of the former's hall for the holding of meetings, with the privilege of erecting in the library room the necessary bookshelves, until such time as the Historical Society would be able to make other provision for itself. This generous offer was, of course, thankfully accepted.

It having been resolved to organize a Catholic historical society in accordance with the call which brought them there, all the gentlemen present consented to become members. The names of the signers of the call not present were also placed upon the roll. A committee was appointed to draft a form of Constitution and By-Laws. Mr. Griffin was named as chairman, the other members being Dr. O'Hara, Dr. Campbell, Mr. Wolff and Mr. B. L. Douredoure. Instruction was given to the same committee to prepare an address explaining the object of the Society. After listening attentively to some general remarks on the necessity of a Catholic historical society and the means for carrying out its purposes, made by Fathers Middleton and McMillan, and Messrs. Wolff, Westcott, Campbell, McWade and Griffin, the meeting adjourned to reconvene in the same place on the following Tuesday evening.

There were sixteen persons present at the second meeting, on the evening of July 29th, when the names of the following gentlemen were added to the roll of membership: Rev. Luke V. McCabe, Philip A. Nolan, James E. Gorman, S. E. Megargee, Ernest L. Douredoure, John F. McMenamin, Samuel Castner, and T. M. Daly.

The committee on Constitution and By-Laws reported, offering a draft of this instrument for the Society's consideration. Each clause was considered separately. The points giving rise to most debate were the name which the Society should bear and the religious qualification for membership. In reference to the latter, some held that none but practical Catholics should be members, while the majority maintained that, the purpose of the Society being the collection, preservation and publication of Catholic American historical documents and other such material, the investigation of Catholic American history, especially that of Philadelphia and the rest of Pennsylvania, and the development of interest in Catholic historical research, non-Catholics who honestly sought to further this interest should not be prevented from becoming members of our Society if they so desired. The Constitution is embodied in the Charter, and the By-Laws, including those enacted since, are to be printed after that instrument in the first volume of the Society's "Records."

Letters approving of the Society were read from Rev. P. Aloysius Jordan, S. J., John Gilmary Shea, LL. D., S. Castner, Dr. Nolan, Father Middleton, and Dr. John O'Kane Murray.

In accordance with a provision in the Constitution, the first quarterly meeting was held on the evening of September 10th, when a few new members' names were added to the roll. F. X. Reuss was elected Curator and Corresponding Secretary *pro tem.*, and William Gorman Treasurer *pro tem.*

At an adjourned meeting held on the evening of October 1st, nominations for permanent officers were made. The offer of the Cathedral T. A. B. Hall to the Society was renewed, for which manifestation of good will a vote of thanks was returned. The resolution passed at a previous meeting, ordering a circular explanatory of the Society's object and soliciting members, was repeated, and a new committee was appointed to attend to the matter. In accordance with this order the following address was prepared and issued :

THE AMERICAN CATHOLIC HISTORICAL SOCIETY.

PHILADELPHIA, November 24th, 1884.

DEAR SIR :—The want of a Catholic Historical Society has long been felt. Many valuable manuscripts and documents have been lost by reason of the non-existence of such an organization. The history of the Catholic Church in America has so much of interest in it, and forms such a bright chapter in the general history of North America, that special efforts should be made to make it more generally known.

There has been so much misrepresentation on the part of writers and speakers, when referring to Catholics and Catholic history, that facts have become obscured and in many instances so distorted that the deductions made from them are the reverse of the truth. To lay these facts before the public in their true light, and to present American Catholic history in its true aspect, are some of the objects leading to the formation of the American Catholic Historical Society.

Others of the objects are the preservation of old books, manuscripts and papers, the formation of a Catholic historical library, the discussion of events connected with American Catholic history, the preparation of papers and essays upon local and general points, and the assembling in one body of all Catholic writers and persons taking an interest in Catholic historical matters.

As Philadelphia was the birth-place of the American Republic, and, as in Pennsylvania alone, in Colonial days, was full freedom of exercising their religion granted to Catholics at all times, in like manner is Philadelphia the appropriate birth-place of an American Catholic historical society.

This Society has been organized under bright auspices. Most Rev. P. J. Ryan, Archbishop of Philadelphia, has given his warm approval of its formation and has enrolled himself as one of the members. By-Laws have been adopted, a nucleus of a library already secured, and the election for permanent officers will take place on Wednesday evening, December 3, 1884.

As it is desired to have as large a membership as possible, the undersigned committee have been appointed to issue this address, for the purpose of calling attention to the formation and objects of the Society, to the end that Catholics interested in the proposed work may be induced to join the Society.

May we not take the liberty of asking you to became a member? The dues are as follows :

> *Active Members,*   .   .   .   . $5 per annum.
> *Life Members,* $50
> *Contributing Members,*   .   . $2 per annum.

If you think well of the objects of the Society, and desire to aid it in its work, you will kindly fill up the enclosed blank and forward it to F. X. Reuss, Curator, Cathedral Hall, 16th St. above Vine, Philadelphia.

> JOHN H. CAMPBELL, President pro tem.
> F. X. REUSS, Cor. Secretary pro tem.
> MARTIN I. J. GRIFFIN, Rec. Secretary pro tem.
> WILLIAM GORMAN, Treasurer pro tem.
> VERY REV. THOS. C. MIDDLETON, O. S. A.
> S. EDWIN MEGARGEE.
> GEO. DERING WOLFF.
> BERNARD DOUREDOURE.
> WM. J. CAMPBELL, M. D.
>
> *Committee on Address.*

With a view to securing, if possible, a larger attendance of members, it was, on the evening of December 3d, decided to hold the next (the second quarterly) meeting in the afternoon, an innovation which has developed into a practice.

On December 10th a letter was read from Dr. John Gilmary Shea, in which he asked that he be enrolled as a member, and informed us that the United States Catholic Historical Society was about to be organized at the New York City office of the Catholic Protectory. Mr. Campbell moved that correspondence be opened with this New York society, with a view to obtaining co-operation in general work and of forming, if practicable, one general organization. Considerable debate ensued, but no decision was arrived at.

Then the first formal step was taken towards the holding of public meetings, which afterwards assumed such wide development;

but the progress towards them was very slow in the beginning. Though a motion, made by Mr. Campbell, "that a public session of the Society be held, and that a committee be appointed to invite gentlemen to read papers on that occasion ;" and though such a committee was appointed and given full power to act, no such public meeting was held for more than four months afterwards.

Far more successful was the effort to effect permanent organization, which took place at this meeting, as provided for in the Constitution; for all the gentlemen then elected are those now holding the respective offices, except in the case of Managers. Father Middleton was at first reluctant, but in due time consented, to accept the Presidency. The names of the officers are given elsewhere, and need not be here repeated ; but as many changes have taken place among the Managers, it may be well to give the names of those originally selected. They were Bernard L. Douredoure, William Gorman, S. Edwin Megargee, Stephen Farrelly, Lawrence Kehoe (New York), George D. Wolff, Andrew Nebinger, M. D., Rev. William Stang (Providence, R. I.), and Prof. Edward Roth. The changes from these names to the present membership of the Board have taken place on account of death, declination, or expiration of term.

In the minutes of the meeting held December 19th, 1884, the significant entry is made that all those present were officers. The same remark may be applied also to some meetings held since then; but this peculiarity did not seem to interfere with the transaction of the Society's business. At said meeting the Secretary read a translation of an editorial paragraph in the *Nord Amerika* criticising our Society for apparently slighting the German element in the Catholic community. The President was instructed by resolution to write to the editor correcting the error into which he had fallen and asking his co-operation in our work. At this meeting also it was resolved that the President be authorized to have St. Joseph's parish records copied at the Society's expense, and that Mr. Philip S. Conner, who, though not a Catholic, was deeply interested, be notified of this action and asked for a contribution. It is but just to say that this gentleman readily responded, and, joining our Society at the following meeting, has ever since been one of its most faithful and active members.

On December 19th, also, the first resolution was adopted looking to the procuring of a Charter, Mr. Campbell being requested to attend to the matter; but as he was then in ill health and resigned from the Society soon afterwards, the resolution had no effect. It was also resolved that two circulars be drafted, one explaining in detail the objects of the Society to persons not yet members, and the second soliciting books, documents, and other articles bearing on our work. These papers were drawn up by the President and reported by him at the next meeting, which was held in Mr. Griffin's office, three weeks later, or on January 9th, 1885. We give them below as they were issued:

THE AMERICAN CATHOLIC HISTORICAL SOCIETY OF PHILADELPHIA.

Founded July 22d, 1884.

THE AMERICAN CATHOLIC HISTORICAL SOCIETY has been founded to supply a long-felt want. Much valuable material relating to the history of the Catholic Church in America has been lost by reason of the non-existence of an association to gather and preserve it.

The history of the Church has so much of interest in it, and forms so bright a chapter in the general history of America, that special measures should now be taken to make it more commonly known. Societies have long been founded in Philadelphia to guard the other many and varied interests of Catholics, viz: for training youth in Christian principles; for aiding poor missions; for relieving the sick, the homeless, the orphans, and for inculcating the virtue of temperance.

To-day is witnessed the rise of another society to guard the memories of their religious and historic past.

These are the chief objects of this Society:

1st, to aid Catholic writers and speakers;
2d, to make the truth known, and,
3d, to found a library and a cabinet.

Up to the present time those who have labored in the field of Catholic history in America have had to rely mainly on their own individual and unaided efforts to collect the material for their work. There has been no one to help them.

For ages every court, cathedral and religious house had its profes-sional chronicler. He kept a record of events. The world then did not turn so fast as it does now. One man was fully competent to keep himself abreast with the times.

To-day the material is too vast, too varied, too intricate, for one alone to handle. Events follow too quickly for him to grasp. To-morrow is upon us almost before we are conscious that to-day has begun.

Concerted action, then, alone can do now what formerly was within the scope of an individual. It is the age of societies. They are recog-nized necessities.

1st. One of the objects, then, of this Society is to aid in their researches writers and speakers who treat on matters relating to the Catholic Church. The Society hopes in time to also republish such works as may be of special value to the Catholic public.

When each diocese in America, or at least each State, has its own local society, working in union with its fellows, the task of the apologist, essayist and historian will be rendered comparatively light, and good results will be more easily assured.

2d. So many inaccuracies of statement have been made by writers and speakers, when referring to Catholic history, that facts have become obscured and in many instances distorted, so that the deductions drawn from them are the reverse of truth.

To lay these facts before the public in their true light is another object that has led to the formation of this Society.

3d. When things of value are in the keeping of an individual they are liable to be forgotten, and even lost. A public body, by reason of its greater experience, ampler means and more systematic care, is a safer fiduciary. Therefore this Society purposes to form a library and a cabinet for the better preservation of books and articles of value that may be entrusted to its keeping. Such are the objects of this Society.

As Philadelphia was the birth-place of American Independence; as in Pennsylvania, in Colonial times, was full freedom of exercising their right of divine worship granted to Catholics; in like manner is Philadelphia the appropriate birth-place of the American Catholic Historical Society. Here occurred events of singular interest to Catholics, as well as those memorable ones attending the foundation of our Republic so well known to every student of our history.

The American Catholic Historical Society was founded during the past year, on Tuesday, July 22d, by a number of gentlemen who met at Cathedral Hall, in pursuance of a call issued July 4th, the 108th anniversary of American Independence; and the venerable Prelate at the head of the Catholic clergy and laity of the diocese, the Most Rev. Patrick John Ryan, D. D., Archbishop, has signified his warm approval of the plans of the Society, and has given a signal proof of his approbation by consenting to be a member.

It has thus started under bright auspices. A Constitution and By-Laws have been adopted, a nucleus of a library and a cabinet secured, and permanent officers elected.

As it is desired to make the aims of this Society known, in order to create public interest in its favor, this paper has been issued for the information of those who may propose to become members of it or to aid it by their contributions.

The Society dues are : FIFTY DOLLARS for life members, FIVE DOLLARS per annum for active members, and TWO DOLLARS per annum for contributing members.

The Society invites all well-wishers to join in its work, even those who may not desire to affiliate themselves formally by membership. Catholic societies particularly have it in their power to render valuable aid by contributing sketches or papers giving an account of their origin and progress and the names of their original officers and members ; writers, especially writers on Catholic topics, by donating to the Society copies of their published or printed works and writings, and all by donations of any kind of value to the Society library or cabinet.

Whoever desires further details regarding the Society may apply to the Corresponding Secretary, F. X. REUSS, No. 3643 Market St., Philadelphia, or the Society's room at the Philopatrian Hall, 211 South Twelfth St., or to any of the undersigned.

(Rev.) Thomas C. Middleton, O. S. A., President, Villanova ; Martin I. J. Griffin, First Vice-President, 711 Sansom St.; Chas. H. A. Esling, Second Vice-President, 208 S. Fourth St.; Atlee Douredoure, Treasurer, 203 S. Front St.; Fras. T. Furey, Secretary, "Catholic Standard" Office; B. L. Douredoure, 203 S. Front St.; Wm. Gorman, 514 Walnut Street ; S. Edwin Megargee, 434 Walnut St.; Stephen Farrelly, N. E. Cor. Fifth and Library Sts.; George Dering Wolff, Editor "Catholic Standard;" Dr. A. Nebinger, 1018 S. Second Street ; Prof. Edw. Roth, 337 S. Broad Street ; Lawrence Kehoe, No. 9 Barclay Street, New York ; Rev. Wm. Stang, Providence, R. I.

PHILADELPHIA, Jan. 9th, 1885.

FOR THE LIBRARY.

a, Narratives relating to Catholics and Catholic missions.

b, Biographical notices of eminent and remarkable persons.

c, Sketches and catalogues of schools, academies and colleges.

d, Copies of records of proceedings of religious, literary, scientific or social bodies.

e, Journals and newspapers.

f, Manuscripts on any subject or of any date.

g, Magazines and pamphlets.

h, Church Almanacs, Directories, Diaries, etc.

FOR THE CABINET.

a, Prints, especially of persons, church buildings, etc.
b, Pictures.
c, Medals.
d, Utensils.
e, Relics.
f, Any article of value from its historical or biographical affinities.

N. B.—Packages for the library or the cabinet may be addressed to the Society, Philopatrian Hall, 12th street, below Walnut, Philadelphia.

The meeting of December 19th, 1884, was the last held in the Cathedral T. A. B. Hall. In order to make it convenient for more members to attend, the next meeting was held, as an experiment, at 711 Sansom street. On this occasion Mr. John J. O'Rourke, who was among those attending for the first time, extended, on behalf of the Catholic Philopatrian Literary Institute, an invitation to the "Historical" to meet at the Institute's Hall, offering the free use of a meeting room and of a small apartment in which to keep books, papers, and other articles of the Society's property. Considering the central location of the place and other advantages, this offer was thankfully accepted, subject, however, to the payment of a nominal rent; and a committee was appointed to make preparations for removal from Sixteenth street.

Mr. Reuss was urged, and he agreed, to copy St. Joseph's parish records; and inquiry concerning those missing—all prior to August, 1758—was requested, Mr. Esling being asked to attend to this matter, and the seeking of aid through the Catholic press being also suggested.

The Committee on Public Meetings merely reporting progress, it was resolved, on the motion of Dr. Flick, that the existing committee be discharged and a new one appointed in its stead. This new committee, which was made to consist of Mr. Wolff, Mr. Esling and Dr. Flick, presented at the following meeting, which was held on February 12th, a report, which was for the most part considered favorably, providing for a public meeting to be held on a day and at a place to be thereafter decided upon, and at which Monsignor Seton was to be invited to deliver an address. Here at last was a promise of practical work and public utility by and on behalf of the Society. It was decided also to invite other gentlemen to prepare papers to be read at other public meetings.

The result is seen in the special committee's report, and in the historical essays printed in the first volume of the Society's "Records."

At the following meeting (on March 26th) the Public Meeting Committee reported having obtained Monsignor Seton's services, and were authorized to engage a hall for him and incur expenses not exceeding $25. On April 14th they reported having secured the lecture-room of the Historical Society of Pennsylvania for the evening of April 30th, and promised to spare no pains to secure a large attendance. By the time the next meeting was held, April 28th, they had completed all the preliminary arrangements, and had obtained promise to attend from Archbishop Ryan, who had spoken to them most approvingly and encouragingly of the important movement and useful work in which they were engaged. The result of this first public meeting was reported on May 14th as very gratifying, and the committee was discharged with thanks.

The question of procuring a Charter was revived at a meeting held on May 28th, when Mr. Atlee Douredoure offered a resolution, which was adopted, to the effect that a Charter fund be established by one dollar subscriptions from members, and the Secretary was requested to inquire of Mr. Megargee the cost of procuring the instrument. The fund project proved abortive, and the charter movement was doomed to lag for a few months yet, the Secretary reporting having ascertained that it would cost $50.00.

This was not a very inspiriting statement to make on the first anniversary of the Society's organization ; but when the work of the year was reviewed by the officers, there was reason for gratification at what had been accomplished and for hope of better results in the near future. The Librarian reported 1117 articles collected, many of them rare and of great value; and the Secretary stated that thirty-two active and fourteen contributing members had paid their dues up to date.

The collecting of articles of historical interest became much brisker and more successful from this time on, the Librarian, for instance, at a meeting held on September 17th, reporting the addition of 367 items since July; and at the annual meeting on December 9th, he stated that this number had increased to 988.

Our Society was all this time doing business without a Charter, thus creating in the minds of some members a feeling of insecurity. But a change was soon to be made in this regard.

On October 6th J. Carroll McCaffrey, Esq., generously offered to procure one at his own expense, and showed the sincerity of his offer by proceeding at once with the preparations therefor. All the requisite legal formalities having been complied with, the instrument was recorded on December 26th, 1885. It serves not only as a shield to the Society, but as a testimonial of the donor's generous zeal and an evidence of the skilful penmanship of his brother, Mr. Henry L. McCaffrey. At a later period the same gentleman donated the seal now used by the Society, which had rewarded his services in the former instance by electing him a life member. Mr. B. L. Douredoure was formally thanked for paying the cost of advertising the Charter.

During the closing months of 1885 efforts were made to secure the possession or use of letters from pioneer bishops and missionary priests, as well as other documents and articles of great historical interest, found among old papers at St. John's pastoral residence, in Thirteenth street. The pastor, Rev. Patrick R. O'Reilly, very courteously permitted them to be examined by a committee appointed for that purpose by the Society; but it being decided that they are diocesan archives, we have so far failed to obtain any of them. Similar efforts have been made at St. Joseph's, St. Mary's, St. Teresa's, and other places, and, except in the case of the first named, with like result. But our efforts will be renewed. Notwithstanding this drawback, the close of the year 1885 found the Society prosperous and hopeful of still better things.

And with the opening of the next year it showed renewed activity. On January 14th the question of public meetings was revived, it being then resolved to hold one the first week in February; and for this and all subsequent such meetings a standing committee of three (Messrs. McCaffrey, Reuss and Douredoure) was appointed. That they have attended to their duties faithfully is unmistakably shown by their special report.

Then also order was given that a pamphlet be prepared,—and 1000 copies of it printed,—setting forth the character of the Society, giving an account of the work it has done, and containing the names of the officers and members, and the Archbishop's

letter of approbation.   This intended *brochure* has been superseded by the volume soon to be published, the plan of which
has matured rapidly during the past few weeks.   On June 3d last
Mr. James A. McCaffrey introduced a motion to the effect that
a circular be issued and addressed to old Catholic families, asking
for material and members.   A lively discussion took place
regarding the plan and cost of this publication, it being strongly
urged by some that it might be well to combine with it the
various papers read at the public meetings, and an amendment to
that effect, introduced by Dr. Flick, was adopted.   The
probable cost provoked a long discussion. Finally a committee on
ways and means was appointed, its members being Dr. Flick,
Mr. Griffin and Mr. Furey.   This committee reported at the
next meeting, on July 2d, an arrangement which seemed satisfactory to all present, for it was then changed into one on
publication and was given full authority to enter into a contract for the getting out of a book of about 350 pages, an
undertaking that was merely hinted at a month before.

Let us hope that similiar success will attend an important project
originating with Mr. B. L. Douredoure, who on the evening of February 1st introduced an amendment to the By-Laws providing for a
hall fund and hall trustees.   This amendment was adopted, however, only on April 28th, and after a very animated discussion.

Our Society was honored on the evening of January 7th of the
present year by a visit from our Most Reverend Archbishop,
who, on the occasion of a reception tendered to His Grace by
the Catholic Philopatrian Literary Institute, extended his courte-
sies to us also and inspected the treasures collected in our room,
manifesting a lively interest therein and most cordially approving
of our work.

Great pleasure and gratification were also shown when the
Rev. President announced, on February 18th, 1886, that he had
received from Rome the document conveying the intelligence
that the Holy Father had bestowed the Apostolic Blessing on our
work and members.   Our constant aim should be to deserve
ever more and more by our active zeal and unswerving honesty
of purpose this signal favor and inestimable privilege.

FRANCIS T. FUREY,

July 22d, 1886.   *Recording Secretary.*

Corresponding Secretary's Report.

THE Corresponding Secretary is pleased to state that the Society is in correspondence with and receiving exchanges from several of the historical societies in the United States, viz., The Historical Society of Lower California, Buffalo Historical Society, Chicago Historical Society, New Hampshire Historical Society, Ohio Valley Catholic Historical Society, Ridgeway Branch of the Philadelphia Library Company, Philadelphia Irish Historical Library of the Cathedral T. A. B. Society, Philadelphia, and others; also with many religious houses, male and female, in the South and West, having by mail privileged access to libraries owned by these institutions ; also to private libraries of clergy and laymen. We are also in receipt of specially written (manuscript) historical sketches of religious orders, biographical sketches, etc. Our correspondence has been generously responded to and in most cases has developed the fact that the idea of historical societies has taken a firm hold in many parts of the country. There is displayed a greater interest in preserving the new and collecting the old books, papers, etc., bearing on the history of the Church in America. The Secretary takes this opportunity of publicly thanking our many friends for their kindness to us, and also solicits a more extended correspondence both with societies and with the people.

FRANCIS X. REUSS,

July 22d, 1886. *Corresponding Secretary.*

Report of the Treasurer.

RECEIPTS.

The Receipts from all sources are as follows.

Active members for 1885, ...	$205 00
" " " 1886, ...	225 00
Contributing members for 1885, ...	28 00
" " " 1886, ...	32 00
Donation from J. H. Campbell, Esq., ...	2 00
" " Very Rev. M. A. Walsh, V. G., ...	25 00
	——— $517 00

EXPENDITURES.

For books, pamphlets, etc., ...	$242 34
" printing and stationery, ...	105 84
" public meetings and rent, ...	84 25
	——— $432 43
Leaving balance, ...	$84 57

Cash on deposit with Beneficial Saving Fund Society as per book in the hands of the Treasurer, ...	$53 26	
Cash in hands of Treasurer, ...	31 31	
	$84 57	$84 57

ATLEE DOUREDOURE,

September 10th, 1886. *Treasurer.*

FORM OF BEQUEST (LEGACY).

I give and bequeath unto "The American Catholic Historical Society of Philadelphia," incorporated in the year 1885, the sum of . . . . .to be paid to the Treasurer thereof, for the time being, for the use of said Society.

FORM OF A DEVISE (REAL ESTATE).

I give and devise unto "The American Catholic Historical Society of Philadelphia," incorporated in the year 1885 [here describe the property or ground rent], together with the appurtenances, in fee simple.

(24)

The Librarian's Report.

The Librarian submits the following report on the condition of the Library at the present date.

SUMMARY.

No. of bound volumes on shelves, ... 458
" " paper covered volumes on shelves, ... 160
" " "Ordos" on shelves (from 1841 to 1886), ... 51
" " bound volumes of magazines, ... 28
" " odd numbers of sundry magazines, ... 75
" " duplicates on hand, ... 200
" " newspapers, volumes unbound, ... 90
" " magazines, volumes unbound, ... 34
" " prints, portraits, bulletins, broadsheets, etc., ... 750
" " relics, ... 55
" " pamphlets, unbound, ... 785

Total, ... 2,686

CLASSIFIED AS FOLLOWS:

MAGAZINES.

Donahoe's,—3 volumes and odd numbers.
Catholic Record, Philadelphia,—complete, 7 volumes.
Catholic Fireside,—2 volumes, complete.
Notre Dame (Scholastic)—1st volume bound, 2 years; nearly complete, unbound.
United States Catholic Magazine,—1843 to 1848, bound.
Weekly Magazine,—1798.
Metropolitan,—1858, 2nd series.
Catholic Miscellany,—1824, bound.
Catholic Magazine (weekly), Cunningham's,—complete, 2 volumes, Philadelphia, 1846 to 1848.
Ave Maria,—bound volumes 1, 2 and 4; unbound odd numbers of 1865, 1869 and 1872; half year, 1873; one-third year, 1874; odd numbers, 1875; nearly complete, 1882; complete, 1883; nearly complete, 1884 and 1885.
Catholic World,—complete, 1881—'83; nearly complete, 1880, '82, '84.
Catholic Quarterly Review,—complete, 1876 to 1886.
Messenger of the Sacred Heart, Published by S. J.,—1886.

(25)

NEWSPAPERS.

The Jesuit,—Boston, 1829, '30 and '31, bound.

Catholic Mirror,—1861 and '62, bound ; unbound and nearly complete, 1856 to 1870—also 1886.

Catholic Diary, N. Y.,—1834 to '36, bound.

Catholic Standard,—complete.

Catholic Knight,—volumes 1, 2 and 3, bound.

Boston Pilot,—1847, '48, '51, bound ; 1852, 1856, nearly complete.

I. C. B. U. Journal,—complete.

Freeman's Journal,—parts of 1846, '47, '48, '49, '50 to '55, '56 to '58, '59 ; nearly complete, 1860 to '70 ; odd numbers of later years.

N. Y. Tablet,—1858 to 1870, nearly complete volumes.

The Churchman,—parts of 1847, 1848 ; nearly complete, 1849 to 1870.

The Advance, C. Y. M. N. U., New York,—filed for 1886.

Sodalist, Cincinnati,—filed for 1886.

The Holy Family, New Orleans,—filed for 1886.

American Celt,—1850 to 1857.

Catholic American,—illustrated, 6 years complete.

Redpath's Weekly,—illustrated, 3 years complete.

McGee's Weekly,—illustrated, 5 years complete.

Harper's Weekly,—illustrated, 1859 complete.

New York Illustrated News,—1853 complete.

Frank Leslie's,—illustrated, 1885 and 1886 to date.

Cincinnati Telegraph,—filed from 1885.

Pittsburgh Catholic,—filed, 1886.

Emerald Vindicator, Pittsburgh,—filed from 1885.

Colorado Catholic,—filed from 1886.

Kansas Catholic,—filed from 1886.

Catholic Sentinel, Portland, Oregon,—filed from 1886.

Native American (Riots of 1844, Philadelphia),—30 numbers.

Many odd numbers of old papers of Pennsylvania, New Jersey, Delaware and Maryland. Also many Catholic papers of 1885 and 1886, and small Sunday School and Sodality papers from different parts of the country.

Number of volumes of pamphlets bound since 1884, 59.

Purchased prints of churches and portraits, etc., over 400 pieces.

Received portraits of Cardinals, all Roman engravings, 150. Presented by R. Coulton Davis (member of Society).

It might be well to give in connection with this report a short list of the most valuable or rare books, pamphlets, manuscripts and relics, in our library and cabinet, for the benefit of the Catholic public who may be interested in knowing where to find just such particular book or pamphlet as may be on our catalogue.

Among the rare and valuable works in the library are:

An almost complete set of Catholic Directories, from the second number issued, in 1822, down to date. The first number (1817) is wanting. A Catholic Directory for 1858.

A set of Ordos from 1841 down.

The "Pious Guide," Georgetown, D. C., James Doyle, 1792.

"Pious Guide," edition of 180-.

"Pious Guide," New York, by B. Dornin, 1808.

The "Key of Paradise," 1804.

A prayer-book (title wanting), by Rev. John Gother; London, P. Coghlan, 1783.

A "Missale Romanum," Antwerp, 1645, once used in the old Maryland missions,—from time immemorial.

Gordon's (Rev. Jas.) "History of the Civil War in Ireland" (first Amer. edit.), Baltimore, 1805, in two vols.

A "Sermon," by Right Rev. Benedict Fenwick, Bishop of Boston, February 25th, 1810, at the Roman Catholic Church, New York.

De Smet's "Travels in North America" (in French), Paris, 1874, with a map of Oregon Territory in 1846.

Baxter's "Meditations," Georgetown, 1822. (This is probably the earliest American edition.)

"Catechism" (in the Dakota language), by Bishop Marty.

"Pastoral Letter from the Apostolic Vice-Prefect, Curate of the Holy Cross Church, Boston, 1789" (pp. 48 in 4to). This letter is by the Rev. Claudius Florent Bouchard de la Poterie, a cleric of abandoned life, who intruded himself on the infant Church in Massachusetts. Finotti says he was the first Catholic Priest who ministered in Boston, whither he repaired toward the close of 1788. He was suspended May 29th, 1789, by Rev. William O'Brien, of New York, sent by Rev. Doctor Carroll, Superior of the missions in the United States, to examine the charges preferred against him.

Carey (Matthew) "On Religious Persecution," Philadelphia, 1827, pp. 68, 8vo.

M. Carey's Bible, 1790.

M. Carey's Bible, 1805.

Lucas' Bible, illustrated, about 182-.

Cummiskey's folio, 1825.

1 Missal, used in early Missions, at Columbia, Pa., by Rev. Bernard Keenan, in 1828.

History of Church,—Joseph Milner.

History of Church,—Rev. C. C. Pise.

"Discourse on the Federal Fast," May 9th, 1798, by Rev. John Thayer, Catholic Missioner, Boston, 1798.

Carey's "General Atlas," improved and enlarged; being a collection of maps of the world and quarters, their principal empires, kingdoms, etc. Philadelphia, published by M. Carey, 1814; T. S. Manning, Printer, N. W. Cor. Sixth and Chestnut Streets. 58 maps, 2 pages each (folio), in bright colors.

Breviary (æstiva), Venetiis, 1822. Used by Jno. Mary Odin, Vic. Ap. of Texas.

Joh—Andr. Danz, P.P., Compendium Grammaticæ. Hebræo-Chaldaicæ, cum privilegio S. R. Maj. Pol. and Elect. Sax., 1722.

Compleat Collection of the Laws of Maryland with index and marginal notes. Collected and printed by authority, Annapolis. Printed by Wm. Parks, MDCCXXVII.

On the schism at St. Mary's Church, Philadelphia, we have very many of the pamphlets and addresses. The trial, issued by Bishop Conwell, Hogan, Rev. Harold and others. The will of Rev. Matthew Carr, dated March 9th, 1824, 4 pp.

Lettre de M. Charles Louis de Haller, membre du Conseil de Berne, à sa famille, pour lui dèclarer son retour a L'Eglise Catholique, Apostolique et Romaine. Turin, 1821.

An Address to the Roman Catholics of the United States of America, by a Catholic clergyman, Annapolis, 1784. Frederick Green, Printer.

"Tremendous Riots in Southwark;" detailed account of the riots in Philadelphia in 1844.

"News from Jerusalem, in a Letter addressed to Rt. Rev. Henry Conwell, Bishop of Philadelphia," by Samuel S. Cooper. Philadelphia, 1825.

Remarkable Prophecy of a certain Hermit who lived 12 years in the desert between Fort Pitt and Salem.

Original Preamble and By-Laws of the Native American Central and Executive Committee of the City of Philadelphia, adopted October 18th, 1844.

Journal of Chas. Carroll, of Carrollton, during his visit to Canada in 1776 as one of the Commissioners from Congress. (Published by Md. Hist. Society.)

A Pamphlet containing letters of Archbishop Maréchal, Bishop Conwell, Rev. Wm. Harold, Matthew Carey, etc., in the case of the trouble with St. Mary's Church, Philadelphia, 1827. This pamphlet is very rare and has seldom met the public eye; it was printed and distributed among a select few friends.

A series of letters relative to the late attempt at reconciliation between St. Joseph's and St. Mary's congregations, etc., etc., etc., Philadelphia, January, 1825.

Argument on behalf of the Catholics of Ireland, by Theobald Wolfe Tone. Dublin, Printed by order of the United Irishmen, 1792.

Imitation of Christ, 1733, containing book-plate and silhouette of Mrs. Eliza Carson, mother of Mrs. Lloyd, wife of Thomas Lloyd, Catholic Stenographer of Congress.

"Key of Heaven" (German), 1750; "Elevation of the Soul," Dornin, Philadelphia, 1817; Paradeiss Gærtlein (German), 1746.

A compilation of the Litanies, Vespers, Hymns and Anthems, as they are sung in the Catholic Church; adapted to the voice or organ; by John Aitkin, Philadelphia, 1787, with an approbation signed by Rev. John Carroll, Rev. Robert Molineux, Rev. Francis Beeston, Rev. Lawrence Græssel, in German and English, and dated Philadelphia, November 28, 1787. Also another edition of the same, dated 1791. Both these were used in the old choirs of the Church of the Holy Trinity, Philadelphia.

MANUSCRIPTS.

Of Manuscripts, the most valuable ones in the possession of the Society are:

Autograph letters of Fathers T. J. O'Flaherty, Charles Ffrench, Daniel Barber, Virgil Barber, Constantine Lee, Michael Heally, all relating to the history of the early Catholics, and the First Parish at Dover, N. H.

A series of "Nine Letters" of Right Rev. Bishop Fenwick, of Boston, to a Mr. Scanlan, of Dover, New Hampshire, with others regarding the establishment of a mission in that State.

A "Stenography" of the learned and patriotic Thomas Lloyd.

A "Universal Arithmetic," (in Italian), an 8vo in three books, by the Rev. Joseph Saragosa, S. J., 1709.

A "Letter" of Right Rev. John Carroll (first Bishop) to the Visitors and Governors of Washington College. Dated Rock Creek, July 1st, 1785.

An "Autograph Letter" of Rev. John McCloskey, dated August 1st, 1835, and countersigned by him, as Cardinal, for this Society, on the same date, 1884, just 50 years after its original date.

Part of the original Rules for the regulation of the oral controversy between the Rev. John Hughes and the Rev. John Breckenridge, in the autograph of Father Hughes.

"Autograph Letters" of Bishop Conwell, Rev. Wm. Hogan, and the original law papers in the celebrated case of Conwell vs. Hogan. The original copy of the Deed of Title to the ground on which St. Joseph's Church, Philadelphia, stands, showing Records, etc. (Published in *Standard* of October 3d, 1885.)

Title to land in western Pennsylvania, purchased by Rev. Michael Egan, upon which to found a house of the Fathers of the Order of St. Francis, bearing signature of Father, afterwards Bishop, Egan, first Bishop of Philadelphia.

RELICS.

Among its relics the Society has the following rare and singular prints, viz :

A profile cut of Thomas Lloyd, the first to report the proceedings of Congress in short-hand, and the inventor of a system of the same.

Two prints (one apparently a caricature) of the notorious Rev. Wm. Hogan, of St. Mary's Church, Philadelphia ; one of the Right Rev. Henry Conwell, Philadelphia's second Bishop; one of the Right Rev. John Carroll, first Bishop in the United States, and one of the Right Rev. Simon Gabriel Bruté, first Bishop of Vincennes.

Also a wood-cut of St. Vincent de Paul, given to Miss Mary Lloyd by Rev. Prince Demetrius Gallitzin ; a plan of the city of Washington, engraved by Thackara & Vallance, Philadelphia, 1792, and a wood-cut (of about 1816) of Loretto Mission buildings in Kentucky. This cut was made in Holland, with the letter-press notes in Dutch, and is a most impressive picture of the hardships of the early missionaries in the far West.

The mitre worn by Right Rev. John N. Neumann, Bishop of Philadelphia, hangs upon the Society's walls. Also the mitre worn by Bishops Egan and Conwell. The Crozier of the first Bishop of Philadelphia.

Also the canvas-patterns of the Mass vestments, cut out by Right Rev. Bishop Bruté himself, and sent to Miss Mary Lloyd, of Philadelphia, to serve as models.

Part of the yellow damask drapings (formerly a bed-cover of a German stadtholder) that served to adorn St. Augustine's Church, Philadelphia, and altar, on the day of its opening, Sunday, June 7th, 1801.

One of the original medals (tin), bearing the bust of Washington on the obverse, worn at the mock funeral of General Washington.

A silver medal—Expulsion of the Jesuits—1¾ inches in diameter, struck by Jansenists. Obverse, head of Clement XIV. Reverse, 3 figures: Christ, St. Peter bearing keys, and St. Paul driving out 3 figures in religious habits and wearing berettas, and legend, "Nunquam novi vos, discedite a me omnes ;" also, "Exaug. Soc. Jesu memor, 1773. Ps. cxvii, 23." Very rare ; there is but one other known, that of the Georgetown College collection.

A small hand-painted picture of the Sacred Heart. The work of Mother Seton.

An autograph signature of Lionell Brittin, the first Catholic convert in Philadelphia, 1707-08.

Two chairs, formerly part of the furniture of the Prince Priest, Rev. Demetrius A. Gallitzin. Also an autograph letter of the same clergyman.

PRINTS AND PORTRAITS.

Portraits of the Bishops of Philadelphia. 2 portraits of Rev. Wm. Hogan, of Philadelphia. 1 portrait of Rev. Wm. Harold, of Philadelphia.

1 portrait of sexton of St. Joseph's Church, 1794.

150 Portraits of Cardinals, all fine Roman work, uniform size.

Portraits of many Bishops of the United States. One old daguerrotype of Bishop David, of Bardstown. An old daguerrotype of Bishop Chabrat. An ambrotype of Right Rev. Michael Portier, first Bishop of Mobile. A copy of this appeared in Catholic Family Annual for 1886. These are from the collection of F. X. Reuss, Philadelphia.

A large Painting, the Crucifixion, on an old oak panel, with a plain frame about the edge. Supposed to have been painted on the large (3 x 3 ft.) panel of a door. It is from one of the early chapels in Maryland.

A set of prints mounted on heavy board, consisting of 6 Stations of the Cross, 9 portraits of Apostles, 2 of a set of pictures (20 x 24) representing the seven Sacraments, and other religious pictures; all fine Italian engravings, and having been used in the early missions of Maryland. For these last we are indebted to Rev. J. P. Neale, S. J.

The Librarian, on behalf of the Society, returns his sincere acknowledgements to our many benefactors and well-wishers. The following list of donors to our Library and Cabinet appears on our books:

Most Rev. P. J. Ryan, D. D., Archbishop of Philadelphia.

Most Rev. W. H. Elder, D. D., Archbishop of Cincinnati.

Rt. Rev. S. V. Ryan, D. D., Bishop of Buffalo, N. Y.

Rt. Rev. Louis de Goesbriand, D. D., Bishop of Burlington, Vt.

Rt. Rev. Richard Gilmour, D. D., Bishop of Cleveland.

Rt. Rev. Martin Marty, D. D., O. S. B., Vic. Ap., Dakota.

Rt. Rev. Abbot Zilliox, D. D., O. S. B., Newark, N. J.

Rt. Rev. Mgr. Corcoran, S. T. D., St. Charles' Seminary, Phila.

Rt. Rev. Mgr. F. M. Boff, Cleveland, Ohio.

Very Rev. Ign. Horstmann, D. D., Chancellor, Phila.

Very Rev. Jos. Wirth, C. SS. R., St. Peter's, Phila.

Very Rev. Joachim Adam, California.

Very Rev. Thos. C. Middleton, D. D., O. S. A., Villanova College, Pa.

Wm. Stevens Perry, (Prot. Ep.), Bishop of Iowa.

Rev. Francis X. Reuss, C. SS. R., General Secretary for the C. SS. R., Rome, Italy.

Rev. A. M. Colaneri, Ep. Secretary, Omaha, Nebraska.

Rev. G. F. Houck, Ep. Secretary, Cleveland, Ohio.

Rev. John A. Morgan, S. J., St. Joseph's Church, Philadelphia.

Rev. J. P. Neale, S. J., St. Inigoes, Maryland.

Rev. Arthur P. Haviland, Philadelphia (deceased).

Rev. Thos. Barry, Philadelphia.

Rev. Wm. Stang, Cathedral, Providence, R. I.

Rev. Chas. P. O'Connor, D. D., Philadelphia.

Rev. A. H. Alerding, Indianapolis, Ind.

Rev. President, St. Vincent's College, Pennsylvania (O. S. B.).
Rev. Thos. A. McMillan, C. S. P., New York City.
Rev. R. S. Dewey, S. J., Philadelphia.
Rev. Jno. F. Kempker, Iowa.
Rev. A. A. Lambing, Pennsylvania (Diocese of Pittsburgh).
Rev. J. B. Meurer, S. J., Pennsylvania.
Rev. E. F. Prendergast, Philadelphia.
Rev. Antonio Isoleri, Philadelphia.
Rev. Joseph Kelly, Philadelphia.
Rev. Geo. Montgomery, Ep. Secretary, San Francisco.
Rev. C. Mahe, Diocese of Nachitoches, Louisiana.
Rev. Luke McCabe, Philadelphia.
Rev. C. Widman, S. J., St. Charles' College, Louisiana.
Rev. M. J. O'Reilly, Columbia, Pa.
Rev. Jos. M. O'Keefe, O. S. F., Santa Barbara Mission, California.
Rev. C. K. Jenkins, S. J., Leonardtown, Maryland.
Rev. A. J. Tisdall, S. J., Maryland.
Rev. J. M. Jones, S. J., Maryland.

Atlee, Walter F., M. D., Philadelphia.
Arnù, Pierre M., Philadelphia.

Buffalo Historical Society, Buffalo, N. Y.
Brown, Thomas, Philadelphia.
Bell, L. H., Louisville, Ky.

"Catholic Standard," Proprietors of, Philadelphia.
"Cincinnati Telegraph," Proprietors of, Cincinnatti, Ohio.
"Colorado Catholic," Proprietors of, Denver, Colorado.
"Catholic Sentinel," Proprietors of, Portland, Oregon.
California Archives, per J. A. Donahue, San Francisco.
Cavenaugh, Miss Mary A., Philadelphia.
Carroll, Daniel, Philadelphia.
Campbell, John H., Esq., Philadelphia.
Campbell, William J., M. D., Philadelphia.
Coad, Miss Elizabeth, Philadelphia.
Carroll, P. E., Esq., Philadelphia.
Cunningham, Peter F. (Cath. Pub.), Philadelphia.
Clarke, Richard H., LL. D., New York City.
Clarke, Mrs. Patrick, Philadelphia.
Coady, M. A., Philadelphia.
Canadian (Department History), Canada.
Castner, Samuel, Jr., Philadelphia.

Davis, Robert Coulton, Philadelphia.
Drexel, Anthony J., Philadelphia.

Douredoure, B. L., Philadelphia.
Douredoure, Atlee, Philadelphia,
Davis, John E., Philadelphia.
Doyle, Richard, Philadelphia.
Duffee, F. Harrold, Philadelphia.
Devine, Miss Mary T., Philadelphia.
Dreer, Ferdinand J., Philadelphia.
Daly, Miss Josephine, Philadelphia.
Durney, Michael A., M. D., Cecilton, Md.

Edwards, Prof. James F., Notre Dame University, Indiana.
Esling, Charles H. A., Esq., Philadelphia.
English, Edmund, Philadelphia.
"Emerald Vindicator," Proprietors of, Pittsburgh, Pa.

Flick, Lawrence, M. D., Philadelphia.
Flick, John, Carrolltown, Pennnsylvania.
Furey, Francis T., Philadelphia.

Griffin, M. I. J., Philadelphia.
Greaves, J. J., Publisher, Cleveland, O.

Hargadon, John, Philadelphia.
Hegner, Geo. Edw., Lancaster, Pa.
Hoffman Brothers (Publishers), Milwaukee.
Hughes, Mrs. Mary, Philadelphia.
Hendry, Miss E. Carmel, Philadelphia.
Hartranft, R. C., Philadelphia.

Johann, John A., Philadelphia.

Kildare, William P., Philadelphia.
Kehoe, Lawrence (Cath. Pub. Soc.), New York.
Keegan, Andrew J., Philadelphia.
" Kansas Catholic " (Proprietors of), Leavenworth, Kansas.

Lyon, Henry F., Philadelphia.
Lucas, Fielding, Baltimore, Md.
Lynch, Mrs., Philadelphia.

McCaffrey, J. Carroll, Esq., Philadelphia.
McCaffrey, James A., Philadelphia.
McCloskey, Henry J., Philadelphia.
McCormack, John D., Trenton, N. J.
McAllister, John A., Philadelphia.
McVey, J. J., Philadelphia.
Magee, Charles B., Philadelphia.
Mackey, James, Philadelphia.
Mitchell, Hon. John I., U. S. Senator, Washington, D. C.

Notson, William, M. D., Philadelphia.
Nolan, P. A., Philadelphia.
New Hampshire Historical Society, N. H.
New Jersey Historical Society, N. J.

Oesterle, H. G., Philadelphia.
O'Dea, Thomas J., Philadelphia.
O'Donell, Mrs. M. H., Brooklyn, N. Y.

Pintard, H. A. (Pres. French Ben. Society), Philadelphia.
Penna. Dept. of Archives, Harrisburg, Pa.
Power, William J., Philadelphia.
"Pittsburgh Catholic" (Proprietors of), Pittsburgh, Pa.

Quinn, Joseph L., Philadelphia.

Roth, Professor Edward, Philadelphia.
Russell, W. E., Kentucky.
Ridgway Library, Philadelphia.
Reed, Joseph, Philadelphia.
Rogers, John P., Philadelphia.
Reuss, Francis X., Philadelphia.

Sisters of Loretto, Loretto, Ky.
Snyder, Miss F. G., Philadelphia.
Smith, J. A., Philadelphia.
Spellissy, Henry, Philadelphia.
Sullivan, David, Philadelphia.
Shea, Mrs. Maria, Philadelphia.

Treacy, James J., Philadelphia.

Ursuline Nuns, Galveston, Texas.

Visitation Nuns, Mobile, Ala.

Wall, John J., Philadelphia.
Williams, William R., Philadelphia.

Young Men's Sodality Library, Cincinnati, O.
"Young Crusader" (Publishers of), New Orleans, La.

Ziegler, Francis, Columbia, Pa.

Also to many Religious Orders and congregations spread over the United States, and the Canadas, who have so kindly and so generously responded to our applications for aid and information.

FRANCIS X. REUSS,
Curator.

Reports of Committees on Public Meetings.

The Committee on Public Meeting, appointed in January, 1885, have the honor to report that they secured, through the courtesy of the officers and council of the Historical Society of Pennsylvania, the hall of that Society at Thirteenth and Locust streets, for the evening of April 30th, 1885, on which occasion the Very Rev. President read an introductory address on Catholic Historical Studies and the Rt. Rev. Monsignor Robert Seton, D. D., read a paper on the Origin and Progress of Historical Societies. The Society was honored that evening by the presence of the Most Rev. Archbishop Ryan and several of the Rev. Clergy. At the close of the meeting resolutions of thanks to the Rt. Rev. Lecturer and the Historical Society of Pennsylvania were offered and passed unanimously.

GEORGE D. WOLFF,

LAWRENCE FLICK, M. D.,

CHARLES H. A. ESLING, *Chairman.*

At a business meeting of the Society held January 21st, 1886, it was decided to hold a series of public meetings for the reading of historical papers, and a standing committee was appointed to make the necessary arrangements. The Committee submits the following report :

Six meetings have been held at the hall, 211 S. Twelfth street, at which various subjects of historical interest were presented to and enjoyed by appreciative audiences.

At the first meeting of this series, it being the second public meeting held under the auspices of the Society, on the evening of February 1st, 1886, Mr. Charles H. A. Esling presided. Mr. Francis X. Reuss read an historical sketch of the religious

(35)

congregation known as the " Sisters of Jesus and Mary." He was followed by Mr. Martin I. J. Griffin, who read an historical paper entitled, "Wm. Penn, the Friend of Catholics.

At the third public meeting of the Society, held on Tuesday evening, February 23d, 1886, Lawrence F. Flick, M. D., read a paper entitled, "The French Refugee Trappists in the United States."

At the fourth public meeting, held on Tuesday evening, March 23d, 1886, Mr. Chas. H. A. Esling read a paper entitled, "Catholicity in the Three Lower Counties, or the Planting of the Church in Delaware."

At the fifth public meeting, held on Wednesday evening, April 28th, 1886, Rev. James J. Bric, S. J., read a paper entitled, "Catholicity in the Public Institutions of Boston, Mass."

At the sixth public meeting, held on Wednesday evening, May 26th, 1886, the Rev. A. A. Lambing, A. M., of the Diocese of Pittsburgh, Pa., read a paper entitled, " The Pioneer French in the Valley of the Ohio."

At the seventh public meeting, held on Wednesday evening, June 2d, 1886, Thompson Westcott, Esq., historian of Philadelphia, read a paper entitled, " The Rev. Michael Hurley, D.D., O.S.A., pastor of St. Augustine's Church from 1820 to 1837, with a history of that Church."

It is the opinion of the Committee that these public meetings form a valuable feature of the Society's work, and that they should be continued, as they have excited and maintained controversies on mooted historical points resulting in the final settlement of some of them.

We take this opportunity to thank the gentlemen who have responded to our invitations, for the care and attention they have bestowed on these occasions, and for the benefits which the Society has derived therefrom.

We also express our appreciation of the kindness of the ladies and gentlemen who furnished us with music upon these evenings.

J. CARROLL McCAFFREY,
FRANCIS X. REUSS,
ATLEE DOUREDOURE,
Public Meeting Committee.

⤞MEMBERS⤝

OF THE

American Catholic Historical Society

OF PHILADELPHIA.

ACTIVE MEMBERS.

Aledo, Edward J., ... Philadelphia, Pa.

Barry, Rev. Thomas J., ... Philadelphia, Pa.
Bradley, Rt. Rev. D. M., D.D., ... Manchester, N. H.
Bric, Rev. James J., S. J., ... Philadelphia, Pa.

Campbell, John H., ... Philadelphia, Pa.
Castner, Samuel, ... Philadelphia, Pa.
Colaneri, Rev. A. M., ... Omaha, Neb.
Conner, Philip S., ... Philadelphia, Pa.
Corcoran, Rt. Rev. James A., D. D., ... Overbrook, Pa.
Cross, Michael H., ... Philadelphia, Pa.

Daly, Timothy M., ... Philadelphia, Pa.
Devine, Mrs. Mark, ... Philadelphia, Pa.
Devine, Miss Mary T., ... Philadelphia, Pa.
Douredoure, Atlee, ... Philadelphia, Pa.
Douredoure, B. L., ... Philadelphia, Pa.

Elcock, Rev. John J., ... Philadelphia, Pa.
Emmet, Rev. John T., O.S.A., ... Philadelphia, Pa.
Esling, Charles H. A., ... Philadelphia, Pa.
Esling, Henry C., ... Philadelphia, Pa.

Fahy, Thomas A., ... Philadelphia, Pa.
Farrelly, Stephen, ... Philadelphia, Pa.
Farren, Bernard N., ... Philadelphia, Pa.
Fasy, Frank A., ... Philadelphia, Pa.
Flick, Lawrence F., M.D., ... Philadelphia, Pa.
Furey, Francis T., ... Philadelphia, Pa.

Gallagher, Rev. A. J., ... Pottsville, Pa.
Gallagher, D. J., ... Philadelphia, Pa.
Glennan, Michael, ... Norfolk, Va.
Gorman, William, ... Philadelphia, Pa.
Griffin, Martin I. J., ... Philadelphia, Pa.

Hardy, Charles A., ... Philadelphia, Pa.
Hookey, Charles G., ... Philadelphia, Pa.
Horstmann, Rev. Ign. F., D.D., ... Philadelphia, Pa.

Junker, Jules, ... Philadelphia, Pa.

Kehoe, Lawrence, ... New York, N. Y.
Kelly, Dennis B., ... Philadelphia, Pa.
Kelly, Rev. Joseph C., ... Philadelphia, Pa.
Kempker, Rev. John F., ... Muscatine, Ia.
†Kennedy, Joseph P., ... Philadelphia, Pa.

Lane, Rev. Hugh, ... Philadelphia, Pa.
Love, Louis F., M.D., ... Philadelphia, Pa.

McCabe, Rev. Luke V., ... Overbrook, Pa.
McCaffrey, James A., ... Philadelphia, Pa.
‡ McCaffrey, J. Carroll, ... Portland, Oregon.
McEnroe, Rev. M. C., ... Manayunk, Phila.
McMenamin, John F., ... Philadelphia, Pa.
McWade, Robert M., ... Philadelphia, Pa.
Mahony, Daniel H., ... Philadelphia, Pa.
Megargee, S. Edwin, ... Philadelphia, Pa.
Meyer, C. Carroll, ... Philadelphia, Pa.
Middleton, Rev. Thomas C., D.D., O.S.A., . . . Villanova, Pa.
Morgan, Rev. John A., S. J. . . . . Philadelphia, Pa.

†Nebinger, Andrew, M.D , ... Philadelphia, Pa.
Nolan, Edward J., M.D., ... Philadelphia, Pa.
Nolan, Philip A., ... Philadelphia, Pa.

Penny, Joseph, ... Philadelphia, Pa.

Quinn, Patrick, ... Philadelphia, Pa.

Reuss, Francis X., ... Philadelphia, Pa.
Roth, Prof. Edward, ... Philadelphia, Pa.
Ryan, Most Rev. P. J., D.D., ... Philadelphia, Pa.

*Shea, John Gilmary, LL.D., ... Elizabeth, N. J.
Sherman, Mrs. Gen. W. T., ... New York, N. Y.
Smith, Walter George., ... Philadelphia, Pa.
Stang, Rev. William, ... Providence, R. I.
Sullivan, Jeremiah J., ... Philadelphia, Pa.

*Treacy, Rev. P. A., ... Burlington, N. J.
Twibill, George A., Jr., ... Philadelphia, Pa.

Walsh, Very Rev. M. A., LL.D.,V.G. . . . . Philadelphia, Pa.
Westcott, Thompson, ... Philadelphia, Pa.
Williams, William R., ... Philadelphia, Pa.
Wirth, Rev. Joseph A., C.SS.R., ... Philadelphia, Pa.
Wolff, George D., ... Norristown, Pa.

Zilliox, Rt. Rev. James, O.S.B., ... Newark, N. J.

CONTRIBUTING MEMBERS.

Campbell, William J., M.D., ... Philadelphia, Pa.
Clarke, Richard H., ... Morristown, N. J.
Conway, William B., ... Livermore, Pa.
Cunningham, Peter F., ... Philadelphia, Pa.

Davis, Robert C., ... Philadelphia, Pa.

Engel, Joseph M., ... Philadelphia, Pa.
English, Edmund, ... Philadelphia, Pa.

Fitzpatrick, T. F., ... Philadelphia, Pa.

Harrity, William F., ... Philadelphia, Pa.
Harson, M. J., ... Providence, R. I.
Heckel, George B., ... Chicago, Illinois.

Keating, J. Percy, ... Philadelphia, Pa.

Lyon, Henry F., ... Philadelphia, Pa.

McDonald, Rev. O., ... St. Louis, Mo.
McHugh, Rev. John A., ... Ashville, N. C.
McVey, John J., ... Philadelphia, Pa.
Murphy, M., ... Philadelphia, Pa.

*Nolan, John J., ... Philadelphia, Pa.

O'Rourke, John J., ... Philadelphia, Pa.

Pequignot, Constant, ... Philadelphia, Pa.
Power, William J., ... Philadelphia, Pa.

Spellissy, P. Henry, ... Philadelphia, Pa.

*Treacy, James J., ... Philadelphia, Pa.

*Resigned.   † Deceased.
‡ Elected a life member on account of services rendered.

IN MEMORIAM.

ANDREW NEBINGER, M. D.,

Died April 12th, 1886.

JOSEPH P. KENNEDY, STATE SENATOR,

Died June 17th, 1886.

Importance of Catholic Historical Studies.

[Summary of the Address read at the First Public Meeting of the Society, in the Hall of the Historical Society of Penna., on Thursday evening, April 30th, 1885, by the REV. DOCTOR MIDDLETON, O. S. A.]

I WILL begin with a principle which I think you all will admit, that all works of vast design are, as a rule, far better carried out by the concerted action of many than by the unaided efforts of a sole individual, first, because a task divided among many workers—each a master of his own branch—is more thoroughly and easily done, and, secondly, because the rivalry of the workmen generally is a spur to genius, and genius is the parent of mighty results.

And should any other reason be required why this Society has thought it well to be established, I may say that this principle of skilful, intelligent, and systematic co-operation in all branches of labor has from the very beginning of Christianity been the fixed, nay, the essential policy, if I may so term it, of the Catholic Church. She formulated her plan of leaguing men together nineteen centuries ago, at Jerusalem, when she commissioned her first societies of missionaries, apostles and disciples to go teach the truth to all the peoples of the earth. Society life is essentially Catholic.

This seems to me to be a very important, even vital, reflection to make, at the outset, on society life. Our Society professes to be wholly Catholic—Catholic in its means, and Catholic in its end. For if we consider the Catholic Church not merely as a supernatural and divine agent, but also as a great civilizing or humanizing power, we must fain confess that in the prosecution of her designs she has ever known how skilfully to enlist in

(41)

her behalf, and combine, the varied faculties and energies and sympathies of men, how to have these all work in common, in one common line of action, under the same common principles of guidance, towards the one common end, whether this be for their own personal good or for that of society at large. This principle of harmonized action underlies all society life in the Church, the different grades of her hierarchy, the various orders of her religious men and women, and her confraternities of the laity.

Gentilism rarely recognized or sought to develop in man the principle of mutual co-operation in labor. Gentilism was in fault. It had its societies, it is true, societies both literary and commercial; but these were few in number, and, as a rule, instead of aiming at purposes of solid and lasting advantage, were employed mainly for mere conquest or greed. But the Catholic Church is wiser than Gentilism. It has been pre-eminently her prerogative to draw men together, no matter how varied in gifts, or different in temperament or age or even race, to labor in union for their spiritual and even temporal interest.

Have men ever sought of her the light of science? or of art? or her aid against the despotism of power? What has been the course of action, the policy of the Catholic Church, but to band her scholars, her merchants, her freemen into guilds and brotherhoods? In her unions has always lain her strength. And what has she not accomplished by them? Where is the science she has not promoted? or the art she has not fostered? or the theory she has not matured? Look at her schools and her universities. Or where is the state under her full and free control that has not been raised to prosperity and happiness? Look at the republics and free cities and towns of the Middle Ages, with their varied industries and pursuits, with their guilds of artisans, tradesmen and citizens, with their franchises and their privileges; look at these homes of peace, the refuge of the student and the freeman, where all enjoyed in common the fullest measure of religious and civil freedom compatible with the public weal, and then say whether the Church has not well known how to league men together in self-defence or self-improvement.

I dwell on this view of the Middle Ages designedly. It gives us the key-note in analysing all social problems, in harmonizing all social discord. For the great social development of Christendom at this—commonly styled the golden—age of the Church, was the age of chivalry, of noble feelings, of lofty ideas, of pure civilization. It is worthy of our study; it has always been the favorite field for the dreams of poets, or the reveries of philosophers, and it is just in these Middle Ages that we can best understand the associating and assimilating power of the Church.

Do you seek to know the source of this power in the Church, the secret of her influence in winning over so many great and noble souls to learning and to holiness? The question is very natural, and the answer is equally as plain.

The Church bids all men alike, no matter what their condition in life, no matter what their desires or aspirations, to come to her in trust, to gather around her altar, and here at the home of the God of truth, within her holy of holies, at the feet of the Redeemer of the world, here within her temple—rich repository of all on earth that is most beautiful, most majestic, most sublime; here in the cradle of the arts, where vie with one another the masterpieces of human skill developed by genius, of genius illumined by divine truth; here within the store-house of tapestries, sculptures, bronzes, marbles, gems, of the pictures and statues of the world's greatest men, of saints and prophets and martyrs, of their likenesses on the walls, on the ceilings, under foot, in the chapels, over the altars, everywhere throughout and throughin the hallowed spot; here amidst these treasures, these memories that reflect the eternal truths of ages, that speak of the sanctity and valor of heroes, of the piety and faith and generosity of their ancestors, whose ashes mayhap lie enshrined around them; here she bids them come, here she hearkens to their prayers, here she tells them lay their offerings on the altar of love—of brotherly love, of truth. What do they ask her for? They ask for an inspiration. What do they get? They get a benediction, and with it an inspiration from on high, and a benediction of a pure and holy purpose; they set about to devote their lives, with all the powers of their mind and heart and soul, to the service of truth, the artist with his pictures, the poet with his fancies, the scholar with his studies, and the priest or the layman with his virtues.

This is the purpose of society life—to unveil the truth; its means —religion, faith, labor, and self-sacrifice. Now, do you recognize the secret of her power? how the Church, ever self-consistent in her aim to civilize man, is everywhere founding societies for his improvement, schools for his intellectual development, guilds for his moral interests, asylums for his physical ailments, churches and missions for his spiritual welfare, a stupendous union everywhere throughout Christendom of many associations, all with their own special ends, varying greatly, maybe, in detail, yet all working intelligently and continually under one common guidance—religion, towards one common end—the perfection of man.

This is the chief and ultimate end of all society life. I have dwelt, perhaps, over long on this presentation of society life in the Catholic Church, but the theme is attractive in displaying the wonderfully brilliant, yet solid, results of systematic co-operation when guided by religion; and it seemed even necessary tonight to show you that this Society, in venturing on, I believe, a hitherto unknown path in social development in this country, must bear well in mind the necessity of understanding thoroughly the fundamental policy of the Church in creating, classifying and directing the various elements among mankind before attempting to write or study her history, that is, we must recognize that she first inculcates among men the truths of revealed and natural science, and then she establishes her societies and brotherhoods of citizens, scholars and workmen, in a word, that she first makes men Christians, then students. We must first be Catholics.

I noted above that, as far as my knowledge ran, this Society is the first one distinctively Catholic ever to be founded in the United States for purely historical researches. I have never heard of any prior to it. However that be, the question now is, What does this Society propose to itself to do? What is its special aim? its plan? I answer, whoever would venture to build, must first clearly fix upon some plan before attempting to gather together the materials for his building ; and so, I may say, whoever would study the history of the Catholic Church in this country, must first gather the many details which concern her history here, her first planting of the Faith, and her subsequent successes and losses. Now, where so numerous and so diverse must necessarily be the details of so vast an undertaking, that has aimed to Christianize not a single petty State, with its few square miles of territory, but the union of all the States reaching from ocean to ocean; that has aimed to convert not merely one tribe or people, but all tribes and all peoples within its borders, peoples not only varying in degrees of civilization, but of different tongues and customs—now what man alone could venture on so huge a task? Who ·else but an association of many men, of earnest, intelligent and faithful co-laborers, could attempt with any chance of success a work so varied and so immense?

For whether we consider the extent or magnitude of the labors of our Catholic forefathers, or the various phases of their activity, we will be at a loss at which most to marvel—their wonderful successes, in spite of drawbacks of every kind, or their persever-ance amid so many difficulties, or the faith and piety that could fire their souls to such heroic deeds.

Time will not allow me to touch, except briefly, even on a few of the very many salient points of interest in our American Catholic history.   I will not go back so far as the landing of the first Christian missionaries on American soil, in 1492 ; nor to the founding of the first great Catholic university in the Northern Continent, in 1551 ;* nor to the ordination of the first native

* Luis Fernandez Guerra y Orbe, in his work entitled *D. Juan Ruiz de Alarcon y Mendoza*, medaled by the Real Academia of Spain, and printed at its expense at Madrid, 1871, at pages 9–10, says that the Emperor Charles V., by decree dated September 21, 1551, ordered a university to be founded in the City of Mexico, that the solemn opening of the same took place January 25, 1553, and that the one who chiefly is deserving of the honor of having planned and executed this idea of establishing a great seat of learning in the New World, which should rival Salamanca and Alcalà, was the Augustinian Father Alonzo of Veracruz, afterwards the first teacher of the Holy Scriptures in the same university of Mexico. Guerra's words are : *"Fray Alonzo de Veracruz ideò, promoviò con el virey Mendoza y agitò la fundacion de la universidad mejicana,"* etc.

I should, perhaps, add that this university was not the first founded in the Americas.   The University of Lima, in South America, dedicated to St. Mark and started by the Dominicans, in 1549, was recognized by royal decrees of May 12th and September 12th, 1551, thus antedating the University of Mexico by a few months.

See also *Coleccion de documentos ineditos*, etc., by Don Luiz Torres y Mendoza, Madrid, 1867, pp. 31–32, for much information regarding the foundation of these two American universities, and also Baluffi *L'America un tempo Spagnuola*, etc., Ancona, 1844, pp. 88–95, for details con-cerning these two universities, besides other schools for the Indians, and

North American priest, about 1650;* nor even to the intervening periods, when Englishman, Spaniard, and Frenchman were racing wildly for the possession of this fair Hesperian garden; but I will merely glance back a hundred years ago, when the Catholic Church in these United States numbered only a few places of worship, possibly a half-dozen scattered far and wide along the eastern sea-board, when Catholics numbered only about twenty-five thousand souls, and for this little flock there was not even a bishop (the first bishop, the Right Reverend John Carroll, being consecrated August 15, 1790), and but only about twenty-four priests in all to serve them. There were no Catholic schools, except one here in Philadelphia, connected with St. Joseph's Church; no convents, no asylums; the Church was weak and struggling

---

the books, catechisms, grammars, etc., written for their use by the early missionaries and civilizers.

* The only mention I have ever discovered regarding the above priest is found in Du Creux's *Historiae Canadensis, seu Novae Franciae Libri decem*, published at Paris, 1664. His words are: "*Obtulit hic idem annus* [that is 1650] *summo Deo primitias gentis Iroquiœ, regenerato per Baptismum eo, quem supra se Gallis ultro dedisse vidimus, ante quinquennium; nisi si primus Iroquiorum omnium, qui in Summi Pastoris alumnis numeratus sit, censendus est is qui etiamnum in Hispania superstes, ex ea gente parvulus abductus in terras regis Catholici, dicitur in venerabili Patrum Augustinianorum familia feliciter militare Deo, jam sacerdos et scilicet summa eruditione. Qui si forte in nostros hosce Commentarios inciderit, non dubito quin jucundissime lecturus sit quo de homine populari itidem in Jesu Christi familiam per lavacrum regenerationis adscito subjicimus.*"

From Father Du Creux's words it appears that this priest was of the Iroquois race, that he had been captured when a child, had been taken to Spain, received into the Augustinian Order, become a priest, and was respectable for his learning.

Mr. John Gilmary Shea, from whom I have received much valuable historical information on this point, says that this priest must have been captured as far back as 1623, or thereabouts; that the French in Canada have never succeeded in getting an Indian priest, and that the Jesuits now [1875] have a Father belonging to the tribe of the Delawares.

Frequent searches in the libraries at Rome and in Spain for more particulars regarding this Iroquois priest and Augustinian, have had no other result than to merely verify Father Du Creux's statement, as given above.

almost for existence against the persecutions of Puritans in New England, of government tyranny in New York, and the bigotry of the Established Episcopal Church in Maryland.

In Pennsylvania only does there seem to have been a chance to live free of systematic and legalized persecution.

I would not wonder much were some aged man, here within the very reach of my words, to rise up and exclaim, "Yes, I well remember the condition of the Church at the time you refer to, a little prior to the beginning of this present century. I myself have seen the venerable John Carroll, the first Catholic bishop in these United States ; he died in 1815, only seventy years ago. I remember that in all the United States there were but five churches open to divine worship—three in Philadelphia, St. Joseph's, St. Mary's and Holy Trinity ; one in New York, St. Peter's ; and one, St. Peter's, in Baltimore." In Pennsylvania, it is commonly stated, the Catholics numbered sixteen thousand, in Maryland seven thousand, and elsewhere scattered about fifteen hundred. Yet now who can number the multitudes within her fold ? Where, in 1790, there was but one bishop, now there are seventy-seven ;* where only five churches, now nine thousand four hundred and twenty-eight places of worship; instead of twenty-four priests, we now have seven thousand and forty-three; instead of no schools, three thousand one hundred and twenty-eight universities, colleges, academies and parish schools ; where at that time there were no hospitals, now we have four hundred and twenty-six foundations for the relief of the sick, the orphan and the homeless, while the number of Catholic souls is variously put at from seven to ten millions. Truly the tiny seed of the Faith has not fallen on stony ground, but in fertile soil, and the harvest has been exceeding great. You yourselves have been witnesses of much of this mighty increase. Yet why should one wonder at it ? Is it not as natural for the Catholic Church to grow as for the sun to shine ? or the tree to bring forth its fruit ? Has not Tertullian most truly said that *every soul is naturally Christian ?* Why, then, should not all men become Catholics ? How can any man refuse to be one ?

I have simply noted the chief events of the last one hundred

* See Sadlier's *Catholic Directory*, for 1886.

years. Time is too brief to go back to the days of the earlier
Catholic missions, when every plain and valley of this vast continent, from Maine, in the far north-east, to Texas, to Mexico, in the
south-west, down across the intervening chains of mountains,
along the valleys of the Mohawk, along the Ohio and the Mississippi, in Florida, up to the borders of British (at that time
French) America, everywhere almost has passed the Catholic
missionary or the Catholic explorer.

Open your atlases and note for yourselves how river, and lake,
and mountain, and headland have been christened with the names
of Catholic saints and martyrs, how they speak in honor of the
Mother of God, or of some Christian doctrine. Silent, yet enduring, records of the olden Faith, of the faith which began in
Jerusalem under the Cæsars of the East, which thrived under the
Christian kings of Europe, and now thrives anew amidst the republics of the New World.

But if the material progress of the Catholic Church in this
country has been marvellous and far beyond any parallel in story,
the variety of her active life causes no less wonder. As in Jerusalem, on Pentecost day, were gathered together peoples from
every clime, so here at a late important assembly, a few months
ago, of the Catholic Church, the Third Plenary Council at Baltimore, were represented congregations of the faithful claiming
kinship with nearly every people of the civilized world. Yet why
should we limit their descent when there were representatives
of Africans, of Asiatics, and even of the aborigines of America?
But this is not so very strange. For what people is there that
does not know the Catholic Church to be its friend? Or where
can a man—be he rich or poor, or king or serf, or learned or ignorant—feel so much at home as at the altar of the true God?
But the variety of the membership in the Catholic Church is
equalled only by the variety of her works. I will not mention
those who have been famous in the department of letters, nor in
civil positions. It would take too long to specify where none
have been exempted. Enough to know that everywhere, whether
in the peaceful walks of civil life, in the chairs of science, in the
studios of artists, in the assemblies of statesmen, in the halls of
justice, or even on the field of battle, there (our annals say) have
Catholics ever been found at the front. May we not, then, again

say with Tertullian: " *We* [Catholics] *came but yesterday, and yet we have filled your cities, your towns, your fortresses, your council-halls, your senates, your tribunals.   We leave you only your temples.*"

What, too, have not been the developments in our midst of the nobler, the more refining and more perfect phases of her character? the religious orders and congregations of pious men and women, all aiming at succoring their neighbor, some by prayer, or teaching, or tending the poor, some one way and some another, and ——? But I must pass along and declare that it is not alone the triumphs of the Catholic Church that form the chief argument of her greatness.   You will understand me.   It is not the prosperous voyage that tests fully the seamanship of the sailor, nor the staunchness of his craft, but the storm, the warring elements of heaven and sea, that bring forth and prove the good qualities of the steersman and the trustworthiness of his bark ; and so we say that the divinity of the Catholic Church—the bark of Peter—is tested not so much by her thriving in the sunshine of power, nor by her growing lusty and strong under the smiles of Cæsar, but by her endurance under suffering, her recovery after defeat. For to prosper where fortune leads may be merely human, but to grow strong in adversity is wholly divine.   If the American Church has had her periods of triumph, so also has she had her full measure of affliction and sorrow, of persecution from bad men without her portals, and of scandals from bad men within them.   Not long ago, not so many years ago but men still living, perhaps even here present with us to-night, may remember, the Catholic Church in this country—in this land of freedom, in the nineteenth century—the age of so-called enlightenment, was grossly maligned and inhumanly oppressed almost beyond what is credible except to those who have witnessed it. In 1834, at Charlestown, Massachusetts, at the dead of night, on August 11, did bands of armed ruffians break down the doors of a peaceful community of women—of Ursuline nuns ; these were driven forth from their quiet home; their pupils scattered, and their convent and school-house burned to the ground.   Again, no farther back than 1844, here in Philadelphia, on Wednesday, May 8, were convents, churches and school-houses burned by an infuriated mob, their inmates driven into concealment, their lives threatened and their property ruined. Again, about 1854, arose a party of self-styled patriots, fanatics would be a far more appropriate term, bent on repeating the infamies of their predecessors, had not the strong arm of the law, and perhaps the still stronger voice of popular disapproval, crushed them dishonored from public gaze; and even no longer ago than last year, in the autumn of 1884, the defeat at the polls of a powerful and popular candidate for the chief office in the gift of the nation by a still more powerful and popular one was brought about by the old-time spite and venom and obloquy against the Catholic Church* displayed by one of his admirers.

Nor is it unknown to you that the Church is even yet most grievously maligned, that she is often styled the arch-plotter against our religious and civil liberties, that she is charged with seeking to hand over our beloved land to a foreign power, that, it is said, she is opposed to the education of the masses, is the enemy of public schools, of the Bible, that every Catholic is an idolater, every priest an emissary of Satan, every nun a victim of priestcraft and wild delusions, and, in a word, that if anything goes wrong in church or state, it is surely set down as the result of some Popish conspiracy, and then usually follows infringement of our civil rights and misconstruction of our motives, even our most innocent ones. It is pretty much the same as to say, " Tolerate all errors, approve all nonsense, let Buddhism with its idols be protected, let Mormonism and its gross breaches of public decency be legalized, let Fetichism with its unclean and horrible rites flourish. America shall be the home of the pagan, the sensualist, the libertine, but shall never be the home of the Christian."

You have been witnesses of her sorrows as well as of her victories, yet who has kept account of all these vicissitudes of her joy not unmingled with pain, of her defeats not unsupported by triumph ? Who has cared for these ? Yet I have given you to-night but a faint, a very faint outline of her history. What, too,

---

* The Republican candidate for the Presidency of the United States, the Hon. James Gillespie Blaine, is said to owe his defeat by the Democratic candidate, the Hon. Grover Cleveland, chiefly to the ill-timed and utterly unwarranted charges against Catholics made by one of his partisans, a Presbyterian minister named Burchard.

must be the details of this long and glorious record? It must be said, I fear, to our shame, that in so far as is concerned a care for the past, we Catholics have, as a rule, shown a grave neglect, an utterly inexcusable neglect for some of our best and holiest interests. We patronize most readily every writer except the Catholic; it is a common cry that we neglect our own. Now, then, you ask : What is the task this Society has set about to do, that has brought together into one fellowship men of varied pursuits and tastes, the cleric and the laic, to join their forces, and by instant and sympathetic co-operation to seek to repair, in so far as may be given them, the past inaction? I reply that now, for the present, our preliminary work will consist chiefly in the rescue, if not too late, from loss or oblivion of whatever records may yet exist of the origin, the progress, and the vicissitudes of the Catholic Church in these United States, but principally in Philadelphia. This is what we are bending all our energies to accomplish; to gather with reverential care the memories and traditions of the pioneers in the Faith, the examples of their piety, their zeal, their learning, the historical details of our missions, churches and schools—to discover, in a word, how the mustard-seed of yesterday has grown into a mighty tree to-day, beneath whose grateful shade, that reaches to the farthest boundaries of this continent, have been assembled men of every condition of life—the scholar, the priest, the workman, the artist, the hero.

Is not this task of ours a noble, a most honorable one? And if by our efforts to fulfil our task we succeed in inspiring in others an earnest love and reverence for the Faith that has worked such wonders, is not this even a still nobler end? And, if besides the purposes I have mentioned, you yourselves be led by sympathy, by a love for scholarly work, to throw in your fortunes with ours and become fellow-workers in our task, a task that cannot fail to redound most honorably to Faith and fatherland,—I put it so designedly,—will not our greatest, our noblest glory be this—that in cherishing true historical studies we will aid morality, in aiding morality we will foster religion, in fostering religion we will promote the best interests of our fatherland, and thus the better the scholar, the more earnest the Christian, and the nobler the patriot.

The Origin of Historical Societies.

[Read before the AMERICAN CATHOLIC HISTORICAL SOCIETY OF PHILADELPHIA on the evening of April 30th, 1885, by MONSIGNOR ROBERT SETON, D. D., and published in the CATHOLIC WORLD for July, 1885.]

"Time antiquates antiquities, and hath an art to make dust of all things."—SIR THOMAS BROWNE.

One of the sure signs that a people is advancing towards a higher state, in which letters, arts and sciences may ultimately flourish, is when a feeling is born among them to perpetuate the memory of former days and to interpret the origin and meaning of ancient things. Then history begins ; and the spirit of history will associate men of similar and conservative tastes—men of patriotism and religion—to preserve the records of the past, to confer upon present occurrences, and to form a rallying-point for future generations. This is the beginning of historical societies; and whatever truth there may once have been in the melancholy words of the old antiquary who has suggested to me the motto of this essay, the enlarged views at present entertained about the benefits of association and the division of labor, and the universal diffusion and almost absolute perfection of the art preservative of all arts (printing), allow us to combat Time itself and dispute the assertion of the "Urn Burial:" "There is no antidote against the opium of time, which temporally considereth all things; our fathers find their grave in our short memories, and sadly tell us how we may be buried in our survivors. Grave-stones tell truth scarce forty years."

Probably the first example of a historical association was the society of the Argonauts. Some writers of an original turn of mind believe that this famous expedition, which was undertaken about one thousand years before Christ, consisted of a number of

(52)

young knights under one celebrated leader, banded together to explore the Euxine with the mingled objects of curiosity and traffic; and that upon their return to Greece they continued their companionship in order to combine their common experiences, sift their various impressions, expose to view the many strange curiosities they had brought back with them, and by the public recital, in the midst of a hall (or be it temple) filled with trophies, of their wonderful adventures, promoted among their countrymen the spirit of geographical discovery and historical research. Their corporate seal can no longer be found, but Shakspeare has preserved for us the legend which it bore :

"We are the Jasons; we have won the fleece."

At such a period of a people's existence the loss of an authentic record of earlier times, and the destruction of old monuments, is always keenly felt, and when expressed, is generally coupled with at least an implied regret that no means had been found to preserve them. Thus the inspired writer, three hundred years before the Christian era, after having praised men of renown and his fathers in their generation, mournfully concludes : "And there are some of whom there is no memorial, who are perished, as if they had never been ; and are become as if they had never been born, and their children with them" (Ecclesiasticus xliv., 9) ; and thus also the Augustan poet sang:

"Vixere fortes ante Agamemnona
Multi ; sed omnes illachrymabiles
Urgentur ignotique longa
Nocte, carent quia vate sacro."
                                        —HORACE, Od., iv., 9.

A house and garden in one of the suburbs of Athens, enclosed by a wall and having the grounds laid out in walks shaded by trees in which the nightingales made music—this was the original Academy. It is thought to have been so called from the name of its first owner, Academus. When his groves were bought by Cimon, the Athenian general, he adorned the place with statues and fountains and works of art, so as to convert it into a retreat for study and meditation amidst the charms of natural scenery and the luxuries of Hellenic refinement. At his death he left the garden to the public, and it immediately became a favorite resort of philosophers. Hither Socrates was wont to repair to converse with his more intimate disciples; and here his most illustrious pupil, Plato, established that school of divine philosophy which took its distinctive name from the surrounding associations, and over which he presided for half a century. Although the speculative sciences were the principal objects of the Platonic Academy, yet the abundant erudition of its founder, the variety of topics treated in his writings, and the special pursuits of so many of his followers, who insisted that history was but philosophy teaching by examples, would seem to justify us in claiming it as the first historical society ever established outside the mythological cycle of the Argonauts and order of the Golden Fleece.

The "Itinerary" of Pausanias, which mainly refers to objects of antiquity in Greece, such as buildings, temples, statues, and pictures, and to mountains, rivers and fountains, with the popular stories connected with them, may be considered as a gift of the Academy to future societies, and entitles the author to be called prince of antiquarians.

Passing over into Italy, we find that the study of history and antiquity is cultivated with eagerness in the atmosphere of freedom. There Varro, and there also Tully, surrounded themselves with friends imbued with their own zeal for the memorials of past ages and the rational interpretation of the remains of other epochs. Both were founders of historical societies ; and both, either by their published writings or their oral discussions on a very wide range of practical subjects, gave a mighty impulse to the study of history and antiquities among the Romans. Marcus Terentius Varro, whose accumulated wisdom in every department of knowledge distinguished him as the most learned man of his age, wrote, among other things, one work which commends him in a special manner to our esteem. It is his "Treatise on Ancient Things," which is divided into two sections—the Human Antiquities and the Divine Antiquities. From this source St. Augustine drew largely for his own admirable treatise "On the City of God." Marcus Tullius Cicero is too well known from his "Tusculan Disputations" and his "Academic Questions"—the fruit of the *conversazioni* (as we might now say) held in his villas at Frascati, near Rome, and at Pozzuoli, in the vicinity of Naples—to need any further mention ; but I would still observe that he is most strongly stamped as a genuine antiquarian by his remark that the Laws of the Twelve Tables—whose language in his time was archaic, and most of whose provisions had long been obsolete—were of greater value than all the libraries of the Philosophers ("De Oratore," i. 44). The "Archæology of Rome," by Denis of Halicarnassus, in which he treats of everything relating to the constitution, the religion, the history, the laws, the public and private life of Rome; the "Acts and Sayings of the Ancient Romans," by Valerius Maximus, in which a miscellaneous amount of curious matter of historical interest is collected in nine books; the "Natural History" of the elder Pliny, in which, attributing a wider sense than moderns would to such a title, he furnishes a great variety of information on human inventions and institutions, and on the history of the fine arts; the "Attic Evenings" of Aulus Gellius, in which he throws a flaming light upon the history and antiquities of the Greeks and Romans—are some only of those classical works of that period which have been saved from the well-nigh universal destruction of ancient literature.

We know little of the Gymnosophists of India, of the Magi of Persia, of the Star-gazers of Babylon and Chaldea, of the Celtic Druids, and of the Egyptian Hierarchs, except that all seemed to have formed in their several countries so many associations of learning and to have been so many members of historical societies. A celebrated association of individuals for the cultivation of history and science was formed by the first Ptolemy, King of Egypt, in the city of Alexandria. Like the Athenian garden which has given the word *academy* to our language, the Alexandrian establishment etymologically survives in the word *museum*. A place dedicated to the Muses, in which poetry, history, and kindred subjects should be studied, and later any place where learning was pursued or which was set apart as a repository for things having some immediate relation to the arts and sciences, was anciently called a museum, from the Greek *mouseion*. The earliest institution which received this appellation was that one founded, as we have said, by Ptolemy Philadelphus about two hundred and eighty years B. C. The buildings of this famous institution were afterwards enlarged by the Emperor Claudius. It was so perfectly adapted for the pursuit of knowledge, and for the comfort, dignity, and cultivated leisure of learned men under monarchical government, that the same plan, only with less magnificence, was adopted by other sovereigns in after ages. Strabo has left us a good description of the Alexandrian Museum (*Geogr.*, xviii. p. 794). It formed part of the royal palace, and contained cloisters, porticos, a public theatre or lecture-room for the more elaborate discussion of appointed subjects, and a large hall where the professors supped together and enjoyed their symposiums unmolested by the presence, and perhaps the criticisms, of the vulgar. The museum was supported by a common fund supplied from the public treasury, and the whole was under the direction of an archpriest, who was appointed by the king, and, when Egypt became a province of the Roman Empire, by the Cæsar. Botanical and zoological gardens and an aquarium were attached to this splendid establishment. The sciences of mathematics, astronomy, and geography were especially cultivated ; but literary criticism, philology, history, and antiquities were also much studied. The Museum was subsequently transferred to the *Serapeion*, or temple of Serapis, in another quarter of the city, and continued to flourish until the end of the fourth century of our era, having existed altogether for upwards of six hundred and fifty years.

In the city of Pergamus, in Asia Minor, a similar academy of learning was established by its wealthy kings, who raised it to prosperity and fame throughout the East. A jealousy having sprung up between Ptolemy Epiphanes and Eumenes, king of Pergamus, about the libraries attached to their respective academies, produced a singular revolution, the effects of which are still perceived after the lapse of two thousand years. The Egyptian king, fearing, or pretending to fear, that the supply of papyrus would diminish on account of the large demand for that article to furnish additional volumes to the rival library,—of papyrus, which is a reed or water-plant growing on the banks of the Nile, upon the thin leaves of which, when cut in strips and glued together transversely, the ancients wrote, and whence we derive our modern word *paper*,—forbade the exportation of it from his dominions. Thereupon the historical society of Pergamus, equal to the occasion, invented a new and better material for writing upon—namely, the skin of an animal, generally a sheep or a lamb, and prepared in a certain manner. It was called *charta Pergamea*, in compliment to the society. From it we derive our word *parchment*. When its use became general the whole perishable papyraceous manuscripts were transcribed anew upon this more durable substance, without which the works of ancient authors would have perished totally. *Vellum* is only a finer, smoother, and whiter sort of parchment, made of the skin of the calf—*vitulus*, " veal."

With the restoration of letters and classical learning in the fifteenth century the term academy was revived in Italy, whence it spread into other countries, but with a somewhat different signification from that which it had borne in former times. Then all the seven sciences of antiquity—viz., grammar, logic, rhetoric, arithmetic, geometry, astronomy and music—were comprehended within the range of encyclopædic knowledge affected by a member of one of the ancient academies, although even these had their specialists. At the Renaissance, however, learned men separated according to their particular tastes or bent of genius, to unite again with others of similar attractions and form together an academy. There were at one time no fewer than six hundred academies in Italy. Almost at the very beginning ot this surprising ferment ot scholars in the fifteenth century the learned, while united in one common and often exaggerated devotion to antiquity, divided themselves into two great schools—those who studied the philosophy and languages (Greek and Latin) of the ancients, and those who sought after and explained their monuments and literary remains, being less interested in the style than in the facts which these contained. Thus rose up on the one side the school of philosophers and humanists of which the Platonic Academy at Florence was the first in point of time and the chief in regard to merit ; and on the other side the school of historians and archæologists of whom the Roman Academy was the proud exponent. At a later period, and at first almost exclusively among the English-speaking races, a distinction was drawn between an academy and a society ; the former being a place where the belles-lettres or fine arts—music, painting, sculpture, architecture or poetry—were cultivated, and the latter one devoted to history, archæology, or the sciences. In this division a society ranks higher than an academy, in so much as the pursuit of that which can instruct mankind in useful knowledge and add to the conveniences and comforts of life is always nobler than that which, however pleasing to our sense of the beautiful or however stongly appealing to the pleasures of the imagination, can serve but for the entertainment of a leisure hour. Compare, for instance, in general usefulness and elevated aim the Royal Society of England, chartered in 1662, for the promotion of mathematical and physical science, of natural and experimental philosophy, with the Royal Academy, incorporated in the year 1768, for the purpose of cultivating and improving the arts of painting, sculpture and architecture. There *is* no comparison.

The oldest society in Europe devoted to historical studies and antiquarian researches is the Pontifical Society of Archæology at Rome. It was naturally in the "Eternal City" that, at the dawn of the Renaissance, the study of antiquities and ancient history was first taken up. Two Italians were particularly engaged in this resuscitation of the past—Petrarch and Poggio Bracciolini. The former was often moved to tears by the sight of the crumbling ruins of Rome, and, wandering alone by moonlight in the chaotic Forum, or sitting by day beneath the shade of some tree growing in soil which ages and neglect had accumulated upon the palace of the Cæsars, he brought back to life in his excited imagination the presence of a mighty people and formed intentions of restoring, at his own expense, some of the monuments around him. It is chiefly as a poet and Latinist that Petrarch is known; yet his familiar epistles and innumerable passages of his Latin poems reveal how much more deeply he was moved by the spirit of history than touched by the grace and beauty of a sonnet; and although the title of poet-laureate and the ceremony of coronation were revived for him on the Capitol on the 8th of April, 1341, it was rather an occasion, by recalling the deeds of the past, to kindle hope for the future and enthusiasm for the Seven Hills and the majestic ruins of Rome, than to confer upon any individual, however renowned, the reward even of an intellectual triumph.

Poggio Bracciolini went to Rome about the year 1402, when Boniface IX. employed him in the Papal chancery as one of the apostolic secretaries—a position which he held for fifty years and under eight successive Popes. The Sovereign Pontiffs were in sympathy with the great revival of studies in the fifteenth century, as is shown, to mention only one of many proofs, by the high and sometimes eminent honors, important and always lucrative offices, conferred by them on account of scholarship and literary merit. Poggio, turning his thoughts

> " To Latium's wide champaign, forlorn and waste,
> Where yellow Tiber his neglected wave
> Mournfully rolls,"   (*Dyer, "Ruins of Rome"*)

made excavations at Ostia and in the Campagna around Rome, and in one of his letters describes his country-house as adorned with statues and other antiquities which he had collected in various places. His merit as a historian and archæologist rests mainly on his treatise—one of his best works—"De Varietate Fortunæ," in which he indulges at the very beginning in a vision of the past, and sadly contrasts the miserable remains of fallen empire with the Roman magnificence of a thousand years before. It was in the last days of Pope Martin V.—that is, about the year 1430— that this discourse was composed. It was then, as Gibbon has described it, that "the learned Poggius and a friend ascended the Capitoline Hill, reposed themselves among the ruins of columns and temples, and viewed from that commanding spot the wide and various prospect of desolation. The place and the object gave ample scope for moralizing on the vicissitudes of fortune, which spares neither man nor the proudest of his works, which buries empires and cities in a common grave ; and it was agreed that, in proportion to her former greatness, the fall of Rome was the more awful and deplorable." ("Decline and Fall," vol. viii., p. 207.)

The Roman Academy, which still exists in usefulness and splendor, was subject at its birth to some mishaps which delayed its growth and withdrew from it the favor of the reigning Pope. About the middle of the fifteenth century a learned professor in the Roman University, Pomponius Lætus, a bastard of the ducal house of San Severino at Naples, gathered around him a number of young men, admirers, like himself, of the ancients and their remains. With these he formed a historical association called the Roman Academy, which met regularly in his dwelling on the Quirinal. The Academy was soon accused of being a centre of licentiousness, treason, and impiety, and when the rumors culminated in a specific charge of conspiring to dethrone the Pope and restore the pagan religion, strong measures were taken against it. During the carnival of 1468 twenty academicians were arrested and imprisoned in Castle Sant' Angelo, the rest saving themselves by a precipitate and (as some argued) a guilty flight. Leto, however, who was then absent from the city, voluntarily returned to Rome and stood his trial. He and his companions were finally set free, and the graver charges against them were declared not proven ; but it can hardly be said that they received an honorable acquittal. This episode is sometimes yet spoken of among the erudite as a brutal example of antagonism between the Papacy, upholding ignorance and barbarism, and the Renaissance, the representative of learning and civilization, the very title of one oi Hallam's chapters, "Paul II. persecutes the learned" (Hist. Lit., vol. l., p. 165), showing the hold such an unjust opinion has still upon men otherwise worthy of respect. Hallam has the boldness to say of the Roman Academy : "Paul II. thought fit to arrest all this society on charges of conspiracy against his life, for which there was certainly no foundation, and of setting up pagan superstitions against Christianity, of which, in this instance, there seems to have been no proof." As regards the charge of treason, the reader is referred to the great work of Tiraboschi, where it is amply discussed ; but concerning the other and more serious charge of impiety, in which even the infidel Gibbon must have believed when he wrote, while treating of the use and abuse of ancient learning, that "some pagan votaries professed a secret devotion to the gods of Homer and Plato," and referred in a note to this very Academy, additional testimony was brought to light a few years ago, quite unexpectedly, from the gloom of the Roman Catacombs. The excavations among these underground and early Christian cemeteries, carried on so successfully by the celebrated archæologist, De Rossi, under the patronage of the late Pope Pius IX., led to the reopening and, as it were, the rediscovery of some parts which had been visited in the fifteenth and sixteenth centuries by a few, but the precise location of and entrance to which had since been choked up and concealed by the *débris* of the Roman Campagna and forgotten even by the peasants.

"The names of Pomponio Leto and other *literati*, his associates in the famous Roman Academy, may still be read in several places of various catacombs, written there by themselves, with the addition of their title as '*Unanimes antiquitatis Amatores*, or '*Perscrutatores.* . . . .' Platina also says that the motive which induced his friends and himself to visit these subterranean places was a religious one ; but it is unfortunate that the inscriptions which they left behind them do not confirm this statement. On the contrary, when taken in conjunction with what is known ot the history of the writers, they suggest or strengthen suspicions of another kind. Those who are familiar with the literary history of that time will remember how the Roman Academy fell into disgrace with the Sovereign Pontiff Paul II., on suspicion both of being affected with heresy and of conspiring against the government. One of the grounds for the first of these charges was their pedantic conceit of taking old pagan classical names in place of their Christian ones ; but it has always been a matter of controversy how far the charge of conspiracy was really supported by evidence, and Tiraboschi hardly mentions any appreciable ground for it at all. We are not here concerned with the religious or political integrity of the Academy ; yet, in elucidation of an obscure point of history, it is worth while to mention that the name of Pomponio Leto is found in these newly-discovered memorials of him, with the title of *Pontifex Maximus*, *Pont. Max. regnans;* that another member, calling himself by the name of Pantagathus, is described as *Sacerdos Academiæ Rom.;* a third is *Æmilius vatum princeps*, and to some of the names other titles are added which show the dissolute habits of the academicians, and that they were not ashamed to perpetuate their own memories as lovers not only of pagan names, but of pagan morals. Another circumstance, too, ought not to be overlooked—viz., that whereas the names of the friars and others who ' came to visit this holy place' are found in the chambers and galleries nearest to the staircase, these 'lovers and investigators of antiquity' uniformly left records of their visits in the most distant and inaccessible parts of the cemetery. But whatever may have been the moral and religious character of this association, it must at least always remain a matter of profound regret and surprise that men whose lives were devoted to the revival of learning, and of whose

chief it is particularly recorded that he applied himself to the elucidation of Roman antiquities, 'which were then being disinterred,'
should have been familiar with these earliest monuments of
the heroic age of Christianity, and yet never have felt sufficient
interest to excite them to investigate their history or to publish
anything at all about them. Whatever they may really have
believed, we cannot wonder at the charge brought against them
by their contemporaries, and which we find addressed to one of
them by a Bishop even after their acquittal—that they were more
pagans than Christians." (Northcote and Brownlow, *Roma Sot-
teranea.*)

The Academy, purged of evil members and corrected in its
chief, rose up again during the pontificate of Paul's successor,
Sixtus IV. The Emperor Frederick III., visiting Rome, granted
many privileges to the Academy by a diploma which was read
amidst great enthusiasm on occasion of the first celebration of the
foundation of Rome (B. C. 753), which took place on the Capitol
on April 21, 1483, and ended with an imperial banquet. This
historic *fête*—still sometimes called, with a lingering trace of
pagan thought, the birthday of Rome—has continued to be kept
ever since ; and I would refer anyone asking for the *rationale* of
such a celebration to the eloquent discourse, entitled *Roma Æterna,*
pronounced on one of these occasions by Cardinal Manning, and
published in a volume of his *Miscellanies.*

Outside of Italy, and particularly in France and Germany, the
study of antiquities was eagerly pursued; but the earliest society
for historical studies and the preservation of ancient monuments,
founded north of the Alps, was the Society of Antiquaries in
England. It was begun in the year 1572 by a few eminent
scholars, and continues to be one of the very best societies of its
kind in Europe, for the rank and erudition of its members, for
the number and costliness of its publications, and for the zeal
with which it has suggested and furthered the study of native
history and the preservation of antiquities in all countries throughout the world to which the power of Great Britain has extended.
In France the oldest society for the study of history and antiquities is the Académie Royale des Inscriptions et Belles-Lettres, established in 1663, in the reign of Louis XIV. In 1701 this Academy was placed upon a new and more extended foundation and

its title changed to Academy of Inscriptions and Medals. From this date it published every year a volume of memoirs, many of great value, until it was suppressed in the year 1792. After the Revolution it was re-organized, and now forms part of the French Institute. The Royal Academy of Spanish History was commenced as a private association at Madrid in 1730, but was incorporated by Philip V. in 1738, and has published some interesing transactions. An Academy of Portuguese History was established at Lisbon in 1720 by King John V. Germany, Russia, Denmark and Sweden have all some distinguished academies, which, although later in the field of historical and antiquarian research, have done good service to archæology.

A BRIEF ACCOUNT

OF THE SOCIETY CALLED

"Sisters of Jesus and Mary."

[Read before the AMERICAN CATHOLIC HISTORICAL SOCIETY OF PHILADELPHIA,
on February 1st, 1886, by FRANCIS X. REUSS.]

IN the year 1816 God inspired the Abbé Coindre,—a missionary of the Diocese of Lyons, and, later, Grand Vicar at Blois (the history of whose life is in preparation at Le Puy, Upper Loire, France),—with the design of founding a society of Religious, the members of which would devote themselves to the instruction of the forlorn children and orphans left in a most wretched condition by godless parents. From among the faithful souls who flocked to him the Abbé Coindre had selected a number whom he deemed chosen by God to act as instruments in the enterprise he meditated. Several pious ladies readily responded to the call of the zealous priest and enrolled under the name of "Association of the Sacred Heart." They began at once their charitable ministry, and their sublime acts of generosity and heroic devotedness soon yielded good fruit. But, contrary to their ardent desire, the fervent associates were compelled to yield to various unexpected impediments and to leave the little orphanage, with its rising industry of flower-making, in the charge of the Sisters of St. Joseph, reserving for themselves the right of contributing to its increasing prosperity by their generous donations.

Four years had elapsed since the first attempt. Among the first members of the Association of the Sacred Heart several had been called by God to tread a special pathway in life. Pauline

Marie Jaricot, one of the number, had been elected by Providence to become the foundress of the "Propagation of the Faith" and of the Living Rosary ; but the Abbé Coindre had not lost sight of his generous band, nor had he relinquished his favorite project. The obstacles which forced the Society to resign the orphanage into the hands of the Sisters of St. Joseph had disappeared, and the Abbé summoned the associates of the original Society and united them by the bond of religious life under the rule of St. Augustine. A modest little house was rented for a space of two years in the Quartier des Chartreux, in the city of Lyons. Poor children were sought and brought to the new home prepared for them. Shortly after, a new industry was started in the manufacturing of Lyons silk. Frames were introduced into the new establishment, and soon the girls of the orphanage were working and the home was self-sustaining.

The foundress of the Congregation was the Venerable Madame Claudine Chevenot, a woman of uncommon energy, eminent piety and incomparable charity, who was born at Lyons in 1774. It is related of her that during the "Terror" of 1793, two of her brothers, sound Catholics and Royalists, were detected, seized by the "Patriots," and sentenced to be guillotined. Madame Chevenot, who was then only nineteen years of age, took courage to solicit the favor of being admitted to her brothers in prison. "Yes, citoyenne," answered the president of the murderous tribunal, "on condition that you drink with me." So saying, he poured out a glass of liquor, and, drinking half of it, offered the dregs to her. The young woman grew pale and faint, shuddering at the thought of drinking the disgusting dregs ; but brotherly love roused her energy, and, with the stern eye of the tribune fixed on her, seeming to gloat over her agony, she lifted the glass to her lips and slowly absorbed the remaining liquor, while the human monster laughed. The next day the two valiant brothers, with a group of noble victims, were cruelly shot at the Place des Brotteaux. Miss Chevenot followed her beloved ones at a distance, in disguise, with the hope of saving their dear remains, but she did not succeed; and the terrible shock told greatly on her delicate frame, and for the remaining years of her life she was afflicted with a nervous shaking of the head. The revolution of 1830-34, and the serious dangers it brought on the new community, found Madame Chevenot no stranger to such scenes. She died in 1836, leaving to the community she had founded the inheritance of the most sublime lessons and virtues, and the example of her heroic generosity in responding to the call of God.

Under her administration, in 1820, the rising community purchased the beautiful property owned by M. Antoine Jaricot—father of Pauline Mary Jaricot—situate on the mountain of Fourvières. This spot ranks next to the mountains of Judea for the memorable facts of its history and the unrivalled beauty of its scenery. It was the bulwark of the Roman power in eastern Gaul, and the theatre of the indomitable constancy of millions of Christian martyrs. From the *Forum* (hence the name Fourvières) the blood of the martyrs gushed like a torrent, and tumbled from rock to rock until it rushed into the river Saone, which was dyed and swelled by the bloody stream.

The mother house—the cradle of the Congregation of Jesus and Mary—is on one side of the square (formerly the ancient Forum) which for centuries has been trodden by pilgrims from the four parts of the globe, directly opposite the once humble and glorious shrine, which is at present the magnificent basilica of our Lady of Fourvières. So near the hallowed sanctuary is the house of the Congregation that the Sisters can catch the strains of the sacred hymns, and see the soft glimmering of the tapers burnt in offering at the feet of the miraculous statue of "Our Lady of Fourvières."

The park surrounding the convent is scattered with groves of chestnut and mulberry trees, with long shady avenues of lime trees. Groups of tall pines overshadowing the statue of some favorite saint, cross, or madonna, seem to keep watch over the solitude and religious silence of the place, while the royal foliage of the vine, the flexible bough of the honeysuckle, the syringa and the clematis, form a beautiful garment for the solid stone walls of the enclosure. From the terminus of the grounds the view is commanding; below lies the beautiful city of Lyons—*the City of Martyrs*—girded by the two rivers, Rhone and Saone; beyond lies a vast undulating campania, decked with vineyards and elegant villas. In the distance the snow-crested summits of the Alps rise. This lovely spot was, no doubt, in olden time the summer residence of some wealthy Roman patrician, who found there the realization of the fairest dreams in the enjoyment of all that is grand and beautiful. In the vicinity is seen the Antiquille, the ancient dwelling-place of the Roman Emperors, where the tourists are admitted to visit the catacombs; where St. Pothin, Bishop of Lyons, and St. Blandina were martyred A. D. 177. In 1821 Madame Chevenot, who was known in religion as Mother St. Ignatius, had a spacious building erected for the orphans, under the title of "La Providence," in a remote part of the extensive property, and an academy was opened for a number of young ladies belonging to the wealthy families in the city. In the same year another academy was founded at Belleville (district of Saone and Loire), and another at Thordistrol, which was later transferred to the episcopal city of Le Puy in Velay.

The political disturbances of 1830–34, as previously mentioned, were times of severe trial for the Sisters. The "*Insurgés*" chose the mountain of Fourvières as their standing point for operations; they sacrilegiously established their barracks in the hallowed chapel; their black flag floated from the top of the steeple; from Bellecour square below the regular troops darted their bombs and bullets at the camp of the rebels. A detachment was directed to turn to the opposite side of the plateau and take the "*Insurgés*" in the rear. Believing the orphanage to be their barracks, they made a large breach in the solid stone wall, and would have sacked the building had it not been for the chaplain, who persuaded them that they were mistaken; but this place being the surest for them, they ordered the Sisters and orphans to shelter in the safest part of the house, while from the windows they fired against the rebels, who, enraged at this unexpected and sudden attack, directed their artillery against the convent; but after a few hours' resistance they could stand it no longer, and retired into the neighboring country, where they hid until they could safely enter the city and seek their poor hearths. It is attributed to the miraculous protection of "Our Lady of Fourvières" that the Sisters had not to deplore the loss of any of their members. An officer of the regular troops, examining the scene after the battle, remarked "that if he believed in miracles he would most certainly say that he had witnessed one, for," he added, "our bullets were strong and numerous enough to pulverize the very stones of your building, and we have been aiming at it for three days." It is also stated that the artillerymen at Bellecour noticed with astonishment that the bombs directed at Fourvières seemed diverted from their natural course, and, hurried by some unaccountable force in an opposite direction, never reached even the precinct of the church of "Our Lady of Fourvières."

In 1842 a convent of these Sisters was opened at Remiremont, in Alsace, at the request of Bishop de Jerphanion, of St. Dié, the Department of the Vosges. About the same time Bishop Borghi, of Agra, East India, asked that a foundation be made in that far-off infidel diocese confided to his care. Cardinal de Bonald, Archbishop of Lyons, who was ecclesiastical superior of the Congregation, consented, and sixteen Sisters of the Order received his blessing and departed, bidding an eternal farewell to sunny France, for the purpose of devoting themselves to the conversion of the Hindoo children. No regular line of communication at this time (1842) existed between Marseilles and Agra. The history of the hardships endured on the journey of eleven months, of the crossing of the desert between Cairo and Suez, the passage of the Red Sea, where their sailing vessel met with contrary winds, would be very tedious.

On their arrival at Agra they were greeted with enthusiastic demonstrations by both the natives and the Europeans. They were led by the Bishop and Clergy to the Cathedral, where a "Te Deum" was chanted. Numerous convents have been founded since under Bishops Carli and Persico.* One academy, on Mount Himalaya, is resorted to by the daughters of the noblest English families settled in the East Indies.

In 1851 Bishop Hartmann, of Pata, and Ablegate of Bombay, made a foundation of the Sisters in that city, and since then several others were founded in adjacent towns.

During the year 1847 the Constitution of the Society now known as the Congregation of Jesus and Mary received the solemn approbation of His Holiness Pope Pius IX. In the letter Cardinal Isoard Vauvenargues, Auditor of the Rota, addressed

---

* Ign. Persico, Titular Bishop of Gratianople, *i. p. i.*, afterwards Bishop of Savannah, U. S.

to the Mother Superioress-General on the subject, that prelate says : "Whenever a code of religious constitutions is brought for approval under the examination of the Sacred Congregation, it is a rule to grant at first only a Brief of Praise, but considering the great amount of good already accomplished by the Sisters of Jesus and Mary, His Holiness was pleased to dispense the petitioners from the usual formalities and to grant at once the Brief of Approbation." This was an exceptional favor, and is kept sacred among the Sisters.

The year 1848 was marked by another terrible outbreak of civil war, which renewed the sad experiences of 1834, with still greater danger and loss for the mother-house at Fourvières. A great excitement pervaded the city of Lyons for a few weeks, and a strike was organized by the workers in the silk factories. No sooner had the Mayor proclaimed the French Republic, in the name of "*La Liberté, l' Egalité, et la Fraternité*," on the 25th of November, 1848—no sooner was this done than the turbulent mob began rioting. A troop of workers who gloried in the names of "Voraces," "Vautours" and "Ventres Creux," ascended the hill of Fourvières by night, burst open and pillaged the orphanage of the Christian Brothers, and proceeded to the orphanage of the Sisters of Jesus and Mary, under the pretence that the little silk factory owned by the Sisters prevented them from obtaining higher pay for their work in the city factories. They committed horrible depredations, tearing the pieces of silk, breaking the frames, venting their rage on the furniture, and heaping the remains in the yard to set them on fire. The plunderers spared nothing but the main building, and, on leaving at daybreak one of the leaders cried out : " We are going to rest now, but we shall come back at night to burn the house. And I don't advise the nuns to wait, for their turn will come next."

Cardinal de Bonald ordered the nuns to leave the place in disguise and seek shelter among their friends in the city. It was only after six months that, peace and security having been restored, the Sisters returned to their desolated convent. This crisis preceded the founding of the new academy at Rodez (Aveyron).

In 1850 Canon de Vionnet y Montfort introduced the Order into Spain. The first colony was sent to Sant' Andre de Polemar, near Barcelona. Soon another house was founded at

Tarragona; a third, in Valencia, and, recently, a fourth in Barcelona.

In 1855 Mgr. Charles François Baillargeon, third Archbishop of Quebec, Canada (died Oct. 13th, 1870), solicited the favor of a foundation of the Sisters in Canada. At his request Bishop Bourget, of Montreal (died June 8th, 1885), who was on his way to Rome, visited Lyons and the convent of Fourvières for the purpose of presenting the petition and making arrangements; and in November, 1855, a colony of eight Sisters left for Canada. They arrived in December, 1855, at the Grand Trunk Station opposite Quebec. The whole population of the adjacent country had gathered to meet them, and a cortege of over sixty sleighs and other vehicles accompanied them to their new convent at Sauryon. Meanwhile, other foundations had been demanded in England. A convent was established in London in 1855, and another at Ipswich in 1860.

In Canada the Congregation has rapidly extended itself. St. Gervais got a convent in 1860; one was established at Trois Pistoles, Province of Quebec, in 1863, another at St. Michael, Province of Quebec, in 1865; a convent and academy at Sillery, in 1870, and it now has the Provincial House for Canada. There have been several houses founded in the United States,—one at Fall River, Mass., in 1877; one at Manchester, N. H., in 1883; and another at Woonsocket in 1884. The Superioress-General for the Sisters in America is Mother Marie St. Cyrille. Thus does God, who works in quiet and might, further His own designs in spite of persecution and wicked opposition, choosing the weakest and the humblest as the instruments in His hands.

WILLIAM PENN,

THE

FRIEND OF CATHOLICS.

[Read before the AMERICAN CATHOLIC HISTORICAL SOCIETY OF PHILADELPHIA, on February 1st, 1886, by MARTIN I. J. GRIFFIN.*]

THE purpose of our American Catholic Historical Society of Philadelphia is amply disclosed by its title. Not only is our concern all that relates to our Church in this country, but in an especial manner all that relates to the history of the Church in our own city, and to that has the work of the Society chiefly been devoted.

Organized as we are to collect and preserve all that will tell the story of the founding and expanding of the Church here, it seems fitting that on our first manifestation of the work of the Society it would best accord with the object declared "especially" that of the Society—the elucidation and preservation of the history of the Church in Philadelphia—if I would speak a word in vindication of the memory of William Penn, the Founder of our State, and defend him from the aspersions cast upon his character as a friend of Religious Toleration.

If the history of our Faith in Philadelphia is ever to be written or its development aided by our Society, surely the first point of historical inquiry and patient and conscientious research must be the principles on which our State was founded, and how these principles and the professions according therewith were applied to the early Catholic settlers in the colony Penn established.

---

* Also read before the Friends' Evening Hour Club, of Germantown, December 7th, 1885.

Who should be lenient in judgment, tolerant in opinion and disposed to fair examination, if not Catholics, who above all others have suffered most reproach because the enemies of the Church have not examined into the truth of the statements alleged against her? Who should not idly speak in derogatory terms of the character or memory of any man unless the truth of history demand, and then judging only by the standard of the times in which the actor was a public character? Yet, in this have Catholic writers offended. They have done injustice to William Penn as the friend of religious liberty. He is charged with denying to Catholics that liberty of conscience which he proclaimed as the right of all who came within the lines of his "Holy Experiment."

Thus the minds of our people have been misled, and worse, our children are being taught that Penn and his people were bitterly hostile to our forefathers in the faith in our city. This, too, in Catholic histories, because our children cannot use other histories without being kept in ignorance of the deeds of Catholics in the settlement and development of our country and in gaining its independence.

If mine be the first words of vindication of the founder of my native city, and such as to show him to have been in act as in name—a Friend—they are so only because serious and patient and conscientious examination has convinced me that injustice has been done; not censurable injustice, because unknowingly, though carelessly done.

Our whole early history is but a romance, and rarely founded upon facts. The very first alleged fact, that in 1686—just 200 years ago—there was a Catholic priest resident in Philadelphia, is not true, and the Catholic writer who first started that historical tale is censurable because he perverted the fact upon which he built a story that has its life still longer lengthened as it appears in the recently issued "Life of Bishop Neumann."

We Catholics regard William Penn as a religious enthusiast, who contended for religious toleration or liberty when he was oppressed, and, when given the opportunity to establish a colony, proclaimed as the corner-stone of its structure the principles which he had advocated when oppressed for conscience sake.

While policy demanded that none should be by declaration "excepted" from the benefits of the principles he proclaimed, yet he was one loath to have religious liberty construed to cover Roman Catholics, or "Papists," as we were generally called in those days.

Though not excluding Catholics, we Catholics believe that we were not desired by Penn, that he spoke disparagingly of us for publicly exercising the rites of our Church, that his course and words influenced his followers, and that they thus made our position an uneasy one in the Province.

In fact, the Catholic opinion regarding Penn is best expressed in the words of Bishop Gilmour, the present respected Bishop of Cleveland, who, in a public discourse in 1880, said: " Even the gentle Penn had his fling at the Catholics."—[The Debt America owes to Catholicity, page 8.]

It is against this stain on Penn that I seek to show that there is no justification for any hesitation on the part of Catholics to express admiration for the Founder of Pennsylvania, nor any reason why his followers, "the people called Quakers," to use the old time words, should not be regarded especially as Friends.

But how did the Catholic misjudgment of Penn's character arise? From Watson, the annalist of Philadelphia. He relates that Penn wrote to Logan, in July, 1708, saying: " Here is a complaint against your Government that you suffer public Mass in a scandalous manner. Pray send the matter of fact, for ill use is made of it against us here."

Then continues Watson: " And in a subsequent letter he returns to it in these terms: 'It has become a reproach to me here, with the officers of the Crown, that you have suffered the scandal of the Mass to be publicly celebrated.'"

This, related by a Protestant, is the basis of the Catholic opinion concerning Penn.

The first extract is well founded. It appears in " The Penn and Logan Correspondence." Though dated 7th month 29th, 1708, Watson and the Catholic writers give the date as July 29th, forgetting that in 1708 September was the seventh month. This letter was sent by the hand of the new Governor—Gookin—by Penn to James Logan, his confidential secretary and friend. It speaks generally of such affairs relating to the young colony as were of concern at the time, and such instructions as Penn might be expected to give by the new Lieutenant-Governor whom he was sending to the Province.

Recall Penn's troubles from 1692. Remember that all the settlers were not Quakers. Remember his financial difficulties, the people's ingratitude, the hostility of "the Hot Church party," and the efforts to dispossess him of his proprietary rights or to prevent him from disposing of them to the Crown. Remember that Mass was not allowed to be publicly celebrated in England; that his enemies invented lies, perverted facts, and misrepresented circumstances in order to obtain the mastery of him. The malcontents here reported everything to London; and Penn simply informed Logan : " Here is a complaint against your Government, that you suffer public Mass in a scandalous manner." Remember that in England the public exercise of the Catholic religion was not permitted. In all her colonies Catholics were "excepted" from the declaration that liberty of conscience should prevail ; and even in Maryland, founded by Catholics, Mass was not publicly allowed even in Father Andrew White's time, and was prohibited by statute in 1692.

Pennsylvania alone did not "except" Catholics, and her statute books contain no prohibition of the public exercise of their religion.

But let us consider "the scandal of the Mass" charge. It is this alleged extract that I attack. I deny its authenticity. It has got into our Catholic histories from *Watson*, because about 30 years ago Henry de Courcy, a French Catholic journalist making a tour of America, wrote sketches of Catholicity in the United States for his paper ; these were translated and published under the title, " History of the Catholic Church in the United States."

I deny the existence of "the Scandal of the Mass" (alleged) extract. It is not in the " Penn and Logan Correspondence." I have searched innumerable books for it, have examined a number of authorities, questioned those who have repeated the statement, and sought diligently, anxiously and faithfully to discover if Penn ever used the language. I can get no other or any farther back than Watson. My position might rest here when the evidence upon which Penn has been charged with "having his fling at Catholics" is not verified nor discoverable.   Proof must be produced before condemnation is pronounced.   No indefinite "subsequent letter" is evidence.   Proof, if it existed in Watson's time, is available now, and even more so in these days of historical research.

But let us examine the probability of any such language having been used.   Even if it had, I claim that it is not a just judgment to take one sentence from a private official letter and hold it as destructive of a life-time of professions and practices totally at variance with the spirit which we Catholics might impute to one who would call the most consoling, the most efficacious and most cherished practice and belief of our faith—the scandal of the Mass, even though these were but the words in every day use. But let us see how Penn regarded Catholics.

From King Charles II. Penn received a grant of this land. He undertook to settle it upon a principle first practised in our country by a Catholic, Lord Baltimore—Religious Liberty. "For the matter of liberty and privileges I propose that which is extraordinary," wrote Penn to Turner, Sharp and Roberts, April 15th, 1681, as cited in Janney's "Life."

It was "extraordinary" to grant religious liberty in any of the colonies to "Papists and Quakers."   Everywhere they were the banned and hunted people, and he who prayed that "the Lord guide me by His wisdom and preserve me to honor His name and serve His truth and His people, that an example may be set up to the nations," would be most likely not to do ill to those who were fellows with him in suffering, who with him were, at home and in the new land, persecuted and oppressed for conscience sake.   But mere toleration would not satisfy Penn.   He made religious liberty a right.   All know of the penal laws of England against Catholics.   They were used to oppress Quakers. He protested against this, but urged that the blow that he desired turned from his people should not fall upon others.

Penn was "a Protestant and a strict one, too," as he declared. He believed not the doctrines of "the Church of Rome."   As a youth at Oxford he had torn the surplice from a fellow student because "it was a relic and a symbol of that Church."

For his religious principles he had suffered imprisonment and under laws designed to oppress Catholics.   The law of 1582,

which imposed on "Papists" a fine of £20 a month for absence
from the Established Church, and the law of 1605, giving the
option to the Sovereign of accepting this sum or all the personal
and two-thirds of the real estate of the accused, were used by
the enemies of the "Quakers" to oppress them.

When the Parliament of 1678 was considering the laws against
"Popery," it was proposed to insert an oath by which the penalty
could be avoided. The Friends objected to the oath. They
wished their word, subject to the penalty for perjury, to be taken.
On the 22d of January, 1678, Penn appeared before a committee
of Parliament in defense of the position of his people. His remarks give the key to his course towards Catholics, and deserve
attention therefor:

"That which giveth me more than ordinary right to speak at
this time and place is the great abuse that I have received above
any other of my profession for a long time. I have not only
been supposed a Papist, but a seminary, a Jesuit, an emissary of
Rome and in pay of the Pope, a man dedicating my endeavors
to the interest and advancement of that party. Nor hath this been
the report of the rabble, but the jealousy and insinuations of persons otherwise sober and discreet. Nay, some zealous for the
Protestant cause have been so far gone in this mistake as not only
to think ill of us and to decline our conversation, but to take
courage to themselves to proscribe us as a sort of concealed Papist. All laws have been let loose upon us, as if the design were
not to reform but to destroy us, and that not for what we are, but
for what we are not. I would not be mistaken.

"I am far from thinking that Papists should be whipped for
their consciences, because I exclaim against the injustice of
whipping Quakers for Papists. No; for the hand pretended to be
lifted up against them hath, I know not by what discretion, lit
heavily upon us, and we complain, yet we do not mean that any
should take a fresh aim at them or that they must come in our
room. We must give the liberty we ask, and cannot be false to
our principles, though it were to relieve ourselves, for we have
good will to all men and would have none to suffer for a truly
sober and conscientious dissent on any hand."

To the charge that he was a Papist he replied: [Letter to Wm.
Popple, Oct. 20, 1688.]

"If the asserting of an impartial liberty of conscience, if doing to others as we would be done by, and an open avowing and a steady practising of these things at all times and to all parties, will justly lay a man under the reflection of being a Jesuit or Papist of any sort, I must not only submit to the character, but embrace it too."

To Archbishop Tillotson, who reported him "a Papist, perhaps a Jesuit," he wrote: "I am a *Catholic*, though not a *Roman*. I have bowels for mankind, and dare not deny others what I crave for myself. I mean liberty for the exercise of my religion, thinking faith, piety and providence a better security than force, and that if truth cannot prevail with her own weapons, all others will fail her . . . . I am no Roman Catholic, but a Christian whose creed is the Scripture." ["Hazard's Register," Vol. ii., pp. 29, 30.] "Two principles of religion I abhor : Obedience upon authority without conviction ; destroying them that differ from me for God's sake." [Wm. Penn to Abp. Tillotson. *Ibid.*]

But that Penn could not object to the public celebration of Mass, take his testimony from his "Persuasion to Moderation :"

"By liberty of conscience I mean a free and open profession and exercise of one's duty to God, especially in worship." [Janney's "Penn," p. 280, 2d Ed. 1882.]

He cites instances of Catholics granting toleration, and asks: "Who should give liberty of conscience like the Prince that wanted it?" And again he repeats even more plainly: "By liberty of conscience I mean a free and open profession of that duty."

That was the "cause I have with all humility undertaken to plead against the prejudices of the times," said he; and shall I, a Catholic, withhold words of justice from him who pleaded that my forefathers in the faith were entitled, beyond all human laws, to enjoy "the free and open profession" of their faith and the practices of their religion? No.

He suffered for his creed and he suffered under laws intended to crush "Popery," and he had to be charged with being a Papist for even attempting to justify the wrong against him. His principles and his sufferings for them taught him "not to vex men for their belief and modest practice of their faith with respect to the other world, into which province and sovereignty temporal power reaches not from its very nature and end."

Such were Penn's professions before the King of England granted him this land. How did he act then?

The Frame of Government granted Religious Liberty. The Great Law passed at Chester, December 10, 1682, also proclaimed it.

"The Great Law declares: All persons living in this Province . . . shall in no way be molested or prejudiced in their religious persuasion or practice, or in matters of faith or worship."

Penn, in "A Further Account of the Province of Pennsylvania and its Improvements," says of the "Government:" "We aim at duty to the King, the Preservation of Right to all, the Suppression of Vice and Encouragement of Virtue and Arts *with Liberty to all People to Worship Almighty God according to their Faith and Persuasion."* [*Pa. Mag.*, Apr., 1885, p. 79.]

Benjamin Furley, Penn's agent at Rotterdam, in his "Explanation concerning the Establishment of Pennsylvania," issued Mar. 6, 1684, says:

"And in order that each may enjoy that liberty of conscience which is a natural right belonging to all men, and which is so comformable to the genius and character of peaceable people and friends of repose, it is established firmly, not only that no one be forced to assist in any public exercise of religion, but also full power is given to each to make freely the public exercise of his own without meeting with any trouble or interference of any kind; provided that he profess to believe in one eternal God all powerful, who is the Creator, Preserver, and Governor of the world, and that he fulfil all the duties of civil society, which he is bound to perform towards his fellow-citizens."

Note that Penn always speaks of the right to practise one's religion as well as to profess it. One is naturally contained in the other, but in Penn's day it was not the profession, but the practice of his creed and that of the Catholics that was punished. It was the Mass that was especially objectionable. As regards Catholics, Protestant opinion was aptly summarized by Cromwell's order that liberty of conscience should prevail in Ireland, but no Mass. So that if Penn really meant anything just or wise concerning Catholics and liberty of conscience, he meant above all things else concerning them that Mass should be celebrated in his colony.   And history proves it so.

There were Catholics in Philadelphia as early as 1686, and one Peter Debuc, who died in 1693, whose will I have examined, bequeathed £50 to Father Smith—supposed to be an alias for Father Harrison, or Harvey, as investigation may show.   Now, if half a dozen Catholics could be gathered together in the new city during this time, they surely had Mass celebrated by the Jesuit who visited them when journeying from Maryland to New York, or on his return.

After 1692, until the Revolutionary War, nowhere else in the British Provinces was Mass allowed to be publicly celebrated but in Philadelphia—or elsewhere in Pennsylvania.   Even in Maryland, founded as it had been by Catholics who welcomed all, Catholics were, as soon as Protestants got the power, oppressed for their religion, and doubly taxed, and the public exercise of their religion prohibited.   Mass could only be said in one of the private rooms of the manors of the well-to-do Catholics.

Penn declared "the first fundamental of the government of my Province to be, that everyone should have and enjoy the free possession of his faith and the exercises of worship, in such way and manner as every such person shall in conscience believe most acceptable to God; and so long as such person useth not his Christian liberty to licentiousness or the destruction of others, he shall be protected in the enjoyment of the aforesaid Christian liberty by the civil magistrate."   So the few Catholics who were here in Penn's time were visited by Priests.   They made no special display ; they kept to themselves and quietly performed their religious duties.

But I judge that at Christmas or New Year's of 1707-8, the few who were here made special manifestation of their faith on the occasion of two converts being received into the Church.   Now, reception into the Catholic Church implies long and serious consideration and instruction, and in this case means that priests had been here frequently, were publicly known and moved among the citizens; else how did one of such prominence as Lionell Brittin come to seek admission to the Catholic Church, whose members must have been very few in 1708, as the highest estimate made of the Catholics at the building of St. Joseph's Chapel in 1732 is forty !

It was this public ceremony of the reception of the two converts that led Rev. John Talbot, afterwards the first Episcopal Bishop (by non-juring consecration), to write to the secretary of the London Society for the Propagating of the Gospel, on January 10, 1708 : "Arise, O Lord Jesus Christ, and help us and deliver us for thine honor ! . . . There's an Independency at Elizabethtown, Anabaptism at Burlington, and the Popish Mass in Philadelphia. I thought that the Quakers would be the first to let it in, particularly Mr. Penn, for if he has any religion 'tis that. But thus to tolerate all without control is to have none at all." This is the earliest direct evidence of the celebration of Mass in Philadelphia.

On February 14 Talbot wrote to Rev. George Keith : "I saw Mr. Bradford in New York. He tells me that Mass is set up and read publicly in Philadelphia, and several people are turned to it, amongst which Lionell Brittin, the church warden, is one, and his son is another. I thought that Popery would come in amongst Friends, the Quakers, as soon as any way." [From "Doc. His. of P. E. Church, U. S. Church Documents." Conn., Vol. I, p. 37. Jas. Pott, publisher, 1863.]

It was this Mass and reception of converts that the Episcopalians so promptly reported to London. Penn was there, harassed with debt and family troubles and battling with "The Hot Church Party" for the retention of his proprietary interest. His enemies and the enemies of his followers were pressing against him that while neither England nor any of the American Colonies gave toleration to Catholics, in Pennsylvania they were not only allowed to live, but were doing an act unlawful in England—publicly celebrating the Mass and receiving converts. Penn simply wrote to Logan to send a true account of the affair. Unfortunately, that account, if sent, has not come down to us.

Catholics have failed to remember that though Penn was the founder, and, with the exception of a brief time, the Governor of the Province, he was not always the controller of its affairs. Nor were his own people always able to direct affairs as he and they desired. Not only had he and they personal and financial difficulties to contend against, but religious controversies and Quaker dissensions thwarted many good works.

But as concerns our question, Penn and his followers had the

Established Church party to contend with.   They strove to have his rights taken from him in order to have the Church of England established.

Religious controversies were rife during Lord Cornbury's time, and others than Catholics, as few as they were, suffered from the attempts to have the Established Church of England made the Church of the Province; for Rev. Francis Makemie, founder of Presbyterianism in America, on March 28, 1707, wrote to Rev. Benj. Colman: "The penal laws are invading our American sanctuary without the least regard to the Toleration Act, which should justly alarm us all." [*Pa.Mag.*, No. 2. vol. v., 1881 p. 224.]

Such were Penn's principles, professions and acts.

How did his followers act?   Did they do as he proclaimed?

Let us take the "History of the United States," one of Sadlier's Excelsior Series of Catholic School Books.

This history has been prepared because the histories in the Public Schools are "a conspiracy against truth," as regards Catholics and their doings in this country.   Yet it contains the following:

"Though William Penn granted religious toleration throughout his own colony, still in maintaining it towards Catholics he was bitterly opposed by his own people."

So while Penn is not saddled with the charge of the big histories, the odium is now placed on his followers.

A few sentences earlier the people are described as "emigrants, mainly Quakers."

Yet there is no foundation whatsoever for this declaration that they bitterly opposed "the maintenance by Penn of religious toleration towards Catholics."

Take these facts as proof:

Pennsylvania was the only colony except Maryland from which Papists were not excluded from the first hour of their settlement. After 1692 it was the only colony that did not prohibit the public exercise of the Catholic religion, and for forty years previous to that time our religion was not free even in Maryland.   It was, indeed, a haven from oppression, and a Catholic, even from the Catholic-founded colony of Maryland, was considered as having reached an asylum or sanctuary when within Pennsylvania's borders; for in April, 1690, Captain Goode, writing to Jacob Leisler, of New

York, about two persons whom he describes as "strangers, Irishmen and Papists," says: "They made their escape towards Pennsylvania."

There is not a sign to show that the Quakers during Penn's time here, or when he was in England, or after his death, at any time "bitterly opposed" Catholics practising their religion.

The truth is, indeed, the reverse of this. The complaint sent to England about the Mass of 1708 amounted to nothing injurious to Catholics. They were here; they came and went, as did others. Priests visited them regularly, and the founder of the little chapel of St. Joseph is traditionally related to have come to this city in the garb of a Quaker. Perhaps so. It was that of Friends in reality, and he could be safe at any rate.

But after Father Greaton concluded to build a little chapel,— and, if we take our Catholic school history as correct, among those who "bitterly opposed" his presence,—where did he build? Why, of all places in our city, the one he would have avoided if that charge were true—right beside the Quaker Almshouse, back of Walnut Street. That alone is proof of the utmost cordiality and friendship existing between the two peoples, and there are people yet living who remember the passage-way between the two. And when in July, 1734, Governor Patrick Gordon informed his Council that a house lately built in Walnut Street had been set apart for the exercise of the Roman Catholic religion, where several persons resorted on Sundays to hear Mass openly cele-brated by a Popish priest,—and he thought "the public exercise of that religion contrary to the laws of England,"—on what grounds did the forty or less Catholics maintain their right to freely and publicly exercise their religion? That they had a right to do so by "the Charter of Privileges granted to this Gov-ernment by the late honorable Proprietor."

The laws of England were against them, but they appealed to the Charter of Penn. Governor Gordon was not a Quaker. It was to a Quaker document Catholics appealed, and they were not molested. To show still further, and perhaps more clearly, that this lesson taught our Catholic children, that Penn's follow-ers bitterly opposed the religious toleration of Catholics, is founded on error, let me cite the testimony afforded by a letter in the *London Magazine and Monthly Chronologer*, dated July 7, 1737, which may be examined at the Ridgway Library. Charges are made against the Quakers. A correspondent endorses them, and adds : "A small specimen of a notable event which the people of that profession have taken towards the propagation of Popery in Pennsylvania. Let the Quakers deny it if they can. In the town of Philadelphia is a public Popish chapel where that religion has free and open exercise, and all the superstitious rites of that Church are as avowedly performed as those of the Church of England are in the Royal chapel of St. James'; and this chapel is not only open upon fasts and festivals, but is so all day and every day of the year, and exceedingly frequented at all hours either for public or private devotions, though it is fullest at those times when the meeting-house of the men of St. Omers is thinnest, and *vice versa*." And one hundred and fifty years afterwards on the same spot is a chapel, not only open on fasts and festivals, but is so all day and every day in the week, and frequented at all hours either for public or private devotions— dear St. Joseph's. "The men of St. Omers," you will remember, is intended as a stigma on the Quakers as being "Papists," from the Catholic college of St. Omers, in France.

The correspondent continues : "That these are truths you may be satisfied of by inquiry of any trader or gentleman who has been there within a few years."

And we know it was the truth, and it remained the solitary instance, until the Revolution, of a Catholic chapel in all the British Provinces, so much so that Rev. McSparran, writing from Narragansett, R. I., in 1752, to a friend in England, mentions the fact that in Philadelphia there was then a Popish chapel, the only one in the British Provinces. At this very time, though the Provincial laws permitted only "Protestants to hold lands for the erection of churches, schools, or hospitals," as Dr. Stillé states in his very valuable paper on "Test Laws in Provincial Pennsylvania," yet the title of the ground on which St. Joseph's chapel stood was then held in the name of a Jesuit priest, and so recorded, as the recently discovered brief of title, now in the MSS. department of the American Catholic Historical Society, shows.

During all this time the Quakers were not without power, and Catholics freely, publicly, and unmolestedly had all the public exercises of their religion as they have to-day; and nowhere is there a trace of a cause for instilling into the minds of our children that Penn's followers "bitterly opposed" them.

Everywhere throughout the Province the friendship existing between Quakers and "Papists" was known.   Even the street ballads prove this, as witness the following lines from "A Poor Man's Advice to His Neighbor.   A ballad.   New York, 1774:"

> "I've Papists known, right honest men,
> Alas ! what shame and pity !
> Ah ! how unlike the *vartus* Penn
> To drive them from our city."

And seventy years before that from Maryland came the report to the London Society *for Propagating the Gospel:* "Popish priests and Quakers equally obstruct a good progress."   [*First Report*, 1703].

Not only had Penn and his people in England to suffer as "Papists," but in this country even, down to the heat of the Revolutionary War, Catholic titles, opprobriously applied, were used to stigmatize the Quakers.   The bigot, John Adams, who on October 9th, 1774, accompanied Washington to Vespers, could at once write to his wife about "the poor wretches fingering their beads, chanting Latin, not one word of which they understood, their *Pater Nosters* and *Ave Marias*—their holy water, their crossing themselves perpetually—everything to charm and bewitch the simple and ignorant,"—could also on September 8th, 1776, write : "We have been obliged to humble the pride of some Jesuits who call themselves Quakers."

Many additional facts on the same line of consideration which I am presenting might be offered if my time or your patience permitted.   Nor do I enter upon the civil disabilities under which Catholics were, though not by name, debarred from public office, had any been aspiring or deemed worthy of official distinction.   This has been fully and accurately shown by Dr. Stillé in his recent paper read before the Pennsylvania Historical Society.   The very production of so learned and historically accurate an essay proves the opportuneness of our Society, as it was an encouragement to our members.   The spectacle is at this time presented of a Protestant showing the civil disabilities Penn allowed (and for a time sanctioned) to be imposed upon Catholics, thus lessening his reputation as a friend to civil liberty, while I, a Catholic, strive to prove him to my fellow Catholics as one who did not oppress Catholics in their religious rights.

But if historical research be now again directed to William Penn, let us be just in our judgment. He was a man proclaiming a principle the world was not then disposed to receive, and we must be careful not to judge his acts by the spirit of to-day. Civil and religious liberty is now the professed and statutably declared principle; but we Catholics know, nevertheless, that in both do we suffer because of our faith.

Pennsylvania alone tolerated the Mass, though many thought it a "scandal" and idolatrous.   To-day, though our State's Constitution declares every man's conscience to be unmolested, yet public officials not Quakers consider the Mass a scandal and deny it to our brethren in faith, though unfortunate they be.

Can we be harsh in judgment even if, in one instance only, it shall be proved that he used but the commonplace language of the time, though to our modern ears it sounds so harsh ?   Yet officers of our municipal institutions, here in the city of Penn— the American Sanctuary, as one hundred and eighty years ago it was called—deride the claim of Catholics to equal and exact justice. Not only is the Cromwellian order of "No Mass" given, but a baser crime than Cromwell's is committed, and Catholics are forced to attend a religious worship hostile to their faith—and Catholics rebuke Penn's followers that he once, if at all, simply spoke unkindly, while this deed of infamy against men's consciences awakens but little concern among us. No follower of Penn now perpetrates this crime; "the Hot Church party" and renegades to our faith, and not "the men of St. Omers," live again to-day, here in the City of Penn, once the only home of our Faith in the English Provinces.

[Signature of the first known Philadelphia convert to Catholicity, 1707–8.]

The French Refugee Trappists

IN THE

UNITED STATES.

[Read before the AMERICAN CATHOLIC HISTORICAL SOCIETY OF PHILADELPHIA, on February 23d, 1886, by LAWRENCE FRANCIS FLICK.]

EVER since the rules of St. Benedict had birth in the piety and wisdom of that great and holy man, they have, in some form or other, drawn men from the world and impregnated their lives with sanctity and wisdom. Time and the perversity of man's inclinations might occasionally relax them, but only again to give them champions, such as Blessed Bernon in 910, St. Robert in 1098, and Armand Jean Le Bouthillier de Rancé in 1662.

The name, *Les Trappistes*, came about in this way. In 1122 a French count, Rotrou du Perche, made what he believed to be a miraculous escape from some great danger. Out of gratitude to the Blessed Virgin, to whom he ascribed his preservation, he vowed to build a church and to place it under her patronage. He fulfilled his vow by building a church in a solitary valley, surrounded by dense forests and in a spot where a number of streams come together and form the river Yton. This place has from time immemorial been called *La Trappe*. When, therefore, the good Count Rotrou afterwards brought monks from Savigny, and established a monastery for them near his church, they were given the name of *Les Trappistes*.

It was here, at La Trappe, that the monks, having gradually forgotten the rigor of their rules, were reminded of it by the saintly Abbé de Rancé. He had just about fully established his reform when he was called to his reward ; but his good work went on until it was disturbed by the French Revolution.

(86)

On February 13th, 1790, all religious orders in France were suppressed by a legislative act of the French government.   There was, however, too much of the spirit of St. Benedict, Blessed Bernon, St. Robert, and Abbé de Rancé at La Trappe, to be dispersed by a mere edict.   Dom Augustin, one of the priests of La Trappe, resolved, since he could not keep his vows in his native land, to establish his Order in some other country.   With twenty-three of his brethren, all volunteers like himself, he formally applied to various governments for an asylum.   He received a favorable answer from the Senate of Freiburg, which, on April 12th, 1791, granted him permission to establish a house in Switzerland.   The twenty-four monks signed a covenant, forming the *Abbaye de Notre Dame de La Trappe de Valsainte* on April 26th, and elected Dom Augustin abbot on May 3d of the same year.   The election, however, was not confirmed, nor the abbey formally established by Rome, until November 27th, 1794.   By this time so many recruits had flocked in that several new houses had gone out from Valsainte, and had sought asylum in different parts of Europe.

One of the day dreams of Dom Augustin, from his first arrival at Valsainte, had been to send a colony to America.   Twice he essayed it, but each time the colony was providentially located elsewhere.   In 1793 Dom Jean Baptiste departed for Canada with some companions.   When he got to Brabant he was so earnestly implored by the people to remain, that he sought the permission of his superior, and established a house there.   In April, 1794, a large number of recruits were sent to Brabant, with the understanding that a colony was to start from there for Canada.   An attempt to carry out the design was made in July of the same year, when Jean Baptiste again started for Canada with several companions, this time by way of England.   A pious Englishman, by name Thomas Weld, offered him a location on his land at Lulworth, Dorsetshire, and pressed him to accept.   Again Dom Jean sought permission to depart from his instructions, and located his colony in England.

Meanwhile the Order grew so rapidly that Dom Augustin had considerable difficulty in supplying asylums for the outgrowths. Already flourishing off-shoots from Valsainte existed in Spain, Italy, Holland and England.   But persecution went hand in hand with success; no sooner were colonies established than the far-reaching influence of the Revolution again routed them, and new asylums had to be sought.   Russia promised a safe retreat, and in 1796 quite a large colony took refuge under its neutrality.   It proved a poor asylum, and in 1800, after the monks of Valsainte had sought shelter in its dominions, on account of outrages committed against their abbey, all Trappists were expelled from the country by a ukase.

This revived in Dom Augustin the great desire to establish his Order in America.   For nearly two years he confided it to his own bosom, striving meanwhile to find homes for his persecuted brethren.   Some were sent to England, some were received by brethren in Germany, and many went back to Valsainte, whither they were invited by the Senate of Freiburg in 1802.   America was not forgotten ; as soon as affairs were somewhat settled, Dom Augustin confided to his brethren his long cherished hope and desire.   His enthusiasm fell not on barren soil.   Père Urbain Guillet, one of the original covenanters of Valsainte, a man of great piety and zeal, but evidently possessing little worldly wisdom, craved permission to undertake the difficult task.   The chief obstacle in the way was the lack of funds ; but great as this obstacle might appear to others, it dwindled into insignificance in the presence of Père Urbain's faith and zeal.   Having obtained permission, he at once proceeded to select his companions, and to seek the means.   He had no difficulty in procuring the former; the latter he got in spite of difficulties.

On January 16th, 1803, after about two years' preparation, his colony came together at Amsterdam, preparatory to setting sail. At first it consisted of five priests, including Père Urbain, six lay-brothers and eight students ; but before departure the number was augmented to twenty-two by the arrival of more members of the Order.   This number was too small for the zeal of Père Urbain.   Knowing that "the vineyard of the Lord was large" in America, and the "laborers therein few," he conceived the idea of taking with him a number of young men and educating them for the priesthood.   He had no difficulty in securing young men in Amsterdam, as many were seeking an opportunity to get to America ; but, unfortunately, he was no student of human nature, and many "tares were gathered in," with a little wheat.   When his Superior, Dom Augustin, came to see him and his colony off, he remarked that he did not like the looks of those young men; poor Père Urbain was astonished, but it was not long until he discovered the meaning of his Superior's words.

The colony, consisting of forty people, set sail on May 29th, and arrived in Baltimore on September 4th, 1803. The voyage was long and full of hardships, as the provisions ran short, though Père Urbain had laid in a special store for his people, and for two months all persons on board had to subsist on two ounces of bread each a day. At Baltimore they were kindly received by M. Nagot, to whom Père Urbain had a letter of introduction, and were comfortably quartered and well entertained at the Sulpician college. But in spite of the kind reception, Père Urbain's first day in America was a sad one. Two of his Amsterdam *protégés*, and one of his own flock, who had been tainted on the way over, took advantage of the confusion in going from the ship to the college, and deserted. Père Urbain now understood the unfavorable comments of his superior.

The faculty of the Sulpician college strove to make their visitors welcome, and even offered them a permanent home in the college. Rev. Father Moranvillers, a parish priest of Baltimore, supplemented these good offices by raising money for them among his parishioners; but Père Urbain, fearing that he and his brethren might be in the way and prove a burden, expressed a desire to depart. Accordingly, after a stay of some weeks at the college, he, by the advice of the Sulpicians, started with his colony for Pigeon Hills, Adams county, Pennsylvania.

Of the trip there is no record, but it was probably made on foot, and over bad roads. The distance is fifty miles, to travel which it must have taken them three or four days. The Sulpicians and Father Moranvillers sent wagon loads of food along, and probably also some furniture.

There is considerable difference of opinion in regard to the time of arrival of the Trappists at Pigeon Hills. Father Lambing says they first went to Cambria county, Pennsylvania, and from there to Pigeon Hills. In this he is undoubtedly mistaken. Archbishop Spalding, both in his "Catholic Missions of Kentucky," and in his "Sketch of the Life, Times and Character of Bishop Flaget," gives August 15th, 1804, as the time. Bishop

Maes, probably copying from Archbishop Spalding, gives the same date.

Gaillardin,* who is the best authority to follow, as he wrote carefully and deliberately, and was probably acquainted with some of the monks who belonged to the colony and afterwards returned to Europe, and likewise had at his command the memoirs written by Fathers Marie Joseph and Vincent de Paul, says they stopped with the Sulpicians at the college some weeks, and then went to Pigeon Hills. His reference to their gathering wild fruits and nuts for food upon their arrival is evidence that they went there in autumn. Probably the correct time, therefore, is October, 1803.

Pigeon Hills† is the name given to a tract of land in the eastern portion of Adams county, Pennsylvania, near the foot of Pigeon Hills, in Oxford township. It is about ten miles from Gettysburg and about four or five from Conewago. Another name given to it, and probably a more familiar one, is the Seminary Farm. This sobriquet it earned by its having been, at various times, the location of the Seminary School. Even as far back as 1794, some young men got their preliminary education there. The farm is quite large and originally consisted of two tracts, one granted to Henry Gearnhardt, on July 26th, 1750, by the Proprietaries of Pennsylvania, and the other to Robert Lorimore, on September 19th of the same year. On September 19th, 1758, Lorimore purchased Mr. Gearnhardt's tract, and on April 4th, 1794, he sold the two tracts to a reputed monk, by name Joseph Heront, for 1000 pounds. Mr. Heront opened a school on his farm, but was probably not very successful; for after a few years he took his departure for France, leaving his property to the superior of the Sulpician college at Baltimore. At least one of his pupils, a Mr. Myers, afterwards became a Catholic priest.

The Trappists, according to Gaillardin, found a comfortable and commodious house awaiting them at Pigeon Hills. As it was autumn, and a winter and spring would have to ensue before they

---

* In preparing this paper, I have taken much of my information from Gaillardin's work entitled, "Les Trappistes," published in Paris.

† Most of my information about Pigeon Hills I have taken from John T. Riley's "History of Catholicity in Adams County."

could reap the fruits of their labor on the farm, they had for the time being to depend for the necessaries of life upon the Sulpicians and Father Moranvillers, who kept sending corn, flour and dried fruits from Baltimore. To economize the charity of their friends, they gathered wild fruits and nuts from the adjacent woods, and tried in a certain measure to subsist on them. They prepared some ground, and in the spring planted an acre of corn, three little patches of potatoes, and a garden. The students gave great trouble; they would not work, on the plea that they had to study, and likewise would not study.

On them Gaillardin lays the blame for the failure of the settlement at Pigeon Hills. They were not only non-producers, but consumed everything they could lay their hands on. The poor monks could do nothing with them; they would not expel them because they had brought them to a strange country and felt in conscience bound to support them.

Of the daily routine life of either the students or the monks Gaillardin makes no mention. Much, however, can be supplied by the imagination. His reference to the complete insubordination of the students during the absence of Père Urbain; their feasting upon meats and vegetables; their sports and games; and the patient submissiveness of the monks, gives us glimpses which we can use as corner-stones, so to speak, whereon to build fuller descriptions.

Students are proverbial for their jolly times. Place them where you will, they will try to enjoy themselves. Situated as were the searchers after lore at Pigeon Hills, they no doubt held high carnival. Short study hours and long sleeping hours, few prayers and many meals, hunting, fishing, games and gymnastics, is the programme that naturally suggests itself to one's mind in trying to picture their probable daily life.

The monks, of course, followed their rules,* and therefore lived as all other Trappist monks live. They observed perpetual silence, except when it was necessary to speak with the superior. They arose at half-past two in the morning,—Father Nerinckx says at one,—and retired at seven in the evening during winter, and at eight during summer. They took two meals a day between

---

* I give here the Trappists' rules as observed at Valsainte.

Easter and the middle of September, and one meal a day during the remainder of the year.   When two meals a day were allowed, one was taken at twelve o'clock, noon, and the other in the evening.   When only one meal a day was permitted, it was taken about three o'clock in the afternoon.   The usual quantity of bread given each monk was one pound a day ; but at the discretion of the Superior an additional ration might be granted of a kind of bread made of three parts of potatoes and twelve parts of bran, called the bread of indulgence.   In summer, when hard manual labor had to be performed, fresh vegetables were added to the diet.   Water was the only drink permissible to the healthy. A beverage made of wild or dried fruits, barley or juniper berries, was at the option of the sick.   They worked from half-past five to half-past eight in the morning, and from a little before two to half-past four in the afternoon, during the summer ; and from nine to half-past eleven in the morning, and from twelve to two in the afternoon, during winter.   During Lent they began work at half-past nine.   The intervals between the working hours were devoted to chanting the office, meditation, and probably to teaching. They dressed in a white habit, a garment in shape something like a Roman toga, and wore a cowl, which, when occasion required, was used as a covering for the head.   They slept in apartments in common, the priests in one and the lay-brothers in another ; and, when they could afford it, had each a straw mattress, a bolster, and a sheet to lie upon and a blanket to cover themselves with.

This is a synopsis of the ordinary life of a Trappist, and if we subtract a little from the privileges and add a little to the deprivations related therein, we will probably get a proximate idea of the every-day life of the Trappists at Pigeon Hills.   An anecdote related by Gaillardin illustrates their poverty and self-denial : A priest from Conewago, seeing the steward distribute bread for supper, expressed surprise at the smallness of the portions. "Sir!" said the steward to him, "this bread is very good and most nourishing ; it is not necessary to give so much of it." "My Rev. Father," responded the priest, "you will change your mind about that ; it is not here like in Europe ; weights and measures are not known here."

As far as we know, the principal events that broke in upon the austere sameness of the monks during their stay at Pigeon Hills, were the to and fro journeyings of Père Urbain to Baltimore, his preliminary trip to Kentucky, and, according to Father Nerinckx, the occasional trip of the monastery wagon to Baltimore and return.   Père Urbain must have spent much of his time on the road and in Baltimore.   He there met many of the missionary priests of the country, and there probably first heard of Kentucky. The description he got of that country placed it uppermost in his mind, and he became seized of the idea of removing his colony thither.   He, however, first visited it, taking with him Brother Placide and a native of the country as interpreter.   The lovely appearance of Kentucky in spring-time, and the persuasive appeals of Father Badin, who wanted more priests in his field of labor, joined hands with the zeal of Père Urbain in blinding him to the great obstacles in the way of removing a community so great a distance, over bad roads and through thinly settled districts, and to the drawbacks which the contemplated new home itself presented.   He was not long in making up his mind to locate in Kentucky, and at once returned for his colony, leaving Brother Placide behind to make some desirable preparations.

In the absence of any reference to sickness or death in the colony by any of the writers on the subject, we may conclude that its members enjoyed good health while at Pigeon Hills. This, unfortunately, cannot be said of them in locations subsequently chosen by Père Urbain.   In the face of this fact, and in the light of our knowledge of the failure of all his later settlements, we may safely say that he had better have remained at Pigeon Hills.   One of his principal reasons for leaving was the inability of the community to support itself there.   This, however, cannot be charged to the place, but must go to the debit side of Père Urbain's qualifications as a leader.   There was plenty of good land to farm, and there were enough men in the community to till it ; all that was wanting was a practical head.   Besides, the Sulpicians and Father Moranvillers seem to have been willing to help the institution along until it was able to take care of itself.

The colony, when it came to Pigeon Hills, probably consisted of twenty-one monks and sixteen lay-people.   Gaillardin says that twenty-two members of the Order, priests and lay-brothers, and eighteen lay-men, students and workmen, came over from France. One lay brother and two lay-men deserted upon their arrival at Baltimore. It is not likely that the Order got any recruits during the short stay at the Sulpician college, though it is on record that at least one of the students felt a call to join it. In his Life of Bishop Flaget, of Kentucky, Archbishop Spalding states that the then young candidate for Holy Orders looked upon the arrival of the Trappists in Baltimore as a stroke of Providence in his behalf, and applied to Rev. Urbain Guillet for admission into the Order, but for some reason or other did not avail himself of the favorable answer received. While at Pigeon Hills the membership of the community was considerably increased. Gaillardin says that the ranks of the renegades, who were frightened away at the prospects of a trip west were more than filled by new-comers. Who these novices were it would now be interesting to know; the only individual spoken of by Gaillardin in this connection is an old planter from San Domingo, who, having lost his reason, was taken in by Père Urbain, and by the kind treatment of the monks and the novel, quiet life, was restored to health. Father Nerinckx,* in one of his letters, speaks of meeting, in the migration west, as a member of the Order, Father Charles Guny, a former Benedictine, and his traveling companion across the ocean. Yet these are but two. In the same letter Father Nerinckx, referring to the departure of the colony from Pigeon Hills and their trip through Pennsylvania, says "the caravan consisted of thirty-seven persons, seven or eight of whom were priests." If his figures are correct, the recruits just about filled the ranks of the disaffected.

How long the Trappists remained at Pigeon Hills is a mooted question. Bishop Maes and Hon. Ben. J. Webb say one year. Gaillardin gives July, 1805, as the time of departure from Pigeon Hills; and Archbishop Spalding, the autumn of 1805 as the time of arrival in Kentucky. Rev. Father Nerinckx, who accompanied them through Pennsylvania, in a letter dated May 6th, 1806, gives the date of departure as June 10th, 1805, and as he writes from personal knowledge, and at so short an interval after the event, he must be accepted as the most credible witness. Accepting,

---

*My quotations from Father Nerinckx's letters are taken from Bishop Maes' "Life of Father Nerinckx."

then, as the most likely time of arrival that given by Gaillardin, and as the most probable time of departure that given by Father Nerinckx, the stay of the Trappists at Pigeon Hills was from October, 1803, to June 10th, 1805, or about twenty-one months.

The casual visitor to Pigeon Hills at the present day would recognize in it nothing to apprise him of the part it played in the early Catholic history of the United States. The pious zeal of Heront, the plaintive midnight chant of the monks, the carnivals of the Dutch students in the Trappists' time, and later the youthful hilarity of the seminarians, never crystallized into monuments ; and so the place must depend upon history for any distinction it may claim. And yet, what prayers have gone up to heaven from there, what penances practised, what inspirations received, what good resolutions formed ! And in antithesis, how boldly stands out the ingratitude of those heartless adventurers, if Gaillardin tells truly, who shamelessly feasted while the monks were suffering want. I cannot help but feel, however, that the poor students are made scapegoats, in a certain measure, for the incompetency of Père Urbain. No doubt they did many things which would not be tolerated in a well-conducted school ; but then there were many mitigating circumstances. Some of them, it is likely, left home with no higher motive than a love of adventure ; they were all cut off from the influence of friends and relatives ; they were away from civilization, so to speak; and they had nothing to occupy their minds but their books and sports. Their young, healthy bodies no doubt made frequent demands for food through craving appetites. Their buoyant spirits must have often overflown in games and tricks. Need we wonder at cause for complaint ! What student could withstand the temptation of truancy, for example, under similar circumstances? With an empty larder at home, with fishing creeks and game-forests that a king might envy close by, and with poor, half-starved monks for disciplinarians, what youth would not flee from the dingy, pent-up, lore-smelling study hall, to the free, exhilarating woods as an amateur Nimrod or a practical admirer of Isaak Walton?

At least all were not recalcitrant. Many of them afterwards braved the dangers and trials of a trip to Kentucky, Missouri, and Illinois, and there continued their studies under the most adverse circumstances. Such perseverance bespeaks a better spirit than deflects from the contrast between austere monks and fun-loving students.

Father Urbain's order, upon his return from Kentucky, at once to break up camp and start for the West, was received with monastic submissiveness by the monks, and with commingled approval and disapproval by the rest of the colony. Some of the students sneaked off, leaving letters of explanation behind. Others demanded recommendations to persons in Baltimore, and then openly took their departure. The hired workmen blankly refused to go west. Under these discouraging circumstances, says Gaillardin, some of Père Urbain's charitable deeds "returned to him as bread cast upon the waters." It was necessary to have a wagon built, and as the mechanics apparently had already left, there was no one to build it. Père Urbain's *protégé*, the San Domingo planter, came to his relief. Unaided he constructed a large wagon. This story, however, does not fit in with Father Nerinckx's reference to the monastery wagons making trips to Baltimore and return, nor with his statement that on account of the slow progress of the four wagons through Pennsylvania he parted company with the Trappists. It may be that the monastery wagon referred to by Father Nerinckx was really owned by the Sulpicians or by Father Moranvillers, or the Trappists may have had three wagons, and required the fourth to convey all that they desired to take with them.

The route they traveled through Pennsylvania was the old state or turnpike road by way of Gettysburg, Chambersburg, McConnellstown, Bedford, Somerset, Union and Brownsville. At Brownsville they sold their horses and wagon or wagons and bought two flat-boats, for which they paid $12.00. On these they placed themselves and goods, and floated down the river to Pittsburg. That this is the route they took can scarcely be doubted. Gaillardin simply tells us that they went on foot until they got to the Monongahela River, where they took flat-boats ; but Father Nerinckx says he left them at Bedford, where he bought a horse and saddle for $75.00 and started ahead by himself. Now, as the state road passed through Bedford, and as there was only one through road in southern Pennsylvania at that time, there can be no doubt about the road they traveled. Brownsville was in those days a kind of port, at which most travelers westward changed their mode of travel from that by land to that by water. Hence we may conclude that it was there the Trappists bought their flat-boats.

Probably about two weeks were required to go from Pigeon Hills to Brownsville. Stretches of twenty miles were made between camping places. When regular stopping places could be reached, if even by an extra effort, they put up at an inn; but generally they had to content themselves with such comfort as a barn afforded, or as mother earth gives her children, under heaven's diamond studded canopy. In addition to their usual diet they were allowed butter, according to Father Nerinckx; and butter, milk and cheese, according to Gaillardin, the latter being the specified traveling diet. Somewhere between McConnellstown and Bedford their wagon broke down, and they were detained a day or two. It was then that Father Nerinckx became impatient, and after having waited for them at Bedford a day and a half, started ahead by himself. While traveling, silence was observed as far as conversation was concerned, although all had the privilege of talking with Father Nerinckx. The office was, however, daily chanted and prayers were said aloud. What a ripple of wonder and excitement must have passed over the adjacent country as this processsion of white-robed monks, chanting and praying, leisurely moved along the highway.

The Monongahela, to the great disappointment of Father Urbain, did not even furnish as easy or as rapid a means of transit as the turnpike had furnished. Instead of making twenty miles a day, they now with difficulty covered fifteen. As the water was quite shallow in places, the boats frequently stuck fast on sandbanks, and all hands had to jump out and help push them off. In this way they finally arrived at Pittsburg, where, owing to the necessity of making considerable change in their river out-fit, they remained for some days.

The principal cause of detention was the unloading and reloading of their goods, as it was necessary to replace their small boats by larger ones. This exchange so drained their treasury that Père Urbain was afraid to venture the further expense of hiring a pilot and some rowers, as apparently was the custom in traveling on the Ohio, and with his monks undertook the voyage, notwithstanding their inexperience. He, however, took the pre-

caution of informing himself about the Ohio river by interviews
with some Pittsburgians, and as a reference for emergencies
purchased a popular almanac in which its author claimed to
lay down explicitly all the necessary instructions for navigating
the Ohio. Unfortunately, what sounded nice in theory did not
work well in practice. Fallen trees obstructed their way, sandbanks and whirlpools were encountered, and sometimes the
swiftness of the current would hurl them against the bank or an
island. On one occasion, one of the boats sprang a-leak and
rapidly began to fill. All on board became terror-stricken, and
cried for help. Their brothers on the other boat, being too far
away to bring them timely assistance, called to them to pull for
the bank, which they fortunately succeeded in doing. Having
landed, they unloaded by the light of a candle, for it was now night,
and temporarily plugged up the holes. On the following day the
boat was thoroughly repaired and the amateur scullers again entrusted to it their lives.

For six weeks the poorly fed monks and students rowed and
floated down the Ohio, apparently running the gauntlet of death
safely at every turn, and yet gradually and surely falling into his
clutches by constantly inhaling the poisonous effluvia arising from
the swamps along the banks of the river. When they finally
arrived at Louisville in the early part of September, 1805, all
hands were sick, and some unto death.

A most cordial reception awaited them. People from all over
the country flocked to the landing place with their wagons,
anxious to render aid. Those who arrived first loaded up the
baggage and hauled it to its destination. Later comers, finding
no more baggage, contended with each other for the privilege of
conveying the monks. Soon baggage, monks and all were safely
landed at a farm house on Pottinger's Creek, in the northern part
of Nelson County, about thirty miles south of Louisville, about
ten north of Bardstown, and about a mile from Holy Cross Church,
where Father Badin then had his headquarters. The property
belonged to a pious lady, who offered the use of it to the Trappists, as long as they might wish to remain, reserving for her own
use only the product of every fourth or fifth fruit tree. Gaillardin
describes the house as a frame building, ornamented by a portico,
and says there were several log houses close by, which could be

used as work-shops. Once at the house, the ovation began. Every farmer had come with his offering, bringing flour, Indian corn, vegetables, potatoes and even poultry. Everything was in abundance. The trees in the orchard adjoining the house were laden with fruit, and Brother Placide's garden was in a most flourishing condition. All were made comfortable, and poverty, for once, had to make a bed-fellow of plenty. But comfort and abundance could not stay the ravages of disease, nor shut out the grim visage of death. Of the entire community but two could present themselves in choir, a religious and a postulant, and one of these, the religious, had hemorrhages from the lungs. Father Badin took two of the priests, who were most dangerously ill, namely, Fathers Dominic and Basil, to his own house, and lavished the greatest care on them. They, however, both soon died. At the farm house all recovered, except Father Robert, whose demise followed closely upon that of his brothers. Poor Father Urbain, himself sick, was almost heart-broken at the loss of his priests. When the news of the first death was brought to him, he tried to bear up under the affliction; but when, two days later, he heard of Father Basil's death, he turned his face to the wall, and gave vent to his grief in tears.

Gaillardin ascribes the dreadful visitation to imprudence, in eating all kinds of fruit after long exposure and want, on the one hand, and, on the other, to the too sudden change from the hardships and fatigues of travel to the ordinary austere life of a Trappist. He especially exonerates the climate. Father Nerinckx, in his common-sense way of looking at things, comes nearer the truth. He says, had he come down the Ohio, as the Trappists did, he would likely have been sick with the same fever.

The clouds that hung over the colony at Pottinger's Creek, after its arrival, were soon dispersed. On the 10th of October, 1805, re-inforcements arrived in the persons of Father Marie Joseph, four other religious, and a priest from Canada, who came to take the habit. Sorrow at once gave place to joy, and discouragement to confidence. A school was opened, and many young men of the country availed themselves of the opportunity to get an education, even though they could spare but a few hours a day from their work. Over twenty children, says Father Nerinckx, were adopted, and the monks bound themselves to educate them and sustain them, until they were twenty-one years of age, without recompense. With mental training was combined mechanical, every boy having to learn a trade; and at the end of the term the boys were to have the choice of going out into the world or becoming postulants. The only obstacle in the way of the success of the school was the inability of the monks to speak English. Yet teachers and scholars struggled along with admirable forbearance.

As yet, Father Urbain had not chosen a permanent location. Plenty of land had been offered, but, it seems, none suited. Toward the latter part of 1806, he heard of a fine tract of land for sale, on Casey Creek, in Casey County. He purchased it, and sent a colony to take charge of it under the leadership of Father Marie Joseph. Father Nerinckx says the tract contained 1500 acres of land, and cost $6000. He describes it as a fine piece of land, well situated, and well watered by streams, and locates it 34 miles from Father Badin's plantation. The colony, consisting of thirteen members, three of whom were Belgians, one a Rev. Mr. Doncke, and another Mr. Henry Rysselman, who later became a Jesuit brother, left Pottinger's Creek, just before Christmas. The weather was extremely cold, and the trip to the new home difficult, on account of the wildness of the country through which they had to pass. When they lit their camp-fires at night, says Gaillardin, all kinds of wild beasts prowled around, attracted by the light and warmth. The hardships did not end with the trip itself. There was little, if any, clear land on the tract, and it is questionable whether there was even a house upon it. When Father Nerinckx visited the place, in 1807, he found fourteen monks "lodged in a double-frame cabin about as large as a ten-horse stable," to use his own words, and which was not even water-proof. Whether or not they built it themselves he does not say. As the warmth of spring thawed out the ground, and they began to dig up the land which they had cleared during the winter, snakes of all kinds, but particularly rattle-snakes, appeared in great numbers. In two days, says Gaillardin, they killed more than 800. Wolves, too, kept prowling about. Yet in spite of all obstacles, the new settlement prospered under the spirited leadership of Father Marie Joseph, who brought to his monastic life the endurance and resoluteness to which he had been inured as a grenadier in the French army. At the time of Father Nerinckx's visit, the monks were already engaged in building a saw-mill. Their comforts, if one can speak of the comforts of a Trappist, were, it is true, as yet very few. Father Nerinckx says "the dormitory, refectory and church" were all in one, and the only other rooms in the house were an apartment for the lay-brothers and a small place for storing provisions. The members of the community all slept on the bare floor. Father Nerinckx and his guide were given the storage room, and Father Nerinckx had a bag of oats to sleep upon. In a short time, however, great improvements were made, and Casey Creek was so transformed, according to Gaillardin, as to merit the appellation of the "place of rest." A chapel was built and a small congregation gathered together from the thinly settled country around, and the name of St. Bernard given to the parish thus formed. Only seven or eight Catholic families lived in close enough proximity to attend mass there, and they had formerly gone to St. Mary's, in Marion county. Some of the Protestant families, however, who lived close by, and who had probably no church of their own, attended services in the chapel. In this way there was generally a good attendance at Mass, both on Sundays and feast days.

In 1807, at the time of Father Nerinckx's visit, the community at Casey Creek had received two novices, one an Irishman and the other an American, and one member had probably gone back to Pottinger's Creek, for Father Nerinckx says they then numbered fourteen people at Casey Creek. How long Father Marie Joseph and his colony remained at Casey Creek is not positively known, as Father Nerinckx does not refer to the place after 1807; and Gaillardin says nothing about the abandonment, although he leads us to infer that it was not before 1809. Inasmuch as Père Urbain consulted Father Marie Joseph about moving to Louisiana, we may conclude that both settlements were kept up until the departure from Kentucky. Indirect evidence of the same fact are the frequent allusions which Mr. Henry Rysselman is said to have made in after life to his residence at Casey Creek, as a Trappist, until 1809.

In regard to the mother colony at Pottinger's there is little more to be said, and nothing, from a worldly point of view, that would add lustre to the name of *Les Trappistes*. Judging from the tone of

Father Nerinckx's letters to Bishop Carroll, its history can be read in the words, *want, patient suffering* and *failure*. Farther Urbain had not yet learned wisdom nor forsaken his Bohemian ways. He was ever looking out for a good location and never making use of present opportunities. Whether or not he ever owned land at Pottinger's Creek I have not discovered, but probably he did not. The farm on which the colony was located was at their command as long as they wished to remain, and Gaillardin positively states that they did not own it.

The graves of five priests and three lay-brothers in the churchyard adjoining Holy Cross Church are a sad commentary on the four years' sojourn of the Trappists in Kentucky. Who the two additional priests and the three lay-brothers were, and when they died, is not stated. A reference to the records of Holy Cross Church, or to the tombstones, if there were any, might reveal the names and dates. The school was probably the redeeming feature of the settlement at Pottinger's; for the influence which its light exerted upon the future generations of Kentucky is acknowledged by Hon. Ben. J. Webb, in his "Century of Catholicity in Kentucky." It, however, had the great difficulty to contend with of a difference of languages between teacher and pupil. The monks did not learn English readily, and even after many years' residence in the country spoke it with great difficulty. To overcome this obstacle in the way of the usefulness of the Order, was the gordian knot which constantly challenged Père Urbain's ingenuity. Need we wonder, then, that while on a business trip to Baltimore, in 1808, he was persuaded, by the eloquent tongue of a son of Erin, named Mullanphy, to again change his base of operations and migrate to Louisiana,* where his own language was spoken, and he would receive encouragement and protection from the government. Mullanphy offered him a house in Louisiana as a gift, if it suited the purposes of the Trappists, and if not, at least as a temporary home. Père Urbain triumphantly returned to Kentucky, laid the matter before his community, took counsel with Father Marie Joseph, and with him started on a visit to Louisiana in November, 1808.

---

*It must be remembered that at the time referred to here Louisiana took in nearly all that portion of country west of the Mississippi.

We can readily imagine what a trip through the West implied at that time, especially if taken in winter. Yet Fathers Urbain and Marie Joseph arrived at St. Louis before Christmas. Both were delighted with the prospects in Louisiana. According to Gaillardin, an old Parisian named Jarrot, who had formerly been a steward with the Sulpicians in Baltimore, and who now lived at Cahokia, a small town in Illinois, about five miles south-east of St. Louis, offered Père Urbain a large prairie enclosed by a dense forest, and situated about six miles from St. Louis. It was then called the Cantine, and contained excellent land, but was most unhealthy. The Jesuit Fathers had occupied it at one time and had a church there, but had to give it up on account of the fatality of the climate. In olden times it had been an Indian burial ground, and it was dotted over with seven or eight pyramids built of earth and measuring about 160 feet in circumference and 100 feet in height. At present the place is called Monks' Mound. Father Urbain accepted M. Jarrot's offer, and having completed his business affairs in St. Louis, prepared for his return trip to Kentucky. Meanwhile Father Marie Joseph had already initiated himself in missionary work, for which he saw a good field in St. Louis, and for which also he had a special taste. He arrived in St. Louis on the vigil of Christmas, and announced at once that he would celebrate midnight Mass. The happy tidings spread rapidly, and Father Marie Joseph, when the hour for celebration arrived, found himself in the midst of quite a large congregation. The unfortunate people were overjoyed at the sight of a priest, as they had been left without one for some time on account of the wickedness of many among them who had mobbed and driven out the Jesuit Fathers.* Gaillardin tells us a story illustrative of the perversity of the people of St. Louis at that time. He says a man sold his wife for a bottle of whisky; the purchaser sold her for a horse; and in a short time she was again sold for a pair of oxen. Yet Father Marie Joseph was kindly received. He was implored to remain, and was asked to take the last sacraments to the sick. Crowds of people accompanied the Holy Viaticum with pious reverence.

---

*Gaillardin says that some of the Jesuit Fathers were murdered and others tied to logs and floated down the Mississippi.

As Father Marie Joseph had, however, come on a visit only, he could not remain. He promised to return soon, and departed to join Father Urbain. They started on the return trip in January, 1809.

If the journey out had been difficult, that going back was much more so. Winter had now fully set in, deep snows had fallen, roads were drifted shut, and in many places bridges had been swept away, and the ice was not strong enough to carry. In these emergencies Father Marie Joseph resorted to a trick, which he had learned from the natives, namely, felling a tree across the stream and using it for a bridge. But as his traveling companion was somewhat stiffened by disease, he invariably had to carry all the baggage and provisions over first, and then return to help him across. Sometimes streams had to be crossed again and again, at others freshets had suddenly so swollen creeks as to make them impassable, and the travelers had to go around them. Finally, after much patient suffering and toil, they arrived at Pottinger's Creek.

The mandate at once was given to prepare for the journey to Louisiana. It being deemed more convenient to travel by water than by land, the first thing requisite was boats; and as Père Urbain did not wish to undergo the expense of hiring professsional boat-builders, he set to work all the brothers who had any practical knowledge of carpentry. Among them was Brother Palemon, an Irishman and an ex-colonel, probably the Irishman of whom Father Nerinckx speaks as having joined the Order at Casey Creek.

About nine miles from the monastery was Salt River, which flows into the Ohio. Though a small stream, it sometimes suddenly swells into an immense river, and as suddenly collapses. The Trappists decided to build their boats on its banks, hoping to be ready with the rise which was then expected, and to float down to the Ohio on its borrowed impulse. In order to push the work as rapidly as possible, a temporary cabin was put up, and the workmen camped at the place, returning to the monastery only on Sunday. The task was soon completed and the flood came. Farmers flocked around to see them embark, and many accompanied them as far as the Ohio.

According to Archbishop Spalding, Father Urbain did not

accompany the colony down the Ohio, but crossed the country to St. Louis, hoping to arrive there in time to send Canadian *voyageurs* down the river to meet his brethren at the junction and row the boats up the Mississippi.

When the monks arrived at Cairo, they looked in vain for the boatmen, and hence had to debark and wait. They camped on the Illinois side of the river, says Spalding, and built a temporary cabin, which they occupied for three weeks. Gaillardin says they waited eight days, and erected an altar under a large tree on which Mass was daily celebrated and before which the office was chanted. He dwells at some length upon the presence of the astonished Indians in their savage costume and with their war paint on. Tired waiting and fearing that the promised aid might not arrive, the monks at last, says Archbishop Spalding, prepared to ascend the river by themselves. They fixed masts on their boats and rigged them out with sail; but as they were ready to start, the boatmen appeared. To the practised eye of the *voyageurs* it was at once apparent that the improvised sailing vessels could not ascend the Mississippi. The masts and sails had, therefore, to be taken down. Even rowing was impracticable, and the boats had to be towed by ropes. In this tedious manner they finally reached St. Louis, one month after leaving the junction.

At St. Louis, Father Marie Joseph and the colony parted company, the former at once assuming his missionary duties, and the latter proceeding to the location which Père Urbain had chosen for them. According to Gaillardin this was Monks' Mound, which has already been described, and according to Archbishop Spalding it was a farm near Florissant, in the northern part of St. Louis county, Missouri. Spalding says the monks continued their slow progress up the Mississippi River to its junction with the Missouri, and then up the Missouri to Florissant, where they landed. At the entrance of the Missouri into the Mississippi the current was very strong, and the ropes broke. None but the disabled were in the boats at the time, and the monks on shore had to look on helplessly while their sick brethren were rapidly carried down the river. After twenty-four hours, however, the boats were checked in their wild progress, and the difficult ascent was again begun. At last they debarked and proceeded to the farm. Here they remained until 1810, when they removed to Monks' Mound. It is strange that Gaillardin says nothing about this settlement. Archbishop Spalding got his information from an old gentleman who had lived with the Trappists for many years, and who, therefore, ought to be a good witness. Yet, as he depended on memory for the reminiscence he gave, he must not be too readily accepted. Besides, he may have confounded the missionary work of Father Marie Joseph, and possibly some of his brethren at Florissant, with a location of the entire colony. Father Marie Joseph's memoirs might throw some light on the subject.

At Monks' Mound the Trappists tried hard to make a permanent establishment. They built seventeen little cabins, one for a church, one for a chapel, one for a refectory, and one indeed for every purpose that might suggest itself. These buildings were probably of logs and very primitive in their construction. Gaillardin says the place looked like an army's camp, from which we may infer that the cabins were very small. The history of this settlement is the same as that at Pigeon Hills, Pottinger's and Casey Creek, only more gloomy in proportion as it was farther removed from civilization, and as the poor monks were more worn out by disease and hardships. Though the community remained there three or four years, nothing is positively known of their doings, except that they strictly observed their rules. Gaillardin, who is usually prolix in his descriptions, dismisses the subject with the statement, in one place, that they went there and built a number of cabins, and in another, that the settlement was a failure. Archbishop Spalding, too, has scarcely anything to say about the place. He tells us that they were there until March, 1813, and that during their stay two priests and five lay-brothers were consigned to their final resting place. Had Father Nerinckx been near, we would know much more. It was the ambition of Père Urbain to carry the Gospel to the Indians ; but in this, as in all his other undertakings in America, he failed. Had he been able to maintain his institution at Monks' Mound, he might finally have accomplished what he desired, for the Indians were his next door neighbors, and were quite friendly with the monks. It was, however, impossible for the community to support itself, and besides, its members were rapidly dying off. When the colony broke up in the spring of 1813, there were probably not more than nine or ten members left. How many had come from Kentucky, and whether any members had entered the Order at Monks' Mound, is not known. We are equally in the dark about what became of the boys whom the monks had pledged themselves to educate at Pottinger's. Probably they remained with their parents and friends in Kentucky. The command to break up camp at Monks' Mound came from Dom Augustin, the Superior of the entire Order, who had arrived in New York in the beginning of 1813, and who had been informed of the condition of Father Urbain's colony. Gaillardin says that Dom Augustin directed Father Urbain to join Father Vincent de Paul's colony in Maryland. He tells us nothing about the departure from Illinois, nor about the trip East, and indeed does not again mention Father Urbain's name until he speaks of the final departure of the Trappists from the United States. Archbishop Spalding enters into some details about the colony's exit from Illinois, its trip down the Mississippi and up the Ohio, but consigns it to oblivion at Pittsburg. He tells us that the property at Monks' Mound was disposed of, that some of the lay-brothers remained in the West, that Père Urbain and his brethren descended the Mississippi in a keel-boat, and that in ascending the Ohio they encountered a great flood and almost fell into the hands of pirates. The information, however, that we would most like to have, namely, how many monks went East, who they were, and whither they went from Pittsburg, he fails to give us. Father Vincent de Paul, in his memoirs, states that Père Urbain and his brethren joined his colony in Maryland shortly before its departure for New York, which was some time in the early part of 1814.

A tradition among the people of the northern part of Cambria county, Pennsylvania, would lead us to believe that Père Urbain and his comrades did not go directly to Maryland, but made one final effort to locate in Rev. Dr. Gallitzin's district. That the Trappists had a settlement in Cambria county cannot be doubted, as a number of men who saw them there give testimony of the fact. There is, however, no known record of the matter. Father Lambing's statement that Père Urbain's colony was in Cambria county before it located at Pigeon Hills, is undoubtedly erroneous. Possibly Dr. Gallitzin's letters may throw some light on the subject at some future time. For the present we must be satisfied with tradition and speculation.

Some years ago two very old gentlemen of Cambria county gave me their reminiscences about the Trappists in Northern Cambria. Although many of their statements are contradictory, some noteworthy information is scattered through them.

Mr. Bernard Byrnes, one of the old gentlemen, said that the Trappists came to Northern Cambria* in 1811, and left in March, 1813, and that they came *from Loretto* to their location, near the present sight of Carrolltown; that they were four or five in number, one of whom was a priest, and that they spoke German; that the brothers were low, heavy-set, awkward men, the priest tall, rather heavy and likewise awkward, and that all were of a dark complexion; that they ate but two meals a day, partook of neither meat nor butter, but subsisted on a paste made of flour and water, and on boiled potatoes and turnips; that his father and others gave them oats wherewith to feed a cow, which they had brought with them; that they located in the woods, on a small spot of clear land, about the size of a large potato patch, and that they planted some potatoes around the house; that the men in the neighborhood were allowed to hear mass in their chapel, but not the women, and that he himself frequently heard mass in their house; that the altar in their chapel was very plain, and made of boards; that the priest often traveled backward and forward between the settlement and Loretto, and frequently stopped with his father over-night. Mr. Luke McGuire, the other old gentleman, stated that the Trappists came to their location in Cambria county in 1814, and remained there a few years; that they were five in number; that they could not speak English, but spoke French; that they lived in a wooden house, to help to build which Dr. Gallitzin had sent members of his parish; that they were accessory to their own deaths, as they exposed themselves to cold and wet; that they started back to France, and that he hauled some of their baggage and one sick brother as far as Bedford, where he left them with a Frenchman; that he had a letter from Dr. Gallitzin to Father Hayden at Bedford; that when they got to Bedford they found the town full of soldiers on their way to Erie; that the Luthers, who were

---

*The land on which the Trappists located in Cambria county belonged at the time to Jacob Downing, a merchant of Philadelphia.

other old settlers of Cambria county, hauled some of their baggage, boxed up, to Loretto in sleds; and that the sick brother was afterwards reported to have died on the way, between Bedford and Lancaster; that two more brothers died at Lancaster, and that all three were buried there.

Both old gentlemen related interesting anecdotes about the monks, which I must omit. What I have cited from my notes, taken almost word for word, as related by them, is sufficient to place beyond dispute the fact that the Trappists were in the northern part of Cambria county, Pennsylvania, and that they were there some time between 1811 and 1814. For their identification nothing is wanting but recorded evidence. I myself feel morally certain that they were Père Urbain and his brethren. The restless disposition of the priest, as described by Mr. Byrnes, exactly fits the character of Père Urbain; and the broken-down, sickly condition of his brothers, implied in Mr. McGuire's account of their departure from Cambria county, is what we would expect in men who had undergone years of hardship. But the strongest argument of all is the fact that it could have been no one else. The whereabouts of all the Trappists who had come to America can be acccounted for between the spring of 1813 and the early part of 1814, except in the case of Père Urbain and his brothers. They left Monks' Mound in March, 1813, and came to Father Vincent de Paul's settlement, in Maryland, in 1814. At the longest, it ought not to have taken more than two months to make the trip. It is quite reasonable to suppose that the interim was spent on the Allegheny Mountains. Dr. Gallitzin may have accidently met them in Pittsburg and taken them to his mountain home; or the little band may have sought out the great missionary. Princess Gallitzin, the reverend doctor's mother, had been a friend and protectress of the Trappists during the troublesome times in Europe,—how natural for this stray remnant of the refugee colony to seek out the illustrious son of their former benefactress.

The history of the Trappists' settlement in Cambria county is a fitting epilogue to the story of Père Urbain's work in America. Its very obscurity adapts it to its place. Much of what Messrs. Byrnes and McGuire have told us about it was no doubt dimmed by time and colored by imagination. Their dates and figures, though probably wrong, serve, nevertheless, as landmarks by which we may find the truth. Mr. McGuire's reference to the soldiers in Bedford gives a reliable clew to the time of departure, placing that event in the latter part of 1813 or the beginning of 1814. Though Messrs. McGuire and Byrnes both state that the Trappists were in Cambria county two or three years, it is probable that they were there only from about May until December in 1813. Mr. McGuire says they came in Spring, and both he and Mr. Byrnes state that they left in cold weather.

The report preserved for us by Mr. McGuire about the death of the three brothers and their burial at Lancaster, must have had its origin in the vivid imagination of some sympathetic individual who had observed their delicate health. It is not likely that the monks even passed through Lancaster. Mr. McGuire left them at Bedford, and as they were on their way to Maryland, the most direct and convenient road would have led them much south of Lancaster. What sad thoughts must have pervaded Père Urbain's mind as he repassed the same road, with his small, sickly band, over which he had led the large, stout-hearted colony nine years before. According to Father Vincent de Paul's memoirs, he arrived in St. Mary's county, Maryland, some time in the early part of 1814. Nothing is said about the number of men he brought with him, nor about their condition. Both himself and his men were merged in Père Vincent de Paul's colony, and we do not again hear his name mentioned by anyone until the final departure from New York.

Père Vincent de Paul, according to his own memoirs, set sail from Bordeaux on June 10th, 1812, and arrived at Boston on August 6th. Strange to say, Gaillardin gives the time of arrival as June 6th, 1811. This is probably a misprint, for Gaillardin appears to be a most careful writer. Père Vincent brought with him three members of his Order, one sister and two brothers. The intention had been to bring five sisters, who were to introduce into America the female branch of the Order, but only one was successful in getting a passport out of France. The little band was kindly received at Boston by the pastor of the town, Father Matignon, who urged them to remain in the diocese of Bishop Cheverus. Père Vincent de Paul, however, had orders to locate along the coast near Baltimore. After remaining at Boston long enough to provide a temporary home for his brethren and get some needed rest, he started for Baltimore on foot. The Archbishop of Baltimore received him kindly and showed a disposition to aid him in his undertakings, but was evidently embarrassed for want of means. After a short while, a farm belonging to the Jesuits was placed at his service as a temporary home. He accepted it and wrote to Boston for the two brothers, making arrangements at the same time to have the sister placed in a convent there. Where this farm was located is not stated, but it is probably in the north-eastern part of St. Mary's county, Md., and near the place where he afterwards bought some land and established his colony. Meanwhile, a wealthy Baltimorean convert to the Catholic faith offered him a tract of land, containing 2000 acres, on the mountains in Pennsylvania. It was situated near Milford, in what is now Pike county. The generous donor offered to send his son along as a guide if Father Vincent desired to go and view it. Father Vincent accepted the proffered services and at once started on his trip. His visit must have been very brief, and his inspection very unsatisfactory, for upon his return he immediately made preparation for a more prolonged visit. This time he took with him two young men who had applied for admission into the Order, permitting them to make the journey as part of their novitiate. The two brothers were left on the farm in Maryland.

A sentence in Père Vincent's memoirs conveys the idea that this second trip was made from Philadelphia. He states that the whole journey was made in silence and on foot, and in the next sentence, referring to Milford, he locates it as sixty miles from Philadelphia, the starting point of the journey. Possibly this refers only to that portion of the trip which was made on foot. If Philadelphia was the *bona fide* starting-point, the two novices were probably Philadelphians. Father Vincent de Paul was in Philadelphia in August, 1813, at which time he stopped with Bishop Egan, at old St. Joseph's, for at least one week. He baptized Rosetta De Silva on August 22d, Jane Havelan on August 29th, and John Paul on August 30th. It was then that he started on his second trip to Pike county, for he says in his memoirs that they made the journey in summer and in very warm weather. The only place along the route of which he speaks is Milford. Here he celebrated mass on a Sunday, and had for his congregation all the people of the town, though there was not a Catholic among them. After mass the two young men gave some instructions on the Catholic faith. The people requested him to remain among them, and offered to take up a subscription for his support. One man promised to give fifty dollars. Father Vincent, however, had not come as a missionary, but to establish his Order. He accordingly proceeded with his companions to the farm, or, more correctly speaking, tract of forest land. The exact location of this piece of land is not known, but might be discovered through the aid of some of the oldest residents of Pike county. It was on the mountain not far from Milford, nor very far from the Delaware River ; hence it must have been north-west of Milford.

Upon their arrival at the place, Père Vincent and his companions built a temporary cabin out of branches of trees. In it they sought shelter at night, and from it they made their excursions through the dense forests to inspect the land. As a guide, they usually had a boy or young man from the neighboring country. One day, when Père Vincent and the boy were out together, they lost their way, and were overtaken by night. Seeing a large flat rock close by, Père Vincent suggested that they camp on it over-night. "If we do," said the boy, "we will be devoured by bears." Soon after, such unearthly howls went up from the dense woods around that Father Vincent was glad to continue his search for the cabin until he found it. Two weeks were spent in examining the tract of land, and two weeks of hardship they were to Père Vincent and his novices. The bare earth had to serve them as beds, and during the first few days they had to depend on wild fruits for their sustenance. On the fourth day a Jew and a Protestant came to their relief with potatoes. The Jew remained with them over Sunday and attended mass, evincing, says Père Vincent, a great interest in the Catholic faith. During the two weeks Père Vincent said mass several times in the cabin. He gave religious instructions to a family consisting of father, mother and three children, and had hopes of receiving them into the Catholic Church ; but owing to the interference of a woman from Milford he was disappointed. One day his companions and himself made a cross and carried it in procession for the distance of a mile, singing psalms all the way. The latter part of the route they walked in their bare feet, though rattle-snakes abounded, and at its terminus they planted the cross. Père Vincent soon discovered that the tract of land at his refusal was not a good sight for a Trappist monastery. It consisted of rocks and marshes, was over-run by snakes and wild beasts, and was too far from large towns and too difficult of approach. He would gladly have remained as a missionary, but, bound as he was by his vows to the interest of his Order, he could not do so. In company with his novices, he accordingly retraced his steps to the shores of Maryland. As on his way up, so on the return trip he tarried for a few days with Bishop Egan at old St. Joseph's, in Philadelphia. He is recorded as having baptized Ann Elizabeth and John Sturges, twins, on October 4th, 1813, Mary Ann Shields and Margaret Dorothea on October 10th, and Mary Ann Norbeck and Edward Russell on October 11th. He acquainted Bishop Egan of the ripening vineyard in the northern part of the State, and advised him to send evangelical laborers into it; but the Bishop had no one to send.

The part of Maryland to which Père Vincent went was the north-east of St. Mary's county, the most southern county of the State. He describes the place as being situated on the coast near the Patuxent River, and not far from the Potomac. The Archbishop of Baltimore and the Sulpicians had long since advised him to establish his colony there. Many statemants in his memoirs would lead one to believe that it was there he left the two brothers, and that he began the settlement before he made his trips to Pike county, Pennsylvania. This view gains additional strength from the fact that three brothers, who arrived from France at the end of 1812, or in the beginning of 1813, are said to have joined the colony in Maryland.

At what time the monks gave up the temporary home on the Jesuit farm and bought land of their own, and what distance the two places were apart, I have not been able to learn. Père Vincent says that land was bought and its clearance at once begun. The colony lodged with a private family in the neigh-borhood until it had time to put up quarters for itself. With the aid of the negroes of the vicinity, who, Père Vincent says, were all Catholics, the brothers completed a log-house eighteen feet square in a short time. Afterwards a chapel was begun, but it was probably never finished. During the winter sufficient land was prepared to make a potato-patch, a garden and a nursery. Père Vincent speaks in terms of praise of the fertility of the soil; hence, no doubt, the efforts at farming were successful. The colony was doing well, but as spring approached unlooked for enemies sprang up, which, as time wore on into summer, grew to be almost unbearable. The effluvia from the marshes along the river breeded disease and pestiferous insects, and the great heat of the summer was most oppressive. The colony, however, held out for one season. Toward the end of 1813 it was augmented by the arrival of Père Urbain and his comrades. Father Vincent says that Père Urbain joined his colony just before its departure for New York. The only clew I have been able to find to the time when the Maryland settlement broke up, is in the baptismal records of St. Joseph's Church, Philadelphia. Father Vincent de Paul is there recorded as having baptised Sarah Ann Johnson on January 18th, 1814, John Peter Scott, adult, on January 23, and Peter Robert Mayot on the same day. These baptisms he must have administered when on his way to New York. Some time before the departure from Maryland two brothers died and were buried in the orchard close to the house. Their surviving brethren, fearing that their graves might be desecrated when the property fell into other hands, before leaving took up the bodies at night, and on the following day buried them in a cemetery at the nearest village. Possibly these were some of Father Urbain's sick comrades.

As already intimated, Dom Augustin, the superior of the Order, and its rescuer in 1790, had come to America, to himself try to establish his Order. After a most unhappy voyage, during which he had been cast into prison at Martinique, upon the accusation of one of his own men, he arrived in New York in the early part of 1813, bringing with him several English and Irish monks from Lulworth. He at once cast about for a site for his monastery, and after a short while found a suitable property, which he purchased for ten thousand dollars. He called to New York the colony in Maryland, thus gathering into one house all the Trappists in America, except Father Marie Joseph, who was still on the mission in Missouri. Barely enough survived to make one community. The exact location of the monastery I have not been able to discover, but Father Vincent says it was situated on the plains not far from New York City.

While looking after the interest of his own house, Dom Augustin did not forget the Sister who was patiently waiting at Boston for an opportunity to establish the female branch of the Order. He had her come to New York, procured for her a house near the monastery, and thus enabled her to establish a convent, though necessarily on a very small scale. Probably other sisters of the Order had meanwhile come over from Europe, and it is not unlikely that recruits had come in from among the natives of the country. Père Vincent de Paul was appointed chaplain to the convent, and also to an Ursuline convent about three and a quarter miles from the monastery. He said mass at both places on Sundays and feast-days. At the Ursuline convent he received three Protestant young ladies, boarding scholars, into the Catholic Church.

For a while the Trappist monastery near New York flourished. Dom Augustin took charge of thirty-three children, most of whom were orphans, to feed, clothe and educate gratuitously. Many persons, both Catholic and Protestant, visited the place, attracted, no doubt, in a great measure by curiosity. Many conversions to Catholicity followed, says Gaillardin, and among those who embraced the faith were some Protestant clergymen. An especially large crowd was drawn to the vicinity of the monastery on the feast of Corpus Christi, when the monks, having erected altars, at intervals, in a large field, carried the Blessed Sacrament around it in public procession. In spite, however, of apparent success, the monastery could not gain a permanent foot-hold at New York. Unexpected opposition sprang up, money was wanting, and there was a yearning on the part of many of the monks to return to France. In the Fall of 1814 it was decided to return to Europe, and steps were at once taken to do so. The members were divided into three groups. One, consisting of twelve members, including the Sisters, was taken charge of by Dom Augustin himself; another, numbering fifteen persons, was placed under the guidance of Père Urbain; and the third, composed of seven people, under the direction of Father Vincent de Paul. The first and second set sail in October, 1814, in two separate vessels. The third remained behind to close up the temporal affairs of the monastery, and did not leave New York until May, 1815, when it set sail for Halifax on its way to Europe. At Halifax the ship was detained, and when it departed for Europe Père Vincent was by accident left ashore. Looking upon the matter as providential, and knowing of no way to get to his brethren, he began at once to devote himself to a missionary life, in which he continued for many years. His life has been recently published by Miss Amy Pope, of Charlottetown, Prince Edward Island, to whom I am under obligations for a transcript of part of his memoirs.

The only Trappist left in the United States, after 1815, was Père Marie Joseph, who continued his missionary work in Missouri until 1820, when he likewise returned to France. At the request of his superior he published memoirs of his work in America. These I have not been able to get the use of, although a copy of them is extant in Canada.

Catholicity in the Three Lower Counties;

OR,

THE PLANTING OF THE CHURCH IN DELAWARE.

[Read before the AMERICAN CATHOLIC HISTORICAL SOCIETY OF PHILADELPHIA, Tuesday Evening, March 23, 1886, by CHARLES H. A. ESLING.]

MY good friends, you must not expect to-night any essay of an elaborate and grandly heroic character or any narration of mighty achievements. It is a simple little pastoral tale, and yet it has an element of grandeur all its own; for this story of the quiet, every-day life of a few scattered rustics in a new and thinly populated country involves within itself the story of the planting of the Church of Jesus Christ in a sovereign State, albeit the smallest, of the American union. Such is generally God's way. The weak things of this world doth He use to confront the powerful, and the foolish things to confound the wise. The shepherds that "came and wondering eyed in Bethlehem born the heavenly stranger," to whom the celestial splendors and choicest favors of Christmas night were alone revealed, what were they but the first evangelists of Christianity? I have, then, no apology to make for the simplicity of my narrative, but will rather say to you, in the words of St. Ambrose, which the Church solemnly sings in the Matins of our Saviour's Nativity, "*Videte ecclesiae surgentis exordium. Christus nascitur; pastores vigilant . . . et bene pastores vigilant quos Bonus Pastor informat.*" "Behold the exordium of the rising Church. Christ is born; the shepherds watch, and well do those shepherds watch whom the Good Shepherd enlightens."

Delaware, as you know, was first settled by the Swedes and Finns; then the Dutch from New York conquered it, and finally the English came in and stayed. I make this brief recapitulation of its civil history to elucidate one or two points in its religious history. The first is somewhat of a coincidence. As William Penn received his charter from a sovereign who died a Catholic, as he granted a religious toleration which subsequently proved more tolerant to Catholics than even that of their own Catholic-founded State of Maryland when it had fallen under Puritan and Episcopalian rule, so Delaware, which subsequently formed a part of Penn's grant, was settled by a colony sent out by Queen Christina of Sweden, who although then herself, as were all her counsel, Protestant, subsequently became a most fervent Catholic, went to Rome, and lived and died there in the Farnesina palace. Now with the advent of the Dutch to Delaware comes another curious incident, for which I am indebted to a profound chronological scholar of our city, who is particularly apt in the fixing of our American dates. It is this: Any Dutch date in Delaware records need not have the usual eleven days added to it to make it coincide with our modern system of chronological computation, because at the time of the entry of the Dutch the Netherlands were under Spanish jurisdiction, and Spain, as a Catholic country, had accepted both for herself and her colonies the Bull of Pope Gregory XIII. rearranging the calendar. In other words, all Dutch dates are N. S. Swedish and English dates, being Protestant, are O. S. So you see Delaware was, even thus early, beginning to call "time!" on Catholicity. The faithful, what few there were of them within the limits of the present State of Delaware, or, as it was then called, "the three lower counties" of Pennsylvania, from which it was separated into an independent State at the revolution in 1776, were, in common with most of the Catholics of this part of the country, attended by the missionaries from Maryland, generally speaking, but more directly from the mission of Bohemia Manor. It is not my purpose in this paper to explain the point of civil history, how these three lower counties, from being an integral part of Penn's territory, were subsequently erected into an independent State, which would include the story of the boundary known as Mason and Dixon's line, a part of which is the peculiar semi-circular division between Delaware and Pennsylvania. That is part of the civic history of the country. Nor do I propose to go into the history of the old mother mission of Bohemia. That belongs to the religious history of Maryland, and I shall have quite enough to do to cover in the limits of one evening's lecture all that I shall have to tell about the planting and progress of the Church in the field I have chosen—"The Diamond State." But I imagine the inquiry, Why have you chosen this special locality? For the very best reason. A man can talk best upon those subjects which he understands best; and as my own ancestors were the planters of the faith in Delaware, I can give you the prehistoric or traditional history of the Church there, which knowledge is the very apple of the historian's eye, the *cor cordium* of his desires and researches.

The next earliest historical record concerning the Church in Delaware, outside of my own family records, which I have been able to find, and up to the date of the commencement of my narrative the only printed record, is taken from the Episcopalian church missions on file in the library of the Pennsylvania Historical Society; and for a knowledge of it I am indebted to Mr. M. I. J. Griffin, who reproduced it in his "Catholicity in Philadelphia" from "Some Account of the Missions in Pennsylvania," under date of May 20th, 1760, by the Rev. Phillip Reading. He says, speaking of Appoquinimink mission, in New Castle county : "But what makes this mission of great consequence to the society, and indeed to every lover of the Protestant cause, is its lying contiguous to a very considerable Popish seminary in the neighboring province of Maryland. This seminary is under the direction of the Jesuits. A priest of this order used formerly to preach and say mass at stated seasons within the mission of Appoquinimink, but, by the blessing of God, a check has been given to their attempts, and no mass has been celebrated in Appoquinimink for a considerable time past." Now here we have positive evidence, and that of the best kind, to wit, the unwilling confession of our religious opponents, that there were Catholics in Delaware prior to 1760, in sufficient numbers to receive the ministrations of a priest, and that mass was celebrated in New Castle county prior to that date. The neighboring Popish seminary was undoubtedly Bohemia Manor, which was a classical seminary of considerable repute from about 1745 till about 1792. It was, moreover, on an almost

direct line with Appoquinimink creek, which flows through that
part of New Castle county rising not far from the Maryland Border,
and emptying into the Delaware, a few miles above the line of
Kent county, In an old Jesuit diary, or rather a copy of it made by
the Rev. John Morgan, S. J., I find this entry : "The Rev.
Christ. von Keating baptized August 10th, 1791, at Appoquinimink."* So although "a check had been given" to the priest's
"attempts" in that mission, yet its effect was only temporary, even
though there be no record of his return until after thirty years. I
have made some effort by consulting old maps to discover the exact territory comprised within the limits of the Episcopalian mission
of Appoquinimink. So far I have been unsuccessful, but I presume
it lay around the locality just mentioned, and probably included
the hundred which took its name from the creek. St. Ann's
Episcopal Church, at Appoquinimink, is near Middletown, and
was built in 1705. In the same copy of the diary, which is
really composed of extracts from a collection of diaries and registers belonging to several of the old missionaries, and immediately following the above entry, is the following list of "out-missions,
as seen (?) from the record," depending on Bohemia Manor.
There is no date given, but while they are evidently of much
later date than the period of which I am treating, probably
as late as 1830, yet are interesting as showing the stations before
there were any churches in Delaware with resident pastors, except
St. Mary's, at Coffee Run (of which I am about to treat), and
Wilmington; and I make this exception, because you will please
observe that that mission of Whitely Creek, or Mill Creek hundred, as it is indiscriminately called in the Jesuit records, is not
mentioned, and this is only another presumptive proof added to
others which I shall presently adduce of the seniority of that
mission in Delaware. The list which I have copied includes

---

* The name of this missionary priest is almost invariably spelled by
writers in this form, yet it must be obvious to all well instructed readers
that it is erroneous, the prefix VON being Teutonic, and the Keating
being decidedly Celtic. It is, in fact, an error. The venerable priest's
name was Christopher Vincent Keating, but he usually signed himself
CHRISTOPHER VIN. In course of time this became corrupted
by copyists into VON, until by long usage the error was lost sight of in
custom.   C. H. A. E.

other stations than those in Delaware, but I will give only the latter: "New Castle, Delaware; Kent county, Delaware; Middletown, Georgetown, Taylor's Bridge, Delaware; Sussex county, Delaware; Smyrna, Delaware; Galena, Kent." It may be just as well to state here that the earliest missionaries to this part of America were nearly all Englishmen, with Anglo-Saxon tastes, sympathies, and methods ; hence they not only coalesced more easily with their fellow settlers, and had more influence over them, but they also brought to bear in the prosecution of their missionary work the same system which the English government has always applied so successfully to its colonial military conquests; for just as the English policy is always to protect such newly acquired settlements by lines of military fortifications and supply stations, so these English Jesuit missionaries established an easily traceable chain of missions or central rendezvous starting from Maryland and running up into Pennsylvania and New York; and I have the authority of a distinguished Jesuit for saying that it is the same policy which the English Jesuit, Father Weld, is pursuing to-day in his missionary evangelization of the English conquests in Africa.

I shall now proceed to discuss the point—who were the Catholics mentioned? and I think to prove, presumptively at least, that Mass was said in New Castle county much earlier than 1760. The first Catholic settlers in the three lower counties were undoubtedly Irish. But why did they come to Delaware instead of going to Maryland? Or did they go to Maryland first and then migrate to Delaware? I think not. The persecution of the Catholics in Maryland was over by that late date. Mr. Griffin's exoneration of the character of William Penn seems to me the true solution. He had a large acquaintance in Ireland, held estates there, as his descendants do to this day, had traveled much therein, and by his own persuasion had induced large numbers of its people to come out to his colony; and the reputation of his mild rule and the well-known tolerance of its government had made it quite as safe a haven for Catholics as Catholic Maryland. Perhaps many of the emigrants were not so punctilious or scrupulous about the exercise of their faith. New adventurers are not apt to be. If they were they were within easy reach of the priests in Maryland, and if they were not, the priests of Maryland

were within easy reach of them. However it be, it is a patent
fact that these Irish did not come up to Philadelphia, but largely
landed at New Castle. Among them most probably came him
whom I feel justified in calling the lay pioneer—planter of the faith
in Delaware—my own maternal great-great-grandfather, Cornelius
Hollahan. I do not say he was the first Catholic in point of time,
but I do say that from what I shall be able to tell you of him I
think you will agree with me that he was the first Catholic layman
of standing, importance and character in the colony, the standard-
bearer of faith to whom the clergy of Maryland subsequently
looked and upon whom they placed their principal dependence to
aid them in the lay work of the Church. He is supposed, and
for very good reasons, to have come from county Kerry, on the
Blackwater river, a little above Cork, probably from the immediate
vicinity of Charleville.

I cannot tell anything definite about his immediate family con-
nections in Ireland. "James Hwolahan, gentleman, county Kerry,"
is the name of a subscriber to an old book in his library, and supposed to have been a relative; but the family or clan from which
the name is derived has been traced by Irish genealogical scholars.
" From Lucan, king of Munster, probably the grandfather of Brian
Boru, of the line of McCarthy More, is descended the Muinter
Wallachain, or O'Hoolaghans. The word "muinter" signifies
household, family, people or posterity of. The name is sometimes Anglicized O'Coulaghan and MacCoulaghan. They were
princes of Ui Mani, a great division of Connaught, the Latin
name for which is Hymania, the full derivation of the name being
given in O'Mahony's translation of Keating's Ireland. But the
O'Houlaghans were, according to O'Dugan, especially termed
lords of Fial Anmchada. The chief of the family is thus described by O'Dugan :

> A noble chief of lasting fame
> Rules over the plain of the Anmchada,
> A valiant rough-fettering warrior
> Of keen-edged weapons is O'Hoolaghan.

There is to be found among the poems of Clarence Mangan
the translations of two Irish Jacobite songs in which the fate of
Ireland is deplored and her future resurrection prophesied, she
being personified in both under the symbolic name of Caithleen

Ni Wallachain, Angelicized Catherine Holahan, One of these is not suited in either style, rhyme or rhythm to the taste of modern readers, but the second is so beautiful that some specimen stanzas will, I am sure, meet with the favor of this audience, especially at this time :

> Let none believe this lovely Eve
>   Outworn or old ;
> Fair is her form ; her blood is warm,
>   Her heart is bold.
> Though strangers long have wrought her wrong,
>   She will not fawn—
> Will not prove mean, our Caitilin Ni Wallachain.
>
> Her stately air, her flowing hair,
>   Her eyes that far
> Pierce through the gloom of Banbo's doom,
>   Each like a star ;
> Her songful voice that makes rejoice
>   Hearts grief hath gnawn,
> Prove her our Queen, our Caitilin Ni Wallachain.
>
> We will not bear the chains we wear,
>   Not bear them long.
> We seem bereaven, but gracious Heaven
>   Will make us strong.
> The God who led through ocean Red
>   All Israel on,
> Will aid our Queen, our Caitilin Ni Wallachain.*

Almost as many liberties were taken with the spelling of Cornelius Hollahan's name by the early settlers in Delaware as with the ancient Celtic version. He himself always signed his Christian name "Con."   His son John was the first of the family to spell the surname with one l, being, according to family tradition, "too lazy to write the other one."   Cornelius Hollahan seems also, from such relics as the family still possess of him, to have been of the better, or gentry, rank of society, and possessed of considerable means and education.   Among these relics are a pair of silver knee buckles and a pair of silver sleeve buttons " linked " exactly in the re-

---

* For a further account of the different branches of the Holahan family and the name since the days of King James II., see O'Hart's " Irish Pedigrees." See also *Catholic World*, February, 1886, p. 680.

vived fashion of the present day. I myself possess a part of his library, consisting mainly of religious works filled with curious old distichs on the fly leaves and margins, which I have described elsewhere.* Among these books is one of the original edition of the Rheims Testament, 1582; "The Life of St. Francis Xavier," from the French of Father Bouhours, S. J., by the great English poet, John Dryden, London, printed by Jacob Tonson, at the Nag's Head, 1688 ; Challoner's "Catholic Christian Instructed," gilt edges, London, 1738. Among the Irish imprints, Parsons' " Christian Directory," Dublin, 1752 ; Monsieur Fleury's " Catechism," Dublin, 1753 ; all in perfect preservation. He certainly wrote, too, what was for those days a fine hand. I may say here, however, that in this he was surpassed by his son John, whose penmanship is a marvel of beauty even in this age of high education. It is almost equal to copper-plate. The date of Cornelius Hollahan's arrival I cannot give, but it was certainly prior to 1754, for I have deeds in his name of that date ; and if the family tradition concerning his marriage be correct, he was here as early as 1747. He settled on what is known even in our day as one of the most beautiful estates in Delaware, or indeed anywhere, Mt. Cuba, or Cuba Rock as it was formerly called, on the Red Clay Creek, about seven miles north-west of Wilmington, which he purchased from Letitia Aubrey, daughter of William Penn, if the tradition be true, or at least from her vendees, it being a portion of her Manor of Stening.† The date of the purchase I am unable to fix, no amount of searching in the New Castle records having enabled me to trace back the title. The estate comprised 148 acres 140 perches, and it is said that the price paid for it was £1 per acre, a good round sum for those days: Here, according to the tradition of the family, was celebrated in Cornelius Hollahan's house the first Mass in New Castle county, and most probably the first in Delaware, since I hardly think the more thinly populated lower counties could have numbered sufficient Catholics to have demanded the services of a priest when the district

---

* See *Catholic Standard*, Philadelphia, of September 16, 1876; also *Catholic Book News*, published by Benziger Brothers, New York, issues of December, 1876, and April, 1877.

† See Addendum No. 1 at the end of this paper.

around New Castle and Wilmington, the very nucleus of Delaware's population, had not yet had any celebration of the Holy Sacrifice. The priest at Appoquinimink was evidently a later missionary than the priest at Mt. Cuba. The fact that the celebration took place in Mr. Hollahan's house, together with other facts which I am about to relate, goes to prove my assertion as to his social and religious prominence among the little band of Catholics in that community. Moreover, the great care with which the story of this first mass was handed down through all the succeeding generations of the family helps to prove not only its truthfulness, but their appreciation of the honor.

Cornelius Hollahan was, according to family tradition, unmarried when he came to America. His wife was Margaret Kelly, a native of the town of Dungevin (?), probably a mispronunciation of Dungarvin, as I have been unable to discover any town in Ireland of the former name. While yet a child she had, together with another little girl, been enticed away from her home by a woman under pretence of getting some "oranges and other dainties," then suddenly carried off and put aboard a ship bound for America, a system of kidnapping quite common in those days, the children thus stolen being bound out to service on their arrival in the colonies, thus furnishing a lucrative source of trade to the traffickers in human beings. The celebrated Charles Springer, afterwards so famous in the annals of Delaware, was kidnapped in this way when he was twenty years old, and carried to Virginia and there bound to service. (We must not, however, confound children thus stolen and bound out with the "redemptioners" of those days. The latter were a class of people who bound themselves out by selling their term of service to a sea captain to pay for their passage.) Family tradition has not failed to record the vociferousness of the screams of these two children when they discovered their deplorable situation; but a kind providence turned their misfortunes into a means of good. The other child mentioned was afterwards known to the families of the neighborhood as Mrs. McCauley. Margaret Kelly was shortly after her arrival discovered by Cornelius Hollahan, who knew her family in Ireland. He most probably redeemed her from those to whom she was bound, and she ultimately became his wife and the mother of his children. These children were five in number, two being daughters, Margaret and Mary, the dates of whose births are unknown. The tradition was given to me that one of these married a man of the name of McLaughlin; the other became Mrs. Spencer. Both emigrated to the West, but not, it would seem, until after their father's death, after which period nearly all traces of them are lost. The tradition about the names of their husbands I am disposed to doubt, although I derived it from their aunt, Mrs. Charlton, nearly all of whose statements, even when extreme old age had impaired her recollection, I have found to be borne out from time to time by discovery of records, and she must have been fully thirteen years old at the last mention of them in these records. My reasons for doubting her recollection in this particular point are these : Cornelius Hollahan in his will, dated October 26th, 1788, refers to them merely as his daughters Margaret and Mary, and makes Margaret a co-executor with his son John, she being then unmarried. In 1793, when his estates were sold, the deed recites that John Holahan, Margaret Craig and Francis Ailcock were heirs and terre tenants of the land, and that certain writs had been served on them. Now, as Cornelius Hollahan left by his will all his estates to his children, then surviving, respectively (naming them), it is most natural to suppose that Margaret had intermarried with a man named Craig and that Mary must have married Francis Ailcock, who in her right as his deceased wife was substituted for her in these writs and deeds as terre tenant. Had the husband been also dead and this Francis Ailcock been a surviving child, the writs would have been served upon and the deeds referred to a third party as guardian for Francis Ailcock, a minor. I would also infer from the fact of the nonjoinder of Margaret's husband in these documents that she was at that time a widow. The sons of Cornelius and Margaret Hollahan were three in number. I. John, born August 8th, 1748, according to an entry made by his son Jacob in his family Bible ; but according to an entry made by himself in the old Rheims Testament, the date given is Sept. 5th, same year. II. James, the date of whose birth is unknown. III. David, the only record of whose birth I discovered on the page of a very old copy of "The Following of Christ" by Thomas à Kempis: "David Hollahan, born January 25th, 1753," and on the fly-leaf of another old book this distich:

> David Hollahan's my name,
> Irish is my nation,
> New Castle is my dwelling place,
> This is my situation.

Of these sons John is the only one who married and survived his father.   James was remarkable for his great physical strength, being "able to lift a barrel of flour with ease."   During the war of the Revolution his eldest brother John was drawn for the Colonial army, but James went as a substitute, and with him went the youngest brother David.   They were both wounded and taken prisoners at one of the battles in South Carolina, Cowpens it is said, but I think more probably Camden.   Cowpens was a very insignificant fight.   Camden, on the other hand, was a heavy battle in which the Delaware line regiments were severely cut up. They were put aboard the odious British prison ships, where they are supposed to have perished, as they were never heard of again.   John I shall speak of more fully hereafter.

With such brief details concerning this family, given to round out my narrative and make it more intelligible, I shall resume the main thread.   Bear in mind that all this time there was no Catholic church in the confines of the three lower counties, or Delaware.   Cornelius Hollahan's house was practically "the mission," as subsequently was his son John's.   Hither came all the priests of the old Maryland mission; Carroll, Molyneux, Lewis, Rossiter, Keating; and all the celebrated missionary names were household words, and not only the Catholic missionaries, but the ministers of other denominations, even the Quakers, among whom John Holahan had married (as we shall subsequently see), assembled there as on neutral ground and held their discussions and rustic theological controversies.   Some reminiscences have been handed down concerning the missionaries.   I have it from the lips of Cornelius Hollahan's granddaughter, Mrs. Martha Charlton, who died so late as 1872 at the advanced age of ninety-two years, that she had heard her mother, I think it was, say that Archbishop, or Father Carroll, as he was then, was a very dignified man, somewhat haughty; and when on one occasion a woman in the neighborhood had with great pains

and care been long preparing some altar linens against the coming
of the missionaries, upon Father Carroll's arrival she offered
them to him, he declined them, saying they were not fine enough
for the service of the altar.   Here at Mt. Cuba Cornelius Hollahan continued to live until, as is said, the first church was built,
when, upon the invitation of the clergy, who desired him to take
charge of it, he left Mt. Cuba and removed to the vicinity of
Coffee Run.   Such is the tradition (as to its verity I cannot
answer); and in the inventory of his effects is an entry, "hay at
the old place on the stable loft," which would indicate a former
residence.   From old deeds and surveys in my possession it
seems evident that he owned other lands in Mill Creek hundred
in the vicinity of Coffee Run, and some of these he owned as
early as 1771, and adjoined his son John's lands, as we shall
presently see, though Mt. Cuba and Coffee Run, or the Old
Homestead, as John Holahan's place was usually called, were
not very far apart.   I am sometimes inclined to think that these
other lands of Con Hollahan's were simply the out-lying portions
of Mt. Cuba; but the records and papers give no definite information, as they merely refer to his lands as bounding others.*   Mt.
Cuba remained in the family certainly for forty years, and Cornelius Hollahan left it by will to his children.   It finally passed out of
the family by sale January 12th, 1793, to Evans Phillips of Christiana hundred, for £165. (See New Castle County Records, Deed
Book M, Vol. II., page 463.)   Whether Cornelius Hollahan removed to his own house on these other lands or to his son John's I
am unable to say, but certainly his interest in the church did not
slacken.   Coffee Run is a small stream crossed about seven
miles from Wilmington on the Lancaster turnpike.   Here stands
a little frame church painted brown, known as St. Mary's, almost
hidden from the road by surrounding trees, save where the little
white cross rises above the foliage to arrest, as it were, the
traveller's attention.   The church is surrounded by a cemetery.
This is indisputably the first, and consequently the oldest, church
in Delaware.   From a mass of correspondence and other manuscript materials collected during the course of several years I will
now proceed to give its history.

---

* See Addendum II.

There was at one time a supposition, for I can scarcely call it a tradition, that the ground for it was given by the Holahans. This I feel safe in positively denying. There is not a shred of evidence to prove it ; indeed, the evidence would seem to clearly disprove it, although they doubtless contributed very materially to its erection.   The cemetery seems to have antedated the church at least twenty-five years. A writer in an old number of the Philadelphia *Catholic Herald*, the date of which I cannot give, speaking of the place in connection with the exercises of the jubilee held there some years ago, says that there are headstones in this cemetery on which can be deciphered inscriptions dated as far back as 1764. Bishop Becker, in a sketch of the Church in Delaware, printed in the *Catholic Standard* of July 30th, 1879, says that the "cemetery dates back to 1786, as appears from the tombstones there." I think the former date is more nearly correct. The Bishop probably did not investigate the tombstones as thoroughly as the jubilee reporter had done. Undoubtedly Catholics died and were buried thereabouts in considerable numbers before 1786.   Those that were not buried there were probably conveyed a long distance to Maryland, for among my great-grandfather's, John Holahan's, papers I found a scrap of paper in his own handwriting, in which he states that £— —d was paid for taking the body of ———— to Bohemia. I know positively that burials took place there in 1788. Bishop Becker also says "the first church was a log building." This is correct. He continues : "At what time precisely it was erected we do not know." Father Reilly, for many years vicar-general of Wilmington, says in a letter to me dated December 28th, 1876 : "St. Mary's Church was built, I think, in 1790 ;" but I do not think so with him, and for this reason: My maternal grandfather, Jacob Holahan, used to go once in a while to Delaware, generally for the express purpose of hearing Mass at Coffee Run, and he usually timed his going by the special Sunday of the month on which the mission Mass was celebrated there. St. Mary's in later days, not having a resident pastor, had Mass only once or twice in the month. My grandfather was getting old, and, as he always expressed it, he wanted "to hear Mass once more in the old church before he died." Moreover, he always expressed a desire to be buried there, and in this connection used to tell a story about some old man down there who always pointed out a certain tree under which he wished to be buried, because after he was dead he wanted to be laid where he could "see the ships going up and down the Delaware." Possibly this spot may have been at Mt. Cuba, from the summit of which there is a superb view not only of the Delaware river, but of the surrounding country for a circuit of at least sixty miles. There is no view of the Delaware from Coffee Run. But my grandfather did not die so soon as he anticipated, but lived till I was over ten years old, and the last time he went to Delaware he insisted on taking me with him, because he would then have seen five generations of his family worship in that church. Now, to count back from me five generations he would have to include his grandfather Cornelius Hollahan, and this he could not have done if the church had only been built in 1790, because Cornelius Hollahan died two years before; and as at that time my own grandfather was over ten years of age, he undoubtedly had seen his grandfather, and was brought up near him, if not with him. Moreover, why did Cornelius Hollahan leave Mt. Cuba to be near the new church (if he did so) if the church was not erected until two years after his death? Still, in order to avoid any possible error, I must say that 1790 is the earliest approximate date given. A good story is told of John Holahan in connection with the building of the church. John was appointed to collect funds for the purpose. One day as he was riding along on horseback he met a Presbyterian neighbor, James Crossin, whose descendants still live in that neighborhood. John asked him to subscribe a dollar. Crossin looked at him a moment undecidedly, and then drawled out: "Well, John, I'll give ye a dollar, but ye know I hate your religion." "So does the devil, Jimmy, and you can keep your dollar," replied John as he whipped up his horse and rode off. Jimmy afterwards went to the priest then in charge of the mission, said to have been Father Rossiter, gave him the dollar and told the story to him as a good joke on himself. The records of the church, if any ever existed, have long since been lost, and I can only give you its history as I have compiled it from various authentic sources. Not being able to trace any title by index at New Castle, I wrote to the Very Rev. Father Reilly, Vicar General of Wilmington. My purpose was partly to discover who gave or sold the lands for this cemetery and church. I was the more anxious, as I had always understood that there was something dubious about the transfer of the title in later times. He replied that the farm or lands originally belonged to the Jesuits, of whom, said he, the Rev. Father Molyneux was one, and that Father Kenny, the last resident pastor, had purchased it from Archbishop Neale of Baltimore, who had been a Jesuit priest, and that the records in Georgetown or Baltimore could give the only reliable information of the original deeds or grants. On application to the Jesuit Fathers at Georgetown, as suggested by Vicar General Reilly, I received the following reply from the Rev. Clement S. Lancaster, of that Order, who, at the request of the Rev. James Pye Neale, S. J., to whom I had directly applied, had made the investigation. Father Neale, in a note accompanying Father Lancaster's reply, said: "Here is Mr. Lancaster's answer. He can do more than any one else."

LOYOLA COLLEGE, January. 30th, 1877.

Rev. J. P. Neale, S. J.:

REV. AND DEAR FATHER IN XTO.—I have looked over the books of the corporation of the Roman Catholic clergymen, and the following is all I find that probably regards the farm at Coffee Run :

"At a meeting of the corporation held December, 1798, the memorial of Rev. L. Neale was presented, asking a grant of $800 for the relief of the farm in Mill Creek hundred, Delaware, purchased by Father Manners."

"August 3, 1799—At a meeting held this day it is entered on their records as the opinion of the representatives of the Roman Catholic clergymen that the farm at Mill Creek hundred, Delaware, should be sold, reserving the church and burying ground. That a house and lot be purchased in New West Chester to accommodate the priest to serve the neighboring congregation, and that the residue of the purchase money be funded for his support.

"October 9, 1799—At a meeting of the corporation a resolution was passed concurring in the above proposal of the representatives."

Some time after it is mentioned that the Rev. Antony Herr was at West Chester and a certain amount of money was paid him.

"June 29, 1808—The agent of the corporation acknowledges the receipt of $752 from the sale of Mill Creek." (Farm, of course.)

The above [says Father Lancaster] is all I can find on the corporation books regarding property in Mill Creek hundred, Delaware, and I think it is the same property bought by Father Kenny on Coffee Run, where stands St. Mary's Church. "About 35 years ago I knew a good old man by the name of Francis Council, living in Talbot county, who frequently spoke of having lived with Father Kenny on a farm on Coffee Run purchased from the Jesuits. He has since died. Father Manners, who purchased the farm, lived at Bohemia, I think, at the time, and probably made the purchase before our [Jesuit] charter was obtained in 1792. If this is so, it will account for no other mention of that property being made on the books of the corporation."

Yours very respectfully and affectionately in Xto.,

C. S. LANCASTER, S. J.

Following out the references, I wrote to his Grace Archbishop Bayley of Baltimore. In a reply dated April 17th, 1877, Father Starr wrote:

The archbishop a few days before his departure for Europe bade me write to you, and say, in reply to yours of March 23d, that he has had all the documents in the archives of this church carefully arranged and docketed, and that in going over them by title he has been unable to find anything that would suggest the matter you speak of. He begs, however, that you will write again on his return from abroad, with the hope that his health will enable him to give the matter some attention.

Yours very truly in Xto.,

WILLIAM E. STARR.

Ten days after this I followed the Archbishop to Europe, but never saw him alive again. He returned, as you know, only to die, and I pursued the matter no further in Baltimore.

Now no one doubts that Father Kenny purchased Coffee Run from the Jesuits. That is in a certain sense contemporaneous history. But when and whence did the Jesuits get it? Father Lancaster's statement would seem conclusive that Father Manners was the purchaser, and that the church and burying ground were part of his purchase. Now the fact of the matter seems to be that the whole plantation forming the Jesuits' property in Mill Creek hundred, including Coffee Run cemetery and church, was the result of several successive purchases, probably made from time to time as need or opportunity presented. For I shall now proceed to show you that the Jesuits owned lands there twenty years prior to the dates suggested by Father Lancaster, and of which Father Manners was not the purchaser. There is in my possession, among other family papers of which I am the owner, an old manuscript without date, written and signed by Rev. Robt. Molyneux, S. J.   Here it is:

My plantation, containing two hundred and eight acres, more or less, begins at a corner black oak tree, being a corner tree of Letitia Penn's manor on the east end thereof; from thence west forty-two perches to an old corner white oak; thence south thirty-seven perches; thence west thirty-six perches to an old corner hickory; thence west one hundred and twelve perches to an old corner white oak by a run; thence up said run north ninety-two perches to a new corner white oak; thence leaving the run and continuing the same course ninety-six perches to a new corner black oak in the woods on manor; thence east sixty-two perches to a small run; thence by the same course one hundred and forty-six perches to a new corner hickory in the manor line; thence by the said line south eleven degrees, west one hundred and sixty-five perches to the place of beginning.

R. MOLYNEUX.

Father Molyneux calls it his plantation. This must be explained. After the suppression of the Jesuits by Pope Clement XIV. the members of that Order purchased and held lands as individuals, which they transferred from time to time, one to the other. On the restoration of the Society in 1792, they obtained a charter, and then the individual priests holding lands conveyed them to "the corporation." But this corporation existed only in the State of Maryland, which accounts for Father Molyneux still holding title in his own name, long after that date, in Delaware; and any exercise of authority by the corporation over him, as to those lands, was simply in their character of his religious, and not his legal, superiors.

The boundaries of the land described in his paper seem to correspond very closely with the site of St. Mary's Church. The stream spoken of therein would answer very well to Coffee Run. But this is not all. Bishop Becker, in his sketch of the Church in Delaware to which I have already referred, said : "The land, it seems, was originally bought by the Catholic clergy of Maryland, since a deed is still extant, signed by the Rev. Robert Molyneux, a well-known missionary of the Society of Jesus." On reading this I at once wrote to the Bishop for information about this deed. He replied under date of August 20th, 1879: "The deed to the Rev. Robert Molyneux is inferred to be extant (that is the word I used) from an indenture in my possession to this effect: 'This indenture made the 25th day of March, in the year of our Lord, 1795, between the Rev. Robert Molyneux, of Georgetown, on the Potomac, in the state of Maryland, on the one part, and Arthur McGough, of New Castle county, in the State of Pennsylvania (?), on the other, showeth that the said Robert Molyneux for good reasons, &c., &c., doth hereby lease, &c., for ten years that parcel of land, &c., in Mill Creek hundred deeded by Samuel Lysle on the 17th of February, A. D. 1772, unto the Rev. John Lewis of St. Mary's county, State of Maryland, containing 208 acres, more or less, for £26 5s., Pennsylvania currency, yearly, for every year, &c.' This proves that the Rev. John Lewis bought the property from Samuel Lysle ; that the Rev. Robert Molyneux either owned it or represented the owners." So far Bishop Becker. The figures given in the above lease, of course, refer to the rental, not the original purchasing price.

I ought to add that the Rev. John Lewis was, for several years prior to the erection of a bishopric here, the religious superior of this country after it had severed its connection with the vicariate apostolic of the London district. In 1772 he was probably acting as superior of the missions of the then Society of Jesus, and in some such capacity made this purchase. But that to which I wish particularly to direct your attention is that the number of acres mentioned in Father Molyneux's paper in my possession agrees exactly with the amount of land named in Bishop Becker's deed, " 208 acres."

Thus far had I written of this essay when I determined to make another inspection of the records at Wilmington. I inferred that if Father Kenny had purchased, his deed at least would be on record, and might show the chain of title back. I was correct in my surmise. I did find the deed to him, and it did recite the title. Here it is: "January 17th, 1772, deed from Samuel Lyle to the Rev. John Lewis, 13th of March, 1788, by will, devised the same to the Rev. Robert Molyneux; will on record in register's office, of Cecil County, Maryland. June 6th, 1809, Rev. Robert Molyneux by will devised the same to Rev. Francis Neale, of Georgetown ; will on record in the register's office at Philadelphia. By deed proved before Judge Cranch of the circuit court in the District of Columbia, May 17th, 1810, and before Mayor

Robert Brent, of Wilmington, Delaware, June 7th, 1810, the Rev. Francis Neale, clerk of Georgetown, in the District of Columbia, in the State of Maryland, sold the same for $1600 to Rev. Patrick Kenny, clerk of Mill Creek hundred, New Castle County, Delaware." Here ends the mystery, except as to Father Manners' purchase, which may have been a mistake in name only on the Jesuit corporation books ; but as Father Kenny's purchase was not until two years after the receipt of $752 by the Jesuit corporation for the sale of Mill Creek, and as the price paid by Father Kenny was a much larger sum, I with reason believe this to be a smaller tract acquired by a different purchase adjoining the church lands, and transferred by a different sale.   The reservation of the church and cemetery by the corporation can easily be accounted for on the supposition that the corporation had but ill-defined notions as to the special properties allotted under the one title—Mill Creek hundred.   I must add, however, that the description in the deed to Father Kenny corresponds verbatim with that in my private papers signed by Father Molyneux, and with the lease made by him to Arthur McGough.*

Our Very Rev. President, Dr. Middleton, O. S. A., made during last October an examination of the church records in Wilmington, and the result of his researches embodied in two compilations is now among our Society's archives.   I have had the use of them, and among the documents shown him was this very "indenture," which is simply an unsigned lease; but it tells much more on a further examination than Bishop Becker told of it.   The conditions, ten in number, recite that McGough will board the clergyman of that district, if the bishop wishes, in a suitable manner, viz., lodging, table, candle light, fire, washing, mending of clothes, taking care of his horse, furnishing him with plenty of grass, hay and seventeen bushels of oats yearly, and all for £25 6s. yearly, days of absence to be counted out; also that McGough "will plant an apple orchard with the trees 25 feet apart," "will fence in all the property," "will plant one lot with chestnut or other timber at 10 feet apart," and "will allow one acre for a church and burying ground," &c., &c.   The fact that this lease is unsigned counts nothing against its descriptive

---

* See Addendum No. II. at the end of this paper.

value. It was evidently meant to be signed. But can any one doubt that the place designated therein is Coffee Run? Now, when we see also that the priest was to live in the vicinity, and when we see, as we shall see from this my paper to-night, that prior to this date the Holahans were probably the only Catholics, or at least the nearest Catholics to this church, can we have any serious doubts about the truth of the tradition that they settled here after leaving Mt. Cuba for the purpose of acting as custodians of the church, and that their house was the head-quarters of the priest? Moreover, among my great-grandfather John Holahan's papers I found a fragmentary scrap in his own hand-writing: "Paid ———— for cleaning the chapel." There was no chapel in that part of Delaware but Coffee Run. At the date of this lease Cornelius Hollahan had been dead several years, and in just one year after the date of the lease John Holahan commenced to sell off his property in that locality, as we shall see later on, and he himself was probably preparing for his departure from Delaware, or for some other reason the clergy were seeking new accommodations. His possession, too, of Father Molyneux's description is another piece of presumptive evidence, albeit however slight. From all of which we may sum up that the farm or plantation known as the Jesuit Farm, in Mill Creek hundred, was the first religious settlement made by the Church in Delaware; that it was acquired from time to time, as necessity or convenience required, by a series of purchases at least two in number; that the earliest known date of these is 1772, although there are indications of a Catholic cemetery on it as early as 1760; that the church was originally a log building, erected probably between 1785 and 1790. We are now out of the mist as far as its subsequent history is concerned, for we have seen, first, that the Jesuits sold the farm or portions of it from time to time, always reserving the church and cemetery, until they finally disposed of that through Father Francis Neale to the seculars in the person of Father Patrick Kenny, about 1808, who continued to own and hold it in his own name until the time of his death in 1842; but he did not retain all of it, for he sold a large portion of his farm long before his death, retaining, however, to the end of his life the church and grave-yard on one side of the road and twenty-eight acres on the other side. This is the statement of Vicar-General Reilly, Father Kenny's successor. "I applied," he continues in his letter to me of December 28th, 1876, "to the Delaware legislature for his escheat or escheatable estate for the Sisters of Charity and got it, and sold it for, I think, $2,800 for the Sisters." Bishop Becker adds to this in his letter to me of August 20th, 1879: "However it came into Father Kenny's hands (the farm, I mean), it was sold by the State of Delaware subject to the limits which granted the church building and grave-yard." This evidently refers to the escheat. All this, however, must be easily discoverable matter of late record, if any future historian will desire to take the matter up where this paper leaves it. But the Bishop adds : " When did the property pass into the hands of the Bishop of Philadelphia or His Grace of Baltimore? I do not know. I take it that in Georgetown all the deeds may be found." Father Reilly also said: "The records in Georgetown can give the only available information of the original deeds or grants;" but we have seen just how much Georgetown could give us and that Baltimore could furnish nothing. It would not be difficult to surmise, however, that when the See of Philadelphia was erected, Delaware being a part thereof, the title at once vested in the Bishop of Philadelphia and in turn passed to the Bishop of Wilmington when that diocese was created in 1868, according to the laws framed 'for the Church in this country. Bishop Becker says that Father Kenny succeeded Father Whalen as pastor about 1796, and that Father Kenny first called the mission Coffee Run. From this we may infer that Father Whalen, or Whelan, was its first regular pastor, although, as I have intimated, Father Rossiter seems to have been in charge at the time the church was built. Who Fathers John Rossiter and William Whelan were I need not tell you. You can learn that from any history of the early church here. They were not Jesuits. The seculars seem to have united their forces indiscriminately with the Jesuits in those days. Perhaps it would be more correct to say that the Jesuits up to 1792 were all seculars; that upon the restoration of the Society of Jesus at that time, the lines were drawn by the former Jesuits returning to the fold ot their Order, while the seculars remained roving missionaries; yet even up to 1830 both classes resided together under the Jesuits' roof at old St. Joseph's, Philadelphia, and at the beginning of the century the distinction was more nominal than real when practical work was the test. I doubt, however, if Father Kenny assumed the pastorate as early as 1796. The Jesuits, we have seen, were still in possession at Mill Creek hundred in 1799, and Father Kenny's purchase seems to have been much later; but the following curious old deposition found among my family papers would, from its contents and the reference to the priest, seem to indicate that Father Kenny's predecessor was still at Coffee Run:

NEW CASTLE COUNTY, SS., STATE OF DELAWARE: Personally appeared Daniel Henery before me, Joseph Burn, Esq., one of the Justices of the Peace, in and for said county, and was sworn upon the Holy Evangelist of Almighty God, that David Vauhan lived three years with this deponent, and in the year 1801, in the month of December, he was took sick and was asked by this deponent if he had no affairs to settle. He said he had, and that John Holahan owed him thirty pounds on bond, and he allowed ten pounds of said sum to be paid to the priest, supposed to be William Wheelan, and five pounds to a Molatoe girl said to be the child of said Vauhan, named Jeny, and the remainder to John Holahan wife Phoebe and to her oldest daughter and no interest to be charged on said bond, and his wearing apparel all but a bigg coat to Daniel, Henery and John Doves and the bigg coat he allowed to Jacob Holla- •han, and to John Coneway he left his bed and bedding. But it is to be observed that this deponent saith he does not swear that said Vauhan was in his reason but was in a violent fever at the time and further this deponent saith not. Sworn this 8th day of August, 1801. Before me, as witness my hand and seal the year and day above written.

JOSEPH BURN.

Certificate and hearing, 75 cents.
Pd by David Hollahan.

The above date is evidently a slip of the pen for 1802, as a deposition could not be made in August, 1801, of what had not yet occurred, to wit, in the following December. A full account of Father Whelan can be found in Mr. Griffin's "History of Catholicity in Philadelphia," and in other works to which he refers. He was succeeded at Coffee Run, according to Bishop Becker, by Father Kenny early in the present century, and from here as from a cathedral church this veritable apostle of the faith built up the Catholic religion in Delaware. He was practically the vicar-general of the diocese of Philadelphia for Delaware, and until 1816 he had no other church than St. Mary's little log chapel at Coffee Run. In that year he built St. Peter's at Wilmington, and subsequently removed thither, but Coffee Run seems to have always maintained its hold upon his affection and care. He continued to visit it as one of the regular missions of his church, and from it we may truly say sprang that series of missions and churches which resulted in 1868 in the erection of Delaware, with the eastern shore counties of Maryland and Virginia, into the diocese of Wilmington, with the Rt. Rev. Thomas A. Becker as its first bishop. It is no part of the scope of this lecture to narrate in detail the growth of this progress, but a few condensed data can hardly be out of place. Father Kenny has left the story of his part of the work in a diary which is now in the possession of the Willcox family of Ivy Mills, which place shared with Bohemia and Coffee Run the honors of the mission for that part of the country. I hope this diary may some day be transcribed for the archives of this Historical Society. Mrs. James Willcox has given me some details about this good old priest, and Mrs. Admiral Dupont has furnished, through Mr. Rowe of Brandywine, some further reminiscences which have been filed in this Society's library. These more properly belong to his personal biography; but there is an amusing secret chapter concerning the "escheat" of Coffee Run, which is not out of place here and which I give on the highest authority. It appears that towards the close of his days Father Kenny's mind became impaired, and while in this mental condition he undertook to write his will. The burthen of it was that he wished to devise his estate to the Sisters of Charity in Wilmington, but he used up twenty-five pages of foolscap to say so, and with this devise he left several bequests in trust for the support and maintenance of several dogs, cats and a particular cow, so long as these animals respectively practised virginity. Of course such a will was easily set aside. Indeed it could not stand, and Father Kenny having no heirs, one of the Duponts succeeded in getting the Legislature to practically carry out the intent of the will by giving the escheatable estate to the Sisters, substantially in the manner stated by Father Reilly in his letter already quoted. As the disinherited cats were Pat Kenny and not Kilkenny cats, they probably took this result with feline equanimity, particularly if they shared any of the matrimonial tendencies of one of their tribe in the neighboring mission of Bohemia. Father Francis Beeston in a diary kept at the manor makes, under date April 17th, 1793, this entry : "Ordered cat to be killed, the dogs having broke her back. She was the oldest cat I ever knew, being near forty years old by the accounts of those who knew her ; a ratter; she had not a tooth in her head, and still I have seen her kill rats; she had kittens last year."

Father Kenny died in 1842 and was buried at Coffee Run. A large marble slab with a suitable inscription covers his grave. After his death no priest attended the mission till the church crumbled down. Meanwhile the Rev. Patrick Reilly, for so many years known as " Priest Reilly," succeeded as vicar-general. He established the Sisters of Charity in charge of a flourishing young ladies' academy of the usual type of those days, and an institution for boys of some celebrity known as " St. Mary's College," under the charge of lay professors, and continued to rule among them like a little pope. Meanwhile he built the second Catholic church, known as St. Mary's. St. Peter's at New Castle was commenced in 1808, but left unfinished until 1830, when it was completed by the Rev. George Aloysius Carrell, afterwards first bishop of Covington. The insurrection of the Blacks in San Domingo and the breaking out of the French Revolution sent many French refugees to Wilmington; and this is the introduction into Delaware of such names as Dupont, Garesché, Bauduy, Noel, etc., etc., whom De Courcy and Shea, in their "History of the Church in the United States," written from a French standpoint, designate as distinguished Catholic families of our American revolutionary history, and whom they seem to honor as being the faith-bearers to Delaware. Yet a very little investigation would have shown those authors that the faith was already there to comfort the refugees. The Duponts de Nemours were a French family and were not Catholics at all, but Huguenots. The earliest record of the family on the church registers gives the name as Dupont de Gault de St. Domingo. The latter were a West Indian family. The two branches are said to be entirely unconnected. The Duponts de Nemours settled on the Brandywine in 1801 and established there their now famous powder mills. Mr. Victor Dupont married a Catholic lady, and his daughters, among whom was Mrs. Admiral Shubrick, were brought up in the faith of their mother. That is how much they had to do with *planting* Catholicity in Delaware. Nevertheless they did give the ground and material aid towards the erection of St. Joseph's Church at Brandywine Village, built, about 1842, for the workmen at the mills, but at the same time erected for themselves a beautiful little Episcopal Church on the other side of the creek. Dr. Middleton's researches among the church registers has thrown some valuable light on these French residents. They prove, first, that they were in Wilmington as early as 1796, August 18th of that year being the first entry. Up to 1804 all the entries are in French, for these refugees brought their priests with them. The first named of these was the Rev. Etienne Faure, deputed as pastor of Wilmington by Rt. Rev. John Carroll, Bishop of Baltimore. Next the Rev. P. Bauduy is mentioned as baptizing in 1797. In 1799 there is baptism by the Rev. ———— Cibot, Vice Prefect Apostolic and Superior General of the missions of the north of St. Domingo, a refugee, and also deputed pastor of Wilmington by Bishop Carroll. From August 5th, 1804, to 1834, a few entries are in Father Kenny's handwriting. On August 17th, 1810, another French priest appears, the Rev. F. X. Brosius. From February 2d to April 29th, 1800, Father Rossiter and Dr. Carr, both Augustinians, sign all the registries, and the latter ventilates his "Corkonian" French by signing himself "Curé de la Paroisse de Ste. Marie de Philadelphie et Vicaire Général de Monseigneur l'Evêque de Baltimore." The first mention of the Gareschés is a baptismal entry in 1796. Then came the Duponts in 1797, closely followed by the Bauduys and Keatings in the same year. I refer to these registries to disprove the insinuation of De Courcy and Shea that any of these refugees, who afterwards acquired a social notoriety as Catholics, had anything material to do with the establishment of the Church in Delaware. We have seen that Catholicity was growing there at least thirty years before they came at all ; and when they did come, Coffee Run was a flourishing station with a resident priest, with Wilmington for an outlying mission. The priests they brought with them undoubtedly relieved somewhat the English-speaking clergy, but they seem to have had but little work to do. Their baptisms all told only amounted to one or two a year ; their marriages, ditto ; yet they had to be provided for, and what more natural than that

they shoud be put over their own people? But their office would
seem to have been a sinecure, as their title, " Pasteur de Wilmington," was an empty honor.   They also appear occasionally on the.
Baltimore registries.   And as for the laity under them, just how
much they advanced the faith in Delaware can be imagined from
the fact that though they came there in 1796, at the latest, yet
Wilmington had no church until twenty years after their arrival.
I question not the piety or zeal of the individuals among the
"Messieurs" and "Mesdames," as the old Wilmington people
called them, but I have shown how little they added as a body to
the strength of the Church in Delaware.

In the old diary to which I referred in the earlier part of my
address I found the following, which, as it refers to the first "pasteur" of Wilmington, is of interest here:

"Aug. 21, 1798, died at Bohemia, Rev. Stephen Faure, a French
priest, residing at Wilmington, Del.   He was about thirty-seven
years old.   His eminent piety, extensive erudition and active
charity made him an object of respect and veneration to those
who knew him.   His remains were buried close to the north
end of the church.   The grave head began at the east side or
border of the gospel window."

Under date of March 21st, 1805, is entered the death of "Rev.
Chas. Whelan, a Franciscan, formerly chaplain to the French
navy, pastor at White Clay Creek.   His remains were buried
next to those of Rev. Mr. Faure by Rev. Mr. Pasquet."   White
Clay Creek is, as I told you, but another name for Mill Creek
hundred or Coffee Run mission, and Charles Whelan and the
" William Wheelan " of the old deposition are probably identical,
although there were several priests named Whelan, and one was
named William ; but it is at least evident that the first pastors of
Coffee Run and Wilmington sleep their last, long sleep together
side by side at the old mother mission church of Bohemia.

Five or six years after Father Kenny's death Father Walsh
began to attend Coffee Run station.   He rebuilt the old church very
neatly and substantially as it now stands.   It was reopened
with considerable ceremony about 1850, and a notice of the
dedication was published at the time in the Philadelphia *Catholic
Herald*, but I cannot give the exact date, either of the fact or
the description.   Since then it has been a mission attended once or

twice a month from Brandywine. Although my grandfather was disappointed in seeing me worship there, having made his last excursion for that purpose on the wrong Sunday, yet I have since frequently heard mass there. The congregation used to be a very large one, much in excess of the church accommodations, and most of the people spoke the native Irish. Father Walsh was succeeded by Father George F. Kelly. With the advent of Bishop Becker the star of Coffee Run began to decline. The Bishop erected St. Paul's church and fixed there his residence. He introduced the Benedictine Order, who erected the Church of the Sacred Heart, speedily followed by St. James' and St. Patrick's, all in the city of Wilmington. Outside churches were erected on missions previously established at Newark, Dover, Smyrna, Georgetown, Middletown, Delaware City and finally at Ashland and its mission of Hockessin. St. Patrick's church at Ashland sealed the fate of Coffee Run. It was built to supplant it, as the change of population seemed to demand, and Coffee Run has within a year or two been finally abandoned, the cemetery being retained and the church probably being used as a mortuary chapel. Wilmington city alone, and for this purpose Wilmington is Delaware, now has about fifteen priests, nine benevolent societies, two orphan asylums,—one for males, in charge of the Sisters of St. Francis, and one for females, in charge of the Sisters of Charity; three academies,—one of the Visitation, one of the Sisters of St. Benedict, and one of the Sisters of St. Francis,—one high-school under the charge of the Benedictine Fathers, and five parochial schools, with a Catholic population of about 10,000, that of the entire diocese being about 15,000, the old Jesuit mission of Bohemia Manor, still under the charge of the Jesuits, being embraced in the diocese. About a year ago "Priest Reilly," the venerable vicar-general and successor of Father Kenny, died; thus in eighty five years Delaware has had but two vicar-generals. Within a month Bishop Becker has been transferred, after an administration of over seventeen years, to the see of Savannah, Georgia, and soon Delaware will welcome her second Bishop in the person, it is believed, of the distinguished Dr. John Foley of Baltimore.* I

* While these sheets were going through the press, the Rt. Rev. Alfred Ambrose Curtis, D. D., was nominated as second Bishop and consecrated in the Cathedral of Baltimore, on November 14, 1886. On

cannot better conclude this brief synopsis of the history of the Church in the Diamond State than by reading for you the full text of a letter written to me by Bishop Becker shortly after taking possession of his see, and on the very day when he set out to plant the cross in the capital town of Delaware:

WILMINGTON, DELAWARE, Nov. 9th, 1870.

Charles H. A. Esling, Philadelphia, Pa.:

Dear Sir :—I have the account you were pleased to forward me in reference to the earlier portion of the Delaware missions and am very thankful to you for them. I propose making up a diocesan statement to be kept in what may be in time the archives of the diocese, and your relation of facts, as well as your name and courtesy to me, will be remembered long after either of us shall have ceased to exist. We have so little of a standing now as Catholics in Delaware, and then there has been so little done for the advancement of the Church that everything almost must be begun. Even in the capital, Dover, there is no church, and we may state that, of all the others, Delaware is the only one of the United States (as far as I know) with no Catholic church at the seat of government. I leave this morning for Dover, where I propose laying a corner stone which may hereafter bear aloft the cross and welcome the immigrant to us.

With many thanks for your kindness and asking pardon for my delay,

I am yours in Xto.

THOS. A. BECKER, Bishop, &c.

We have seen the mustard seed become a flourishing tree, and the birds of the air beginning to gather in the branches. Would it be right or proper for me to close this narrative without telling you of the fate of those who planted this, indeed, "the least of all seeds?" Bear with me, then, yet a little, while I recur briefly to them. Long before the date of this portion of my paper Cornelius Hollahan had far advanced in age. For several years he had walked with a crutch, having been lamed by a wheel running over

---

November 21 he was installed by his predecessor, Dr. Becker, in the Pro-Cathedral of his see, in the presence of several distinguished prelates, and a large concourse of the laity, the city and diocese of Wilmington having also on that occasion the honor of receiving for the first time within its limits an American Cardinal, in the person of His Eminence Archbishop Gibbons, of Baltimore, who preached the installation sermon. C. H. A. E.

his leg. His wife, Margaret Hollahan, died suddenly on the 16th of August, 1788. "She had gone to the meadow fence to call her son John, and on his coming to the house he found her choking to death." She was buried on the 17th or 18th of August, most probably the latter date, that being the Sunday after her death. A vast concourse of people of all denominations, particularly Quakers and Presbyterians, attended the burial. Father Molyneux preached the funeral sermon, "and I mind," said Mrs. Charlton, her grand-daughter, from whose lips when she was at the age of ninety years I heard the narration, and who was present on the occasion, she being at that time about eight years old, "I mind to have heard him say that she never let the poor go empty handed from her door." Her husband survived her but ten weeks. The celebrated Dr. Latimer attended him in his sickness. He died on the 1st of November, 1788. Beneath the old trees at Coffee Run, in the shadow of the venerable church, lie these founders of the American family which bear their name, and most of whose descendents still profess the faith which they bore to these shores, and planted here, with what success we have seen. The Church in Delaware, cradled and reared in the log chapel of Coffee Run, reigns now from the cathedral throne of Wilmington.

But I would omit one of the most interesting incidents in the history of the faith in Delaware did I fail to add, even at the risk of detaining you a little longer, the vicissitude which it experienced in the very household which nursed it, and how by that very vicissitude that household was saved to it. About thirteen years before Cornelius Hollahan's death, his only surviving son John violated all the religious proprieties and family traditions by marrying a Quakeress. Of course no Catholic priest did or could perform the ceremony, and of course the Quaker meeting would not. How his family took the matter we can only surmise from one little incident. How the Quaker meeting regarded it we are not left in doubt, as I shall presently give you some of the record. Phoebe Way was the youngest child of Jacob Way, who lived on the hills overlooking the west bank of the Brandywine just above Chadd's Ford, Pa. She was of an ancient and high family. Her mother was Judith, daughter of William Harvey, and her maternal great-grandfather that Francis Hickman whose will is one of the earliest on record in Pennsylvania, 1682. On her

father's side the family of Way, which takes its name from the
river Wey, was originally of Somersetshire, but removed in the
reign of Henry VII., or early in that of Henry VIII., to Torrington, in Devonshire. William Way of Great Torrington, who was
a yeoman of the guard to Henry VIII., was a son of Alexander
Way and had a confirmation of arms from Robert Cook, Claren-
cieux, 1574. This coat of arms bears the six "lucies hauriant,"
or salmon running up streams, a feat which that fish performs
with great difficulty and persistency, the family motto being "*Fit
via vi—a way is made by labor.*" This William Way had four
sons, of whom the eldest, William, was the ancestor of the family
that afterwards removed to Bridport, in Dorsetshire. From the
Dorsetshire branch the American Ways are descended; and they
brought the coat of arms with them. Henry Way, the Puritan,
born in England, 1583, emigrated to America with Governor
John Winthrop in 1630. The Governor's fleet was a large
one, and the particular ship in which Henry Way "came through
the deeps comfortably," to quote the old chronicle, was the Mary
and John, the same vessel that bore among the company Matthew
Grant, the first American ancestor of General Grant. Henry
Way is frequently referred to by Governor Winthrop in his journal and other Massachusetts records.* The entire family is
illustrious in New England annals. Henry settled at Dorchester,
Mass. He was the father of many sons and daughters. From
his eldest son, George, who was one of the pioneers of Roger
Williams' colony, are descended all the Ways of Connecticut.
From James, another son, are decended all the Ways of
New York and Canada. From Aaron, whose sons first
put a stop to the Salem witchcraft frenzy, are decended
the Ways of South Carolina and Georgia. Three of Henry's

---

* See, for a full account of the Ways, Blake's Annals of Dorchester,
Mass.; Clapp's History of Dorchester, Mass.; Young's Chronicles of
Mass.; Mass. Colonial Records; Suffolk Co., Mass., Records; Caulkin's
History of New London, Conn.; Kirker's Annals of Newtown, New
York; Danvers and Salem Mass. Church Registers; Ferris' History of
Early Settlements on the Delaware; Miss Montgomery's Reminiscences
of Wilmington; Minutes of the Early Quaker Meetings of Delaware and
Chester Cos., Penna.; Savage's Geneological Dictionary; Savage's Win-
throp; Wood's New England Prospect.

sons left, as far as known, no issue surviving them : Henry, who came over with Roger Williams and was lost at sea on the passage ; another son killed by the Indians ; and Lieutenant Richard Way, of the Ancient and Honorable Artillery of Massachusetts, who was also Governor of Castle Island, Farmer-General of the Imposts, and was urged for Post Master of Boston about 1765 ; there was also another son Robert and two daughters.

Within seventy years after the arrival of Henry Way not one of his name could be found in Massachusetts, but they could be found abundantly elsewhere ; and so perfectly has the family genealogy been written out that to-day over 10,000 of Henry Way's descendants can be located, and their ancestry traced back to the particular son of Henry from whom they are descended. The Pennsylvania Ways are believed to be descended from Henry's son William. The earliest known ancestor in Pennsylvania is Robert, suppositive grandson of Henry, born in Boston in 1651, and who was settled in Pennsylvania as early as 1636. He purchased lands on the Brandywine in 1691, and there settled finally in 1711. The family is famous also in the Pennsylvania and Delaware records, but it would not be in my power to give in the limits of this paper any of the historic records or the quaint and amusing traditions connected with them, of which I have myself compiled almost a volume. Suffice it to say that they owned a portion of the land on which Wilmington now stands, and the adjacent county nearly fifty years before Wilmington was settled; and when the town was built and incorporated, they were among its most prominent citizens. Phoebe Way, who married John Holahan, was Robert's grand-daughter and her father's youngest child. Her cousin Ann was the grandmother of Bayard Taylor. Another cousin, the celebrated Dr. Nicholas Way, was first Treasurer of the United States Mint. She is described by her own children as exceedingly pretty and vivacious. The story of the courtship as told by her Quaker relatives is that he had "kept company" with her for some time, but that she refused to have him until she knew how to make a shirt. One day she took a sheet, cut it up in proper form, and when she had properly accomplished the Penelopian test, she accepted him. The meeting records told a less poetic tale. The charge, involving as it did the fact of her being married out of meeting, and that not even by a "priest," as they called all ministers in those days, to say nothing of her wedding "a papist," naturally demanded official action, and so "at Kennett monthly meeting held 1776, 11th of 4th month," Kennet preparative meeting lodged complaint against Phoebe Way, * * * who was married to her husband by a magistrate. This meeting appoints Mary Swayne and Hannah Russell to treat with her for the same and report to the next meeting."

On the same day and place the same " complaints are brought by women Friends against Phoebe Hooligan (formerly Way). William Lamborn and Caleb Pierce are appointed to join with women Friends in treating with her for the same, and make report to our next meeting."

" 1776, 16th, 5th mo.   At our monthly meeting held at Kennett, the Friends appointed to visit Phoebe Hooligan, formerly Way, report that they, with men Friends, answered the appointment and think she is not in a proper disposition to condemn her disorder, neither did she desire longer time; therefore her case is left to men Friends to testify against her."

" 1776, 5th mo., 16th.   The Friends appointed report they with women Friends had a seasonable opportunity with Phoebe Hooligan, and she doth not appear capable to condemn her misconduct. The same Friends are desired to prepare a testimony against her, and produce to our next monthly meeting, informing her thereof."

" 1776, 6 mo., 13th.   The Friends appointed, not having complied with the directions of the last meeting in Phoebe Hooligan's case, are continued in the service."

" 1776, 7th mo., 11th.   The Friends appointed produced a testimony against Phoebe Hooligan, which was read and approved and signed.   The same Friends are desired to let her know the same, give her a copy if she desire it, also inform her of her privilege of an appeal, which if she desire it, get it read in Kennett First-day meeting and return it to our next."

The seventh and last record is "the testimony." My hearers, however, must not be misled.   "Testimony" in the sense of the Quaker meeting does not mean evidence or proof in the legal or popular idea of the term, but merely the statement of the meeting's action, just as the word "priest" so constantly used in those records, does not mean a Catholic priest, but any minister, not of the Society of Friends. To judge from the frequent use of this term in the records, an unsophisticated reader would imagine that nearly all the Quakers married Catholics. The testimony, after repeating the charge, goes on to say that, being treated with, she did not seem capable to condemn the same to Friends' satisfaction. "Therefore we account her no member of our religious society until by repentance and amendment of life she doth come to make suitable satisfaction, which that she may is our sincere desire. Given forth from Kennett monthly meeting the 11th day of the 7th mo., 1776, and signed by order of the same by

CALEB PIERCE, Clerk."

The name of Phœbe Holahan does not appear again on the Quaker records. The subsequent portion of this narrative will show that the copy of the testimony which was ordered to be given to her was never "desired." The "disownment" was mutual. The marriage with a Catholic does not, however, seem to have affected her family. John Holahan held land at the time in Pennsbury township, near her father's home, on the Brandywine, and in his will, dated 6 mo. 21st, 1776, old Jacob Way left "to son-in-law John Holahan and Phœbe, his wife, the sum of £70." But there is a tradition in the family that Phœbe Holahan would never consent to have any of her sons named Cornelius after their grandfather Holahan. Whether the tradition is correct I cannot say, but certainly the fact sustains it, for all her children bore scriptural or Quaker names and not one Cornelius. But if this fact was indicative of any hostility to the marriage on his part, it must have blown over very soon, as we shall shortly see. After their marriage they resided at Chadd's Ford. . Their house was Washington's head-quarters at the battle of Brandywine, and Phœbe was his hostess. My own grandfather, who was their second child, was born in the same room in which the general had lodged the night before the battle, and all the traditions of the battle have been carefully preserved in our family. These I have already detailed to the public in a paper read before the Pennsylvania Historical Society in March, 1877. At the same time that the daughter was entertaining Washington, her father's house was the very centre of the British lines. About two years after the battle John Holahan and wife removed back to Delaware, where, on March 24th, 1784, he purchased for £440 two tracts of land from Samuel Dixon, wheelwright, and Amy his wife, one of one hundred acres, and another of sixteen acres, evidently contiguous ; the descriptions in the deeds and surveys seem to plainly indicate proximity to both Mt. Cuba and Coffee Run. The deed is recorded in New Castle County, Deed Book P., vol. ii., page 474. The smaller tract was bounded in part by his father's lands. This purchase was also originally a part of Letitia Penn's Manor of Stening, and some of the original deeds are in my possession. On April 16th, 1796, he sold about thirty-three acres of this tract, and on April 14th, 1801, another portion of twenty-four acres. The whole tract is marked as being divided by the public great road to Wilmington, and at the time of sale partly bounded " by the priest's land." It was also bounded by the other lands of Cornelius Hollahan.* After the latter's death John maintained his father's custom of receiving the missionaries of all denominations, and his house was also a neutral ground for their religious argumentations. Phœbe used to listen, and quietly conceived her own impression. One day, while one of the missionary priests, Dr. Carroll, it is said, was at the house, she went to him and said she would like to become a Catholic. He asked her reasons for thinking upon such a course of action. She replied that she thought a woman ought to be of the same religion as her husband. He told her that was not a sufficient motive, and that until she could say she was convinced of the truth of Catholicity she could not be received into the Church. Here the matter seems to have dropped, but it is a noteworthy fact, which I have from the lips of my grandfather Holahan, that it was she and not her husband that looked after the religion of her children, and that she herself taught them all to the best of her ability out of the Catholic Catechism. Among the most valued relics preserved in our family are two catechisms, from one of which she trained her children, the other being surmised to be her own "questing book," as declared in what seems to be her own handwriting on the title page, from which she herself, perhaps, imbibed later the truths of the Catholic religion, though it may have been her daughter Phœbe's. Under the signature, another little daughter has written

---

* See Survey given.

the following distich :   "Susanna is my name holahan came by
Neture heven is my poarshun and god is my Creator."
And with this I have an old copy of the " Pious Guide," published at "Georgetown on the Powtomack, 1792," which was presented to her by her husband.   There is nothing further to note
in the matter of Phœbe's religious convictions until about the
time of the removal of the family to Philadelphia, and the issue is
best told by transcribing the following from the baptismal records
of St. Joseph's Church, in this city :

"*Jan. 13, 1799.   A Rev. Leonardo Neale, Phœbe Holigan, alias
Tremula, 44 circa annos nata.   Patrinus fuit baptizans.*"

The only comment reported by tradition upon Phoebe's conversion was the simple remark of some of her Quaker relatives,that
she was a fool to have become a Catholic, for if she had tried she
could easily have made her husband a Quaker.   In 1801, John
and Phoebe Holahan sold the remainder of their property near
Coffee Run.   Their eldest son, Amos, who afterwards became
one of the most prominent citizens of Philadelphia, together
with a younger brother, David, had already settled here, and now
Jacob, their second and favorite son, proposed to emigrate to the
west.   He was a favorite with both his father's and mother's
family.   Among the latter a rich Quaker uncle had said to him,
"Jacob, I will leave thee all I possess, if thee wilt give up that
cursed religion." Jacob refused, and now his father said to him,
"Jacob, if you will stay with me I will leave you everything.
Jacob replied: "That would be unjust to my brothers and sisters,
and I will not stay now on any account."   So he came to Philadelphia with the intention of going west, but finally determined
to stay here.   Then he purchased ground of Edward Shippen
Burd, at what is now the corner of Tenth and Locust streets, and
built a house there with a large garden and a forge on the rear, for,
like most of the male portion of the early Quakers, he was a blacksmith, which in those days corresponded to what is now called an
iron manufacturer.   Through the influence of Mr. Burd he soon
had all the patronage of the city, and did all the iron work for the
public institutions.   Tenth and Locust streets was then the country.   At Eleventh street was a creek with a bridge over it, and
where the lately demolished Unitarian Church stood was a corn-
field.   This was in 1801.   Then he became a pew-holder in St.

Mary's, and his family have lived on the same property and continue to hold the pew to this day. As soon as he was established and his father had sold his property, in the spring of 1801 his parents and sisters came to Philadelphia and lived with him. John Holahan, however, lived but a few months after coming here, dying December 21st, 1801. In St. Mary's burial register, under date of December 31st, 1806, I find this entry: "*Phoebe Huligan died suddent. Paid 6s 6d*" (for burial of course), which was true. She choked to death with asthma in her chair. And this is, in brief, the story of the little daughter of the Puritans and Quakers, who restored to her own family and maintained in that of her Catholic husband the faith which her ancestors had surrendered more than two hundred years before, at the bidding of Henry VIII.

John and Phoebe Holahan were both buried in St. Mary's burial ground, at Thirteenth and Lombard streets, Philadelphia, the existence of which place of sepulture has only recently been made known to most of our Catholic people through Mr. Griffin's notes on "Catholicity in Philadelphia." It seems strange that they should have left Coffee Run just in time, as it were, to fail of burial there.

When Cornelius Hollahan died, John Holahan was one of the executors of his will, and when John died, Jacob, his son and my grandfather, was his administrator, hence the accumulated papers of each generation have descended to me, and from them and the family traditions I have compiled this sketch. I suppose if we could especially designate as Catholics the different people mentioned in them, we could get the names of nearly all the early Catholics of Delaware. Thus Arthur McGough, who is mentioned in Father Molyneux's lease, and David Vaughan, mentioned in the old deposition, were both witnesses to Cornelius Hollahan's will, which, I may add incidentally, was admitted to probate under the signature and official seal of the celebrated Gunning Bedford. I think now I have told enough to claim for myself the authorship of the initial chapter and to suggest much more for those who in some future day shall write the subsequent chapters of the history of the Church in Delaware.

ADDENDA.

I.

The publication of the foregoing lecture in the *Every Evening*, of Wilmington, Delaware, some time after its delivery brought out one or two comments on certain statements contained in it which I have deemed advisable to notice.   The first objection is this:

"Mt. Cuba is not a part of the old Manor of Stening, but the Manor line ran at least a mile further up the Red Clay Creek." My answer to this is that certain deeds *in my possession* connected with that estate expressly mention that part of its boundaries were "*to a white oak standing on the Manor line, and thence along the Manor line 11¼ West, 333 perches.*" This would be impossible if the Manor line were "a mile above," as has been stated.

Secondly. Mr. Amos C. Brinton, of Wilmington, who gives evidence of much knowledge and research of the New Castle County Records, writes me further that no move was made towards building a place of Roman Catholic worship "until after 1784, at which time *John Holahan, a blacksmith, bought ground on which was built St. Mary's at Coffee Run, some distance from Mt. Cuba Mill Creek hundred.*"

I inquired on what ground he made the statement that the church was built on lands owned at any time by John Holahan. His reasons, though not perfectly conclusive, lead rationally to that conclusion.   It will be observed by reference to my paper "that there was at one time a supposition, for I can scarcely call it a tradition, that the ground on which Coffee Run church was built was given by the Holahans.   This I feel safe in positively denying.   There is not a shred of evidence to prove it : indeed the evidence [by which I meant certain deeds afterwards quoted] would seem to clearly disprove it."   But here now is a shred of evidence brought to light, and by a totally disinterested person ; and, taken into consideration with the point I am about to make, is a very considerable shred. We have seen that on March 24th, 1784, John Holahan purchased for £440 two tracts of land from Samuel Dixon, wheelwright, and Amy, his wife, one of 100 acres and another of 16 acres. Recorded in New Castle county, Deed Book P, vol. ii, page 474. I have before me the original draught of the survey of these two adjoining tracts made May 1st, 1788,* and they show much the same boundaries as the deeds, except that Cornelius Hollahan's land seemed to have bounded, on two sides of the road, the larger as well as the smaller tract, and his name would seem to be substituted for that of Joseph Cannon, at least the latter does not appear on the survey. There is an increase on the survey, which was probably a re-survey after the purchase, of an acre or two to the larger tract, while the smaller one is increased from 16 to 24 acres ; at least that is my surmise, for that is the quantity of land given in the draught, and there is no evidence that John Holahan acquired by deed or otherwise any more land at that time.   ·

Now, on April 24th, 1796, John and Phoebe Holahan sold to James Rice, farmer, for the sum of £150 a certain portion of the above 100 acre tract containing 31 acres, 3 quarters and 7 perches and recorded in New Castle county, Book O, vol. ii., page 444 ; and Mr. Brinton says : "Rice's land joined the Roman Church lands, that makes me think that St. Mary's church was built on the land that John and Phoebe Holahan bought from Isaac Dixon."

On April 14, 1801, John and Phoebe Holahan sold to John Valentine Webber, paper maker, for the sum of £50 one of these two tracts containing 24 acres, 1 rood, 12 perches. This was partly bounded by the priest's land, or to quote the deed, " 24 acres beginning where an ancient corner hickory stood of now Moses McKnight's land, and of the priest's land, *and of the aforesaid other piece of land.*" New Castle Records, Deed Book Z, vol. II, page 247. Now, by comparing the survey with the boundaries given in the deed I am very well assured, first, that the 16 acre tract and the 24 acre tract are the same, the discrepancy resulting, as I have already suggested, because, too, the deeds say 16 acres, *more or less,* as by

---

* See plan of survey given.

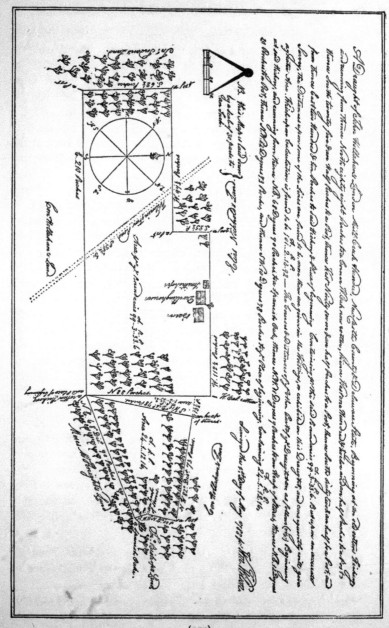

the survey thereof *may* more fully appear. Secondly, because the boundaries of the two tracts, 16 and 24 acres, are precisely the same, as near as I can get at them, at the time of John Holahan's purchase. The draught of survey would seem to indicate that the *priest's* land must have cut in between the lands of both the Hollahans and Moses McKnight. As the priest does not appear as one of the boundary owners at the time of John Holahan's purchase, and he does appear as such at the date of the sales, what more reasonable than to conclude that this priest's land was acquired from either Cornelius or John Holahan, especially as from its supposed position as inferred above, from the survey, it could not well have been obtained from any of the other boundary owners? And this is strengthened by the fact that while John Holahan appears to have purchased altogether 124 acres of land, yet there *is no record* of his having sold in all more than 56 acres. *Query.* What became of the other 69 acres? Were they sold to the priest? Who can produce the record deed? And if they were sold to him, then my theory about the Jesuits having made up their Mill Creek mission by several purchases is correct. Again, is this missing 69 acres the tract purchased by Father Manners? It was certainly not a part of the Samuel Lysle tract, for of that we have the entire record. Father Kenny's purchase of the 208 acres, some years later, did not necessarily include this, nor necessarily include the church and burial ground, but only the farm; and we have seen that the Manners tract passed out of the Jesuits' hands by a transfer earlier by two years. If the Manners tract contained the church and burial ground, then Father Kenny was probably also the purchaser of that tract, and in part of the whole Jesuit estate. Now, if my theory be correct, and Father Manners purchased from John Holahan, and St. Mary's Church was erected on those 69 acres, then the chain of title to St. Mary's Church at Coffee Run will read as follows:

OCT. 23, 1701, PATENT. William Penn to Letitia Penn for Manor of Stening, recorded in the Rolls office at Philadelphia in Patent Book A, vol. II, page 404.

Deed Letitia Penn Aubrey by her agent James Logan to David Cloyd.

APRIL 2, 1733. Deed. David Cloyd and Margaret, his wife, conveying 100 acres of said land to James Crege, Recorded in New Castle in Deed Book K, page 147. [Note—the original deed of this transfer is in my possession.]

DEC. 14, 1769. Last will and testament of James Creage, Sr., devising his estate including these 100 acres to James Creage, Jr., his son.

APRIL 27, 1771. Deed from James Creage or Craige, Jr., devisee of James Creage, Sr., and Janet, his wife, to Joshua Jackson Yeoman, for the above tract of 100 acres. Recorded in New Castle County Deed Book Z, page 395.

Eo Die. Deed from same to same for a second tract containing 16 acres, more or less. Recorded in New Castle county, Deed Book Z, page 395.

[This last part is bounded in part by lands of Con Hollahan, which is a proof that Cornelius Hollahan owned other lands besides Mt. Cuba *and near the church lands* in New Castle county and Mill Creek Hundred. The other boundary owners were John Bishop, Moses McKnight *and others.* The original deed of this transfer is likewise in my possession.]

MARCH 25, 1776. Deed from Joshua Jackson and Dina his wife to Isaac Dixon for both tracts conjointly, 116 acres. Recorded in Rolls office of said county, Book C, vol. II, page 153. Price paid £115.

MARCH 24, 1784. Deed from Isaac Dixon and Anny (?), his wife, to John Holahan of Mill Creek Hundred, blacksmith, for the same 116 acres. Price paid £440 [an amazing increase in value in eight years]. Recorded in New Castle county Deed Book P, vol. II, page 474.

The remainder of the record is before the reader, who must draw his own conclusions as to the church having acquired title from John Holahan.

II.

COPY OF THE LAST WILL OF REV. JOHN LEWIS.

In the name of God, Amen.

I, John Lewis, of Cecil County, Maryland, though afflicted with sickness at present, yet of sound mind and judgment, do make this, my last will and testament in manner and form following, viz : Imprimis, I bequeath my soul to God, hoping, through the merits of my Saviour, the forgiveness of sins, and future and eternal happiness.

Second. I bequeath my body to the earth, to be interred in such manner and decency as my executors shall seem meet.

Third. I bequeath wholly and solely to my worthy friend, Robert Molyneux, of the City of Philadelphia, gentleman, all my real and personal estate, of what denomination soever ; namely, my plantation in Talbot county, Maryland, now in the tenure of John Bolton, gentleman.

Item. A plantation in New Castle county, State of Delaware, now in the tenure of Con. Hollahan.

Item. The Roman Catholic Church, of St. Mary's, in Fourth Street; also the Roman Catholic Chapel, in Walnut Street ; together with the lot or lots of ground thereunto belonging ; and, also my two houses in Chestnut Street, all in the City of Philadelphia, State of Pennsylvania.

Item. All my estate in Hereford township, late in the tenure of R. J. Baptist De Ritter, now of Rev. Peter Helbron, Berks county.

Item. All my estate in York county, now in the the tenure of R. J. Pellentz.

Item. The Roman Catholic Church, together with the lots and messuages thereunto belonging, in the Borough of Lancaster, in Lancaster county, State of Pennsylvania, together with all my other estate or estates, real and personal, whatsoever or wheresoever in Maryland, Pennsylvania or elsewhere, and in case of his death before mine, I then bequeath all my said real and personal estate, in the same ample manner, to John Bolton, of Talbot County, gentleman, in final token of my esteem and affection, to be disposed of in such a manner as to the one or other shall seem best, and as I have bequeathed all my whole estate aforesaid, both real and personal, to Robert Molyneux, aforesaid, so do I constitute and appoint the said Robert Molyneux not only my sole heir, but also my executor of this my last will and testament, hereby revoking and annulling all other wills by me heretofore made, desiring this, and this only, made on the twelfth day of March, one thousand seven hundred and eighty-eight, to be deemed my last will and testament. In witness and testimony whereof I have set my hand and seal, and now finally published, executed and declared the same this thirteenth day of March, anno domini one thousand seven hundred and eighty-eight.

JOANNES LEWIS.

IN THE PRESENCE OF
{
JAMES O'DONALD,
BENJAMIN FLINTHAM,
Her
ALICE x O'DONALD.
Mark

Proved April 7th, 1788, and Rev. Robert Molyneux qualified as an executor the same day.

Recorded in the Register's office, at Elkton, Cecil County, Maryland.

All the persons named in the above will were Roman Catholic Clergymen and noted missionaries, with the exception of Con. Hollahan, who was a layman. This fact goes to prove the statement made in the foregoing essay, that Cornelius Hollahan had charge of the church lands and mission at Coffee Run, or the old Jesuit mission of Mill Creek hundred, New Castle county, Delaware, the only one of all the Jesuit missions in the charge (as to its temporalities, of course) of a layman.

The full brief of title to this mission of 208 acres is as follows:

1701. Oct. 23. Patent of William Penn to his daughter, Letitia, of 15,500 acres known as the Manor of Stening.

1701. Oct. 31. Power of attorney to sell and convey by Letitia Aubrey to James Logan.

1702. Nov. 2. Deed from James Logan for 208 acres of above tract, commonly known as the Lovel Estate, to George Reed, of Mill Creek hundred. Recorded in Rolls office, Philadelphia, Lib. B, vol. 3, page 100.

1719. February 17. Deed from George Reed, late of Kent county, Delaware, son and heir of George Reed, for the same, to Richard McDonald.

1733. Aug. 12. Will of Richard McDonald, registered in New Castle county, devising the same to his five daughters, Martha, Rebecca, Margaret, Mary, Rachel, with William Witherow, husband to Martha.

1754. November 5. Deed from same for same to Samuel Lysle. Recorded at New Castle county, Lib. R, page 494.

1772. January 17. Deed from Samuel Lysle for the same to Rev. John Lewis, of Newtown, St. Mary's county, Maryland, for the sum of £565. Recorded in New Castle county, Del. Then follows the devise to Rev. Robert Molyneux, who in turn, by will dated June 6, 1809, devised it to Rev. Francis Neale, of Georgetown. Registration office at Philadelphia. In May, 1810, Rev. Francis Neale sold the same to Rev. Patrick Kenny for $1600, at whose death what remained unsold by him, which includes the church and burial ground, escheated to the State of Delaware; his will having been set aside; but the escheat was purchased for a nominal sum by Rev. Patrick Reilly for the Sisters of Charity, reserving the church and burial ground for the Diocesan estate.

The fact that Cornelius Hollahan had these lands "in tenure" accounts probably for the statement made in old deeds and surveys of the time that he owned other lands in Mill Creek hundred besides Mt. Cuba, his own individual estate, and first settled place of residence.

At this late date it is impossible to state exactly what was meant by the words "in the tenure of" used by Father Lewis, whether the lands so held were in trust or merely in rental. If in trust, there should be deeds of trust on record, which there are not. If in rental, the term, while applicable to Mr. Hollahan, as a layman (which probably was the case), was totally inapplicable to the others, who, as clergymen, certainly did not rent church lands held, as these were, for church purposes. Moreover, one of the above deeds proves that Mr. Hollahan held lands outside of Mt. Cuba, and exactly in this locality, nearly one year before the date of Father Lewis' purchase, which, as we have seen, was made January 17, 1772, while the deed referring to Con. Hollahan's land is dated and recorded April 27, 1771; consequently it is to be inferred that not all the lands in his tenure at Coffee Run were exclusively ecclesiastical property.

An Account of Catholicity

IN THE

PUBLIC INSTITUTIONS OF BOSTON.

[Summary of a paper read before the AMERICAN CATHOLIC HISTORICAL SOCIETY OF PHILA-
DELPHIA, on the evening of April 28, 1886, by Rev JAMES J. BRIC, S. J.]

THE Rev. Lecturer entered upon his subject by stating that the religious history of the Boston prisons might, for convenience sake, be divided into three periods. The first was when the officers assumed full power to exclude priests, who, however, were sometimes allowed to administer the sacraments to the sick, the officers thinking that the friendship of the priest was more desirable than his displeasure. The second period began with the passing of the statute known as the Liberty of Worship Bill, which opened the prisons to the ministrations of Catholic clergymen, and gave them legal right to say Mass in the prisons, preach there and administer the sacraments. While Catholics, however, were free to go to Mass or absent themselves therefrom, they were compelled to attend Protestant worship. The third part of the history of Catholicity at the prisons he dated from the time when they were placed on perfect equality with the Protestant element and the compulsion to attend Protestant services was stopped.

In speaking of the first period he described the efforts made to pervert the children in the House of Refuge or Reformation. He said that what Mrs. Sadlier states in one of her books of the New York prisons for juveniles could be applied in the fullest extent 'to the Boston prisons. All Catholic books were taken from the children, whose names were changed and who were placed in the most Protestant districts of New England or sent to the West to be entrusted to the most bigoted Protestant families there. He gave as testimony a paper read before the Governor by one of the Prison Commissioners, and also the recollections of some prominent Boston people on the subject. He stated, however, that he found it hard to believe that there was so much bigotry in Boston, whose people are so high-minded and generous, and that in his intercourse with them he was treated with the greatest liberality and kindness.

As to the second period, he remarked that about fourteen years ago a prominent preacher and politician, a distinguished member of the Legislature of Massachusetts, brought before that body a measure that would open the prisons of the State to Catholic priests, and would give them the right to say Mass and perform the other functions of the ministry in these institutions. The bill passed the Legislature, and by statute law the prisons of the State were opened to the ministrations of priests of the Catholic Church. The city authorities soon followed the example of the State Legislature. Great opposition was shown to the measure by many members of the Legislature, but the majority followed the example given by the minister.

But although state law gave the priests full power and liberty to visit the prisons, say Mass there, etc., many of the Catholics absented themselves from Mass owing to the fact that they had to attend the Protestant worship. They complained that they had to work hard during the week and also on a good part of Sunday, besides having to attend the Protestant service; so that if they went to Mass they had no time for recreation whatever. The children stated that every effort was made to pervert them. Here the lecturer remarked that he believed the children exaggerated. He had found the officers very kind and willing to co-operate with him. He described at considerable length the consolations afforded him in the hospitals, where many sincere conversions were made. He also gave an account of the manner of his life in prison from Saturday until Monday, and the difficulty he experienced in getting the children to go to confession. He stated that he succeeded, nevertheless, in getting them to go.

After relating a number of anecdotes concerning prison life he passed to the third part of his subject. Reports of cruelty at the prisons, and complaints that Catholics were forced to attend Protestant service—reports which were made by some of the poor prisoners—led to an investigation of the prisons by a special committee of the city government. The gentleman who called for the investigation openly stated in the City Council that he had grave charges to make against the management of the city institutions. These charges he reduced to two, namely, brutality and interference with the rights of conscience. His attacks created quite a sensation.

Shortly after the investigation began the city prison officials brought the matter to the notice of the Corporation Counsel, asking an opinion as to the legality of compelling Catholics in the prisons to attend Protestant service. He gave at full length the arguments brought forward by the Catholic directors on the Board against compelling Catholics to attend Protestant service. He showed how it was unconstitutional, as it made the Protestants a privileged class and was in every way objectionable to Catholics.

The Corporation Counsel's decision was all that could be desired. It stated that the prison officials had no right to compel Catholics to attend Protestant services. This ruling was published in the prisons, and the result was a much better attendance at Mass on Sundays. Another result of Mr. Fraser's investigation was that the prisoners were thenceforward treated much more mildly than they had been. Permission was given also to have a corps of Catholic Sunday School teachers go to the prison every Sunday. About twenty gentlemen and ladies accordingly visited the institution at two o'clock every Sunday afternoon. They assisted the priest in catechising the children, and after these were pardoned out or had served their time in prison, the Sunday School teachers assisted them in getting employment, and protected, guided and watched over them as much as possible. The friends of Mr. Fraser, who called for the investigation, stated that he met with great opposition, and that it was owing to his ability, persistency and earnestness that the matter was settled in such a satisfactory manner. To the credit of the officers at the Island, the lecturer heard them state that they were pleased that the custom of forcing Catholics to attend Protestant service had been stopped ; also that so many highly educated Catholics took such an interest in the poor prisoners, that no matter how stormy the weather, they were always at their post, and that their self-sacrificing conduct went far towards removing the old-time and deep-seated prejudices against Catholics.

The Pioneer French in the Valley of the Ohio.

[Read before the AMERICAN CATHOLIC HISTORICAL SOCIETY OF PHILADELPHIA, May 26, 1886, by REV. A. A. LAMBING, A. M.]

The non-appearance of Father Lambing's paper in this volume is explained by the following abstract from a letter addressed by the author to Mr. McCaffrey, Chairman of the Committee on Public Meetings, dated Wilkinsburg, Pa., July 26, 1886:

"I sent the only copy of my 'Pioneer French in the Valley of the Ohio,' that I had to the Society in New York, at whose request I prepared it.

"If I had it you would be welcome to it, but I regret that I have no longer control of it."

A MEMOIR

OF THE

Very Rev. MICHAEL HURLEY, D.D., O.S.A.,

Sometime Pastor of St. Augustine's Church, Philadelphia,
Prior of St. Augustine's and Vicar-General of the
Province of Our Lady of Good Counsel (now
St. Thomas of Villanova).

WITH A

SKETCH of the HISTORY OF ST. AUGUSTINE'S CHURCH.

[Prepared for the American Catholic Historical Society of Philadelphia by Thompson Westcott, and read by his son, Dr. Thompson S. Westcott, June 2d, 1886].

IN the year 1800 there were only three Catholic churches in Philadelphia. Two of these, St. Joseph's and St. Mary's, were served by the Rev. Philip Stafford, O. S. A., Rev. Bartholomew Augustine McMahon, O. S. A., Rev. George Staunton, O. S. A., and Rev. John Rosseter, O. S. A.* With these resided, and officiated in both churches, Rev. Matthew Carr, also of the Order of St. Augustine. The third congregation was the German Roman Catholic church of the Holy Trinity, at the corner of Sixth and Spruce streets, the services of which, at that time, were conducted by the Rev. John Nepomucene Goetz and Rev. William Elling, and were held irregularly. The congregation was in contempt

---

*It was stated by counsel for the church of St. Augustine, on the trial in 1847 to recover damages for the destruction of the property, that Rev. John Rosseter was an officer of the French Army, and came to the United States in the Revolutionary War, with the troops under Rochambeau. After peace was declared he entered the Order of St. Augustine.

(165)

of the authority of Bishop John Carroll, and under excommunication, in accordance with the order that Goetz and Elling should not
exercise the functions of priests within that church. The cause of
this difficulty, which was the first in Pennsylvania between the superior and subordinate clergy, was a claim on the part of the trustees and congregation of a right to choose their own pastors.
They had selected Goetz and Elling in 1796 or '97, and maintained them in the exercise of their clerical duties during the interval, in spite of the disapproval of the Bishop. In 1802, Goetz
having withdrawn, Elling made his submission. His faculties
were restored and the excommunication of the trustees removed.

This much is introductory and merely to show the condition
of the diocese at that period. The Rev. Dr. Matthew Carr, who
was residing at St. Joseph's, had come to America in 1795, with
authority to establish a church which was to be under the control of the Brothers of the Order of St. Augustine. Whilst he
did his duty for the congregation of St. Joseph's and St. Mary's,
he was busy in his efforts to establish the new church. He began shortly after he came to the city to solicit contributions and
make collections towards the purchase of ground and the construction of a building. On the 11th of July, 1796, Jonathan Meredith and wife conveyed to the Rev. Matthew Carr and the Rev.
John Rosseter, of New Castle, Del., a lot of ground on the west
side of Fourth street, below Vine, 75 feet front and 175 feet deep
to Crown street, subject to a ground rent of 340 Spanish milled
dollars. The witnesses to the deed were the Rev. Michael
Ennis and the Rev. Leonard Neale. Dr. Carr thought that in
the prosecution of a work like this the funds could only be obtained by the help, good will and liberality of others. It was not
his policy to wait until all that was necessary had been procured.
He believed, wisely, that it would require a long time to obtain
sufficient money under such circumstances. He believed that the
shortest way to success was to take the risk of beginning the
work, although he might have but little on hand with which to
continue it. In accordance with this philosophy the cornerstone
of the new church, to be called the Church of St. Augustine, was
laid in September, 1796, on the lot in Fourth street. The experiment certainly assisted the project, although the progress
was very slow. Subscriptions began to come in more plentifully.

The proposed building, it was represented, would be an ornament to the city. Dr. Carr was, fortunately, popular with all classes of people, and Protestants added their mites to the general fund. Among the subscribers were President George Washington, who put his name down for $50; Governor Thomas McKean is represented to have been a contributor, although his name does not appear upon the list in Dr. Carr's handwriting; John Vaughan, one of the best known and most benevolent men in the city, gave $30; Samuel Blodget added $50; Peter Blight, merchant, $50; Jared Ingersoll, lawyer, $30; Col. Francis Johnston, a Revolutionary officer, $20; Thomas Leiper, tobacconist, $20; Samuel Meredith, grandfather of the eminent lawyer, William Morris Meredith, once Secretary of the Treasury of the United States, $30; Michael Morgan O'Brien, merchant, $20; Henry Pratt, merchant, afterwards known by his ownership of Lemon Hill, $20; Jesse and Robert Waln, merchants, $20. The contributions from the Catholics were quite liberal, considering the condition of the people. The Hon. Thomas Fitzsimons, merchant and member of Congress, who for a very long time represented Philadelphia, gave $500; Commodore John Barry, of the Revolution, gave $150; Redmond Byrne, $200; Patrick Byrne, $140; John Carrell, $100; Matthew Carey, $150; Timothy Collins, $150; Viscount Louis de Noailles, brother-in-law of General Lafayette, $200; Kerin Fitzpatrick, $100; James Gallagher, $200; John Leamy, $200; Patrick Linehan, $100; Neal Ginnis, $300; George Meade, $50; James Miller, $300; Jasper and John Moylan, $50 each; James Ryan, $200; John Taggert, $200; Don Jose Viar, Consul of Spain, $100; and Stephen Girard, $40.

A considerable amount was thus obtained; but, unfortunately, not enough to meet necessities. The principal reason for the slow progress of the work was the condition of trade at the time. Mechanics were receiving high wages, and there was a brisk demand for their services. Collections toward the expense of building the church were slow. As far as possible Dr. Carr preferred to get along without running into debt. In 1799 the Legislature gave authority for the management of a lottery by which $10,000 could be raised to assist in the completion of the building. This method of raising money, which would now be considered objectionable, was at that time a common method of procedure. Many religious congregations of all denominaations had profited by it. The grant was of some assistance.

The managers of the lottery were Thomas Fitzsimons, John Leamy and Edward Carrell.

During five years Dr. Carr was unremitting in his efforts to obtain funds and make progress in the building of the church. He was gratified by reaching an important point in the history of his endeavor, by the dedication of the Church building, on the 7th of June, 1801. It could not be said to be finished. Various conveniences were added from time to time. There were originally no galleries, no cupola, and no vestibule. At first the altar was of plain construction. In the year 1809 an altar of the florid Corinthian order, with fluted columns, was planned and executed by Thomas Carstairs. The vestibule was arranged in 1824. Before that time the doors opened into the body of the church. The architect of this building was Nicholas Fagan, a carpenter and a member of the congregation. The building was 62 feet wide on Fourth street, by 125 feet long from east to west. It occupied the centre part of the lot on Fourth street, leaving open on the north and south narrow spaces to be used as passage ways. The front of the building presented two square tower-like projections, at the north and south ends. They were no higher than the roof, and were connected by a curtain, which ran between them. In each tower space at the first story was a door, with pediment head and Doric pillars, placed in an arched recess. At the second story in each tower space was a triple Venetian window. In the centre of the curtain, at the first story, was a door in a semi-circular arched recess, flanked with a circular head window on each side. There were arched windows in the curtain of the second story ; a balustrade protected the front of the roof. The building stood back 6 or 8 feet from Fourth street and was guarded from intrusion by a low wall with coping and railings. The first floor was reached by steps, and was some 3 or 4 feet above the sidewalk. The building on the sides contained five windows in each of the stories, with closed window spaces in the towers. The front of the church was improved in 1826, when, it is supposed, the rough-casting of that part of the building was first made. A small cupola formed a portion of the design of the church by Nicholas

Fagan. It is believed it was not erected. In 1829 a cupola of three stories, surmounted by a cross, was built, according to the designs of William Strickland, architect. About that time there were alterations at Independence Hall. City Councils had resolved to erect a steeple on the tower attached to the original building. In the course of alterations it was necessary to furnish a new clock and bell. The old State House clock constructed by Peter Stretch, in 1753, was to be removed and replaced by a new and better instrument. The Rev. Michael Hurley, who was then pastor of St. Augustine's, took advantage of the opportunity to purchase the old State House clock, which bargain was effected by payment of $250. Having got the clock, the next question with Father Hurley was what he should do with it. It was his expectation to place it in the new cupola of St. Augustine's. Upon inquiring the cost of the necessary work and alterations, it was estimated that they would amount to $1200. The attention of the people residing in the north-eastern section of the city was attracted to the matter, and, in 1830, they sent a memorial to Councils, in which they set forth the great advantage which would be afforded by a public clock to be placed in that neighborhood. They said "it would be of great advantage to the citizens, as well for giving the correct time as for affording a suitable bell to be rung on alarm of fire." They spoke with approbation of the cupola placed upon St. Augustine's church, and stated "they considered that from the circumstance of its being upon the highest ground within the city plot, and elevated to a degree affording a view second to none in the city, it is a very superior situation for the clock so long desired by them." They declared they had themselves collected contributions, but the total amount required would be greater than the sums expected to be obtained. They therefore asked Councils "for a remission of the price of the old clock, and such further aid as Councils might be pleased to extend," adding, "your memorialists are authorized to state that the clock and bell when completed are to be considered public property, and will be placed under the constituted authorities, if desired by them." At a later period in the same month the committee to which the subject had been referred reported that the cost of a clock and bell would be $1285. The bell was to be 1500 pounds in weight. The citizens had

already collected $800, leaving a deficiency of $485. A remission of the cost price of the old bell was recommended. The
committee was of opinion that "by such a course Councils would
promote an object of public utility." A precedent for such a
disposition was alluded to as having taken place in the placing
of a clock and bell on the building at the head of the market
house at the intersection of Pine and Second streets. Citizens had
subscribed over $600 ; and Councils gave $600. The committee
added: " This grant is not to be considered in favor of, or for the
special benefit of, the congregation of St. Augustine's church,
but it is designed for the convenience of such of our fellow-citizens as reside in the north-east part of our city. It is free from
sectarian feelings, and the cupola of the church is made use of as
being peculiarly adapted to the object." It seems that the bell
of the State House must have been considered to be in the bargain with Dr. Hurley. The resolution which was recommended
to Councils stated that the clock had been sold to Dr. Hurley,
and that the purchase money for the same be remitted. Further,
"that the clock and bell about to be placed in St. Augustine's
church be, and the said bell and clock are, hereby vested in the
pastor of the said church of St. Augustine and his successors
forever, on lease, for the use and benefit of the citizens of Philadelphia : provided that in case of removal or demolition of the
said church, and provided, also, that unless the said clock be
kept in order and repair without any expense to this corporation,
this grant shall cease and be void; and the property of the said
clock and bell shall be vested in the Mayor, aldermen and citizens of the city of Philadelphia." This resolution was adopted.
In February, 1835, a petition was sent to Councils by citizens,
asking that a suitable person should be appointed to take charge
of St. Augustine's clock on Fourth street, "the organization being unable to attend to the same any longer." In the succeeding
month the committee of Councils reported that "the cost of attending the clock has been $50 a year, and the congregation can
no longer afford it." The committee then recommended that
the clock be taken care of in the same manner as other city clocks.
In accordance with the recommendation an ordinance was subsequently passed concerning the establishment and the appointment
of a person to take charge of all the public clocks and bells, at a

salary of $200 per annum. The bells were declared to be those at the State House, the old Court House, Second and Market, at Second and Pine, at the market west of Broad street, and at St. Augustine's church, whenever an agreement shall be made not to charge rent for the use of the cupola and access thereto.''

The church was directly opposite New street and presented a fine appearance from Second and Third streets. Over the altar there was placed, probably in 1809 or '10, a crucifix with the full length size sculpture of the body of our Saviour. This was cut in wood by the famous Philadelphia sculptor, William Rush. It was an exceedingly impressive figure. The agony of the sufferer was skilfully expressed upon the countenance, and upon the person who saw the figure for the first time the impression was one of awe.

In 1836 the church was newly decorated, the designs being by Uberti, an Italian artist. A description at this time said: "The ceiling has been richly clouded with suitable figures along the division of the various compartments. The top of the principal arch, over the organ gallery, is ornamented with a burning heart on a rich field, over which is the motto, *inde lucet, unde ardet*. The walls of the galleries were painted with pilasters, and the walls of the lower part of the church were correspondingly decorated. Over the sanctuary was a richly arched recess, over which was an eye surmounted by the motto, "THE LORD SEETH." Corinthian columns supporting the arch are clouded to represent dark variegated porphyry. The door of the tabernacle is a representation of the burning heart, stuck through with darts, the badge of the Order of St. Augustine. The rear of the sanctuary is colored like French marble."

The building of the church caused an immigration from other Catholic churches and filled up St. Augustine's, probably to its full capacity. An account of the pew holders between 1801-1808 shows that there were 237 pew renters. These with their families made up a congregation probably of five or six hundred. Among those who held pews at that time may be mentioned :

Commodore John Barry, John Ashley, Matthew Carey, Garrett Cottringer, Lewis Desauque, Don Fatio, the Spanish Consul; Thomas Fitzsimons, Anthony Groves, Thomas Hurley, Sr., John Leamy, Robert and Richard W. Meade, Jasper Moylan, Captain John Rosseter, Stephen Sicard and Don Jose Viar.

Among the pew holders between 1814-1820 were John J. Borie, Dr. Peter Pares, an eminent practitioner of medicine in the Northern Liberties, and John Troubat.

Some time after the original lot was purchased, an additional piece of ground on the north, running through to Crown street, was bought. It was 20 feet front by 175 feet deep. This was the first burying-ground of the church. It served its purpose until 1836. On the 25th of May, 1824, a piece of ground was bought from Andrew Hamilton and others, for the purpose of establishing a graveyard for the congregation. It was situated on Bush Hill, at that time in Penn township, at the north-east corner of Schuylkill Seventh (Sixteenth street) and St. Andrew (Wallace street). By a declaration of trust made shortly afterwards, this property was declared to belong to the Order of Hermits of St. Augustine, consisting of Rev. Louis de Barth, Rev. Demetrius A. Gallitzin, Rev. Patrick Kenny, and Rev. Michael Hurley. The ground was not put in use for some years. The first interment was on September 1st, 1836, and the last, August 20th, 1853. It was abandoned when extensive building improvements were set up in the neighborhood. The lot was sold, and is now covered with handsome houses.

The residence of the clergy of St. Augustine's was back of the church, on Crown Street, on which the house fronted, and had a private entrance. It was probably built in 1801. The *Philadelphia Directory* for 1802 gives the residence of Rev. Matthew Carr as *"near* No. 39 Crown Street." This building in after years was mentioned as at No. 39 Crown Street. Rev. Dr. Matthew Carr, the pastor, was assisted by the Rev. George Staunton, O. S. A. This clergyman went with Dr. Carr from St. Joseph's to St. Augustine's. Messrs. Carr and Staunton were also aided by the Rev. Raphael Fitzpatrick, a secular priest, who died May 25th, 1803, and was buried in St. Mary's.

The services of Mr. Fitzpatrick were taken up by a new priest, a young man aged twenty-three years, who went into the church in the same year. The name of Rev. Michael Hurley appears on the church records for the first time in the administration of baptism, September 26th, 1803, and at a marriage December 22d, 1803. At St. Joseph's his first ministry was a baptism, April 25th, 1804.

The memory of the Rev. Michael Hurley was associated with the old congregation for thirty-four years. He was pastor during the most important period of its history, and he was (in the community) a man of influence, not only as a clergyman, but as a citizen.

Concerning the birth-place of Michael Hurley there are conflicting statements. His half-sister, Mrs. Mary Cross, widow of Benjamin Cross, believes he was born in Philadelphia; Mary Lloyd, daughter of Thomas Lloyd, states in her diary, extracts of which have been kindly furnished by the Rev. Thomas C. Middleton, that Michael was born in Ireland, and that Thomas Hurley, the father of Dr. Michael Hurley, had married, in Tipperary, Catherine Fogarty. Thomas Hurley had three brothers, John, Joseph and Edward. Baptisms of the children, John and Edward, are found on the registries of St. Joseph's church. Thomas Hurley's wife, "Catherine Fogarty," says Mary Lloyd, "was the most beautiful woman I ever saw." She was buried in St. Mary's church graveyard, at what date has not been ascertained. Thomas Hurley, senior, the father of Michael, married, a second time, Mary Rogers, a Protestant lady, probably in 1794 or '95, as we find a registry of the baptism, by Rev. Leonard Neale, of his oldest child by his second marriage, Catherine Hurley, October 14th, 1795. By his first marriage he had Michael and Thomas Hurley, junior. When the Rev. Michael Hurley died May 14th, 1837, his age was recorded as 56 years, which would have made the year of his birth either 1780 or 1781.*

---

*Relating to the Hurley family the following account has been ascertained. Thomas Hurley, Jr.. brother of Michael Hurley, married Anna Louisa Carrell, and had nine children, Louis Neil, born February 6th, 1811; Elizabeth Lucas, born 1812; Mary, born August 23d, 1814, and married to Ambrose White, April 23d, 1833; Thomas, born October 17th, 1816; Anna Louisa, born November 28th, 1817, afterwards a Visitation nun ; John Carrell, born September 28th, 1819; Michael, born December 12th, 1820; Eleanor, born December 24th, 1821; and Catherine, born August 14th, 1823.

The children of Thomas Hurley, Sr., by Mary Rogers were Catherine, born September 16th, 1795, married Augustus Taney, of Maryland, a brother of Chief Justice Roger B. Taney, of the U. S. Supreme Court, February 1st, 1821; John, born November 8th, 1798; Mary, born June 10th, 1809, married Benj. Cross, July 10th, 1832; Edward, born April

If Michael Hurley was born in Ireland, in 1780 or 1781, he must have been brought to America in his infancy. Thomas Hurley was by trade an upholsterer. His name appears in the *City Directory* for 1785 as an upholsterer on Third street, between Arch and Race. In 1791 he resided at 21 Pewter Platter alley, the name given to the passage called Jones alley, and latterly Jones street, running from Front to Second street, and north of Market street. The addition, "paper hanger," is made after Mr. Hurley's name in the *Directory* of 1793. In 1795 he was living at No. 16 Carter's alley, running from Second to Third street, south of Chestnut. He remained there until 1803, when, having been successful in his business, he established himself as a paper hanger at No. 68 Chestnut street, between Second and Third. By this time he had become a manufacturer of paper hangings, and had an establishment of large size in the District of Southwark. In 1802 he advertised that he had for sale "French paper of his own manufacture." In 1806 he advertised that at his manufactory in Southwark he had colorists, printers, print cutters and designers. He died January 25th, 1817, aged 58 years.

The Rev. Michael Hurley was the administrator of his father, who at the time of his death owned some fine property. He owned a lot 90 feet deep on the west side of Tenth street, extending from Cherry street to Race street, 283 feet, and also a lot on the east side of Eleventh street north of Cherry, 60 feet front by 198 feet in depth. The properties were disposed of by sale in 1818 to John Carrell, merchant, of Philadelphia, for $31,700.

When Father Matthew Carr arrived in Philadelphia in 1795, Michael Hurley was 14 or 15 years old. His father was a member of St. Mary's church, and was a pew-holder in the same in

---

20th, 1812. In 1817, after the death of Thomas Hurley, Sr., it appears, by petition presented to the Orphans' Court, of Philadelphia, that the children over the age of fourteen were John, Joseph, and Robert, and those under that age Mary and Edward. The date of the births of John, Mary and Edward appear by registries already cited. Mentions of the baptism of Joseph and Robert have not been found; being over fourteen years old, the dates of their births must have been before the year 1803.

1787. Michael must have attracted the attention and interest of Father Carr, and to his advice and assistance may be attributed the determination of the boy to enter the priesthood. His father may have had other views for him, and intended to bring him up in his own trade. Indeed, in the *City Directory* for 1797, when Michael was only seventeen years old, his name appears and is marked "paperhanger," 16 Carter's alley, which was the residence of his father. It is likely enough that he had learned the trade. It was not usual to put the names of minors in the directories. Michael must have been of sufficient importance in conducting the business of the family to give his name to the canvasser of the *Directory*. His name is not found in the subsequent volumes of that valuable publication until he had become a clergyman.

We have no particulars of his early days; how he came to devote himself to the subject of theology, under whose patronage he went abroad, who were his teachers, and not even with certainty where he studied. The Rev. Dr. Carr forwarded the undertaking. Young Hurley completed his studies, it is supposed, either at Rome or Viterbo in Italy, and was ordained a priest in 1802 or 1803. On his return to the United States he came at once to his friend Dr. Carr, and entered into the service of the church of St. Augustine. He soon acquired the confidence of his seniors in the clergy. In 1804 he was made one of the corporators of the *Fratres Ordinis Eremitarum Sti. Augustini*, Brothers of the Society or the Order of the Hermits of St. Augustine, which was incorporated by the Legislature of Pennsylvania, November 10th, 1804. There were but five corporators, Rev. Matthew Carr, Rev. John Rosseter, Rev. Michael Hurley, Rev. Demetrius Gallitzin and Rev. Louis de Barth. They had authority to elect annually two, but at the most five, additional members, "being clerks in the order of the Roman Catholic Church, citizens of the state and exercising their ministerial functions according to the rules and discipline of the said Church." Three members were sufficient for a quorum for transacting the business of the Brothers aforesaid. Although they had a right to elect other members of the corporation, they appear not to have done so. After Father Rosseter ceased to serve there was not a legal quorum. The authority of the corporation, it may be presumed, was asserted whenever it was necessary in the service of the church.   Matters remained this way until 1832, when Father Hurley found himself the only surviving member of the corporation, with no power to continue it.   Under this stress the Legislature was appealed to, and on June 11th, 1832, a supplement to the original act was passed, by virtue of which the Rev. Michael Hurley was allowed to elect two or more additional or permanent members of the corporation.   It was directed that thereafter a majority of the members should be sufficient to constitute a legal quorum.   The direction that an annual election of members of the corporation should be held, was discontinued.   Privilege was granted that when the corporation was reduced to two members, the survivors might elect permanent members not exceeding five, providing that the persons elected had the necessary qualifications.   In 1820, according to the statement in the will of Rev. Dr. Carr, the members of the corporation of Hermits of St. Augustine were Rev. Michael Hurley, pastor of St. Augustine's church, Philadelphia; Rev. Prince Demetrius Gallitzin, of Bedford County, Pa.; Rev. Louis de Barth of St. Mary's, Philadelphia; Rev. Patrick Kenny, of Coffee Run, Chester county, Pa.; and Rev. J. B. Holland, Lancaster county, Pa.

One of the first acts of Father Hurley outside of his religious duties was to unite himself with "the Hibernian Society for the Relief of Emigrants from Ireland."   This society was composed of Irishmen and their sons.   Rev. Michael Hurley joined this association in 1803, shortly after his return to the city.   He continued in membership until his death.

Father Hurley soon found a better field for the display of his benevolent feelings and the exercise of charity.   He was not the founder of St. Joseph's Orphan Asylum, but the institution languished until he became interested in its affairs.   The charity dates its foundation from the yellow fever period in 1797.   By that dreadful calamity many children in Philadelphia were left orphans.   Those who were of Roman Catholic parentage naturally obtained the sympathy and assistance of members of the same denomination and religious faith.   A few persons made themselves responsible for the support of the Catholic children. They were confided to the care of a pious lady and were lodged in a house on the west side of Sixth street, north of Spruce, and adjoining the German Catholic church of the Holy Trinity. The building stood back from the street; there was a yard in front of it enclosed by a wall, the entrance to which was by a wooden gate. The place seemed very secluded, and it was suitable in arrangement for the management of the children. In the course of six or seven years the original supporters of this benevolence had diminished and the funds were somewhat scarce, and therefore more liberal assistance was demanded. The institution seemed to be destitute of friends until young Father Hurley, prompted by his religious duty, and sympathizing with distress, undertook to interest the Roman Catholic community in the institution. In this he was generously and ably assisted by Cornelius Tiers, a block and pump maker, a man of means and of influence, and an industrious and respectable citizen. Hurley and Tiers set to work in hope of gaining all the assistance that was required for the asylum. They succeeded so well that in 1807 "the Society of St. Joseph's for maintaining and educating Roman Catholic orphan children of both sexes" was effectively constituted by a better organization than it had previously. In 1808 Matthew Carey was chosen president and Thomas Hurley, father of the Rev. Michael Hurley, treasurer. In 1810 there were fifteen orphan children under the care of the society, the capital then being $4,397.90. The president at that time was the Right Rev. Michael Egan, Bishop of Philadelphia; vice-president, Edward Carrell; treasurer, James Oellers; secretary, J. Maitland.

In 1814 the Trustees resolved to ask the Sisters of Charity, who had been recently established at Emmittsburg by Mother Seton, to take charge of St. Joseph's Asylum. It was the first colony that Mother Seton sent out, and the invitation was welcomed with joy. Sister Rose White as Superior, with two other Sisters, was detached for this work. They left St. Joseph's convent, Emmittsburg, September 29, 1814, and took possession of the asylum October 6, 1814, which contained "thirteen children in rags, groaning under the burden of a debt of $4000." Their early efforts were crossed by trials, but three years afterward they had paid the debt (De Courcy and Shea, page 226).

Sister Rose White was a pious widow, born in Maryland in 1784, and was at this time thirty years old. She was one of the first American ladies who joined the order of Sisters of Charity.

She became Superior General of the Order in the United States on the death of Mother Seton, and was re-elected as often as the constitution of the Society allowed. She died in Maryland, July 25, 1841 (DeCourcy and Shea, page 226). The officers of the asylum in 1824 were : President, Rev. Michael Hurley ; Vice-President, John Keating, Sr. ; Chaplain, Rev. Francis Roloff, of the church of the Holy Trinity ; Treasurer, Anthony Groves ; Secretary, Joseph Snyder. The Society was aided by the people and the clergy. Charity sermons were frequently preached for the benefit of the orphans. On October 27, 1816, such a sermon was preached at St. Augustine's by the Rev. Michael Hurley. On the same day the Rev. Dr. Carr preached for the same purpose at St. Mary's.

In the disastrous controversies attendant upon the introduction of Rev. William Hogan to the pastorship of St. Mary's, which resulted in the deprival of his faculties and excommunication, the Rev. Michael Hurley was loyal to the Church. He seems to have gauged Hogan at his proper worth from the first. He denounced the pastor of St. Mary's as the " fop who had made himself a priest." It was at St. Augustine's on Sunday, May 27, 1821, that the decree of excommunication of Rev. William Hogan was first read. It was said of Hogan " that he had not hesitated to rend and tear the seamless garment of Christ by causing a confusion in the Church and endeavoring to establish a schism." He had continued to exercise priestly functions, although forbidden by the Bishop. It was declared "that he was cut off by the sword of excommunication as a putrid member and forbidden from having any share in the work of the Church," and was pronounced to be "no longer a member of the Holy Roman Catholic Church." This judgment was concurred in by Archbishop Ambrose Maréchal, of Baltimore ; Bishop John Cheverus, of Boston; and Bishop John England, of Charleston, South Carolina.

The College of the Propaganda Fide, at Rome, to which the decree against Hogan had been sent, on August 20th, 1822, transmitted to Archbishop Maréchal, of Baltimore, an apostolic letter from Pope Pius VII., with directions to have it printed, and to transmit a copy to every Catholic church in the United States.

The Sacred Congregation, upon review of all the facts, declared that "these disorders have originated principally from two causes, viz., from the senseless arrogance and nefarious proceeding of the priest, William Hogan, and also from an abuse of power in those that do administer the temporal properties of the church." The conduct of Hogan was declared to be "execrable." Another source of evil was named in the "immoderate and unlimited right which the trustees or administrators of the temporal properties of the churches assume independently of the diocesan bishops. "The letter was intended as much to set the seal of disapprobation of the Holy Father on the conduct of Hogan, as to repress the ambition of the trustees of St. Mary's to administer the property of the church in opposition to the will of the Bishop." The bitter controversy that ensued between the adherents and opponents of Hogan was carried on under circumstances of great scandal, during the course of which the faith of many of the friends of Hogan, and those, too, of families of great wealth and influence, was undermined. They abjured the faith of their fathers and went over to Protestantism. Hogan remained in the exercise of his priestly duties, notwithstanding his excommunication, for three years. He professed to have become a convert to the doctrines of the Greek Church, and made some attempt to form an American Catholic Church. As the Greek Church allows marriage to its priests, he showed the sincerity of his conversion in August, 1824, by his marriage at Wilmington, North Carolina, to Mrs. McKay, a widow who possessed, in addition to her personal charms, the agreeable merit of owning property. Indeed, so warm was his attachment to the principles of his new faith that, his first wife having died a few months after his marriage, he as soon as possible contracted another matrimonial engagement with a rich widow, Mrs. Lydia White Gardner, the relict of a rich planter who owned slaves and cotton plantations.

The unfortunate results of this schism continued at St. Mary's after the withdrawal of the recreant priest. His successors were some of them weak, and some disposed to be rebellious, although they did not go the extent in their conduct that had distinguished that firebrand Hogan. The troubles were partially overcome and settled in 1828. Bishop Conwell was then called to Rome and the Rev. Wm. Matthews named administrator of the diocese of Philadelphia. The confusion was ended during the term of

Bishop Francis Patrick Kenrick, Coadjutor of Philadelphia, with right of succession to Bishop Conwell, who was consecrated in 1830.

The Rev. Dr. Carr died September 29th, 1820, and was succeeded as pastor by the Rev. Michael Hurley. By his will, dated September 3, 1820, Dr. Carr named as his executors the Rev. Michael Hurley and the Rev. Patrick Kenny. He devised all the property belonging to the order of the Society of *Fratres Ordinis Eremitarum Sti. Augustini,* or Brothers of the Order of Hermits of St. Augustine, incorporated September, 1804, consisting of the following clergymen: Rev. Michael Hurley, of St. Augustine's, Philadelphia; Rev. Prince Demetrius Gallitzin, of Bedford county, Pa.; Rev. Louis de Barth, of St. Mary's, Phila.; Rev. Patrick Kenny, Coffee Run, Chester county, Pa.; and Rev. J. B. Holland, Lancaster county, Pa. Among the devises was the lot on which the church stood on Fourth street below Vine, 65 feet front and 175 feet deep to Crown street; also the adjoining property on the north used as a grave-yard, 20 feet front and running through to Crown street. All the church property of the said Society, the income of sixteen shares from stock in the Farmers' and Mechanics' Bank of Philadelphia, was designated to be for the education and support of one or more fit and suitable clerical member of the said Order of *Fratres Ordinis Eremitarum Sti. Augustini,* or for the expenses of sea voyages of any clerical member or novice of the said Order from any part of the United States, or beyond the seas, whom the said Society shall deem expedient to join the said Order of Brother Hermits of this State and for the purpose of keeping up the succession of said Order for the service and worship of Almighty God in the City of Philadelphia and other parts of the United States.

Dr. Carr bequeathed his books to various persons and made a special bequest of a piece of wood from Penn's Treaty Tree to his friend Edward Hudson. By the death of Dr. Carr Father Hurley became pastor of the church, and was appointed Superior of the Province, with the title of " Prior of St. Augustine's and Vicar-General of the Province of Our Lady of Good Counsel.'' The title of the Province has since been changed to that of St. Thomas of Villanova.

In 1811 the clergy of St. Augustine's founded an educational institution in connection with the church. It was called "St. Augustine's Academy," and was held in Crown street, in the rear of the church, and possibly in the pastoral residence. In a prospectus printed in English and Spanish it is termed " a literary and ecclesiastical institution;" there is evidence of an effort to make this school of superior character. The course of studies included Latin, Greek, modern languages, drawing, music, mathematics, geography, book-keeping, etc. The charges were to be $250 per annum, for board, tuition, washing, mending, paper, pens, and ink. This must have been intended to be made a boarding school, but it failed in the attempt. The accounts, which are still extant, were kept by Dr. Hurley. It appears that the pupils were then charged from $12 to $16 per quarter, and therefore could not have been boarders. The Drs. Hurley and Carr were among the teachers. The writing-master was named Patterson, probably Thomas Patterson, there being a teacher of that name in Philadelphia at the time. He received for his services as writing-master $160 for six months and two weeks' tuition. There were thirty-nine students in all when the school was opened. It was commenced December 9, 1811, and was closed June 19, 1815, most probably on account of the small number of students.

In 1805, during the yellow fever epidemic in the city of New York, Dr. Hurley went there and aided the clergy of the church in their dangerous and laborious work. In 1807, according to the papers, he preached " an eloquent sermon " in St Patrick's church, Baltimore.

In 1823, chiefly through the efforts of Denis Kelly, of Haverford township, Delaware county, the church of St. Denis was founded at Haverford. In consequence of a disagreement with Bishop Conwell the building remained unopened for two years. In 1825 authority was given to Father Hurley to open the church. He said the first Mass there in July, and managed to officiate in it and also at Villa Nova for several years. The church of St. Denis was considered an out-mission of St. Augustine's until 1831. It was then transferred to the Bishop of Philadelphia, and remained under his control for twenty-two years. In 1853 it was again transferred to the Augustinians.

In 1827 Bishop John Dubois, of New York, conferred upon Dr. Hurley faculties for missionary work within his diocese. In pursuance of that authority Dr. Hurley went to Binghampton, in Broome county, N. Y. Here his labors were directed towards the establishment of a congregation, and they culminated in the foundation of the church of St. James. During his stay there of two weeks he visited half a dozen Catholic families, married two couples, and drew together a sufficient number of communicants to found a church. His work was continued by the Rev. William Quarter. Hurley enjoyed this sort of excursion, and occasionally would make journeys to the benighted regions on missionary service. The church records (of St. Augustine's) show that he officiated frequently at Trenton, Lambertville, Cape Island, New Jersey, in the neighborhood of Philadelphia, at Bustleton, Germantown, Frankford, Darby, and Norristown.

On the 22d of July, 1814, the funeral services of Bishop Michael Egan, of Philadelphia, took place at St. Mary's. The religious services were attended by all the clergymen of the diocese. The Rev. Michael Hurley preached the funeral sermon.

At the trial of the suit brought in 1847, on behalf of the church, by the Hermits of St. Augustine, to recover damages for the destruction of property in the riots of 1844, it was stated that the members of the congregation during the "War of 1812" worked upon the trenches erected in Blockley for the defence of the city.*

---

* One fortification and three redoubts were built in August and September, 1814, under the supervision of the Committee of Defence, a body of citizens. The fort was on the southeast side of the Darby road, near the intersection of the road from Gray's Ferry ; the Hamilton redoubt was opposite Hamilton's seat of the Woodlands; another redoubt was on the Lancaster road, and a third on the southern side of the hill at Fairmount, which commanded the road from Haverford, crossing the bridge at Callowhill street ; and the roads and approaches to the Market street bridge were constructed at this time. These extensive works could not have been accomplished except by the voluntary help of citizens in digging the earth and forming the bulwarks. They organized themselves in parties and went down to the trenches. Societies, workers in trades, and church congregations assisted. In the lists of these parties, which have been preserved, the aid given by the congregation of St. Augustine's is not mentioned. They probably marched down with "The Sons of Erin," citizens of the United States who went to work one day twenty-two hundred strong, and on another with three hundred and fifty persons.

In 1816 Lieutenant Richard Smyth, formerly of the United States army, was executed at Philadelphia for the murder of Captain John Carson, of the merchant service. This execution was memorable because it was the first one that had occurred in the city since the close of the preceding century. The cause was wild passion and infatuation which the criminal felt towards a wicked and misguided woman, the wife of Carson. Smyth was of good family; he was a nephew of Daniel Clark, of New Orleans, the father of the celebrated wife of General Edmund Gaines, of the United States army, and in after years the claimant of a great amount of property, as the heir of her father, in that city. Father Hurley administered the consolations of the church to Smyth, who was hanged on the northwest, now Logan, square, on the 10th of August, 1816.

In 1830 Father Hurley accompanied Bishop Kenrick to Wilmington, Delaware, on the occasion of the first visit of that distinguished prelate to that place. Whilst there he preached an "eloquent and impressive discourse."

The pastors of St. Augustine's were patrons of music. The choir of the church was well filled with respectable talent. Benjamin Cross was the organist for many years. The pleasure taken in music by the clergymen led to their granting in June, 1810, permission for the use of the church for the perfect production of the finest concert that had yet been held in the city. Accommodations for such purposes, sufficient for large audiences, did not exist at that time. There was no public music hall, no concert room. Whenever attempts were made to produce works of the best composers, either the theatre or the church was the only place that could be obtained for such uses. Occasionally the hall of the University, Ninth street below Market, a room forty or fifty feet square, was used, although entirely unfit for orchestral or choral effects. The necessity was not met until some years afterward, when the grand saloon of the Masonic Hall, in Chestnut street between Seventh and Eighth, the assembly room of Washington Hall, in Third street near Spruce, and the fine hall of the Musical Fund Society, in Locust above Eighth street, were available for such purposes. These considerations no doubt led to the favor with which the clergymen of St. Augustine's regarded the propositions of Benjamin Carr, René Taylor and

George Schetky, the directors of the concert, that they should be allowed the use of the church building for the production of selections from the great oratorios, Haydn's "Creation" and Handel's "Messiah." The vocal performers were forty in number, most of them being amateurs. The principal soprano was described in the bills as " a young lady amateur pupil of Messrs. Carr and Schetky;" the principal tenor was Thomas Carr, of Baltimore; the organists were Benjamin Carr, Thomas Carr, René Taylor and Mr. Minecke, of Baltimore. The orchestra was strong in professional musicians, who were members of the orchestra of the Chestnut Street Theatre. They were led by George Gillingham. There were twenty-one violins, six violas, four clarionets, six flutes, six violoncellos, three bassoons, three double basses, four trumpets and horns, and one kettle drum. The conditions were embarrassing, owing to the want of trombone performers. They were supplied by players from the Moravian Seminary, in Bethlehem. Altogether there were over one hundred performers. The newspapers of the day give no account of the performance. It was then rare that much space was allowed to matters of local interest. It may be presumed, however, that the affair was entirely successful; the professional talent was the best to be had in the cities of New York, Philadelphia and Baltimore. The amateurs were respectable and fairly trained.

On the 31st of July, 1814, a solemn "Te Deum" was sung in thanksgiving for the restoration of Pope Pius VII. On the 16th of December, 1824, a requiem service was celebrated for the repose of the soul of his late Majesty Louis XVIII. of France. The church was draped in mourning. In the centre was a mortuary catafalque "three stories high." Dr. Hurley was the celebrant, and was assisted by the Rev. Fathers Smyth, Ryan and Harold. Bishop Conweil was present.

In 1833, January 3d, was issued under the editorship of the Rev. Nicholas O'Donnell, O.S.A., assistant clergyman of the church, aided by Dr. Hurley, pastor, the initial number of *The Catholic Herald*. This was the first Catholic newspaper in Philadelphia. Father O'Donnell was a man of learning, of extensive theological training, and had at his elbow the fine library of the Province, which was stored in the residence adjoining the church. Father O'Donnell is credited with having supplied the Rev. John

Hughes, afterward Archbishop of New York, with pertinent extracts from the works of the Fathers, and logical deductions founded thereon, which were used with effect by Hughes in his discussion, upon the merits of the Catholic religion and doctrines, with the Rev. John Breckenbridge, of the Presbyterian church, which took place in Philadelphia in 1833 and 1834, and occupied some weeks.

During the time Dr. Hurley was pastor of the church it was customary to celebrate with more than ordinary ceremony the festival of the patron saint, *i.e.*, St. Augustine. Frequently the services were performed by Mr. Hurley and his associate clergymen. At times efforts were made to obtain the assistance of some eminent Catholic divine to give more than ordinary importance to the occasion. On the saint's day (the Sunday within the octave of the feast), August 29th, 1830, the services at the altar were conducted by the Rev. Father Hurley. The venerable Bishop Conwell occupied a canopied seat and joined in a portion of the ceremonies. The panegyric was delivered by Bishop Kenrick. The principal part of the music of the Mass was composed by a Philadelphian whose name was not announced. In 1831 the panegyric was pronounced by the Rev. Father Kenny. In 1834 the Right Rev. Bishop Kenrick pronounced the eulogy of the saint, and in 1835 the same duty was performed by the Rev. J. H. Hoskyn, president of St. Mary's College, Baltimore.

In 1832, June 17th, there was performed an original mass composed by Charles Taws, Jr., of Philadelphia, and dedicated to Dr. Hurley. It was probably the first entire mass composed by a native Philadelphian. Taws was the son of Charles Taws, who, if not a native, was a resident of the city for many years. The son succeeded the father in the business of manufacturing organs and musical instruments. He was also an accomplished musician and organist. His services were often found valuable in the orchestras of the period.

The church was peculiarly fortunate in securing the best musical talent in connection with the administration of the religious services. The most distinguished organist of the time went into the service of the congregation at the opening of the church in 1801. This was Benjamin Carr, professor of music, and for thirty-eight years the most prominent member of that profession

in the city. Mr. Carr was a brother of Sir John Carr, an Englishman of some literary reputation.   Mr. Carr studied music
under the celebrated Dr. Samuel Arnold, in London, and afterward with John Wesley, a nephew of John Wesley, the founder
of the sect of Methodists. Wesley the music teacher was considered a superior man in his knowledge of harmony and of musical
science. Benjamin Carr came to Philadelphia in 1793, and was
prominent in all musical affairs down to his death. He was a
teacher and a composer, and many of his compositions may be
found in the portfolios of musical collectors. Carr died in May,
1831. To his memory the choir of St. Augustine's erected a
tablet bearing the following inscription :

"This tablet was erected by the members of the choir of St.
Augustine's church, in grateful and affectionate remembrance of
Benjamin Carr, its founder, and for thirty years organist and director, who died in this city on the 28th of May, 1831, in the
sixty-fourth year of his age. May he rest in peace. Amen."*

Benjamin Cross, who had married Mary Hurley, was, during
the latter part of Mr. Carr's time, his assistant, and succeeded
him as organist and musical director in 1831. He was there
until after Dr. Hurley's death, and until some time in 1837 or
1838, when, in consequence of some disagreement with the Rev.

---

* Mr. Carr, although so many years an organist in a Catholic church,
was not a Catholic. His remains were interred in the graveyard of St.
Peter's P. E. church at Third and Pine streets. The Musical Fund
Society erected a monument to his memory bearing the following inscription :

BENJAMIN CARR,
A distinguished musician,
Died May 21st, 1831.   Aged 62 years.
Charitable without ostentation, faithful and true in friendships.
To the intelligence of a man he added the simplicity of a child.
This monument is erected by his friends and associates of
The Musical Fund Society.

This monument was designed by Strickland and executed by Struthers.
There is some difference between the monument and the tablet as to
the statement of the age of Mr. Carr at the time of his death, and also
as to the day of his death. The published notice of his death in the
United States Gazette states that the age of Mr. Carr was 61 years ; the
date of death was May 21st.

Nicholas O'Donnell, then rector, he left the service of the church. In 1839 Antonio F. Dos Santos was the organist. From 1841 to 1843 Benjamin Cross, reinstated, was organist. It is believed that for a comparatively short period, probably about 1844 or 1845, William A. Newland was organist. George J. Corrie was engaged as organist September 1, 1846, and was succeeded about 1852 by Henry Gordon Thunder, who served for twenty-four years. After three years, in which Mr. Thunder officiated in other churches, he returned to St. Augustine's about 1879, and remained until his death, December 14, 1881. His son, Henry Thunder, succeeded him, and still holds that important position.

The services of the choir were gratuitous. The organist received a certain fixed salary. In 1837 it was $200 a year. In 1841 Benjamin Cross was paid $300 a year. In 1846 Geo. J. Corrie was engaged at only $150 per annum. The choir singing master received fifty dollars a year in 1837. The tuner of the organ, C. Knauer, held that position in 1843 and was paid thirty dollars a year, and the organ-blower obtained the same amount.

Once in a while the choir was given a dinner. The account books of the church show that on December 30th, 1811, the cost of the feast was $26.00. On the same day of that month, 1837, a dinner was given to the Rev. Dr. John Hughes and the choir, and was charged in the books at an expense of $24.93½. The next day Dr. Hughes preached a charity sermon, and, sorry to relate, the collections received were only twenty dollars, not enough to pay the cost of the feast the day before.

Occasionally the congregation of the church, for the purpose of raising funds, resorted to the device of holding a fair. A memorable incident of that kind occurred in April, 1840. Masonic Hall, on Chestnut street, was engaged for the purpose, and through the efforts of all concerned there was netted the handsome amount of $3,896.47. On the 13th of April, 1846, another fair was opened at the Chinese Museum building, Ninth and Sansom streets, to secure funds towards the erection of the new church. It was open ten days, and after paying all expenses it was found that the large amount of $5,120.00 was realized.

Towards the close of Dr. Hurley's administration the Roman Catholic Church, which for nearly thirty years after St. Augustine's was finished had only four church buildings in Philadelphia, began

to increase. It had been delayed and kept back by the unfortunate controversies arising under the Hogan schism. It began to
be stimulated to progress and prosperity after the effects of that
trouble had been allayed. The first church constructed in the new
order of things was at Manayunk. It was called St. John the
Baptist's church. The corner-stone was laid May, 1830, Manayunk then being eight years old. There was a peculiarity about
the celebration which was considered worthy of remark. The
ceremonies at the foundation were conducted by Rev. John
Hughes and three other priests. They proceeded to the place
where the church was to be built from the house of Mr. Keating
near by. After these formal ceremonies were gone through, the
clergymen in full vestments repaired to the neighboring Presbyterian church building. There was no other place in the neighborhood at which the address proper on such an occasion could be delivered. The trustees of the Presbyterian congregation tendered
the use of their building for the occasion. A writer who saw the
procession and described the scene, said: "It presented to my mind,
as it passed, under all the circumstances, something more than
mere novelty. If I might make use of the word, I would call it
religiously romantic. There was old age moving with a celerity
of footstep quickened by the dread of losing a seat ; there was
boyhood in all his glee making the most of a holiday; there were
the gentlemen and ladies, and close by them the man of labor
who 'went not back to take up his coat,' the whole variegated
with a proportionate sprinkling of beauty and fashion ; it seemed
to be a miniature of mankind. But that which struck me most
was the *agitans molem*, the Roman Catholic priest, shedding
from the glittering robes in which religion had arrayed him the
broken rays of a setting sun that beamed full upon his vestment
and countenance. Where was he going ? He was going to preach,
by permission both Divine and human, in a Presbyterian church,
and to a congregation of all religions. It was altogether a sight
the like of which I had never before seen." The Rev. Mr.
Hughes preached from Genesis 28th, "And this stone which I
have set up for a title shall be called the House of God." The
church was finished in eleven months and dedicated April 4th,
1831.

On the 6th of May, 1831, the cornerstone of the church of St. John the Evangelist, on Thirteenth above Chestnut, was laid. On that occasion there were impressive ceremonies. Bishop Kenrick conducted the service, assisted by several clergymen, including Rev. William O'Donnell, Rev. N. O'Donnell, of St. Augustine's, with their pastor, Rev. Dr. Hurley ; Rev. Jeremiah Keily, of St. Mary's ; and Rev. T. J. Donahoe, of St. Joseph's. This church was founded by the Rev. John Hughes, who was at that time a clergyman at St. Joseph's. It was intended to be the finest church in the city, and it was, when finished, considered an elegant building. St. John's was completed and dedicated on the 8th of April, 1832. Father Hughes was proud of the building, which he considered to be designed more nearly in the correct ecclesiastical style than any that had yet been built in the city. In a letter to the late Archbishop Purcell, dated September 31st, 1832, he said, concerning this edifice : '' It will cause those who give nothing toward its construction to murmur at its costliness, and those who do contribute to be proud of their own doings. As a religious edifice it will be the pride of the city. The leading Protestants and infidels proclaim it to be the only building entitled to be called a church, inasmuch as its appearance indicates its use, and there is no mistaking it for a workshop.''

On Easter Monday, April 8th, 1833, the foundations of another church were laid in Kensington. This was St. Michael's, at the corner of Second and Jefferson streets. Bishop Kenrick laid the cornerstone, and was assisted by Dr. Hurley, Revs. John Hughes, Terence J. Donahoe, Jeremiah Keily, William Whelan, Tolentine Da Silva, James Foulhouze, Francis Gartland, and N. O'Donnell, O. S. A. This was the first Catholic church established in the Northern Liberties. It was dedicated September 20, 1834.

In 1825 one of the assistant clergymen of St. Augustine's was the Rev. John Hughes, afterwards Archbishop of New York. Father Hurley had become acquainted with him whilst he was still in the seminary of Mt. St. Mary, at Emmittsburg, Maryland, where, after having studied, he was for some time a teacher. In expectation of his ordination as deacon, Hurley wrote to Hughes in 1825, advising him before his admission to orders to consider and prepare at least sermons enough to last six months, to be delivered on occasion, assuring him that he would find such forethought to be to his advantage. By such means he would be ahead of his work whenever he would be called upon to perform it. The wisdom of this well-meant advice was either not apparent to Hughes or his time was taken up so that he had not opportunity to prepare his sermons. It was determined that he should come to Philadelphia in the service of St. Augustine's church. Unluckily or luckily, it would be hard to decide which, on his way to this city he encountered, at Chambersburg, Bishop Conwell.

The latter was upon an episcopal visitation to the churches in the western part of his diocese. He was very much pleased with young Hughes, and invited him to go with him during the remainder of his trip. This, coming from the Ordinary, was a favor and, besides, a command. Hughes turned aside in his journey and went with the Bishop. At the first church at which they stopped the bishop requested the young priest to preach. Then the latter found the wisdom of Hurley's advice, and regretted that he had not taken it. Instead of having twenty-five or thirty sermons, he only had one. He was ready enough to preach that one, and did very well. But at the next church on the circuit he was again asked to preach, and, very much to his dissatisfaction, was compelled to enlighten the congregation with the same sermon. This he repeated at every church during the visitation, and caused the dry remark from the Bishop, on their return, "that it was a very good sermon, but he thought he knew it by heart." At Philadelphia, Hughes at once went to St. Augustine's, where he remained a few weeks, when he was transferred to St. Joseph's. There was always a strong feeling of friendship between Hughes and Hurley. (See "Life of Archbishop Hughes," by J. R. G. Hassard, page 46.)

In 1832 the Asiatic cholera, a dread pestilence, which in former years had seemed to march with deadly virulence through Europe and Asia, destroying in its progress hundreds of thousands of lives, approached the western continent. A lively interest had been taken in former years in the accounts from foreign countries of the progress of the awful visitation. There was some hope that the great ocean would be a barrier to its coming to this country. These expectations were dissipated. In the early part of the summer of 1832, the Board of Health sent a communication to the City Councils of Philadelphia, June 2d, requesting that particular attention be given to the cleansing of the streets, and removal of nuisances from houses and enclosures. In less than a week information was received that the cholera had broken out on the 8th of June at Quebec in Canada. It made its appearance two days afterward at Montreal. In all parts of the United States there was an immediate alarm. In this city ward meetings were held and Citizens' Committees of Vigilance were appointed. A sanitary board of twelve members was appointed by City Councils. The Board of Health dispatched a medical commission, composed of Drs. Samuel Jackson, Charles D. Meigs and Richard Harlan, to Canada, to obtain information of the character and means of prevention and cure of this disease. Bishop Francis Patrick Kenrick issued an address to the clergy of his diocese, recommending humility, submission and prayer, and directing that certain offices should be observed in addition to the usual religious services. The Bishop added : ''Since the use of fish and vegetables is considered by eminent members of the faculty to predispose the system to the disease, the obligation of abstinence from the use of meat during the continuance of the alarm or the prevalence of the malady shall be dispensed with.'' The Protestant clergy in meeting assembled on the 6th of July, the venerable Bishop White, of the P. E. Church, acting as chairman. It was determined to set aside ''a day of fasting, humiliation, and prayer, to entreat the God of Providence to avert the awful disaster of his righteous judgment.'' July 19th was fixed for that purpose, and was duly observed. A month afterward, August 19, an official fast was observed by all denominations by recommendation of Governor George Wolf. The establishment of hospitals for the nursing and care of those stricken down with the disease was the first necessity. Twenty-one buildings were appropriated for that purpose, and a staff of physicians and nurses was assigned to them. Of these places of refuge for the sick ten were school-houses, two were buildings used as carpenter shops, six were houses occupied as dwellings, but at that time vacant, one was the City Hospital at Bush Hill, south of Coates street (Fairmount avenue), between Nineteenth and Twentieth streets ; one was the session room of a Presbyterian church, Cherry street west of Fifth ; and the last which we shall mention was the dwelling house of a Catholic priest, the residence of the Rev. Dr. Hurley, in Crown street below Vine. For the purpose of assistance to the community during this great calamity, Father Hurley gave up the comfort of his own residence and took lodgings elsewhere ; the furniture was removed. The St. Augustine's Hospital was under the control of Dr. Oliver H. Taylor, assisted by Sisters of Charity. Indeed, so great was the alarm and fear of the contagious character of the disease that the full available force of the sisterhood volunteered their services, and were at the bedside of the sick and dying in other hospitals. John Binns, in his "Personal Recollections," says, speaking of that dreadful time : "At that awful period a minister of the Gospel in Philadelphia, who had a large house and a school-house adjoining, caused to be removed out of them every article of furniture that could be dispensed with, and converted the building into a hospital. He had it admirably arranged, fitting it up with all necessaries and supplied with fearless and tender nurses, women religiously devoted to the faithful discharge of their duties. I was acquainted with this benevolent individual ; he was an Irishman and a Catholic. Although we thought widely different on many subjects of religious moment, yet we worshipped the same God and adored the same Redeemer. I was, by him, invited to walk over this new establishment for cholera patients. The whitewashed walls and nicely-sanded floors exhibited its neatness and cleanliness. A plentiful supply of medicine and everything required was provided. There were sedan chairs, with spring poles of the easiest possible construction, to convey patients to this hospital. It was so judiciously adapted to its purpose, its doors were thrown so hospitably open, and its superintendent was so intent on doing good, that many patients were collected within its walls. The whole number of patients was three hundred and seventy. Of these sixty-three were Catholics and three hundred and seven were Protestants. Having no faith myself in the contagious character of the disease, I went through the rooms, and while memory holds her seat I can never forget the impression made upon me by the affectionate solicitude of all who were in attendance on the sick. There are hundreds now in this city who have more or less knowledge of the intense and anxious care and untiring solicitude with which the poor and afflicted were there watched over by day and by night. Many a parent, husband, and wife were, through the instrumentality of that hospital, restored to their afflicted families.''

It does not appear that the services of Dr. Hurley on this occasion were ever specially the subject of thanks, or that the expenses incurred were remunerated. After the ravages of the pestilence had ceased, City Councils, in October, 1832, received the report of the special committee appointed to consider and prepare resolutions of thanks to the physicians who tendered their services during the prevalence of the cholera. In reference to that subject the committee, of which William J. Duane was chairman, said : " They will not depart without manifesting their grateful sense for those eminent members of an enlightened, liberal, and essential profession who at the moment of general dismay gave their voluntary and gratuitous services in the cause of humanity. In ordinary cases medical practitioners incur only the perils incident to the prevalence of the disease ; but during the existence of the recent pestilence in this city it is with mortification recollected that they had to encounter resistances and menaces from the timid, ignorant, uninformed, and deluded, which were calculated to produce alarm as well as disgust ; yet those who had undertaken to act, persisted unto a happy termination to their labors, overcoming disease by their skill and assiduity, and prejudice by firmness and moderation. Nor can the present Councils without impropriety omit an expression of their cordial thanks to those individuals of the tender sex who, under a sense of religious obligation, as well as from an impulse of their own pure hearts, performed at once the duties of kindred and those as nurses to the poor and destitute in the abode of disease and death.'' A resolution was therefore adopted tendering the grateful thanks of the committee to twelve physicians who had charge of the hospitals which were located within the bounds of the city proper, and to the medical assistants who served with them. The following was also adopted :

Resolved, That the citizens of Philadelphia entertain an adequate sense of the courageous devotedness, assiduity and zeal of those women, and especially of the Sisters of Charity, who risked their lives and exerted all their energies to restore the sick to health, to give comfort to the dying, and to protect the bereaved orphan.

"An appropriation of $2000 was made to the Mayor and Presidents of Councils, 'to cause an adequate number of pieces of plate, with an appropriate inscription on each, to be prepared and presented, one to each of the physicians aforenamed, and one to each of the Sisters of Charity who served in the Cholera Hospitals, as a mark of esteem and thankfulness of the citizens of Philadelphia.' ''

In consequence of the passage of this resolution, John Swift, the Mayor, received the following communication on the 26th of October:

To his Honor, the Mayor of the City of Philadelphia:

RESPECTED SIR:

The Sisters of Charity beg leave to submit respectfully to the City authorities, that it would be at variance with the spirit of their institution, and contrary to the rules by which they are governed as a religious community, for them to receive anything as a consideration for their services, except mere personal expenses. They are induced to make your Honor acquainted with the circumstances, in consequence of its being stated to them that a piece of plate with an appropriate inscription was voted to each of the Sisters who served as nurses in public hospitals during the prevalence of cholera. They are aware that this was not to be presented as a recompense for their services, but as a mark of approbation of their conduct. If their exertions were useful to their suffering fellow-beings, and satisfactory to the public authorities, they think it sufficient reward, and indeed the only one consistent with their vocation to receive. For the motives which prompted the offering they are sincerely grateful—and we trust your Honor and the members of City Councils will not be displeased (considering the motives which influence them as a *religious community*) at their declining to accept any further testimony of that kindness and respect which, in their intercourse in the hospitals and elsewhere, they have not ceased to experience.

After the reception of this communication, Councils resolved that the money which would have been spent for silver plate to be presented to the Sisters should be given for the support of orphans in those institutions over which they presided. One half of the whole sum was to be given to the Asylum, at Broad street, and the other half equally between St. Joseph's Asylum, at Sixth street near Spruce, and the Female Free School, in Prune near Fourth.

Among the marriages registered on the church books were some which may be mentioned as of interest, from the names of the parties. Among them were:

1808, Feb. 12, by Rev. Father Hurley, John Jos. Borie to Sophia Beauveau.

1810, Feb. 15, by the same, Fielding Lucas to Elizabeth Carrell.

1814, Dec. 24, by Dr. Carr, John Baptist Bernadou to Henrietta Fontaine.

1817, Oct. 28, by the same, Henry Dominic Lallemand to Henrietta Maria Girard.

The witnesses on this occasion were Stephen Girard, Joseph Bonaparte (Count de Survilliers, ex-king of Naples and Spain), Marshal Count de Grouchy, General Charles Lallemand, and others.

1818, May 28, by Dr. Hurley, Franklin Bache, grandson of Benjamin Franklin, to Aglaie Dabadie.

Witnesses were William Duane and Hartmann Bache.

1819, Jan. 21, by Dr. Hurley, Henry C. Carey to Martha Leslie, a Protestant.

Witnesses were Mathew Carey, father of the groom, Isaac Lea, his partner, Mr. Carey and Thomas Jefferson Leslie.

1820, Nov. 2, by Father Hurley, Robert Ewing to Sarah Y. Davis.

1821, Feb. 21, by the same, Augustus Taney to Catharine, half sister of Dr. Hurley.

The witnesses were Mathew Carey, William Hawkins and Patrick Burns.

1821, Feb. 26, by Dr. Hurley, Isaac Lea to Frances Anna Carey, daughter of Mathew Carey.

1821, Nov. 29, by Father Hurley, Robert Meade to Elizabeth Nice, widow, maiden name Holcomb.

1822, Oct. 10, by Father Heyden, Titian Rembrandt Peale to Elizabeth Laforgue.

1824, Dec. 23, Father Hurley, Dr. Aaron B. Tucker* to Elizabeth Henrietta Carroll.

The witnesses were Charles Carroll, the Revolutionary patriot, Samuel Chew, Joseph Cabot, Samuel Tucker, Harriet and Louisa Carroll.

1829, February 10, by Dr. Hurley, George Edwards to Elizabeth Whelan.

1829,——, by the same, Dr. John Y. Clark to Henrietta Maria Lallemand, widow of Henry Dominic Lallemand, married in 1817.

Among the baptisms were the following :

1801, Dec. 1, Caroline Eugenie, daughter of John Girard, a brother of Stephen, born in Burlington, N. J., 1797, and Henrietta Maria, twin to Caroline Eugenie Girard.

---

* Is this name *Aaron* B. or *Abner* B. ? See below in baptisms. The Philadelphia Directory only gives the name A. B.—T. C. M.

1803, Nov. 20, Augusta Virginia Peale, daughter of Rembrandt Peale, born at Reading, England.

1819, June 3, Charles Louis Borie, son of John Joseph Borie.

1820, Feb. 21, Mary Jane Henrietta Cora, daughter of Peter A. Frenaye.

1822, March 6, Matthew Carey Lea, son of Isaac Lea.

1823, April 6, Caroline Adelaide Stephanie Girard Lallemand, daughter of Henry Dominic Lallemand. The sponsors were Stephen Girard and Adelaide Segoigne.

1826, July 17, Mary Louisa Caroline, daughter of James A. Bayard, of Delaware, by his wife Mary Carroll, daughter of Charles Carroll, of Carrollton, Md.

1826, May 4, Henrietta Sophia Tucker, daughter of Abner B. Tucker* by his wife Elizabeth Carroll, daughter of Charles Carroll.

1833, May 8, Michael Hurley Cross, son of Benjamin Cross and Mary Hurley.

It appears from the books of St. Augustine's that the number of baptisms between the opening of the church in 1801 and the close of 1883, inclusive, was 18,203. The number of marriages was 4540 for the same period, and the confirmations 5807.

There was no record of confirmations until 1838, when one hundred and one persons were confirmed by Bishop Francis Patrick Kenrick, on October 7th. In 1844, one hundred and three were confirmed in St. Joseph's on July 7th.

After St. Augustine's was burned, Bishop Francis Patrick Kenrick gave confirmation in 1846 and '47, and Peter Richard Kenrick, Archbishop of St. Louis, officiated in 1848; Bishop John Timon, of Buffalo, N. Y., in 1849; Bishop Francis Patrick Kenrick, of Philadelphia, in 1850-1; Bishop John Nepomucene Neumann, in 1852-3-5 and '57. In 1858, '61-3-5-7-9, '70-3, Bishop James Frederic Wood officiated.

During Dr. Hurley's time the following societies were established amongst the worshippers of the church:

(1) St. Augustine's Beneficial Society.
(2) Confraternity of Saints Monica and Augustine.
(3) Library Society.
(4) St. Augustine's Temperance Society.
(5) Ladies Benevolent Society.
(6) Rosary Society.

---

* See query Fr. Middleton on preceding page.

The career of Dr. Hurley was active and continuously useful until within a short time of his death. On May 2d, 1837, he administered for the last time the rite of baptism and made his entry on the register in his own hand writing. On May 7th he sang Mass for the last time. On Pentecost Sunday, May 14, he received the last sacraments at 9 o'clock, and died three hours afterward, a little before midnight. It was stated in the *U. S. Gazette* of May 16 that the cause of his death was acute bronchitis and effusion of the lungs.

The notices of his death in the public journals are somewhat scant. He died at an unfortunate period in our local history. Philadelphia, and indeed the whole country, had been turned upside down, financially; great anxiety prevailed, and there were with many people gloomy forebodings of poverty and ruin. Trade was dull. Thousands were out of employment, and the collection of debts was a difficult matter. On May 10, while Dr. Hurley was in his last sickness, the banks of the city of New York suspended specie payment. On the 11th this action was followed by the banks of Philadelphia and by others all over the country. The sudden stoppage of the circulating medium by the refusal of banks to cash their notes created great embarrassment; there were anxious consultations as to adopting the best methods about it. Before expedients could be resorted to, the pastor of St. Augustine's had ceased to live. The event of his death caused scarcely any thought in a community deeply engaged in other affairs. No public announcement was made of his death until Tuesday the 16th, and the notices on the occasion were brief. The only reference to the bereavement on that day which appeared was in the ordinary advertisement.

The *Philadelphia Inquirer*, on the 17th of May, noticed the fact of Dr. Hurley's death, and said: "He was charitable and philanthropic in an eminent degree. Hundreds of Philadelphia's poor, to whom he administered mental as well as pecuniary relief, will mourn his departure to the land of the spirits. His death will also be deeply deplored by his large and respectable congregation, while Christians of all denominations who were acquainted with his virtue will pay the proper tribute to his memory." An obituary notice signed "B." appeared, March 17, in the *U. S. Gazette* and *Poulson's Advertiser:* "The heart which but recently beat in that—now tenement of clay—was as warm and generous a heart as ever beat in human bosom. The writer of this has known him for thirty years, and is thoroughly assured that there never was a period in which Michael Hurley would not have divided his dollars or his loaves and fishes with the poor or the stranger. His heart and hand were ever open to the claims of the afflicted. The whole human family he regarded as brothers and sisters, and esteemed the worthy and good, whatever may have been their creed. He has raised monuments of gratitude in the hearts of widows and the fatherless, and of those who had none save him to help them. The sod covering his grave will often be wet by the tears of orphans whom he has provided with food and raiment."*

The solemn obequies took place at St. Augustine's church, May 17. The body was raised on a platform in the middle of the church. Around it were sixteen priests chanting the office of the dead. The Rev. John Hughes, of St. John's, afterward Archbishop of New York, sang the Mass of Requiem, and Rev. Dr. James Ryder delivered the panegyric.

The body of Father Hurley was interred in an ordinary grave, just as his predecessors, Dr. Carr and Father Lariscy, had been, in the little churchyard in the rear of the church, usually known as the Garden Graveyard, on Crown street. After his death, in 1837, the members of St. Augustine's choir held a meeting to provide a suitable burying-place for the deceased clergymen attached to the church. A committee was appointed to receive collections. John Brown was president and John Walsh was treasurer. The other members were Benjamin Cross, the organist, John Huneker, Matthew Brown, John Sinnet, Charles G. Hookey, Miss Cross, Miss Ellen Roland, Miss Margaret McCormick, Miss Louisa Guibert, and Mrs. John Brown, all members of the choir. A few others contributed to the fund. Enough money was obtained to go on with the work without delay. A vault was built back of the church, and in it were placed the remains of the clergymen,—Rev. Matthew Carr, D. D., who died Sep-

* The newspapers place the date of his death as May 15. This is shown to be a mistake by the diary of Mrs. Mary Lloyd, a lady who was an earnest member of St. Augustine's congregation. She says he died "twelve minutes before midnight of May 14."

tember 29, 1820; Rev. Philip Lariscy, who died April 6, 1824; and Rev. Michael Hurley, who died May 14, 1837. Since that time other clergymen have been interred in the vault. In 1869 the marble coping, iron railing, and inscriptions of the names of persons deposited in the vault were finished.

In reference to the personal appearance of Dr. Hurley, there are some differences of description among those who knew him in his lifetime, which are scarcely reconcilable. His sister, Mrs. Mary Cross, says "he was tall, stout, large limbed, and of full face —a very fine, dignified man, of pleasing features and kind expression; a man of culture, eloquent and courtly; though brusque on some occasions, yet he was exceedingly generous—giving away everything he had; and very hospitable, always having some friend or other at table; while very abstemious himself, he loved to give others whatever good cheer was in his power. Father Jordan ("Sketch of St. Joseph's Church") says of Hurley that "he was not eloquent" and "was brusque and unpolished * * * He instructed by his works, and preached most eloquently by his actions * * * Whenever there was a scandal to be corrected in either of the parishes of St. Joseph or St. Augustine, Father Hurley was to be found. He did not believe in wearing kid gloves while scouring the ink. His speech on such occasions was loud and caustic."

A gentleman who was brought up under the shadow of St. Joseph's, over fifty years ago, writes: "Father Hurley was about five feet ten inches in height, large boned and muscular, weighing about 200 pounds. His complexion was florid, his voice was clear, strong and musical, and gave satisfaction during his high Masses to all. He was a holy and amiable man, and was the leading priest of Philadelphia."

Two portraits of Dr. Hurley are still in existence, painted for his father and for his brother Thomas. Both are by Sully. The first now belongs to the Taney family, of Maryland. It is of half figure size, and represents Dr. Hurley in surplice and stole. The second belongs to his half sister, Mrs. Mary Cross, of this city. It is of the same size, and portrayed him in black soutane.

Perhaps it was a happy thing, in consideration of Dr. Hurley's devoted service at St. Augustine's, that he did not live long enough to suffer the pain which he would have felt could he have

witnessed the scene of desecration and destruction a few years
after his death which happened to the church he had loved so
much. He could not have anticipated that in the city of his childhood and manhood, inhabited, as he knew, by a population subject to many creeds, but moving harmoniously together, the
spirit of religious animosity could attain such strength that it
dared to apply the incendiary torch to God's Holy Temple. Yet
all this happened within seven years after his death. The church

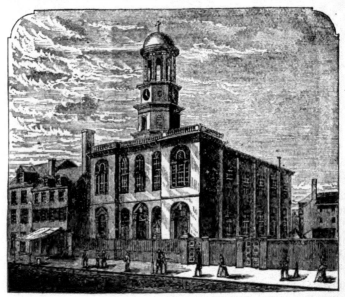

ST. AUGUSTINE'S CHURCH BEFORE ITS DESTRUCTION IN 1844.

of St. Michael and the seminary on Second near Master were
first burned. On the same night, May 8th, 1844, the church of
St. Augustine was attacked, and was soon destroyed by the mob.

Amidst all this riot and desolation, the remains of Dr. Hurley
lay quiet in the vault adjoining the church and residence, which
were totally destroyed. If on that dreadful occasion his spirit
could have looked down the next day on the scene which he had
loved so well, there would have appeared to his vision, as it did to
the eyes of living persons who looked upon the evidence of destruction, on the blackened walls of the chancel above the high

altar, the inscription appearing as fresh and unsoiled as when it was first painted, the startling words, and such as they now appeared to be, "THE LORD SEETH."

Dr. Hurley, as one of the Brethren of the Order of Hermits of St. Augustine, by his last will devised all his property to the Rev. John Hughes, pastor of St. John's church, and the Rev. Nicholas O'Donnell, O. S. A., "my coadjutor in the ministry." He also forbade "any one claiming kindred in any degree" from having anything. The witnesses to his will were the Rev. Terence J. Donahoe, pastor of St. Michael's, and Dr. Bernard McNeil. The executors were Messrs. Hughes and O'Donnell.*

With the death of Dr. Hurley the task of the writer properly ceases; but as considerable material has been collected illustrating the subsequent history of St. Augustine's church, up to the present time, it is thought proper to add it in the shape of a sketch in this place.

On the death of Dr. Hurley, the pastorship of St. Augustine's remained in charge of the Rev. Nicholas O'Donnell, O. S. A., who served from 1837 to 1839. He was succeeded by the Very Rev. Patrick Eugene Moriarty, D. D., O. S. A., who remained from 1839 to 1844. Dr. Moriarty was exceedingly popular as an ecclesiastic and orator. He was the foremost clergyman of the Roman Catholic Church in Philadelphia at that time. He was not only noted for his attention to his pastoral duties, but shone in a sphere outside of the Church. He was ready to speak on all public occasions; he was a noted orator on behalf of the Irish cause when, then as now, it was in agitation amongst sons of the Green Isle and American citizens. Public lectures on literary and historical subjects were then much in vogue. They were encouraged by the highest and most intelligent class of citizens and ran through courses of twelve or sixteen weekly lectures. The brightest scholars, the most eminent speakers of the legal and medical professions, with divines of various denominations, par-

---

*The devise to Father Hughes vested him, in connection with Father O'Donnell, of the Order of Hermits of St. Augustine, with the title in the church, and made it necessary for Father Hughes, who was in 1844 Bishop of New York, to join in the suit subsequently brought against the county of Philadelphia, for the recovery of damages for the destruction of St. Augustine's church during the riots of 1844.

ticipated on such occasions, under the auspices of the Athenian Institute and Mercantile Library Company. Dr. Moriarty was usually to be found as a speaker in each annual course. His topics were either historical or philosophical, and usually chosen with such good taste that they were attractive to all classes of hearers. Dr. Moriarty was pastor at the time the church was burned, but he was soon afterward transferred to another field of usefulness. He was succeeded in 1844 by the Rev. John Possidius O'Dwyer, O. S. A., upon whose shoulders fell the hard task of keeping the congregation together and endeavoring to rebuild the despoiled edifice.

After the church of St. Augustine was burned the clergy were dispersed and the congregation worshipped at St. Joseph's in the afternoon of Sundays until some means were taken to assemble them together again. The pastors and congregation consulted as to what was best to be done. The loss was heavy, and the Brothers of St. Augustine were without the means to rebuild the church immediately. The first measure was to erect some kind of building in which they could assemble. This was done by the building of a chapel, using the bricks and material, that were suitable for building, from the ruins of the old church. The chapel was dedicated to Our Lady of Consolation and stood back of the graveyard on the north side of the church, extending to Crown street. The architect was P. A. Topinard. The chapel was dedicated on Sunday, October 27th, 1844. The sermon was delivered by the Rev. Dr. Ryder, of Georgetown College.

There was a considerable delay in the suit to recover damages for the destruction of the church which was brought against the County of Philadelphia by the Revs. Nicholas and James O'Donnell, O.S.A., and Rt. Rev. John Hughes. In January, 1846, the County Commissioners, who were at that time members of the Native American party, petitioned the Supreme Court for a writ of *quo warranto* to be issued against Messrs. O'Donnell and Hughes, demanding to know by what authority they claimed to exercise the franchise of a corporation as Brothers of the Order of Hermits of St. Augustine. The petition declared there was no such corporation, that the records of the Acts of Assembly passed by the Legislature had been searched, and that no such law was in existence.*

The petition also advanced the ordinary political argument of the day, that if there was such a corporation it was composed of foreign ecclesiastics who owed allegiance to the Pope of Rome, which allegiance was averred to be more binding upon them than the laws of the United States or of Pennsylvania.

There was much delay about the decision of this question. The machinery which the law sometimes uses to delay and defeat justice was abundantly resorted to. There were motions of various kinds affecting the proceedings. Upon each, when made, there was necessity of argument and delay. One of the notable occurrences connected with the affair was that in 1846, when the first skirmish occurred before the Supreme Court on a preliminary matter, Peter A. Browne, the solicitor for the County Commissioners, who had instituted the proceedings, appeared to argue the question, while Horn R. Kneass, who had been elected by the County Commissioners after Browne,—there being at that time a majority of Democrats in the Board of Commissioners,—appeared and informed the court that he had received no authority to go on with the case. Browne claimed under his former authority, and proceeded to argue the question which he himself had raised. The cause came on finally to be argued in the spring of 1847. The court heard argument upon six issues of law, which involved what might be denominated the religious questions raised about the authority of the Pope and the rights of the clergymen to exercise the functions of American citizenship. These were all disposed of by decisions in favor of the defendants. There remained three issues of fact to be determined by the jury. The cause was called before the Supreme Court at *Nisi Prius* on November 22, 1847. By that time the County Commissioners had been entirely reorganized politically, and they had ordered their solicitor to discontinue the proceeding. Consequently he entered a formal

---

*It is the fact that the printed copies of the Laws of Pennsylvania passed in 1804, commonly called the Pamphlet Laws, do not contain any act chartering the Order of Hermits of St. Augustine. Yet it is also the fact that in the Act of Assembly of June, 1832, which is entitled a Supplement to the Act of 1804, the latter is expressly referred to and some of its provisions quoted.

withdrawal on record.   The counsel for the church, who had been put to great inconvenience and delay in the recovery of a just claim, were not disposed to submit to such a policy.   They demanded a trial upon the issues framed.   The court decided that the county had no right to discontinue a proceeding on *quo warranto*, which was a prerogative writ of the commonwealth. The counsel for the church—Messrs. William A. Stokes, William Morris Meredith, and Henry J. Williams—pressed for trial, and the right was awarded them.   The issues were these :

1. That there had never been such a corporation.
2. That the succession of corporators had not been regularly kept up.
3. That the charter was forfeited by the corporation holding more real estate than the charter allowed.

Upon all these issues the verdict was given for the defendant. Two days afterward the long delayed suit for damages came up for trial.

The claim which was made on behalf of the church for damages was as follows :

Library of 3000 volumes, collected by the Rev. Drs.
  Carr and Hurley, Fathers Staunton, Kyle and
  James O'Donnell * $13,000
Damage to church furniture $5,370 87
  "   " Rev. John P. O'Dwyer's effects 9,225 00
  "   " " James O'Donnell's effects 6,916 75
  "   " " Thomas Kyle's effects 570 00
  "   " " Francis Ashe's effects, ⎫
  "   " " William Harnett's, " ⎬ 150 00
  "   " Four servants'   " 170 00
  "   " Six Trombones 300 00
  "   " House Furniture. 3,650 07

             Total $39,372 69
Damages to buildings 44,255 06
Total amount to buildings and personal property . . 83,627 75

* The library was one of the most valuable theological collections in the country.   It contained the complete works of the Fathers from the third century down.   There were over five hundred Bibles, one of them printed in 1480.   Another was in forty volumes and written in six languages.   The complete works of Luther were in it, and Protestant, Catholic and Infidel works.   Some of these were rescued from the flames, but the greater portion were destroyed.

A verdict was given in favor of the church in the Court of *Nisi Prius* on November 29th of that year for $47,433.87.

There was a stubborn opposition to the claim on behalf of the County. It was asserted that the amount of damages was far less than the claim, and that there was exaggeration in all the items. Perhaps there might have been political or religious prejudice also. The amount of the verdict was peculiar, and shows that there must have been some attempt among the jury to average the various amounts which the individual members of that body were willing to give.

St. Michael's church, the case of which was tried on December 8th, made out much better. They claimed $19,391 for the destruction of the church, $4,066.55 for the destruction of the parsonage, and $61.73 for the destruction of church furniture, making a total of $29,631.07. The jury gave a verdict in favor of the church for $27,090.02. St. Michael's also recovered, in 1844, a verdict for the value of the seminary and school house on Second street, destroyed by the mob, of $6,468.98.

Before this verdict was secured the congregation of St. Augustine's found itself very much crowded in the little chapel, and efforts were made to rebuild the church. The corner-stone was laid by Bishop Kenrick and several other clergymen on May 23d, 1847. The sermon was to have been delivered on the occasion by Rev. Dr. Ryder, S.J. That part of the ceremony, in consequence of stormy weather, was postponed until the next day. The collections on laying the corner-stone were $1,050, which, together with contributions already obtained, amounted to $10,000.

The details of the building are thus described : "It is of brick, 61 feet wide by 152 feet in depth, an addition of 26 feet to the length of the old church. A tower in front extends 8 feet beyond the line of the old front. The sanctuary in the rear extends 18 feet from the line of the former rear wall. The architecture is of the Roman Palladian school. The front consists of a tower 200 feet high to the summit of the *dome*, flanked on each side* by niches at the angles of the walls and projections, strengthened, protected and ornamented by granite quoin stones of alternate

---

*This part of the design was not carried out. The tower is only about 165 feet from the ground to the cross.

lengths. The tower is in four grand divisions: The lower one occupies the whole height of the main story of the church ; the second is a square ornamented with windows, stone dressing, etc.; the third is of octagonal form, the bases ot which will exhibit clock dial faces on the four cardinal points, decorated with Attic wreaths. The order of this story is Ionic, the four sides are to be pierced with circular-headed openings and the angles to be decorated with statues of the Evangelists elevated on pedestals. The fourth story is circular, resting on an octagonal base, and decorated with eight Corinthian pillars supported on an enriched entablature. The sides towards the cardinal points are pierced with semi-circular openings, and the other sides are embellished with niches and panels. The whole is surmounted by a domical panelled roof, above which on an ornamental base is planted the cross. The sanctuary in the west end of the building is in a rectangular recess of 18 by 25 feet, ornamented by Corinthian columns, the whole representing a triumphal-arch. "The architect was Napoleon le Brun. The church was so far finished that it was opened on Christmas Day, 1847, when Mass was sung for the first time by Bishop Kenrick, assisted by the Reverend Messrs. Hartnett, Mullen, Meagher and O'Dwyer. It was consecrated, being free of debt, on Sunday, November 5th, 1848, by Bishop Kenrick. The sermon on this occasion was delivered by Bishop John Hughes, of New York. Father O'Dwyer died soon after the new church was built, May 24th, 1850. The Very Rev. P. E. Moriarty, D.D., returned from Ireland to the church, and served until 1855. The Rev. Patrick Augustine Stanton succeeded him."

The Rev. Mark Crane became pastor in 1862. He died January 19th, 1871, aged 39 years. His successor was Rev. Peter Crane, who is still in the service of the church. Since the erection of the new edifice the history of the congregation has been unmarked by any unusual event. The services have been administered attentively and faithfully, and the efforts of the clergymen have been justly valued by the congregation. The communicants have been steady in the discharge of their religious duties, obedient to pastoral admonitions and liberal in contributing for good purposes whenever occasion might arise.

ADDENDA.

I.

LIST OF PASTORS, ASSISTANTS AND VISITING CLERGYMEN WHO OFFICIATED AT ST. AUGUSTINE'S CHURCH, INCORPORATORS OF THE CHURCH, AUGUSTINIAN MISSIONS, 1778-1841.

[Tables furnished by REV. THOMAS C. MIDDLETON, O. S. A.]

LIST OF PASTORS OF ST. AUGUSTINE'S CHURCH, PHILADELPHIA, WITH THE YEARS OF THEIR PASTORATE, 1801-1886.

(1) Matthew Carr, D.D., O.S.A., 1801-1820; (2) Michael Hurley, D.D., O.S.A., 1820-37 ; (3) Nicholas O'Donnell, O.S.A., 1837-39 ; (4) Patrick Eugene Moriarty, D.D., O.S.A., 1839-44 ; (5) John Possidius O'Dwyer, O.S.A., 1844-50 ; (6) Patrick Eugene Moriarty, D.D., O.S.A, 1850-55 ; (7) Patrick Augustine Stanton, O.S.A., 1855-62 ; (8) Mark Crane, O.S.A., 1862-71 ; (9) Peter Crane, O.S.A., 1871-86.

LIST OF ASSISTANTS AND VISITING CLERGYMEN AT ST. AUGUSTINE'S CHURCH, PHILADELPHIA, FROM 1801 TO 1850 (WITH THE NAMES OF THOSE WHO WERE NOT AUGUSTINIANS IN BRACKETS), AS RECORDED IN THE PARISH REGISTERS.

1801. George Staunton, [Raphael Fitzpatrick, secular].
1802. G. Staunton, Philip Stafford.
1803. G. Staunton, P. Stafford, John Rosseter, Michael Hurley, [Thomas Flynn, Trappist monk].
1804. P. Stafford, M. Hurley, [T. Flynn].
1805. M. Hurley.
1806. [Peter Helbron (or Heilbron), secular ; Matthew O'Brien, ditto ; Balthassar Torelli, ditto].
1807. M. Hurley, [B. Torelli, secular ; Peter Babade, a Sulpitian ; Michael Lacy, secular].
1808. M. Hurley, [P. Babade, P. Helbron].
1809. M. Hurley, [Matthew Hérard, secular].
1810. M. Hurley.
1811. M. Hurley, [Patrick Kenny, secular ; Michael Byrne, ditto].
1812. M. Hurley, [P. Kenny, M. Byrne, Michael Egan, a Franciscan, and Bishop of Philadelphia].
1813. M. Hurley, [M. Egan, Franciscan ; James Harold, a Dominican].
1814. M. Hurley.

1815. M. Hurley.

1816. M. Hurley, [Terence McGirr, secular].

1817. M. Hurley, P. Stafford.

1818. M. Hurley, [T. McGirr, John Egan, secular].

1819. M. Hurley, [T. McGirr, P. Rosetti, secular].

1820. M. Hurley, [P. Babade, T. McGirr].

1821. [P. Rosetti, George Sheufelter, secular; Henry Doyle, ditto; John Tuomy, ditto; Thomas Heyden, ditto].

1822. Philip Lariscy, [T. Heyden, secular; William Vincent Harold, Dominican].

1823. P. Lariscy, [T. Heyden, secular; John Walsh, ditto; John Fitzpatrick, ditto; Samuel Sutherland Cooper, ditto].

1824. P. Lariscy, [James Smith, secular].

1825. [J. Smith].

1826. [S. S. Cooper, secular; J. Smith, ditto; J. Fitzpatrick, ditto].

1827. [M. Egan, Franciscan; J. Smith, secular; Michael Curran, ditto; John Larkin, ditto; John Reilly, ditto; Edward F. Mayne, ditto].

1828. William C. O'Donnell, Nicholas O'Donnell, [E. F. Mayne, secular; George Aloysius Carrell, ditto (afterwards Bishop of Covington); Thomas Butler, ditto; Michael Whelan or Wheler, ditto].

1829. W. C. O'Donnell, N. O'Donnell, [M. Curran, secular; Vincent Heuberger, ditto].

1830 W. C. O'Donnell, N. O'Donnell, [G. A. Carrell, secular; M. Curran, ditto; Wm. Joseph Clancey, ditto (afterwards Coadjutor of Bishop England, of Charleston); John Hughes, ditto (afterwards Bishop of New York)].

1831. W. C. O'Donnell, N. O'Donnell, [Thomas Gegan, secular].

1832. N. O'Donnell, [T. Gegan, secular; E. F. Mayne, ditto; G. A. Carrell, ditto; E. V. Burke, ditto; Francis Patrick Kenrick, ditto (Bishop of Philadelphia); Bernard O'Cavanaugh, ditto; M. Whelan, or Wheler, ditto].

1833. N. O'Donnell, [G. A. Carrell, secular; Terence J. Donaghoe, ditto; Patrick Michael Costelloe, ditto].

1834. N. O'Donnell, [T. J. Donaghoe, secular].

1835. N. O'Donnell, [T. J. Donaghoe, secular].

1836. N. O'Donnell.

1837. N. O'Donnell, [Edward J. Sourin, secular (afterwards Jesuit); John O'Reilly, ditto].

1838. James O'Donnell, Thomas Kyle, [J. O'Reilly, secular; Stephen Chartier, ditto].

1839. J. O'Donnell, T. Kyle, Patrick Eugene Moriarty, [Francis Baker Jamison, secular].

1840. T. Kyle, John Possidius O'Dwyer, [F. B. Jamison, secular; P. P. Kroes, ditto].

1841. T. Kyle, J. P. O'Dwyer.

1842. T. Kyle, J. P. O'Dwyer.

1843. T. Kyle, J. P. O'Dwyer, Francis Ashe.

1844. T. Kyle, J. P. O'Dwyer, F. Ashe, J. O'Donnell, William Hartnett.

1845. F. Ashe, J. O'Donnell, W. Hartnett.

1846. F. Ashe, J. O'Donnell, W. Hartnett, George Augustus Meagher.

1847. F. Ashe, J. O'Donnell, W. Hartnett, G. A. Meagher, T. Kyle.

1848. F. Ashe, J. O'Donnell, W. Hartnett, G. A. Meagher, Michael Francis Gallagher, Edward Michael Mullen, Patrick Augustine Stanton.

1849. P. A. Stanton, G. A. Meagher, E. M. Mullen, M. F. Gallagher, W. Hartnett.

1850. P. A. Stanton, G. A. Meagher, W. Hartnett, E. M. Mullen, P. E. Moriarty, M. F. Gallagher.

NOTE.—The names given on the previous pages of the officiating clergymen include many who were not assistants, *i. e.*, regularly appointed assistants of the pastor ; they were merely friends, or visitors, who, "dropping in" now and then, were requested to officiate.

LIST OF INCORPORATORS OR TRUSTEES OF ST. AUGUSTINE'S CHURCH, UNDER THE NAME AND TITLE OF *Brothers of the Order of Hermits of St. Augustine*, WITH THE YEAR OF THEIR ELECTION.

1804. First Incorporators—Rev. Dr. Carr, O.S.A., President ; Rev. John Rosseter, O.S.A., of St. Mary's church, Fourth Street ; Rev. Michael Hurley, O.S.A., Secretary ; Rev. Demetrius Prince Gallitzin, *alias* Augustus Smith, secular, of Westmoreland county ; and Rev. Louis de Barth, secular.

1807. Rev. Michael Egan, O.S.F., of St. Mary's Church, Fourth Street.

1812, November 14. Rev. Patrick Kenny, secular, of Coffee Run, Delaware, *vice* Rosseter, deceased.

1820, March 25. Rev. John B. Holland, secular, of Lancaster, Pa.

1837, May 18. Revs. James O'Donnell, O.S.A., William Hartnett, O.S.A. and Nicholas O'Donnell, O.S.A.

LIST OF MISSIONS FOUNDED OR ATTENDED BY AUGUSTINIANS FROM 1778 TO 1841.

In MAINE, the *Passamaquoddy Indians*, near Machias, visited by Rev. H. de la Motte in 1779.

In NEW YORK, *New York City*, visited by Rev. H. de la Motte in 1778; *Staten Island*, visited by Rev. Philip Lariscy about 1821; *Newburg-on-the-Hudson*, visited by the same at the same time; *Binghampton*, in

Broome county, first visited by Rev. Dr. Michael Hurley in 1834; *Salina* (now Syracuse), visited by Rev. James O'Donnell in 1837; *Brooklyn*, St. Paul's church, attended by Revs. Nicholas and James O'Donnell in 1837; *Long Island.* missions as far east as Montauk, visited by Rev. James O'Donnell in 1839; *Williamsburg*, St. Mary's church, founded by Rev. James O'Donnell in 1841; *Albany*, visited by a "Dr. Stafford" at the beginning of the century, maybe Rev. Philip Stafford.

In PENNSYLVANIA, *Philadelphia*, St. Augustine's church, founded by Rev. Dr. Matthew Carr in 1795; *Westchester*, attended by Rev. John Rosseter in 1794, who resided there; *Lancaster*, visited by the same in 1800; *Lamberton*, visited by Rev. Philip Stafford in 1804; *Conewago*, in Adams county, visited by Rev. Dr. Carr in 1807; *Villanova* (then Belair), visited by several of the Fathers of St. Augustine's, probably as early as 1805; *Haverford*, St. Denis', founded by Denis Kelly in 1822, and blessed by Rev. Dr. Michael Hurley in 1825; *Silver Lake*, in Susquehanna county, visited by the same in 1834; *Frankford, Darby, Bustleton*, and *Germantown*, visited by the Fathers of St. Augustine's; *Norristown*, visited by the same in 1837; *"Poor House,"* visited by the same in 1839.

In DELAWARE, *Coffee Run*, visited by Rev. John Rosseter about 1788; *Wilmington*, visited by the same and Rev. Dr. Matthew Carr in 1800.

In NEW JERSEY, *Cape May Island*, visited by Rev. Michael Hurley about 1803; *Trenton*, visited by Rev. Dr. Matthew Carr in 1805; *Paterson*, first visited by Rev. Philip Lariscy about 1821.

In MASSACHUSETTS, *Boston*, Church of St. Augustine, founded by Rev. Philip Lariscy in 1818; *New Bedford*, attended first by the same in 1820.

In MARYLAND, *Bohemia Manor*, in Cecil county, visited by Rev. George Staunton in 1801; *St. Thomas' Manor*, visited by Rev. John Rosseter in 1812.

In GEORGIA, *Augusta*, attended by Rev. Robert Browne in 1808.

In SOUTH CAROLINA, *Charleston*, attended by the same about 1815.

In NEWFOUNDLAND, *St. John's*, attended by Rev. Philip Lariscy and Rev. Timothy Brown about 1816.

II

St. Augustine's Academy, Crown Street, Philadelphia, Founded in 1811.

[The following memoranda have been gathered from a Circular or Prospectus of the Academy, and the account books of the same. Here follows a copy of the Circular.]

ST. AUGUSTINE'S ACADEMY.

The flourishing and widely extended commerce of the United States of America with all civilized nations of the earth, but particularly with the Spanish Territories of the Old and New World, no longer allows an acquaintance with the language, manners and customs of Federal America to be a matter of indifference to any enlightened commercial country. The United States, already become, by their brilliant advancement in the liberal arts and sciences, the illustrious rivals of the most polished nations, challenge their esteem and must excite the desire of a liberal intercourse. Hence, with great satisfaction, we already find in almost every part of the Confederation, the polite languages, and especially the Spanish, cultivated with the greatest zeal and success. Emboldened by these auspicious evidences of intellectual ardor for improvement, the Superior-General and Brethren of the Order of St. Augustine, in the city of Philadelphia, assisted by professors of distinguished abilities, under the cordial approbation and patronage of the Right Reverend Michael Egan, Bishop of Pennsylvania, etc., present their literary and ecclesiastical Institution to the favor and encouragement of the lovers of polite literature in every part of the Spanish Territories. In this plan they wish to combine all the advantages of classical science with enlightened instruction in our Holy Faith, and the practical observance of its religious duties.

Their System and Terms comprise the following:

Boarding and education per annum....................$220 00
Washing and mending............................... 24 00
Paper, pens and ink............................... 6 00
                                                   ‾‾‾‾‾‾‾
                                                   $250 00

Payable quarterly in advance.

Letters addressed to the Rev. Dr. Carr, Superior-General of St. Augustine's, Philadelphia, shall be treated with due attention.

[The above circular is printed in two columns in Spanish and in English on one side of a folio (10 inches by 7½ inches), evidently torn from some book or pamphlet.

At St. Augustine's church is still preserved an old vellum register of those who held pews or sittings in the church during the early part of the present century. In this register were kept also the accounts of the Academy with the students in the same. From these it appears (1) that the Academy opened December 9, 1811, and closed June 19, 1815; (2) that thirty-nine (39) students in all were taken; (3) that these studied Latin, Greek, French, Spanish, book-keeping, mathematics, etc.; (4) that the charges for tuition per quarter were from $12.00 to $16.00; and (5) that a certain —— Patterson, writing-master, was paid the sum of $116.00 for six months and two weeks instruction.

The names of the students are given as entered in the register referred to above.]

LIST OF STUDENTS IN ST. AUGUSTINE'S ACADEMY, CROWN STREET, PHILADELPHIA, FROM DECEMBER 9, 1811, TO JUNE 19, 1815.

1. Bedford, James.
2. Berton, Augustus.
3. Blackwell, Rom.
4. Blane, William.
5. Blaney, Willis.
6. Cauffmann, Robert.
7. Coleman, John.
8. Connery, Michael.
9. Cox, Edward.
10. Coxe, Theodore.
11. Desauque, Louis.
12. Desmond, Daniel.
13. Desmond, James.
14. Donath, Joseph.
15. Doran, Joseph.
16. Dunn, Edward.
17. Hope, Thomas.
18. Hurley, John.
19. Hurley, Joseph.
20. Hurley, Robert.
21. Jordan, Francis.
22. Keasely, John.
23. Keefe, Michael.
24. Ladoveze, ——.
25. Leib, George.
26. Linehan, Dennis.
27. Lyons, Matthew.
28. McQuaid, John.
29. O'Conway, Columbkill.
30. Pennington, Edward.
31. Pennington, William.
32. Sartori, Charles.
33. Schneiller, Joseph.
34. Scravendyke, James.
35. Sneller, Joseph.
36. Taggart, Gerald.
37. Thackara, William.
38. Trenor, John.
39. Waltman, Samuel.

Report of Committee on Prize Essay.

We the undersigned Committee on Essay report that we have thoroughly examined the several papers submitted to us and have been well satisfied with them. The merits of these papers were so nearly equal that we found some difficulty in deciding, but we finally selected the work of Mrs. Vogel as the best, Miss Ducie being second. The facts are as follows :

The competitors for the medal were :

Mrs. Ettie M. Vogel, Post Graduate, Boerne, Texas.
Miss Lorena Marie Ducie, Ursuline Academy, Galveston.
   "   Florence de Zavala, Post Graduate, Shevano, Texas.
   "   Mamie J. Lyons, Academy Graduating Class.
   "   Olivia M. Tuttle de Willrich, Post Graduate, Flatonia, Texas.
   "   Clara M. Pritchard, Academy Graduating Class.
   "   Lou. M. Schwartz, Academy Sub-Graduating Class.

We have found the result of the examination to be :

Medal : Mrs. Ettie M. Vogel.
Next in m--rit : Miss Lorena Marie Ducie, and Miss Florence de Zavala, *ex æquo.*
Meritorious : Misses Mamie J. Lyons, Olivia M. Tuttle de Willrich, Clara M. Pritchard, Lou. M. Schwartz.

BERNARD DOUREDOURE,	MARTIN I. J. GRIFFIN,
ATLEE DOUREDOURE,	FRANCIS X. REUSS,
CHAS. H. A. ESLING, ESQ.,	J. CARROLL MCCAFFREY, ESQ.,

Committee.

THE AMERICAN CATHOLIC HISTORICAL SOCIETY OF PHILADELPHIA.

TO ALL WHOM IT MAY CONCERN, GREETING :

Whereas, This Society, in its desire to foster a love for Catholic History, has offered for competition, by the pupils of the Academy under the charge of the Ursuline Nuns of Galveston, Texas, a Silver Medal donated for this purpose by the Corresponding Secretary and Librarian, Mr. Francis X. Reuss, of Philadelphia, to be awarded to the one submitting the best historical paper on the subject proposed by the donor of the medal, namely, "The Ursuline Nuns in America;" and *whereas,* the Committee named by the Society to examine the papers submitted has reported that the one signed by Mrs. Ettie M. Vogel is the most deserving for accuracy of statement, conciseness and literary expression ; *therefore,* the Society has resolved that the medal be awarded to her.

        Attest: FRANCIS T. FUREY, *Rec. Secretary.*

Philadelphia, June 10, 1886.

The Ursuline Nuns in America.

[Written for the AMERICAN CATHOLIC HISTORICAL SOCIETY OF PHILADELPHIA by MRS. ETTIE MADELINE VOGEL, of Boerne, Texas.]

IN response to the honor conferred by the gentlemen of the American Catholic Historical Society of Philadelphia upon our worthy and beloved Alma Mater, I enroll myself among the ladies who will take up the pleasant task assigned; and, whilst I cannot hope to either interest or instruct as perhaps others will do, I will observe that brevity which is said to be the "soul of wit" and the priceless jewel of poor essays.

The Ursuline Order of Nuns is devoted exclusively to the education of youth, and as such possesses, above all other religious women, untold of power for good or evil; and what a source of pride, then, should it be to all true lovers of the human race to point to the present work and past history of this noble sisterhood !

The Order was founded by Angela Merici, at Brescia, in Italy, and so called from St. Ursula, under whose protection it was placed. The saintly foundress was born at Desanzano, near Lake Garda, in Italy, in 1474. From her tenderest years she was noted for her exalted piety and the many manifestations of Divine favor revealed in her behalf. In 1495, under Divine inspiration, she established the BASIS of the Institute of St. Angela, an order of virgins till then unknown in the Church. The company, composed of twelve members, was solemnly inaugurated November 25, 1535; confirmed by Pope Paul III. June 4, 1544; and erected into a monastic order by brief from Paul V. June 13, 1612. In 1546 the religious dress or habit was adopted, which, with some minor modifications, has been worn to the present day.

From Italy, which now possesses thirty houses, the Order was carried, in 1594, by Mother Bermond, into France; thence it ex-

(214)

tended into Belgium, which country counts at this date thirty-three houses; Germany, 28; Austria, 22; Great Britain, 10; Holland, 10; Poland, several; East Indies, 3; West Indies, 2; Grecian Archipelago, 3; British Guiana, 1; Australia, 1. In France, where now one hundred and fifty communities flourish, there were at the time of the revolution, in 1792, upwards of three hundred houses of the Order.

The Ursulines are cloistered. The Order has never been subject to provincial governors or superiors, except in Italy whilst it was still in congregational form.

All Ursulines agree in the essentials of the original institute, but owing to local necessities may differ in minor points of the constitutions. The Order follows the rule of St. Augustine, according to brief by Pope Pius V.

FOUNDATION IN AMERICA.

Whilst we praise the self-forgetful heroism of all those mighty apostles whom the Church has commanded to go forth in every age since the days of the inspired fishermen, let us not overlook the Ursulines. These heroic apostles have gone forth to strange and ofttimes inhospitable shores by dozens and scores—high-bred, delicate women, hiding their personality under the simple dress of their Order, casting aside the names that would recall their rank in the world, unencouraged in their beneficence by blazoned paragraphs, and unrewarded save by the sweet consciousness of duty done—these noble women, risking their lives when need be, or devoting themselves to the evangelical ministry within the peaceful seclusion of cloister walls, present a fine contrast to some of the world's noisy theorists, and compare favorably with any of the distinguished known philanthropists. To France belongs the honor of having sent out, toward the middle of the seventeenth century, the first company of these missionaries across the seas, to labor for the salvation of the Indians in the wilds of newly discovered America.

CANADA, 1639.

The Ursulines of Quebec, founded exclusively for the religious instruction and education of young persons, have the oldest establishment of the kind in North America.

They owe their establishment in Canada to the piety and generous devotedness of a noble widow of Normandy, the celebrated Mme. de la Peltrie.

The name of their first superior, Mother Marie Guyart de l'Incarnation, a widow, and afterwards a nun of Tours, is held in veneration in this country. She was a woman distinguished by a rare and highly cultivated intelligence, but more so by her remarkable virtue. The introduction of the cause of her beatification into the Court of Rome has shed a new light on one of the purest glories of both old and new France.

Linked to these two revered names are Mother Marie de Torche (in religion St. Joseph), and Mother M. de Flécelles, (in religion St. Athanasius), the former from Tours, the latter from Paris. By their zeal these holy religious vied with their foundresses in the work of civilization and charity. Quebec had been founded by French Catholics under Champlain in 1608. In 1639, just 31 years later, this little company of Ursulines landed, and prostrating themselves upon the new soil, invoked God's blessing upon their future labors. These were *the first nuns* to set foot upon America's soil.

During the life-time of the venerable Mother of the Incarnation, eleven nuns from France joined the community in America. Toward the close of the seventeenth century the community was composed principally of subjects of Canadian origin, and belonging to the best families of New France.

Founded while the whole of North America was yet uncivilized, these Ursulines have, necessarily, since greatly modified their system of education.

During the first half century they were obliged to not only instruct the Indian children in four different languages, but also to catechise a great number of the parents. At the same time they educated young girls of French families, and prepared them to take the lead in the society of the young colony. This continued until the Indians gradually withdrew altogether.

The period following was exclusively French ; in 1681, therefore, the Ursulines of Quebec adopted the regulations of the first houses of their Order in Europe. Already at Quebec a college under the direction of the Jesuit Fathers gave diplomas and degrees to its pupils, and the Seminary of Foreign Missions, founded by Bishop Montmorency-Laval, prepared young ecclesiastics for their heavy labors in the new country. Such was the ardor religion evinced for the good organization of America. France did her part by choosing the colonists for Canada, while the local government instituted wise laws calculated to uphold these generous views :

In the second century of their existence, the Ursulines of Quebec found themselves confronted with needs of another kind. The conquest of the country by England, in 1759, opened to their zeal a new field of labor by bringing in a population of strangers in religion, customs and language. The Ursulines understood the mission that devolved upon them with the arrival of the conquerors, and prepared themselves for it. On their side, the new masters of the country evinced great esteem for the community, and confided their children to its care. In this way have English names multiplied in the convent records, and to day those of English speaking nationalities form a considerable part of the population of the cloister, although the prevailing element is French among both nuns and pupils.

The work of the Ursulines of Quebec was interrupted at three different times, in 1650 and in 1686, when the monastery was completely destroyed by fire, and the third time at the capitulation of Quebec, in 1759.

Through the encouragement of their ecclesiastical superiors, and particularly the assistance afforded by the rev. gentlemen of the Seminary of Quebec and well-known lay authorities, the Ursulines of Quebec have been enabled to revise their course of study to meet the advanced requirements of each successive period, until to-day their curriculum embraces all the higher branches and sciences taught in the leading female colleges of England and America. This institution is, no doubt, a very favorable example, yet is a representative of all the leading Ursuline schools in America. Their buildings, twelve in number, are four stories in height, and present a front 1324 feet in length. These spacious buildings allow separate rooms and classes for the pupils of each department, boarders, normal students and day scholars, as well as the pupils of the different grades. No insignificant feature of their system is the education of the pupils with reference to their varied future pursuits in life. Thus specialists are·

engaged to teach the sciences, language, book-keeping and other industrial branches, music, penmanship, etc. Their pupils number—boarders, 375 ; half boarders, 130, who pursue the same courses of study as boarders, music excepted ; normal students, (boarders having professors named by the government), 62; day scholars (gratis), with whom the normals are exercised in teaching, 350.

The community numbers eighty-eight religious, of whom nine are novices, three postulants, and twenty-six lay Sisters, the last named employed in manual labor.

In 1863 the Ursulines of Quebec issued their "History" of their own Order in the Provinces (in the French language). Their other work, "Glimpses of the Monastery," appeared later. We may well call the former of these works a magnificent History of Canada.

In 1697 the Ursulines of Quebec founded the Ursulines of Three Rivers, Canada, which soon became a "mother house," and even sent religious to other convents of the Order in America. The Ursulines of Three Rivers are the only known religious of their Order who conduct a hospital. The community in this work carries out a primitive idea of the institute, inasmuch as St. Angela undertook the care of the needy and distressed as a branch of her main work.

These Ursulines are abundantly blessed with subjects fitted for the task of education. Their schools number—boarders, 201 ; day scholars, 280. The community possesses 73 members. Their hospital contains about 18 beds.

In 1882 the Ursulines of Quebec built a convent 80x40 feet on the borders of Lake St. John, and sent there seven professed nuns. The house is prosperous. Their school consists of—boarders, 40 ; day scholars, 80.

In 1884 the Ursulines established a convent 80x50 feet at Stanstead Plains, near the Canadian boundary of Vermont. The Quebec monastery sent nine professed nuns. They have at this date forty-nine boarders and over ninety day scholars. The house gives promise of great success. There is also a convent at Sherbrooke, Canada, where eight professed nuns carry on flourishing schools.

The community at Chatham, Upper Canada, was transferred

thither, in 1860, from Sault Ste. Marie, Michigan, where the community had labored since 1853.   These Ursulines conduct flourishing boarding, select day, and parochial schools.

NEW ORLEANS, LA., U. S. A., 1727.

The first convent of Ursulines in the United States was founded at New Orleans, La., in 1727, by ten Sisters from France, under Mother Marie Tranchepain, than whom a more beautiful type of saintly womanhood neither poet nor historian hath described.

This undertaking was supported by the West India Company, which was pledged to erect a monastery at New Orleans, and provide for the support of a specified number of religious. The royal approbation which the venerable superior obtained is dated September 18, 1726.   It was, however, seven years before the Ursulines came into possession of their building.   In the meantime a house was hired for them by the company.

At that date New Orleans was but a spongy swamp, exhaling miasma and teeming with insects peculiar to semi-tropical localities.   The city proper consisted of something over one hundred wooden houses scattered amidst rank vegetation over the driest parts of the town tract.   This tract was fenced in by sharp stakes and surrounded by a wide ditch.   A smaller ditch ran along the four sides of every square.   The Blessed Sacrament was kept in a warehouse, which did duty as the church.   The town had been settled by the French in 1717.   The territory of Louisiana was under the spiritual jurisdiction of the Bishop of Quebec.   He had appointed Capuchins to minister to the spiritual necessities of the white settlers and several tribes of Indians at New Orleans—viz., Choctaw, Chickasaw, Yoloff and Mandigoes.

Educational facilities were limited to one school, opened for boys by Father Cecil, a monk.   But as civilization depends more upon the education of the future mothers of a country, the work progressed slowly until the Ursulines arrived.

During their first year they devoted themselves to the education of French and Indian girls, catechising the negro and Indian races, instructing French adults, and in attendance at the military hospital.

During the following year, to their multiple duties they added the care of a colony of orphans, whose parents had been massacred by the Natchez tribe of Indians; also to the care of several installments of *filles de cassette*, girls with trunks whom the king of France had sent out as wives for his soldiers. Later their charity was further called upon to provide for a large number of women and children of the wandering Acadians, whose homes had been laid waste by English wars. It is not a little singular that, in the earlier years, among so many women, they never found a religious vocation, but were dependent upon the mother country for subjects.

In 1728 the Ursulines lost a most efficient member in Sister Madeline Mahein; in 1731 Sister Marguerite Judde followed, and in 1733 Sister Marguerite Talon. During the same year the heroic and gentle superior, Mother Marie Tranchepain, passed to her heavenly reward. The year following Sisters from France arrived to fill the void thus caused by death; but ever fragrant must be the memory of these early founders, who had in their hearts a place alike for unprotected innocence and abandoned sinners, and sacrificed their lives in their labor of love.

During the French Revolution, in 1792, large numbers of religious were put to death in France. With these horrors vividly in mind, the Ursulines of New Orleans were filled with consternation when Spain ceded Louisiana back to France, in 1802; and the following year, in spite of every assurance of safety, twenty of the Ursulines departed for Cuba and founded the now prosperous convent of Havana. The Ursulines of New Orleans had shared in full the ill fortunes which the territory of Louisiana suffered through the frequent changes of masters — alternately French, British, Spanish, French—and were naturally alarmed whenever a change of government took place.

Upon the purchase of the territory of Louisiana from France by the United States in 1803, the mother superior appealed to President Jefferson for protection of their rights of property. The President gave her every assurance which the Constitution of the United States and the power of his office conferred, and ever afterward proved himself their sincere friend.

Upon the repulse of the English forces by Gen. Jackson at New Orleans in 1815, a service of thanksgiving was solemnized in the Catholic cathedral. Young girls from the Ursuline school, attired in costumes symbolic of every State in the Union, with stars upon their foreheads and flags in their hands, occupied the centre of the church, and strewed the way with flowers as the victorious hero passed up the aisle. Gen. Jackson afterwards visited the Sisters at the convent and testified his appreciation of this mark of distinction, and assured them of his continued friendship. During his famous struggle the Ursuline convent was converted into a hospital for disabled soldiers, and the Ursulines gave their services for three months.

In 1788 the first convent building owned by the nuns was destroyed by fire, and of the second one not a vestige remains; but the street upon which it stood is now called Nun street, in commemoration of the early missionaries who prayed and labored here for the good organization of the infant colony. Their present monastery, three miles below the city, was erected in 1824, and is a magnificent structure.

During the civil war the Ursulines of New Orleans suffered the full force of all the vicissitudes of life in a land in open warfare. Their resources decreased until they were barely able to keep in repair the vast buildings formerly crowded with the flower of the South.

When the North had conquered, misery of every kind, resulting from civil war, occasioned a certain apathy for education in the population.* However, the course of studies adopted by the Ursulines in 1867 shows how eager and prompt they were in following the movement which was not long in showing itself in the country.

During the war the Ursulines of New Orleans compiled a correct and comprehensive " General History," ancient and modern, for use in the convents in the South. The volume was published by a French printer in New Orleans, and although far from being up to the standard of typographical excellence, was right gladly received in the South, where scarcity had made the value of books obvious to all.

With its roots planted in the early part of a by-gone century, this institution has developed by slow and tedious processes.

---

* This state of things continued until 1870, when a prodigious movement again took place in the South toward progress in commerce, immigration, agricultural pursuits, etc.

The early founders labored under difficulties of which to-day we can form no adequate idea. The results, however, of their labors are no less gratifying to the Ursulines than to the citizens of the State. In education, as in every other matter of human interest, progress is marked by successive adaptations of means to ends. This principle these Ursulines have admirably illustrated. I will not, however, expose myself to the just ridicule of intelligent judges by saying that their system of education or instruction is now perfect (which is a degree, I believe, not yet reached for the benefit of the female sex); but the comparisons that might be instituted are highly flattering to the Ursulines. Above all are they worthy of honor for having been the first to demonstrate to the people of this section the propriety of combining deep religious interest with high-toned literary acquirements.

Of late years public interest has again awakened in behalf of this once flourishing institute, and we may feel assured that its darkest hour is past.

The community numbers forty members; the academy, fifty boarders, in addition to which about forty orphans are cared for. The day school enrolls one hundred and fifty pupils. It is remarkable that through so many years of exceptional vicissitudes the work of these Ursulines has never been interrupted. Their corps of teachers includes a number of noted specialists, and all are well qualified for the task of education.

BOSTON, MASS., 1818.

In 1818 an Ursuline convent was founded at Boston, Mass., by Mother Mary Ryan and three other ladies from Limerick, Ireland, under the care of the saintly Bishop, afterwards Cardinal, Cheverus. Here the health of the Sisters gave way. In 1826, therefore, the community removed to Charlestown, in the same State, where it enjoyed great prosperity until 1834; but fanaticism was rife, and a mob, only too ready to give credence to some silly stories afloat, plundered and destroyed the house. It is not a little singular that the Ursulines have not re-established themselves in the State, as perseverance in the face of difficulties has always distinguished this chosen Order.

CHARLESTON, S. C., 1834.

The Carolinas had been settled in the middle of the seventeenth century by Protestants who sought to escape religious persecution in Virginia.   In 1834 Bishop England brought a number of Sisters from Cork, Ireland, to found an Ursuline convent at Charleston, S. C., but these, for some reason, departed in 1851.   Bishop Lynch, however, immediately after his consecration, gathered the dispersed members, and on September 1, 1858, established them at Columbia, the capital of South Carolina, where they opened an academy now known as Valle Crucis.   The Sister founders were Mothers Mary Molony, Borgia McCarthy, Antonia Hughes and Mary Joseph de Sales Woulfe.

Under the direction of the illustrious prelate this institute attained a standard of excellence and reputation that at once ranked it among the leading academies in the South.   It derived its patronage from the upper classes of South Carolina and surrounding States.   In 1859 they removed the community to more extensive buildings.

At Columbia other sects had profited by the beautiful location, and erected schools; but soon the Ursulines eclipsed them all. The eminent qualifications of the ladies thus made widely known in a State where but 12,000 of the 800,000 inhabitants were Catholics, excited jealousy in certain directions against them, which the influence of the clergy, General Wade Hampton, Hon. John S. Preston, and many other illustrious friends was powerless to dispel.   In 1860 this hostile feeling was at the highest pitch.   On the night of June 25 a mob had collected in the town hall to proceed in a body to pull down the convent buildings.   Upon learning its object all the worthier citizens refused to participate in the organization of the meeting.   Impatient of delay, a speaker was called for.   General Macey-Gregg (himself a non-Catholic) responded.   He addressed the assembly for over an hour—appealed to Southern manhood and the chivalric spirit of old South Carolina to cherish these distinguished women, "whom," to quote the words of the illustrious speaker, "we hold to be a blessing to our State, a treasure in our social community, and whose influence, once withdrawn, can never be replaced."   The magic of his eloquence created a sudden revulsion of popular feeling.   The

Ursulines were protected, and from that time regarded with additional respect.

During the years of civil war this convent was the haven of refuge to which many families, regardless of sect or creed, confided their daughters, to shield them from the society of the swarms of adventurers that drifted to southern cities during the political tumult. Young ladies of all ages were admitted; and right sacredly did the holy Sisters guard their trust, until the destruction of Columbia by Sherman's army in 1865 rendered the community shelterless.

South Carolina had taken the lead in the rebellion. The Secession Act was passed at Columbia, its capital, December 20, 1860. Hence, when the fall of Chattanooga, "the gate of the South," was announced in 1865, every one believed that Columbia was doomed. Sherman's army had rapidly stretched across Georgia, and on the 16th of February occupied the heights of Lexington, and subjected Columbia to a destructive siege and bombardment, which lasted twenty-four hours. The Ursuline school at this time was crowded. The Sisters removed their pupils safely beyond the city limits, and they themselves remained. The mother superior appealed to the commander of the Union forces to spare her house and shield her cloistered charges. General Sherman at once sent a guard, but when the conflagration spread *not one* of these soldiers raised a hand to ward off approaching danger, even when implored to do so. At three o'clock on the morning of the 17th, the agonized occupants, exposed to biting cold in the open churchyard, beheld the greedy flames lick up the last vestige of their beautiful cloister. Two young Sisters, Gertrude Spann and Patricia Reynolds, prostrated by the terrors of that memorable night and the succeeding days of privation, never recovered, and died soon after. General Sherman subsequently visited the sorely tried Ursulines in the churchyard, with words of comfort; and all attest to the dignified, lady-like deportment and Christian fortitude of the Sisters upon this trying occasion. When the war ended, its effects gradually ceased to be apparent in the South; but around the community at Valle Crucis, like that at New Orleans, the shade still lingers to perfect their virtue and enhance their merits.

The Ursulines of Valle Crucis have twice been obliged to

separate. The last time, in 1866, a body repaired to Tuscaloosa, Ala., in the diocese of Bishop Quinlan, where they labored for thirteen years, but which they at last relinquished for lack of subjects. The heroic and saintly Mother Charles White was superioress. Aside from her vigorous, cultivated intellect, she is held as a pattern of exalted virtue.

The Ursulines of Valle Crucis, in spite of adverse fortune, have by extreme self-denial been enabled to save money, which they have lavished upon whatever pertains to the intellectual training of the rising generation. This self-denial, generosity and large wisdom have been fully rewarded by the issue. Their graduates are famous for solid and refined education, and many hold responsible public positions.

Notable among the ladies whose piety and learning have endowed this institute is Mother Mary Baptiste Lynch, sister of Bishop Lynch, by whom she was directed until his death, which occurred in 1882. She has governed the community for twenty-eight years. The religious number about twenty. In addition to the academy in the suburbs, they conduct a large day school in the city of Columbia.

ST. MARTIN'S, BROWN CO., OHIO, 1845.

In 1845 Bishop Purcell secured a number of Sisters from the celebrated convent at Boulogne, France, and founded the Ursulines at "St. Martin's." This home was begun under favorable auspices, and has since met with no reverses. Mother Julia Assumption Chatfield, who died in 1878, was the first superioress. She was an English lady of brilliant attainments, a convert, and noted for her prudence, simplicity, fortitude and meekness. The present superior is Mother Ursula. She has done much to maintain the standard of excellence which the schools have attained. The community numbers sixty-one religious; the academy, sixty-five boarders ; the free school, fifty pupils.

In 1849 a second installment of five Ursulines from the convent of Boulogne arrived, and entered the convent at Cleveland, prepared for them by Bishop Rappe, who was tireless in his zeal for the promotion of education. The Ursulines of Cleveland conduct boarding academies in Cleveland and Nottingham, besides seven parochial schools in the city of Cleveland, and teach over

3,000 children. There are fifty-seven professed Sisters, seven novices and six postulants in the community.

These Ursulines at first suffered some of the privations incident to a new foundation, but have happily overcome every obstacle; and when I say that they have applied the knowledge of principles, methods, and manners gained by actual experience in the training of youth, in full satisfaction of the advanced demands of the age, I say more than these words seem to imply. We may estimate the result by the fact that in 1860 their schools numbered seven hundred pupils, against over three thousand to-day. This in a city where the public schools are numerous and know no superiors as far as the actual requirements of literary schools are concerned.

The Ursuline convent of Cleveland has been a fruitful parent, and has contributed greatly to the good of religion throughout the diocese by the houses it has established. They are the Ursulines of Tiffin, Toledo, Youngstown and Nottingham.

In Toledo, besides the large academy and select day school, these Sisters direct six parochial schools where 1700 children are taught. The community numbers fifty professed nuns.

In Youngstown the Ursulines have an academy, and teach two parochial schools attended by 1023 pupils.

In 1863 the Ursulines of Tiffin were estbalished. The superior was Mother St. Joseph, aided by Sisters St. Maxime, St. Alexis, St. Scholastica, and the venerable and beloved Mother Mary of the Annunciation, late superior of the Cleveland house. The foundation was begun under great discouragement. No preparation had been made to receive the Ursulines, who were dependent upon the charity of Catholics, until Rev. Father Bihn generously vacated his presbytery for their accommodation.

On the 29th of September, immediately after their arrival, they took charge of the two parish schools of Tiffin, St. Joseph's and St. Mary's; the former with one hundred and fifty, the latter with fifty pupils. The academy was opened shortly after with seven pupils. Two of these, Sister Ursula, daughter of the late Judge Johnson, and Sister St. Liguori Houck, are now useful members of the Ursuline community. Their first postulant, a sister of Rev. Mr. Kirsch, was received in 1866.

In 1865 the meek and holy superior, Sister St. Joseph, was stricken with typhoid fever, and expired after a brief illness. So poor were the Tiffin Ursulines at this time that her funeral expenses devolved upon the Cleveland house.   In their crowded house all felt symptoms of malignant fever, but the vigorous precautions taken by Sister St. Ignatius, who arrived to govern the orphaned community, prevented an epidemic.

This zealous and fervent religious, Sister St. Ignatius, who had entered the monastery of Cleveland almost at its commencement, was sent as a missionary to establish the house in Toledo, and after seven years of fruitful labor there, returned home, hoping to end her days in the holy quiet of regular community life, when she was appointed to conduct the still more laborious mission of Tiffin.   The results of her prudent management are seen to-day.

In 1865 the Ursulines of Tiffin erected a small brick monastery; in 1870 a handsome and substantial structure was built, 60x50 feet, three stories in height, with Mansard roof.   In 1879 an exhibition hall, 70x35 feet was added, and over this a handsome chapel.

In 1878 the institution was incorporated and chartered under the title, "College of Ursuline Sisters."   In 1873 the last of the devoted band of Cleveland Ursulines returned home, leaving the community of Tiffin fourteen members, with the beautiful legacy of their good example, zeal and devotedness to the glory of God.

The present community numbers thirty religious.   The average attendance at their academy is 175 pupils.   At their parochial schools several hundred are enrolled. The present superior is the excellent Mother Ursula.

The history of the Ursulines of Ohio shows the merciful and especial providence of God toward the Order.   In this State they number 150 members, and train over 5000 children; and their devotedness, great acquirements and rare personal worth have combined to soften prejudice and do away with much irreligious animosity.

ST. LOUIS, MO., 1846.

In 1846 Rev. Mother Magdalen Stehlin, accompanied by Mothers Ann Pan and Augustine Schragel, arrived from Landschut, Bavaria, and founded the Ursulines of St. Louis. These on their arrival occupied a small wooden building, and labored under many disadvantages. This house, founded with three religious, now numbers one hundred and twenty-five members, and their small wooden cottage has grown to many buildings, vast in size ; and hundreds of pupils now attend their schools to the tens that were first admitted. In the progress of civilization, the series of differentiations is almost infinite, and education must vary to meet the demand. Nor have these Ursulines been unmindful of this, as shown by their school curriculum.

Besides the large academy and day schools in the suburbs of St. Louis, they maintain twelve affiliated convents in the diocese dependent upon the "mother house" in St. Louis, and presided over by its superior.

There are enrolled in St. Louis:

At the Academy, ...	190 pupils.
At Parochial Schools, ...	195 "
At Dog Prairie, St. Charles Co., ...	80 "
At Kirkwood, St. Louis Co., ...	75 "
At Portage des Sioux, ...	90 "
At the Arcadia Seminary, ...	60 "
At Fredericktown, Madison Co., ...	70 "
At Jackson, Cape Girardeau, ...	40 "
At Perryville, Perry Co., ...	60 "
At Boonville, ...	105 "
Making a total of . . . . :	985 pupils.

The present large communities of New York City and Alton, Ills., were colonized from the St. Louis Ursulines.

GALVESTON, TEXAS, 1847.

History asserts that Catholic missionaries were not only the forerunners of civilization in Texas, but the first white men to penetrate the primeval wilds of Texas proper. Resplendent are the pages of history that tell how here, in the days before An_ glo-American colonization, the saintly Franciscan brothers labored and prayed for the spiritual welfare and temporal amelioration of the Indian race. About the commencement of the present century the citizen soldiers commanded by Col. Uralde, being left for a short time without their leader, invaded the religious hamlet of San Antonio, and by their brutal conduct gave the lie to the beneficent teachings of the holy Fathers and destroyed the work of years. This led to the recall of the Franciscans to their principal house in Zacatecas, and all the archives of value were sent to the same city. Religion was thus stamped out, and the Indians soon relapsed into their original condition.

It was about 1838 when the second religious era dawned in Texas. It was then that Fathers Clarke, Heyden, Timon and others from the States volunteered their services to relieve the spiritual destitution of the few Catholic settlers in Texas. Of all the illustrious names of that period handed down to us, none is so revered as that of Bishop John Odin. He was nominated for the Vicariate of Texas in 1842. Galveston was the episcopal city, but, unhappily, it was the rendezvous of pirates and malefactors of every class. Texas was admitted into the Union in 1845, and the attitude of Mexico, which regarded her as a revolting province, was alarming. Events of the most startling nature were happening. The dauntless Odin, however, had come to plant the Church of God in the wilds of Texas, and was not to be discouraged by the unsettled state* of society and politics. He at once saw the necessity of establishing schools, and with the view of introducing a religious teaching Order, he visited the leading Catholic seminaries for young ladies in the United States. His choice fell upon the Ursulines. He applied to the New Orleans Ursulines for subjects to found a branch house at Galveston, Texas, and set out to Europe for postulants. At Rome he unfolded his plans to the Pope, who approved of the foundation, and accorded a plenary indulgence to young persons who should make their first Communion in the proposed convent.†

In 1847 the Ursulines of Galveston were founded by Sisters Arsene Blin, Stanislas Truchet, St. Bruno and Ambroise, from New Orleans, aided by three postulants from France. Bishop Odin had arranged all preliminaries, and the Ursulines were received with favor in the new colony.

---

*Even though the subject in hand does not seem to demand or justify my bringing these points to notice, I have thought it well not to omit some account of the rise and progress of the Faith in Texas, to which more than usual interest attaches from its size, growing importance and past achievements.

†This decree, bearing the seal and signature of Pope Gregory XVI., hangs in their present sacristy in Galveston.

Their first years were full of trials—drought and yellow fever epidemic combined to deplete their schools, and in '54 fire threatened them with ruin. It was then resolved to erect a brick monastery, which was solemnly blessed in 1855. In 1849 Sisters de Chantal White and St. Thomas Burke arrived from the Quebec Ursulines to organize the higher classes in the Galveston school.

In 1850, their chaplain being called elsewhere, for six weeks the Ursulines were without spiritual resources. In the meantime the renovations of vows were performed, notwithstanding the absence of the usually required dignitaries attending the ceremony.

In 1861 this convent was converted into a hospital for disabled soldiers, and the meek Sisters, recognizing the will of God, devoted themselves heroically to Christ's suffering members. Their sacrifices were rewarded by the conversion and baptism of a number of soldiers. During this and the succeeding year, by events of the civil war, these Ursulines were reduced to the extreme of poverty, corn bread and potatoes being often the only diet served at their tables. On January 1, 1863, General Magruder, commander of the Confederates, planned his disastrous attack upon the Federal naval fleet, which had taken possession of and blockaded Galveston harbor. The General had, previous to the battle, sent wagons to convey the Ursulines beyond danger, but the heroic band crowded these vehicles with the panic-stricken citizens, who had flocked to the convent, themselves remaining behind. The convent halls were soon lined with dead and dying soldiers, and for many days every inmate of the monastery was employed in relieving the afflicted and preparing souls for eternity. Federal reinforcements arrived and the siege was continued. During the bombardment of the city, on the 10th of May, every shell seemed directed toward the convent, but upon hoisting a yellow flag the ships slowly moved off. In 1861 the work of the Ursulines was interrupted for a short time by the removal of the Sisters to San Antonio, on account of their exposed situation upon the Island, subject to siege and bombardment. This change was urged by their ecclesiastical superiors, much against the will of the Ursulines. The summer of '63 found the pecuniary resources of the Ursulines thoroughly drained, but in September of this year applications poured in from all parts of Texas, and before winter every class was filled, and boarders were refused for want of accommodations. During the three years of stormy trial the community was governed by Mother St. Pierre Harrington, and fully was her wisdom and benevolence proven. This eminent religious was elected Superior in 1859, at the age of thirty years. She was a Canadian by birth, of English and Irish parentage, and educated by the Ursulines. Tall in stature, commanding in form, and possessing a strong personal magnetism, to which was added great universality of acquirements and natural genius, she was one of the most successful educators the South ever possessed. During her régime the fashionable exodus of students from the State received a check, and filled to overflowing the Galveston academy. Her piety, meekness and ingenius affability won all hearts, and the influence of her virtues extends over the community to the present day. Texas valued her highly, and her decease, which occurred in 1872 (in the twenty-sixth year of her religious profession), was mourned as a public calamity.

· In 1865 the Ursulines of Galveston were called upon to mourn the death of their senior lay-sister, St. Ambrose. She was a Bostonian by birth, distinguished for her wit, powers of observation and strong sense of duty, but more so by her remarkable virtue. At an early age she had felt a yearning for something more than her own religious creed offered. From sect to sect she sought the Faith, and found her object in the Catholic Church, at that time almost ignored in Boston. She was instructed by the holy Bishop (afterwards Cardinal) Cheverus; was at the Charlestown convent when the riotous plunder and destruction there took place; was transferred to New Orleans, and subsequently went with the founders of the Galveston Ursulines.

Among the religious who labored most zealously and successfully among the pupils during the early years of this foundation were Sisters St. Thomas Burke and St. Bruno, the former from Canada and the latter from New Orleans. Many conversions were wrought through the instrumentality of these learned and virtuous ladies. The former returned, after seven years, to Canada.

Until 1866 the Ursulines of Galveston were the only religious Order of women in Texas. Several of the most useful members of the present community were pupils of the Rev. Mother St. Pierre Harrington.

For all that regards education, the Ursulines of Galveston have drawn information from the best sources, and have received valuable assistance from lay authorities. Their chaplains also have never ceased to watch over their interests with all the solicitude with which religion surrounds the sacred depository of mind and heart. Neither the agitation of modern ideas nor the tendency of the age to popularize all the sciences has escaped these wise mentors.

The regular correspondence of these Ursulines with the most prosperous houses of their Order in Europe and America is a source of valuable information to them.

In the last fifteen years the establishment has increased three-fourths. It now comprises a handsome church and several other spacious buildings of two or three stories each, and all possible hygienic ameliorations have been introduced. Calisthenics and other exercises are in vogue, being favorable to good deportment no less than to development of physical strength among their pupils. The government in their schools is by tact rather than by force, means of emulation being found preferable as calculated to promote the happiness and elevate the mind of youth. The departments of their school are divided into academy boarders, half boarders, select day school, and two parochial schools, the latter attended by three hundred pupils.

The brief granting this community dispensation from cloister life for parochial school purposes bears the seal of Pius IX., dated February 10, 1876. The community numbers twenty-nine members. The superior is Mother St. Agnes McClellan, whose gentle womanly dignity and exalted virtue have alike been the admiration and veneration of her grateful pupils for nearly a quarter of a century. Mother St. Augustine de Lassaulf has been the only other superior since the death of Mother St. Pierre.

In 1851 the Ursuline convent at San Antonio, Texas, was founded by Sisters from the Galveston and New Orleans Ursulines, viz., Mothers Mary Delury, St. Anthony, Angela Noyé, Marie de Lacy and St. Augustine Melton. Bishop Odin had erected for them a house proportionate to his means, but was absent in France at the time the Sisters set out from Galveston.

They arrived at San Antonio at midnight on the feast of the Holy Cross, and found their humble adobe monastery destitute of everything save carpenter chips and mason rubbish. Their baggage failed to arrive, and for six weeks their only couch was the bare floor. Nor was this the greatest of their hardships. But in the midst of such trials these noble ladies, reared in affluence, preserved great cheerfulness, and thanked God that they had been called upon to practise the poverty of Bethlehem. After four months they found themselves in possession of tables and chairs, and thus were enabled to open school. The population of San Antonio was then largely of the poorer Mexican class; and, although the Ursuline school numbered over three hundred pupils, the majority were charity scholars, and until after the civil war the income of their school barely supported the community in the common necessaries of life.

We may designate the first fourteen years of the Ursulines in San Antonio as an exclusively Mexican period.

The rapid colonization of the State during the succeeding years led the late Bishop Pellicier, for the better advancement of all the pupils, to advocate the establishment of separate parochial schools for the English-speaking and Mexican children, placed under the direction of uncloistered congregations, thus reserving the Ursulines exclusively for boarding and select day schools. The change was welcomed by the citizens, and has been advantageous to all the establishments. The results that have accrued to the Ursulines give them the largest attendance of any academy in the State. Their boarders number ninety pupils, their day school many more.

The Spanish element predominates among the religious in the cloister, who number twenty-nine members. Since 1870 great improvements are perceptible in the temporal affairs of the Ursulines of San Antonio. A church and an academy have been erected and the monastery enlarged. Now they have as many paying pupils as the original number of charity scholars. To these toiling missionaries, it may be truly said, have the saintly Franciscans bequeathed their apostolic spirit. The abundant fruits derived from their arduous labors is a subject of consolation to them and glory to the Church.

To the clergy of San Antonio are due both the progress of religion and, in no small measure, the present prosperous condition of the religious communities. The Ursulines of San Antonio cherish with veneration the memory of Rev. C. M. Dubuis, for many years their chaplain. His incessant labors and sacrifices knew no limit; so exalted was his esteem for the Ursulines, that upon his elevation to the episcopal dignity it was his desire to propagate the Order throughout his vast diocese.

Within late years the authorities of San Antonio assumed the right to tax the Ursuline establishment. The matter was referred to the Supreme Court, where exemption from taxation was granted the Ursulines, in view of their eminent services to the State in the cause of education.

The convent at its foundation, and for many years after, was governed by Mother Marie Truard, whose tact and knowledge of the world admirably fitted her for the charge. She died at the advanced age of seventy, after a life of great piety and usefulness.

The late Mother St. Augustine Xavier Melton exercised the functions of superior. In 1877, after twenty-six years of arduous labor, she returned to the house of her profession, in Galveston, where she is at present the only survivor of the original founders of the two communities.

In 1868 Mother de Chantal White returned to the house of her profession in Quebec, after seventeen years of suffering and toil spent in founding the houses of Galveston and San Antonio.

The Ursulines of Laredo, Texas, owe their establishment to the zeal of the holy Mother St. Joseph, of Brignolles, France. In 1868 this noble missionary was *en route* to the house of her profession, in France, hoping to spend her remaining days in quiet retirement, after her labors in founding the San Antonio Ursulines, when she was called upon by Bishop Dubuis to undertake the laborious mission of Laredo. Here, fifteen years before, the zealous Bishop Odin had set apart grounds and erected a stone house for the foundation of an Ursuline convent.

Accompanied by one young Spanish-American Sister, she set out in the summer of '68. When the Laredoites learned that she was *en route*, a deputation of leading citizens was sent to escort her into town. The Ursulines were enthusiastically received. One old man, who had attained the age of 150 years, rushed forth and exclaimed, like Simeon of old: "Now that I have seen this day, I die willingly."

Laredo is an antiquated Texan-Mexican border town, and, until the advent of the railroad in 1876, had an exclusively Catholic population. A unique feature of this unique town is the marvellous manner in which the ancient faith has been preserved, amidst the many half Spanish half Aztec traditions to which the people tenaciously cling. Thus, for instance, although Catholics, they think nothing of eating meat on Friday, and trace this abuse generations back, to the time, probably, when their forefathers were dispensed from abstinence on account of the poverty of the country or inability to procure other food save wild game and buffalo meat. Their code of etiquette requires mourners to seclude themselves for thirty days after the death of a relative; hence they do not attend Mass on Sundays within that period. Left for years without proper guidance, ignorance has thus merged many holy and religious doctrines into superstitious practices; but with time and patience the Ursulines will overcome many of these peculiarities, which prevail in this part of Texas and Mexico. I have not forgotten that I am writing about the "Ursuline Nuns in America," but have brought forward these examples to convey an idea of the magnitude of the evangelical mission that still devolves in great part upon the Ursulines of Laredo.

Hundreds of children have attended the Ursuline school since its foundation. The average attendance at the academy and day school is one hundred and fifty pupils.

The community has been reinforced by members from France, and now numbers nineteen professed nuns.

Their buildings have been enlarged and are adequate to present needs. The house has sustained none of the reverses incident to the other foundations in Texas.

In 1874 the Ursulines of Galveston founded the Ursulines at Dallas, and sent there six Sisters, with Mother St. Joseph Holly as superior, and Sister St. Paul Kaufman as treasurer. This colony had been equipped with what was needed to set them up in housekeeping, by the community they were leaving. But their new lodgings at Dallas were poor and much exposed. During the first few severe winters it was not uncommon for them to arise in the morning to find their beds covered with snow, and the same spot-

less flakes served as a table cloth at their frugal repasts. These
ladies never before endured hardships, but a charming gayety
made light of the privations which their poverty now entailed.
By arduous labor, and perseverance in this generous spirit of self-
sacrifice, in a few years they were enabled to erect a handsome
monastery and academy. The community now numbers nineteen professed, presided over by the excellent Mother Paul
Kaufman.

The academy has a large and select attendance of pupils, less
than one-third of whom are Catholics. Their parochial schools
enroll three hundred day pupils.

Their first superior, Mother St. Joseph Holly, during the first
years of poverty and exposure contracted a pulmonary disease,
which terminated her usefulness in 1884, at the age of forty-two
years. This eminent religious was educated by the Ursulines of
Galveston, and was no less distinguished by her cultivated intellect than by her religious virtues.

I regret exceedingly that I cannot adequately represent the
vast amount of good the Ursulines have accomplished in Texas.
It would involve a history of the social conditions and educational development in the State since 1847. Having conducted for
almost thirty years the leading schools, attended by pupils from
all sections of the State, the Ursulines have exerted no insignificant control; and hosts of reliable witnesses would gladly testify
to the happy influence of the discipline, instruction and moral
training acquired in the Ursuline schools upon the social condition of the people of Texas.

NEW YORK, 1855.*

The present Ursulines of New York City owe their foundation
to the zeal of the venerable Mother Magdalen Stehlin, who had
inaugurated her work of civilization and charity in 1846 by founding the Ursulines of St. Louis.

In 1854 she purchased nine acres of ground at East Morrisania, more modernly East One Hundred and Fiftieth street, New

---

* In 1812 a convent was founded in New York by Ursulines from Cork;
but gaining no subjects, the nuns returned, after three years, to Ireland,
according to previous agreement.

York City, and the following year, with a colony from St. Louis, began her mission in New York by erecting a building one hundred by sixty feet, and opened her school under the patronage of St. Joseph. The usual privations incident to a new foundation were felt here in full force, and in 1856 so great was their poverty that the superior sought aid in Europe. Pope Pius IX. headed her subscription list, and added a number of spiritual indulgences, with his pontifical benediction, for the establishment in New York. At Prague Ferdinand I., at Vienna the Empress Caroline, Archduchess Sophia and the Archduke Francis, by their generous donations, are regarded as benefactors of the house.

In 1868 a second building, one hundred and twenty by fifty feet, was erected. Nor did the Sisters exhaust themselves in the building of a fine house with all the modern improvements; they also revised their course of study to correspond with the grades of the larger schools of their Order in Europe. The time that the Rev. Mother Stehlin spent in visiting the leading seminaries for young ladies in Europe was particularly favorable to them. To the present date the number of graduates from their academy is fifty.

In 1872 the Rev. Mother Stehlin returned to the house of her profession in Europe, and Mother Dominick Weiss, a saintly and beloved religious, was elected in her place, and has governed the community twenty-four years.

In 1871 these Ursulines undertook a neighboring parochial school with four hundred boys and girls, on One Hundred and Thirty-seventh street. So well did this undertaking succeed, that in 1884 a beautiful convent building was erected on this site, and thirteen Sisters from the mother house, with Mother Claire as superior, opened an academy for girls and small boys. This house is now known as St. Jerome's. The community has fourteen professed, the academy one hundred girls, and the parochial school, which they still conduct, 350 pupils.

In 1873 Rev. Father Boyce, late pastor of St. Teresa's Church, purchased large, commodious dwellings adjoining the pastoral residence, and invited the Ursulines of Morrisania to his parish. Rev. Mother de Sales and eight Sisters were sent to organize an academy and parochial school for about 850 girls.

This continued to be a mission or dependant house upon that

of Morrisania till 1881, when a novitiate was opened, and St. Teresa's became an independent institution. The number of graduates from this academy is twelve, and a number of young ladies from both schools, although not remaining to receive the honors of graduation, are now engaged in responsible positions in the public and other schools, or as book-keepers, etc.

The work of the Ursulines of New York has never been interrupted. Established without opposition, they have encountered none since; and the excellence of their work has overcome even the force of the great Protestant tradition of enmity toward those of their vocation, as far as their influence has extended.

The present community numbers twenty-two professed, governed by the beloved Mother de Pazzi; and 135 young girls attend their academy, known as St. Teresa's, and 600 pupils attend their parochial school.

Another offshoot from the Ursulines of Morrisania is in Providence, R. I. Rt. Rev. Bishop Hendricken, of this diocese, desirous of securing the eminent services of these Ursulines for the youth under his spiritual jurisdiction, offered them the gift of the academy building adjoining his Cathedral, and negotiated with the pastor for them to teach the parochial school.

The foundation was begun in 1878, by Mother Rose and twelve Sisters from the mother house. They opened school in September, and the attendance has steadily increased, and now numbers over 400 pupils.

In 1879 it was found necessary to enlarge the house, and last year ('85) a handsome academy and monastery were built by this new colony of Ursulines.

In 1880 Mother Rose returned to Morrisania, and was succeeded by the present superior, Mother Gonzaga, whose excellent qualities of head and heart have aided in no small degree in elevating the condition of these schools. The present community numbers thirteen professed.

LOUISVILLE, KY., 1858.

The Ursulines of Louisville were established in 1858, through the efforts of Rev. L. Streuber. He succeeded in gaining three Sisters under Mother S. Reitmeier, from Bavaria, his native land. These upon their arrival occupied a two roomed cottage, and lived in great poverty. After they opened school, so rapidly did the number of pupils multiply that they applied for additional force to their house in Europe. Three more Sisters were granted them, and during this time several young ladies asked for admission into the Order. In 1860 five novices were received, and Bishop M. J. Spalding performed the ceremony of bestowing the religious habit.

In 1861 suitable buildings were erected and the foundation laid for a church; but ere the completion of this beautiful edifice the virtuous and zealous Mother Reitmeier was called to her reward, having directed the Ursulines of Louisville for ten years. Mother Martina Mekalas was her successor in office, and finished the work inaugurated by her predecessor.

The twenty-fifth anniversary of the Ursulines in Louisville was celebrated with great pomp, a large concourse of the laity joining in the commemoration of the event. Pontifical High-Mass was celebrated by Rt. Rev. G. McCloskey, present Bishop of Louisville.

The present community numbers 129 members, governed by the estimable Mother Leandra. Besides the academy, they conduct five parochial schools in the city and two beyond the suburbs, and teach over 1000 children. These Ursulines began their school, in 1858, with twenty pupils.

In 1872 the Ursulines of Louisville responded to the invitation of Rev. P. Volk, of West Louisville, Daviess County, and founded a colony in his parish. The founders were five in number. The community now counts seventeen professed.

Their academy contains forty boarders and a number of day pupils. Ninety-five girls attend the parochial school. This house gives promise of great success.

ALTON, ILLINOIS.

The Ursulines of Alton, like those of Cleveland, although not counting more than twenty years' existence, have several affiliated houses in the State. The community at Alton is presided over by Mother Teresa Gillespie. There are fifty-two members, with branch houses at Litchfield, Decauter, Springfield, and Collinsville, where academies are established, besides the parochial schools, eight in number, that count 1,380 children, exclusive of the academies. There are also houses of the Order in Peoria, Bloomington, Pekin, and Metamora, in the diocese of Rt. Rev. J. L. Spalding, whose solicitude and watchful care have greatly advanced the prosperity of their institutions.

PITTSBURGH, PA.

The year 1866 witnessed, in addition to the fruitful Alton house, the foundation of the Ursulines of Pittsburgh, Pa.

The venerable superior, Mother St. Liguori, came from France in 1866, in company with a colony for Texas, where she remained for some years.

In 1870 she returned to Europe, and in England associated with herself the four daughters of Mr. Burns, of the well-known Catholic publishing-house of Burns & Oates, London. After Mr. Burns' death in 1879, his widow also withdrew to the retirement of this convent, which institution she endowed. The community numbers twenty members. These conduct a select academy for boarders and day pupils.

OTHER CONVENTS AND SCHOOLS.

In 1880 the Ursulines of Santa Rosa, California, were founded by a colony from St. Martin's, Ohio. Their school is divided into preparatory and collegiate departments, and gives promise of success.

In 1883 Mother Amadeus, with six Ursulines from Toledo, Ohio, founded the convent at Miles City, Montana. These Ursulines conduct one school at St. Labre's mission among the Cheyenne Indians, and one at St. Peter's mission among the Blackfeet tribe of Indians. Both of these last-mentioned houses are dependent upon the mother convent at Miles City. The combined communities governed by Mother Amadeus number fifteen religious. Their missionary work has effected much good in Montana.

Besides these Ursulines, a convent of the Order is established at Lake City, Minnesota, where a community of eleven professed conduct an academy and parochial school. One at Cumberland, in the archdiocese of Baltimore, and one at Memphis, Tenn., are recent foundations.

In the State of Indiana the parochial schools of Madison, Jeffersonville, Evansville, St. James, Haubtstadt, and St. Bonifice are taught by Ursulines. At Bloomington, Ill., is a convent of German Ursulines.

This list concludes the enumeration, and includes, I believe, EVERY Ursuline convent and school in the United States and Canada, numbering in all nearly fifty houses, peopled, according to rough estimate, with about 2,500 religious, who train over 50,000 children in the paths of virtue.

CHARACTER OF THE URSULINES' WORK.

The public school question, during the last fifteen years, has excited so much attention in this country that the Ursuline nuns of the United States have obtained dispensation from cloister life for school purposes, and conduct free schools in many States of the Union, effecting incalculable good. I regret that it does not come within the limits of this faint outline sketch to adequately represent the finer features of their system of education, or its best products, as, for instance, well trained reasoning faculties, logical memories, gentle manners, noble aspirations, and God-fearing, pure hearts. From the first crude, unclassified Ursuline school, taught in a log cabin in the wilds of Canada, two and a half centuries ago, to the model institutions that exist to-day in America, with diversified departments looking to the preparation of girls for home, or students for college, or training of teachers and others in industrial and scientific pursuits, the Ursulines have, with commendable zeal, striven to excel in the work of education. Is it to be wondered at, therefore, that, as the art of teaching has become each year more of a skilled profession, they have faithfully met every advancing requirement?

The constant correspondence between the Ursuline ladies of the different houses of the Order in America and Europe is a source of precious information to them all. They are thus enabled to keep up, as far as local necessities permit, a uniform grade in their system of education; and with the sympathy of numbers, tangible encouragement, and generous opportunities opened, are led to strive for a self-culture and education beyond that actually required by the necessities of their work.

CONCLUSION.

In the foregoing pages I have endeavored to give in chronological order a correct history (as far as space permits) of the "Ursuline Nuns in America." Such a history, in its very nature, must be a collection of statistical information, a recapitulation of names and dates; and whilst my method of treating this entertaining subject may fail to interest from its seeming dryness, I will express the hope that these pages are free from any anachronisms and errors. To attain this end, I have left no opportunity untried; spared no effort to gain information upon the subject from the most reliable sources. I will here take occasion to thank those ladies of the Order who have kindly rendered me valuable assistance by furnishing me with corrrected names, dates, and items of occurrence, relating to their various houses, both in the United States and in Canada.

In tracing the history of the Ursuline Order through the different European countries and America, the most casual student cannot fail to be impressed with the exalted character of its members in all ages and countries, and the earnestness with which they have battled for those principles, old as the human heart and broad as civilization's bounds, the religious enlightenment and intellectual advancement of the human race. So perfect is the reality of their religion, so broad their culture, that in all countries we find even those who have least sympathy with the Church to which those holy Sisters devote their lives, willing to forget doctrinal differences when weighed against the invaluable acquirements which these zealous educators bestow upon youth. It would be impossible for any one pen to record the benefits accruing to mankind through the moral and religious instruction imparted by these pious women. Innumerable are the homes in America that are blessed by the sweet chastity, the exalted moral and intellectual virtues of the pupils trained in these institutions. Correspondingly numerous are the social evils that have been rectified by the purer, higher and holier living thus introduced. It is in no small degree gratifying to note the steady enlargement and perpetuation of the Order, which, as God revealed to St. Angela, should exist to the end of time.

Of the early Ursuline founders in America, who delved and quarried in the mines of faith and of knowledge, and who suffered for the good of religion and the glory of God, alas ! but few survive ! Their mantles have, however, fallen upon worthy successors, whose influence continues to control, in no small degree, the intellectual and religious destinies of the country, type of the wise who

> " Do noble things, nor dream them all day long,
> And thus make life divine, and that great forever
> One grand sweet song."

The Genealogical Department

OF THE

AMERICAN CATHOLIC HISTORICAL SOCIETY

OF PHILADELPHIA.

THIS section consists of a committee of five gentlemen members, whose office it is to register and arrange for preservation in the archives of the Society any presented and accepted genealogies of our old Catholic families. Many of these are rapidly dying out; others, by intermarriage, are losing their distinctive character and family names. As regards the families themselves, the Committee deems it prudent to limit the expression "old" to families settled in America prior to 1820. This is deemed essential, in order to prevent abuses which would render the work of the department a historical absurdity. This does not mean, however, that contributions of this character from families of later date will be unacceptable, for all are cordially invited to join in this work; but the Committee reserves more especially to itself the criticism, rejection, or acceptance of such contributions, unless from their very special character they should be regarded as historically valuable. Neither by the term CATHOLIC does the Committee wish to be considered as limiting its work exclusively to families who are now in actual communion with the Roman Catholic Church, but it extends its labors also to those Protestant families whose ancestry was notably Catholic. For these also, the period fixed, 1820, is for obvious reasons most opportune, as marking for such families, at least in Philadelphia, the date of their separation from the Church. There is a much larger field of work here than most persons imagine. Many of our Catholic families can easily trace their pedigrees, in America alone, as far back as the beginning of the eighteenth century; some, far beyond that date. The Rev. Ferdinand Farmer's registries at St. Joseph's church, Philadelphia, are themselves an invaluable mine of undeveloped genealogical information. It ought to be a source of great pride in all to aid this Committee by every means in their power ; either by having their own family genealogy prepared by a thoroughly competent person and filing them with the Society, or by placing in the hands of the Committee such family records, papers, *memoranda*, and *data*, as will enable the Society to do the work for them. All family *traditions*, too, should be carefully noted, for, even when they are mainly incorrect, they are generally founded on some leading FACT, and contain within themselves germs of truth and historical information which, when properly investigated, are of invaluable service to the trained historian. They are often key-notes to the most important imformation. All such papers placed in the hands of the Committee will be carefully preserved, and, if desired, safely returned. It is the purpose of the Committee to ultimately issue these genealogies in the more permanent form of publication. The Committee cannot too earnestly appeal for the assistance of friends, Catholic and Protestant, in the matter. Of the gentlemen comprising the Commitee, Mr. Atlee Douredoure will have special charge of the French genealogies, and Dr. Lawrence Flick of the German pedigrees.

> THOMPSON WESTCOTT,
> PHILIP S. P. CONNOR,
> ATLEE DOUREDOURE,
> LAWRENCE F. FLICK,
> CHARLES H. A. ESLING,
> *Chairman.*

LIST OF BAPTISMS

REGISTERED AT

ST. JOSEPH'S CHURCH, PHILADELPHIA.

(FIRST SERIES.)

From August 29, 1758, to December 31, 1775.

Copied from the Original Records by Francis X. Reuss, Corresponding Secretary and Librarian of the American Catholic Historical Society of Philadelphia. With Introduction and Bracketed Notes by Rev. Dr. Middleton, O.S.A., President of the Society.

THE value and importance of vital statistics from an ecclesiastical as well as a civil point of view is beyond dispute. Legal tribunals in all ages have accorded to them, whether public or private, the greatest weight in determining questions relative to the rights of inheritance, of name, of power or of property. In Holy Writ, in the Gospels of Saints Matthew and Luke, we have, set down in detail, the lineage of Christ our Saviour.

Both Church and state, being interested, have equally provided for the keeping of registers of births, baptisms, marriages, deaths, burials, holy orders, profession of vows, and other events, sacred or political, that effect the individual or social welfare.

Cantù, the eminent historian, is authority for saying that baptismal registers were not generally in use before the fourteenth century, that at Florence (Tuscany), at the famous baptistery of S. Giovanni, the parish priest kept a box in which he tossed a bean for every baptism administered by him, a white bean for a male child, a black one for a female, and at the end of the year he counted the beans and recorded their number.   The same historian is also authority for stating that the earliest registers (known) are those of Siena in 1379, of Pisa in 1457, and of Piacenza in 1466.   (See "Storia degli Italiani," edit. Palermo, 1858, Tom. II., p. 659.)

The Council of Trent (sess XXIV., chapt. II.) enjoins on all in care of souls the duty of registering in a proper book the names of those who stand as god-parents at baptism.

According to the Councils of Rouen, in 1581, and of Bordeaux, in 1583, those who were in charge of souls were bound to keep four registers: one for baptisms, another for those who had confessed and communicated at the time prescribed by the Church, a third for marriages, and a fourth for burials.   (See Glaire's "Dictionnaire des Sciences Ecclésiastiques," art. *Registre.*)

The "Roman Ritual" requires parish priests to keep the parochial registers, of which there are five, viz : (1) of baptisms, (2) of confirmations, (3) of marriages, (4) of every family with its members, noting the sacraments received by each, called "Liber Status Animarum," and (5) of the faithful departed.

In the United States, the first attempt to publish Catholic church or mission registers was by John Gilmary Shea in New York, in 1859.   In that year this zealous and learned writer, so well deserving of the esteem of scholars for his many and laborious researches in Church history, had printed one hundred copies of the "'Register of the Baptisms and Interments" which took place at Fort Duquesne, in Western Pennsylvania, during the years 1753 4-5 and 1756.   This Register was republished by the Rev. Father A. A. Lambing in his *Historical Researches*, etc., Pittsburgh, Pa. 1884-5.

The American Catholic Historical Society (of Philadelphia) has here undertaken to publish the mission registers of baptisms, marriages, and burials kept at St. Joseph's church, Philadelphia, during the last century. In this present volume, it contents itself with publishing transcripts from the baptismal register only, leaving it to the future to determine whether the work shall be continued.

This church, it may be said, is one of the oldest missions in

Pennsylvania, or, for that matter, in any of the English-settled parts of the United States. It was founded in 1732, by Fr. Josiah Greaton, S. J. Other old churches of the last century in Pennsylvania are at Conewago, in Adams county (The Sacred Heart), founded about 1730 ; Goshenhoppen, in Berks county (The Blessed Sacrament), in 1741 ; Reading (St. Peter's), in 1751; St. Mary's (Philadelphia), in 1763 ; Holy Trinity, do., in 1787 or '9 ; St. Augustine's, do., in 1796 ; Haycock, in Bucks county (St. John the Baptist's), in 1798, and Elizabethtown, in Lancaster county (St. Peter's), in 1799.

The registers of St. Joseph's church were kept from the beginning—from Fr. Greaton's time. Unfortunately, the earliest volume, containing the records from 1732 to 1758, was lost some fifteen years ago, and the earliest records now known to be extant begin with a baptism conferred August 29, 1758.

The registers from which the following transcripts have been made are all in fair condition. Despite the destructiveness of time and the vicissitudes of the church, they display a neat and scholarly handwriting ; the letters are well formed, and, with the exception of a missing page here and there, the records are clearly readable, except in a few places where the fading of the ink or the wearing away of the margin has rendered all attempts to decipher them unavailing. The earliest register, a small quarto of one hundred pages, running from 1758 to 1768, is almost wholly in Fr. Ferdinand Farmer's hand, as appears from an attestation made by himself on the first page, and another on page eleven, which reads, " *Baptizati a me Ferdinando Farmer Soc. Jesu Missionario nisi aliter notetur.*" Besides him, the names of five other priests are given, namely : Rev. Robert Harding, who is first met with August 28, 1762 ; Rev. Jacob Pellentz, in November, 1765 ; Rev. Luke Geisler, April 1, 1769 ; Rev. —— Hattersky, October 21, 1770 ; and an Anthony Carroll, in the register immediately following September 3, 1774, whom I take to be a priest from the letters R.D. preceding his name, that is, *Reverendus Dominus,* meaning Rev. Mr. Anthony Carroll. In the "Notes" column, opposite the baptisms for March 25 and November 15, 1767, mention is made of two Protestant ministers who had conferred baptism, one a Presbyterian and the other a Lutheran. The Presbyterian baptism seems to have been adjudged invalid, or at least doubtful, as the note remarks that the baptism was conferred by the priest under condition, while the Lutheran was recognized as being valid, since the priest supplied the ceremonies only.

In the registers at the end of each year the baptisms for the year have been summed up apparently by the one in charge, but not always does the sum total as given in the registers correspond with the true number of persons baptized. This discrepancy seems to arise from the fact that the accountant recorded at the end of each year the number of times baptism was conferred, and not the number of persons baptized. Hence when two or more were baptized at one and the same time, the registers seem to count them as only one baptism. The whole number of baptisms or of persons baptized for the eighteen years here published amounts to eighteen hundred and sixty-five.

The registers do not always name the place where baptism was administered. The Fathers of St. Joseph's traveled far and near, to say Mass and give the sacraments. A glance at the registers themselves will show how wide a field bore witness to their sacred labors. We find mention of places in Pennsylvania, New Jersey, and, it has been suggested, since many names are no longer recognizable with certainty, even in Maryland and Delaware. I have noted the places named in the registers now being published, and find them to number forty-three in all. They are here given just as set down, with the supposed or known location in brackets, together with the date of their first appearance in the register. They are:

(1) Philadelphia; (2) Concord [Del. Co., Pa.], Nov. 5, 1758; (3) Matthew Geiger's house [in New Jersey], March 15, 1759; (4) Adam Geiger's [New Jersey], Jan. 2, 1760; (5) Geiger's [ditto], June 27, 1759; (6) the glass-house [Salem Co., N. J.], May 14, 1761; (7) in New Jersey frequently; (8) Thomas Maguire's house, Chester [Pa.], July 27, 1762; (9) Chester [do.], July 4, 1763; (10) in Chester Co. [do.], May 6, 1764; (11) Goshenhoppen [Berks Co., Pa.], July 1, 1764; (12) while traveling, *in itinere*, Nov. 6, 1764; (13) Haycock [Bucks Co., Pa.], Nov. 18, 1764; (14) Pikesland [Chester Co., Pa.], March 3, 1765; (15) Berks Co [Pa.], April 19, 1765; (16) Ringwood [Passaic Co., N. J.], April 26, 1765; (17) while returning home, *in reditu*, May 1, 1765; (18)

near Yellow Springs [Chester Co., Pa.], Dec. 15, 1765; (19) New Castle [Del.], Feb. 8, 1766; (20) Jacob Eck's house, March 4, 1766; (21) Basconridge [Somerset Co., N. J.], April 24, 1766; (22) Salem [N. J.], Aug. 28, 1766; (23) John Broc's house [Philadelphia], Feb. 3, 1767; (24) Gothland [N. J.?], June 20, 1767; (25) Reading Furnace [Chester Co., Pa.], June 18, 1768; (26) Charlottenburg [N. J.?], Oct. 23, 1768; (27) Pilesgrove [Salem Co., N. J.], March 19, 1769; (28) Nicholas Wochman's house [Burlington Co., N. J.?], April 10, 1771; (29) Burlington Co. [N. J.] Nov. 12, 1771; (30) Cohansey [Cumberland Co., N. J.], Nov. 18, 1771; (31) Longpond [Sussex Co., N. J.?], Nov. 18, 1772; (32) during a mission from April 24 to May 4, 1774; (33) near Millstown [?] after May 29, 1774; (34) Springfield [Essex Co., N. J.?], Sept. 3, 1774; (35) Middleton [N. J.?], Sept. 6, 1774 ; (36) Sandy Run, Sept. 7, 1774 ; (37) Hunterdon Co. [N. J.], Oct. 6, 1774; (38) Morris Co. [N. J.], Oct. 13, 1774, (39) Mt. Hope [Morris Co., N. J.], Oct. 23, 1774; (40) Pottsgrove, March 22, 1775; (41) Sussex Co. [N. J.], May 17, 1775; (42) near Haycock [Bucks Co., Pa.]. June 1, 1775; and (43) Greenwich [Cumberland Co., N. J.?], Oct. 11, 1775.

The larger number of these places are so well known as to call for no further description. Others present certain difficulties, apparently insuperable, to determine their location with precision. I therefore leave them without any other note except what is contained within the brackets, with one exception, and that is the Geigers, who, from the frequency with which they are met, seem to deserve something more than a passing notice. It has been suggested that Geiger's was near New York city, somewhere near the state boundary line, between New York and New Jersey. This I am forced to consider as wholly untenable, and to maintain, on the contrary, that the Geigers lived near Philadelphia— maybe at Frankford, or at Salem, N. J. In support of this conclusion, the registers themselves present three plain facts: first, that on May 14, 1761 (q. v.) two baptisms were conferred—one at Adam Geiger's and the other at "the glass-house."

As the baptisms were conferred on the same day, these two places could not have been far apart, at least not more than a day's journey. (This is on the supposition that the same minister conferred baptism in both cases.) Now glass-making was especially carried on in and near Philadelphia, as well as at Salem, N. J. In 1683, Wm. Penn alludes to a glass-house in Frankford (See Scharf and Westcott's "History of Philadelphia," vol. III., p. 2298); in 1740, as we learn from a letter from the custom-house, London, dated July 31, there was "a glass-house" within eight miles of Salem [N. J.] (see "N. J. Archives," First Series, vol. VI.), and in 1769, Richard Wistar transferred his glass-factory from New Jersey to Philadelphia. (See "History," above.) Glass-making was then no rarety in or near Philadelphia. The location of "the glass house" seems more definitely put near Salem rather than Philadelphia, from the second fact that two baptisms again were conferred on immediately successive days, one on March 17, 1771, at Pilesgrove, and the other the day after at "the glass-house." Here, then, we have three places given, one located with precision—Pilesgrove, the second—''the glass-house," not far from it, and the third—Geiger's, not far from either. Pilesgrove is in Salem county, a little southeast of Philadelphia, and therefore Geiger's could not have been very far from this latter place.

The third fact only serves to confirm the vicinity of Geiger's to Philadelphia or Salem the more plainly, and this is that baptism was again conferred on two successive days, namely, August 27, 1766, at Geiger's, and on the day following at Salem, N. J. For these three reasons I am led to infer that Geiger's must have been in or near Philadelphia, and that by no possibility could it have been in the neighborhood of New York.

As to the method employed in copying the registers, I believe it only fair to state that the copyist, as he assures me, has transcribed the various entries in the original faithfully, in the same order in which they read, and without any attempt to change names or dates. Even the peculiarities in spelling have been preserved, except in the case of Christian names. and only these have all been rendered according to modern fashion. As regards family names, although they, as is very evident, have been in many instances mis-spelled, still it has been thought better to preserve them, mistakes and all, without any change. Wherever the words have proved indistinct and have baffled the copyist, the probably true way of spelling them has been supplied in brackets, sometimes with the addition of a question-mark.

The letters L. C. that is, *legitime conjugati*, or lawfully married, are often met with in the old registers, after the names of parents or god-parents. They have been left out altogether in this volume, principally because, while their mention in comparatively but a few instances certifies no doubt to the fact that the parties named were married, their absence or omission can in no manner be taken to imply that the far greater number of parents and others who are not so marked, were unmarried.

Fr. Thomas C. Middleton, O. S. A.

Villanova College, Pa.,
    December, 1, 1886.

N. B.—The inserton of (P.) after a name in the following records, indicates that the person was a Protestant. It is also to be noted, that whenever the place at which the baptism took place is not named, Philadelphia is generally understood.

REGISTER OF BAPTISMS FOR 1758.

Kauffman, James, of Joseph and Anna Catherine (P.) Kauffman, born August 14, baptized September 17, the sponsors being John Gatringer [Cottringer?] and Catherine Spengler.

Carroll, Augustus Patrick, of Morris Carroll and Margaret Canon, born August 24, baptized September 27.

Troy, Daniel and Patrick (twins), of Paul Troy and Maria le Blanc, baptized September 27.

Lancely, Eleanor, of Isaac Lancely and Eleanor Croaglan, born June 21, baptized September 3.

Fitzpatrick, James, of James (P.) and Elsie Fitzpatrick, born October 31, 1757, baptized August 29, sponsors Garret Cavernoy and Susie Mequiet.

Buttler, Mary, of Richard and Rebecca Buttler, born April 25, 1756, baptized October 15, sponsors Darby and Bridget Savage.

Carroll, John, of Timothy and Elizabeth Carroll, born October 7, baptized October 17, sponsors Edmund Buttler and Margaret Arnold.

Becker, Joseph, of Bartholomew and Elizabeth Becker, born October 18, baptized October 24, sponsors Joseph and Catherine Kauffman.

Keeth, Cornelius, of William and Margaret Keeth, born October 17, baptized October 28, sponsor Eleanor Keeth.

Godon, Charles, of Charles and Mary Godon, born October 26, baptized November 2, sponsor Susanna Conelin.

Lewis, Mary, of David Lewis and —— ——, born May 13, 1756, baptized November 5, sponsors James and Elizabeth Wilcox, at Concord, [Delaware county, Pa.].

Wiester, Mary Salome, of Peter and Mary Wiester, born October 29, baptized November 19, sponsors Adam and Salome Wilhelm.

Dumb [Thum?], Mary Margaret, of Caspar and Eva Dumb [Thum?], born November 4, baptized November 19, sponsor Mary Margaret Cunin.

Bower, Robert, of Robert (P) and Mary Bower, born March 20, baptized November 20, witnesses Michael Crowley and Tiranes Kramer, sponsor Mary Scandlan.

Buttler, Jeremiah, of William and Jane Buttler, born November 20, baptized November 22, sponsor Thomas Ryan.

Haffert, Mary, of Jacob and Mary (P.) Haffert, born November 10, baptized November 23, sponsors Bryan Carty and Anna Kelly.

[Philips?], Catharine Elizabeth, of John and Elizabeth [Philips?], born November 19, baptized November 23, sponsors Bartholomew and Catharine Elizabeth Becker.

Lassher, Mary Catharine, of Leonard and Mary Ann Lassher, born November 28, baptized December 8, sponsor Catharine Vole.

Makan, Arthur, of John and Jane (P.) Makan, born November 16, baptized December 24, sponsors Andrew Foley and Elizabeth Burke.

Whole number of baptisms—twenty.

REGISTER OF BAPTISMS FOR 1759.

Meyern, Anthony, of Elizabeth Margaret Meyern (P.), born December 27, 1758, baptized January 2, sponsors Elizabeth and James Welsh.

Fitzgerald, John, of David and Phœbe Fitzgerald, born January 6, baptized January 17, sponsors Joseph and Judith Fitzharald.

Schilling, Peter, of Philip and Eva Schilling, born January 14, baptized January 18, sponsors Peter and Elizabeth Hegner.

Schneider, Anna Regina, of Henry and Barbara Schneider, born January 15, baptized January 21, witnessed by Anton Ottman and Anna Regina, his wife.

——, Sarah, born December —, 1758, baptized January 21.

Schene, Barbara, of Lawrence and Mary Magdalen Schene, born January 27, baptized February 1, sponsors Anton Graf and Barbara Waltrich.

Geck, Peter, of Adam and Catharine (P) Geck, born February 6, baptized February 12, sponsors Peter and Elizabeth Hegner.

Kelly, James, of John and Hannah Kelly, born February 21, baptized February 22, sponsors Thos. and Anna Fitzsimmons, Jr.

White, Charles and Francis (twins), of Chas. and Jane White, born February 9, baptized February 23, sponsors Francis and Barbara Sener.

Holzhauser, Christian, of Dietrich and Christina (P.) Holzhauser, born February 20, baptized February 25, sponsors Christian Bub and Barbara Costin.

Hely, Anna, of John and Catharine Hely, born July —, 1756, baptized March 8, sponsor Catherine Dakin.

Hely, Margaret, of the same parents, born April, — 1758, baptized March 8.

Halder, Anna Maria, of Martin and Margaret Halder, born December 20, 1758, baptized March 15, sponsors Philip Jacoby and Susanna Geiger, in Mathew Geiger's house.

McDead, Mary, of John and Margaret McDead, born February 3, baptized March 15, sponsors Jacob and Mary Eva Cassa.

Friets, Mary Margaret, of Daniel and Joanna Friets, born March 22, baptized March 25, sponsors Peter and Mary Margaret Friets.

Farrell, Thomas, of Robert Farrell and ———, born March 18, baptized March 31, sponsors Francis Farrell and Eleanor Swan.

Stahler, Anna Maria, of John and Christina Stahler, born March 19, baptized April 1, sponsors John Stahler and Anna Maria Wilhelm.

Esling, Mary Eva, of Paul and Christina Esling, born March 25, baptized April 1, sponsors Philip and Eva Schilling.

Kennedy, James, of James Kennedy and Debora (P.) Stephens, born April 25, 1758, baptized April 8, sponsors Thos. Leanon and Catherine Welsh.

Lederman, Francis Joseph, of John and Mary Catherine Lederman, born April 10, baptized April 15, sponsors Francis Joseph Lederman and Charlotta Miller.

Hoffman, John George, of Christian and Cunegunda Hoffman, born April 6, baptized April 15, sponsors Valentine Cori and Barbara Weber.

Waas, Paul Francis Xavier, of Sebastian and Anna Mary Waas, born February 27, 1757, baptized April 17, sponsors Paul and Dorothy Miller.

Waas, Anthony Ignatius, of the same parents, born November 9, 1758, baptized April 17, sponsors Anthony and Anna Mary (P.) Gabriel.

Schad, Francis Joseph and John George (twins), of John Peter and Mary Elizabeth Schad, born April 13, baptized April 19, sponsors John George and Anna Mary Martz.

Villar, Mary Elizabeth, of Anthony and Mary Eva Villar, born Nov. 5, 1758, baptized April 22, sponsor Mary Elizabeth Stauter.

Nicholson, John, of John and Sarah Nicholson, born Dec. 26, 1758, baptized April 29, sponsors Edw. Hughes and Bridget Hunt.

Gräser, Mary Martha, of Frederic and Mary Elizabeth Gräser, born May 1, baptized May 5, sponsors Herman and Mary Martha Faust.

Hugh, Henry, of Patrick and Thamar [Hannah ?] Hugh, born April 5,
   baptized May 6, sponsors Bernard Martin and Catharine Duken, at
   Concord [Del. Co., Pa.].

Malleben, Mary, of Thomas and Christina Malleben, born April 26,
   baptized May 19, sponsors William Gallagher and Magdalen Malleben.

————, Thomas.   (No particulars.)

Viel, Christopher, of Christopher Viel and ————, baptized May 25.

Riechart, Dorothy, of Lothaire and Elizabeth Riechart, born Oct. 3,
   1753, baptized June 2, sponsors Paul and Dorothy Miller.

Riechart, John, of same parents, born March 1, 1758, baptized June 2,
   sponsor John Heiser.

David, Charles, of Anthony and Maria Theresa David, born May 29,
   baptized June 10, sponsors, Gerard and Catharine Mead.

English, Elizabeth, of Francis and Elizabeth English, born April 2,
   baptized ————, sponsors Firman Pow[*dern ?*] and Elizabeth Franks.

Picket, Sarah, of Edmund and Mary Picket, born Dec. 21, 1757, baptized
   July 2, sponsor Thomas Clark, at Concord [Del. Co., Pa.].

Fleur, Martin, of Dominic and Nanon Fleur, born Dec., — 1758, baptized
   June 27, sponsors Martin Halder and Regina Meyer, at Matthew
   Geiger's.

Eyenson, Sarah, of John and Elizabeth Eyenson, born April 7, baptized June 27, sponsors Christopher Thurnbach and Susan Catherine
   Geiger [probably at Geiger's].

Krumholz, Anna Barbara, of John Charles and Anna Maria Krumholz,
   born June 30, baptized July 8, sponsors Francis and Barbara Sener.

Allison, John, of Richard and Eleanor Allison, born ————, baptized
   July 23.

Savage, Thomas, of Jeremiah Savage, born ————, baptized July 25,
   sponsor Bridget Savage.

Essling, John, of Peter and Maria Essling, born June 20, baptized July
   29, sponsors John and Anna Maria Gross.

Rohrer, Mary Catharine, of John (P.) and Anna Gertrude Rohrer, born
   May —, 1755, baptized Aug. 4, sponsors Bartholomew and Catherine
   Elizabeth Becker.

Rohrer, Catharine Elizabeth, of same parents, born Feb. 19, 1757, baptized
   Aug. 4, sponsors Andrew and Mary Catharine Englehardt.

Rohrer, Peter, of same parents, born Jan. —, baptized Aug. 4, sponsor
   Peter Dietrich.

Essling, Paul, of Nicholas and Mary Joanna Essling, born July 30, baptized Aug. 4, sponsors Paul and Christina Essling.

Weidman, Henry, of John and Anna Barbara Weidman, born July 27,
   baptized Aug. 4, sponsors Henry and Mary Catharine MacGray.

Hunecker, Anna Sibylla, of Mark and Anna Hunecker, born Aug. 6,
   baptized Aug. 7, sponsors Anna and Sibylla Walter, near Philadelphia.

Barry, John and James (twins), of William and Mary Barry, born June 7, baptized August 9, sponsors Mary Cook and Bridget Hunt.

[Charlie ?], Mary Barbara, of Joseph and Barbara [Charlie?], born August 14, baptized August 15, sponsors Humbert and Barbara Benoit.

Fox, Anna, of William and Rosina (P.) Fox, born August 1, baptized August 15, sponsor Catherine Ryan.

Viet, Bartholomew, of Henry and Ottilia Viet, born August 7, baptized August 19, sponsors Bartholomew and Catharine Elizabeth Becker.

Geiger, Elizabeth, of Adam and Agnes Geiger, born July 10, baptized August 22, sponsors Christian Thurnbach and Susan Catharine Geiger, at Geigers'.

Schnable, James, of Andrew and Eva Schnable, baptized August 23, witnessed by Joseph and Mary Magdalen Hanckaun.

England, Elizabeth, of Thomas and Anne England, born September 9, baptized September 15, sponsors John Moor and Eliza Doyle.

Hoffman, Anthony, of John and Constantia (P.) Hoffman, born September 8, baptized September 16, sponsors Anthony and Regina Ottman.

Connor, Bridget, of Peter and Dorothy Connor, born September 17, baptized September 19, sponsor Mary Hefferman.

LeBlanc, Mary, of Henry and Mary LeBlanc, born September 8, baptized September 30, sponsors Michael Litle and Mary Hefferman.

Schreiner, Mary Anna, of Anselm and Elizabeth Schreiner, born September 27, baptized September 30, sponsors Leonard and Mary Anna Lasher.

Benner, Susanna, of Christian and Magdalen Benner, born September 16, baptized October 3, sponsors Peter Halder and Mary Catharine Griesmeyer, at Geiger's.

Rudolph, John, of John and Margaret (P.) Rudolph, born October 4, baptized October 8.

Hussey, John, of William and Eleanor Hussey, baptized October 8, sponsors Mary Catharine Griesmeyer and Brian O'Harra.

Baldrich, John, of Robert and Mary Baldrich, born September 6, baptized October 21, sponsors John and Sarah Heasy.

McDonald, Mary, of John and Bridget McDonald, born August 1, baptized October 21, sponsors William Buttler and Thomas Groaly.

————, Sarah, baptized November 1.

Hirst, John Peter, of Nicholas and Barbara Hirst, born November 1, baptized November 2, sponsors Peter and Elizabeth Hegner.

Foy, Elizabeth, of Patrick and Margaret Foy, born November 1, baptized November 8, sponsors Martin Welsh and Catharine Foaley.

Poth, John Adam, of John and Eva Poth, born September 9, baptized November 11, sponsors John Adam and Elizabeth Poth.

Spiess, Anthony, of Wolfgang and Anna Catharine Spiess, born ————, baptized November 21, sponsor Margaret LeBlanc.

Freeman, John, of Wm. and Elizabeth Freeman, baptized December 2, sponsors Peter and Mary Weisser.

Moor, Elizabeth, of John Moor and Catharine Nigart, born November —, baptized December 2, sponsor Rachael Therry.

Zeis, John, of John Adam and Mary Anna Zeis, born December 12, baptized December 19, sponsors John and Anna Barbara Weidman.

Ungar, Mary, of Jacob and Anna Margaret Ungar, born December 15, baptized December 29, sponsors Mark and Anna Hunecker.

Lasher, Frederic, of Leonard and Mary Ann Lasher, born December 19, baptized December 26, sponsors Frederick and Elizabeth Gräser.

Slevin, Margaret, of Patrick and Elizabeth (P.) Slevin, born December 26, baptized December 28, sponsors Neàl Heart and Eleanor Kennelly.

Whole number of baptisms—seventy-eight.

REGISTER OF BAPTISMS FOR 1760.

Bub, Susanna, of Melchior and Barbara Bub, born December 10, 1759, baptized January 1, sponsors Christian Thurnbach and Susan Catherine Geiger.

Kelty, John, of Bartholomew and Catharine Kelty, born December 17, 1759, baptized January 2, sponsors John McGill and Susan Catharine Geiger.

Galvin, Catharine, of Jeremiah and Mary Galvin, born November 9, 1759, baptized January 2, sponsors Patrick Edward Colman and Anna Delaney, at Adam Geiger's, in New Jersey.

Vanhost, Mary, of Isaac and Susanna Catharine (P.) Vanhost, born December 2, 1759, baptized January 13, sponsors Jacob and Anna White.

Viel, John Henry, of Rudolph and Magdalen Viel, born January 17, baptized January 20, sponsors Henry and Mary Barbara Schneider.

Dunn, Daniel, of Nicholas and Anne Dunn, born July 2, 1758, baptized January 28, sponsors Henry Arnold and Joanna Welsh.

Metzgar, Francis, of John and Cecilia Metzgar, born February 10, baptized February 12, sponsors Francis and Barbara Somer [Sener?],

James ——, baptized February 17.

Thum, Anna Mary, of Caspar and Eva Thum, born February 17, baptized February 24, sponsors Michael and Eva Kheun.

Schilling, John Michael, of Philip and Eva Schilling, born February 8, baptized February 24, sponsors John Michael and Catherine Wolff.

Uhlein, George Joseph, of Francis Louis and Mary Ursula Uhlein, born February 28, baptized March 9, sponsors Joseph Dientz and Barbara Kornin.

Foratch, John Bartholomew, of Joseph and Anna Maria Foratch, born February 28, baptized March 9, sponsors Bartholomew and Catharine Elizabeth Becker.

Clerck, Thomas, of John and Elizabeth Clerck, born September 14, 1759, baptized March 12, sponsors James McGill and Hannah Machantlen, at Geiger's.

Huber, James, of Michael and Hannah Huber, born January 18, baptized March 12, sponsors Michael Zartel and Catharine Schülz.

Leanan, James Patrick, of Thomas and Anna Leanan, born March 18, baptized March 20, sponsors William Gallagher and Bridget Savage.

Gerstenberger, Michael, of Andrew and Magdalen Gerstenberger, baptized March 30, sponsors Michael Sauerwald and Charlotte Miller.

Lenox, Martha, of John and Mary Lenox, born January 8, 1758, baptized April 6, sponsors Dennis and Elizabeth Dunn.

Lenox, Mary, same parents, born March 31, 1759, baptized April 6, sponsors Dennis Dunn and Nellie O'Bryan.

[Herrih?], Mary Gertrude, of Nicholas and Sophia [Herrih?], born March 15, baptized April 7, sponsors John and Gertrude Stauter.

Allen, Thomas, of Richmond and —— Allen, baptized April 13, sponsors, Thos. Fitzsimmons, and Catharine Spengler.

Allen, Esther, of the same parents, baptized April 13.

Allen, Mary, of the same parents, baptized April 24.

Wilcox, George, of Jacob and Prudence Wilcox, born April 28, baptized May 5, sponsors Eliza and Thomas Wilcox, at Concord [Del. Co., Pa.].

Daniel, John, of John and Margaret Daniel, born March 10, baptized May 5, sponsors Michael and Jane Robinson.

Kheun, Mary Elizabeth, of Michael and Eva Kheun, born April 28, baptized May 5, sponsors Caspar and Mary Eva Thumb.

Heling, Elizabeth, of John and Magdalen Heling, born Nov. 17, 1756 baptized May 5, sponsors Paul and Dorothy Miller.

Goff, Anna, of Peter and Mary Goff, born April 20, baptized May 5, sponsors Thomas and Henrietta Maria Fitzsimmons.

Weisser, Mary Catharine, of Peter and Anna Mary Weisser, born April 29, baptized May 18, sponsors Michael and Mary Catharine Wolf.

Denetter, John, of John and Anna Mary Denetter, born May 4, baptized May 25, sponsors George and Anna Mary Mertz.

Hegner, Peter, of John and Anna (P.) Hegner, born April 3, baptized May 25, sponsors Peter and Elizabeth Hegner.

Stumpf, Christopher, of Christopher and —— (P.) Stumpf, born Dec. 16, 1759, baptized June 11, sponsors Adam and Agnes Geiger, at Geiger's.

Harrison, Frances, of Lancelot and Joanna Harrison, born July 4, baptized July 27, sponsors John Gatringer and Mary McCarty.

Hely, Edward, of John and Catharine Hely, born March 10, baptized

June 15, sponsors Edward Morry, or Morris and Susanna Isarden, witnesses Andrew Connor and Eleanor Burck.

Schad, John George, of John Peter and Mary Elizabeth (P.) Schad, born July 2, baptized July 22, sponsors John George and Anna Mary Mertz.

Cassin, John, of John and Elizabeth Cassin, born July 16, baptized August 4, sponsors Thomas Thynon and Margaret Brazil.

Rischhart, Joseph, of Lothaire and Elizabeth Rischhart, born March 11, baptized Aug. 24, sponsors Joseph Wirth and Charlotte Miller.

Bane, Gilbert, of Gilbert (P.) and Mary Bane, born June 20, baptized August 27, sponsor Mary Shean.

Villare, Mary, of Anthony and Mary Eva Villare, born Aug. 1, baptized Aug 27, sponsor Mary Taubenhauer.

Gräser, Paul, of Frederick and Elizabeth Gräser, born Aug. 25, baptized Aug. 28, sponsors Paul and Christina Essling.

Welsh, Hannah, of John and Rebecca (P.) Welsh, born May 16, baptized Aug. 30, sponsor Hannah Grogan.

Meyer, John, of John and Mary Rosa Meyer, born Sept. 2, baptized Sept. 14, sponsors George and Mary Mertz.

Holtzhauser, Francis, of Dietrich and Christina (P.) Holtzhauser, born Sept. 11, baptized Sept. 21, sponsors Christian Bub and Mary Barbara Bifar.

Feighen, Daniel, of Patrick and Margaret Feighen, born April 23, baptized Oct. 1, sponsors Adam and Agnes Geiger, at Geiger's.

Banks, Samuel, of Samuel and Susanna Banks, born January —, baptized October 5, sponsor Daniel Hely.

[Philips?], Anthony, of John and Elizabeth [Philips?], born October 18, baptized October 19, sponsors Anthony and Barbara Graff.

Dienstman, Mary Christina, of John Peter and Anna Mary (P.) Dienstman born September 12, baptized October 21, sponsors Michael and Elizabeth Christ.

O'Neill, Elizabeth, of James and Elizabeth O'Neill, born October 21, baptized October 22, sponsors Wm. Farrell and Anna Mary [Bimpel?].

Becker, Bartholomew Francis, of Bartolomew and Elizabeth Becker, born October 18, baptized October 26, sponsors, Francis and Barbara Sener.

Coleman, Catharine, of John and Joanna Coleman, baptized November 2, sponsors John Gogin and ——McCarty.

Martin, Anne, of Anthony and Anna (P.), Martin born November 3, baptized November 3, sponsors Emmanuel Fero and Joanna Welsh.

Sexton, Mary, of John and Catherine Sexton, born October 23, baptized November 10, sponsors Samuel Watts and Placentia Sexton.

Landry, Josephine Mary, of Peter and Anna Landry, born November 26, baptized Noeember 27, sponsors Oliver and Mary Josephine O'Kain.

Tscharte, Mary Elizabeth, of Christopher and Mary Dorothy (P.) Tscharte, born November 30, baptized December 6, sponsor Mary Elizabeth Hauser.

Schöne, Mary Magdalen, of Lawrence and Mary Magdalen Schöne, born December 6, baptized December 7, sponsors John Sauerwald and Mary Magdalen Essling.

Mallaben, Christina, of Thomas and Christina Mallaben, born November 23, baptized December 7, sponsors John Morris and Deborah Doyle,

Lederman, Michael, of John and Mary Catherine Lederman, born December 7, baptized December 7, sponsors Michael Sauerwald and Anna Catharine Becker.

Sweetman, Christopher, of Richard and Bridget Sweetman, born November 30, baptized December 7, sponsors Rudolph Meyer and Anna Catharine Spun.

Hirt, John, of George and Anna Barbara Hirt, born November 28, baptised December 7, sponsors John and Mary Rosa Meyer.

Cumberland, William, of Robert (P.) and Mary Cumberland, born November 28, baptized December 20, sponsor Elizabeth Morry,

Christ, Mary, of Michael and Elizabeth Christ, born November 27, baptized December 20.

Whole number of baptisms—sixty.

REGISTER OF BAPTISMS FOR 1761.

Schneider, Anthony, of Henry and Barbara Schneider, born January 7, baptized January 11, sponsor Anthony Ottman.

Heinrich, Anna Mary Catharine, of John and Mary Catharine (P.) Heinrich, born December 6, 1760, baptized January 11, sponsors George and Anna Mary Mertz.

Schreiner, Catharine, of Anselm and Elizabeth Schreiner, born January 17, baptized January 25, sponsors Joseph and Catharine Eck.

Galater, Anna Barbara, of Michael and Elizabeth Catharine Galater, born February 6, baptized February 8, sponsors Andrew Kestner and Anna Barbara Begern.

Carroll, Daniel, of Timothy and Elizabeth Carroll, born January 28, baptized February 8, sponsors Owen Macarty and Mary Carty.

White, Elizabeth, of James and Anna White, born February 10, baptized February 15, sponsors Dudley Dougherty and Deborah Doyle.

Babin, Margaret Pelagia, of Zachary and Margaret Babin, born February 19, baptized February 20, sponsors John Babin and Pelagia Galerm.

Bony, John Baptist, of Joseph and Mary Bony, born February 19, baptized March 1, sponsors Peter Landry and Josephine Bourg.

————, Rebecca, of Eva ————, baptized privately, March 6.

————, Francis, a slave, baptized March 9.

Miller, Simon, of Matthias and Anna Mary Miller, born January 20, baptized March 11, sponsor Agnes Greismeyer, witness Peter Sauter, at Adam Geiger's, New Jersey.

Martin, Elizabeth, of John Martin and Margaret Halder, born February 8, baptized March 11, sponsors Adam Geiger and Catharine Jacobi, *ibid.*

Waas, Mary, of Sebastian and Anna Mary Waas, born January 14, 1760, baptized March 21, sponsors Henry Arnold and Magdalen Hamin.

Ryan, John, of Thomas and Catharine Ryan, born January 28, baptized March 22, sponsors Thomas Leanan and Deborah Doyle.

Landron, John Charles, of Jean and Blanche Landron, baptized March 25, sponsors John Barbin and Isabella Godrot; baptized privately, ceremonies supplied.

Gatringer [Cottringer?], George, of John and Catharine Gatringer, born March —, baptized March 24, sponsors George Meade and Catharine Spengler.

Wilhelm, Joseph, of Gerard and Elizabeth Wilhelm, born April 2, baptized April 12, sponsors Joseph and Anne Mary Senaur.

Hoffman, Mary Barbara, of Sebastian and Cunegunda Hoffman, born April 2, baptized April 12, sponsors Valentine and Barbara Korn.

Smith, Thomas, of William (P.) and Sarah (P.) Smith, born March —, baptized April 26, sponsors Peter and Elizabeth Weissburger.

David, Lucy Frances, of Anthony and Mary Theresa David, born April 24, baptized May 3, sponsors Thomas and Anna Fitzsimmons.

Hirt, Peter, of Nicholas and Barbara (P.) Hirt, born April 22, baptized May 7, sponsors Peter and Elizabeth Hegner.

Kauffman, Anna Mary, of Joseph and Catharine (P.) Kauffman, born April 25, baptized May 10, sponsors John Gatringer and Catharine Spengler.

Walter, Catharine, of Paul and Magdalen (P.) Walter, born March 25, 1758, baptized May 10, sponsors Adam and Catharine Meyer.

Walter, John, of the same parents, born March 1, 1760, baptized May 10, sponsors John and Catharine Gatringer.

Kelty, William, of Bartholomew and Catharine Kelty, born March 1, baptized May 14, sponsors James and Joanna Magill, at Adam Geiger's, New Jersey.

Wentzel, John Adam, of John William and Anna Mary (P.) Wentzel, born April 27, baptized May 14, sponsors John Adam Geiger and Anna Abel, at the glass house.

Essling, Frederic, of Paul and Christina Essling, born May 8, baptized May 12, sponsors Frederick and Elizabeth Gräser.

Forêt, John Baptist, of Ferdinand and Margaret Forêt, born October 20, 1755, baptized May 12, sponsors —— Babin and Mary M. ——, ceremonies supplied.

——, Catharine, born Sept. 22, 1759, baptized May 26, sponsors Sebastian and Cunegunda Hoffman.

McDonald, Anna, of John and Sarah McDonald, born Aug. 8, 1759, baptized May 30, sponsor Elizabeth O'Neil.

Lee, Thomas, of James and Anna Lee, born April 6, baptized May 30, sponsors Elizabeth and Patrick O'Neil.

Bisar, Francis, of Sebastian and Mary Barbara Bisar, born May 24, baptized May 31, sponsors Francis and Barbara Sener.

Dussonds, Elizabeth, of Thomas Dussonds and —— ——, born May 28, baptized May 31, sponsor Elizabeth Gräser.

Baudoin, James, of Alexander and Mary Josephine Baudoin, born May 28, baptized June 2, sponsors James Alexander Finnet and Mary Bourg.

Macarty, Mary, of Owen and Elizabeth Macarty, born May 27, baptized June 7, sponsors Edmund Buttler and Mary Carty.

Collins, John, of James and Eleanor Collins, born Aug. 11, 1760, baptized June 8, sponsor Jeremiah Shea.

Hunecker, Joseph, of Mark and Anna Hunecker, born June 8, baptized June 11, sponsors Joseph and Catharine Eck, near Philadelphia.

Kelty, Owen, of Owen and Hannah Kelty, born Oct. 9, 1760, baptized June 17, sponsors John and Margery Magill, in New Jersey, at Geiger's.

Geiger, Agnes, of John Adam and Agnes Geiger, born June 11, baptized June 18, sponsors Lawrence Caspar and Agnes Griesmeyer.

McDonald, Thomas, of Jeremiah and Mary McDonald, born June 27, baptized June 28, sponsors James Francis and Elizabeth Murray.

Moran, James, of Patrick and Eleanor Moran, born June 7, baptized July 11, sponsors Martin Welsh and Mary Makra.

Riechart, Mary Magdalen, of John and Mary Apollonia Riechart, born June 28, baptized July 12, sponsors Anna Mary Freddeia [Fredder?] and Mary Magdalen Ambipère.

Welsh, Peter, of Peter Welsh and Margaret Roadge, born Nov. 7, 1759, baptized July 12, sponsors Eustace Daniel and Euphrosyne Daigle.

Kelly, William, of —— and Anna Kelly, born June 13, baptized July 12, sponsors James Smith and Mary Brazil.

Buttler, Elizabeth, of Thomas and Rosa Buttler, born July 10, baptized July 19, sponsors Peter and Elizabeth Weisenberger.

Greanaus, Anna, of Jonathan and Joanna Greanaus, born Nov. —, 1760, baptized July 19, sponsors Wm. Murray and Catharine Ryan.

Smith, Anna, of James and Elizabeth Smith, born May 5, baptized July 19, sponsors Joanna Welsh and Margaret Ryan.

McMahon, Mary, of Patrick and Elizabeth McMahon, born June 25, baptized July 26, sponsor Catharine Arnold.

Sluman, Robert, of Robert Sluman and —— ——, born Aug. 16, 1754, baptized Aug. 2, sponsor Catharine Arnold.

Walker, George, of Emas [Enos?] and Catharine Walker, born March 5, baptized Aug. 9, sponsor Austin Villars.

Magill, John, of Michael and Mary Magill, born August 31, 1758, baptized August 12, sponsors John Magill and Mary Roberts, in New Jersey.

Benner, Margaret, of Christian and Magdalen Benner, born July 12, baptized Aug. 12, sponsors James Philip Wenzel and Margaret Halder, *ibid.*

Thurnbach, Henry, of Christian and Susan Catharine Thurnbach, born July 9, baptized Aug. 12, sponsors Henry Geiger and Agnes Griesmeyer, *ibid.*

————, Elizabeth born ————, 1759, baptized August 27, sponsor Anna Elizabeth ·————, a slave of Peter Hegner, *ibid.*

Guet, Simon Joseph, of Simon Joseph and Magdalen Guet, born September 8, baptized September 10, sponsors Peter Gigitry and Mary Melanson, *ibid.*

Halder, Francis, of Francis and Margaret Halder, born August 6, baptized October 9, sponsors George and Christina Viet, *ibid.*

Walsh, Catharine, of James and Rosa Walsh, born October 2, baptized October 9, sponsors John Murphy and Catharine Duken.

Coleman, Edward, of Edward and Anna Coleman, born November 8, 1760, baptized October 14, sponsors Peter Magill and Mary Kelly, in New Jersey.

Magill, Susanna, of John and Catharine Magill, born June 25, baptized October 14, sponsors Adam and Agnes Geiger, *ibid.*

Graff, Mary Magdalen, of Anthony and Barbara Graff, born October 13, baptized October 19, sponsors Joseph Würth and Catharine Miller.

Sagetson, Anne Margaret, of John Sagetson (P.) and Eva Schreiner, born October 13, baptized October 16, sponsor Elizabeth Schreiner.

Göck, Mary Catharine, of Adam and Anne Mary Göck, born October 18, baptized October 21, sponsors Carl and Anna Catharine Schmidt.

Boirg, Anna, of John and Magdalen Boirg, born October 28, baptized October 28, sponsors Joseph de Bautan and Mary Galerm.

Tscharte, Mary Elizabeth, of Christopher and Mary Dorothy (P.) Tscharte, born October 8, baptized November 1, sponsor Mary Elizabeth Stauter.

Haug, Sophia, of Anthony and Mary Haug, born October 21, baptized November 1, sponsors Nicholas and Sophia Viel.

Turner, Daniel, of John Turne and Mary Bristlin, born October 20, baptized November 3, sponsor Michael Kelly, witness Rebecca Parker.

Murphy, John, of Philip and Margaret Murphy, born November 10, baptized November 11, sponsors Timothy Carroll and Barbara Arnold.

McDonald, Reynold, of Roderic and Anna (P.) McDonald, born October 17, baptized November 14, sponsors James White and Magdalen Gerstenberger.

Nihill, James, of Edmund and Mary Nihill, born October 19, baptized November 16, sponsors Thomas Fitzsimmons and Mary Gatringer.

Goff, Thomas, of Thomas and Alice Goff, born November 8, baptized November 22, sponsors John and Anna Mary de Wetter.

Bourg, Judith, of Paul and Judith Bourg, born November 8, baptized November 26, sponsors Peter Landry and Anna Bourg.

Ruhl, Adam, of George and Barbara Ruhl, born December 5, baptized December 8, sponsors Adam and Catharine Meyer.

O'Brien, Anna, of Matthew and Elizabeth O'Brien, born December 7, baptized December 10, sponsor Mary Galerm, ceremonies supplied.

Jeneker, Joseph Charles, of Ephraim and Maria Jeneker, born November 10, 1760, baptized December 11, sponsor Mary Magdalen Russel.

Hahn, John Valentine, of Christopher and Christina (P.) Hahn, born November —, baptized December 26, sponsors John Valentine and Barbara Korn.

Whole number of baptisms—seventy-five.

REGISTER OF BAPTISMS FOR 1762.

Schnable, Mary Magdalen, of Andrew and Eva Schnable, born Dec. 19, 1761, baptized Jan. 3, sponsor Joseph Huneker, Mary Magdalen Huneker witness.

Kneut, Elizabeth, of John and Elizabeth Kneut, born Nov. —, 1761, baptized Jan. 7, sponsor Catharine Hefferin.

Foaley, Mary, of Peter and Judith Foaley, born Nov. 8, 1761, baptized Jan. 17, sponsors Richard Sweetman and Mary Duffy.

Essling, Anna Christina, of Peter and Mary Elizabeth Essling, born January —, baptized Jan. 17, sponsors Peter and Christina Essling.

Bichau, John Baptist, of Paul and Mary Bichau, born —— ——, baptized Feb. 1, sponsors Gregory Chenne and Magdalen Chenne, ceremonies supplied.

Feinaur, John George, of Joseph and Anna Mary Feinaur, born Jan. —, baptized February 8, sponsors John George Lamb and Catharine Spengler.

Schilling, Anna Catharine, of Philip and Eva Schilling, born —— ——, baptized Feb. 11, sponsor Catharine Wolff.

Weisenburger, Catharine, of Peter and Elizabeth Weisenburger, born Jan. 20, baptized Feb. 22, sponsors Andrew Gallagher and Catharine Duken, in vicinity of Philadelphia.

Bosran, Miriam Modesta, of John and Anna Bosran, born Nov. 25, 1761, baptized March 3, sponsors Anthony Baudard and Margaret Doiron; baptized conditionally.

Mullen, William, of Daniel and Catharine Mullen, born March 3, 1756, baptized March 10, sponsor Thos. Buttler, in vicinity of Philadelphia.

Mullen, Hannah, of the same parents, born Feb. 6, 1758, baptized March 10, sponsor Anna Huneker.

Mullen, John, of the same parents, born Aug. 8, 1760, baptized March 10, sponsor Mary Huneker.

Landry, Miriam Margaret, of Peter and Josephine Landry, born —— —, baptized March 13, sponsors Peter O'Kain and Margaret Landry; baptized conditionally.

Frietz, John, of Caspar and Mary Frietz, born March 15, baptized March 28, sponsors John and Mary Stebing.

Baldrich, William, of Robert and Mary Baldrich, born Feb. 15, baptized April 11, sponsors William Heasy and Joanna Neal.

Herrick, John Anselm, of Nicholas and Sophia Elizabeth Herrick, born March 20, baptized April 12, sponsors John Stauter and Elizabeth Schreiner.

Armstrong, William, of John and Mary Armstrong, born March 28, baptized April 13, sponsors —— Baudon and Mary Benoit.

Connor, Patrick, of Daniel and Eleanor Connor, born Oct. 20, 1761, baptized April 14, sponsors Richmond and Mary Allen.

Eck, Joseph, of Jacob and Anna Eck, born Oct. 10, 1761, baptized April 18, sponsors Joseph and Catharine Eck.

O'Kain, Mary, of Oliver and Mary O'Kain, born May 3, baptized May 4, sponsors Oliver de Cotau and Magdalen le Prince.

Rühl, John George, of Joseph and Anna Mary Rühl, born May 6, baptized May 9, sponsors Adam and Anna Mary Göck.

Metzgar, Mary Elizabeth, of John and Cecilia Metzgar, born May 5, baptized May 9, sponsors John Hoffner and Elizabeth Cöchler.

Nicholson, Owen, of John and Sarah Nicholson, born autumn, 1761, baptized May 15, sponsor Rudolph Essling.

O'Harra, Mary Anna, of Bryan and Mary (P.) O'Harra, born Feb. 7, baptized May 15, sponsors Darby and Anna Savage.

Stahler, John Frederic, of John and Christina Stahler, born February 11, baptized May 16, sponsors Frederick and Elizabeth Gräser.

Hoffman, Mary Magdalen, of John and Christina Hoffman, born Feb. 9, baptized May 16, sponsors Valentine Korn, Jr., and Mary Magdalen Essling.

Ford, John Peter, of John Stanislaus and Anna Ford, born May 18, baptized May 18, sponsors Peter Ford and Margaret Babin.

Ball, George, of William Ball and Elizabeth Smith, born March 8, baptized May 23, sponsors George Nagle and Barbara Kneulin.

Galather [Galater?], Mary Elizabeth, of Michael and Elizabeth Catharine Galather [Galater?], born May 31, baptized June 1, sponsors Joseph Kientz and Elizabeth Stauter.

Hiner, John William, of Peter and Mary Josephine Hiner, born June 1, baptized June 1, sponsors John le Prince and Magdalen Caporon.

Gatringer, [Cottringer?] James, of John and Catharine Gatringer [Cottringer?], born May 20, baptized June 6, sponsors James Thompson and Catharine Spengler.

Sauerwalt, Elizabeth, of Michael and Margaret Sauerwalt, born June 6, baptized June 7, sponsors John and Elizabeth Walter.

Kennedy, Rachael, of Patrick and Flora Kennedy, born May 11, baptized June 10, sponsors Cornelius Scantlen and Catharine O'Brien.

Le Blanc, John Charles, of Charles and Anna le Blanc, born June 21, baptized June 21, sponsors Alexander le Prince and Magdalen Gliche.

Stump, John, of Christopher and Margaret Stump, born December 3, 1761, baptized June 24, sponsors John and Regina Mayer, in New Jersey, as above.

Huber, Francis, of Michael and Hannah Huber, born April 19, baptized June 24, sponsors Francis Franks and Margaret Halder, *ibid.*

Butin, Susan Catharine, of Paul and Ursula Butin, born December 17, 1761, baptized June 24, sponsors Peter Dietry and Christina Geiger, *ibid.*

D'Aigle, Joseph, of Alline and Euphrosyne D'Aigle, born May 22, baptized June 27, sponsors Joseph and Judith de Champs.

Miller, Mathias, of John and Mary Miller, born June 12, baptized June 29, sponsor Mathias Jager, witness Catharine Brehm.

Ungar, Gertrude, of Joseph (P.) and Margaret Ungar, born June 14, baptized July 4, sponsors Andrew Schwartzman and Gertrude Hegner.

Kheun, Catharine, of Michael and Eva Keuhn, born June 17, baptized July 11, sponsors Caspar and Mary Thum.

McKollom, Elizabeth, of James and Mary McKollom, born July 5, baptized July 11, sponsors Edward and Susanna Kearney.

Mullen, Mary and Anna, twins, of Thomas and Anne Mullen, born July 13, baptized July 13, sponsor James Mullen, witness Hannah Maglochlin, for Mary, John O'Donnell and Margaret O'Donnell sponsors for Anna.

Makoy, Margaret, of Enos and Sarah Makoy, born May —, baptized July 27, in house of Thomas Maguire, Chester, Pa.

Lennox, John, of John and Margaret Lennox, born July 19, 1761, baptized August 8.

Blanchart, Mary Margaret, of Oliver and Euphrosyne Blanchart, born August 9, baptized August 11, sponsors Daniel and Mary le Blanc.

Sterling, Francis, of Joel and Mary Magdalen Sterling, born July 27, baptized August 17, sponsors Francis Waltrich and Mary Magdalen, daughter of Paul Essling.

Green, Thomas, of Thomas and Margaret Green, born December 24, 1761, baptized August 22, sponsors Michael Bryan and Anna Deally.

Fitzharold, Mary, of David and Phœbe Fitzharold, born —— 16, baptized August 22, sponsors Darby McDonald and Margaret Conway.

Warren, Mary, of Peter and Mary Warren, born July 20, baptized August 24, sponsors Dennis and Mary O'Harra, in New Jersey.

Ruh [Ruhl?], Lawrence, of Melchior and Barbara Ruh [Ruhl?], born August 8, baptized August 24, sponsors Lawrence Caspar and Mary Catharine Greismeyer, *ibid*.

Ribau, James, of Joseph and Margaret Ribau, born August 19, baptized August 28, sponsors James and Sophia Robinson, by Father Robert Harding.

DeWetter, Mary Catharine, of John and Anna Catharine de Wetter, born August 22, baptized August 29, sponsors Joseph Würth and Catharine Spengler.

Waas, Mary Elizabeth, of Sebastian and Anna Mary Waas, born April 17, baptized August 29, sponsors Henry and Anna Mary Fredder.

Hely, Catharine, of John and Catharine Hely, born February 22, baptized August 29, sponsors Matthew and Catharine Lenny.

McBike, Benjamin, of Daniel and Margaret McBike, born August 26, baptized September 2; had been privately baptized; ceremonies supplied.

Schmidt, Anna, of Charles and Catharine Schmidt, born September 2, baptized September 3, sponsors Marius and Anna Hunecker.

Viehl, Mary, of Nicholas and Catharine Viehl, born September 15, baptized September 16, sponsors Anthony and Mary Haug.

Cassin, Joseph, of Joseph and Elizabeth Cassin, born September 4, baptized September 19, sponsors John Sheridan and Margaret Conway.

Freeman, Anna Mary, of William and Elizabeth Freeman, born June 21, baptized September 19, sponsors Peter and Anna Wiester.

Fevron, Augustine, of Augustine and Margaret Fevron, born September 19, baptized September 19, sponsors Louis Gentre and Elen [Ellen] Deboutere.

Doiron, Joseph, of Paul and Mary Doiron, born September 20, baptized September 20, sponsors Paul Blanchard and Josephine Bourg.

Arnold, Barbara, of Henry and Agnes Arnold, born September 20, baptized September 20, sponsors Anthony and Barbara Graff.

Allen, Richmond and James (twins), of Richmond Allen and ———, born September 21, baptized September 21, privately.

Bauer, Mary Elizabeth and Mary Magdalen (twins), of Leonard and Ursula (P.) Bauer, born September 22, baptized September 26, sponsors John and Elizabeth Phillips for Mary Elizabeth, Paul Bischoff and Magdalen Ansperger for Mary Magdalen.

Becker, Stephen, of Bartholomew and Elizabeth Becker, born September 22, baptized September 26, sponsors Stephen and Mary [Foratch?].

Reichart, Adam, of Frederic and Elizabeth Reichart, born September 17, baptized September 26, sponsors Adam and Catharine Mayer.

Sexton, Elizabeth, of John and Catharine Sexton, born April ———, baptized September 26, sponsors Anthony and Barbara Graff.

Neukomm, Barbara Catharine, of Henry and Mary Neukomm, born August 1, baptized by Father Robert Harding September 12, sponsors Adam Mayer and Barbara Knewlin.

Babin, Joseph Michael, of Zachary and Margaret Babin, born September 29, baptized September 30, sponsors Peter Babin and Pelagia Galerm.

Viehle, Catharine, of Robert and Sibylla Viehle, born October 3, baptized October 4, sponsors Christopher and Catharine Viehle.

Morris, Mary, of Andrew and Rebecca Morris, born October 6, baptized October 10, sponsors Patrick Marcum and Martha Levy.

Graff, John George, of Anthony and Barbara Graff, born October 6, baptized October 10, sponsor Catharine Spengler.

Kientz, Martin John, of Andrew and Eva Kientz, born October 10, baptized October 11, sponsor Martin Weberan, near Philadelphia.

Makay, James, ot William and Catharine Makay, born October 5, baptized October 17, sponsors Thomas Ghill [Gill?] and Mary Brown.

Hely, Thomas, of Daniel and Mary Hely, born October 18, baptized October 18, sponsors Thomas Derry and Catharine Francis.

Daniel, Margaret, of Eustace and Margaret Daniel, born October 18, baptized October 22, sponsors Paul Bourg and Anna Bosron.

Camel [Campbell?], Daniel, of John and Mary Camel [Campbell?], born October 12, baptized October 24, sponsors Michael and Anna Davis.

Rudolph, Catharine, of Tobias and Margaret Rudolph, born October 22, baptized October 25, sponsors Peter and Gertrude Hegner.

Gliche, Louis Joseph, of Louis and Magdalen Gliche, born October 26, baptized conditionally, October 26, sponsors Simon O'Kain and Anna le Blanc.

Makra, [Fegentius?], of John and Anna Makra, born September 22, baptized October 26, sponsors Thomas Murphy and Margaret Menin, Michael Cronin witness.

Cahel, John, of Thomas and Mary Cahel, born November 1, 1757, baptized October 30, sponsors Dennis Faulon and Margaret Brazil.

Cahel, Thomas, of same parents, born September 3, 1760, baptized October 30, sponsor Hugh Makeny.

Collins, Sarah, of Daniel and Isabella Collins, born July 22, baptized November 2, sponsors John and Margaret Reding.

Walter, Francis, of John and Elizabeth Walter, born November 6, baptized November 7, sponsors Francis Waltrich and Barbara Steling.

Kelty, Michael, of Bartholomew and Catharine Kelty, born October 6, baptized November 10, sponsors Louis Murphy and Mary Tynan.

Murphy, Robert, of John and Mary Murphy, born November 2, baptized November 10, sponsors John Barret and Margaret Murphy.

Lery, Elizabeth, of Daniel and Mary Lery, born September 11, baptized November 10, sponsors Edmund and Barbara Buttler.

Martin, Peter Firmian, of Peter and Frances Martin, born November 10, baptized November 11, sponsors Joseph Dieri [?] and Mary Martin.

Nikol, William, of William and Johanna Nikol, born November 9, baptized November 13, sponsor Mary Brady.

Gräser, Laurence, of Frederick and Elizabeth Gräser, born November 10, baptized November 14, sponsors Laurence and Magdalen Schöne.

Martin, Anthony, of Anthony and Anna (P.) Martin, born November 12, baptized November 14, sponsors Mathew Power and Margaret Brazil.

Dunn, Peter, of Hugh and Elizabeth Dunn, born September 29, 1760, baptized November 17, sponsor William Morry, in vicinity of Philadelphia.

Thumb, Catharine, of Caspar and Eva Thumb, born November 7, baptized November 21, sponsors Michael and Eva Khue.

Brooks, James, of James and Mary Brooks, born April 4, baptized November 22, sponsors Charles and Mary Queen.

Miller, Christian, of Matthias and Anna Mary Miller, born September 22, baptized November 23, sponsors Christian and Magdalen Benner, at Geiger's, in New Jersey.

Eyenson, Mary, of John and Elizabeth Eyenson, born September 26, baptized November 23, sponsors Patrick and Margery Magill, *ibid*.

Lascher, Mary Catharine, of Leonard and Mary Anna Lascher, born November 30, baptized December 8, sponsor Mary Catharine Engelhardt.

Bridy, John, of John and Dorothy Bridy, born November 18, baptized December 12, sponsors George and Barbara Haug.

Baily, John Henry, of Richard Baily (P.) and Catharine Frick, born about September —, 1757, baptized December 12, sponsors Henry Kramer and Catharine Arnold.

Göck, Charles, of Adam and Mary Göck, born December 12, baptized December 13, sponsors Charles and Catharine Schmid.

Miller, Barbara, of Mathias and Anna M. Miller, born December 13, baptized December 16, sponsors Andrew and Magdalen Gerstenberger.

Uhla [Uhler?], John Anthony, of Francis Louis and Mary Ursula Uhla [Uhler?], born December 10, baptized December 27, sponsors John Ehreman and Barbara Korn.

Moor, Elizabeth, of John and Elizabeth Moor, born December 4, baptized December 30, sponsor Anna Fitzsimmons.

Whole number of baptisms—one hundred and seven.

REGISTER OF BAPTISMS FOR 1763.

Bell, William, of William and Mary (P.) Bell, a young man, baptized January 5, sponsors William and Eleanor Hussy.

Babin, Mary Margaret, of Charles and Frances Babin, born January 9, baptized January 9, sponsors Peter Vincent and Margaret Babin.

Hesteron, Elizabeth, of John and Elizabeth Hesteron, born January 11, baptized January 16, sponsors Samuel Watts and Mary Connor.

O'Kain, Peter, of Oliver and Anna O'Kain, born January 21, baptized January 21, sponsors Francis Savoy and [Ogithea ?] Dupries.

Wallis, Mary Magdalen, of Michael and Anna Mary Wallis, born January 20, baptized January 23, sponsors Christian Schütz and Mary Magdalen Wallis.

Schreiner, Mary Christine, of Anselm and Elizabeth Schreiner, born January 16, baptized January 23, sponsors Paul and Anna Christina Essling.

Foratch, Frederika Catharine, of Stephen and Anna Mary Foratch, born January 23, baptized January 23, sponsor Valentine Schalin, witness Frederika Catharine, his wife.

Savoy, Mary Margaret, of Francis and Margaret Savoy, born February 16, baptized February 16, sponsors Joseph Debotan and Anastatia Leblanc.

Vincent, Margaret, of Joseph and Genevieve Vincent, born February 3, baptized February 3, sponsors Peter Vincent and Mary Magdalen Babin.

Vincent, Joseph, of the same parents, born —— —, baptized February 3, sponsors Marin Leblanc and Margaret la Vache.

McKnight, John, of John and Catharine McKinght, born January 3, baptized February 9, witness Elizabeth O'Neal.

Geiger, Laurence, of Adam and Agnes Geiger, born February 10, baptized February 20, sponsors Laurence Caspar and Susanna Catharine Thurnbach, in New Jersey.

Leblanc, Mary, of Henry and Mary Leblanc, born January 29, baptized February 25, sponsors Nicholas Bernard and Catharine Swan.

O'Doran, James, of Hugh and Rosa O'Doran, born February 26, baptized February 27, sponsors Joseph Eck and Catharine Spengler.

[Glontia?], Mary Margaret, of Louis and Mary Magdalen [Glontia?], born March 7, baptized March 7, sponsors Oliver O'Kain and Mary Josephine Dupries.

Hoffman, John Valentine, of Sebastian and Cunegunda Hoffman, born March 8, baptized March 13, sponsors Valentine Korn, Jr., and Elizabeth Löchler.

McDonald, Mary, of James and Bridget McDonald, born December 31, 1762, baptized March 13, sponsors John and Anna Lion.

Böhm, Francis, of Joseph and Mary Catharine Böhm, born March 19, baptized March 19, sponsors Francis and Anna Barbara Sener.

Schoch, Margaret, of William (P.) and Catharine Schoch, born January 4, baptized March 22, sponsor Margaret Halder, witness Andrew Roth (P.), in New Jersey.

Schad, Anna Mary Elizabeth, of John Peter and Mary Elizabeth (P.) Schad, born February 16, baptized March 27, sponsors George and Anna Mary Metz.

Stoneman, Joanna, of William and Gertrude Stoneman, born May 17, 1753, baptized March 27, sponsor Susanna Kearney.

Stoneman, Sarah, same parents, born June —, 1756, baptized March. 27, sponsors Owen Sullivan and Mary Lauville.

Stoneman, Henry, same parents, born October 6, 1758, baptized March 27, sponsor John Lions.

Stoneman, Salome, same parents, born September —, 1761, baptized March 27, sponsor Mary Lauville.

Pierie, Mary, of John and Mary Pierie, born December 23, 1741, baptized April 2, sponsor Christina Mullabi.

Lederman, John, of John and Mary Catharine Lederman, born March 29, baptized April 3, sponsors John Becker and Christina Elizabeth [Umessin?].

Brehmen, Anthony, of Anthony and Catharine Brehmen, born February 8, baptized April 3.

Green, Anna, of Thomas and Margaret Green, born March 9, baptized April 10, sponsors Edward Murray and Susanna Kearney.

Daniels, Hugh, of John and Margaret Daniels, born February 2, baptized April 10, sponsors Thomas and Elizabeth Griswold.

Frietz, Anna Barbara, of Daniel and Joanna Frietz, born March 9, baptized April 10, sponsors Nicholas and Barbara Hirt.

Welsh, Christopher, of Solomon and Mary Welsh, born April 6, baptized April 10, sponsors John and Magdalen Steling, Mary Mills witness.

Kelly, William, of —— and Anne Kelly, born March 26, baptized April 16, sponsor John Moor, witness Catharine Shephard.

Bisar, Peter, of Sebastian and Rosina Bisar, born April 10, baptized April 17, sponsors William Dorf and Mary Custer.

Maguire, Mary, of Richard and Rosa Maguire, born March 6, baptized April 17, sponsors John Rediger and Mary Hughs.

Hunecker, Mark, of Mark and Anna Hunecker, born April 13, baptized April 18, sponsors Joseph and Catharine Eck.

White, Catharine, adult, baptized April 21.

Mullen, James, of Daniel and Catharine Mullen, born Sept. 7, 1762, baptized April 21, sponsor Mark Huneker.

Schilling, John Philip, of Philip and Eva Schilling, born April 15, baptized April 24, sponsors Michael and Catharine Wolf.

Bosran, John Baptist, of John and Anna Bosran, born April 17, baptized conditionally April 24, sponsors John Baptist Sinere and Anne Vincent.

Essling, Anna Elizabeth, of Paul and Christina Essling, born April 17, baptized April 26, sponsors Frederick and Anna Mary Elizabeth Gräser.

Reding, Thomas, of John and Catharine Reding, born January 6, baptized May 7, sponsor William Welsh, witness Abigail Moor.

Heath, Thomas, of John and Rebecca Heath, born February 26, 1762, baptized May 15, sponsors James Morris and Joanna O'Brian, witness John Lion.

Benner, Anna Mary, of Christian and Magdalen Benner, born March 18, baptized May 18, sponsors Matthew and Anna Mary Miller, in New Jersey.

———, John baptized May 23, sponsor Margaret Redmond.

Jäger, Anna, of Mathew and Mary Jäger, born April 20, baptized May 23, sponsors John Miller and Anna Siat.

Barry, Margaret, of William and Mary Barry, born February 21, baptized May 23; the mother acted as god-mother in default of another.

McKenny, Margaret and Anna, twins, of Hugh and Mary McKenny, Margaret born May 25, Anna born May 26, baptized May 26, sponsors, John Casey and Honora Conely for Margaret, John Kennelly and Mary Kennedy for Anna.

Viel, Catharine, of Christopher and Catharine Viel, born May 30, baptized June 5, sponsors Charles and Catharine Schmid.

———, Anna, of Anthony and Catharine ———, born January —, baptized June 12, sponsors Joseph [Ribari?] and Susanna Robinson.

Wilhelm, Anthony, of Gerard and Elizabeth Wilhelm, born June 11, baptized June 13, sponsor Anthony Ottman, witness Regina —— (P.).

[Gräser?], Elizabeth, of Louis and Mary Grosar [Gräser?], born June 18, baptized June 18, sponsors Firmian and Elizabeth Bodoin.

Klein, Elizabeth, of James and Elizabeth (P.) Klein, born May 11, baptized June 19, sponsor William Schwerber, witness Mary Gertrude Tschuster.

McDonald, John, of Darby and Mary McDonald, born June 17, baptized June 19, sponsors William Fitzharris and Rebecca Evet.

Wilcox, Mary, of James and Prudence Wilcox, born June 11, baptized July 4, sponsors John Gatringer and Catharine Spengler, in Chester [Pa.].

Keanan, Rebbecca, of Bryan and Susanna Keanan, adult, baptized July 11, sponsors Terence Fitzpatrick and Barbara Haug.

Beale, Mary, of George (P.) and Catharine Beale, born May 31, 1761, baptized July 13, sponsor Mary Hefferman.

[Juwel?], Mary, of Philip and Mary [Juwel?], born June —, 1761, baptized August 2, sponsors Daniel Mignati and Mary Bridy.

O'Cain, Mary Magdalen, of Oliver and Margaret O'Cain, born August 6, baptized August 6, sponsors Simon O'Cain and Magdalen Doiron.

Buttler, George, of Edmund and Barbara Buttler, born August 7, baptized August 7, sponsors Timothy Carroll and Margaret Murphy.

Mignati, Joseph, of Daniel and Mary Mignati, born July 21, baptized August 7, sponsor Christina Archbold.

[Caujemi?], James Cajetan, of Peter and Dorothy [Caujemi?], born July 25, Baptized August 7, sponsor James Lion.

Kessler, Frederika Catharine, of Andrew and Catharine Kessler, born

July 25, baptized August 11, sponsor Frederika Catharine Schlausen, witness Valentine Tschalus.

Villar, John, of Anthony and Eva Villar, born June 24, baptized August 21, sponsors Joanna Haug and Elizabeth Stauter.

Siran, Josephine Mary, of Peter and Mary Siran, born August 26, baptized August 26, sponsors Joseph Leblanc and Mary Magdalen Babin.

Metzgar, Catharine, of John and Cecilia Metzgar, born August 23, baptized August 28, sponsors John Hoffner and Catharine Dun [Dunn?].

Haug, John Nicholas, of Anthony and Mary Haug, born August 24, Baptized August 28, sponsors Nicholas and Sophia Viel.

Keanan, Elizabeth, of Henry Keanan and [Latiss?] ———, born August 4, baptized September 6, sponsor Mary Kennedy, witnesses John Macaghan and John Wilson.

———, Mary Magdalen, born September 10, baptized September 10, ceremonies supplied September 11, had been baptized in danger of death by Paul Miller, an intelligent man.

Maglon, Hugh, of Laghlan and Mary Maglon, born September 11, baptized September 15, sponsors Andrew Maglon and Mary Willson.

Bodoin, Catharine, of Firmian and Elizabeth Bodoin, born September 13, baptized September 17, sponsors Stephen and Catharine Schwerber, in the vicinity of Philadelphia.

[Mir?], Anna Mary, of John Baptist and Magdalen [Mir?], born September 18, baptized September 18, sponsors Francis Mouton and Anna Savoy.

Wiester, Nicholas, of Peter and Anna Mary Wiester, born September 14, baptized September 18, sponsors Nicholas Raub and Margaret Halder.

Landry, Peter Matthew, of Peter and Anne Landry, born September 21, baptized September 22, sponsors John Broc and Margaret la Vache.

Imfeld, Anna Caroline, of Sebastian and Mary Clara Imfeld, born September 29, 1759, baptized September 24, sponsor Caroline Hornesser.

Lechler, John George, of George Ernest and Mary Lechler, born September 11, baptized September 25, sponsor Catharine Spengler.

Raulater, John, of Peter and Judith Raulater, born February 1, 1761, baptized September 30; the mother acted as godmother in default of another.

Würth, Charles Joseph, of Joseph and Barbara Würth, born October 2, baptized October 6, sponsors Charles and Catharine Schmid.

Reichart, Joseph, of Joseph and Mary Apollonia Reichart, born October 4, baptized conditionally October 16, sponsors Joseph Kientz and Elizabeth Stauter.

Kramer, Francis, of Henry and Catharine Kramer, born October 16, baptized October 20, sponsors Francis and Barbara Sener.

Connor, Mary, of Michael and Mary Connor, born August 15, 1762, baptized October 21, sponsor Susanna Kearney, in New Jersey.

———, Joseph Simon, of Alexis and Catharine ———, born October 28, baptized October 29, sponsors Susanna Debotan and Mary Babin.

Barry, John, of James and Esther Barry, born September 5, baptized September 29, witness Mary Hughes; the mother acted as god-mother in default of another.

Heling, Mary Magdalen, of John and Mary Magdalen Heling, born Nov. 2, baptized Nov. 3, sponsors Lawrence and Mary Magdalen Schöne.

———, William, of parents unknown, baptized Nov. 4, witnesses Michael and Margaret Schonaltz.

Mayer, Elizabeth, of Joseph (P.) and Gertrude Mayer, born Oct. 31, baptized Nov. 3, sponsors Peter and Elizabeth Hegner.

Schnable, Michael, of Andrew and Eva Schnable, born Oct. 22, baptized Nov. 6, sponsors Michael and Eva Khuen.

Holzhauser, Francis, of Dietrich (P.) and Christina Holzhauser, born Nov. 3, baptized Nov. 6, sponsors Francis and Barbara Sener.

Babin, Joseph, of Simon and Anastatia Babin, born Nov. 6, baptized Nov. 6, sponsors Joseph Babin and Mary Leblanc.

Hirt, John, of Nicholas and Barbara Hirt, born Nov. 9, baptized Nov. 9, sponsors John and Elizabeth Walter.

Jones, Ruth, adult, baptized Dec. 2, sponsor Catharine Lemy.

Thurnbach, Adam and Mary Catharine (twins), of Christian and Susanna Catharine Thurnbach, born Nov. 25, baptized Dec. 6, sponsors Adam and Margaret Geiger for Adam, Philip Wrentzel and Catharine Griesmeyer for Mary Catharine, in New Jersey.

Reardon, John, of Daniel and Credely [Cordelia?] Reardon, born Feb. 28, 1761, baptized Dec. 8, sponsors Peter Magill and Magdalen Dietry, *ibid.*

Reardon, Catharine, same parents, born July 2, baptized Dec. 8, sponsors Peter Dietry and Susanna Butin, *ibid.*, ceremonies supplied.

Leblanc, John Baptist, of Daniel and Margaret Leblanc, born Dec. 9, baptized Dec. 10, sponsors Joseph Leblanc and Mary Babin.

Haug, Paul, of James and Mary Magdalen Haug, born Dec. 6, baptized Dec. 10, sponsors Paul and Christina Essling.

Hirt, Anna Barbara, of George and Barbara Hirt, born Dec. 3, baptized Dec. 11, sponsors Michael and Barbara Hirt.

Murray, Catharine, of William and Eleanor Murray, born Oct. 17, baptized Dec. 11, sponsors Mathias Lemy and Catharine Mackey.

O'Brian, John, of Mathew O'Brian and ——— ———, baptized Dec. 13, conditionally.

[Schmidt?], James, of James and Elizabeth Shmith [Schmidt?], born Oct. 2, baptized Dec. 25, sponsors Patrick O'Neil and Bridget Pointon.

Russ, Rachael, of Eleanor (Nelly) Russ, baptized Dec. 27, privately.

Mullabi, Francis Xavier, of Thomas and Christina Mullabi, born Dec. 10, baptized Dec. 29, sponsor Anna White.

Crowley, William, of William and Mary Crowley, born Dec. 26, baptized Dec. 29, privately.

Whole number of baptisms—one hundred and four.

___

REGISTER OF BAPTISMS FOR 1764.

Essling, Helen, of Peter and Mary Essling, born December 11, 1763, baptized January 1, sponsors John Sauerwald and Helen Villars.

Mignon, John Charles, of Charles and Anastatia Mignon, born December 25, 1763, baptized conditionally January 1, sponsors Francis and Mary Galerm.

Burgeois, Joseph, of Claude and Catharine Burgeois [Bourgeois?], born December 13, 1763, baptized January 8, witnesses John and Magdalen Boutoux.

Wealin, Elizabeth, of Thomas and Mary Wealin [Whelan?], born January 9, baptized January 15, sponsors Gallahan Morarty [Moriarty?] and Catharine Dun.

Becker, Mary Elizabeth, of Bartholomew and Elizabeth Becker, born January 16, baptized January 22, sponsors Leonard and Mary Anna Lascher.

Göck, Anna Mary, of Adam and Mary Göck, born January 28, baptized January 31, sponsors Joseph and Anna Mary Rühl.

Eck, John, of James and Anna Eck, born January 22, baptized February 1, sponsors Marius [Mark?] and Anna Hunecker, in the vicinity of Philadelphia.

Viel, Peter, of Rudolph and Sibylla Viel, born February 13, baptized February 15, sponsors Peter and Catharine Viel.

Stuart, Joseph, of Thomas and Phœbe Stuart, born February 15, baptized February 19, sponsors Jacob Welsh and Rebecca Morris.

Le Blanc, Mary Genevieve, of Marin and Isabella le Blanc, born February 22, baptized conditionally February 26, sponsors Charles le Blanc and Genevieve Vincent.

Harrison, John, of Lancelot and Joanna Harrison, born February 25, baptized February 26, sponsors Henry McAdam and Catharine Swan.

Mayer, Anthony, of John and Elizabeth Mayer, born February 9, baptized March 3, sponsors Anthony Lechler and Margaret de Wetter.

Sexton, Sarah, of John and Catharine Sexton, born February 26, baptized March 7, sponsors Mark and Mary Connor.

Landry, Anna, of Peter and Anna Landry, born March 9, baptized March 9, sponsors Paul Doiron and Mary Josephine Bourg.

O'Hara, Charles, of Brian and Mary O'Hara, born March 9, baptized March 11, sponsors Timothy and Elizabeth Carroll.

Freelan, Barnaby, of James and Joanna Freelan, born March 8, baptized

March 12, sponsors Barnaby Mullholan and Margery McBride, witness William Callaghan.

Hunecker, Elizabeth, of Mark and Anna Hunecker, born March 18,
baptized March 20, sponsors Joseph and Catharine Eck, in vicinity
of Philadelphia.

Sauerwald, Catharine, of Michael and Margaret Sauerwald, born March
19, baptized March 20, sponsors John and Elizabeth Walter.

O'Kain, Mary Magdalen, of Simon and Isabella O'Kain, born March 26,
baptized March 27, sponsors Peter Fore and Mary Landry.

[Stone?], Margaret, of Elizabeth [Stone?], born April 27, 1763, baptized
March 28.

Kheun, Elizabeth, of Michael, Jr., and Eva Kheun, born March 9, baptized March 29, sponsors Andrew and Eva Schnable.

Feinauer, Mary Regina, of Joseph and Anna Mary Feinauer, born March
31, baptized March 31, sponsor Anthony Ottman, witness Regina
———.

Grogan, Anna, of James (P.) and Hannah Grogan, born March 7, baptized April 10, sponsor Judy Bond, witness Terence Doud.

Hueber, Christian, of Michael and Hannah Hueber, born March 9, baptized April 11, sponsors Christian and Magdalen Benner, in New
Jersey.

Goff, James, of Thomas and [Elsie?] Goff, born April 5, baptized April
15, sponsors Joseph Feinauer and Catharine Spengler.

Schmid, Anna Barbara, of Charles and Catharine Schmid, born April 14,
baptized April 15, sponsors Joseph and Barbara Würth.

Hoffman, Francis, of John and Christina Hoffman, born April 7, baptized April 22, sponsors Francis Louis and Mary Ursula Uhla
[Uhler?].

Coghran, Hannah, of William and Mary Coghran, born September 16,
1760, baptized April 15, sponsors James Reynolds and Anna
———zell.

Henrich, John Nicholas, of Nicholas and Sophia Henrich, baptized
April 25, sponsors John Lechler and Anna Mary Weber, near
Philadelphia.

Kauffman, John, of Joseph and Catharine Kauffman, born April 30, baptized May 1, sponsors John Gatringer and Catharine Schalusin.

Landry, Joseph, of Peter and Josephine Landry, born May 3, baptized
May 3, sponsors Peter Landry, Sr., and Margaret Savron.

Hair, Thomas, of Agnes Hair, born April 28, baptized May 3,
privately.

Fury, Martha, of Jacob and Mary Fury, born October 31, 1763, baptized
May 6, sponsors Daniel McMenamin and Sarah [Tin——?],
in Chester County, [Pa.].

Gist, Thomas, of Simon and Mary Gist, born April 13, baptized May 7,
Sponsor John Wilcox, *ibid.*

Corman, Mary, of Cornelius and Hannah Corman, born June 28, 1763, baptized May 7, sponsor John Hanley, *ibid.*

Ryan, John, of Thomas and Catharine Ryan, born April 11, baptized May 13, sponsors James Macra and Bridget Hunt, *ibid.*

Bird, Anna Emily, of Jonathan (P.) and Mary Bird, born April 13, baptized May 16, sponsors Joseph and Euphrosyne Ribau, *ibid.*

Dewitter, Mary Magdalen, of John and Anna Mary Dewitter, born May 18, baptized May 20, sponsors John Sauerwald and Mary Magdalen Wegfort, *ibid.*

[Connelly?],Sabina, of John and Rebecca Cornely [Connelly?], born May 10, baptized May 21, sponsors Martin Pendigast [Prendergast?] and Eva Haug, *ibid.*

Schilling, Mary Catharine, of Philip and Eva Schilling, born May 9, baptized May 23, sponsor Mary Catharine Böhm, *ibid.*

Gerstenberger, Joseph, of Andrew and Magdalen Gerstenberger, born May 24, baptized May 24, sponsors Joseph and Catharine Eck.

Budan, Paul, of Paul and Ursula Budan, born December 26, 1763, baptized June 6, sponsors Peter Oliver Budan and Magdalen Quietry, in New Jersey.

Stump, Regina, of Christopher and Mary Margaret Stump, born December 3, 1763, baptized June 6, sponsors Peter Halter and Regina Mayer, *ibid.*

Zeis, John, of George and Eva Zeis, born May 29, baptized June 10, sponsor John Mayer, witness Anna Margaret Wolf.

Henrich, John, of John and Margaret Catherine Henrich, born June 7, baptized June 24, sponsors George and Anna Mary Mertz.

Sweetman, John, of Richard and Bridget Sweetman, born June 22, baptized June 24, sponsors Bartholomew Kelsey and Anna Dougherty.

Haug, George, of David (P.) and Catharine Haug, born April 10, baptized July 1, sponsors Joseph and Catharine Ehrman, at Goshenhoppen [Berks Co.].

Leibich, Mary Eva, of John Leibich and ——, baptized July 1, sponsors Joseph Lorentz and Mary Bischoff, *ibid.*

Miller, Barbara, of Michael and Elizabeth Miller, born June 18, baptized July 8, sponsors Theobald Miller and Barbara Kuhn, *ibid.*

Russell, John Bernard, of Matthew and Christina (P.) Russell, born May 28, baptized July 8, sponsors Melchior and Catharine Ziegler, *ibid.*

Lebaune, Joseph, of Joseph and Mary Lebaune, born May 27, baptized July 16, sponsors Catharine [Boudro?] for Anastatia le Blanc; had been privately baptized.

Lechner, Peter Christian and Veronica Gertrude (twins), of Mathew and Barbara Lechner, born July 14, baptized July 18, sponsor Mary Gertrude Stauter; had been baptized privately, near Philadelphia; ceremonies supplied.

Schneider, Joseph, of Henry and Barbara Schneider, born July 18, baptized July 22, sponsors Joseph and Anna Mary Feinauer.

Vogel, Magdalen, of Adam (P.) and Magdalen Vogel, born April 2, baptized July 22, sponsors John Sauerwald and [Mary?] Magdalen Wegfort.

Lenox, Catharine, of John and Margaret Lenox, born July 15, baptized July 23, sponsors Joseph and Catharine Eck.

Furlon, Catharine Elizabeth, of Robert and Catharine Furlon, born about November 17, 1763, baptized August 2, sponsor Mary Anna Lescher.

Hoffman, Catharine, of Sebastian and Cunegunda Hoffman, born August 2, baptized August 4, sponsors Caspar Körn and Catharine Haug.

Connor, Elizabeth, of John and Eleanor Connor, born August 27, 1760, baptized August 8, sponsors Patrick and Margery Magill, in New Jersey.

Kelty, James, of Bartholomew and Catharine Kelty, born August 6, baptized August 9, sponsors Patrick and Margery Magill, *ibid.*

Kässer, James, of Peter and Mary Barbara Kässer, born June 25, baptized August 15, sponsors James Kuhn and Mary Elizabeth Hartman, at Goshenhoppen.

[Tscharte?], Mary Dorothy, of Christopher and Mary Dorothy [Tscharte?], born August 22, baptized August 24, sponsor Mary Gertrude Stauter, in vicinity of Philadelphia.

Kellar, Mary Elizabeth, of John and Barbara Kellar, born August 29, baptized September 2, sponsors John and Elizabeth Philips.

McBike, Margaret, of Daniel and Margeret McBike, born August 7, baptized September 2, sponsors Christopher O'Brien and Catharine Shaw.

Cainere [?], Mary Josephine, of Thomas and Susanna Cainere [?], born July 17, 1763, baptized September 2, sponsors Erne Chasse and Mary Josephine Benoit.

Watts, John, of Samuel and Mary Watts, born August 11, baptized September 4, sponsors John and Christine Mallaben.

Forest, Mary Modesta, of Peter and Margaret Forest, born September 4, baptized September 5, sponsors Simon O'Kain and Anna Landry.

Nagel, Nicholas, of George and Anna Mary Nagel, born September 11, baptized September 11, sponsors John Heiser (for Nicholas Swan) and Anna Fichtler.

Hely, John, of John and Catharine Hely, born February 3, baptized September 30, sponsors Andrew and Eleanor Connor.

Mackey, William, of William and Catharine Mackey, born September 23, baptized October 7, sponsor John Camel, witness Mary Camel [Campbell?].

Delitle, Hannah, of Hugh and Catharine Delitle, born March 2, baptized October 7, sponsor Mary Kennedy, witnesses Henry Keanan and James Corman.

Boudrot, ———, of Peter Vincent and Catharine Boudrot, born October

22, baptized October 23, sponsors Francis Cire and Margaret la Vache.

Schreiner, Anna Margaret, of Anselm and Elizabeth Schreiner, born October 21, baptized October 24, witness Francis Wolf, sponsor Anna Margaret, his wife.

Danhauer, Anna Barbara, of James (P.) and Mary Danhauer, born September 7, baptized October 28, sponsors Christian and Anna Barbara Viel.

McKay, Elizabeth, of Brian and Margaret McKay, born October 3, baptized November 11, sponsors Nicholas and Sophia Viel.

Bodan, Theodore, of Anthony and Barbara Bodan, born November 6, baptized November 11, sponsor Theodore Holzhauser, Eva, his wife, witness.

Blanchart, Josephine Miriam, of Oliver Blanchart and Euphrosyne Leblanc, born November 9, baptized conditionally November 14, sponsors Paul Blanchart and Margaret Debotan ; ceremonies supplied.

Herberger, Philip, of John Peter and Anna Mary Herberger, born November 5, baptized November 15, sponsors Philip and Eva Schilling.

Poulton, Ambrose, of Charles Poulton and Ruth [Enoch?], born August 26, 1758, baptized November 6, sponsor Edward Macarty ; baptized while traveling.

Beck, Joseph, of Nicholas and Apollonia Beck, born November 1, baptized November 18, sponsors Joseph Kohl and Alberta Kohl, at Haycock [Bucks Co., Pa.].

Fegan, Hugh, of Patrick and Margaret Fegan, born November 6, 1762, baptized condtionally November 21, sponsor Nicholas Boyl [Boyle?]; had been privately baptized.

Boehm, Joseph, of Joseph and Mary Catharine Boehm, born November 17, baptized November 25, sponsors Joseph and Anna Mary Feinauer.

Miller, Mary Catharine, of Matthew and Anna Mary Miller, born July 11, baptized November 28, sponsors Peter Halder and Mary Catharine Greismyer, at Geiger's, in New Jersey.

Jäger, John, of Matthew and Mary Jäger, born May 7, baptized December 1, sponsors George and Mary Nagel.

Donely, Margaret, of Philip and Catharine Donely [Donnelly?], born October 20, baptized December 2, sponsors John Haug and Margaret de Wetter.

Followe, Margaret, of Michael and Mary Followe, born November 5, baptized December 14, sponsors Richard Allen and Rachael White, by Rev. Robert Harding.

King, Alice, of James (P.) and Margaret King, born November 28, baptized December 2, sponsors Henry McAdam and Mary Dohe.

Hertz, John, of John and Barbara Hertz, born December 5, baptized December 6, sponsors Michael and Margaret Sauerwald.

Barry, Margaret and Eleanor (twins), of William and Mary Barry, born November 15, baptized December 22, sponsors, for Margaret Christopher O'Brien, for Eleanor Mary Carey.

Mullen, Elizabeth, of Thomas and Anna Mullen, born November 3, baptized December 22; had been baptized privately.

Charso, Anna Mary, of Joseph and Christina [Charso or Chasso?], born December 25, baptized December 25, sponsors Joseph and Anna Mary Feinauer.

Whole number of baptisms—ninety-two.

REGISTER OF BAPTISMS FOR 1765.

——, Anna and Sarah (sisters), baptized January 3, sponsor Magdalen Mallaben·

Conel, Elizabeth, of John and Honora Conel [Connell?], born January 4, baptized January 10, witness Roger Heferman, sponsor Dorothy Connor.

[Savage?], Catharine Elizabeth, of Stephen and Anna Mary Sorage [Savage?], born January 3, baptized January 13, sponsors Bartholomew and Elizabeth Becker.

Macra, John, of James and Bridget Macra, baptized January 13; had been baptized privately.

Mackay, Mary, of Patrick and Mary Mackay, born January 12, baptized January 17, sponsors Michael Kelley and Salome Wilhelm.

Boyd, Robert, of Patrick and Anna Boyd, born January 7, baptized February 4, sponsors Patrick Conley and Catharine Spengler.

[Gaghard?], John Caspar, of John and Mary [Gaghard?], born January 25, baptized February 8, sponsors Caspar [Colombo?] and Eleanor Redgecock.

Hirt, Annie Barbara, of Nicholas and Barbara Hirt, born January 28, baptized February 10, sponsors George and Barbara Hirt.

Haug, Mary, of George and Margaret Haug, born February 3, baptized February 10, sponsors Anthony and Mary Haug.

Mayer, Mary Eva, of John and Elizabeth Mayer, born February 8, baptized February 11, sponsors Christopher Grebert and Anna Eva Lechler.

Kneul, Anna Catharine, of Balthasar and Christina Elizabeth Kneul, born February 11, baptized February 15, sponsors George Kneul and Catharine Frankenfield.

Haug, Margaret, of Anthony and Mary Haug, born February 14, baptized February 19, sponsor George Haug, witness Margaret Haug.

Rühl, Susanna, of Joseph and Anna Mary Rühl, born February 25, baptized February 28, sponsors Rudolph and Susanna Sibylla Viel, in vicinity of Philadelphia.

Vale, John James, of John and Anna Mary Vale, born February 15, baptized March 3, sponsors James and Elizabeth Weisenburger, at Pikesland [Chester Co., Pa.].

Gräser, Joseph, of Frederic and Elizabeth Gräser, born March 3, baptized March 5, sponsors Paul and Anna Christina Essling.

Stahler, Cathararine Elizabeth, of John and Christina Stahler, born February 24, baptized March 10, sponsors Bartholomew and Catharine Elizabeth Becker.

McKillam, John, of Archibald and Margaret McKillam, born May 6, 1764, baptized March 26, sponsor Dennis Lafferty, witness Hannibal McKensey.

Viel, John, of Christian and Barbara Viel, born March 23, baptized April 1, sponsors, John and Eva Hasner.

Schreiner, James, of Henry and Sarah Schreiner, born January 1, baptized April 7, sponsor James Trein, witness Mary Margaret Trein.

——, Mary Magdalen, of Christopher and Mary Magdalen ——, born February 19, baptized April 7, sponsors David Gogg and Mary Magdalen Mayer.

Walliser, John, of Michael and Anna Mary Walliser, born December 4, 1764, baptized April 9, sponsors John Schutz and Anna Mary Walliser.

Archdeacon, Mary, of Patrick and Joanna Archdeacon, born April 10, baptized April 12, sponsors William Nunan and Mary Theresa David.

Babin, Mary Margaret, of Peter Vincent and Mary Magdalen Babin, born April 15, baptized conditionally April 16, sponsors Charles le Blanc and Mary Josephine Babin ; had been baptized privately, ceremonies supplied.

Feinauer, Joseph, of Joseph and Anna Mary Feinauer, born April 15, baptized April 18, sponsors George Joseph and Mary Catharine Böhm.

Fagan, Mary, of Patrick and Margaret Fagan, born April 12, baptized April 19, sponsor John Poulton, in Berks Co. [Pa.].

David, Mary Theresa, of Anthony and Mary Theresa David, born February 28, baptized March 3, sponsors Jacob Burns and Catharine Gatringer, by Rev. Robert Harding.

Miller, Mary Barbara, of Philip and Elizabeth Miller, born December 6, 1764, baptized April 21, sponsor Mary Ruplin, at Haycock [Bucks Co., Pa.].

Horn, Catherine, of John George (P.) and Margaret Horn, born November 1, 1764, baptized April 21, sponsors Jacob Rus [Russ?] and Catharine Gressir [Gräser?], *ibid.*

Heitzman, Mary Magdalen, of John George (P.) and Agatha Heitzman, born September 29, 1764, baptized April 21, sponsors Jacob Glass and Elizabeth Miller, *ibid.*

Merrick, Anna Dorothy, of Henry and Catharine Merrick, born December 8, 1764, baptized April 21, sponsor Anna Dorothy Weinburn, *ibid.*

Wean, Elizabeth, of Isaac and Rosina Wean, born February 21, baptized April 22, sponsors Hugh and Cecilia McNagh, while traveling, in New Jersey.

Kean, Jubal, of John and Mary Kean, born January 9, 1763, baptized April 23, sponsor Philip McDead, *ibid.*

Durst-Reider, Anna Mary, of Francis Joseph and Anna Mary Durst-Reider, born October 29, 1764, baptized April 26, sponsors John Mayer and Mary Juliana Abtin ; had been privately baptized, at Ringwood [Passaic county, N. J.].

Sullivan, Daniel, of Dennis and Catharine Sullivan, born May 5, 1762, baptized April 28, sponsors John Brown and Catharine Fichterin, *ibid.*

Sullivan, George, of the same parents, born December 23, 1763, baptized April 28, sponsors George Sly and Mary Brown, *ibid.*

McAllister, Daniel, of John and Mary McAllister, born September 6, 1762, baptized May 1, sponsors Isaac and Rosina Wean, while returning.

McAllister, Anna, of the same parents, born July 5, ——, bapt. May 1, sponsor Francis Honey, witness Margaret (his wife), while returning.

McGill, Patrick, of James and Joanna McGill, born February 9, baptized May 8, sponsors Stephen Magill and Catharine Kelty, at Adam Geiger's, New Jersey.

Kolb, Simon, of Andrew (P.) and Catharine Kolb, born February 19, baptized May 8, sponsors Adam and Margaret Geiger, *ibid.*

Ruh, Peter, of Melchior and Peter Ruh [Ruhl ?], born April 18, baptized May 8, sponsors Peter Halder and Christina Geiger, *ibid.*

Lin, Sarah, of Hugh and Anna Lin [?], born September 19, 1764, baptized May 10, sponsors Peter Goff and Mary Quinn.

O'Neil, Elizabeth, of Terence and Eleanor O'Neil, born January —, baptized May 11, sponsor Edward Hanlin.

Scantlin, Cornelius, of Cornelius and Mary Scantlin, born April 28, baptized May 11, sponsors Dennis Hood and Winifred Cooper ; had been baptized privately, ceremonies supplied.

O'Hara, Arthur, of Henry and Bridget O'Hara, born April 26, baptized May 13, sponsors Timothy Maginnis and Margaret Roge.

Makra, James, of James and Bridget Makra, born January 11, baptized May 19, sponsors John Hargin and Joanna Pornor.

Viel, Catharine, of Nicholas and Sophia Viel, born May 16, baptized May 19, sponsors Charles and Catharine Schmid.

Naval, Margaret, of John and Nancy Naval, born April 22, 1761, baptized May 25, sponsors Neal Shaw and Judith Bond.

Essling, James, of Peter and Mary Essling, born April 26, baptized May 26, sponsors Peter Rice and Mary Magdalen Essling, Jr.

Schumacher, John, of Christian and Anna Mary Schumacher, born May 3, baptized July 9, sponsors John Kheun and Magdalen Cupser, at Goshenhoppen.

Keintz, Margaret, of Mathew and Margaret Keintz, born May 8, baptized July 16, sponsors James and Eva Hönig [König?], at Haycock.

Wilhelm, Catharine Elizabeth, of Gerhard and Elizabeth Wilhelm, born May 16, baptized July 23, sponsors Bartholomew and Catharine · Elizabeth Becker.

Schmid, John, of William James (P.) and Catharine Schmid, born May 5, baptized July 23, sponsors Christian and Elizabeth Schültz.

Eyenson, Louis, of John and Elizabeth Eyenson, born May 1, baptized July 26, sponsors Thomas Eyenson and Esther Eyenson, at Adam Geiger's, New Jersey.

Kelty, Anna, of Walter Kelty and Judith Cotter, born June 8, baptized July 8, sponsor Mary Connor.

Will, Sarah, of Phillip and Elizabeth Will, born November —, 1764, baptized July 8, sponsors Anthony and Sarah Aman; the sponsor, Anthony Aman, had given it private baptism, ceremonies supplied.

Hoeffner, John Joseph, of John and Eva Hoeffner, born July 10, baptized July 12, sponsors Valentine Korn and Eva Lechler.

Connor, John, of Andrew and Eleanor Connor, born July 1, baptized July 14, sponsors John Connolly and Catharine Brian.

Borson, Peter, of Joseph and Anna Borson, born July 18, baptized July 18, sponsors Oliver Debotan, Jr., and Anna Bourg.

Leblanc, John, of Henry and Mary Leblanc, born July 27, baptized July 30, sponsor Mary Frances [Esconveman?], Jacob Gilotan witness.

Rieger, Godfrey, of Simon and Anna Margaret Rieger, born July 28, baptized August 1, sponsor Anna Cassin, witness Godfrey Schisler.

Wealin, Catharine, of Thomas and Margaret Wealin [Whelan?], born August 1, baptized August 3, sponsor David Clancy, Barbara Burkhart witness.

Hauck, Elizabeth, of James and Mary Magdalen Hauck, born July 28, baptized August 4, sponsors Frederic and Elizabeth Gräser.

Lascher, Eva, of Leonard and Mary Anne Lascher, born August 8, baptized August 11, sponsors Anselm and Elizabeth Schreiner.

Mignati, Francis, of Daniel and Mary Mignati, born May 27, baptized August 11, sponsor Francis Wollin, Margaret Steward witness.

Klein, Theresa, of James and Elizabeth Klein, born August 7, baptized August 15, sponsors Anthony and Barbara Graff.

———, Elizabeth, about two years old, baptized August 16; had been baptized privately.

Waltrich, Andrew, of Francis and Catharine Waltrich, born August 14, baptized August 18, sponsors Andrew and Charlotte Schwartzman.

Sexton, John James, of John and Catharine Sexton, born August 19, baptized August 25, sponsors James Forage and Barbara Kneulin.

Renigar, Anne Margaret, of Anthony and Eva Renigar [Reniger?], born August 7, baptized conditionally August 30, sponsor Anna Angela Schwartzman.

[Cancenny?], Dorothy Margaret, of Peter and Dorothy [Cancenny?], born August 30, baptized September 1, sponsor James Lyons, Dorothy Lyons witness.

McFadden, John, of John and Margaret McFadden, born July 24, baptized September 8, sponsor Henry McAdam.

Benner, Agnes, of Christina and Magdalen Benner, born May 20, baptized September 11, sponsors Agnes Roth and Adam Geiger, at Adam Geiger's, N. J.

Essling, Catharine, of Paul and Christina Essling, born September 12, baptized September 20, sponsors Frederic and Elizabeth Gräser.

Ledermann, Andrew, of John and Mary Catharine Ledermann, born September 19, baptized September 22, sponsors Andrew and Eva Schnable.

Sailer, Mary Salome, of Sebastian and Elizabeth Sailer, born September 22, baptized September 24, sponsor Mary Salome Schwartz.

Becker, John Michael, of Bartholomew and Elizabeth Becker, born September 29, baptized October 6, sponsors Michael and Catharine Wolff.

Blanchart, Paul, of Paul and Cecilia Blanchart, born October 7, baptized October 7, sponsors Oliver Blanchart and Magdalen Dibotan.

Ryan, Prudence, of —— Ryan and Elizabeth O'Donagh, born August —, baptized August 10, sponsors John Carr and Joanna Dedy.

Christi, Martin, of Martin and Hannah Christi [Christy?], born October 11, baptized October 13, sponsors Dennis Dogherty and Barbara Buttler.

Zeis, Elizabeth, of George and Eva Zeis, born October 8, baptized October 13, Michael Schreiner witness, sponsor Eva Schreiner.

Dogherty, George, of Dennis and Margaret Dogherty, born October 13, baptized October 13, sponsors James Byrne and Barbara Buttler.

Kinslow, Catharine, of John and Elizabeth Kinslow, born October 6, baptized October 17, sponsors William Kelly and Winifred Cooper.

Schultz, Anna Elizabeth, of John and Eva Schultz, born October 1, baptized October 20, sponsors John Schultz, Sr., and Anna Schultz for Elizabeth Schultz.

Schöneck, Charles Joseph, of Lawrence and Magdalen Schöneck, born October 14, baptized October 20, sponsors Charles and Catharine Schmid.

Jackson, Catharine, of William and Margaret Jackson, born September 20, baptized October 27, sponsor Magdalen Gerstenberger.

[Matson?], Mary, adult, baptized October 27, sponsor Catharine White.

Schwartzman, Anthony, of Andrew and Charlotte Schwartzman, born October 27, baptized October 28, sponsors Anthony and Barbara Graff.

Greanaus, Catharine, of Cornelius and Elizabeth [Greanaus?], born November 4, baptized November 4.

Ryan, Mary, of Thomas and Catharine Ryan, born September 7, baptized November 4, sponsors Martin Christi [Christy?] and Joanna Dedy ; had been baptized privately.

Philips, Elizabeth, of John and Elizabeth Philips, born October 24, baptized November 3, sponsors Gerard and Elizabeth Wilhelm.

Seilers, Hannah, of Joseph and Mary Seilers, born May 2, 1764, baptized November 4.

Crämer, Anna Mary Julia, of Mathias and Mary Catharine Crämer, born August 10, baptized November 9, sponsors John Mayer and Mary Juliana Abtin, at Ringwood [Passaic Co., N. J.].

Sullivan, Mary Juliana, of Dennis and Catharine Sullivan, born August 13, baptized November 10, sponsors Redmund Welsh and Mary Juliana Abtin, *ibid*.

Hogan, Mary, of John and Rosina Hogan, born February 26, 1764, baptized November 12, sponsors John Wider and Juliana Abtin, *ibid*.

Feniger, Mary Gertrude, of John and Elizabeth Feniger, born August 23, baptized November 14, sponsor Gertrude Abtin.

Caroll, Edward, of Timothy and Elizabeth Caroll, born November 6, baptized November 17, sponsors Jerome (Darby) Savage and Ailie Clark.

Rudolph, John George, of Tobias and Margaret Rudolph, born November 13, baptized November 18, sponsors George Ernest and Mary Magdalen Lechler.

——, Festus, baptized November 20, sponsor Mary Clary, a mulatto servant of James Byrne.

Magill, James, of John and Catharine Magill, born January 21, baptized November 27, sponsor James Magill, witness his wife, Joanna, at Adam Geiger's, in N. J.

Roth, Catharine, of Andrew (P.) and Agnes Roth, born September 15, baptized November 27, sponsors Peter Halder and Catherine Griesmeyer, *ibid*.

Thurnbach, Mary Anna, of Christian and Susanna Catharine Thurnbach, born October 10, baptized November 27, sponsors Simon Geiger and Regina Meyer, *ibid*.

Sullivan, Mary, of Owen and Mary Sullivan, 10 years of age, baptized November —, sponsors Thomas Green and Anna Broc, by Father Jacob Pellentz.

Bullock, George, of Timothy and Catharine Bullock, 12 years old, baptized November —, sponsor Arthur John O'Neil, by the same.

Bullock, Timothy, Anna, and Joanna, of same parents, born respectively about August —, 1755, July —, 1758, and —— —, 1760, baptized December 2, sponsor for all three, Arthur John O'Neil, in Chester Co. [Pa.].

Gorman, Eleanor, of Cornelius and Hannah Gorman, born September 8, 1764, baptized December 2, sponsor Joanna Hanlon, *ibid.*

Hely, William, of Daniel and Mary Hely, born December 5, baptized December 5, sponsors Oliver Hunt and Anna Cusic.

Stuart, Richard, of Thomas and Phœbe Stuart, born December 7, baptized December 7, sponsors Louis Luke and Margaret ———; baptized privately on 7th, and ceremonies supplied on the 8th.

Schmatzga, John Michael, of James and Eva Mary [Schmatzga?], born October 24, baptized December 8, sponsor John Michael Wolf.

Späth, John Matthew, of John and Anna Margaret Späth, born December 3, baptized December 8, sponsors John Mathew Göck and Eva Lechler.

Schneider, James, of Burchard and Catharine Schneider, born September 11, baptized December 15, sponsors Jacob and Frances Walter, near Yellow Spring [Chester Co., Pa.?].

Whole number of baptisms—one hundred and thirteen.

REGISTER OF BAPTISMS FOR 1766.

Kramer, Christian, of Henry and Catharine Kramer, born January 2, baptized January 2, sponsors Christian Bub and Catharine Arnold.

———, Susanna, of unknown parents, born December 28, 1764, baptized January 8, sponsor John Baptist Theole, witness Susanna Oge (?).

Meyer, Peter, of I—— (P.) and Gertrude Meyer, born January 8, baptized January 13, sponsors Peter and Elizabeth Hegner.

Mahoni, Mark, of Anthony and Hannah Mahoni [Mahony?], born January 10, baptized January 14, sponsor Catharine Talley.

Landry, Mary Modesta, of Peter and Josephine Landry, born January 19, baptized January 20, sponsors Peter Savoy and Mary Martin.

Connel, Robert, of John and Honora Connel, born January 20, baptized January 20, sponsors John Keasy and Dorothy Connor.

Sparrow, Mary Ann, of Samuel and Grace Sparrow, born January 22, baptized January 26, sponsors John Donely and Anna McDonald, witness ——— Dougherty.

Dunbar, James, of ——— ——— and Catharine Dunbar, born January 23, baptized January 27, sponsors Adam Mayer and Winifred Cooper.

Gorman, Bridget, of Cornelius and Hannah Gorman, born January 17, baptized January 28, in Chester Co [Pa.].

Burton, John, of John and Esther Burton, 9 years old, baptized February 8, in New Castle [Delaware].

Leaman, James, of Thomas and Esther Leaman, 1 year old, baptized February 8, by Rev. Robert Harding, *ibid.*; ceremonies supplied.

Bullock, Thomas, of Timothy and Catharine Bullock, 14 years old, baptized February 10, sponsor Arthur John O'Neal, in Chester Co. [Pa.].

Karns, Elizabeth, of Hugh and Anna Karns, 8 years old, baptized February 10, sponsors Arthur John O'Neal and Bridget Leary, *ibid.*

Karns, Benjamin, of same parents, 6 years old, baptized February 10, sponsors Arthur John O'Neal and Bridget Leary, *ibid.*

Karns, John, of same parents, 3 years old, baptized February 10, sponsors Arthur John O'Neal and Bridget Leary, *ibid.*

Karns, Margaret, of same parents, born March 26, 1764, baptized February 10, sponsors Arthur John O'Neal and Bridget Leary, *ibid.*

Tscharte, John, of Christopher and Mary Dorothy Tscharte, born February 12, baptized February 16, sponsor John Schneider, witness Elizabeth (his wife).

Le Prince, Joseph, of John and Mary le Prince, born February 17, baptized February 17, sponsor Joseph Davoit, ceremonies supplied.

Viel, Christopher, of Rudolph and Susanna Viel, born February 13, baptized February 18, sponsors Christopher and Catharine Viel, in vicinity of Philadelphia.

Rearton, Dennis, of Cornelius and Susanna Rearton, 6 years old, baptized February 23.

Bodouin, James, of Firmian and Elizabeth Bodouin, born February 21, baptized February 23, sponsor Jacob Lion, Dorothy (his wife) witness.

Burgois, Margaret Rosa, of Claude and Catharine Burgois [Bourgeois?], born February 9, baptized February 23, sponsors Joseph and Margaret Ribau.

Schneider, Ottilia, of Henry and Barbara Schneider, born February 19, baptized February 26, sponsors William Dorg and Ottilia Viet, in vicinity of Philadelphia.

———, William, born January —, baptized March 4, sponsors Jacob Eck and wife, in the house of Jacob Eck.

Nagel, Anna, of George and Mary Nagel, born March 2, baptized March 6, sponsor Mary Walburga Bremick for Anna Fichtler.

Ridiger, Mathew Anthony, of John, Jr., and Margaret Ridiger, born March 2, baptized March 9, sponsors John Ridiger, Sr., and Anna Mary ———.

Welsh, William, of James and Rosa Welsh, born March 9, baptized March 9, sponsors Joseph Cassin and Margaret Harkins.

Scheimer, Bartholomew, of Frederic and Mary Magdalen Scheimer, born November 23, 1765, baptized March 16, sponsors Francis and Apollonia Sohl, in Pikesland [Chester Co., Pa.].

———, Margaret, of Joanna ———, born March 13, baptized March 24, sponsor Mary Clary, servant of James Burns.

Weade, Mary, of Michael Weade [Meade?] and Elizabeth Nugent, born

January 14, baptized March 25, sponsors William Fitzharris and Catharine Shaw.

——, Mary, of Hannah ——, born March 24, baptized March 25, sponsor Catharine Nunan, servant of James White.

Eustace, Mary Josephine, of Daniel Eustace and Margaret Doiron, born April 3, baptized April 4, sponsors Joseph Ribau and Genevieve Boudrot.

Weider, Anna Mary, of Joseph and Margaret Weider, born March 17, baptized March 19, sponsors John Nicholas Jungfleisch and Anna Mary Reider, at Ringwood [N. J.].

Weibl, Conrad, of Charles and Susanna Weibl, born March 14, baptized March 19, sponsors Conrad Welsh and Catharine Demuth; had been baptized privately, ceremonies supplied, *ibid*.

Mentzenbach, John Anthony, of Nicholas and Helen Mentzenbach, born April 5, baptized April 19, sponsors Anthony Schumers and Clara Legohn, *ibid*.

Potter, Susanna, of Joseph and Margaret Potter, born January 17, 1762, baptized April 20, sponsors Michael Forrester and Catharine Sullivan, *ibid*.

Fechter, John, of Philip and Mary Eva Fechter, born November 18, 1762, baptized April 20, sponsors John Mayer, Jr., and Mary Catharine Cramer, *ibid*.

Call, Mary Elizabeth, of John Nicholas and Anna Margaret Call, born October 20, 1764, baptized conditionally April 21, sponsors James Demuth and Mary Elizabeth Hoffman, *ibid*.

Farrell, Mary, of Richard and Charlotte Farrell, Born December 1, 1764, baptized April 22, sponsors James Curran and Catharine Sullivan, *ibid*.

Borm, John Peter, of John and Anna Mary Borm, born July 29, 1764, baptized conditionally April 22, sponsors John Peter Heilsamer and Elizabeth Schmid, *ibid*.

Hoffman, George Louis, of Paul and Anna Magdalen (P.) Hoffman, born April 6, baptized April 24, sponsor Gertrude Abtin, witnesses Louis Fischer and George Hupacher, at Bascon Ridge [Somerset Co., N. J.].

Reichman, Mary Theresa, of —— Reichman and —— ——, born April 24, baptized April 30, sponsors ·—— and —— Reichman, near Philadelphia.

Lamy, Stephen, of James Lamy and Hannah Ludek, born December 26, 1765, baptized May 7, sponsors Matthew Lamy and Sarah Tim, in Chester Co. [Pa.].

Walter, John, of James and Frances Walter, born February 5, baptized May 8, sponsor John Schieler, in Pikesland [Chester Co., Pa.].

Walter, Francis, of same parents, born February 4, baptized May 8, sponsors Francis and Apollonia Sohl, *ibid*.

Roth, Anna, of Christian and Elizabeth Roth, born February 4, baptized May 8, sponsor Peter Einold, *ibid*.

Farrell, Isidore, of Patrick and Alice Farrell, born April 27, baptized May 3, sponsors James Byrne and Mary Murphy, by Rev. Robert Harding.

Eimold, James, of Peter and Mary Ann Eimold, born March 2, baptized May 8, sponsor Christian Weisenberger, in Pikesland.

O'Neil, Andrew, of Arthur and Mary O'Neil, born March 12, baptized conditionally May 9, sponsors Thomas Ryan and Catharine Ryan.

Gleman, Mary Catharine, of John Dewald and Mary Eva (P.) Gleman, born April 19, baptized May 14, sponsors William and Mary Catharine Schoch, William being witness, at Geiger's.

Archdeacon, Catharine, of Morris and Bridget Archdeacon, baptized May 25, sponsor Adam Mayer.

Schreiner, Mary Agatha, of Anselm and Elizabeth Schreiner, born March 10, baptized April 25, sponsors James Otts and Mary Agatha Hart.

Rischart, Elizabeth, of Lothaire and Elizabeth Rischart, born March 10, baptized May 28, sponsor Walburger Brennich.

McCaffrey, Luke, of Edward and Sarah McCaffrey, baptized May 31, sponsors Luke and Mary Dun, witness James Smith.

Savage, John, of Darby and Anna Savage, born May 30, baptized June 1, sponsors Brian O'Harra and Elizabeth Carroll.

Mayer, Mary Magdalen, of John and Elizabeth Mayer, born May 3, baptized June 8, sponsors Anthony Lechler and Mary Agatha Hart, by Rev. Robert Harding.

Haug, Christian, of George and Margaret Haug, born May 30, baptized June 8, sponsor Anthony Haug, witness Margaret Miller.

Heits, Laurence, of John and Barbara Heits, born June 17, baptized June 22, sponsors Laurence Göck and Catharine Haug.

Shortel, Mary, of Richard and Margaret Shortel, born June 17, baptized June 22, sponsors Jude Thaddeus Salasar and Margaret Mallabi.

Brian, Catharine, of —— Brian and —— ——, born February —, baptized conditionally June 24.

Kelty, Mary, of Bartholomew and Catharine Kelty, born June 19, baptized June 29, sponsors Stephen Magel [McGill?] and Joanna Johns, in New Jersey.

Miller, Matthew, of Matthew and Anna Mary Miller, born May 21, baptized June 29, sponsors Christian and Magdalen Benner, *ibid*.

Bucher, Henry, of John and Catharine Bucher, born June 8, baptized June 29, sponsors Henry and Barbara Geiger, *ibid*.

Foulon, Margaret, of Michael and Mary Foulon [Fowler?], born August 3, baptized by Rev. Robert Harding, sponsors Richard Allen and Rachael White, *ibid*.

Kean, Anna, of Miles and Catharine Kean, born April 1, 1765, baptized conditionally July 10.

Glancy, Mary, of Dennis and Susanna Glancy, born July 7, baptized July 13, sponsors Philip Campbell and Susanna Glancy.

Koch, Peter, of John and Anna Mary Koch, born June 22, baptized July 13, sponsors Peter and Anna Maria Wiester.

McDearmot, Bridget, of Dennis and Mary McDearmot, born July 9, baptized July 13, sponsors William Nunan and Mary Theresa David.

O'Davelin, James, of Roger and Susanna O'Davelin, born April 4, 1765, baptized July 20, sponsors Thomas Riley and Sarah Tim, in Pikesland [Chester Co., Pa.].

Schue, John, of John Bartholomew (P.) and Mary Crescentia Schue, born July 12, baptized July 22, sponsors John Kramer and Mary Magdalen Mayer.

Goff, Andrew James, of Thomas and Mary Goff, born July 3, baptized July 22, sponsors William Connor and Mary Macarty.

Delaney, Mary, of Michael and Honora Delaney, born May 4, 1765, baptized August 6, sponsors John Carrel and Margaret Green.

Hely, William, of John and Catharine Hely, born July 17, baptized August 10, sponsors William and Honora Murray.

Hoffman, Simon, of John and Christina Hoffman, born August 1, baptized August 10, sponsors Simon and Magdalen Haug.

Trelan, John, of James and Joanna Trelan, born October 17, 1765, baptized August 13, sponsors Philip and Anna Ryan.

Geiger, Anna Mary, of Henry and Barbara Geiger, born July 8, baptized July 27, sponsors Adam and Margaret Geiger, at Adam Geiger's.

Huber, Peter and Catharine (twins), of Michael and Hannah Huber, born July 25, baptized July 27, sponsors Peter Halder and Mary Catharine Griesmeyer for Peter, Laurence Caspar and Catharine Schoch for Catharine, *ibid.*

Navel, John, of John and Anna Navel, 11 years old, baptized August 31, sponsors Solomon Welsh and Mary Lewis, at Salem [N. J.].

Dugan, John, of Jacob and Sarah Dugan, born August 17, baptized August 31, sponsors Philip Lynch and Elizabeth Sohl, at Pikesland [Chester Co., Pa.].

White, Mary Magdalen, of Dennis and Catharine White, born August 13, baptized August 31, sponsors Cormick [Macatea?] and Mary Miller, *ibid.*

Allen, Mary, wife of Richard Allen, baptized September 8, at Concord [Del. Co., Pa.].

Veil, Mary Susanna, of Christopher and Catharine Veil, born September 8, baptized September 9, sponsors Charlotte Engelbrand and Sibylla Rudolph.

Graff, Aloysius, of Anton and Barbara Graff, born September 14, baptized September 15, sponsors Paul Miller and Catharine Spengler.

Johnston, Joseph, of Hugh and Eustatia Johnston, born November 22, 1765, baptized conditionally September 17.

Brady, Mary, of John and Dorothy Brady, born August 10, baptized August 20, sponsors Anthony and Mary Haug.

Bodart, William, of Anton and Barbara Bodart, born September 20, baptized September 21, sponsors William Dorff and Anna Siere.

Leblanc, Mary Magdalen, of Daniel and Margaret Leblanc, born October 8, baptized October 8, sponsors Anthony Landry and Barbara Leblanc.

Haugh, John Frederick, of Simon and Mary Magdalen Haugh, born ' October 10, baptized October 12, sponsors John Frederick and Elizabeth Gräser.

Williams, Moses, of Francis and Eleanor (P.) Williams, born July 12, 1765, baptized October 14; the mother was sponsor in default of another.

Collins, Elizabeth, of Thomas and Sabina Collins, born October 2, baptized October 19, sponsors Patrick Dealy and Mary Gatringer.

Birt, Marianne, of Jonathan (P.) and Mary Birt, born October 17, baptized October 23, sponsors Charles O'Harra and Anna Broc.

Fitzgerald, Joseph, of James and Mary Fitzgerald, born October 30, baptized October 26, sponsors George Coffey and Mary Lamb.

Becker, John Michael, of Bartholomew and Elizabeth Becker, born October 18, baptized October 26, sponsors Michael and Catharine Wolf.

Kelly, John, of Luke and Margaret Kelly, born February 8, 1759, baptized November 2, sponsors Martin Lawless and Eleanor Ulaghan [Hoolihan?], at Ringwood [Passaic Co., N. J.].

Kelly, Luke, of same parents, born December 27, 1760, baptized November 2, sponsors Martin Lawless and Eleanor Ulaghan [Hoolihan?], *ibid.*

Kelly, Frances, of same parents, born February 12, 1763, baptized November 2, sponsors Martin Lawless and Eleanor Ulaghan [Hoolihan?], *ibid.*

Kelly, Mary, of same parents, born December 4, 1765, baptized November 2, sponsors Martin Lawless and Eleanor Ulaghan [Hoolihan?], *ibid.*

Strach, John Anthony, of John William and Anna Elizabeth Strach, born May 21, baptized November 2, sponsors John Mayer and Mary Eva Fichter, *ibid.*

Deal, Elizabeth, of John and Mary Deal, baptized November 3, sponsors Laghlin Burns and Margaret McCollom, *ibid.*

Etinger, Charles Frederic, of —— and Mary Etinger, born October 19, baptized November 4, sponsors Charles and Catharine Schmid, *ibid.*

Burk, John, of Adam and Mary Burk, born November 5, baptized conditionally November 11, *ibid.*

——, Sebastian, born November 13, baptized November 15, sponsors Sebastian and Elizabeth Seibert, *ibid.*

Tims, Sarah, of Henry and Anna Tims, born September 11, baptized November 30, sponsors John King and Sarah Tims, at Pikesland [Pa.].

Hely, Thomas, of Thomas and Margaret Hely, born November 24, baptized December 4, sponsors Dennis Dun [Dunn?] and Anna Savage.

Haug, Joseph, of Anton and Mary Haug, born November 29, baptized December 7, sponsors Joseph and Anna Mary Feinauer.

Finey, William, of John and Mary Ottilia Finey, born October 19, baptized December 7, sponsor Anna Mary Hirsch.

Lorentz, Mary Catharine, of Caspar and Margaret Lorentz, born August 23, baptized December 11, sponsors Simon Geiger and Catharine Halder, at Adam Geiger's.

[Ruhl?], Michael, of Melchior and Barbara Ruh [Ruhl?], born October 25, baptized December 11, sponsors Michael Huber and Margaret Lorentz, *ibid.*

Magill, Margaret, of James and Joanna Magill, born November 3, baptized December 11, sponsors Stephen Magill and Christiana Mullabe [Malleben?], *ibid.*

Watts, Samuel, of Samuel and Mary Watts, born December 13, baptized December 14, sponsors Hugh Quigley and Christiana Mullabe.

Christ, John, of Michael and Elizabeth Christ, born August 31, baptized December 23, sponsors John and Catharine Schreiber.

Davis, Margaret, of Thomas and Isabella (P.) Davis, born November — baptized December 23, sponsors Solomon Welsh and Margaret Roage.

Whole number of baptisms—one hundred and thirteen.

REGISTER OF BAPTISMS FOR 1767.

Sauerwald, Mary Magdalen, of John and Magdalen Sauerwald, born January 4, baptized January 11, sponsors Lawrence and Mary Magdalen Schöne.

Kientz, Sophia, of Joseph and Catharine Kientz, born January 19, baptized February 1, sponsors Nicholas and Sophia Veil.

Herberger, Tobias, of Peter and Anna Mary Herberger, born January 29, baptized February 2, sponsors Tobias and Anna Margaret (P.) Rudolph.

Maglochlin, Joanna, of William and Mary Maglochlin, born December 20, 1766, baptized February 2, sponsors Margaret Lucas and Francis Hughs [Hughes?].

Arnold, James, of Henry and Agnes Arnold, born January 28, baptized February 2 ; the priest was godfather.

————, Mary of unknown parents, baptized privately February 3, in house of John Broc.

Reinhold, Rebecca, of James and Mary Reinhold, born January 12, baptized February 3, sponsors Timothy and Elizabeth Carroll.

Wilhelm, John, of Gerhard and Elizabeth Wilhelm, born February 2, baptized February 8, sponsors John Wilhelm and Catharine Gerstenberger.

Dillon, Rudolph, of —— and Judy Dillon, born October 26, 1766, baptized conditionally February 11.

Holtzhauser, Mark, of Theodore and Christiana (P.) Holtzhauser, born February 11, baptized February 15, sponsors Mark and Anna Hunecker.

Donely, Eleanor, of Philip and Catharine Donely, born February 5, baptized February 15, sponsors John and Eva Hoffman.

Connor, Mary, of Mark and Mary Connor, born February 9, baptized February 15, sponsors Henry Hughs [Hughes?] and Dorothy Connor.

Kenedy, Mary, of —— and Mary Kenedy, born February 26, baptized February 27, sponsor Catharine Arnold, widow.

Hoffner, Mary Magdalen, of John and Eva Hoffner, born February 23, baptized March 1, sponsors Caspar and Mary Magdalen Korn.

Böhm, Mary Catharine, of John and Catharine Böhm, born February 23, baptized March 1, sponsors Joseph and Anna Mary Feinauer.

——, Dinah, of Nicholas and Flora ——, born ——, 1764, baptized March 1, sponsor Anna Mary Wiester, negro servants of Warwick Coats.

Jacobs, James, of William (P.) and Catharine Jacobs, born February —, baptized March 10, sponsors Henry and Agnes Arnold.

Maher, Anna, of —— and Mary Maher, born February 2, baptized March 17; the mother acted as godmother in default of another.

Beal, Henry, of George (P.) and Catharine Beal, born February 9, baptized March 19, sponsor Charlotte Engelraid.

Murray, Margaret, of Hugh (P.) and Elizabeth Murray, born April 12, 1763, baptized conditionally March 25, sponsors James Welsh and Anna Roage; had been baptized by a Presbyterian minister.

Zeigler, Anna Elizabeth Sarah, of Henry James and Mary Catharine Zeigler, born July —, 1765, baptized March 25, sponsor Regina Catharine Nagel, witness Anna Elizabeth Betsin.

Benner, Simon, of Christian and Magdalen Benner, born February 18, baptized March 29, sponsors Simon and Christiana Geiger, at Geiger's [N. J.].

Magill, Stephen, of Peter and Barbara Magill, born February 15, baptized March 30, sponsors Stephen Magill and Margaret Delaney, near Geiger's.

Dun, Mary, of William and Bridget Dun [Dunn?], born March —, baptized April 5, sponsors John Farron and Elizabeth Donaghy.

Lynch, John, of John and Elizabeth Lynch, born March 19, baptized April 5, sponsors Jeremiah Lynch and Anna Hanlon.

Gallagher, Mary, of John and Anna Gallagher, born March 20, baptized April 7, sponsors Patrick Daly and Bridget Doyle.

Joyce, Anna, of Albert and Sarah Joyce, born about January 20, baptized April 9, sponsors Bryan O'Harra and Barbara Buttler.

O'Harra, Anna and Catharine (twins), of Bryan and Mary O'Harra, born April 11, baptized April 13, sponsors John and Catharine Gatringer, for Anna, Timothy Carroll and Barbara Buttler for Catharine.

Will, Margaret, of Philip and Elizabeth Will, born March 17, baptized April 19, sponsors John and Margaret Späth.

Cancemi, Peter Firmian, of Peter and Dorothy (P.) Cancemi [Cancerni?], born March 14, baptized April 19, sponsors Firmian and Elizabeth Bodoin.

Feinauer, Mary Catharine, of Joseph and Anna Mary Feinauer, born April 25, baptized April 26, sponsors Joseph and Catharine Böhm.

Jacobi, Christian, of Philip and Margaret Jacobi, born March 25, baptized April 28, sponsors Christian and Susanna Catharine Thurnbach, at Geiger's.

———, Lucie, of Sylvester and ——— ———, born April 7, baptized May 4, sponsors Thomas and Elizabeth Wilcox, at Concord ; servant [or slave] of Wilcox.

O'Donel, Anna, of Hugh and Rosa O'Donel, born March 31, baptized May 5, sponsors James Klein and Catharine Spengler.

David, Winifred Catharine, of Anthony and Mary Theresa David, born April 26, baptized May 3, sponsor Catharine Swan, by Rev. Robert Harding.

Sauerwald, Barbara, of Michael and Margaret Sauerwald, born May 5, baptized May 6, sponsors Anthony and Barbara Graff.

Haug, Mary, of John and Catharine Haug, born May 3, baptized May 8, sponsors Anthony and Mary Haug.

———, Flora Rosa, 20 years old, baptized May 10, sponsor Mingo Coats, servant to Warren Coats; witness Flora, servant to Timothy Caroll.

Lery, Henry, of Daniel and Mary Lery, born February 21, baptized May 14, sponsors Timothy and Elizabeth Caroll.

Conwell, James, of James Conwell and Jane Stephenson, born April 13, baptized May 17, sponsors Edward Murray and Mary Kenedy.

Hald, Mary, of John Hald and Catharine Manin, born December —, 1755, baptized conditionally May 21, sponsor Judith Hatton.

Späth, Joanna Catharine, of John and Margaret Späth, born May 15, baptized May 22, sponsors John and Joanna Catharine Wagner.

Conor, Susanna, of Michael and Mary Conor, born February 28, baptized May 30, sponsors Robert White and Mary Crowley.

Larcon, Susanna, of ——— ——— and Anna Larcon [Larkin?], born October 31, 1766, baptized May 31, sponsors Anthony Murray and Sarah Dugan, at Pikesland [Pa.].

Sohl, John, of Francis and Apollonia Sohl, born April 9, baptized May 31, sponsors John Bernard Brown and Mary Elizabeth Sohl, *ibid.*

Sherman, Elizabeth, adult, baptized June 6, sponsors John and Catharine Smith ; wife of Philip Morrison.

Thompson, John, of John Thompson and Hannah Ryan, born April 21, baptized June 7, sponsor Daniel Hely, witness Margaret M'Clean.

Juson, Mary Martha, of Thomas and Catharine Juson, baptized June 8, sponsors Adam and Martha Poth.

Deleany, Elizabeth, of Michael and Honora Deleany [Delaney?], born April 19, baptized June 14, sponsor Mary Bussye, witness Patrick Linard.

O'Kain, Simon Joseph, of Simon O'Kain and Cecilia Dibotan, baptized conditionally June 14, sponsors John Gatringer and Catharine Schmid.

Welch, John James, of Conrad and Elizabeth Catharine Welch, born November 18, 1766, baptized conditionally June 18, sponsors James Walter and Susanna Waibe, at Ringwood [N. J.].

Butz, John George, of John William and Mary Magdalen Butz, born April 3, baptized June 18, sponsors John Els and Anna Elizabeth Walker, *ibid*.

Fichter, John, of Philip and Eva Fichter, born February 10, baptized June 18, sponsors John Mayer, Jr., and Susanna Waibe, *ibid*.

Reider, Joseph, of Francis Joseph and Anna Mary Reider, born December 25, 1766, baptized June 19, sponsors Joseph Wingart and Anna Mary Borm, *ibid*.

Hoffman, Mary Eva, of Lambert and Elizabeth Hoffman, born January 5, baptized June 19, sponsors John Mayer, Sr., and Mary Eva Fichter, *ibid*.

Crämer, Anna Mary, of Matthew and Mary Catharine Crämer, born April 9, baptized June 19, sponsors Joseph Wingart and Anna Mary Reider, *ibid*.

Pfältzer, John, of Eugene and Mary Margaret Pfältzer, born December 13, baptized June 20, sponsor John Cobole, at Gothland.

Schmid, Anna Sophia, of Adolph (P.) and Elizabeth Margaret Schmid, born January 6, baptized June 20, sponsors John Cobole and his wife (for Sophia Schneider), *ibid*.

Cobole, John, of John and Catharine Cobole, born May 13, 1765, baptized June 20, sponsors John Burn and Magdalen Butz, *ibid*.

Schneider, Anna Margaret, of Henry (P.) and Mary Sophia Schneider, born June 3, baptized June 21, sponsors Nicholas Mentzenbach and Wilhelmina Butz, at Ringwood [Passaic Co., N. J.].

Miller, Robert, of David and Mary Miller, born March —, 1763, baptized June 21, sponsors Wendelin Kramer and Elizabeth Warle, *ibid*.

Miller, James, of same parents, born November 24, 1765, baptized June 21, sponsors James Dun and Mary Lehre, *ibid*.

Bachman, Henry, of Martin and Anna Barbara Bachman, born February 24, baptized conditionally June 21, sponsors John Mayer (for Henry Strable) and Mary Anna Welker, *ibid*.

Schreiner, Mary Christina, of Henry and Anna Sarah Schreiner, born

—— —, baptized June 24, sponsor Mary Barbara Wolf, witnesses James Zein and Christina Pfister, at Basconridge [Somerset Co., N. J.].

Barefoot, Anna, of John and Anna Barefoot, born ——, baptized June 28, sponsor Bridget O'Neil.

Matley, James, of Walter and Mary Matley, born April 11, baptized June 28, sponsors Adam Mayer and Anna Savadge [Savage ?].

Seibert, Francis Joseph, of Sebastian and Elizabeth Seibert, born June 28, baptized June 29, sponsors Peter Bremich (for Francis Joseph Schwartz) and Mary Salome Schwartz.

McHughin, Anna, of John and Martha McHughin [McCuen ?], born April 9, 1764, baptized July 19, sponsors John and Eleanor Conor, at Adam Geiger's.

O'Neal, Mary, of John Arthur and Rose O'Neal, born July 15, baptized August 2, sponsors William Moran and Susanna Fitzsimmons, at Concord [Del. Co., Pa.].

Barry, Robert, of James and Esther Barry, born June 22, 1766, baptized August 8, sponsors Patrick and Joanna Brady.

Migno, Mary Isabelle, of Charles Migno and Pelagia Galerm, born August 12, baptized conditionally August 12, sponsors Paul Bichan and Josephine Daroit.

Bagnel, John, of Edward Bagnel and —— ——, born —— —, baptized conditionally August 12.

Kessler, Valentine, of Andrew and Catharine Kessler, born March 4, baptized August 12, sponsors Valentine and Frederika Catharine Schalus.

Treim, Mary Dorothy, of James and Elizabeth Treim, born August 4, baptized August 16, sponsors Christopher and Mary Dorothy Tscharte.

Doyle, Anna Mary, of James and Mary Christina Doyle, born July 4, baptized August 23, sponsors Peter and Anna Mary Weister.

Dugan, Catharine, of John and Mary Dugan, born July 13, baptized August 25, sponsors Richard Garrety and Catharine Lemy.

Glangley, Elizabeth, of William and Elizabeth Glangley, born December 25, 1764, baptized August 30, sponsors John McHughin [McCuen ?] and Margery Magill, at Adam Geiger's.

Glangley, Catharine, of same parents, born July 23, 1762, baptized August 30, sponsors Owen Kelty and Regina Mayer, *ibid.*

Neal, William, of Cornelius and Elizabeth Neal, born February 18, baptized August 30, sponsors Hugh Magines and Margery Magill, *ibid.*

McHughin, Barnabas, of John and Martha McHughin [McCuen ?], born October 17, 1765, baptized August 30, sponsors John Osmund and Margery Magill, *ibid.*

Hamilton, Mary Felicia, of William, Hamilton and —— ——, born

November —, 1766, baptized September 3, sponsor Mary Felicia Escher.

Cahel, Eleanor, of John and Catharine Cahel, born August 16, baptized September 6, sponsors Daniel Caroll and Joanna Nichols.

Ridiger, Anna Mary, of Matthew Anthony and Mary Anna Ridiger, born June 24, baptized September 6, sponsors John and Mary Anna Ridiger.

Frelan, John, of James and Joanna Frelan, born July 30, baptized September 7, sponsors Dennis and Bridget Dun [Dunn?].

Schneider, Mary Gertrude, of John Christian (P.) and Mary Elizabeth Schneider, born August 24, baptized September 7, sponsors John and Mary Gertrude Stauter, near Philadelphia.

Gerstenberger, Anthony, of Andrew and Mary Magdalen Gerstenberger, born September 8, baptized September 11, sponsors Anthony and Barbara Graff.

Senner, Mary, of Francis and Mary Senner, born September 8, baptized September 13, sponsors John and Mary Gatringer.

O'Davelin, Susanna, of Roger and Susanna O'Davelin, born July 19, baptized September 20, sponsors James Hickey and Eleanor Karker, at Pikesland [Chester Co., Pa.].

Mackey, Francis, of William and Mary Mackey, born August 20, baptized conditionally September 26.

Zeis, Mary Anna, of George and Eva Zeis, born September 19, baptized September 27, sponsors Leonard and Mary Anna Lascher.

Schwartzman, Joseph, of Andrew and Charlotte Schwartzman, born September 30, baptized October 1, sponsors Peter Eck (for his father Joseph Eck) and Catharine (wife of Joseph).

Patterson, Hannah, of John and Mary Patterson, born August 9, baptized October 4, sponsors William Sherlock and Rosa O'Neal, at Concord [Del. Co., Pa.].

Summer, Mary Catharine, of John and Anna Margaret Summer, born September 29, baptized October 13, sponsor Catharine Spengler.

Welsh, James, of David and Mary Welsh, born July 8, 1760, baptized October 16, sponsor Sophia Dogherty.

McAdam, Sarah, of Henry and Mary McAdam, born October 17, baptized October 17, sponsor Rebecca Clark.

Egan, Charles, of John and Margaret Egan, born September 23, baptized October 18, sponsors Thomas Fitzsimmons and Mary Clarey.

O'Brian, William, of M—— O'Brian [O'Brien?] and —— ——, born June —, 1767, baptized October 20, sponsors Martin Pendegras [Prendergast?] and Catharine Swan.

Linard, Catharine, of Patrick and Margaret Linard [Leonard?], born September 3, baptized October 25, sponsors Dennis Sullivan and Christina Mullabi.

Anderle, Mary Elizabeth, of Michael and Mary Anna Anderle, born June 8, 1764, baptized October 25, sponsors Peter and Mary Schad.

Schlosser, Mary Magdalen, of Joseph and Anna Mary Schlosser, born October 2, baptized October 26, sponsor Mary Magdalen Mallock.

Rush, Joanna, of Patrick and Margaret Rush, born October 27, baptized October 30, sponsors John Lennox and Mary Farrell.

Eck, Barbara, of James and Elizabeth Eck, born October 30, baptized November 1, sponsors Anthony and Barbara Graff.

Sig, Mary Magdalen, of John George (P.) and Mary Magdalen Sig, born February 19, baptized November 15 ; had been baptized by a Lutheran minister ; ceremonies supplied ; at Ringwood [N. J.].

Perkins, Benjamin, of Benjamin and Mary Perkins, born September 22, 1766, baptized November 16, sponsors Joseph and Margaret Patterson, *ibid.*

Patterson, John, of Joseph and Margaret Patterson, born August 20, baptized November 16, sponsors William Fitzgerald and Elizabeth Freeman, *ibid.*

Burns, Mary Margaret, of Laghlin and Margaret Burns, born July 4, baptized November 16, sponsors Henry Philips and Margaret Schwefel, *ibid.*

Glä, Anna Catharine, of Charles and Anna Eva Glä, born June 28, baptized November 16, sponsors John Reider and Anna Catharine Demuth, *ibid.*

Bremignon, Thomas, of William and Catharine Bremignon, born February 25, 1755, baptized November 26, sponsors Thomas Byrnes and Rebecca Clark.

Bremignon, Margaret, of same parents, born December 12, 1758, baptized November 26, sponsors Thomas Byrnes and Rebecca Clark.

Bremignon, Eleanor, of same parents, born September 15, 1760, baptized November 26, sponsors Thomas Byrnes and Rebecca Clark.

Bremignon, John, of same parents, born September 15, 1764, baptized November 26, sponsors Thomas Byrnes and Rebecca Clark.

Kolb, Catharine Margaret, of Andrew and Catharine (P.) Kolb, born November 1, baptized November 29, sponsors Adam and Margaret Geiger, in New Jersey.

Eyenson, Simon Peter, of John and Elizabeth Eyenson, born October 18, baptized November 30, sponsors Patrick Magill and Esther Eyenson, *ibid.*

Schöne, John James, of Laurence and Mary Magdalen Schöne, born December 3, baptized December 6, sponsors James and Elizabeth Klein.

——, William, born October —, baptized December 6, sponsor Margaret Vincent Blanchard (widow), a mulatto.

Essling, Margaret, of Peter and Anna Mary Essling, born November 24, baptized December 6, sponsors Henry Lechler and Margaret Stolls.

Koempf, Matthew, of Matthew and Susanna Koempf, born November 27, baptized December 6, sponsor Matthew Bremich.

McMullen, Matthew, of John and Margaret McMullen, born November 4, baptized December 11, sponsor Elizabeth Maddon.

Rider, Robert, of Christopher and Anna Rider, born ——— —. baptized December 14, sponsor Catharine Gordon.

Albrecht, Anna Eva, of James and Anna Mary Albrecht, born December 13, baptized December 16, sponsors John Westermeyer and Anna Eva Miller.

Lederman, John, of John and Mary Catharine Lederman, born December 21, baptized December 26, sponsors John Becker and Barbara Wolf.

McKegg, John, of Brian and Margaret McKegg, born June 7, baptized December 27, sponsors Peter Heffner and Anna Lechler.

Whole number of baptisms—one hundred and twenty-three.

REGISTER OF BAPTISMS FOR 1768.

Hall, Margaret, of Philip and Elizabeth Hall, born December 23, 1767, baptized January 2, sponsors Joseph Feinauer and Margaret Egan.

Nagel, Mary Barbara, of George and Mary Nagel, born January 3, baptized January 6, sponsors Francis Joseph and Mary Barbara Hirt.

Mignati, Dorothy Elizabeth, of Daniel and Mary Mignati, born January 6, baptized January 10, sponsor Peter Caputh, Dorothy, his wife, witness.

Ummerzetter, Regina Catharine, of Conrad (P.) and Anna Margaret Ummerzetter, born October 30, 1767, baptized January 17, sponsors Jacob and Regina Nagel.

Burgeois, Mary Magdalen and Mary Eva (twins), of Claude and Catherine Burgeois, born January 18, baptized January 19, sponsors George and Mary Magdalen Lechler for Mary Magdalen, Peter Heffner and Eva Lechler for Mary Eva.

Frühwirth, John Adam, of John George and Catharine Frühwirth, born January 14, baptized January 21, sponsors Adam Göth and Catharine Spengler.

De Witter, Mary Catharine, of John and Anna Mary de Witter, born January 19, baptized January 24, sponsors Joseph Kauffman and Catharine Spengler.

Lenox, David, of John and Margaret Lenox, born January 22, baptized January 29, sponsors Patrick and Margaret Rush.

McCullough, Duncan, adult, baptized February 6, conditionally.

Göck, John, of Adam and Mary Göck, born February 5, baptized February 9, sponsors John Frühwirth and Catharine Spengler.

Schwerber, Susanna Catharine, of William and Ottilia Schwerber, born February 11, baptized February 16, sponsors Christopher and Catharine Viel ; in the vicinity of Philadelphia.

———, Anna, of Hannah and ——— ———, born February 3, baptized February 10, sponsor Anna Fichtler, servant of James White.

———, Timothy, 13 years old, baptized February 18, sponsor Anna Fichtler, a slave (or servant) of James White.

Kidd, Anna, of John (P.) and Susanna Kidd, born April 30, 1765, baptized February 21, sponsors Francis Sohl and Eleanor Karker, at Pikes-land [Chester Co., Pa.].

Kidd, Francis, of same parents, born August 31, 1767, baptized February 21, sponsors Francis Richard Smith and Apollonia Sohl, *ibid*.

———, Mary, of ——— and Rebecca ———, born September —, 1761, baptized February 25, sponsors George and Catharine Coffa.

Joyce, Anna, of Patrick and Anna Joyce, born February 4, baptized February 26, sponsors David and Margaret Glancey.

Morrison, Mary, of Philip and Elizabeth Morrison, born February 18, baptized February 28, sponsors Patrick Neave and Margaret Nihil [Niel?].

Frederick, George Frederic, of Philip and Alice Frederick, born February 21, baptized March 5, sponsor Peter Derry, Margaret Hely witness.

Conely, Anna, of Robert and Anna Conely, born February 19, baptized March 6, sponsors John Wallace and Eleanor Buttler.

Hussy, Margaret, of William and Eleanor Hussy, born March 4, baptized March 11, sponsors Patrick Flanigan and Elizabeth Carroll.

Bodar, William, of Anthony and Barbara Bodar, born March 5, baptized March 13, sponsors William Dorff and Eleanor More.

Klein, James, of James and Elizabeth (P.) Klein, born March 6, baptized March 13, sponsors Michael and Margaret Sauerwald.

Thurnbach, Margaret, of Christian and Susanna Catharine Thurnbach, born December 16, 1767, baptized March 20, sponsors Adam and Margaret Geiger, at Adam Geiger's [N. J.].

Stehling, Anna Barbara, of John and Mary Magdalen Stehling, born March 21, baptized March 23, sponsors Joseph and Barbara Wirth.

Haug, Mary Margaret, of George and Margaret Haug, born February 7, baptized March 24, sponsors George Ernest and Mary Magdalen Lechler.

McCaffrey, (Phila?), of Edward and Sarah McCaffrey, born February 23, baptized April 2, sponsors Philip and Margaret Campel [Campbell?].

Aman, John Adam, of Anthony and Sarah Aman, born December 8, 1767, baptized April 3, sponsor John Adam Bremich.

Hegner, Catharine, of John and Anna Hegner, born September 19, 1767, baptized April 3, sponsor John Mayer, witness Gertrude (his wife).

Bremich, Joseph, of ——— and Eva Bremich, born April 1, baptized April 3, sponsors Joseph and Catharine Egg [Eck?].

Bordt, John, of Francis and Catharine Bordt, born February 27, baptized April 14, sponsors John Ells and Anna Elizabeth Welker, at Ringwood [N. J.].

Mentzenbach, Charles Michael, of Nicholas and Helen Mentzenbach, born February 28, baptized April 16, sponsor John Mayer.

Stalter, Mary Elizabeth, of Nicholas and Elizabeth Stalter, born February 23, baptized October 27, sponsor John Mayer; ceremonies supplied; had been baptized privately at Charlottenberg [in New Jersey].

Sullivan, Catharine, of Dennis and Catharine Sullivan, born April 17, 1767, baptized April 17, sponsors Joseph Wingart and Anna Margaret Reider.

Miller, John and William (twins), of William and Helen Miller, born April 12, baptized April 24, sponsors Catharine Fox and Elizabeth Gräf.

West, Catharine, of ——— ——— and Elizabeth West, born April 12, baptized April 24, sponsor Eleanor Hanlon.

Macarty, Anna, of ——— ——— and Margaret Macarty, born April 18, baptized April 24, sponsor Hannah Ryan.

Veil, Charles Joseph, of Rudolph and Susanna Sibylla Veil, born April 19, baptized April 26, sponsors Charles and Catharine Schmid.

Metzgar, Christina Catharine, of John and Cecilia Metzgar, born February 28, 1766, baptized conditionally April 28, sponsor Catharine Hoffner.

Haug, William, of John and Catharine Haug, born April 24, baptized May 1, sponsors William and Catharine Buttler.

Kneul, Mary Magdalen, of Balthasar and Christina Elizabeth Kneul, born April 16, 1767, baptized May 1, sponsors George Ernest and Mary Magdalen Lechler.

Watts, James, of Samuel and Mary Watts, born April 27, baptized May 10, sponsors John Farren and Elizabeth Pierce.

Magill, James, of John and Catharine Magill, born April 21, baptized May 2; bad been baptized privately.

Burns, William, of ——— ——— and Margaret Burns, born May 20, baptized May 23, sponsors Patrick Neave and Catharine Barry.

Vincent, Cecilia, of Peter and Genevieve Vincent, born May 26, baptized May 26, sponsors Eustace Daniel and Anna Cierene (?) Vincent.

Scheimer, Mary Magdalen, of Frederic and Mary Magdalen Scheimer, born March 25, baptized May 29, sponsor Patrick McFall, witness Elizabeth Bamberger, at Pikesland [Pa.].

McHughin, Anna, of John and Martha McHughin [McCuen?], born January 10, baptized June 19, sponsors Arthur McHollin and Mary Roberts, at Adam Geiger's.

Geiger, Catharine Margaret, of Henry and Barbara Geiger, born April 6, baptized June 19, sponsors Adam and Margaret Geiger, *ibid*.

Caspar, Christina, of Laurence and Margaret Caspar, born June 15, baptized June 19, sponsors Michael and Hannah Huber, *ibid*.

Miller, Catharine, baptized conditionally June 24; servant [or slave] of Tobias Rudolph.

Kelly, Archibald, of ——— ——— and Anna Kelly, born May 17, baptized June 25, sponsor Margaret Carty.

Neal, William, of William Neal and Catharine Grafford, born June 1, baptized June 25, sponsor Helen Karn.

——, Flora, adult, baptized July 1, sponsor Elizabeth, wife of Timothy Carroll; slave of Timothy Carroll.

Waas, Mary, of Sebastian and Anna Mary Waas, born April 6, 1767, baptized July 3, sponsors Francis and Mary Agatha Senner.

Boyton, Anna Mary, of Daniel and Sarah Boyton, born September —, 1767, baptized June 18, sponsors Balthasar Gans and Mary Weiseburger, at Reading Furnace [Chester Co., Pa.].

Schneider, Mary Catharine, of Burchard and Catharine Schneider, born April 7, baptized June 18, sponsors John Henry Kuentz and Mary Weiseburger, near the same place.

Anderson, Margaret, of Charles and Joanna Anderson, born June 12, baptized June 23, sponsor Mary Berd [Baird?].

Hauck, Mary Catharine, of Anthony and Mary Hauck, born July 6, 1767, baptized June 24, sponsors Joseph and Anna Mary Feinauer, by Father Robert Harding.

Metzgar, Joseph, of John and Cecilia Metzgar, born June 30, baptized June 31, sponsors John and Anna Mary Rüh.

Freund, Sebastian, of Stephen and Salome Freund, born August 6, baptized August 9, sponsors Sebastian and Elizabeth Seibert.

Cullins, James, of William and Mary Cullins, born July 21, baptized August 13, sponsors Edward Malloy and Catharine Fox.

Reinolds, Sarah, of Brod (?) Reinolds and Catharine Coghlin, born July 3, baptized August 13, sponsor Anna Kelty.

Caghagan, James, of Patrick and Sarah Caghagan, born December 24, 1767, baptized August 24, sponsors Charles and Mary Quin.

Otto, Charles Joseph, of James and Mary Ann Otto, born August 21, baptized August 28, sponsors Charles and Catharine Schmid.

Conley, John, of Thomas and Mary Conley, born August 13, baptized August 28, sponsors Daniel and Mary Hely.

Veil, Anna Ursula, of Nicholas and Sophia Veil, born August 30, baptized September 2, sponsors Charles and Catharine Schmid.

Hoffman, Sebastian, of John and Christina Hoffman, baptized September 2, sponsor Sebastian Kehl, by Father Robert Harding.

Graff, John, of Anthony and Barbara Graff, born September 1, baptized September 5, sponsors John Gatringer and Mary Ohara [O'Hara?].

Krapf, James, of Peter and Claudina Krapf, born May 21, baptized September 8, sponsor James le Compte.

Mayer, Gertrude, of Isidore (P.) and Gertrude Mayer, born September 5, baptized September 8, sponsors Peter (for John) Hegner and Ann Elizabeth Barthman.

Christi, Mary, of Hugh and Catharine Christi, born July 25, baptized September 8, sponsors Dennis Sullivan and Mary Scantlin.

Dogan, George, of James and Sarah Dogan, born September 6, baptized September 18, sponsor James Griffin, at Pikesland [Pa.].

Dealy, William, of Charles and Margaret Dealy, born August 16, baptized September 22, sponsors Dennis Flood and Catharine Heiky.

Stephenson, Anna, of —— Stephenson and Mary McClean, born September 11, baptized September 22, sponsor Catharine Heiky.

Dogherty, Mary, of Dennis and Margaret Dogherty, born September 22, baptized September 25, sponsors Patrick Flanigan and Mary O'Hara.

Göck, Adam, of Lawrence and Christina Göck, born August 26, baptized September 29, sponsors Adam and Margaret Geiger, at Adam Geiger's.

Magill, Marchery [Margery?], of James and Joanna Magill, born September 5, baptized September 29, sponsors John Linton and Catharine Kelty.

Makay, Anna, of William and Catharine Makay, born September 30, baptized October 2, sponsor Catharine McDonald.

Fichter, Joseph, of Philip and Mary Eva Fichter, born September 23, baptized October 3, sponsors John and Anna Mary Feinauer.

Wood, Henry, of Patrick and Margaret Wood, born September 25, baptized October 4, sponsors Joseph and Barbara Würth.

Bell, Elizabeth, adult, baptized October 16.

Tussy, Mary, of John and Joanna Tussy, born March 15, 1762, baptized October 16, sponsor Mary Haselwood.

Mather, Anna Mary, of Peter and Anna Mather, born September 30, baptized October 16, sponsor Peter Jones, Margaret Duffy witness.

Migno, John, of Charles and Pelagia Migno, born October 16, baptized October 16, sponsors John la Viola and Anna Blanchart.

Darmoty, Mary, of Edward and Esther Darmoty, born July 21, 1765, baptized October 23, sponsors Alexander McConaghy and Mary Elizabeth Halter, at Charlottenburg [N. J.].

Darmoty, Barnabas, of same parents, born May 10, 1767, baptized October 23, sponsors Patrick Burk and Mary Catharine Kramer, *ibid.*

Demuth, Matthew, of James and Anna Catharine Demuth, born September 29, baptized October 23, sponsors Matthew Kramer and Juliana Miriam, *ibid.*

Scholtzer, Elizabeth, of Martin and Susanna Scholtzer, born January 19, baptized conditionally October 23; had been baptized by Nicholas Stalter, an intelligent man, his wife being witness, living at Charlottenburg [N. J.], the ceremonies afterwards supplied.

Cobole, John James, of John and Catharine Cobole, born October 9, baptized October 25, sponsors John Mayer and Mary Margaret Schwable, at Ringwood [N. J.].

Pfältzer, Anthony Louis, of Eugene and Susanna Pfältzer, born September 27, baptized October 25, sponsors Anthony May and Anna Catharine Elizabeth Call, Louis Texheimer witness, *ibid.*

Wohlleben, Mary Sophia, of John and Catharine Wohlleben, born October 20, baptized October 25, sponsors John James and Mary Susanna Walter, Mary Sophia Schneider witness, *ibid.*

Harrison, John Anthony, of Samuel (P.) and Mary Harrison, born October 15, baptized October 26, sponsors John and Hannah Ettinger, *ibid.*

Lawless, John, of Martin and Mary Lawless, born May 29, baptized October 26, sponsor Catharine Elizabeth Call, Michael Schneider witness, *ibid.*

Philips, John, of John and Elizabeth Philips, born October 20, baptized October 30, sponsors John and Catharine Lederman.

Schnell, Stephen, of Francis and Mary Ann Schnell, born September 11, baptized conditionally November 2, sponsors Stephen Felix and Elizabeth Probst.

McCann, Benjamin, of John and Margaret McCann, born July 29, baptized November 6, sponsors Arthur John O'Neil and Elizabeth Blood, at Concord [Del. Co., Pa.].

Fitzsimmons, Thomas, of Michael and Mary Fitzsimmons, born April 2, 1763, baptized November 14, sponsor Patrick Kearnan.

Blum, Anthony, of Anthony and Barbara Blum, born November 14, baptized November 19; the record seems to say that Catharine Weit was sponsor for Joseph Rühl, who was absent; near Philadelphia.

Hunecker, Elizabeth, of Mark and Anna Hunecker, born November 22, baptized November 22, sponsor Catharine Eck, near Philadelphia.

Homes, James, of Emmanuel and Mary Magdalen Homes, born November 20, baptized November 22, sponsors Simon and Mary Magdalen Haug, by Father Robert Harding.

Rerig, Stephen, of —— and Sophia Louisa Rerig, born November 18, baptized November 23, sponsor Stephen Forage.

Buch, Anna Elizabeth, of Joseph Buch and Hannah Ring, born October 22, baptized November 23, sponsor Ann Elizabeth Bartman.

Becker, John, of Bartholomew and Elizabeth Becker, born December 4, baptized December 6, sponsors John Becker and Elizabeth Lascher.

O'Brien, Sarah, of Dennis and Frances O'Brien, born January 14, 1767, baptized December 9, sponsor Catharine Fox.

O'Brien, Henry, of same parents, born August 8, baptized December 9, sponsor Catharine Fox.

Dunbar, Peter, of Peter Dunbar and Agnes Steling, born December 4, baptized December 10, sponsors Joseph and Barbara Würth.

Schreiner, Elizabeth, of Henry and Sarah Schreiner, born December 7, baptized December 11, sponsors James and Elizabeth Trimm.

Proc, James, of Nicholas and Flora Proc, born October 15, baptized December 11, sponsor Flora, a slave of Timothy Carroll, slaves.

Reynolds, John, of John and Margaret Reynolds, born November 14, baptized December 12, sponsors Charles Ganderin (represented by the priest) and Winifred Theresa David.

Haug, Joseph, of Simon and Magdalen Haug, born December 10, baptized December 18, sponsors Frederic and Elizabeth Gräser.

Sauerwald, John Patrick, of John and Magdalen Sauerwald, born December 17, baptized December 22, sponsors Patrick Travers and Anna Fichtler.

Schad, Mary Agnes, of Peter and Mary Elizabeth Schad, born October 21, baptized December 26, sponsors John and Mary Agnes Heisser.

Gallagher, Anna, of John and Anna Gallagher, born December 13, baptized December 31, sponsors William Gallagher and Mary Hair (for Mary Murphy), in Chester County [Pa.].

Whole number of baptisms—one hundred and fifteen.

REGISTER OF BAPTISMS FOR 1769.

Ryan, Deborah, of Thomas and Catharine Ryan, born December 17, 1768, baptized January 2, sponsors Thomas States and Deborah Patton, in Chester County [Pa.].

Bird, Margaret, of Jonathan (P.) and Mary Bird, born December 10, 1768, baptized January 3, sponsors Thomas and Anna King.

Sener, John, of Francis and Mary Sener, born January 1, baptized January 4, sponsor John Rudolph, Mary Margaret Rudolph witness.

Bridy, Edward, of John and Dorothy Bridy, born November 15, 1768, baptized January 12, sponsor Elizabeth Murray.

Cahill, John, of John and Catharine Cahill, born December 28, 1768, baptized January 15, sponsors Thomas Badge and Margaret Vealan.

Burns, Catharine, of Edward and Elizabeth Burns, born January 25, baptized January 27, sponsors Peter Gallagher and Agnes Arnold.

O'Donel, Mary Catharine, of Hugh and Rosa O'Donel, born January 27, baptized February 2, sponsors Anthony Graff and Catharine Spengler.

Doyle, George, of James and Mary Christina Doyle, born January 29, baptized February 4, sponsors Peter and Anna Mary Weister.

Purcel, Eleanor, of —— and Elizabeth Purcel, born November 27, 1768, baptized February 4, sponsor Eleanor Brunnen, Robert Taylor witness.

Schreiner, Elizabeth, of Cornelius and Elizabeth Schreiner, born February 3, baptized February 4, sponsors Lothaire and Elizabeth Rischart.

Griffin, James, of Thomas and Joanna Griffin, born February 1, baptized February 19, sponsors James Hickey and Eleanor Karker.

Wertmayer, Ann Eva, of John and Ottillia Wertmayer, born February 23, baptized February 27, sponsors John and Eva Miller.

Ottenauer, Regina Catharine, of Henry and Elizabeth Ottenauer, born January 14, baptized February 28, sponsors Anthony Reniger and Regina Catharine Nagel.

Cassin, Dennis, of Joseph and Elizabeth Cassin, born February 30, baptized March 2, sponsors John Maloney and Elizabeth Cassin.

Rischer, William, of —— —— and Mary Rischer, born February 15, baptized March 6, sponsor Catharine Fox.

Maglaghlin, James, of James and Mary Maglaghlin, born March 11, baptized March 11, sponsor Catharine Fox.

Brown, Margaret, of ———— Brown and Margaret Harris, born about August, 1768, baptized March 11, sponsor Catharine Fox.

Franks, Catharine, of Samuel and Elizabeth Franks, born January 23, baptized March 11, sponsor Catharine Fox.

Bradford, Mary, of Thomas (P.) and Anna Bradford, born December 5, baptized March 17, sponsor Catharine Fox.

Hueber, Laurence, of Michael and Hannah Hueber, born October 13, 1768, baptized March 19, sponsors Laurence and Christina Göck, at Pilesgrove [Salem Co., N. J.].

Miller, Anna Mary, of Matthew and Anna Mary Miller, born August 26, 1768, baptized March 19, sponsors Laurence and Margaret Caspar, *ibid.*

Glancy, Thomas and William (twins), of William and Elizabeth Glancy, born November 1, 1768, baptized March 19, sponsors Eleanor Conor (for William) and Mary Langley (for Thomas), *ibid.*

Ernstdorf, Barbara, of Henry (P.) and Elizabeth Ernstdorf, born March 8, baptized March 21, sponsors Henry and Barbara Geiger, *ibid.*

Morrey, John, of Patrick and Margaret Morrey, born July 21, 1768, baptized March 22, sponsors James and Catharine McCormic.

Harkins, Rosa, of William and Eleanor Harkins, born March 19, baptized March 26, sponsor Joanna Nicols, witness John Madden.

Caugemy (?), Peter Caspar, of Peter and Dorothy Caugemy (?), born March 22, baptized March 26, sponsors Caspar and Elizabeth Hayle.

Davis, Susanna, of Edward Davis and Anna Donohi, born March 11, baptized March 26, sponsors S———— Riddle and Anna Power.

Flemming, John, of Thomas and Mary Flemming, born March 22, baptized March 26, sponsor Elizabeth M—ey (?).

[NOTE.—Here can barely be traced remnants of letters of one or two baptisms. The edges at the bottom of the page are quite worn off.]

Tattles, Elizabeth, of ———— Tattles and Anna ————, born August 1, 1768, baptized April 1, sponsor Ottilia Schweiberin, by Father Luke Geisler.

Reading, Joseph, of John and Margaret Reading, born February —, baptized April 1, sponsors Henry Hughes and Catharine Foh—(?).

Holtzhauser, Theodore, of Theodore and Christina (P.) Holtzhauser, born April —, baptized April 16, sponsors William Dorff and Catharine Hon—(?), by Father Luke Geisler.

Herts, Joseph, of John and Barbara Herts, born April 14, baptized April 18, sponsor Joseph Rübel, by Rev. Luke Geisler.

Bachman, Mary Barbara, of Martin and Anna Barbara Bachman, born April 6, baptized April 15, sponsors Nicholas Jungfleisch and Barbara Her—(?), at Charlottenburg [N. J.].

Schott, John Peter, of Philip and Mary Catharine Schott, born December

6, 1768, baptized April 15, sponsors Peter Walker and Ann Eva Jungfleisch, *ibid.*; ceremonies supplied.

Strack, Henry Philip, of William and Ann Elizabeth Strack, born December 29, 1768, baptized April 16, sponsors Philip and Ann Elizabeth Fichter, at Ringwood [N. J.].

Ettinger, Ann Elizabeth, of John (P.) and Hannah Ettinger, born March 27, baptized April 16, sponsors John and Elizabeth Ditz, *ibid.*; ceremonies supplied.

———, Hannah, of Philip and Catharine ———, born April 3, baptized April 23, sponsors John and Eva Hoeffner.

Lynch, Catharine, of Jeremiah and Elizabeth Lynch, born April 10, baptized April 23, sponsors Michael Ryan and Catharine Readall.

Pulfred, Joseph, of Thomas and ——— Pulfred, baptized, by Rev. Luke Geisler, April 29.

Finey, Susanna, of John and Mary Finey, baptized, by the same, April 30, sponsor Cormack Donaghy.

Shiney, Catharine, of Laurence and Mary Magdalen Shiney, born April 30, baptized, by the same, May 3, sponsors Anthony and Barbara Graff.

Tims, Eleanor, of Henry and Anna Tims, born March 15, baptized April 30, sponsors Patrick McFalls and Catharine McDonald, at Pikesland [Pa.].

Walter, James, of James and Francis Walter, born November 20, 1768, baptized April 30, sponsors James and Anna Mary Weisenburger, *ibid.*

Griffin, Eleanor, of James and Elizabeth Griffin, born April 9, baptized April 30, sponsors James Hickey and Magdalen Hanley, *ibid.*

Hedinger, Mary Margaret, of John and Magdalen Hedinger, born April 2, baptized May 4, sponsor Margaret Butz, by Rev. Luke Geisler.

Gilgare, John, of George and Prudence Gilgare, born April 4, baptized May 7, sponsors Michael and Joanna Robinson.

Sauerwald, Margaret, of Michael and Margaret Sauerwald, born April 8, baptized May 8, sponsors Anthony and Barbara Graff.

Barrett, George, adult and servant, baptized May 11, his wife acted as godmother.

Linn, Bridget, of George and Loeta Linn, born March 17, 1768, baptized May 15, sponsor Mary Holland.

Campbell, Rosina, of C——— and Barbara Campbell, born March 21, 1768, baptized May 18, sponsors John Harkins and Catharine Tolly.

Späth, John, of John and Margaret Späth, born May 14, baptized May 21, sponsors John and Catharine Wagner.

Mannin, Walter, of Peter and Eleanor Mannin, born May 24, baptized May 29, sponsors James White and ——— Malony.

Bauer, John Leonard, of George and Christina Bauer, born February 24, baptized June 3, sponsors Leonard and Mary Ann Lascher.

Donaughey, John, of Cormack and Elizabeth Donaughey, born May 6, baptized June 4, sponsors John Robinson and Margaret Harkins.

Harvey, James, of James and Hannah Harvey, born March 12, baptized June 4, sponsors Owen and Susanna Glancy.

Mahan, John, of Jeremiah and Judith Mahan, born May 11, baptized June 4, sponsors James Robinson and Sarah Gromley.

Zeis, Anna Margaret, of George and Eva Zeis, born May 30, baptized June 4, sponsor Anna Margaret Wolf.

Hoffner, Mary Magdalen, of Peter and E——— Hoffner, baptized June 11, sponsors Michael and Margaret Sauerwald.

[NOTE.—The register for the months of July, August, September and October is missing.]

Mannin, Joseph, of ——— and Catharine Mannin, born October 14, baptized November 5, sponsor Bridget Archdeacon.

Tscharte, John Adam, of Christopher and Mary Dorothy (P) Tscharte, born October 25, baptized November 5, sponsors Adam and Mary Poth.

Göck, Anna Christina, of Adam and Mary Göck, born October 30, baptized November 5, sponsors Paul and Christina Essling.

Holt, Sampson, of Abel and Mary Holt, born February 8, baptized November 6, sponsors William Gallagher and Mary Farrell.   •

Crowley, Eleanor, of David and Mary Crowley, born March 6, baptized November 12, sponsors Christopher Fitzpatrick and Anna Christi [Christy?].

Caldwell, Daniel, of Patrick and ——— Caldwell, born 176—, baptized November 14, sponsor Dennis Fowlon.

Magill, Bridget, of John and Catharine Magill, born October 15, baptized November 16, sponsors Patrick McLaughlin and Joanna Magill, at Adam Geiger's [N. J.].

Kessler, Anna Mary, of Andrew and Catharine Kessler, born September 24, baptized November 28, sponsor Frederica Catharine Schalus, while returning home.

Reichman, Anna Mary Magdalen, of John and Mary Reichman, born July 22, 1767, baptized November 29, sponsors Matthew and Joanna Benner.

Reichman, Anna Mary Elizabeth, of same parents, born April 20, baptized November 29, sponsors Martin Benner and Elizabeth Brown.

Bell, Mary, of Alexander and Mary Bell, adult, baptized December 1, sponsor Anna Kling.

O'Neill, Hannah, of Arthur and Mary O'Neill, born November 6, baptized December 3, sponsors John Davelin and Elizabeth Blood, in Concord [Pa.].

———, Thomas, of ——— and Hannah ———, born Nov. 9, baptized December 12, sponsor Anna Fichtel; the mother was a slave of James White.

Christman, Mary Catharine, of Francis and Mary Elizabeth Christman, born November 12, baptized December 17, sponsors Charles and Mary Catharine Christman.

Mignot, Francis, of Daniel and Mary Mignot, born November 6, baptized December 17, sponsor Francis Vollin.

Hughson, Alice, of Thomas and Catharine Hughson, born November 17, baptized December 24, sponsor Elizabeth Gross.

Gleason, Mary, of Robert and Joanna Gleason, born January 12, 1766, baptized December 25, sponsors John Hardnut and Hannah Hampton.·

Miller, Antony, of John and Eva Miller, born November 22, baptized December 26, sponsors Anthony Gräff and Elizabeth Hegner.

Reichart, Anna Mary, of Joseph and Mary Apollonia Reichart, born July 4, 1767, baptized December 27, sponsors John and Gertrude Stanton.

Reichart, John, of same parents, born October 14, baptized December 27, same sponsors.

Rediger, John, of Anthony and Mary Anna Rediger, born December 26, baptized December 27, sponsors John and Margaret Rediger.

Lariole, Mary, of John and Anna Lariole, born December 30, baptized December 30, sponsors Emanuel and Mary Ohms.

Maddon, Mary, of John (P.) and Elizabeth Maddon, born December 25, baptized December 31, sponsors Matthew and Mary Gatringer.

Whole number of baptisms—eighty-two.

REGISTER OF BAPTISMS FOR 1770.

Aigan [Egan?], Mary, of John and Margaret Aigan [Egan?], born December 11, 1769, baptised January 1, sponsors Nicholas Bernard and Mary Gatringer.

Hall, Elizabeth, of Dennis and Frances Hall, born December 31, 1769, baptized conditionally, January 5.

——, Cæsar, servant of Thomas Wilcox, adult, baptized Junuary 10, sponsor Mark Wilcox, in Chester Co. [Pa.].

Leblanc, Susanna, of Henry and Mary Leblanc, born December 10, 1769, baptized January 14, sponsors John Lehy and Anna Leblanc.

Bray, William, of George and Susanna Bray, born January 2, baptized January 18, sponsors Joseph Cassin and Elizabeth Caroll.

Bray, Sarah and Susanna, of same parents, adults, baptized January 18, same sponsors.

Tudor, Henry, of Henry (P.) and Eva Catharine Tudor, born December 21, 1769, baptized January 24, sponsors Caspar and Elizabeth Nagle, near Philadelphia.

Essling, John George, of Peter and Mary Essling, born January 20, baptized January 30, sponsor Ann Mary Gross.

Savage, Margaret, of Jeremiah and Anna Savage, born January 29, baptized January 30, sponsors Timothy Caroll and Elizabeth Cassin.

Graff, Catharine, of Anthony and Barbara Graff, born January 29, baptized January 31, sponsors Timothy Caroll and Mary O'Haia (for Catharine Spengler).

Rischart, Mark, of Lothaire and Elizabeth Rischart, born January 31, baptized February 3, sponsors Mark Hunecker and Catharine, his daughter.

Kehl, John Christopher, of Sebastian and Catharine Kehl, born January 27, baptized February 4, sponsors Christopher and Mary Dorothy Tscharte.

Babin, John Baptist, of Simon and Anna (Trahan) Babin, born February 6, baptized conditionally, February 8, sponsors Francis Vallin and Margaret Trahan.

Keas, James, of James and Sarah Keas, born March 24, 1767, baptized conditionally, February 9.

Keas, Thomas, of same parents, born May 8, 1769, baptized February 9.

Hönig, Mary Magdalen, of Jacob and Catharine Hönig, born February 14, baptized February 25, sponsors George Kohl and Catharine Grieser, at Haycock [Bucks Co., Pa.].

Leblanc, Isabel Josephine, of Daniel and Margaret (Babin) Leblanc, born March 11, baptized March 11, sponsors Charles Leblanc and Josephine Deroit.

Colaghan, John, of John Colaghan and Ann Murphy, born February 3, baptized March 12, sponsor Sarah Tims.

Campbell, Sarah, of James and Elizabeth Campbell, adult, baptized conditionally, March 13, sponsor Sarah Tims.

Levy, Hannah, of Daniel Levy and Eleanor Fitzgerald, born March 5, baptized March 25, sponsors Michael Dorey and Elizabeth Burns.

Connelly, John, of Laurence Connelly and Anna Roanny, born March 10, baptized March 31, sponsors Thomas and Catharine Ryan, in Chester Co. [Pa.].

Worrell, Hannah, of Josue Worrell and Eleanor Tenson, born November 5, 1768, baptized April 1, sponsors Arthur O'Neil and Judith Wills, *ibid.*

———, Ruth, of Sylvester and Margaret ———, born March 5, baptized April 1, sponsor Deborah Sutton, *ibid.;* were servants or slaves of Thomas Wilcox.

Hoy, Mary, of John and Catharine Hoy, born August 17, 1768, baptized April 13, sponsors John Scot and Mary Barbara Harmon.

Ryan, Louis, of Dennis and Agnes Ryan, born November 24, 1769, baptized April 14, sponsor John Bray.

Stephen, John, of Matthew and Catharine Stephen, born March 24, baptized April 16, sponsors John Dart and Catharine Wagner.

[Badge?], Frances, baptized conditionally, April 22.

Würth, John Andrew, of Joseph and Barbara Würth, born April 17, baptized April 22, sponsors Michael Bremich and wife for Andrew and Catharine Kessler.

Brown, George, of John and Mary Brown, born November —, 1765, baptized April 29, sponsors William Fitzgerald and Catharine Fowler, at Charlottenberg [N. J.].

Rice, John, of James and Esther Rice, born November 30, 1769, baptized April 29, sponsors Thomas Price and Elizabeth Campbel, *ibid.*

Sutton, Mary Margaret, of William and Anna Sutton, born December 26, 1769, baptized April 29, sponsors Margaret Engelhardt and Henry Gläs, *ibid.*

Aussom, Henry, of John and Ann Elizabeth Aussom, born October 4, 1769, baptized conditionally, May 1, sponsors William Butz and Catharine Walke, at Ringwood [N. J.].

Bussy, Judith, of Moses and Elizabeth Catharine Bussy, born April 30, baptized May 6, sponsors John Lehey and Eleanor Noonan.

Christy, Catharine, of Martin and Hannah Christy, born May 3, baptized May 6, sponsors Andrew McClone and Mary Finney.

Faris, John and Eleanor (twins), of Bernard and Hannah Faris, born April 15, baptized May 7, sponsor Patrick Lanagan.

Rattisheim, Mary Ann Elizabeth, of John and Catharine Rattisheim, born December 29, 1769, baptized April 13, sponsors Philip Will and Mary Ann Roth.

Schilling, John Philip, of Philip and Eva Schilling, born April 25, baptized May 14, sponsors John Schrieber and Catharine, his wife.

McHughin, Mary, of John and Martha McHughin, born April 9, baptized May 24, sponsors James Bennet and Margaret Deleany, at Pilesgrove [Salem Co., N. J.].

Caspar, Adam, of Lawrence and Margaret Caspar, born February 8, baptized May 24, sponsors Adam and Margaret Geiger, *ibid.*

Thurnbach, Simon, of Christian and Susanna Catharine Thurnbach, born May 6, baptized May 24, sponsors Simon and Mary Geiger.

Garrety, Catharine, of Richard and Anna Garrety, born May 1, baptized May 27, sponsors Bernard Faris and Anna Land.

Fullon, Patrick, of Daniel and Mary Fullon, born May 11, baptized May 27, sponsors Dennis Sullivan and Eleanor Green, by Rev. Robert Harding.

Dartoit, Anna, of Bonaventure and Venanda Dartoit, born May 18, baptized May 20, sponsors Peter Savoy, Jr., and Anna Brau, by the same.

[Cloverin ?], Mary, adult, baptized June 7, sponsor Mary Queen.

Hewson, Anna Elizabeth, of John and Elizabeth Hewson, born June 19, baptized June 24, sponsors Nicholas Cappel and Anna Hewson.

Kagan, Rachael, of Brian and Susanna Kagan, adult, baptized June 28, sponsors John and Rebecca Connelly.

Seid, John, of —— —— and Catharine (P.) Seid, born this year, baptized June 28.

Montgomery, Deborah, of John (P.) and Mary Montgomery, born March 3, baptized July 1, sponsors Mark Wilcox and Deborah Sutton, at Concord, [Pa.].

Mignot, Mary Josephine, of Charles and Pelagia (Galerm) Mignot, born July 3, baptized July 3, sponsors Bonaventure Dartoit and Anna O'Kain (Kandry).

Campbel, Elizabeth, of James and Elizabeth Campbel, 8 years old, baptized July 6, sponsor Sarah Tims.

Lederman, Mary Elizabeth, of John and Mary Catharine Lederman, born June 27, baptized July 8, sponsors John and Mary Elizabeth Philips.

Kean, Mary, of Francis and Bridget Kean, born June 25, baptized privately, July 8.

Harvey, Susanna, of Job and Elizabeth Harvey, 13 years old, baptized July 9, sponsor the priest, in default of any one else.

Haynes, John, of Philip and Elizabeth Haynes, born June 25, baptized July 21, sponsor Anna Hethorn (Kelty).

Hethorn, Daniel, of Archibald and Anna Hethorn, born July 18, baptized July 21, sponsor Elizabeth Haynes.

Bray, Mary Anna, of John and Judith Bray, born July 18, baptized July 22, sponsors Dennis Foulon and Margaret Morrey.

——, Richard, baptized privately August 8.

Keanan, William, of John and Elizabeth Keanan, born about 1766, baptized August 8, sponsors Patrick and Elizabeth Keanan, witnesses David Barry and Thomas Flemming.

Staler, Joseph, of John and Christina Staler, born July 22, baptized August 12, sponsors Joseph and Catharine Eck.

Musson, Sarah (P.), infant, baptized privately August 12.

McLaughlin, William, of John and Margaret McLaughlin, born August 5, baptized August 13, sponsors Matthew Felding and Leah Jones.

Mahaney, Daniel, of Jeremiah Mahaney and Judith Fitzsimons, born August 11, baptized August 16, sponsor Eleanor Doyle.

Griffin, Mary, of Thomas and Joanna Griffin, born June 27, baptized August 19, sponsors Patrick McFall and —— Hickey, at Pikesland [Chester Co., Pa.].

Hedingder, Mary Magdalen, of John and Mary Magdalen Hedingder, born August 26, baptized August 31, sponsors George Ernest and Mary Magdalen Lechler.

Schneider, Mary Magdalen, of Henry and Barbara (P.) Schneider, born August 8, baptized August 9, same sponsors.

Schimp, Ann Elizabeth, of Philip and Elizabeth (P.) Schimp, born August 9, baptized August 16, sponsors Peter and Elizabath Haas.

Barry, Margaret, of Edmund and Eleanor Barry, born July 11, 1769, baptized September 29, sponsors Nicholas and Catharine Tuit.

Kean, Thomas, of Francis and Eleanor Kean, born October 26, 1758, baptized September 30, sponsors Francis and Apollonia Sohl, at Pikesland [Pa.].

Kean, Margaret, of same parents, born January 11, 1761, baptized September 30, sponsors James Griffin and Sarah Sohl, *ibid.*

Patterson, Mary, of John and Mary Patterson, born June 3, baptized September 30, sponsors James and Joanna Griffin, *ibid.*

Scheimer, James, of Frederic and Magdalen Scheimer, born September —, baptized October 1, sponsor John George Adla, in Chester Co., [Pa.].

McFall, Margaret, of Patrick McFall and Elizabeth Bamberger (P.), born July 5, baptized October 1, sponsor Frederic Scheimer, his wife witness, *ibid.*

——, Martha, of Sebastian and Anna Mary ——, born August 27, baptized October 10, sponsors Philip Branon and Martha McHenry.

Walton, Elizabeth, of John (P.) and Sarah Walton, born November 3, 1769, baptized October 12, sponsor Honora Fitzsimmons.

Reilly, John, of Jeremiah and Anna Reilly, born September 7, baptized October 14, sponsors Timothy Reilly and Joanna Nicols.

Pemberton, William, of William Pemberton (P.) and Bridget Fraser, born October 14, baptized October 16, sponsor Mary Bird.

Macarty, John, of John and Mary Macarty, born August 16, baptized October 18, sponsors James Lecomte and Anna Bijan.

Lewis, Mary, of Manuel and Margaret Lewis, born September 30, baptized October 21, sponsors Anthony Martin and Mary Homes, by Rev. —— Hattersky.

——, Mary, baptized conditionally October 22, sponsor Catharine Keasy; was the wife of Patrick Gallagher.

Muney, [Mooney?] Mary, of Neal and Mary Muney, born January 17, baptized October 26' sponsors John Lery and Dorothy Connor.

Sauerwald, Mark, of John and Magdalen Sauerwald, born October 22, baptized October 28, Mark and Apollonia Wegford witnesses.

Landry, Margaret, of Anthony Landry and Barbara Leblanc, born October 29, baptized October 29, sponsors Charles Braw and Margaret Bijan.

Keanan, John, of Robert and Martha Keanan, born October 28, baptized October 29, sponsor Mary Kennedy.

Sexton, Daniel, of John and Catharine Sexton, born December 1, 1767, baptized October 30, sponsor Barbara Gräss.

Sexton, Matthew, of same parents, born September 18, baptized October 30, sponsor Barbara Schultz.

Anderson, Hugh, of Charles and Joanna Anderson, born October 27, baptized October 30, sponsor Bridget Fraser.

Göck, Matthew, of Laurence and Christina Göck, born September 27, baptized November 1, sponsors Matthew and Anna Mary Miller, at Adam Geiger's.

Miller, Laurence, of Matthew and Anna Mary Miller, born October 2, baptized November 1, sponsors Laurence and Christina Göck, *ibid*.

Harrison, Mary, of Lancelot and Joanna Harrison, born September 25, baptized November 4, sponsors William Nunan and Margaret Kallahan.

Hayes, Anna, wife of John Hayes, baptized November 9, sponsor Anna Glingham.

Forest, Robert, of James and Margaret Forest, born October 25, baptized November 11, sponsors Michael Green and Margaret Veal.

Ridiger, Julia and Margaret (twins), of John and Mary Ridiger, born November 11, baptized November 11, sponsors John and Ottilia Vanie for Julia, Anton Ridiger, Sebastian Vanie and Margaret Vanie for Margaret.

Mitchell, Rachel, adult, baptized November 10, sponsor Christina Mullabi.

Weber, John, of James and Anna Catharine Weber, born October 28, baptized November 18, sponsors John and Anna Catharine Cobole, at Ringwood [N. J.].

Wider, John, of Joseph and Margaret Wider, born August —, baptized November 18, sponsors John Cobole and Eva Fichter, *ibid*.

Murphy, Martin, of Richard and Mary Murphy, born November 15, baptized November 18, sponsor Mary Susanna Walter, witness John Folk, *ibid*.

Butz, John Joseph, of William and Mary Magdalen Butz, born May 6, baptized November 18, sponsors John Mayer and Anna Catharine Cobole, *ibid*.

Wohlleber, Susanna Margaret, of James and Catharine Wohlleber, born October 17, baptized November 18, sponsors Joseph Stecher and Susanna Pfaltzer, witness Nicholas Call, *ibid*.

Call, Mary Eva, of John Nicholas and Anna Margaret Call, born August 3, baptized November 19, sponsors Philip and Eva Fichter, *ibid*.

Conrad, Henry Frederic, of Nicholas (P.) and Mary Conrad, born November 3, baptized November 19, ceremonies supplied, *ibid*.

Schot, Mary Magdalen, of Philip and Mary Catharine Schot, born September 30, baptized November 21, sponsors Martin Bachman and Magdalen Welker, at Charlottenburg [N. J.].

Cobole, Anna Barbara, of Daniel and Mary Ann Cobole, born September 5, baptized November 21, sponsors Bartholomew Cobole and Catharine Welker, *ibid*.

Kean, Anna Eva, of William and Eleanor Kean, born June —, baptized November 22, sponsors James Brown and Eva Jungfleisch, *ibid*.

Butz, Anthony James, of Christian and Catharine (P.) Butz, born November 20, baptized November 25, sponsors Anthony Schumers and Barbara Bachman, *ibid*.

Tscharte, Mary Elizabeth, of Christopher and Mary Dorothy Tscharte, born November 22, baptized December 2, sponsors Sebastian and Elizabeth Seibert.

Hayle, Elizabeth, of Caspar and Elizabeth Hayle, born December 4, baptized December 6, sponsors James and Elizabeth Klein.

Farron, Catharine, of Thomas and Dorothy Mary Farron, born October 24, baptized December 10, sponsors Andrew and Catharine Kessler.

Dionellos, Airis [?], of Alvaro and Susanna Dionellos, born October 22, baptized December 23, sponsors Alfred and Frances Clifton.

Schad, Francis Joseph, of Peter and Mary Elizabeth Schad, born October 24, baptized December 26, sponsors Anthony and Barbara Graff.

Lechler, John, of Anthony and Catharine Lechler, born December 22, baptized December 26, sponsors John Lipp and Magdalen Mayer.

Barry, Elizabeth, of David and Mary Barry, born July 3, baptized December 30, sponsors John and ——— Nickel.

Lynch, Thomas, of Jeremiah and Elizabeth Lynch, born December 21, baptized December 30, sponsors John Brunan and Mary McCan.

Whole number of baptisms—one hundred and fifteen.

REGISTER OF BAPTISMS FOR 1771.

Laride, Anna Margaret, of John and Anna Laride, born January 1, baptized January 1, sponsors Madalino Lequeal (?) and Mary Vincent.

Reuter, Margaret, of ——— and Apollonia Reuter, born December 17, 1770, baptized January 2, sponsor Margaret Späth.

Mahanny, Samuel (a mullatto), of ——— and Catharine Mahanny, born December 10, 1770, baptized January 2, sponsor Mary Bird.

Lennox, John, of John and Margaret Lennox, born December 10, 1770, baptized January 6, sponsors Patrick and Elizabeth Hogan.

Cook, Elizabeth, of Laurence and Catharine Cook, born January 8, baptized January 9, sponsors Dennis Foulon and Elizabeth Carrol.

Byron, Bartholomew, of William and Lydia Byron, born January 4, baptized January 13, sponsor Thomas Burk, Parnell Humphry White witness.

Albrecht, John Adam, of James and Anna Mary Albrecht, born January 13, baptized January 14, sponsors Adam and Mary Göck.

Buttler, Thomas, of Matthew and Sarah Buttler, born January 11, baptized January 27, sponsors Edmund McDonald and Susanna Kearney.

McDermott, Honora Mary, of Dennis and Mary McDermott, born January 21, baptized January 27, sponsors George Coffee and Mary Theresa David.

Sylvester, Elizabeth, of Thomas and Margaret Sylvester, born January 27, baptized January 31, sponsors John Joseph and Anna ———.

Kientz, Joseph, of Joseph and Catharine Kientz, born January 15, baptized February 3, sponsors Joseph and Mary Apollonia Reichart.

Ryan, Michael, of John and Margaret Ryan, born February 10, baptized February 12, sponsors Timothy Carrol and Catharine Casey.

Ring, Mary Magdalen, of John (P.) and Mary Ring, born October —, 1766, baptized February 15, sponsor Mary Magdalen Lohrman.

Griffin, Francis, of James and Elizabeth Griffin, born January 29, baptized February 17, sponsors Francis and Sarah Sohl, at Pikesland [Chester Co., Pa.].

Watts, Christian, of Samuel and Mary Watts, born February 21, baptized February 25, sponsors Edward Hines and Margaret Mullabi.

Schreiner, Joseph, of Anselm and Elizabeth Schreiner, born February 24, baptized March 3, sponsors Joseph and Catharine Eck.

Mannota, Bonaventure, of Ferdinand and Catharine Mannota, born January 25, baptized March 11, sponsors Bonaventure and Venanda Dartoit.

Huber, Michael, of Michael and Hannah Huber, born December 1, 1770, baptized March 17, sponsors Joseph and Regina Mayer, at Pilesgrove [Salem Co., N. J.].

Halder, David, of Peter and Dorothy (P.) Halder, born February 3, baptized March 18, sponsor Henry Geiger, at the glass house.

Veit, Mary Magdalen, of Christian and Barbara Veit, born March 15, baptized March 24, sponsors Caspar and Anna Mary Korn.

Schmid, John, of Patrick and Mary Schmid, born January 29, baptized March 31, sponsors Daniel Fitzpatrick and Eleanor Prior.

Connor, Michael, of Michael and Rosa Connor, born September 17, 1770, baptized April 7, sponsors Timothy and Mary Connor.

Connor, Thomas, of Timothy and Mary Connor, born August, 1770, baptized April 7, sponsors Michael and Rosa Connor.

McDonald, Mary, of Edmund and Margaret McDonald, born March 22, baptized April 7, sponsors Matthew and Rachel Bremich.

Charmelin, Rosanna, of John and Mary Margaret Charmelin, born April 10, 1761, baptized April 10, sponsors Nicholas and Anna Wochman, at Nicholas Wochman's.

Brown, Ann Elizabeth, of William (P.) and Margaret Brown, born May 23, 1770, baptized April 10, sponsors Nicholas and Anna Wochman, *ibid.*

Sauerwald, Daniel, of Michael and Margaret Sauerwald, born April 13, baptized April 14, sponsors John Sauerwald and Catharine Schmid.

Brown, Margaret, of James and Grace Brown, born March 27, baptized April 20, sponsors James Brown and Grace McDead, at Charlottenburg [N. J.].

Harris, Elizabeth, of Samuel Harris and —— Joice, born March 31, 1767, baptized April 21, sponsors Philip McDead and Grace Brown, *ibid.*

Harris, Samuel, of same parents, born May 9, 1769, baptized April 21, sponsors Philip McDead and Grace Brown, *ibid.*

Barr, Mary Ann, of George and Catharine Barr, born December 23, 1770, baptized April 21, sponsors Hugh Dougherty and Margaret Engelhardt, *ibid.*

Fichter, John Nicholas, of Philip and Mary Eva Fichter, born April 14, baptized April 23, sponsors Nicholas Call and Margaret Wider, at Ringwood [N. J.].

Alderman, Peter, of Peter and Mary Alderman, born March 22, baptized April 21, sponsors William and Mary Smith, by Rev. Luke Geisler.

McCan, John, of Gabriel and Mary McCan, born April 21, baptized April 22, sponsors John Stäler and Margaret Wilcox, by the same.

Göck, Paul, of Adam and Mary Göck, born February 14, baptized February 18, sponsors Paul and Anna Christina Essling, by Rev. Robert Harding.

Haas, Mary Martha, of Peter and Elizabeth Haas, born March 27, baptized April 28, sponsors Adam and Martha Poth.

Beats, Mary, of —— and Mary Beats, about 3 years old, baptized April 29, privately.

Smith, Amy [Amata?], of —— and Elizabeth Smith, born January 1, baptized May 1, sponsor Mary Heart.

——, Charlotte, born about January 10, baptized May 1, sponsor Mary Heart.

Honeiker, Barbara, of Mark and Christina Honeiker, born May 1, baptized May 5, sponsors Anthony and Barbara Graf.

Hennings, Henrietta, of Benjamin and Mary Hennings, born February 28, baptized April 12, sponsors John Lehy and Phœbe Pendercrast.

——, Margaret, adult negro, baptized April 22, sponsor Anna ——, a negro, and formerly a slave of N. Meredith (Catholic).

Gallagher, Andrew, of John and Anna Gallagher, born March 30, baptized May 23, sponsors Andrew Gallagher and Elizabeth England, at Chester [Pa.].

Trahan, Mary Margaret, of Charles and Agnes Trahan, born May 30, baptized May 31, sponsors Joseph Trahan and Anna Bijan.

Mayer, Mary Margaret, of Joseph (P.) and Gertrude Mayer, born June 3, baptized June 5, sponsor Tobias Rudolph, Margaret Rudolph witness.

Klein, Frederica Catharine, of James and Elizabeth Klein, born June 5, baptized June 9, sponsors Anthony Frederic Graff and Catharine Schalus.

Welte, George Philip, of Bernard and Mary Welte, born May 29, baptized June 9, sponsors George Philip Kitzinger and Mary Zeigler.

Senner, Barbara, of Francis and Mary Agatha Senner, born June 5, baptized June 10, sponsors Anthony and Barbara Graff.

Becker, Peter, of Bartholomew and Elizabeth Becker, born June 4, baptized June 10, sponsors Peter and Elizabeth Hegner.

Shanon, James, of Quintin (P.) and Mary Shanon, born June 8, baptized June 20, sponsor Peter Haire.

Holt, Anna Theresa, of Abel and Mary Holt, born June 17, baptized June 22, sponsor Lydia Morland.

Mackey, Thomas, of N—— N—— and Catharine Mackey, born June 22, baptized June 25, sponsor Mary Heart.

Babin, Anna Margaret, of Simon and Anna (Trahan) Babin, born July 6, baptized July 6, sponsors Patrick O'Kain and Margaret Bourg.

——— Andrew, born March —, baptized July 13, sponsor Anna Kelty (the child's nurse).

Magill, Sarah, of James and Joanna Magill, born June 5, baptized July 16, sponsor Anna Boyd.

Connor, Eleanor, of David and Mary Connor, born July 11, baptized July 21, sponsors Patrick Connor and Mary Hughs.

———, Mary, of Nicholas and Flora ——— (negroes), born June 9, baptized July 21, sponsor Flora ——— (a slave of Timothy Carroll).

Arachar, Mary Anna, of Louis and Mary Ann (Medec) Arachar, born July 23, baptized July 24, sponsors John Baptist Hubert la Croix and Anna Blanchard.

O'Hara, Catharine, of ——— and Catharine O'Hara, born July 25, baptized July 27, sponsor Elizabeth Laller.

McCauley, Hugh, of John and Margaret McCauley, born July 14, baptized July 28, sponsors John Nowlan and Margaret Veal.

Lery, Cornelius and Henry (twins), of Daniel and Mary Lery, born July 28, baptized July 28, sponsors Timothy and Elizabeth Carrell.

Kramp, Anna, of Valentine and Ottilia Kramp, born July 29, baptized July 30, sponsors Leonard Bremich and Anna Klein.

Henley, Timothy, of Thomas and Rachel Henley, born July 28, baptized July 30, sponsors Peter Byrne and Margaret Conely.

McCarry, William, of J—— and Margaret McCarry, born April 1, baptized August 5, sponsors John Arthur O'Neil and Prudence Wilcox, at Concord [Pa.].

Cassin, James, of Joseph and Elizabeth Cassin, born July 19, baptized August 8, sponsors John Dugan and Mary O'Hara.

Dogherty, Mary Catharine, of Dennis and Margaret Dogherty, born August 12, baptized August 13, sponsors Patrick Dogherty and Barbara Kauffman.

Feinauer, Mary Barbara, of Joseph and Anna Mary Feinauer, born August 10, baptized August 15, sponsors Stephen and Mary Ann Forage.

Dugan, Joseph, of James and Sarah Dugan, born November 18, 1770, baptized August 18, sponsor Eleanor Karker, at Pikesland [Chester Co., Pa.].

Hanley, Elizabeth, of Thomas and Mary Magdalen Hanley, born July 12, baptized August 18, sponsors Frederic Scheimer and Sarah Sohl, *ibid.*

McFall, Sarah, of Patrick and Catharine McFall, born July 8, baptized August 18, sponsors James and Joanna Griffin, *ibid.*

Boosee, Mary, of Moses and Elizabeth Boosee, born August 22, baptized August 25, sponsors Patrick Hogan and Judith Connor.

Roderigo, Emmanuel Joseph, of —— and Joseph Roderigo, 4 years old, baptized August 26, sponsors Emmanuel and Mary Magdalen Ohms.

Miller, Eva, of John and Eva Miller, born August 27, baptized September 1, sponsors George Philip Kitzinger and Eva Catharine Rathaus, by Rev. Robert Harding.

Haug, John, of Simon and Magdalen Haug, born September 6, baptized September 8, sponsors John Thadd and Elizabeth Essling.

Kearns, Henry, of John and Mary Kearns, born August 11, baptized September 19, sponsor Philip Campbell, witness Catharine Jackson.

Hercule, John Lewis, of Francis and Pelagia (Douret) Hercule, born September 20, baptized September 20, sponsors Amandus Douret and Catharine Boudrot, by Rev. Robert Harding.

Morisy, Anna, of Philip and Elizabeth Morisy, born March 22, baptized September 22, sponsors John and Catharine Smith.

O'Hara, Margaret, of Robert Got and Mary O'Hara, born June 27, baptized September 29, sponsor Apollonia Sohl, witness Robert Karker, at Pikesland [Pa.].

Burns, Thomas, of Thomas and Margaret Burns, born August 2, baptized October 3, sponsors Andrew Minchaucer and Joanna Moore.

Metzgar, Thomas, of John and Cecilia Metzgar, born September 25, baptized October 4, sponsors Thomas and Elizabeth Tisdall.

McDonald, Robert, of Alexander and Honora McDonald, born September 24, baptized October 6, sponsors Edward Macoy and Eleanor Smith.

Keys, William, of James and Sarah Keys, born August 17, baptized privately October 6.

Dealy, William, of Charles and Mary Dealy, born January 1, baptized October 7, sponsors John Heling and Joanna Archdeacon.

Townsend, Mary, adult, baptized October 13, sponsor Barbara Graff; was wife to Joseph Preiss, and after her baptism renewed her marriage consent.

Welsh, Mary Magdalen, of Conrad and Elizabeth Welsh, born September 4, baptized October 20, sponsors Thomas Kauffman and Magdalen Butz, at Ringwood [N. J.].

Davis, Margaret, of Walter and Catharine (P.) Davis, born January 3, baptized October 24, sponsors Daniel and Mary Anna Kobole.

Halter, Joseph, of Nicholas and Elizabeth Halter, born June 18, baptized October 26, sponsors Joseph Wingart and Anna Catharine Demuth; ceremonies supplied; at Charlottenburg [N. J.].

Demuth, Anna Elizabeth, of James and Anna Catharine Demuth, born

July 5, baptized October 26, sponsors Ernest Glä and Anna Elizabeth Marian ; ceremonies supplied, *ibid.*

Reider, Anna Elizabeth, of Francis Joseph and Anna Mary Reider, born May 18, baptized October 26, sponsors Joseph Wingart and Anna Elizabeth Marian, *ibid.*

Scholtzer, of Martin and Elizabeth Scholtzer, born October 22, baptized October 26, sponsors Nicholas and Elizabeth Halter, *ibid.*

Harkins, Catharine, of William and Eleanor Harkins, born October 22, baptized November 3, sponsors Moses Boosee and Anna Rush.

Agan [Egan?], John, of William and Eleanor Agan [Egan?], born March 11, baptized November 10, sponsors Peter Agen and Margaret Agen.

Muny, Mary (Meredith), of John and Margaret Muny, born April 8, 1768, baptized November 12, sponsors Nicholas and Anna Wochman, in Burlington Co. [N. J.].

Muny, John, of same parents, born October 31, 1769, baptized November 12, sponsors Nicholas and Anna Wochman, in Burlington Co. [N. J.].

Duffee, John, of John and Anna Duffee, born November 6, baptized November 14, sponsors Tobias and Margaret Rudolph, Elizabeth Ireland witness.

Caspar, Laurence, of Laurence and Margaret Caspar, born November 3, baptized November 18, sponsor Henry Schreiner, at Cohanzey, now Cohansey [Cumberland Co., N. J.].

Bennet, Elizabeth, of John (P.) and Margaret Bennet, born August 31, baptized November 22, sponsor Catharine Schreiber.

Preiss, Samuel, of Joseph Preiss and Mary Townsend, born October 25, baptized November 27, sponsors Anthony and Barbara Graff.

Kneul, George Ernest, of Balthasar and Christina Elizabeth Kneul, born November 20, baptized November 29, sponsors George Ernest and Mary Magdalen Lechler.

Hoffert, Peter, of John and Mary Hoffert, born October 8, baptized December 8, sponsors John Mollan and Margaret Wealin.

Zeis, John Francis, of George and Eva Zeis, born December 1, baptized December 8, sponsors Francis and Margaret Wolf.

Litzelnoder, Michael, of Michael and Margaret Litzelnoder, born December 8, baptized privately, December 10, in vicinity of Philadelphia.

——, Josue, about 10 years old, baptized privately and conditionally at point of death.

Veil, John, of Nicholas and Sophia Veil, born December 14, baptized December 19, sponsors John and Mary Stiller.

Bremich, John Adam, of Matthew and Regina Bremich, born December 17, baptized December 22, sponsors John Adam Bremich and Eva Elizabeth Keil.

Seibert, Elizabeth, of Sebastian and Elizabeth Seibert, born October 10, baptized October 31, sponsor Salome Schwartz, by Rev. Robert Harding.

Crew, Catharine, of Edward and Margaret Crew, born September 7, baptized December 23, sponsors Francis McFarlon and Elizabeth Henry.

Bray, Catharine, of John and Judith Bray, born December 25, baptized December 29, sponsors Patrick Dogherty and Bridget McNamara.

Whole number of baptisms—one hundred and nine.

REGISTER OF BAPTISMS FOR 1772.

Devenach, Elizabeth, of Joseph and Magdalen (Galerm) Devenach, born January 12, baptized January 12, sponsors Charles Vignot and Venanda Dartoit.

McManus, John, of —— and Bridget McManus, born January 17, baptized January 18, sponsor Dennis Clansey.

Häffner, Catharine, of Peter and Eva Häffner, born February 9, 1771, baptized conditionally February 2, sponsors John and Eva Häffner.

Sweeney, James, of Edmund and Elizabeth Sweeney, born November 26, 1771, baptized February 9, sponsors Patrick Dogherty and Anna Morning.

Tisdall, Mary, of Thomas and Elizabeth Tisdall, born February 3, baptized February 9, sponsors Nathaniel Preston and Mary Farrell.

Plusch, Dorothy, of Joseph and Dorothy Plusch, born February 10, baptized February 11, sponsors Caspar and Elizabeth Hayle.

Casey, Dennis, of Dennis and Catharine Casey, born February 8, baptized February 13, sponsors Timothy and Elizabeth Caroll.

Carrol, Margaret, of Daniel and Mary Carrol, born February 5, baptized February 20, sponsor the mother, in default of another.

Champain, Mary Josephine, of Stephen and Mary (Benoit) Champain, born February 20, baptized February 21, sponsors Joseph Ribau and Catharine Boudrot.

Soderick, Elizabeth, of John and Margaret Soderick, 14 years old, baptized February 24, sponsor Margaret Dogherty.

Göck, Anna Mary, of Matthew and Charlotte Göck, born March 4, baptized March 5, sponsors Andrew and Anna Mary Leiphart.

Forage, Josephine Elizabeth, of Stephen and Mary Ann Forage, born February 24, baptized March 8, sponsors Sebastian and Elizabeth Seibert.

Bender, Joanna Elizabeth, of Martin and Christina Bender, born March 8, baptized March 9, sponsors Matthew and Joanna Bender.

Jung, Catharine, of Francis and Catharine Jung, born February 24, baptized March 16, sponsors Anthony and Barbara Blum, near Philadelphia.

Lennox, Margaret, of John and Margaret Lennox, born March 4, baptized March 18, sponsors Francis Farrell and Mary Hogan.

Laviole, Anna, of John and Anna Laviole, born March 21, baptized March 22, sponsors Joseph O'Kain and Margaret Bourg.

Glancey, John, of Dennis and Susanna Glancey, born March 14, baptized March 22, sponsors Patrick Murphy and Esther Eyenson.

Bremegeon, Eleanor, of John and Margaret Bremegeon, born February 22, baptized March 22, sponsors Thomas Quill and Eleanor Smith.

Landry, Elizabeth, of Joseph and Sarah Landry, born March 17, baptized March 22, sponsors Charles and Mary Bowman.

Macalgen, Mary, of Michael and Mary Macalgen, born November 1, 1771, baptized March 29, sponsors Martin and Anna Miller, at Pikesland, [Chester Co., Pa.]

Miller, Anna Mary, of Martin and Anna Miller, born December 18, 1771, baptized March 29, sponsors Bernard Brown and Margaret Sohl, *ibid*.

Tims, Anna, of Henry and Anna Tims, born January 7, baptized March 30, sponsor Francis Sohl, in Chester Co. [Pa.].

Graff, Joseph, of Anthony and Barbara Graff, born April 4, baptized April 12, sponsors Joseph Kaufman and Catharine Spengler.

Will, Elizabeth, of Philip and Elizabeth Will, born April 9, baptized April 12, sponsors John Späth and Anna Hewson.

Bucher, Catharine Elizabeth, of John and Anna Catharine Bucher, born January 18, baptized April 15, sponsors Bartholomew and Catharine Elizabeth Becker.

Hardnet, Elizabeth, of James and Joanna Hardnet, born January 3, baptized April 19, sponsor Samuel Griffin.

O'Neil, Elizabeth, of Arthur John and Rose O'Neil, born November 6, 1771, baptized April 19, sponsors John Fagan and Anna Rush.

Aman, Leonard, of Anthony and Sarah Aman, born September 20, 1771, baptized April 20, sponsors Leonard Bremich and Magdalen Mayer.

Magill, John, of Peter and Barbara Magill, born April 2, baptized April 23, sponsors Patrick Barret and Mary Geiger, at Pilesgrove [Salem Co., N. J.].

Geiger, Barbara, of Henry and Barbara Geiger, born November 26, 1771, baptized April 23, sponsors Adam and Margaret Geiger, *ibid*.

Herberger, Mary Ottilia, of Peter and Mary Herberger, born February 14, baptized April 26, sponsors John and Mary Ottilia Manderfeld.

Chambers, John, of John and Eleanor Chambers, born November 28, 1771, baptized April 26, sponsors Thomas Kearns and Susanna Kearney.

O'Brien, Margaret, of Thomas and Judith O'Brien, born April 16, baptized April 26, sponsor Sarah Tims.

Maconvill, Margaret, of Anthony and Rosa Maconvill, born April 20, baptized April 26, sponsors John Magefran and Mary Corcoran.

Macanna, Thomas, of John and Sarah Macanna, born October 24, 1771, baptized May 1, sponsors James Weiseburger and Sarah Sohl, at Pikesland [Chester Co., Pa.].

Hertz, Michael, of John and Barbara Hertz, born May 5, baptized May 6, sponsors Michael and Margaret Sauerwald.

Haynes, Philip, of Philip and Elizabeth Haynes, born April 13, baptized May 9, sponsors Christopher Kelty and Joanna Archdeacon.

Powel, John, of —— and Anna Powel, born January 29, baptized May 12, sponsors John and Elizabeth Hanley.

Applegate, Mary, of Benjamin and Elizabeth Applegate, born April 5, baptized May 17, sponsor Mary Brown.

Ryan, Michael, of Philip and Anna Ryan, born April 20, baptized May 18, sponsors Michael and Joanna Robeson.

Devlin, Anna, of Henry Devlin and Mary Maher, born April 22, baptized May 19, sponsor John Steling.

North, Thomas, of Thomas and Margaret North, born February 16, baptized May 21, sponsors Brian and Mary O'Hara.

Bachman, Francis Anthony, of Martin and Anna Barbara Bachman, born April 20, baptized May 28, sponsors Francis Anthony and Anna Catharine Zech, at Charlottenburg [N. J.].

Burns, Martha, of Laghlin and Mary Burns, born November 8, 1771 baptized May 28, sponsors James Marniny and Eleanor Callaghan, *ibid.*

Coble, Anna Elizabeth, of John and Catharine Coble, born April 14, baptized May 31, sponsors Daniel Coble and Anna Catharine Welker, at Ringwood [Passaic Co., N. J.].

Butz, John Henry, of William and Mary Magdalen Butz, born March 25, baptized May 31, sponsors John Henry Ells and Elizabeth Welsch, *ibid.*

Buttler, Hannah, adult, baptized May 31, sponsor Judy Power, *ibid.*

Karker, Peter, of Anthony and Mary Karker, born June 15, 1770, baptized May 31, sponsors James and Elizabeth Walls, *ibid.*

Maginnis, John Nicholas, of Edward and Mary Maginnis, born March 15, baptized May 31, sponsors Nicholas and Anna Margaret Call, *ibid.*

Jamison, Henry, of John and Mary Jamison, born March 4, baptized privately May 31, sponsor Daniel Coble, *ibid.*

Campbel, Joanna, of Peter (P.) and Anna Campbel, born June 5, baptized June 8, sponsors Timothy McCanlas and Mary Flin.

Lechler, Mary Magdalen, of Anthony and Mary Lechler, born June 3, baptized June 8, sponsors Peter and Mary Magdalen Regimenter.

Dartoit, Bonaventure and Christopher (twins), of Bonaventure and Venanda Dartoit, born June 11, baptized June 11, sponsors Christopher Schultz, Antonia Swaine and Barbara Schultz.

McCarty, Jeremiah, of Daniel and Honora McCarty, born May 18, baptized June 18, sponsor Catharine Boudrot.

Kappel, Elizabeth Margaret, of Nicholas and Magdalen Kappel, born

June 17. baptized June 18, sponsors Matthew and Margaret Elizabeth Bremich.

——, Anna, of —— and Hannah ——, born June 16, baptized June 18, sponsor Anna Fichtler; the mother was a slave of Robert White.

Magill, Peter, of John and Catharine Magill, born February 18, baptized June 21, sponsors Edward Coleman and Barbara Magill, at Pilesgrove [Salem Co., N. J.].

Becker, Michael, of John and Barbara Becker, born May 24, baptized June 21, sponsors Michael and Hannah Huber, *ibia*.

Morris, Joanna and Jane, of —— Morris and —— Bensh, sisters (adults), baptized June 21, sponsors Adam and Margaret Geiger, *ibid*.

Kean, Barnabas, of Francis and Bridget Kean, born September 20, baptized privately June 22.

Savoy, Mary Margaret, of Peter and Mary (Lequeul) Savoy, born June 24, baptized conditionally June 25, sponsors James Forester and Margaret Lequeul.

Walter, John George, of James and Frances Walter, born February 18, baptized June 28, sponsors Peter Eimold and Sarah Sohl, at Pikesland [Chester Co., Pa.].

Scheimer, John Bernard, of Frederic and Magdalen Scheimer, born May 30, baptized June 28, sponsors John Bernard Brow and Catharine Weisenberger, *ibid*.

Jones, Daniel, of John and Mary (Lery) Jones, born January 29, baptized June 28, sponsors Edward Brady and Mary Full, *ibid*.

O'Hara, Charles and Elizabeth (twins), of Brian and Mary O'Hara, born July 3, baptized privately July 3.

——, John, of parents unknown, about 2½ years old, baptized July 7, sponsor John Cahil.

——, John, of —— and Margaret, free negroes, born July 5, baptized July 7, sponsor Anna (a negro).

Viel, Rudolph, of Paul and Mary Viel, born July 9, baptized July 12, sponsors Rudolph and Sibylla Viel.

Swiney, Mary, of Patrick and Catharine (Hurley) Swiney, born June 28, baptized July 12, sponsors Philip Neal and Mary Fitzgerald.

Babin, Isabella Josephine, of Simon and Anna (Trahan) Babin, born July 13, baptized July 14, sponsors John Baptist O'Kain and Josephine Daroit.

Foy, Abigail, of Matthew and Mary Foy, born January —, baptized July 17, sponsors Michael Murphy and Anna McDonald.

Page, Henry, of William and Elizabeth Page, born July 14, baptized July 18, sponsors Walter Fitzgerald and Mary Callaghan.

Schreiner, Anna Christina, of Anselm and Elizabeth Schreiner, born July 21, baptized July 23, sponsors Paul and Christina Essling.

Winter, Elizabeth Sarah, of Patrick and Eleanor Winter, born July 18, baptized July 26, sponsors George and Eleanor Conely.

Maly, John, of Jeremiah and Eleanor (P.) Maly, born August 7, 1771, baptized July 26, sponsor Miles Welsh.

Westermayer, Mary Magdalen, of John and Ottilia Westermayer, born about March, baptized August 9, sponsors Sebastian and Cunegunda Hoffman.

Heuson, Anna, of John and —— Heuson, born August 4, baptized August 12, sponsors the minister and the maternal grandmother, Catharine Magg witness.

McHughin, Sarah, of John and Martha McHughin, born April 1, baptized August 16, sponsor Eleanor ——, at Pilesgrove [Salem, Co., N. J.].

Thurnbach, John, of Christian and Susanna Catharine Thurnbach, born Aug. 4, baptized Aug. 16, sponsors Henry and Barbara Geiger, *ibid.*

Sauerwald, Catharine, of Michael and Margaret Sauerwald, born August 21, baptized August 22, sponsors Anthony and Barbara Gross.

Hoffman, Michael, of John and Christina (P.) Hoffman, born August 19, baptized August 25, sponsors Michael and Walburga Bremich, near Philadelphia.

Schilling, Stephen, of Philip and Eva Schilling, born August 26, baptized September 4, sponsors Stephen, Jr., and Mary Ann Forage.

Roth, Nicholas John, of —— and —— Roth, born August 31, baptized September 6, sponsors Nicholas and Anna Schnaller.

McCunigham, Mary, of —— and Jemima McCunigham, born July 9, baptized September 8, sponsor Mary Heart.

Borris, Anna, of Thomas and Margaret Borris, born July 30, baptized September 8, sponsor Mary Heart.

Magarry, John, of —— and Catharine Magarry, born August 12, baptized September 8, sponsor Margaret Borris.

Senner, Mary Ann, of Francis and Anna Mary Senner, born September 8, baptized September 11, sponsors James Klein and Anna Klein.

Schlotz, Susanna Catharine, of Philip and Susanna Schlotz, born March 11, baptized September 15, sponsor Catharine Spengler.

Springer, Catharine, of John and Mary Springer, born September 19, baptized September 20, sponsors Nicholas Essling and Catharine Miller.

Williams, Peter Benjamin, of Joseph and Eleanor Williams, born June 15, baptized September 24, sponsor Mary Rosa Jaquier, witness Mary Mosel.

Cahil, Peter, of Peter and Elizabeth Cahil, born October 15, 1771, baptized September 25, sponsors Arthur and Elizabeth Donoho.

Meade, Henrietta Constance, of George and Henrietta (P.) Meade, born August 15, baptized September 27, sponsors Thomas and Catharine Fitzsimmons.

Lone, Mary, of Henry and Catharine Lone, born September 27, baptized October 4, sponsors Barnaby Higgins and Catharine Ragan.

——, Anna, born August 9, baptized October 6, sponsor James Gallagher, witness Frances Yorkson.

Mignot, Elizabeth, of Charles and Pelagia (Galerm) Mignot, born October 8, baptized October 8, sponsors Bonaventure and Venanda Dartoit.

Weidman, Christian, of John and Barbara Weidman, born October —, 176-, baptized October 14, sponsors Philip Schilling and Tobias Rudolph, near Philadelphia.

Weidman, Joseph, of same parents, born October —, 176-, baptized October 14, sponsors Philip Schilling and Tobias Rudolph, *ibid.*

Weidman, William, of same parents, born October —, 176-, baptized October 14, sponsors Philip Schilling and Tobias Rudolph, *ibid.*

Weidman, Mary Magdalen, of same parents, born October —, 177-, baptized October 14, sponsors Philip Schilling and Tobias Rudolph, *ibid.*

Hanley, Timothy, of John and Elizabeth Hanley, born October 23, baptized November 1, sponsors Jeremiah Lynch and Lydia Byron.

Krombel, Tobias, of Philip and Mary Krombel, born November 1, baptized November 2, sponsor Tobias Rudolph, witness Mary Margaret Rudolph.

Holms, Mary, of Emmanuel and Mary Holms, born November 3, baptized November 5, sponsors Francis Varrel and Catharine Keasey.

Schöne, Laurence, of Laurence and Magdalen Schöne, born November 4, baptized November 5, sponsors Bartholomew Becker and Barbara Graff.

Ledermann, Peter, of John and Mary Catharine Ledermann, born October 30, baptized November 8, sponsors Adam Mayer and Magdalen Pigmenter.

Grapf, Nicholas, of Peter and Claudina Grapf, born October 20, baptized November 10, sponsors Nicholas and Alberta Carty, at Haycock [Bucks Co., Pa.].

Wider, John David, of Joseph and Margaret Wider, born July 26, baptized November 15, sponsors David Fechter and Mary Ann Walter, at Ringwood [Passaic Co., N. J.].

Murphy, Mary, of Richard and Mary Murphy, born September 3, baptized November 16, sponsors Thomas Fowler and Mary Susanna Walter, *ibid.*

Dentz, Joseph, of Charles and Mary Dentz, born September —, 1764, baptized November 18, sponsors Joseph and Margaret Wider, at Longpond.

Dentz, Anna Catharine Magdalen, of same parents, born September —, 1770, baptized November 18, sponsors John and Catharine Cobole, *ibid.*

Dentz, Dominic, of same parents, born October 26, baptized November 18, sponsors Dominic Andler and Catharine Zech, *ibid.*

Weber, John Bartholomew, of James and Anna Catharine Weber, born

October 8, baptized November 18, sponsors Daniel Cobole (for Bartholomew Cobole) and Elizabeth Welsh, *ibid.*

Navil, Elizabeth, of John and Anna Navil, 14 years old, baptized November 18, sponsors Richard Murphy and Margaret Wider, *ibid.*

Sheridan, William, of William and Bridget Sheridan, born March 14, 1767, baptized November 19, sponsors Edward Cahel and Anna Jung, *ibid.*

Schott, Anthony, of Philip and Catharine Schott, born August 30, baptized November 20, sponsors Anthony Schumers and Catharine Demuth, at Charlottenburg [N. J.].

Miller, Anna Margaret, of Matthew and Anna Mary Miller, born November 8, baptized December 3, sponsors Laurence and Margaret Caspar, at Cohanzey [Cumberland Co., N. J.].

Göck, Mary, of Laurence and Christina Göck, born November 17, baptized December 3, sponsors David Göck and Mary Geiger.

Fitzgerald, Thomas, of Thomas and Mary Fitzgerald, born November 5, baptized December 6, sponsors Thomas Cunningham and Eleanor Burk.

Stähler, Caspar, of John and Anna Mary Stähler, born December 4, baptized December 6, sponsors Gabriel Macan and Barbara Stähler.

Hayle, Barbara, of Caspar and Elizabeth Hayle, born December 4, baptised December 7, sponsors Joseph and Dorothy Plusch.

Lenard, Margaret and Anna (twins), of Patrick and Margaret Lenard, born December 11, baptised December 11, sponsors Christopher O'Brien and Elizabeth Murray.

Grosley, John, of ———— ———— and Susanna Grosley, born September —, baptized December 13, sponsors James and Catharine Nagel.

Nelson, James, of William and Mary Nelson, born November 27, 1769, baptized December 14, sponsor John Bray, witness Anna Coghran.

Crene, John, of Timothy and Mary Crene, born May 6, 1771, baptized December 20, sponsors Edward Crene and Margaret Agan.

Macabe, Mary, baptized December 20, sponsor Margaret Agan.

Dewitter, Anna Catharine, of ———— and Margaret Dewitter, born December 5, baptized December 20, sponsors Philip and Anna Catharine Donely.

Matson, Mary, adult, baptized December 21, sponsors Moses and Elizabeth Boosee.

Schneider, Mary Barbara, of John George and Elizabeth Schneider, born December 14, baptized December 24, sponsors Henry and Barbara Schneider, near Philadelphia.

Smith, Mary, of Patrick and Mary Smith, born October 4, baptized December 25, sponsor John Heling.

Finey, John, of John and Mary Finey, born November 25, baptized December 27, sponsors John Faran and Bridget Dun.

Ryan, John, of John and Margaret Ryan, born December 28, baptized December 28, sponsors John White and Elizabeth Carrol.

Whole number of baptisms—one hundred and thirty-four.

REGISTER OF BAPTISMS FOR 1773.

. Gordon, Abraham, of William and Barbara Gordon, born January 1, baptized January 3, sponsors John Maginnis and Susanna Kearney.

Cäffert, Richard, of Richard and Elizabeth Cäffert, born October 27, 1772, baptized January 5, sponsor Anna Makra.

Brooks, Anna, of Joseph and Anna Brooks, born December 27, 1772, baptized February 28, sponsor Anna Heusin.

Philips, George Conrad, of John and Elizabeth Philips, born February 13, baptized February 28, sponsors George Kleiderle and Catharine Schäffer.

Stahler, Elizabeth, of John and Christina Stahler, born February 23, baptized February 28, sponsors Thomas and Elizabeth Tisdall.

Brooks, John, of Thomas and Mary Brooks, born August 10, 1769, baptized privately March 2.

Mathes, William, of John (P.) and Jane Mathes, born March 11, 1772, baptized privately March 2.

——, John Francis, of unknown parents, born April 10, 1772, baptized March 2, sponsor Mary Heart.

Schneider, Mary Barbara, of Henry and Barbara Schneider, born March 3, baptized March 7, sponsors George Ernest and Mary Magdalen Lechler.

Stafford, John, of James and Mary Stafford, born January 15, baptized March 7, sponsors Patrick Jennan and Bridget McNamara.

Campbell, John, of Barnaby (P.) and Mary Campbell, born February 27, baptized March 8, sponsor Eleanor McCarty.

Ware, Elizabeth, of Thomas and —— Ware, born May 19, 1772, baptized March 9, sponsor Anna Kelly.

Griffin, Eleanor, of Thomas and Jane Griffin, born December 27, 1772, baptized March 21, sponsors Michael Spelley and Catharine Weisenburger, at Pikesland [Chester Co., Pa.].

Horn, Mary Magdalen, of Henry and Justina Horn, born March 24, baptized March 26, sponsors George Ernest and Mary Magdalen Lechler.

Huber, William, of Michael and Hannah Huber, born December 16, 1772, baptized March 28, sponsors Laurence and Margaret Casper, at Pilesgrove [Salem Co., N. J.].

Mayer, Regina, of Joseph and Jane Mayer, born January —, baptized March 28, sponsors Henry Geiger and Mary Ann Halder, *ibid.*

Coyle, Michael, of John and Anna Coyle, born April 2, baptized April 4, sponsors James Gallagher, Mary Madden and Catharine Cook, witness Barnaby Coil.

Wurtzer, Mary Magdalen, of George and Eva Wurtzer, born January 28, baptized April 12, sponsors George Ernest and Mary Magdalen Lechler.

Kitzinger, Philippina, of Philip and Judith Kitzinger, born April 10, baptized April 12, sponsors John and Philippina Lipp.

Waas, Francis Joseph, of Sebastian and Anna Mary Waas, born November 3, 1772, baptized April 12, sponsors Francis and Agatha Senner.

McDonald, Anna, of Edmund and Margaret McDonald, born April 16, baptized April 25, sponsors John Brannon and Catharine Atkinson.

Ridiger, Anna Mary, of John and Margaret Ridiger, born April 19, baptized April 25, sponsors John Vanie and Anna Mary Nagel.

McLoughlin, Elizabeth, of William and Mary McLoughlin, born November 25, 1772, baptized April 30, sponsor Phoebe Pendergast.

McCarty, Thomas and William (twins), of —— and Margaret McCarty, born April 30, baptized privately April 30, sponsor Mary Carty.

Würth, Philip James, of Joseph and Barbara Würth, born April 30, baptized May 1, sponsor Catharine Schmid.

Fitzpatrick, John, of John and Honora Fitzpatrick, born April 26, baptized May 2, sponsors Dennis Glansey and Mary Welsh.

Winters, William, of —— —— and Mary Winters, born September 11, 1772, baptized privately May 4, sponsor Eleanor Conneley.

Macatee, Elizabeth, of —— and Eleanor Macatee, born March 27, baptized May 5, sponsor Elizabeth Makenley witness, Thomas Carfol.

Späth, John Christopher, of John and Margaret Späth, born May 5, baptized May 9, sponsors Christopher and Catharine Frances Wagner.

[Zig?], Miriam Catharine, of John George (P.) and Gertrude Sig [Zig?], born January 31, baptized May 14; ceremonies supplied; in New Jersey.

Cobole, Anna Eva, of David and Mary Cobole, born March 31, baptized May 15, sponsors Nicholas and Anna Eva Jungfleisch.

Reider, Daniel, of Francis Joseph and Anna Mary Reider, born May 12, baptized May 15, sponsors Daniel Cobole and Barbara Welker.

Grown, John, of James Grown and —— ——, born February 3, baptized May 16, sponsors Edward McCoughlin and Catharine Mentzebrach.

Cahil, Mary Ann, of Thomas and Eleanor Cahil, born April 17, baptized May 19, sponsors Bartholomew Cobole and Mary Ann Walter.

Walter, Francis, of John and Rebecca Walter, baptized May 20, sponsors Francis Kirk and Susanna Doyle.

Wex, James, about 18 years old, baptized May 20, sponsors James Walter and Margaret Wider.

Shaw, James, of Moses and Bridget Shaw, born July 21, 1771, baptized May 21, sponsors Patrick Howlan and Elizabeth Ruger.

Flemming, Edward, of Michael and Abigail Flemming, born January 17, baptized May 23, sponsors Francis Dealy and Margaret Engelhard.

Williams, Robert, of George and Margaret Williams, born April 13, 1771, baptized May 23, sponsors Patrick Grin and Anna Manan.

Wingart, Anna Catharine, of John and Anna Elizabeth Wingart, born April 21, baptized May 23, sponsors Hubert Marian and Catharine Demuth.

Fichter, Anna Margaret, of Philip and Mary Eva Fichter, born January 14, baptized May 23, sponsors Anthony Schumers and Mary Engelhard.

Hanlon, Elizabeth, of ——— and Martha Hanlon, born February —, baptized May 29, sponsor Catharine Gordon.

Price, Hannah, adult, baptized June 4, sponsors James and Elizabeth Boosee ; Hannah was wife of Michael Ryan.

Fitzwater, Elizabeth Magdalen, adult, baptized June 9, sponsor Catharine Gatringer.

Rittisheim, Anna Sarah, of John and Catharine Rittisheim, born May 16, baptized June 16, sponsors Anthony and Anna Sarah Aman.

Dugan, Rebecca, of James and Sarah Dugan, born February 18, baptized June 20, sponsors Francis and Sarah Sohl, at Pikesland [Chester Co., Pa.].

Griffin, Mary, of James and Elizabeth Griffin, born May 14, baptized June 20, sponsors Bartholomew Tool and Apollonia Sohl, *ibid.*

Strack, Daniel, of William and Elizabeth Strack, born June 16, baptized June 21, sponsors Daniel and Annie Dogherty, while traveling.

Benner, Matthew, of Martin and Christina Benner, born June 25, baptized June 27, sponsors Henry and Joanna Benner.

Watts, Elizabeth, of Samuel and Mary Watts, born June 3, baptized June 27, sponsors Francis Mullabi and Elizabeth Murray.

Regimenter, Peter, of Peter and Mary Magdalen Regimenter, born June 28, baptized June 29, ssponsor Peter Eck.

Macan, Mary, of Gabriel and Mary Macan, born June 21, baptized July 3, sponsors Magnus Sonhollen and Margaret Lynch.

Sauerwald, Laurence, of John and Magdalen Sauerwald, born June 26, baptized July 4, sponsors Laurence and Magdalen Schönus.

Sharp, Robert, of Robert and Mary Sharp, born June 30, baptized July 4, sponsors James Mullen and Catharine Dardis.

Savoy, Anna Josephine, of Peter and Mary Savoy, born July 9, baptized July 9, sponsors John Gatringer and Margaret Josephine Blanchard.

Baxter, John, of John (P.) and Eleanor Baxter, born July 9, baptized July 10, sponsor Elizabeth Carrol.

Hendrehan, John, of Sylvester and Eleanor (McCarty) Hendrehan, born June 26, baptized July 11, sponsors Abraham McCoy and Mary Murphy.

Boosee, Mary Magdalen, of Moses and Elizabeth [Bussey?] Boosee, born July 9, baptized July 12, sponsors John Aitkins and Barbara Graff.

McCarty, Margaret, of Nicholas and Elizabeth McCarty, born February 21, baptized July 12, sponsors William and Lydia Biron.

O'Hara, Charles, of Brian and Mary O'Hara, born June 24, baptized July 12, sponsors Michael Clark and Margaret Dougherty.

Harity, James, of Connel and Catharine Harity, born July 14, baptized July 16, sponsors Edward Freal and Elizabeth Parker.

Burns, Edward, of Edward and Alice Burns, born March 19, 1772, baptized July 17, sponsor Matthew Foy.

Korn, John Michael, of Caspar and Anna Mary Korn, born January 16, baptized July 21, sponsors John and Catharine Haug.

Tally, Mary Ann, of ——— and Catharine Tally, 6 years old, baptized July 21, sponsor Catharine Tally; a slave of Catharine Tally.

Low, Elizabeth, of Robert and Elizabeth Low, born October 14, 1762, baptized July 25, sponsor Lydia Biron.

Brothers, Susanna, of William and Eleanor Brothers, born April 9, 1772, baptized August 4, sponsors Timothy McAulif and Hannah Clark.

Albrecht, Joseph, of James and Anna Mary Albrecht, born August 4, baptized August 8, sponsors Joseph and Mary Springer.

Coleman, Daniel, of Edward and Catharine Coleman, born April 10, baptized August 10, sponsors John and Eleanor Connor, at Pilesgrove [Salem Co., N. J.].

Connor, Susanna, of Timothy and Mary Connor, born May 31, 1770, baptized August 20, sponsor Elizabeth Bauman.

Hoffman, George Ernest, of Sebastian and Cunegunda Hoffman, born August 12, baptized August 22, sponsors George Ernest and Magdalen Lechler.

Hoy, John, of John and Catharine Hoy, born January —, 1763, baptized conditionally August 26, sponsors Patrick and Rosa Kearns, in Burlington County, N. J.

Hoy, Margaret, of same parents, born May —, 1767, baptized conditionally August 26, same sponsors, *ibid.*

Hoy, John, of same parents, born August 17, 1770, baptized conditionally August 26, same sponsors, *ibid.*

Ryan, Mary, of James and Sarah Ryan, born June 8, 1765, baptized conditionally August 26, sponsors John and Catharine Hoy, *ibid.*

Agan [Egan?], William, of William and Eleanor Agan [Egan?], born May 29, baptized August 26, sponsors John Davelin and Anna Kearns, *ibid.*

Bradshaw, Elizabeth, of John and Hannah Bradshaw, born October —, 1755, baptized conditionally August 26, sponsors John and Catharine Hoyle, *ibid.*

Ferri, Mary, of James and Eleanor Ferri, born July 14, baptized August 29, sponsor Daniel Mignati, witness Mary (his wife).

Mignati, Sarah, of Daniel and Mary Mignati, born August 29, sponsor James Ferri, witness Eleanor (his wife).

Dogherty, Letitia, of George and Mary Dogherty, born September 2, baptized September 2, sponsors Dennis and Margaret Dogherty.

Clarke, Sarah, of Agno and Catharine (Mahany) Clarke, born August 30, baptized September 3, sponsor Mary Heart.

Barnville, John, of Matthew and Isabella Barnville, born August 22, baptized September 5, sponsors John Kirk and Anna Kallahan.

Faran, Margaret, of John and Mary Faran, born September 2, baptized September 5, sponsor John McKeaver, witness Mary Dun.

Coffey, Mary Ann, of George and Catharine Coffey, born August 16, baptized September 5, sponsors Nicholas and Anna Wochman.

Becker, Laurence, of Bartholomew and Catharine Elizabeth Becker, born August 31, baptized September 5, sponsors Laurence and Mary Magdalen Schöne.

Wilcox, Elizabeth, of John and Rebecca Wilcox, born March 15, baptized September 5, sponsor Rebecca Wilcox.

Schreiner, Anna Christina, of Anselm and Elizabeth Schreiner, born August 29, baptized September 5, sponsors Paul and Christina Essling.

Ruck, William, of Samuel (P.) and Christina Ruck, born June 24, baptized September 7, sponsors Anthony and Catharine Lechler.

Cunningham, Anna, of James and Eleanor Cunningham, born September 9, baptized September 9, sponsor Joseph Ebair.

Conelly, Eleanor, of John and Rebecca Conelly, born September 2, baptized September 12, sponsors Timothy Donoho and Rachel Hanly.

Davis, Rebecca, of ——— and Hannah Davis, born March 15, baptized September 19, sponsors Owen Kelty and Christina Göck, at Pilesgrove [Salem Co., N. J.].

Hans, Andrew, of Christopher and Catharine (Vankeisen) Hans, born July 29, baptized September 20, sponsor Alfred Clifton, witness Mary Henry.

Clear, Robert, of Thomas and Catherine Clear, born September 21, baptized September 22, sponsor Anthony Schneider, witness Martha Bass.

Dogherty, John, of George and Anna Dogherty, born August 19, baptized September 22, sponsors John Gatringer and Catharine Veil.

Huskins, Anna, of Richard and Hannah (Kean) Huskins, born August 10, baptized September 26, sponsors Martin and Anna Miller, at Pikesland [Chester Co., Pa.].

Anderson, Margaret, of John and Elizabeth Anderson, born September 5, baptized October 7, sponsors Caspar and Elizabeth Hayle.

Tisdall, Catharine, of Thomas and Elizabeth Tisdall, born October 8, baptized October 10, sponsors Stephen and Catharine Bardin.

Varrel, Matthew, of Francis and Elizabeth Varrel, born February 22, baptized October 10, sponsors Emmanuel and Mary Ohms.

Stalter, Martin, of Nicholas and Elizabeth Stalter, born May 24, baptized

October 21, sponsor Martin Bachman; ceremonies supplied; at Charlottenburg [N. J.].

McDonald, James, of John and Anna McDonald, born June 23, baptized October 23, sponsors James and Anna Catharine Weber, at Long-pond.

Simons, James Francis Patrick, of James and Mary Simons, born October 10, baptized October 24, sponsors Francis and Hannah Doyle.

Monck, John, of John and Margaret Monck, born September 3, baptized October 24, sponsors John Rüger and Bridget Shaw.

Walker, William, of Samuel and Mary Walker, born April 20, baptized October 24, sponsors Elizabeth Walle, William Ledgert witness.

May, Elizabeth, of James and Christina (Keiner) May, born December 12, 1770, baptized conditionally October 24, sponsor Anthony May, at Ringwood [N. J.].

Sealy, William, of Michael and Elizabeth Sealy, born December 18, 1772, baptized privately October 25, sponsor Anna Mary Merschler.

Gibson, Mary, adult, baptized October 13, sponsor Barbara Kaufman.

Schilling, John Theodore, of Philip and Eva Schilling, born November 6, baptized November 7, sponsor John Rudolph, Mary Margaret Rudolph witness.

Halfpenny, Anne, of Thomas and Margaret Halfpenny, born October 25, baptized November 7, sponsors John Finn and Mary McCarty (for her mother, Elizabeth McCarty).

Motley, Elizabeth, of Walter and Mary Motley, born August 4, baptized November 8, sponsors John Hanna and Jane Motley.

Motley, Mary, wife of Walter Motley, baptized November 8 ; the minister was sponsor.

Lynch, Thomas, of Jeremiah and Elizabeth Lynch, born November 12, baptized November 21, sponsors John Hanley and Margaret Trahan.

Cronin, Sarah, of James and Bridget Cronin, born June —, baptized November 25, sponsor John Cronin.

Kauffman, Margaret, of Joseph and Barbara Kauffman, born November 24, baptized November 25, sponsors Dennis and Margaret Dogherty.

Caspar, Henry, of Laurence and Margaret Caspar, born October 27, baptized November 30, sponsors Henry and Barbara Geiger, at Pilesgrove [Salem Co., N. J.].

Geiger, Henry, of Henry and Barbara Geiger, born October 14, baptized November 30, sponsors Simon Geiger and Susanna Thurnbach, *ibid.*

White, John, of John and Rachel White, born November 21, baptized December 12, sponsors Thomas Donaho and Sarah Greswold.

Trim, Martin, of James and Mary Elizabeth Trim, born December 5, baptized December 12, sponsors Martin Wiber and Catharine Wagner.

Haug, Mary Margaret, of John and Catharine Haug, born November 28, baptized December 12, sponsor John Santoz, Margaret Santoz witness.

Price, John, of John and Mary Price, born November 29, baptized December 14, sponsors John Lahy and Elizabeth Fitzpatrick.

Bamfeils, Catharine Elizabeth, of Basil (P.) and Anna (Broc) Bamfeils, born December 2, baptized December 19, sponsors Bonaventure Dartoit and Catharine Boudrot.

Hayle, James, of Caspar and Elizabeth Hayle, born December 18, baptized December 19, sponsors James Klein and Anna Martin, near Philadelphia.

Lechler, Mary Magdalen, of Anthony and Catharine Lechler, born December 19, baptized December 21, sponsors John and Mary Honecker.

Gallagher, Prudence, of John and Anna Gallagher, born November 12, baptized December 25, sponsors James Gallagher and Mary Cotringer.

Aman, Anna Catharine, of Anthony and Sarah Aman, born December 18, baptized December 26, sponsors Peter Bremich and Anna Catharine Waltrich.

Whole number of baptisms—one hundred and twenty-four.

REGISTER OF BAPTISMS FOR 1774.

Murry, Sarah, of Hugh and Eleanor Murry, born December 17, 1773, baptized January 1, sponsors Maurice Kean and Margaret Murry.

Adams, Anna, of John and Grace Adams, born March 13, 1773, baptised January 4, sponsors Thomas and Eleanor Carrol.

Essling, Laurence, of Peter and Mary Essling, born January 1, baptized January 6, sponsor Mary Grosin.

Roberts, Joseph, of Joseph and Anna Roberts, born January 4, baptized January 6, sponsors Peter Field and Margaret Nihil.

Bauman, Joseph, of George and Elizabeth Bauman, born January 8, baptized January 8, sponsors Augustine and Margaret Dreun.

Lort, Anna, of Isaac and Anna Lort, born January 9, baptized January 16, sponsors Bernard Fearis and Elizabeth Greswold.

Bremich, Joanna, of Leonard and Margaret Bremich, born January 19, baptized January 22, sponsors John Hearty and Joanna Nickols.

French, Dominic, of Dominic and Margaret French, born January 14, 1771, baptized January 23, sponsor Robert Waters, Margaret Catiere witness.

Mulhollin, Henry, of Philip and Elizabeth Mulhollin, born August 17, 1769, baptized January 30, sponsor Philip Campbel.

Mulhollin, Edward, of same parents, born November 12, 1773, baptized January 30, sponsor Philip Campbel.

Mulhollin, Mary, of same parents, born December 16, 1771, baptized January 30, sponsor Philip Campbel.

Haug, Elizabeth, of Simon and Mary Magdalen Haug, born January 27, baptized January 30, sponsors John Tart and Elizabeth Esling.

Graff, Mary, of Anthony and Barbara Graff, born January 27, baptized January 31, sponsors Bryan O'Hara and Catharine Spengler.

Hughin, Catharine, of William and Catharine Hughin, born November 14, 1773, baptized February 5, sponsor Margaret McCarty.

O'Neil, John, of Barnaby and Barbara O'Neil, born December 2, 1773, baptized privately February 6.

Viel, Joseph, of Paul and Mary Viel, born February 16, baptized February 20, sponsors Joseph and Anna Mary Rübel.

Davern, Honora, of William and Rosa Davern, born December 11, 1773, baptized February 23, sponsors James Magee and Anna Hussy.

La Riole, Catharine, of John and Anna la Riole, born February 25, baptized conditionally February 27, sponsors Dennis and Catharine Casey.

Boudrot, Mary Ann, of Michael and Anna Boudrot, born February 27, baptized March 13, sponsors John Hany and Margaret Josephine Blanchart.

Morse, Mary, of Thomas and Jane Morse, baptized March 14, sponsors Lancelot Harrison and Margaret Lynch.

Klein, George Ernest, of James and Elizabeth Klein, born March 13, baptized March 17, sponsors George Ernest and Magdalen Lechler.

Elliott, William, of Samuel Elliott (P.) and Bridget Downey, born December 1, 1772, baptized March 20, sponsors Martin Miller and Mary Cary, at Pikesland [Chester Co., Pa.].

Macalgen, Margaret, of Michael and Mary Macalgen, born October 2, 1773, baptized March 22, sponsors Martin and Anna Miller, in Chester County [Pa.].

Kean, William, of Francis and Bridget Kean, born February 14, baptized March 27, sponsors John Mullen and Mary Wagg.

Veit, Catharine, of Christian and Anna Barbara Veit, born March 23, baptized March 26, sponsors George and Catharine Coffey.

Bennet, Hannah, of John and Margaret Bennet, born September —, 1773, baptized March 28, sponsors Thomas McEnery and Catharine Schreiber.

Pola, Mary Elizabeth, of Peter and Anna Pola, born March 20, baptized April 3, sponsors George and Mary Elizabeth Schneider.

Zeiss, John George, of George and Eva Zeiss, born March 20, baptized April 3, sponsor Francis Wolff, Anna Margaret Wolff witness.

Jung, James, of Francis and Catharine Jung, born April 6, baptized April 10, sponsors James and Magdalen Christman.

Jones, Jane, of Peter and Magdalen (P.) Jones, born March 3, baptized April 10, sponsor Magdalen Regimenter.

Brown, James, of James and Catharine Brown, born December 25, 1773, baptized April 24, sponsors William Grady and Catharine Mentzebach, on a mission.

Fischer, John, of John and Margaret Fischer, born November 11, 1773, baptized April 24, sponsor Joseph Wingart, witness John Taylor, *ibid.*

Bachman, Anna Catharine, of Martin and Anna Barbara Bachman, born November 14, 1773, baptized April 24, sponsor Daniel Cobole, ceremonies supplied, *ibid.*

Lafferty, Margaret, of John Lafferty and Margaret Bennet, born May 10, 1771, baptized April 27, sponsors Michael Lamy and Eleanor Cahil, *ibid.*

Lafferty, Anna Catharine, of same parents, born March 18, 1766, baptized April 27, sponsors John and Catharine Cobole, *ibid.*

Lafferty, Daniel, of same parents, born July —, 1773, baptized April 27, sponsors Dominic Audler and Anna Young, *ibid.*

Lawless, Samuel Martin, of Martin Lawless and Mary Allen, born May 13, 1773, baptized April 27, sponsors Arthur Murphy and Bridget Shaw, *ibid.*

Ridal, William, of Thomas and Hannah Ridal, born December 20, 1773, baptized April 27, sponsors William Lefevre and Sarah Morris, *ibid.*

Fitzgerald, Anna Catharine, of William Fitzgerald and Margaret Griskell, born August 9, 1772, baptized April 27, sponsors John Swiney and Catharine Cobole, *ibid.*

Haycock, Sarah, wife of Thomas Haycock, adult, baptized April 27, *ibid.*

Haycock, James, of Thomas and Sarah Haycock, born August 10, 1773, baptized April 27, sponsors Edward Welsh and Bridget Shaw, *ibid.*

Ryan, Willlam, of Timothy and Rebecca Ryan, born February 4, 1773, baptized April 27, sponsor John Simpson, *ibid.*

Macon, William, of William Macon and Barbara Carman, born December 1, 1773, baptized April 28, sponsors William Smith and Bridget Shaw, *ibid.*

Gray, Elizabeth, of John and Anna Gray, born January 8, baptized April 28, sponsor Edward Murphy, Elizabeth Murphy, witness, *ibid.*

Burns, Daniel, of Laghlin and Margaret Burns, born February 20, baptized April 28, sponsor Daniel McShafrey, witness Elizabeth Murphy, *ibid.*

Rüger, Mary, of John and Elizabeth Rüger, born March 18, baptized April 28, sponsors Bartholomew and Mary Ann Cobole, *ibid.*

Audie, Joseph, of John Audie and Mary Josaphine Bawn, born March 19, 1766, baptized April 28, sponsors William Fitzgerald and Sarah Haycock, *ibid.*

Audie, Peter, of same parents, born February 19, 1768, baptized April 28, same sponsors, *ibid.*

Audie, Charles, of same parents, born October 22, 1770, baptized April 28, same sponsors, *ibid.*

Macra, William, of Patrick and Lydia Macra, born March 4, baptized

April 29, sponsor Joseph Wider ; had been baptized privately May 21, 1773 ; ceremonies supplied, *ibid.*

Cobole, Catharine, of John and Catharine Cobole, born April 28, baptized April 29, sponsors Catharine Schoten and John Kauffman, *ibid.*

Kean, Hugh, of William and Eleanor Kean, born December 24, 1773, baptized May 1, sponsors Hugh and Mary Quig, *ibid.*

Zech, Anna Barbara, of Francis and Anna Catharine Zech, born March 21, baptized May 1, sponsors John Mayer and B. Walker for B. Bachman, *ibid.*

Waldman, Mary, of Joseph and Margaret Waldman, born August 7, 1773, baptized May 4, sponsors Anthony Schumers and Frederic Bohn and wife, *ibid.*

O'Neal, Anna, of Henry and Mary O'Neal, born March 20, baptized May 4, sponsors Thomas Welsh and Grace Brown, *ibid.*

Horn, Anna Margaret, of John George (P.) and Anna Margaret Horn, born April 4, 1773, baptized May 4, sponsors Thomas Griffin and Margaret Lallin, *ibid.*

Cooper, Mary, of Thomas and Joanna Cooper, born April 16, baptized May 9, sponsors William and Elizabeth Hardin.

Malowny, Mary, of John and Catharine Malowny, born May 16, baptized May 17, sponsors Timothy Carrol and Margaret Rush.

Cels, Sarah, of Henry (P.) and Magdalen Cels, born February 11, 1766, baptized May 22, sponsor Apollonia Wegfort.

Cels, James, of same parents, born August 21, 1768, baptized May 22, sponsor Joseph Hahn.

Cels, John, of same parents, born February 14, 1771, baptized May 22, sponsor John Peter Krapf.

Cels, Christina, of same parents, born February 24, baptized May 22, sponsor Christina Hahn.

Herold, Mary, of James and Anna (P.) Herold, born April 10, baptized May 22, sponsors Thomas and Margaret Halfpenny.

Negel, Margaret, of John and Alice Negel, born April 16, baptized May 22, sponsor Susanna Glansey.

Magill, John, of John and Catharine Magill, born February 10, baptized May 25, sponsors Christian and Susan Catharine Thurnbach, at Pilesgrove [Salem Co., N. J.].

Kerl, Anna, of John Kerl and Anna Gibson, born May 7, 1769, baptized May 27, sponsor Barbara Kauffman.

McCana, Francis, of John and Sarah McCana, born November 14, 1773, baptized May 29, sponsors Daniel Scheimer and Sarah Sohl, at Pikesland [Chester Co., Pa.].

Miller, Catharine, of Martin and Anna Miller, born April 16, baptized May 29, sponsors Peter Luther and Catharine Eck, *ibid.*

O'Devlin, Samuel, of Roger and Susanna O'Devlin, born August 8, 1772, baptized May 29, sponsors John and Sarah McCana, near Millstown [?].

Keys, Francis, of James and Sarah Keys, born March 17, baptized June 3, sponsors Lewis Griffin and Sarah Wessel.

McCanary, Thomas, of John and Joanna McCanary, born May 20, baptized June 5, sponsors Lewis Byrne and Anna Macarthy.

Lynch, Mary, of Philip and Sarah Lynch, born March 10, 1772, baptized June 6, sponsor John Arthur O'Neal.

O'Neal, Mary, of John Arthur and Margaret O'Neal, born June 2, baptized June 6, sponsors Philip Lynch and Anna Ducre.

Dougherty, Agnes, of Patrick and Esther Dougherty, born June 7, baptised June 9, sponsor Mary Heart.

Davis, William, of —— and Anna Davis, born January —, baptized June 12, sponsors Bonaventure Dartoit and Magdalen Davenac.

Hoy, Asa Joseph, of John and Catharine Hoy, born March 25, baptized June 15, sponsors William and Eleanor Agan, in Burlington County [N. J.].

Lequeul, Aloysius, of Francis Lequeul and Pelagia Douzet, born June 21, baptized June 21, sponsors the minister and Margaret Leblanc.

Mayer, John, of Joseph (P.) and Gertrude Mayer, born June 24, baptized July 2, sponsors Philip Barthman and Mary Ridiger, near Philadelphia.

Lee, Thomas, of Thomas (P.) and Mary Lee, born June 23, baptized July 7, sponsor Eleanor Baxter.

Cunningham, Margaret, of Paul and Margaret Cunningham, born July 1, baptized July 9, sponsor Judith Power, John McEnery witness.

Cooley, Anna Margaret, of Abraham and Anna Cooley, born June 3, baptized July 10, sponsor Mary Poth.

Gans, Margaret, of Balthasar and Sarah Gans, born June 26, baptized conditionally July 24, sponsors James Weisenburger and Margaret Walter, at Pikesland [Pa.].

Magill, Anna, of Peter and Barbara Magill, born May 29, baptized July 31, sponsors Simon Geiger and Susan Catharine Thurnbach, at Pilesgrove [Salem Co., N. J.].

Magill, James, of Stephen and Elizabeth (P.) Magill, born April 1, baptized July 31, sponsors Peter and Barbara Magill, *ibid*.

Savoy, John Peter, of Peter Savoy and Mary Lequeul, born August 1, baptized August 2, sponsors John Lequeul and Josephine Brasan.

Fegan, William, of Patrick and Margaret Fegan, born June 5, 1767, baptized August 10, sponsors Florence McCarty and Mary Goff.

Fegan, Catharine, of same parents, born February 2, 1772, baptized August 10, same sponsors.

Long, Anna, of John Long and Elizabeth Clark, born July 4, baptized August 12, sponsor Dennis McCoghlin, witness Luther Jackson.

Smith, Daniel, of Daniel and Mary Smith, born August 1, baptized August 14, sponsors Samuel Ridney and Anna Triskel.

Lenox, Joseph, of John and Margaret Lenox, born August 12, baptized August 19, sponsors Joseph and Catharine Eck.

Kneul, Mary Elizabeth, of Balthasar and Christina Kneul, born August
17, baptized August 21, sponsors George Ernest and Mary Magdalen
Lechler.

Meade, George (Strich), of George and Henrietta Constance (P.) Meade,
born August 26, baptized August 26, sponsors Thomas and Catharine
Fitzsimons.

Preston, Mary, of Samuel (P.) and Margaret Preston, born March 3,
baptized August 29, sponsor Mary Heart.

Silly, Mary, of William [?] and Joanna Silly, born March —, 1772, baptized August 29, sponsor Margaret Brown.

Zangerte, George Ernest, of Ignatius and Elizabeth Zangerte, born
August 31, baptized September 1, sponsors George Ernest and
Mary Magdalen Lechler.

Humes, John, of Samuel and Margaret Humes, born November 6, 1770,
baptized September 3, sponsor Edward Hughs, at Springfield.

Humes, Alice, of same parents, born December 16, 1771, baptized September 3, sponsor Edward Hughs, *ibid*.

Ryan, Daniel, of Michael and Hannah Ryan, baptized in Philadelphia,
apparently by a Rev. Anthony Carroll, sponsors James Gildmar and
Margaret Hall.

Babet, Elizabeth, of —— and Catharine Babet, born June 16, baptized
September 6, sponsor Prudence Willcox, at Middleton.

Connor, John, of Michael and Rosa Connor, born May 31, baptized Sep
tember 7, sponsor Anna McCarty, at Sandy Run.

Eustâce, Genevieve, of Daniel Eustace and Margaret Doiron, born Sep--
tember 7, baptized September 8, sponsors John Raubin and Mary
Vincent.

Prickel, Elizabeth, of Henry and Margaret Prickel, born September 9,
baptized September 11, sponsors Laurence Gräser and Elizabeth
Chuson.

Crosby, Peter, of Francis and Margaret Crosby, born August 27, baptized September 11, sponsor Patrick McDonogh, witnesses Edward
McDonogh and Catharine Chastin.

Savage, Joseph, of Jeremiah and Anna Savage, born September 4, baptized September 12, sponsors Brian O'Hara and Elizabeth Carrol.

Boosee, Elizabeth, of Moses and Elizabeth Boosee, born September 12,
baptized September 13, sponsors Andrew McLone and Barbara
Graff.

Broderick, Susanna, wife of Richard Broderick, adult, baptized September 14.

Broderick, Margery, of Richard and Susanna Broderick, born August
18, baptized September 15, sponsors Michael Green and Margaret
Forest.

Bastian, Wilhelmina, of John William and Magdalen Bastian, born September 16, baptized September 25, sponsors Charles Anthony Maas
and Wilhelmina Webern.

Grandell, Sarah, of Elias and Rebecca Grandell, born July 25, 1769, baptized September 25, sponsor Bartholomew Bailey, Eunice (his wife) witness.

Grandell, Lydia, of same parents, born October 22, 1772, baptized September 25, same sponsors.

Greswold, Mary, of Joseph and Mary Greswold, born September 15, baptized September 26, sponsors the minister and Anna Hill.

Hueberk, Venanda, of Cassian and Anna Mary Hueberk, born September 21, baptized October 2, sponsors Bonaventure and Venanda Dartoit.

Kurtz, Dorothy, of John Paul and Agatha Kurtz, born September 29, baptized October 2, sponsors John Vadler and Dorothy Richart.

Talbot, Catharine Mary, of James and Catharine Talbot, born May 27, 1773, baptized October 2, sponsors Adam Lechler and Catharine Waltrich.

Schneider, George Adam, of George and Mary Elizabeth Schneider, born September 30, baptized October 5, sponsors Adam Lechler and Regina Schneider.

Flanegan, John, of Patrick and Mary Flanegan, born August 30, baptized October 6, sponsors Roger and Catharine Flahaven, in Hunterdon Co. [N. J.].

Wingart, John, of Joseph and Anna Elizabeth Wingart, born August 15, baptized October 13, sponsors James and Anna Catharine Demuth, in Morris Co. [N. J.].

Haycock, Daniel, of Thomas and Sarah Haycock, born August —, 1763, baptized October 16, sponsor Patrick McLoghlin, at Longpond.

Shaw, Catharine, of Moses (P.) and Bridget Shaw, born August 13, baptized October 16, sponsors John and Elizabeth Rüger, *ibid.*

Vanderoof, David, of Henry and Margaret Vanderoof, born June 19, baptized October 16, sponsors David and Mary Eva Fichter, *ibid.*

Scarboro, John, of William and Catharine Scarboro, born September 23, baptized October 16, sponsors John and Catharine Cobole, *ibid.*

May, Margaret, of James and Magdalen May, born August 30, baptized October 16, sponsors Anthony May and Margaret Waiblin, *ibid.*

Green, Susanna, of Peter and Susanna Green, born March 25, 1770, baptized October 16, sponsor William Fitzgerald, *ibid.*

Green, Peter, of same parents, born July 25, 1772, baptized October 16, sponsor Bridget Shaw, witness Moses Shaw, *ibid.*

Marsele, Peter, of Peter and Tabé Marsele, born September 28, 1761, baptized October 16, sponsor Charles Dentz, witness Mary Anna Dentz, *ibid.*

Marsele, John, of same parents, born May 29, 1768, baptized October 16, sponsors John Baptist and Margaret Oudrie, *ibid.*

Marsele, [John?], of same parents, born July 30, baptized October 16, sponsors John Rüger and Sarah Haycock, *ibid.*

Marsele, Charlotte, of same parents, born January 26, 1773, baptized October 16, sponsors Michael Favene and Susanna Green, *ibid*.

Fichter, Mary Elizabeth, of Philip and Mary Eva Fichter, born May 28, baptized October 17, sponsors John Cobole and Elizabeth Stalter, *ibid*.

Power, John, of Thomas and Susanna Powr [Power?], born August 28, 1773, baptized October 23, sponsors Peter Boyle and Sarah Christy, at Mount Hope [N. J.].

Olls, John James, of John and Ann Elizabeth Olls, born August 10, baptized October 23, sponsors John James Walker and Elizabeth Welsch [Welsh?], *ibid*.

Kirk, Peter, of John Kirk and Joanna Alleton, born June 4, baptized October 24, sponsors Peter Joseph and Anna Catharine Grips, *ibid*.

Kirk, Joanna (Alleton), wife of John Kirk, adult, baptized October 24, sponsor Anna Catharine Zech, *ibid*.

Senner, Margaret, of Francis and Mary Agatha Senner, born October 13, baptized October 30, sponsors Joseph and Margaret Ribau.

Burns, Matthew, of John and Elizabeth Burns, born October 27, baptized October 30, sponsors Thomas Callen and Mary Jonston.

Landry, John Baptist, of Anthony and Barbara Landry, born October 3, 1773, baptized November 3, sponsors Joseph and Margaret le Blanc.

Holt, Francis, of ———— and Mary Holt, born October —, 1774, baptized November 3, sponsor Joanna Nicols.

Hardnet, William, of James and Joanna Hardnet, born February 9, baptized November 6, sponsors Edward Cavenaugh and Elizabeth Snell.

Horn, Mary Elizabeth, of Henry and Christina Horn, born November 5, baptized November 7, sponsors George Ernest and Magdalen Lechler.

Sauerwald, John, of Michael and Barbara Sauerwald, born November 7, baptized November 10, sponsors John Aitkin and Charlotte Engelraid.

Foy, William, of Matthew and Anna Foy, born August 24, baptized November 12, sponsors Michael Shanly and Catharine Barn.

Byrne, Catharine, of Redmond and Anna Byrne, born November 9, baptized November 13, sponsors Tobias Rudolph and Mary Price.

Kessler, John, of Andrew and Catharine Kessler, born September 17, baptized November 13, sponsors John Sigfried and Catharine Spengler.

Donaho, Thomas, of Laurence and Bridget Donaho, born November 12, baptized November 13, sponsors Patrick Daverick and Anna Crowley.

Gallagher, John, of James and Anna Gallagher, born November 9, baptized November 16, sponsors Patrick and Mary Byrne.

Shaw, Genevieve, of Joseph (P.) and Sarah Shaw, born October 1, baptized November 20, sponsors George Gans and Catharine Weisseburger, at Pikesland [Chester Co., Pa.].

Anderson, Lorette (Laureta), of Thomas and Susanna Anderson, born May 29, baptized November 24, sponsor the minister.

Brimigeom, William, of John and Margaret Brimigeom, born November 10, baptized November 27, sponsors John Calanan and Anna O'Hara.

Denetter, James, of Conrad and Catharine Elizabeth (P.) Denetter, born October 30, baptized November 27, sponsors Joseph and Anna Mary Feinauer.

Kelly, Mary, of Patrick and Margaret Kelly, born December 3, baptized December 3, sponsors Stephen Champain and Dorothy Rischartin.

Champain, Charles, of Stephen Champain and Mary Benoit, born November 27, baptized December 4, sponsors Charles Berget and Margaret Benoit.

Donahay, George, of Cormack and Elizabeth Donahay, born November 18, baptized December 4, sponsors Michael and Mary Fowlon.

Ryan, Richard, of John and Margaret Ryan, born December 4, baptized December 5, sponsors Thomas Mullen and Judy Connor.

Bray, Anna, of John and Judith Bray, born November —, baptized December 8, sponsors Daniel Fitzpatrick and Joanna Motley.

Rice, Anna, of James and Esther Rice, born October 17, baptized December 11, sponsors Manes Connor and Margaret McConigl.

Murray, Mary, of Peter and Joanna Murray, born December 3, baptized December 11, sponsor Patrick Landry, Mary Landry witness.

Connor, Hugh, of Michael and Mary Connor, born December 14, baptized December 14, sponsors Thomas and Catharine Fitzsimons; ceremonies supplied.

Lindaus, John, of Michael Lindaus and Eleanor McGued [McQuaid?], born January 14, baptized December 15, sponsor Catharine Boudrot.

Bodar, Peter, of Anthony and Barbara Bodar, born December 3, baptized December 18, sponsors Peter Hegner and Gertrude Mayer (for Mrs. Elizabeth Hegner).

Buch, Gertrude, of Joseph and Hannah Buch, born November 27, baptized December 18, sponsors Joseph and Mary Gertrude Mayer.

Forage, Tobias, of Stephen and Mary Anna Forage, born December 10, baptized December 18, sponsor Tobias Rudolph, Mary Margaret Rudolph witness.

Talbot, William, of James and Catharine Talbot, born January 19, 1771, baptized December 19, sponsors George Ernest and Mary Magdalen Lechler.

Whole number of baptisms—one hundred and sixty-two.

REGISTER OF BAPTISMS FOR 1775.

Rees, Margaret Elizabeth, of Martin and —— Rees, born April 13, 1774, baptized January 1, sponsors Philip Kitzinger and Margaret Ridiger.

Kitzinger, Anna, of Philip and Matilda Kitzinger, born December 15, 1774, baptized January 1, sponsors John Venie and Anna Levingston.

McDermot, Mary, of Dennis and Mary McDermot, born December 18, 1774, baptized January 1, sponsors John and Mary Kean.

Treasy, Andrew, of Matthew and Mary Treasy, born February 5, 1769, baptized January 7, sponsors Laurence Dugan and Ann Fitzpatrick.

Treasy, Jesse, of same parents, born October 26, 1771, baptized January 7, sponsors Owen and Mary Ryan.

Fisher, Robert, of John and Eleanor Fisher, born December 13, 1774, baptized January 7, sponsor Honora Rush.

Blum, Nicholas, of Anthony and Barbara Blum, born January 10, baptized January 15, sponsors Nicholas and Anna Wochman.

Crosby, John, of —— and Mary Crosby, born November 19, 1774, baptized January 16, sponsor Mary Heart.

——, James, of —— and Hannah, slaves of Thomas Fitzsimons, born January 2, baptized January 16, sponsor Anna, slave of Elizabeth Meredith.

Lothier, Benjamin, of Andrew and Charlotte Lothier, born 1769, baptized privately January 20, sponsor Joseph Ribau.

O'Hara, Bridget, of Brian and Mary O'Hara, born January 17, baptized January 27, sponsors Anthony Graff and Mary Byrne.

Stafford, Mary, of James and Margaret Stafford, born January 25, baptized February 12, sponsors John Redin and Bridget Timins.

Doyle, Anna Regina, of James and Mary Christina Doyle, born February 11, baptized February 16, sponsor Anna Regina Kesser.

Dugan, James, of James Dugan and Mary Halfpeny, born about August, 1774, baptized February 20, sponsor Catharine Jacobs.

Durenac, Josephine Magdalen, of Joseph and Magdalen Durenac, born February 22, baptized February 25, sponsors Charles Leblanc and Osithea [?] Brassan.

McDonald, Thomas, of John and Eleanor McDonald, born February 19, baptized February 25, sponsors Patrick Mallon and Mary Tool.

Sexton, Catharine Barbara, of John and Catharine Sexton, born December 24, 1773, baptized February 26, sponsor Barbara Schultz.

Haug, Anna Christina, of Simon and Magdalen Haug, born February 20, baptized March 5, sponsors Paul and Christina Essling.

Schöne, Joseph, of Laurence and Magdalen Schöne, born March 5, baptized March 8, sponsors Joseph and Elizabeth Cassin.

Coock, Charles, of Laurence and Catharine Coock, born March 9, baptized March 12, sponsors Timothy Carrol and Catharine Welsh.

Rue, John, of Thomas (P.) and Anna Rue, born December 24, 1773, baptized March 15, sponsors James and Elizabeth Klein.

Dugan, Sarah, of James and Sarah Dugan, born January 18, baptized March 19, sponsors George Gans and Mary Walter, at Pikesland [Chester Co., Pa.].

Ermold, John, of Peter and Anna Mary (P.) Ermold, born October 7, 1774, baptized conditionally March 19, sponsors James and Anna Mary Weisenburger, *ibid.*

Schindler, William, of Henry (P.) and Catharine Schindler, born October 18, 1774, baptized conditionally March 19, same sponsors, *ibid.*

Gans, Anna Mary, of John and Catharine Gans, born October 16, 1774, baptized March 19, sponsors George and Anna Mary Gans, *ibid.*

Scheimer, Barbara, of Frederic and Magdalen Scheimer, born January 16, baptized March 21, sponsors John Stout and Hannah Christy, at Pilesgrove [Salem Co., N. J.].

Cullin, Anna, of John and Sibylla Cullin, born February 19, baptized March 22, sponsor Catharine Hughs, at Pottsgrove.

Coleman, Anna, of Edward and Catharine Coleman, born October 16, 1774, baptized March 26, sponsors Henry Monro and Susanna Thurnbach, at Pilesgrove [N. J.].

Miller, Christina, of Matthew and Anna Mary Miller, born January 15, baptized March 26, sponsors Joseph Miller and Catharine Benner, *ibid.*

Hueber, Mary, of Michael and Hannah Hueber, born December 21, 1774, baptized March 26, sponsors Simon and Mary Geiger, *ibid.*

Bucher, John, of John and Anna Catharine Bucher, born December 8, 1774, baptized March 30, sponsors Stephen and Catharine Barden.

Hanley, William, of Thomas and Rachael Hanley, born December 16, 1774, baptized April 2, sponsors Philip and Grace McDead.

Agan [Egan?], Thomas, of Nicholas and Anna Agan [Egan?], born January 20, baptized April 2, sponsor Joanna Nicoli.

January, Thomas, of Thomas and Margaret January, born about October, 1774, baptized April 10, sponsor Elizabeth Grace.

——, Mary, a foundling a few months old, baptized April 10, sponsor Anna French.

Klein, Joseph, of John and Anna Mary Klein, born April 14, 1774, baptized April 15, sponsors Joseph and Ursula Haag.

Waas, Anna Margaret, of Sebastian and Anna Mary Waas, born August 15, 1774, baptized April 16, sponsors John and Margaret Ridiger.

Price, Anna, of Joseph and Mary Price, born April 14, baptized April 16, sponsors William Shay and Anna Byrne.

Talbot, Elizabeth, of James and Catharine Talbot, born March 27, baptized April 23, sponsors Adam Bremich and Elizabeth Lascher.

McDonald, James, of Edmund and Mary McDonald, born February 18, baptized April 23, sponsors James Quin and Joanna Kennedy.

Tims, Henry, of Henry and Anna Tims, born March 14, baptized May 7, sponsors James Lamy and Joanna Hotton, at Pikesland [Chester Co. Pa.].

Humphranville, David, of Timothy and Rebecca Humphranville, born April 22, 1770, baptized May 10, sponsor Lydia Biron.

Honecker, John Henry, of John and Mary Honecker, born April 24, baptized May 10, sponsors Henry and Mary Ann Norbeck.

Dippens, John, of Richard and Abigail Apollonia Dippens, born May 3, baptized May 10, sponsor Mary Lee.

Mignot, Mary Josephine, of Charles and Pelagia (Galerm) Mignot, born May 13, baptized May 14, sponsors John Lequeul and Josephine Daroit.

Lany, John, of Michael and Martha (P.) Lany, born October 7, 1774, baptized May 17, sponsor Patrick Campbel, in Sussex County [N. J.].

Weber, Francis, of James and Anna Catharine Weber, born April 8, baptized May 20, sponsors Francis Anthony and Anna Catharine Zech, in Morris County [N. J.].

Brown, Philip, of James and Grace Brown, born February 17, baptized May 21, sponsors William Halfpeny and Mary Pickets, *ibid*.

Sig, Frederic, of John George (P.) and Gertrude Sig, born April 4, baptized May 21, sponsor Peter Grips, Frederic Böhm witness, *ibid*.

Wider, James, of Joseph and Margaret Wider, born February —, baptized May 21, sponsors James and Anna Catharine Demuth, *ibid*.

Darmoty, Edward, of Edward and Esther Darmoty, born February 11, baptized May 21, sponsors Peter Joseph Grips and Hannah Dirk, *ibid*.

Keiner, Peter, of —— and Christiana (P.) Keiner, born February 2, 1774, baptized May 21, sponsors Peter Joseph Grips and Anna Elizabeth Olls, *ibid*.

Price, Anna, of Thomas and Magdalen Price, born March 13, baptized May 23, sponsor Sarah Christy, Adam Mailgan witness, at Charlottenburg [N. J.].

Par, William, of Sophronia and Catharine Par, born March 19, baptized May 24, sponsor Anna Mary Merzbach, Edward Magill, witness, *ibid*.

Schot, Anna Catharine, of Philip and Mary Catharine Schot, born December 1, 1774, baptized May 25, sponsors Daniel Cobole and Mary Anna Quinx (for Catharine Cobole) *ibid*.

Merchler, Mary Margaret, of John and Mary Anna Merchler, born February 12, baptized May 25, sponsors Dominic Andler and Mary Catharine Schot (for Margaret Pfaltzer) *ibid*.

Dentz, Mary Ann (Kelly), wife of Charles Dentz, baptized May 26, sponsor Mary Anna Cobole, at Longpond.

Dentz, John, of Charles and Mary Ann (Kelly) Dentz, born April —, baptized May 26, sponsors John and Catharine Cobole, *ibid*.

Thomas, David, of David (P.) and Frances Thomas, born December 23, 1774, baptized May 27, sponsor Margaret Long, David Fichtler witness, *ibid*.

Stalter, John Bartholomew, of Nicholas and Elizabeth Stalter, born April 8, baptized May 27, sponsors Bartholomew and Mary Eva Cobole, *ibid.*

Cahel, Patrick, of Thomas and Eleanor Cahel, born January 1, baptized May 28, sponsor William Harrison (for Patrick Howlan), Bridget Bridy witness, *ibid.*

Hanlon, Elizabeth, of James and Rachael Hanlon, born April 14, baptized May 28, sponsor Sarah Hedgecock, *ibid.*

Elsworth, Mary Anna, of William and Bridget Elsworth, born October 19, baptized May 28, sponsor Arthur Murphy, Sarah Kelly witness, *ibid.*

Fitzgerald, William, of William Fitzgerald and Margaret Triskel, [Driscoll?] born October 9, 1774, baptized May 28, sponsor John Cobole, Joanna Swinney witness, *ibid.*

Marsele, David, of Peter and Tabese [?] Marsele, born May 8, baptized May 28, sponsors David Fichter and Mary Eva Fichter, Jr., *ibid.*

Call, John Nicholas, of John Nicholas and Anna Mary Call, born December 27, 1774, baptized May 28, sponsors Eugene Pfaltzer (for John Nicholas Calsen) and Margaret Pfaltzer, *ibid.*

Green, Margaret, of Peter and Susanna Green, born March 5, baptized May 28, sponsor Bridget Shaw, *ibid.*

Connely, Margaret, of James and Margaret Connely, born May 26, baptized May 31, sponsor Francis Dealy, Margaret Brown witness, at Mt. Hope [N. J.].

Skelly, Robert, of Robert and Anna Skelly, born May 9, baptized June 1, sponsors Thomas Griffin and Margaret Callan, in Hunterdon County [N. J.].

Cramer, Caspar, of Mathias and Mary Catharine Cramer, born May 13, baptized June 1, sponsors Caspar and Margaret Engelhard, near Haycock [Pa.].

McDonough, Michael, of Michael and Elizabeth McDonough, born April 24, baptized June 4, sponsors Patrick Landy, Eleanor Murry and Mary Griffin, John Welsh witness.

Wurzer, Mary Margaret, of George and Mary Eve Wurzer, born February 28, baptized June 5, sponsors George Ernest and Magdalen Lechler.

Murphy, John, of John Murphy and Mary Miller, born May 1, baptized June 15, sponsors Cassian Hueber and Catharine Netzelnoder.

Coghlan, William, of Robert Coghlan and Elizabeth Russell, infant at the point of death, baptized privately June 16.

Rane, William, of Patrick and Elizabeth Rane, born May 5, baptized privately June 16, sponsors William McKensy and Martha Bass.

More, Sarah, of Stephen and Eva More, born June 10, baptized June 17, sponsor Salome Freundin.

Dugan, James and Anthony (twins), of John and Elizabeth Dugan, born June 18, baptized June 18, sponsors Timothy and Elizabeth Carrol for James,.Anthony and Barbara Graff for Anthony.

Davis, Mary, of Thomas (P.) and Catharine Davis, born April 26, baptlzed June 19, sponsors Patrick and Margaret Rush.

Mahony, William, of William and Catharine Mahony, born June 19, baptized June 19, sponsors John and Elizabeth Bagley.

Foster, James, of John Foster and Catharine Mahana, born June 26, baptized June 29, sponsor Mary Hart.

Courtney, Francis, of Francis Courtney and Judith Barry, born June 24, baptized June 29, sponsor Mary Hart.

Tool, Hannah, of James and Sarah Tool, born June 29, baptized July 2, sponsors Christopher Teas and Mary Smith.

Barry, Eleanor, of·Patrick and Mary Barry, born June 30, baptized July 2. sponsors John and Elizabeth Carrol.

Kearney, John, of Hugh and Sarah Kearney, born July 2, baptized July 9, sponsors John Murray and Sarah Campbel.

Croghan, Joseph, of Dennis and Margaret Croghan, born July 5, baptized July 10, sponsors Michael Connor and Christina Mullabi.

Viel, Mary, of Peter and Lucretia Viel, born July 7, baptized July 16, sponsors Christopher and Catharine Viel.

Griffin, Margaret, of James and Elizabeth Griffin, born July 13, baptized July 30, sponsors Martin and Anna Miller, at Pikesland [Chester Co., Pa.].

Dogherty, John, of Anthony Dogherty and Anna Mealy, born April 17, baptized July 30, sponsors John William and Elizabeth Strack, *ibid*.

Fowhey, Hope Hewitt, wife of John Fowhey, baptized August 3, sponsor Margaret Glass.

McDonald, James, of Edmund and Margaret McDonald, born July 27, baptized August 6, sponsors Timothy and Elizabeth Carrol.

McHughin, Margaret, of John and Martha McHughin, born about April, 1773, baptized August 10, sponsors Henry Morris and Mary Calgen, at Pilesgrove [Salem Co., N. J.].

Thurnbach, Elizabeth, of Christian and Susanna Catharine Thurnbach, born August 3, baptized August 10, sponsors John and Anna Catharine Bucher, *ibid*.

Martin, Mary, of Patrick and Mary Martin, born August 6, baptized August 13, sponsors John Viel and Mary Johnson.

Tisdal, Thomas, of Thomas and Elizabeth Tisdal, born August 8, baptized August 13, sponsors Patrick and Margaret Rush.

Lequeul, Mary Esther, of Francis Lequeul and Pelagia Douzet, born August 13, baptized August 13, sponsors Joseph Leblanc, Jr., and Mary Vincent.

Heany, Margery, of John and Elizabeth Heany, born July 29, baptized August 13, sponsors Joseph Carrol and Anna Rush.

Thorp, Elizabeth, of John and Elizabeth (P.) Thorp, born May 4, 1773, baptized August 17, sponsor Hannah Clark.

Thorp, Sarah, of same parents, born July 29, baptized August 17, same sponsor.

Pola, George Adam, of Peter and Anna Pola, born August 7, baptized August 20, sponsors George Adam Lechler and Magdalen Rauch.

Delie, Charles, of Charles and Mary Delie, born July 14, 1774, baptized conditionally August 20, sponsor James Prouchier, Anna Harty witness.

Roderics, Anna, of John and Charlotta Roderics, born March 31, baptized August 23, sponsors Daniel Cross and Eleanor Crawford.

Neagle, John, of John and Alice Neagle, born August 2, baptized August 27, sponsors John and Margaret Ryan.

Gillen, Sarah, of James and Mary Gillen, born August 25, baptized August 27, sponsors John Brook, Anna Shaw and Margaret Conoly, Jeremiah Hays witness.

Williams, Elizabeth, of Joseph and Eleanor Williams, born August 2, baptized August 28, sponsors Matthew Hyne and Anastasia Devan.

Burns, Mary, of Archibald and Joanna Burns, born August 22 baptized September 3, sponsors John Fitzpatrick and Catharine Conelly.

Burns, John, of same parents, born June 16, 1772, baptized September 3, sponsors Timothy Dorgan and Elizabeth Fitzpatrick.

McFall, Catharine Benson, wife of Patrick McFall, baptized September 7, sponsor Eleanor Crawford.

Springer, Francis Joseph, of Joseph and Magdalen Springer, born September 3, baptized September 10, sponsors Francis Joseph Rübel and Catharine Viel, daughter of Rudolph Viel.

Davis, Mary, of Samuel and Elizabeth Davis, born July 26, baptized September 11, sponsor Elizabeth McKenley.

McMahan, Mary, of Barnaby and Anna McMahan, born September 8, baptized September 21, sponsor Mary Johnson.

Lederman, Anna Mary, of John and Catharine Lederman, born September 9, baptized September 24, sponsors Francis Joseph Lederman and Anna Mary Philips.

Ridiger, Anna Margaret, of John and Margaret Ridiger, born September 17, baptized September 24, sponsors Philip Kitzinger and Anna Mary Nagle.

Caspar, John, of Laurence and Margaret Caspar, born September 2, baptized September 29, sponsors John Bucher and Anna Mary Schnaller; at Pilesgrove [Salem Co., N. J.].

Barnhouse, Mary, of Edward (P.) and Juliana Barnhouse, born December 13, 1773, baptized October 9, sponsor Timothy Downing, in Philadelphia County.

Butz, Catharine Elizabeth, of Christian and Catharine Butz, about five years old, baptized October 11, at Greenwich.

Horn, George Henry, of John George (P.) and Margaret Horn, born July 1, baptized October 12, sponsors George Henry and Catharine Call, in Hunterdon County [N. J.].

Coble, Anna Catharine, of Bartholomew and Mary Coble, born July 5, baptized October 15, sponsors John Kauffman, James Walker and Catharine Cobole, ceremonies supplied, at Longpond.

Swiney, John, of John and Joanna Swiney, born October 4, baptized October 15, sponsors John Glub and Margaret Burns, *ibid*.

Oudie, Mary, of John and Josephine Oudie, born May 20, baptized October 15, sponsors William Fitzgerald and Mary Dentz, *ibid*.

McCormick, George, of Edward and Charity (P.) McCormick, born December 22, 1770, baptized October 15, sponsors James Fichter and Mary Burk, *ibid*.

McCormick, Michael, of same parents, born September 21, 1773, baptized October 15, sponsors David and Eva Fichter, *ibid*.

McCormick, Deborah, of same parents, born June 19, baptized October 15, sponsors John and Anna Larkin, *ibid*.

McKinzy, Charles, of Charles and Christina McKinzy, born August 17, baptized October 17, sponsors Neal Dogherty and Mrs. Mary Margaret Pfaltzer, at Ringwood [Passaic Co., N. J.].

Stecher, Mary Catharine, of Joseph and Anna (P.) Stecher, born August 16, baptized October 18, sponsors William Graty and Mrs. Mary Mentzenbach, at Charlottenburg [N. J.].

Bachman, Helen, of Martin and Anna Barbara Bachman, born September 11, baptized October 18, sponsors Nicholas Mentzenbach, Joseph and Helen Wingart, *ibid*.

Cobole, Mary Anna, of Daniel and Mary Ann Cobole, born July 26, baptized October 18, sponsors Peter Wilkes and Elizabeth Welsh (for Mary Ann, wife of Bartholomew Cobole), *ibid*.

Robertson, Anna, of Dominic and Mary Catharine Robertson, born July —, baptized October 21, ceremonies supplied, *ibid*.

Kamber, Ellzabeth, of Valentine and Ottilia Kamber, born October 24, baptized October 29, sponsors Jacob and Elizabeth Klein.

Halfpenny, Barnaby, of Thomas and Margaret Halfpenny, born October 15, baptized October 29, sponsors Owen Ryan and Joanna Motley.

Meade, Robert, of George and Henrietta Constance (P.) Meade, born September 20, baptized October 29, sponsors Thomas and Catharine Fitzsimons, Garret Meade and wife, and Thomas Straka.

Flanagan, Bridget, of Patrick and Mena (?) Flanagan, born October 16, baptized November 2, sponsors Brian and Mary O'Hara.

Harold, James, of James and Anna Harold, born October 1, baptized November 11, sponsor Thomas Halfpeny.

Donely, Margaret, of Dennis and Mary Donely, born January 8, 1774, baptized November 19, sponsors William Hanan and Catharine Pope, at Pikesland [Chester Co., Pa.].

Byrne, James, of Patrick and Mary Byrne, born December 4, baptized December 10, sponsors Mark Willcox and Elizabeth Carrol.

Hughs, Joseph, of Charles and Anna Hughs, born November 11, baptized December 28, sponsors Daniel Mignati and Eleanor McHollogh.

Binerman, Benjamin, of Benjamin Binerman and Elizabeth Carrol, born December 5, baptized December 30, sponsor Catharine Gordon.

Abt, Adam, of Henry and Mary Elizabeth Abt, born December 4, baptized December 31, sponsors Adam and Mary Margaret Hoffman.

Donaho, Margaret, of Lawrence and Bridget Donaho, born December 28, baptized December 31, sponsors John Sullivan and Anna Crowley.

Whole number of baptisms—one hundred and thirty-nine.

Whole number from August 29, 1758, to December 31, 1775—one thousand eight hundred and sixty-five.

NOTE.

The foregoing registers are, as has been said in the introduction, a translation and adaptation, done with strict fidelity and great care. For the convenience of those who may wish to consult the original books at St. Joseph's Church, we append a list of signs and abreviatins used therein :

C.—Catholicus, Catholic, a Catholic.

A. C.—Acatholicus, non-Catholic.

N. C.—Neo-Catholicus, a neophyte, one newly converted; or it may stand for non-Catholic, according to the context.

P.—Patrinus, a sponsor or godfather.

Pr.—Protestans, a Protestant.

T.—Testis, a witness.

h. a.—hoc anno, in this year.

L. C.—Legalis conjux, lawful wife; or legitimâ conjugatione, in lawful marriage ; legitime conjuncti, lawfully joined—according to the context.

M.—Mater, mother.

l. c.—loco citato, in the place before cited.

c. l. c.–cum. ⎱ Licentiâ præsenti, by immedite license, or license
Lic–Praes. ⎰ presented—at hand.

†—Mortuus, dead.

₊—Quakerius and Tremulus stand for Quaker, that is, a member of the Society of Friends.

T. p. p.—Tribus præmissis promulgationibus, by three previous announcements, that is, marriage by banns.

REGISTERS

OF

ST. AUGUSTINE'S CHURCH,

PHILADELPHIA.

ALPHABETICAL LIST OF THE SUBSCRIBERS TOWARDS THE BUILDING
OF ST. AUGUSTINE'S CHURCH, IN PHILADELPHIA, COMMENCED
JUNE 12, 1796.

[From an old register in Rev. Dr. Carr's writing, with General Washington's name added by a
subsequent hand.]

Alher, John	$ 75	Bready, Peter, two Holy		
Alibone, Thomas	20 00	Water pots		
Allison, David	20 00	Briggs, Francis	$ 5 00	
Alvarez, M.	50 00	Brennan, Laurence	30 00	
App, Michael	10 00	Brown, Clement D.	50 00	
Ash, James	20 00	" Joseph	30 00	
Ashley, John	250 00	" Mrs. Margaret	50 00	
Ashton, George	1 00	" Peter	10 00	
Baker, Jacob	1 00	Burke, Theobald	20 00	
Ball, Joseph	40 00	Burn, Maurice	10 00	
Barclay, James	20 00	Butler, ——	20 00	
Bardon, Stephen	20 00	Byrne, Patrick	140 00	
Barry, Commodore	150 00	" Redmond	200 00	
Barry, Capt. John	20 00	" Terence	10 00	
Bebsau, Mortier	1 00	Bousquet, ——	50 00	
Beck, Paul	20 00	Callaghan, David	50 00	
Bell, Wm.	50 00	Carrell, John	100 00	
Bell, Wm.	10 00	Carey, Mathew	50 00	
Bernard, Martin	20 00	Cassidy, Nicholas	10 00	
Beus, Fridric	2 00	Cassin, John	20 00	
Benson, Peter	20 00	Cazenowe, Theophilus	30 00	
Blair, —— (Isle of Mar-		Christy, Hugh	60 00	
tinique)	50 00	Clarke. Joseph	20 00	
Blight, Peter	50 00	Clifford, Thos. and John	20 00	
Blodget, Samuel	50 00	Cochran & Thursby	20 00	
Bond, I. B.	25 00	Colhoun, Gust.and Hugh	20 00	
Bosler, Joseph	2 00	Collins, Timothy	150 00	
Boureau, ——, (nephew)	3 00	Cemegys, Cornelius	10 00	

Conner, Michael	$ 4 00	Hall, I.	$ 25 00
Conway, Mathias	8 00	Hamilton, Gavin	30 00
Cottringer, Garrett	50 00	Harkin, Neale	5 00
Cress, George	50	Harper, Christopher	50 00
Cronan, Dennis	10 00	Harvey, Sampson	5 00
Crousillat, Lewis	50 00	Hawthorne, Thomas	20 00
Cunningham, John	1 00	Hayes, Laurence	30 00
Clothier, Samuel	1 00	" Patrick	20 00
D'Arcy, John N.	30 00	Henderson, Mrs. Mary	10 00
Delany, Maurice	20 00	Higby, Joseph	50 00
Deneye, John	2 00	Himanus, Conrad C.	1 00
Dennick, Joseph	30 00	Hiney, A.	50 00
De Noailles, Vicomte		Hoare, Capt.	10 00
Louis	20 00	" James	25 00
Desmond, Timothy	30 00	Holmes & Rainey	20 00
Diamond, Mrs. Mary		Hookey, Anthony	6 00
Catharine	15 00	Hoy, John	2 00
Dougherty, Mrs.	10 00	Hurley, Thomas	20 00
" Martin D.	20 00	Imlay & Harper	10 00
Dowling, John	5 00	Ingersoll, Jared [Attor-	
Doyle, John	40 00	ney General of Penn-	
Duffield, Abraham	7 00	sylvania]	30 00
Dugan, ——	50 00	Inskeep, John	20 00
Dumoutet, ——	25 00	Irvine, James	20 00
Dunn, ——, member of		Johnson, John	10 00
the Irish House of Par-		Johnston, Francis [Col-	
liament	20 00	onel and Revolutionary	
Dunn, Daniel	30 00	Officer]	20 00
Durney, Michael	20 00	Jones, Isaac	15 00
Dutilh & Wacksmuth	24 00	" Mrs. (Pottsgrove)	15 00
Eck, Mrs. Catharine	100 00	Kean, Roger	30 00
Faulkner, Capt.	10 00	Keen, L. Patrick	1 00
Fearis, Bernard	30 00	Kennedy, Andrew	20 00
Fenno, John	5 00	" John	5 00
Ferrall, Luke	30 00	Kenney, Charles	10 00
" Patrick	50 00	" Thomas	10 00
" Thomas	20 00	Knell, Polthes	1 00
Fitzpatrick, Keirin	100 00	Kreen, Henry	1 00
Fitzsimons, Thomas	500 00	Lalor, Dennis	30 00
Flahavan, Roger	50 00	" John	60 00
" Thomas	20 00	Lapsley, David	10 00
Ford, Mrs.	2 00	Latimer, George	20 00
Fortune, ——	20 00	Leahy, Michael	26 67
" Nicholas	20 00	Leamy, John	200 00
" Walter	10 00	Leiper, Thomas	20 00
Fox, John	5 00	Linehan, Patrick	100 00
Frazier, Arnold	13 33	Long, James	20 00
Fry, Mrs.	10 00	Lynch, James	5 00
Furlong, John	8 00	Madden, Patrick, (besides	
Gallagher, James	200 00	printing work to a con-	
Gallaudet, ——	5 00	siderable amount)	50 00
Gill, Peter	100 00	Magee, Robert	10 00
Girard, Stephen	40 00	Magrath, Michael	20 00
Glentworth, James	10 00	Maher, Lawrence	10 00
Graaff, Balser	1 00	Mayer, Nicholas	2 00
Green, Mrs. Eleanor	20 00	Mazurié, James	20 00
Halker, Leonard	1 00	McDermott, John	50 00

McDermott, Mrs. Martin	$ 50 00	Rossiter, John	$ 30 00
McEwers, —— (Isle of St.		Rudolph, John	100 00
Thomas)	10 00	Rundle, Richard	30 00
McEwing, Thomas	50 00	Ryan, James	200 00
McGinnis, Neale	300 00	Sanchez, Philip	50 00
McGregor, John	14 00	Scravendyke, Peter	40 00
McIntire, Michael	2 00	Seguin, Andrew	4 00
" Patrick	2 00	Shaughnessy, John	2 00
McNeilis, William	10 00	Shaw, Archibald	8 00
Meade, George	50 00	Shebe, Andony	50
Meaney, John	50 00	Shortall, Thomas, (be-	
Meeker, Cochran & Co.	10 00	sides $150 00 in lumber)	100 00
Melles, John, and Rather		Shugart, Simon	9 00
Flar	2 00	Sibert, Conrad	3 00
Meredith, Samuel	30 00	Sleahort, ——	18 00
Miller, James	300 00	Smith, Edward	10 00
" James, Jr.	5 00	" Robert	20 00
Montgomery & Newbold	20 00	Smitt, Peter	1 00
Morgan, Benjamin R.	20 00	Snyder, John	22 22
Morrell, John	20 00	" Joseph	25 00
Moylan, Jasper	50 00	Stafford, Robert	50 00
" John	50 00	Sterret, ——	50 00
Murgatroyd, Thomas	20 00	Stockdale, Gerald	15 00
Murphy, James (Isle of		Summers, Andrew	50 00
St. Thomas)	100 00	Sweetman, Richard	60 00
Musgrove, Joseph P.	50 00	Taggart, John	200 00
Norris, Joseph	1 00	Telles, Mrs. Margaret	40 00
Nottnagell, Leopold	30 00	Toland, Henry	20 00
Nowlan, Patrick	9 72	Town, Thomas	1 00
Nugent, Edmond	30 00	Tybout, Andrew	20 00
" George		Tansey, Morgan	8 00
O'Brien, Michael Morgan	20 00	Vanuxem, James	20 00
O'Connor, Capt.	10 00	Vaughan, John	30 00
O'Hagan, Charles	10 00	Viar, Joseph	100 00
O'Hara, John	10 00	Waln, J. and R.	20 00
O'Reilly, Thomas	20 00	Walsh, John	53 33
Painter, John	1 00	Warwick, Thomas	1 00
Peacan, ——, Jr.	20 00	Washington, George, (ex-	
" Thomas	30 00	President)	50 00
" Valentine	100 00	Waters, Michael	2 00
Pères [Paris?] Peter [M.		" and son, Mrs.	15 00
D.]	20 00	Wells, John	10 00
Pratt, Henry	20 00	Whelen, Israel	30 00
Preston, ——	100 00	Whelan, James	8 00
Reilly, Thomas	50 00	White, Charles	50 00
Richardet, Samuel	20 00	" Isaac	1 00
Robertson, William	1 00		

NOTE.—The subscribers number two hundred and forty-six, and the sums subscribed amount to eight thousand five hundred and sixty-seven dollars and two cents.

ALPHABETICAL LIST OF THE PEW HOLDERS, TWO HUNDRED AND
THIRTY-FIVE IN NUMBER, OF ST. AUGUSTINE'S CHURCH, PHILA-
DELPHIA, FROM JUNE 7, 1801 TO 1808.

(From the Registers.)

Anderson, Daniel
Angue, John
Ashley, John
Armat, Thomas
Baker, Mrs.
Barber, Louisa
Barron [or McBarron], Michael
Barry, Commodore Jno.
Barry, Mrs. John
Barry, Patrick
Beasly, Mr.
Beaty, Mrs.
Bedford, John
Bouvyer, Michael
Boyle, Philip
Brady, Peter
Briggs, Francis
Briggs, John
Brown, Mrs.
Burke, Captain
Burke, Thomas
Butler, Capt. James
Butler, Michael
Byrne, Arthur
Byrne, Bridget
Byrne, Gerald
Byrne, Maurice
Byrne, Patrick
Byrne, Redmond
Byrne, Terence
Callaghan, David
Carey, Mathew
Carr, John
Cassiday, Nicholas
Cauffmann, Margaret
Christy, Hugh
Clarke, Neal
Clements, Joseph
Cline, Mary
Connoly, Hugh
Connor, Mrs. Agnes
Conry, Thomas
Conway, Arthur
Conway, Bernard
Conway, Mathias
Corran, Hugh
Cottringer, Garrett
Coyle, Edward
Cross, Joseph
Cromer, William

Cronin, Dennis
Cross, Mrs.
Daly, Capt. John
Darquey, P.
De Brie, Mr.
Delahunt, ——
Desauque, Louis
Desmond, Timothy
Divan [or Devan], Wm.
Doran, Michael
Doyle, Bartholomew
Doyle, John
Duffy, Michael
Duggan, Joseph
Duguet, Monsr..
Dumoutet, ——
Dunn, Daniel
Durney, Michael
Eck, Joseph
Ennis, Lawrence
Esling, Nicholas
Fagan, Augustine
Fagan, Mary
Fagan, Michael
Fatio, Don
Fitzsimons, Thomas
Flahavan, Mrs.
Flahavan, Roger
Flahavan, Thomas
Flannagan, John
Flinn, William
Flood, Matthew
Fogarty, Thomas
Ford, Mrs.
Fortune, Daniel
Fortune, Michael
Fortune, Nicholas
Fortune, Walter
Fox, James
Frazer, Andrew
Gallagher, James
Gallagher, John
Gallet, Mr.
Garland, John
Gartland, John
George, Martin
Gilbert, Thos. Augustine
Green, Mrs. Eleanor
Groves, Antony
Griffin, John

Guilleau, Mrs.
Hammer, Lewis
Harison, Charles
Harkin [or Harkens], Neal
Harrison, C. P.
Hartley, Peter
Haughey, William
Hays, Lawrence
Hearn, Edmund
Hickey, John
Hickey, Thomas
Holland, Hannah
Hore, George
Howling, Patrick
Hudson, Mr.
Hurley, Jr., Thomas
Hurley, Sr., Thomas
Johnston, John
Jones, Isaac (?)
Joyce, Thomas
Kean, Roger
Kelly, Hugh
Kennedy, John
Laland, Bert
Lalor, John
Leahy, Michael
Leamy, John
Lees, Mrs.
Le Favre, Nicholas
Lewis, William
Linehan, Patrick
Lloyd, Mrs.
L'Orange, Louis
Lynch, James
Magrath, James
Magrath, Michael
Maguire, Thomas •
Maher, Laurence
Maher, Pierce
Maitland, William
Mallon, Patrick
Malon, James
Malon, Mrs.
Malone, P.
Mason, Mr.
Maurissy, Cornelius
McArthur, Daniel
McCaron, Bernard
McCormick, John
McDermot, John

McDole, James
McGinnis, Neal
McGowan, James
McMullen, George
McNab, James
McNeales, William
McRobbins, Mrs.
McSorley, John
Mead, Mr.
Meade, Richard W.
Meany, John
Miller, James
Miller, Mrs.
Minguil (?), Benjamin
Montgomery, Mr.
Moylan, Jasper
Moynehan, Maurice
Mulcahy, William
Mulligan, Patrick
Murry, Michael
Murry, Patrick
Musgrave, J. P.
Myers, George
Myers, Peter
Nowlan, Patrick
Nugent, George
O'Connor, Mrs.
Parker, John
Parmentier, Mr.

Peacan, Jr., Thoms
Pères, Dr. Peter
Perotteau, Basil
Peters, John
Rademaker, Mr.
Rafferty, D.
Regimenter, William
Renaud, Augustine
Richard, Adam
Ritterson, John
Rosseter, Dominick
    Thomas
Rosseter, Capt. John
Ryan, James
Ryan, Lewis
Ryan, William
Rudolph, John
Scally, Patrick
Scravendyke, Peter
Seguin, Andrew
Serra, Ann
Shade, Peter
Sheehan, Michael
Shields, William
Shortal, Thomas
Sicard, Stephen
Sleahort, William
Smith, Alexander W.
Smith, John

Snyder, John
Snyder, Thomas
Sorin, John
Spurck, Peter
Stafford, Robert
Strahan, Joseph
Suigan, Andrew
Sullivan, Jeremiah
Taggart, John
Tilton, Mrs.
Toner, James
Toner, Philip
Troubat, John
Viar, Don Joseph
Vouchai, Mdme.
Walsh, John
Wealsh, James
Whealan, James
Whelan, Isaac
Whelan, Maurice
Whelan, Mrs. (Maurice?)
Whelan, P. E.
White, Charles
Wickam, James
Wickham, William
Wood, Cornelius
Ysnarte, Don
Zigler, William

LIST OF PEW HOLDERS, TWO HUNDRED AND TWENTY-THREE IN
NUMBER, OF ST. AUGUSTINE'S CHURCH, PHILADELPHIA, FROM
1814 TO 1820.

[NOTE.—The registers for the years 1808 to 1814 are missing.]

Angue, John
Astolfi, Laurence
Balordo, Philip
Barry, Patrick
Basely, Mr.
Bateson, Mr.
Bernard, John
Bernard, Mary
Bogan, John
Bolou, Mdme.
Borie, John J.
Boyle, Bartholomew
Brady, Bartholomew
Brady, Laurence
Brady, Patrick
Brown, Mrs.
Bryan, James
Burke, Thomas
Byrne, Eleanor

Byrne, Gerald
Byrne, James
Byrne, William
Carey, Mathew
Carrol, Walter
Cauffmann, Margaret
Christy, Hugh
Clarke, Eneas
Clinet, James
Coleman, Thomas
Collins, Peter
Cooper, Mr.
Conway ——
Conway, Bernard
Corrigan, Peter
Coy, Maris
Craft, Mrs. John C.
Cragg, Mrs. Rose
Cross, Mrs.

Cunningham, John
Dancé, Simon
Daly, Capt. John
Davis, Mrs.
DéAngelis Giacinto
Decosta, Mr.
Desauque, Louis
Desilver, Joseph
Desmond, Timothy
Develin, Fernando
Donath, Stephen
Donnegan, Thomas
Donnelly, Ann
Donnelly, Eleanor
Donnoly, Nicholas
Doran, Michael
Dornan, Bernard
Dougherty, Hugh
Dougherty, William

Duff, Mrs. Elizabeth
Duff, John
Duffey, Michael
Duffield, Edward
Ducoign, P.
Dugan, Joseph
Dumas, Mr.
Dumoutet, Mrs.
Edwards, Thomas
Ennis, Cornelius
Ewing, Robert
Fagan, Michael
Figaro, John
Finn, Stephen
Finour, George
Flinn, Robert
Fortune, George
Fortune, Walter
Frazer, Antony
Fougeray, René
Fow, Mrs.
Fox, James
Fox, John
Gartland, John
Geoghegan, Mr.
Groves, Antony
Guilleau, Mrs.
Hall, John
Hammel, Henry H.
Hammer, Lewis
Harkins, Neal
Harrison, Francis
Harrison, William
Hearn, Antony
Hoffman, Gaspar
Hookey, Antony, Sr.
Hookey, Antony, Jr.
Hughes, John
Hurley, Thomas, Jr.
Hurley, Thomas, Sr.
Jacob, Mrs.
Jacques, Elen J.
Kaim, Mrs.
Kane, Alexander
Kelly, Mrs,
Kennedy, John
Kenny, James
Lacombe, ——
Lacy, Edward
Lalor, John
Laplante, Lewis E.
Lechler, George
Lewis, Francis
Linehan, James
Long, James
L'Orange, Louis

Love, —— M. D.
Lloyd, Mrs.
Luhn, Jacob
Lynch, Hannah
Lyons, Mrs.
Maison, John A.
Maitland, Thomas
Malon. Mrs.
Manae (?), Mrs.
Mandeville, Henry
Mark, John
Martin, John
Martine, Fanny
Martin, Thomas
Matthews, Capt. John
Mazurie, James J.
McArann, Mr.
McCormick, Philip
McCreedy, Bernard
McDermott, Mrs. Catharine
McDonough, Charles
McDonough, Charles
McDonough, William
McEwin, Patrick
McGawley, James
McGill, Michael
McGinnis, Margaret
McGowan, James
McGowan, Patrick
McGrath, Michael
McGuire, John
McGuire, Michael
McGuire, Thomas
McKenny, James
McLeran, Duncan
McNeil, Thomas
McNulty, Eneas
McNulty, Hugh
McQuaide, Felix
Meade, Richard
Miller, Adam
Miller, William
Molloy, Nicholas
Monroe, Peter
Montgomery, Mrs
Mulligan, Patrick
Murphy, John
Nagle, James
Nagle, Michael
Newland, Margaret
Nugent, George
O'Brien, Daniel
O'Brien, James
O'Connor, Nicholas
O'Connor, Petre

O'Donnel, Mrs.
O'Mealy, Patrick
Page, Joanna
Pères, M. D. Peter
Parker, John
Parmentier, Mr.
Peterson, John
Phillip, Peter
Pichetti, Andrew
Quin, Charles
Rebel, Mrs. Hannah
Reily, Bernard
Reily, Luke
Reily, Patrick
Reily, Paul
Reily, Philip
Richards, Adam
Richardson, Mr. C. A.
Ritterson, John
Rouvert, Mr.
Ryan, James
Ryan, Lewis
Sarmiento, Don
Saville, John
Scally, Patrick
Scanlon, Patrick
Scanlon, William
Scot, William
Seguin, Andrew
Shade, Peter
Sharkey, John
Sheridan, Bernard
Sicard, Stephen
Simmons, Rosanna
Smith, James
Smith, Philip
Smith, William
Smith, William
Snyder, Elizabeth
Snyder, General
Taggart, Mrs. C.
Tanguy, John
Thibaut, Mdme.
Tisdall, Charles
Tracy, Hugh
Troubat, John
Vernou, Elizabeth
Wade, John
Ward, Charles
Warnock, William
Waters, Thomas
Whelan, William
White, Charles
Williamson, Michael

SELECTIONS FROM THE MARRIAGE AND BAPTISMAL REGISTERS OF
ST. AUGUSTINE'S CHURCH, PHILADELPHIA, PA.

NOTE I.—For brevity's sake the officiating clergymen are named in these selections by their last names only. Their full names are : Thomas Matthew Carr, Philip Stafford, George Staunton, William C., Nicholas, and James O'Donnell, Michael Hurley, and Thomas Kyle, Augustinians ; Thomas Flynn, Trappist, and Henry Doyle, Thomas Heyden, Samuel Sutherland Cooper, John O'Reilly, and Edward F. Mayne, seculars.

NOTE II.—The names are given also of all those who are registered as witnesses or god-parents.

MARRIAGES.

Mulcahy—Green. 1801, October 20, by Dr. Carr, O.S.A., William Mulcahy to Margaret Green ; the witnesses were Patrick Linehan, Gerald Byrne, John Taggart and others.

[This is the first marriage recorded in St. Augustine's Church.]

Maher—Burns. 1803, January 11, by the same, Pierce Maher to Eleanor Burns ; the witnesses were Mathew Carey, Raymund Byrne, and others.

Campbell—Stuart. 1803, August 16, by the same, James Campbell to Jane Stuart ; the witnesses were John Hauffman, Robert Campbell, Teresa Care, Peter N. Dorey, and T. G. Agez.

Sartori—Woofouin. 1804, March 8, by Fr. Stafford, O.S.A., at Lamberton, N. J., John Baptist Sartori (Italian) to Mary M. Henrietta l'Official de Woofouin, born in Hispaniola [St. Domingo], of Maria[?] Basil l'Official and N. Salnave ; the witnesses were N. Belleville[?], Rostignol de Grandmont, Ls. Grand Dulteüilh, and Louis Rostignolth.

Hudson—Byrne. 1804, April 1, by Dr. Carr, O.S.A., Henry Edward Hudson [M. D.] to Bridget Byrne ; the witnesses were Patrick Byrne, James Malon, and others.

Sulauze—Beauveau. 1804, June 28, by Dr. Hurley, O.S.A., John Claude Sulauze to Susanna Rose Beauveau ; the witness was John Baptist Serezin.

Fagioli—Ellis. 1805, April 23, by Dr. Carr, O.S.A., at Trenton, N. J., Lawrence Fagioli to Mary Magdalen Ellis [baptized the same day] ; the witnesses were John Baptist Sartori and Mary Magdalen Woofoin.

Fagan—O'Brien. 1805, May 28, by the same, Michael Fagan to Elizabeth O'Brien ; the witnesses were James and John Gallagher.

Whelan—Clark. 1805, June 9, by the same, Pierce Whelan to Catharine Clark (widow) ; the witnesses were John and Benjamin Cross.

McGee—Corbett. 1805, August 24, by the same, James McGee to Martha Corbett ; the witnesses were James Bradley and Philip McRevy.

Guibert—Sulauze. 1807, September 12, by Dr. Hurley, O.S.A., Elias Guibert to Susanna Rose Sulauze [widow, see above, 1804, June 28]; the witnesses were G. B. Gabalde, Peter Lacombe, and Teresa Care.

Borie—Beauveau. 1808, February 12, by the same, John Joseph Borie, Jr., to Sophie Beauveau; the witnesses were Peter Lacombe and Peter Latapié.

Lucas—Carrell. 1810, February 15, by the same, Fielding Lucas [publisher, of Baltimore, Md.] to Elizabeth Carrell; the witnesses were Thamas Hurley, Daniel Carrell, and others.

Laborde—Richard. 1812, February 28, by the same, John Francis Laborde to Mary Victoria Richard; the witnesses were John Joseph Borie and Margaret Byrne.

James—Rose. 1813, June 13, by Dr. Carr, O.S.A., John James (colored) to Mary Rose (colored); the witnesses were Samuel Cooper and Hannah Rebel.

Hoskins—Girard. 1813, September 9, by Dr. Hurley, O.S.A., John Hoskins to Catharine Girard; the witnesses were John Valle and daughter.

Reynoldi—Beauveau. 1814, June 12, by the same, John Reynoldi [Rainoldi?] to Emily Beauveau; the witnesses were John Borie and Eliza Januarius.

Bernadou—Fontaine. 1814, December 24, by Dr. Carr, O.S.A., John Baptist Bernadou to Henrietta Fontaine; the witnesses were Peter Lacombe and Germain Combes.

Meade—Lucas. 1815, March 12, by the same, David P. Meade to Lydia Lucas (widow); the witnesses were Hannah Rebel and Mary Gartland.

Priestman—Dumoutet. 1815, June 17, by the same, William Priestman to Emma Dumoutet; the witnesses were Rev. M. Hurley, William Priestman, and William O'Brien.

Lallemand—Girard. 1817, October 28, by the same, Henri Dominique Lallemand to Henriette Maria Girard; the witnesses were Stephen Girard, Joseph Bonaparte, [Count de Survilliers, ex-king of Naples and Spain], Marshal Emanuel Count de Grouchy, General Charles Lallemand [one of Napoleon's soldiers], and Mesdames Carpentier and Georges.

Bache—Abadie. 1818, May 28, by Dr. Hurley, O.S.A., Franklin Bache to Aglaie Dabadie [perhaps better d'Abadie]; the witnesses were William Duane, Hartman Bache, and Edward Cox.

Hookey—Shoemaker. 1818, October 25, by Dr. Carr, O.S.A., Antony Hookey to Mary Shoemaker; the witnesses were John James Shoemaker and Elizabeth Hookey.

Carey—Leslie. 1819, January 21, by Dr. Hurley, O.S.A., Henry C. Carey to Martha Leslie (Protestant); the witnesses were Mathew Carey, Isaac Lea, and Thomas Jefferson Leslie.

Koecher—Donath. 1819, February 22, by the same, Leonard Koecher to Mary Donath; the witnesses were Joseph Donath, Sr., Joseph Donath, Jr., and John Ruvert.

Ewing—Davis. 1820, November 2, by the same, Robert Ewing [afterwards Sheriff of Philadelphia] to Sarah Y. Davis; the witnesses were Joseph White, Thomas Hurley, and Anna Clark.

Taney—Hurley. 1821, February 1, by the same, Augustus Taney [brother of Roger Brooke Taney, Chief Justice of the United States] to Catharine Hurley [half-sister to the officiating priest]; the witnesses were Mathew Carey, William Carey, William Hawkins and Patrick Byrne.

Lea—Carey. 1821, February 6, by the same, Isaac Lea to Frances Anna Carey [daughter of Mathew Carey, the publisher]; the witnesses were Mathew Carey, Henry Carey, and Samuel Bell.

Laguerenne—Beauveau. 1821, June 5, by Fr. Doyle, Peter Louis Laguerenne to Eliza Helen Beauveau; the witnesses were John A. Dutilh and E. J. Guieu.

Meade—Nice. 1821, November 29, by Dr. Hurley, O.S.A., Robert Meade to Elizabeth Nice [maiden name Holcomb]; the witnesses were Francis Redon and John Reilly.

Peale—Laforgue. 1822, October 10, by Fr. Heyden, Titian [Rembrandt] Peale to Elizabeth Laforgue.

Baird—Carey. 1822, November 19, by the same, Thomas Baird to Elizabeth C. Carey; the witnesses were Henry C. Carey, John Diamond and Thomas [Diamond?].

Chamberlain—Hookey. 1824, May 30, by Dr. Hurley, O.S.A., William Chamberlain to Elizabeth Hookey; the witnesses were James Power and Mary Sneeringer.

Tucker—Carroll. 1824, December 23, by the same, Aaron B. Tucker [M. D.] to Elizabeth Henrietta Carroll; the witnesses were Charles Carroll [of Carrollton, Md.], Samuel Chew, Joseph Cabot, Samuel Tucker, Harriet and Louisa Carroll, and Susanna and Juliana Nicklin.

Russell—Kelly. 1827, September 6, by the same, John Russell to Hannah Kelly; the witnesses were Dennis Kelly [of Haverford, Delaware County, father of the bride], Eugene Cummiskey [the publisher] and Mary McAnulty.

Beauveau—Vernou. 1828, May 29, by the same, John Beauveau to Louise Catharine Vernou; the witnesses were John Vernou and wife.

McElroy—Repplier. 1828, October 8, by the same, Archibald McElroy to Sophia M. Repplier; the witnesses were John George Repplier, Cochran Forbes, Elizabeth O. Betts, Elizabeth Nagle and Mary Ann Coleman.

Edwards—Whelan. 1829, February 10, by the same, George Edwards to Elizabeth Whelan; the witnesses were Thomas Edwards, Catharine and William Whelan, and Samuel Wood.

Clarke—Lallemand. 1829, June 30, by the same, John Y. Clarke to Henrietta Maria Lallemand [maiden name Girard]; the witnesses were E. D. Whitney, James G. Clarke, Adelaide Segoigne, and Jane Carter.

Petre—De Lois. 1830, April 15, by Fr. W. O'Donnell, O.S.A., Alphonse Petre to Marie Françoise De Lois; the witness was John Mitchell.

McElhone—Lawton. 1830, June 26, by Dr. Hurley, O.S.A., James McElhone to Rebecca Lawton; the witnesses were Dennis Lawton, James Tuomy, and Elizabeth Rogers.

Streeper—Fletcher. 1830, August 26, by Fr. N. O'Donnell, O.S.A., Leonard B. Streeper to Elizabeth Fletcher; the witnesses were Margaret Streeper and William Bell.

McGrath—Gill. 1830, December 1, by Dr. Hurley, O.S.A., Thomas McGrath to Mary Gill; the witnesses were John Dickens and Bridget Trenor.

Keating—Hart. 1831, June 7, by the same, Philip Keating to Margaret Hart; the witnesses were Thomas Keating and Bridget Trenor.

Kelly—Kelly. 1831, June 20, by the same, Charles Kelly to Margaret Kelly; the witnesses were Dennis Kelly [of Haverford, Delaware County, father of the bride], Mary, Cornelius, William, Margaret, and Ann Kelly, and Mary Hurley.

Scravendyke—Whelan. 1831, July 25, by the same, John Scravendyke to Lucy Gertrude Whelan; the witnesses were Joseph Donath, Rev. John Hughes [afterwards Archbishop of New York], Susan Whelan, and Peter Scravendyke.

Ryan—Duke. 1831, August 21, by Fr. W. O'Donnell, O.S.A., Antony Ryan to Mary Duke; the witnesses were Bernard and Catharine Duke.

McCawley—Priestman. 1832, May 10, by Dr. Hurley, O.S.A., John McCawley to Emma Priestman [maiden name Dumoutet]; the witnesses were William J. Birch and John E. Destouet.

Cross—Hurley. 1832, July 10, by the same, Benjamin Cross [the celebrated musician] to Mary Hurley [half-sister to the officiating priest]; the witnesses were Rev. John Hughes [afterwards Archbishop of New York], Samuel Jackson, M. D., and George Carrell.

Archer—Corcoran. 1833, February 12, by the same, Pierce Archer to Juliana Corkran [should read Judith Elizabeth Corcoran]; the witnesses were William Murphy and Catharine O'Leary.

White—Hurley. 1833, April 23, by the same, Ambrose White [of Baltimore, Md.] to Mary Hurley [niece of Dr. Hurley, O.S.A.]; the witnesses were Basil Elder, Jr., Edward Lucas, and Mary White.

Newland—Colgan. 1834, June 12, by the same, William Newland [musician] to Sarah Colgan; the witnesses were —— Woolrich and Catharine Colgan.

Bedloe—Holland. 1834, December 24, by the same, Thomas Bedlow [better, Bedloe] to [Anna Holland].

Rudolph—Lloyd. 1836, January 7, by the same, John Rudolph [merchant, and organist of St. Mary's Church] to Jane Abeel Lloyd [daughter of Thomas Lloyd, author]; the witnesses were Mary, Elizabeth and Hannah Lloyd [sisters of the bride], Charles Mackie, and at least five hundred others.

Donnelly—Bloomer. 1838, May 24, by Fr. J. O'Donnell, O.S.A., Peter Donnelly to Anna Bloomer; the witnesses were John Boyland and Thomas [Boyland?].

BAPTISMS.

Amabili. 1801, October 18, by Dr. Carr, O.S.A., Emily Frances Brasier, born at Philadelphia, April 18, 1799, of Claude Amabili and Elizabeth Peyrusse La Fleur; the god-parents were Joseph Ludovic Gaschet De Lisle and Mary Peyrusse La Fleur, for Francis Philippon and Mary Maux Peyrusse La Fleur.

[This is the first baptism recorded at St. Augustine's Church.]

Girard. 1801, December 1, by Fr. Staunton, O.S.A., Caroline Eugenie, born at Burlington, N. J., June 20, 1797, and Henrietta Maria Girard, born at the same place, June 21, 1799, of John Girard and Eleanor; the god-parents of Caroline were Remi La Toche and Eugenie Howard, and of Henrietta, Francis Bourgeois and Marie Bourgeois.

Peale. 1803, November 20, by the same, Augusta Virginia, born at Reading, near London (England), daughter of Rembrandt Peale (Protestant) and Eleanor Mary; her god-parents were Nicholas Barrabino and Julia Guennetau.

Sourin. 1804, April 3, by Fr. Flynn, James, born March 19, 1804, of John Soran [better, Sourin] and Bridget Carr [niece of Dr. Carr, O. S. A.]; the god-mother was Bridget Byrne. [This James was brother of the venerable Father Edward J. Sourin, S.J.]

Montgomery. 1805, February 2, by Fr. Staunton, conditionally, Rachel Montgomery, adult.

Ellis. 1805, April 23, at Trenton, N. J., by Dr. Carr, O.S.A., Mary Magdalen Ellis; her god-parents were John Baptist Sartori and Mary Magdalen Woofoin. [Mary Magdalen Ellis was married the same day to Lawrence Fagioli.]

Fagan. 1805, July 2, by the same, the ceremonies of baptism were supplied over Margaret, born May 5, 1805, and privately baptized on May 10, daughter of Nicholas Fagan and Mary Walsh. [Nicholas Fagan was the architect and builder of St. Augustine's Church, and Mary Walsh was daughter of Captain John Walsh, lumber merchant.]

Hudson. 1805, July 21, by the same, Mary Catharine, born July 6, 1805, of Henry Edward Hudson [M.D.] (Protestant) and Bridget Byrne.

Borie. 1806, March 20, by the same, Mary Francis Borie, born September 6, 1805; her god-parents were Fs. Laborde and Aurora Corneille.

Albright. 1806, May 8, by the same, Jacob, born at Philadelphia, April 8, 1806, of Frederic Albright and Mary Talbot (Protestant); his god-father was Jeremiah O'Sullivan.

Gartland. 1806, November 11. by the same, John, born at Philadelphia, October 31, 1806, of John Gartland and Mary Murphy; his god-parents were Edward and Mary Harland.

Albright. 1808, February 14, by Dr. Hurley, O.S.A., Peter, born January 11, 1808, of the same parents as Jacob, above; his god-parents were Louis and Catharine Hammer. [Among the "Native Americans" concerned in the destruction of St. Augustine's Church, in 1844, was Colonel Peter Albright; he led the riot at St. Michael's Church, in Kensington, and exulted that the record of his Catholic baptism was destroyed at St. Augustine's. But the awful judgment of God on authors of sacrilege is as evident in Philadelphia as elsewhere. Colonel Albright died soon after, very wretchedly, in an oyster-cellar; his brother Jacob perished at a fire, and his widow and daughter were drowned in the Delaware River, January 26, 1856. The record of his baptism still lives. See Shea's "History of the Catholic Church," N. Y., 1857, p. 257.]

Cross. 1808, May 24, by the same, conditionally, Sarah Ann Cross; her god-mother was ―――― Baker.

Cross. 1808, August 3, by the same, conditionally, Robert, born September 27, 1795, Joseph, born October 3, 1798, Mary, born May 28, 1800, and Charles, born August 8, 1803, of John Cross and Elizabeth Baker. [These were brothers and sister of Benjamin Cross, the musician.]

Longstreth. 1809, January 27, by the same, Catharine Anna, born December 3, 1808, of William Longstreth (Protestant) and Mary Rudolph; her god-father was John Soares. [Mary Rudolph was a daughter of John Rudolph, merchant, and organist at St. Mary's.]

Hurley. 1809, June 18, by the same, Mary [his half-sister], born June 10, 1809, of Thomas Hurley and Mary Rogers; her god-parents were Thomas Hurley, Jr., and Anna Carrell.

Borie. 1810, September 13, by the same, Adolph Edward [afterwards Secretary of the Navy under President Grant], born November 24, 1809, of John Joseph Borie and Sophie Beauveau; his god-parents were Francis Laborde and Susanna Guibert, for Emily Beauveau.

Da Costa. 1810, November 11, by the same, Mary Ann, born October 13, 1810, of Charles Da Costa and Anna Bayard (Protestant); her god-parents were James Meade and Elizabeth Da Costa.

Hurley. 1811, February 17, by the same, Louis Neil [his nephew], born February 6, 1811, of Thomas Hurley, Jr., and Anna Louisa Carrell; his god-parents were the minister and Eleanor Maher.

Jordan. 1811, September 22, by Dr. Carr, O.S.A., Henry, born at Philadelphia, September 17, 1811, of Patrick Jordan and Susanna Evans; his god-father was Charles Doyle.

Cross. 1811, November 17, by Dr. Hurley, O.S.A., John Talbot, born October 19, 1811, of Benjamin Cross [musician] and Elizabeth Beatty [error for Betagh]; his god-parents were John and Sarah Cross.

Hurley. 1812, May 26, by the same, Edward H. [his half-brother], born April 30, 1812, of Thomas Hurley and Mary Rogers; his god-parents were the minister and Mary Carrell.

Da Costa. 1812, September 9, by the same, Charles Da Costa, born August 17, 1812, of Charles and Anna (as above); his god-mother was Anna Powel.

Longstreth. 1812, November 6, by Dr. Carr, O.S.A., John Rudolph Longstreth, born August 19, 1812, of William and Mary (as above); his god-father was John O'Connor.

Hurley. 1812, November 29, by Dr. Hurley, O.S.A., Elizabeth Lucas Hurley [his niece], born November 3, 1812, of Thomas and Anna (as above); her god-parents were Thomas Hurley, Sr., and Mary Carrell, Sr.

Cross. 1814, April 24, by Dr. Carr, O.S.A., Thomas Betagh Cross, born at Philadelphia, April 2, 1814, of Benjamin and Elizabeth (as above); his god-parents were John and Sarah Cross.

Hurley. 1814, October 4, by Dr. Hurley, O.S.A., Mary Hurley [his niece], born August 23, 1814, of Thomas and Anna (as above); her god-parents were John Carrell and Elizabeth Lucas.

Lucas. 1814, October 4, by the same, John Carrell, born September 10, 1814, of Fielding Lucas [publisher in Baltimore, Md.] and Elizabeth Carrell; his god-parents were Thomas Hurley, Jr., and wife.

Longstreth. 1814, October 7, by Dr. Carr, O.S.A., George [Rudolph], born August 16, 1814, of William Longstreth and Mary (as above); his god-parents were Bernard Fearis and Julia Groves.

Borie. 1816, June 4, by Dr. Hurley, O.S.A., Sophie Elizabeth, born December 29, 1813; Emily Mary, born November 24, 1811, and Charles Beauveau Borie, born December 26, 1814, of John Joseph Borie and Sophie (as above); the god-parents of Sophie were Napoleon Louis Borie and Elizabeth Beauveau; of Emily, ——— Guibert, for Peter Cedie, and Emily Rainoldi; and of Charles, Charles Pommez, for Napoleon Louis Borie, and Mary Beauveau.

Hurley. 1817, January 2, by the same, Thomas [his nephew], born October 17, 1816, of Thomas Hurley and Anna (as above); his god-parents were John Carrell, Jr., and Catharine Hurley.

Singerly. 1817, July 7, by the same, George Washington, born May 24, 1817, of George Singerly and Catharine Morooney; his god-mother was Catharine Hadder.

Hurley. 1818, March 15, by the same, Anna Louisa [his niece], born

November 23, 1817, of Thomas Hurley and Anna (as above); her god-parents were;William Hawkins and Mary Carrell. .

Borie. 1819, June 3, by the same, Charles Louis, born January 6, 1819, of John Joseph Borie and Sophie (as above); his god-parents were Louis Borie and Emily Rainoldi.

Albright. 1819, June 6, by the same, Emily, born February 23, 1819, of Frederic Albright and Mary (as above); her god-mother was ——— . Albright.

Frenaye. 1820, February 21, by the same, Mary Jane Henrietta Cora, . born February 22, 1819, of Peter Frenaye and Henrietta Elizabeth Gibson (Protestant); her god-parents were Henry Bartholemy Himely and Marie Jeanne Devaure.

Hurley. 1820, June 14, by the same, John Carrell, born September 28, 1819 ; and 1821, July 16, Michael [his nephews], born December 12, 1820, of Thomas Hurley and Anna (as above).

Hookey. 1820, July 16, by the same, George Shoemaker, born June 13, 1820, of Anthony Hookey and Mary Shoemaker; his god-parents were Christian and Elizabeth Shoemaker.

Da Costa. 1820, November 19, by the same, Louisa Augusta, born October 25, 1820, of Raymund Da Costa and Susette Berard; her god-parents were Augustus Aspinette and wife.

Ewing. 1821, November 17, by the same, John Davis, born August 18 1821, of Robert Ewing [afterwards Sheriff of Philadelphia] and Sarah Y. Davis (Protestant); his god-parents were Thomas Hurley and Elizabeth Davis.

Lea. 1822, March 6, by the same, Mathew Carey, born December 30, 1821, of Isaac Lea (Protestant) and Frances Anna Carey [daughter of Mathew Carey, the publisher]; the god-parents were Mathew and Bridget Carey.

Hurley. 1822, March 27, by the same, Eleanor Mary [his niece], born December 24, 1821, of Thomas Hurley and Anna (as above); her god-parents were William and Eleanor Carrell.

Lallemand. 1823, April 6, by the same, Caroline Adelaide Stephanie Girard, born August 27, 1819, of Henri Dominique Lallemand and Henriette Marie Girard ; the god-parents were Stephen Girard and Adelaide Segoigne.

Peale. 1823, August 13, by the same, Bertrand, born ——, of Titian [Rembrandt] Peale and Elizabeth Laforgue; the god-parents were Louis and Mary Leforgue.

Gillingham. 1823, September 1, by Fr. Cooper, Joseph Horace, born June 8, 1822, of Edwin Gillingham and Elizabeth Clemens; the god-mother was Mary Lloyd.

Borie. 1823, September 19, by Dr. Hurley, O.S.A., Mary, born February 21, 1821, and Peter Henry, born April 7, 1823, of John Joseph Borie and Sophie (as above); the god-parents of Mary were John

Theodore Laguerenne and Mary Louise Beauveau; and of Peter Henry, Peter Louis Laguerenne and wife.

Laguerenne. 1823, September 19, by the same, Mary Adele, born August 13, 1823, of Peter Louis Laguerenne and Elizabeth Helen Beauveau; her god-parents were John Joseph Borie and wife.

Hurley. 1823, November 20, by the same, Catharine [his niece], born August 14, 1823, of Thomas Hurley and Anna (as above); her god-parents were John Carrell, Sr., and Sarah Cauffman.

Peale. 1825, September 2, by the same, Mary Florida, born July 22, 1825, of Titian [Rembrandt] Peale and Elizabeth (as above); the god-parents were Louis and Mary Laforgue.

Tucker. 1826, May 4, by the same, Henrietta Sophia, born September 18, 1825, of Abner B. Tucker [M.D.] and Elizabeth Henrietta Carroll; the god-parents were Charles Carroll, Jr., John Muynie (?) and Henrietta Carroll.

Borie. 1826, July 10, by the same, Elizabeth, born April 18, 1825, of John Joseph Borie and Sophie (as above); the god-parents were Adolph and Emily Borie.

Bayard. 1826, July 17, by the same, Mary Louisa, born —— 18, 1822, Caroline, born September 25, 1824, and Elizabeth, born July 7, 1826, of James Bayard and Mary Carroll [daughter of Charles Carroll, of Carrollton, Md.]; the god-mother of Mary Louisa was Louisa Carroll, of Caroline, Henrietta Carroll, and of Elizabeth, Elizabeth Tucker. [The baptism of Elizabeth is recorded for the 7th of July, but this seems to be an error.]

Peale. 1827, July 2, by Fr. Mayne, Cybelia, born May 18, 1827, of Titian [Rembrandt] Peale and Elizabeth (as above); the god-parents were Louis Laforgue and Anna McNally.

Bernadou. 1828, October 4, by Dr. Hurley, O.S.A., Frances Adelaide, born February 12, 1828, of John Bernadou and Henrietta Fontaine; her god-parents were Francis Houard (?) and Eloise Bernadou.

Murdock. 1828, December 31, by the same, Mary, born December 3, 1828, of George D. Murdock and Frances Harrison; the god-mother was Mary Lloyd.

Peale. 1829, September 6, by the same, John Godman, born July 27, 1829, of Titian [Rembrandt] Peale and Elizabeth (as above); the god-parents were Louis and Mary Laforgue.

Borie. 1830, February 27, by the same, Louisa, born March 22, 1828, o John Joseph Borie and Sophie (as above); the god-parents were John C. B. Borie and Sophie Elizabeth.

Edwards. 1830, April 15, by the same, Rosalie, born February 16, 1830, of George Edwards and Elizabeth R. Whelan; her god-parents were Rev. John Hughes [afterwards Archbishop of New York] and Lucy Whelan.

Pizzini. 1831, June 12, by Fr. N. O'Donnell, O.S.A., Angelo Francesco, born May 22, 1831, of Antonio Pizzini and Catarina Malliotti; the god-parents were Joseph Oliveri and Anna Clarke.

Borie.   1831, July 24, by Dr. Hurley, O.S.A., John Joseph, born December 20, 1830, of John Joseph Borie and Sophie (as above); the god-mother was Emily Rainoldi.

Bernadou.   1831, November 24, by the same, Napoleon George Washington, born February 22, 1830, of John Bernadou and Henrietta (as above); the god-parents were Napoleon Helié and Henrietta Bernadou.

McElhone.   1832, April 22, by Fr. N. O'Donnell, O.S.A., John, born April 19, 1832, of James McElhone and Rebecca Lawton; his god-parents were John Regan and Ellen Lawton.   [John McElhone is now chief stenographer in the House of Representatives at Washington.]

Cross.   1833, May 8, by Dr. Hurley, O.S.A., Michael Hurley [his nephew], born April 13, 1833, of Benjamin Cross and Mary (as above); his god-parents were the minister and Sarah Thibault.

Borie.   1834, May 12, by the same, Josephine Louisa, born March 8, 1834, of John Joseph Borie and Sophie (as above); her god-parents were Charles and Margaret Borie.

Ewing.   1834, June 24, by the same, Thomas, born March 24, 1834, of Robert Ewing and Rebecca Smith; the god-parents were Rev. John Hughes [afterwards Archbishop of New York] and Helen Wiseman.

Meade.   1834, August 31, by the same, Sarah Ann, born August 12, 1834, of James Meade and Mary Matthews; her god-parents were Dennis Collins and Bridget Cahill.

Cross.   1834, December 7, by the same, Mary [his niece], born October 31, 1834, of Benjamin Cross and Mary (as above); her god-parents were Francis Thibault and Catharine Taney.

Murdock.   1835, September 7, by Fr. N. O'Donnell, O.S.A., Emma, born July 10, 1835, of George D. Murdock and Frances (as above); her god-mother was Mary Lloyd.

Newland.   1835, September 29, by Dr. Hurley, O.S.A., Mary Ann, born September 20, 1835, of William Newland [musician] and Sarah Colligan [error for Colgan]; her god-parents were John Murray and Jane Cole.

Cross.   1836, October 9, by the same, Edward [his nephew], born September 11, 1836, of Benjamin Cross and Mary (as above); his god-parents were Francis Thibault (for Edward Hurley) and Elizabeth Cross.

Luciani.   1837, June 12, by Fr. N. O'Donnell, O.S.A., Pasquale Paolo, born January 16, 1837, of Pasquale Luciani and Rose Wently; his god-father was the minister.

Morris.   1837, July 24, by Fr. O'Reilly, William Bicknel, born ——, of Robert Morris (Protestant) and Amanda Miller; his god-mother was Malinda Bicknel.

Augustin. 1838, October 1, by Fr. J. O'Donnell, O.S.A., Francis Timothy, born October 1, 1838, of Francis Augustin and Henrietta Luciani; his god-mother was Maria Luciani.

Archer. 1838, October 31, by the same, Pierce Ambrose, born September 28, 1838, of Pierce Archer and Judith [Elizabeth] Corcoran; his god-parents were Patrick Carroll and Catharine Archer.

Bedloe. 1839, March 2, by the same, Thomas, born January 30, 1839, of Thomas Bedloe and Anna Holland; his god-mother was Anna Robinson.

Abel. 1839, June 24, by the same, William Childs, born March 24, 1839, of Isaac Abel and Martha Quigg; his god-father was Philip McCormick.

Eagle. 1839, September 5, by Fr. Kyle, O.S.A., Emma Maud, born ——, 1839, of Stephen Eagle and Elizabeth Quest; her god-parents were Dominic Eagle and Caroline Hossin (?).

NOTE.—Besides the foregoing, the following names are frequently met in the register, namely:

Lambert, Le Breton, De la Croix, Brasier, Champenois, Condé, Lamburié, Montague, Guesnard, Belair, Devereux, Pettit, Andrade, Tarrascon, Cooper, Bournanville, Chevalier, Parmentier, Bogia, Sartori, Guignon, Rebel, De Silver, Dumoutet, Coste, Lefevre, Fitzsimons, Oram, Wickham, Trueman, Gibbons, Pierce, Snyder, Hamilton, Hedges, Donath, Latapié, L'Orange, Vernou, Bouvier, Streeper, Clement, Ewing, and Lloyd.

ST. PETER'S CHURCH,

WILMINGTON, DEL.

[The Registers open 1797 ; the Church was founded in 1816.].

The following items of interest were taken from the registers of baptisms and marriages of St. Peter's Church, Wilmington, Delaware, the 20th October, 1885, by a member of the American Catholic Historical Society :

The earliest registries, now extant, belonging to this mission, are all in one book, headed as follows : "Registres de L'Église Catholique de la Ville de Wilmington, État de la Delaware, Amérique."

Up to 1804, the entries are all in French. The earliest one recorded is a baptism, as follows : " 1796, August 18th, by Rev. Etienne Faure, a French priest, deputed pastor by Rt. Rev. John Carroll, bishop of Baltimore." The sponsors were Jean Garésché du Rocher, I. P. Garésché and M. V. M. Garésché.

1797, April 14th, is the earliest record of the Dupont family. I have preserved the old-fashioned way of spelling their name. The entry runs as follows : (date as above) Baptized by Rev. Etienne Faure, minister, Marie Françoise Jeanne Louise Angelique, born August 25th, 1795, at Wilmington, of Pierre Henry du Pont de Gault, of San Domingo, and Marie Catherine Elizabeth, both refugees.

1797, March 26th, Rev. P. Bauduy administers baptism. I suppose he, too, was a refugee from San Domingo. The name Bauduy is frequently met in the early registries.

1797, November 5th, a baptism at which the sponsors were Alexandre François Bretton Deschapelles, Eulalie Bretton Deschapelles, Bauduy Bretton Deschapelles, Bretton Deschappels Bauday, J [ohn] Keating.

179—, is a marriage between Francis Breuil, in business at Philadelphia, and Jeanne Vidal.

1797 [?], October 15th, baptized, Marie Michel, twenty years old, a negress of the Mandingo tribe, formerly slave of Mr. Lally de la Neuville, of San Domingo, but now freed in reward for her faithful services. The god-mother was Elizabeth Garésché.

1797, December 11th, married, by Rev. Etienne Faure, John Keating, son of Valentine Keating and Sarah Creagh, born at Limerick,

Ireland,to Eulalie Victoire Mathurine Claudine Bretton Deschapelles. [Before many witnesses.]

1798, April 15th, baptized, Pierre Marie Jean Elie Auguste, son of Pierre Henry Dupont de Gault and Marie Catherine Elizabeth Vienot de Vaublanc.

1798, April 15th, baptism of the daughter of Basile d'Orbigny, refugee from the western part of San Domingo.

1799, November 10th, a baptism by Rev. ——— Cibot, "vice-prefect apostolic and superior-general of the missions of the northern part of San Domingo, a refugee and pastor of Wilmington by appointment of Bishop Carroll." [This Rev. ——— Cibot was at St. Peter's Church, Baltimore, 1794, April 5th, where he signs the registries.] The god-parents were Jerome and John Keating.

1800, June —, married, by the same, James Devinney [Irish] and Mary Winterbottom [English]; witnesses, John Keating and John McGurk.

[From 1804, August 5th, to 1834, the entries in the register are all, with few exceptions, in one and the same hand, and apparently copies. Father Patrick Kenny, the rector, enters a few of the records; the others seem to have been written by a clerk.]

1810, August 17th, a baptism by Rev. Francis Xavier Brosius.

1814, September 29, baptism of Mark, son of James Willcox and Eliza Orn, born 1814, August 24, at Concord Hundred, Delaware county, Pa. [The book of registries, at page 13, is headed "Westchester, Chester county, Pa.," and the first entry is dated August 5, 1804.]

1800, February 2, a marriage contracted February 9, 1794, before a Protestant minister, is validated by Rev. John Rosseter, O.S.A.

1800, February 10, a marriage by Rev. Matthew Carr, O.S.A. [Dr. Carr signs himself as "curé de la paroisse de Ste. Marie de Philadelphie et Vicaire Général de Monseigneur l'Eveque de Baltimore."] From February 2, to April 19, Fathers Rosseter and Carr sign all registries.

1815, March —, the baptism of Anna Caroline, daughter of Outerbridge Horsey, "senator in Congress."

1818, September 13, baptism of Anne, born August 31, 1818, at Du Planty's mill, in Christiana Hundred, Brandywine, New Castle county, of John McDermott and Rosanna McCusker. [This was the first baptism administered in St. Peter's Church, Wilmington.]

1824, a baptism by Rev. Patrick Duffy, of Emmittsburg, Md.

1829, February 11, a baptism by Rev. Bernard Keenan, of Lancaster, Pa., sponsor Rev. Terence Donoghoe.

1829, May 31, a baptism by Rev. George Aloysius Carrell, afterwards bishop of Covington.

1832, April 22, a baptism by Rev. T [homas?] R. Butler.

1834, December 7, a baptism by Rev. Patrick Reilly, successor to Rev. P. Kenny.

1838, May 27, a baptism by Rev. Peter Richard Kenrick [afterward archbishop of St. Louis].

1835, April 22, is the earliest record of confirmation administered in this
church. The prelate officiating was Rt. Rev. Francis Patrick
Kenrick. In 1838, May 29 [or 27], he administered confirmation
the second time, and in 1840, June 14, the third time.

The early dead of this mission lie in the graveyard of the now desolate
church of St. Mary, at Coffee Run, a few miles out of Wilmington.

In the yard adjoining St. Peter's Church are many gravestones, the
most of them broken and the inscriptions unreadable. The earliest
date I could make out was "1810, April 17(?), of Marie Adelaide Morin
———, born at Mt. Pleasant, in the Isle of S. Domingo, 1780, and died
at Wilmington;" the next earliest is 1810, December 10, of "Margaret,
daughter of ——— Dougherty, aged 16 years and ——— months," and
the third is "1811, August 9, of John Plunkett."

I here give the number of baptisms and marriages as I found them
summed up in the registers. The totals are given in the register for
only a few years. They are, for

1800 . . . . marriages 10		
1801–2–3 . . . . " . . . . . . [missing]		
1804 . . . . " 1		
1805 . . . . " 1		
1806 . . . . " 6		
1807 . . . . " 1		
1808 . . . . " 3		
1809 . . . . " 6		
1810 . . . . " 2		

                                                    ——
                                                    30

The baptisms, for

1804 (dating from August 5) 4	
1805 43	
1806 35	

                                                    ——
                                                    82

On the first page of the oldest register is a memorandum, in very old
handwriting, of a suggestive and singular character. It runs thus,
without a word of comment to tell what it means; here it is:

"Rev. Mr. McGuire's father, John McGuire, lived before the Revolution near Chester Co. poor house, Brandywine, and withdrew from there
with the British on their retreat. John McGuire's brother Andrew
settled in Londonderry township, Chester Co., died about 15 years ago,
and left issue James, John, George, Mary, Susan, all living in same place,
first cousins to the above Rev. Mr. McGuire of Quebec.

[Dated and signed.]   "June 1st, 1823. PATRICK KENNY."

Among the many curious old papers shown me, on the occasion of my visit to St. Peter's, by the Rt. Rev. Bishop Becker and the Rev. Father Kiely, was one of which I took only a condensed copy. The document in full is a draft of what was meant to be a lease of land, and is dated "1795, March 5," but is unsigned. The parties to the contract were "Rev. Robert Molyneux of George Town on the Pottomac in the State of Maryland and Arthur McGough of Newcastle County, Pa."; the lease was to run ten years, and the yearly rent to be 26£ 5s. Pennsylvania currency; the property was of 208 acres, lying in Mill Creek Hundred, and had been deeded, January 17, 1772, by Samuel Lysle to Rev. John Lewis, of St. Mary's Co., Md. Father Molyneux, to whom it descended in line of title, now rents it to McGough, under ten conditions. These are substantially that McGough shall board the clergyman of the district, if the bishop wishes, in a suitable manner, viz.: "lodging, Table, Candle light, Fire, washing, mending of Cloathes (*sic*), Taking care of his horse, furnishing him with plenty of grass, Hay and 17 bushels of Oats yearly," and all for 25£ 6s. a year (days of absence to be counted out); also, that McGough shall "plant an apple orchard with trees 25 feet apart," fence all the property, plant one lot with chestnut or other timber at 10 feet apart, and allow one acre for a church and burying-ground, &c., &c.   T. C. M.

OLD ST. PETER'S CHURCH,

BALTIMORE, MD.

Opened in 1782.

The following is a transcript from the registries of Old St. Peter's church, Baltimore, the first place of Catholic worship opened in that city, made by a member of the American Catholic Historical Society.

The Church of St. Peter's apparently was opened in 1782, the registries beginning with that year. This church has disappeared long ago, its site now being occupied by "Calvert Hall;" the registries—all in excellent condition and most carefully looked after—are kept at the Cathedral, where they were shown to the writer of this by the rector, Rev. Thomas S. Lee.

The following items I have copied from the registries, viz.: "1782, December 25th, baptism of Mary Treaner, born November 8th, 1782, by Rev. Charles Sewall." This is the earliest record of a baptism appearing on the registries, and is followed by the marriage, "1783, April 20th, of Peter Gerard to Magdalen Momillon, and of Cosme Constant Milleret to Mary Ann Granger ; witnessed by Rev. Charles Sewall." The earliest record in the marriage registry.

From 1782, December 25th [the earliest date], to 1793, May 20th, all the entries in the registries are in one and the same hand, and at the end is the following certification, viz.: "I, Francis Beeston, priest and rector of St. Peter's, Baltimore, certify that the preceding pages have been faithfully transcribed from the original register kept by my predecessor, Rev. Mr. Charles Sewall; also that no regular register of marriages was kept before the said Sewall's time."

The "original register" mentioned above is lost. I now add, from the registries, the names of priests ministering the sacraments, whose signatures appear there with their earliest entry, viz.:

1782 to 1793 (as above), Rev. Charles Sewall, rector.

1792, November 5, Rev. Francis Xavier Brosius.

1793, May 20, Rev. Francis Beeston, second rector.

1794, April 5, a marriage by Rev. —— Cibot, who signs himself "Pastor of Cape François and apostolic prefect of San Domingo."

1794, June 22 and 29, Rev. F. X. Brosius signs the marriage registry as "priest of Conewago."

(372)

1795, June 12 and 21, Rev. William Du Bourg (afterwards bishop of New Orleans).

1795, August 26 and 29, Rev. F. X. Brosius signs the marriage register.

1797, February 28, Rev. Fred. Cæs. Reuter.

1797, May 14, Rev. John Floyd.

1798, June 13, Rev. John Tessier.

1799, February 5, Rev. Gregory Kellhoffer.

1800, May 29, Rev. John Francis Moranvillé.

1800, July 3, Rev. Marcel Guillaume Pasquet de Leyde, "priest and former almoner of the government and of the general hospital of Port-au-Prince, in San Domingo, now exile and missionary at St. Ignatius', in Harford Co."[Md.].

1800, August 7, Rev. Angadrème Le Mercier, "rector of St. John's in Savannah, Georgia."

1802, November 18, Rev. Peter Babade.

1803, June 9, Rev. John Dubois (afterwards bishop).

1803, December 27, Rev. Nicholas Zocchi.

1804, September 20, Rev. F. X. Brosius.

1807, April 15, Rev. Wm. Du Bourg.

1808, May 12, Rev. Nicholas Mertz, "pastor of St. John's."

1809, December 31, Rev. Enoch Fenwick, "rector vice Rev. F. Beeston."

1810, June 23, Rev. Matthew O'Brien.

I have found the following totals for the years noted in the registrie
They are, for

1782–93 . . . . marriages . .		[figures wanting]
1794	"	 63
1795	"	 60
1796	"	 71
1797	"	 41
1798	"	 60
1799	"	 53
1800	"	 57
1801	"	 52
1802–8	"	. . [figures wanting]
1809	"	 39
1810	"	 33

529

T. C. M.

ST. PATRICK'S CHURCH,

BALTIMORE, MD.

FOUNDED 1805.

The following is a transcript from the registries of St. Patrick's Church, at Fell's Point, Baltimore, Md., the second Catholic place of worship opened in that city, made by a member of the American Catholic Historical Society, July 22, 1886.

St. Patrick's was founded in 1805, apparently, as the registries open in 1806, and was incorporated January 30, 1807, with

JOHN FRANCIS MORANVILLÉ, *President,*
PATRICK BENNET,
EDWARD HAGTHROP,
GARRET PRENDERVILL,
JAMES CLONEY,
CHARLES FEINOUR,
THOMAS CONWAY, *Secretary,*

as officers and members of the Board of Trustees.

The books of registries, from 1806 to 1823, are three—two of baptisms, marriages and deaths, and one of the minutes of the trustees' meetings. They are all in good condition, neatly written, well bound, and carefully kept. The entries in all three books are in English, except a few in French. There is no mention, so far as noticed, of the Sacrament of Confirmation having been given at this church.

The following are the priests whose names are met in the registries, with the date of their first entry, viz.:

1st—Rev. John Francis Moranvillé, January 10, 1806.
2d—Rev. Peter Babade, January 27, 1811.
3d—Rev. C. Woutters, April 4, 1814.
4th—Rev. Nicholas Kerney, April 14, 1818.
5th—Rev. J [ohn?] Hickey, August 15, 1819.
6th—Rev. J. O'Brien, November 6, 1819.

[Father Moranvillé invariably signs his name with the accent on the final letter, as given above. Father Babade frequently officiated in Philadelphia, his name appearing on the books of registries at St. Augustine's (Fourth street) in 1807–8–20.]

The first record is a marriage, dated 1806, January 10th, of John Fene-

(374)

gan, lawful son of John Fenegan and Mary, and Rosetta Neary, lawful daughter of Peter Neary and Mary, and signed "Moranvillé past. of St. Patrick's church."

The first burial, dated 1806, January 15, is a child eight days old, daughter of Victoire, a free mulatto woman.

The first baptism, dated 1806, January 19, is Joseph, lawful son of Joseph Ryly [Reilly?] and Mary, born September 19, 1805.

Father Moranvillé, who alone signs the registries up to the coming of Father Babade, signs himself variously, as a rule merely "Moranvillé," and occasionally as "J. F.," or "J. Fr.," or "J. Francis," or "John Fr." Moranvillé. In 1806, July 1, he subscribes his name as "pastor of Fell's Point."

The number of baptisms, etc., for each year, is very carefully given in the handwriting of Fr. Moranvillé at the end of each year's registries. The returns by years are as follows:

	BAPTISMS.	MARRIAGES.	BURIALS.
1806	68	18	26
1807	87	17	28
1808	77	13	45
1809	82	27	25
1810	94	23	37
1811	104	17	50
1812	123	14	45
1813	100	13	44
1814	122	9	53
1815	91	18	48
1816	133	23	60
1817	144	25	79
1818	110	24	86
1819	109	14	181
1820	104	19	84
1821	126	19	149
1822	121	30	183
1823	99*	19	110
Total,	1894	342	1333

* A marginal note states that some baptisms for this year are not recorded.

T. C. M.

INDEX.

(377)

ERRATA.

The editors, desiring to make this volume as nearly perfect as possible, here note the errors, most of them not very serious, detected since the sheets have come from the press:

Page 9, second line of Article I. of By-laws, for "February" substitute "March." This is an error of the original record which has recently been officially corrected by the Society.

Page 23, sixth line, for "Ridgeway" read "Ridgway."

Page 27, tenth line from bottom, and elsewhere, for "Matthew" Carey) read "Mathew."

Page 29, fourteenth line from bottom, for "1835" read "1834." Also note that the Father Egan mentioned at the foot of the same page was not the Bishop of Philadelphia, but his nephew, Rev. Michael De Burgo Egan, at one time President of Mt. St. Mary's College, Emmittsburg, Md.

Page 30, fifth line, omit the words in parenthesis, "one apparently a carricature."

The statement made on page 83, that in 1752 the title of old St. Joseph's, Philadelphia, was in the name of a Jesuit, is withdrawn, subsequent examination showing the date of the record to be 1781.

Page 89, third line of second paragraph, and elsewhere, for "Moranvillers" read "Moranvillé." This mistake is Gaillardin's.

Page 108, third line from bottom, for "Hayden" read "Heyden."

Page 127, eighth line of second paragraph, and elsewhere, for "Rossiter" read "Rosseter."

Lest a statement made on the middle of page 133, and repeated on page 137, may mislead the reader, we venture to suggest that Mr. Esling does not refer to the general restoration of the Society of Jesus, which did not take place until August 7th, 1814, but to an arrangement peculiar to the United States.

Middle of page 141, for "French," as applied to Father Brosius, substitute "German."

Page 167, near end of first paragraph, for "Kerin" (Fitzpatrick) read "Keirin ;" for "Neal Ginnis" read "Neale McGennis," and for (John) "Taggert" read "Taggart."

Page 181, seventh line from bottom, for "Villa Nova" read "Villanova."

Page 189, sixth line, and wherever else the name occurs, for "Donahoe" read "Donaghoe."

Middle of page 195, for (Patrick) "Burns" read "Byrne;" and same page, sixth line from bottom, for "———" after 1829, substitute "June 30."

Page 196, tenth line, for "Mary Louisa Caroline, daughter," read "Mary Louisa and Caroline, daughters;" and about the middle of the same page, where mention is made of those confirmed in 1844, for "one hundred and three" read "one hundred and thirty-three."

Page 198, seventh line (of text) from bottom, for "Huneker" read "Hunneker;" and in the following line for "Roland" read "Boland."

Page 204, first line of figures, for "$13,000" read "$13,020."

About the middle of page 206, and several times afterwards, for "Hartnett" read "Harnett."

Page 208, opposite year 1827, after "M. Egan," omit "|Franciscan."

Page 252, in first line of note, for "inserton" read "insertion."

Page 350, in fourth line of note, for "abreviatins" read "abbreviations;" and in the key, for "Mater, mother," after "M," read "Matrina, god-mother."

Page 351, for "Bond, I. B.," read "Bond, J. B.;" and for "Cemegys" read "Comegys."

Page 352, for (Dutilh and) "Wacksmuth" read "Wachsmuth;" for "Hall, I.," read "Hall, J.;" for "Hawthorne" (Thomas) read "Hawthorn;" for "Madden" (Patrick) read "Maddan," and for "$50," after "Hiney, A.," read "$30."

Page 353, for "McGinnis" (Neale) read "McGennis;" and for "Warwick" (Thomas) read "Warwich."

Page 355, in first list, insert "McGowran, Maria;" for "McNeales" (William) read "McNealis," and for (Montgomery) "Mr." read "Mrs."

On page 356, the typesetter has dealt unfairly with "O'Connor, Peter," and "Taggart, Mrs. C."

In the list of marriages and that of baptisms at St. Augustine's Church there are a few variations from the original, such as "Rostignol de" for "Rostignolde;" "De Lois" for "D'lois;" "Bourgeois" for "Bourgoeis." Besides these please note:

Page 358, tenth line, for "Thamas" (Hurley) read "Thomas."

Page 359, tenth line, omit "William Carey."

Page 360, fourteenth line from bottom, for William J. Birch" read "William Y. Birch."

Page 361, fifth line of baptisms, for "Mary" (Maux) read "Anna."

Page 362, first line, for "Francis" (Borie) read "Frances."

Page 364, eleventh line, for "Bartholemy" read "Barthlemy;" and in the seventh line from the bottom, for "Leforgue" read "Laforgue."

Page 368, eleventh line, for "I. P." (Garésché) read "J. P.;" in the tenth line from the bottom, for "Deschappels" read "Deschapelles," and for "Bauday" read "Bauduy."

Page 369, sixth line from the bottom, for "Donoghoe" read "Donaghoe."

ADDENDUM.

Mr. Francis X. Reuss, furnishes the following additions to the "key" to St. Joseph's Registers printed on page 350 :

Bapt. priv.—Baptizatus privatim, (had been) baptized privately.

Cer. sup.—Ceremoniis suppletis, baptismal ceremonies supplied subsequently.

C. C.—Catholici, Catholics.

Gem.—Gemelli, twins.

H. A.—Hujus anni, of this year, as well as hoc anno, in this year.

P. P.—Patrini, god-parents.

Sp. and ss.—Sponsor, sponsores : god-father, god-parents.

T. T.—Testes, witnesses.

M.—Most frequently matrina, god-mother, rather than mater, mother.

RECORDS

OF THE

American Catholic Historical Society.

OF

PHILADELPHIA.

Vol. II.—1886-88.

PUBLISHED BY THE SOCIETY.

1889.

NOTICE.

Responsibility for opinions expressed and statements made in the various historical essays contained in this volume is to be attributed to their authors only, and not to the Society or its Publication Committee. But we call to the reader's attention the following errors detected after the sheets had come from the press:

On pages 13, 16 and 17, for "Baird" read "Biard;" pages 41 and 44, for "Fitzsimons" read "FitzSimons;" page 41, 4th line from bottom, for "Augustinans" read "Augustinians;" page 122, 10th line from bottom, for "Gardini" read "Giardini;" page 125, 11th line from bottom, for "Gradual," "Vesperal;" page 145, 3d line from bottom, for "fathers," "Fathers;" next page, 4th line from top, for "Befugio," "Refugio;" page 215, for "Retsch," "Petsch;" page 226, 2d line from top, insert "one" after "ninety;" same page, 10th line from bottom, for "Dutchess," "Duchess;" page 314, last line, for "Hancock," "Haycock;" page 316, 5th line of text, for "Connor," "Conner;" same page, in Latin quotation near the foot, for "interrogovi," "interrogavi;" and for "presenti," "præsenti;" and page 373, for "Colonel David Chambers" read "Captain Robert Chambers."

The list of members on pages 386–388 is complete only to December 12th last. Those who have paid their first year's dues since that time will understand, therefore, why their names do not appear in this volume.

JULES JUNKER,
FRANCIS X. REUSS,
FRANCIS T. FUREY,
Committee.

January 23, 1889.

FORM OF BEQUEST (LEGACY).

I give and bequeath unto "The American Catholic Historical Society of Philadelphia," incorporated in the year 1885, the sum of.................... ...., to be paid to the Treasurer thereof for the time being, for the use of said Society.

FORM OF A DEVISE (REAL ESTATE).

I give and devise unto "The American Catholic Historical Society of Philadelphia," incorporated in the year 1885 [here describe the property or ground rent], together with the appurtenances, in fee simple.

(2)

CONTENTS.

(3)

Organization of the Society,

December 12th, 1888.

OFFICERS.

PRESIDENT,
REV. THOMAS C. MIDDLETON, D. D., O. S. A.

FIRST VICE-PRESIDENT,
LAWRENCE F. FLICK, M. D.

SECOND VICE-PRESIDENT,
FRANK A. FOY.

RECORDING SECRETARY,
EDWARD J. ALEDO.

CORRESPONDING SECRETARY,
FRANCIS T. FUREY.

TREASURER,
JOHN F. McMENAMIN.

MANAGERS.
(For one year.)

MARTIN I. J. GRIFFIN,   BERNARD L. DOUREDOURE,
C. CARROLL MEYER.

(For two years.)

JULES JUNKER,   REV. ERNEST O. HILTERMANN,
FRANCIS X. REUSS.

(For three years.)

CHARLES H. A. ESLING,   REV. JOSEPH C. KELLY,
JOSEPH M. ENGEL.

LIBRARIAN.
FRANCIS X. REUSS.

(4)

PREFACE.

After an interval of nearly two years since the first volume of original " Records " of our Society was given to the public, a second instalment is now submitted. The editor takes advantage of this occasion to express his own gratification, as well as that of his colleagues in the work, and of the other interested and really active members of the Society, at the success attending our first effort, whose result has been received with marked favor by all those best qualified to judge of its merits. This verdict has encouraged us in our present work, which we have therefore undertaken with much less diffidence ; but it has not blinded us to defects in the former volume, which we have endeavored to correct here as far as possible and as they have come to our notice.

While the general plan adopted in the first instance is pretty closely followed in the present, yet some modifications are introduced. As before, the book is made up chiefly of original historical papers, read at our public meetings, and church registers heretofore unpublished. Cognate with the latter is a new feature that is now introduced, or rather one at which only a mere glimpse was had before, that of genealogies of old Catholic families, in making out which indispensable aid is rendered by the registers referred to. This is a very important factor in our local annals. Reports of officers and committees, except that of the Recording Secretary, which

5

forms a historical introduction to the volume, are now given place at the end instead of the beginning of the book ; and so also with the list of members, in order to make it complete to date. Our Charter needs not to be copied here again, and our By-Laws will be printed and circulated after the work of revising them, which is now in progress, shall have been completed.

Every member or other person wishing to consult our books, pamphlets and unprinted documents, should carefully study the rules governing the library. In lieu of a detailed report from the Librarian, which does not appear in this volume, a catalogue will shortly be issued.

It is earnestly hoped that Volume II. will be received with at least as much favor as was accorded to its predecessor. It contains equally valuable historical material, and no pains have been spared to give it as perfect and presentable a form as possible.

FRANCIS T. FUREY,

Chairman of Publication Committee.

RECORDS OF

The American Catholic Historical Society.

INTRODUCTION.

A SOMEWHAT detailed sketch of the organization and growth of this Society appeared in the first volume of its " Records," in the form of a report from the then Recording Secretary, under date of July 22d, 1886.*

Following the example thus set, this report is respectfully submitted as the continuation of a narrative, the first instalment of which has been already published. At the above-mentioned date the Society had passed safely through the purely experimental and formative stage, and had become established on a firm basis. To parody a cant phrase, there is nothing so stimulating as success, and it is needed only that the members should realize that their efforts had so far proved successful to induce them to continue the work in hand with renewed zeal and activity.

Prior to September, 1886, all business had been transacted at the regular and special meetings of the Society; the regular meetings being held quarterly, and special meetings being called as often as business would require. Hence meetings of the Society were held at least once and sometimes twice a month. Such a plan would naturally work well while the

---

* See Records of American Catholic Historical Society, Vol. I., pp. 10–22.

Society consisted of only charter members, who were for the most part Philadelphians; but as the organization widened and extended in membership, it was deemed unwise to allow its control to remain so entirely in the hands of a local section, who alone could find it convenient to attend the frequent meetings. Moreover, the Constitution had provided for a Board of Managers, consisting of the officers of the Society and nine others, three of whom should be elected at the members' meeting in December of each year.* Such a Board, it was thought, would the better execute the will of the large body of membership now widely scattered throughout the United States; at least it would be their duty, as the trusted agents of the members generally, to administer the affairs of the Society in the interest of all, and to preserve the broad aim and high principles of its founders. Happily the Society had elected an Executive Board in accordance with the Constitution, but it was found very difficult to arouse it from the " innocuous desuetude " into which it had fallen. Finally, however, a quorum was convened and the Board entered upon its duties as the executive arm of the corporation. This was on September 29th, 1886, and since that time the Board of Managers has been a very important part of the working organization of our Society. The Board has held a meeting regularly every month, with the single exception of July, 1887, when on account of the warm weather a quorum could not be obtained. It has assumed almost the entire direction and management of the Society's affairs, acting at all times in accordance with the Society's wishes as indicated at its quarterly meetings. It appoints all committees and exercises supervision over them, acts upon reports of officers, elects members, and in general transacts any business which may be presented touching the interests of the Society, barring an amendment to the Constitution or By-Laws. The officers perform no important act outside their routine duties without the express sanction of the Board of Managers. It should be stated that the Society retains concurrent jurisdiction over the above subject matters

---

* See Constitution, Vol. I., p. 7.

and transacts similar business at its quarterly meetings, though on account of the more frequent meetings of the Managers, the control of its affairs has virtually passed into their hands. So as to insure the success of the work of the Society, whose affairs it has undertaken to manage, the Board has caused itself to be represented by its own members on the most important committees. This has been found to be for the best interests of the Society, as the Board is thus enabled to gain information at any time of the work of these committees, and to co-operate with them. Thus stimulated and assisted, the committees have performed much valuable work. The committee on genealogy has compiled a number of important genealogies, and that on reminiscences has collected a great deal of valuable information by interviewing the older members of the clergy and laity. The committee on public meetings has caused a number of public meetings to be held from time to time, at which papers have been read and the public kept informed of the Society's work and progress. The publication committee has devoted much time and attention to the preparation and publication of this volume.

Some very important work has been done by the committee on ways and means to procure a hall. As far back as November, 1886, the Society began to look around for more ample quarters, and a committee was then appointed by the Board to inquire into the matter and report. But it was not until March, 1887, that the idea took the form of a practical movement. The former committee was then discharged, and the present committee on ways and means to procure a hall was appointed. The work of this committee has been necessarily slow, owing to the fact that the original suggestion of leasing has been abandoned and the committee has decided to make an earnest endeavor to raise sufficient funds to erect a building or purchase one already erected which would be suitable for the Society's purposes. The members of the committee fully realize the magnitude of their undertaking; but, nothing daunted, they have been making heroic efforts; they have been favorably received by the clergy of the archdiocese of Phil-

adelphia, amongst whom they have been making a personal
canvass, and they anticipate even more substantial recognition
from the laity; and may they not indulge the hope that the
Catholics of the United States, in whose interest the work of
this Society is prosecuted, will take kindly to the suggestion
that they should manifest a practical interest in this particular
project?

The Society has not allowed the inconvenience of cramped
quarters to retard the increase of its library and cabinet, to
both of which numerous additions have been made; and no
opportunity is ever neglected to procure a valuable accession for
either.   Only recently a whole library of over twelve hundred
volumes and fully as many pamphlets, the property of the late
Rev. A. P. Haviland, was purchased, and it has been placed
in storage pending the acquisition of more commodious quarters.   We have also purchased nearly one hundred volumes
of the earliest Catholic newspapers in the United States.
Persons holding such material, and being willing to part with
it, are requested to communicate with the Society.   A noble
example in this direction has been set by the Rev. Father Lane,
Rector of St. Teresa's Church, Philadelphia, who has presented
over one hundred volumes, many of them very rare prints.

At a meeting of the Board of Managers on July 25th, 1888,
it was resolved to adopt the system of Memorial Libraries, and
the newspapers on the following day contained an account of
the proceedings.   It happens frequently that the owner of a
choice library has devoted many years to the careful and dis-
criminative selection of books, and then will contemplate with
a sad reluctance the fact that on his decease they may be
prized only for their commercial value and perhaps scattered
to the winds under the auctioneer's hammer.   Our Society
would gladly come to the rescue in such a case; if authorized
by the owner's will, it would become the custodian of his
library, would keep it intact and would bestow upon it the
same care and solicitude that he would if living.   When a
deceased scholar has neglected to make such a provision in
his will, no better monument could be erected to his memory

than his library presented as a memorial to the American Catholic Historical Society.

Our Society has also established a custom of celebrating important historical events touching the history of the Church in America. Such an event was the death of Rev. Ferdinand Farmer, S. J., on the 17th of August, 1786. The celebration of the centenary of Father Farmer's death was postponed from August 17th to Sunday, December 26th, 1886, and was held at old St. Joseph's Church in this city. A delegation from the Society attended High Mass, Rev. John A. Morgan, S. J., being the celebrant. An excellent discourse was delivered by Rev. J. J. Bric, S. J., at the Gospel, and another by the celebrant, Father Morgan, S. J., at the close of the Mass.

Of a more secular nature was the celebration of the one hundredth anniversary of the framing of the Constitution of the United States, but it seemed to our members peculiarly appropriate that this Society should join in the commemoration of that important event; accordingly special exercises were held at the Society's hall on the evening of September 15th, 1887, and a goodly part of this volume is devoted to an account thereof.

The Society does not lose sight of the fact that while it is Catholic, it is also American in aim and spirit, and therefore it is the intention to celebrate in a fitting manner the anniversary of every important national event that may be worthy of commemoration. To this end, preparations are now being made to observe the centennial anniversary of Washington's first inauguration as President, and a paper on Thomas Lloyd, the official stenographer of Congress at that time, and a staunch Catholic, is being prepared for the occasion.

More ample details of the work of the society will be found in the special reports of officers and committees which appear elsewhere in this volume.

The American Catholic Historical Society is still in its infancy, and a vast field of work lies before it. While the success of the undertaking seems assured, it appeals more than ever to the generous spirit of those who may be incited to an interest in its work by a perusal of this and the preceding volume. The great problem so far has been how to accomplish the most beneficial results with the limited means at our disposal.

FRANK A. FOY,

Recording Secretary.

SKETCH

OF

THE ABENAQUIS MISSION

[Summary* of a Paper read before the AMERICAN CATHOLIC HISTORICAL SOCIETY OF PHILADELPHIA, on Friday evening, February 18th, 1887, by REV. JAMES J. BRIC, S. J.]

FATHER BRIC began by saying that the Abenaquis† Mission was one of much interest. It was the first French mission in this country; it witnessed the martyrdom of Father Rasle in the last century, and in the present the labors of Father Bapst, who was tarred and feathered by the Know-Nothing descendants of those who had murdered Father Rasle.

Before narrating the history of the Abenaquis Mission Father Bric, in order to show the priority of Catholic discovery, conquest and claims on this continent, alluded at some length to the life of Columbus, the discoverer of America, and to Cortez, Lord Baltimore, Cartier and Champlain, the pioneers of civilization and Christianity in America. It was a pleasure to contemplate their noble and pure lives. Everything about them was grand and elevated, because they were thoroughly Catholic. Then, again, the early missionaries of this country, Brébœuf, Jogues, White, Baird, Dreuillettes and Rasle, were exceptionally holy and apostolic men. It is im-

---

* It is to be regretted that the author has not seen fit to give the whole of his valuable essay to the public.—ED.
†Also spelled Abnakis, which means "Men of the Eastern Land."—ED.

possible to read the history of their labors and sufferings without being inflamed with piety and zeal for the salvation of souls.

Of Columbus a distinguished writer has said that only believers in the supernatural can comprehend him, that his figure rises above all the discoverers, ancient and modern. He is distinguished among them by the depth of his genius, by the beauty of his character, by the frankness of his faith and piety, and by the crown of sorrow and affliction which ungrateful Spain placed on his brow. " God led him by the path of his own natural character to the sublimest apostolate." And Irving says of him : " Throughout his life he was noted for his strict attention to the offices of religion. Nor did his piety consist in mere forms, but partook of that lofty and solemn enthusiasm with which his whole character was strongly tinctured." It is worthy of remark that when addressing himself to Genoa and Venice he held out temporal motives to tempt them ; but knowing the piety of Isabella, he spoke to her of spreading the kingdom of Jesus Christ and of His Holy Church. Isabella, won by his piety, elevated views and enthusiasm, became his friend for life. The service of God had always the first place in his esteem. To Isabella and Columbus the great things of this world were very trifling. They looked beyond the stars. God, heaven, religion—these were the supernatural ideas that filled their capacious intellects, raising them far above the low plane of common thoughts, thus imparting an iron resolution to wills naturally strong, and giving marvellous elevation to characters naturally grand and fearless. " The discoverer of America was indeed a true son of the old Crusaders, pious and enthusiastic as Peter the Hermit, bold as Richard Cœur de Lion, patient and dauntless as Godfrey de Bouillon, and a partaker in the holy wisdom of St. Louis and St. Bernard." Another writer, speaking of him, says : " The superiority of Columbus, of his genius, and of his grandeur, was owing to his religious faith."

If from Columbus we pass to Cortez, the conqueror of Mexico, we find much to admire. A Spanish writer, speaking of him, says he desired for God numberless souls. With the great French Catholic, Champlain, of North America, the devout Spaniard of that day deemed the salvation of his soul more glorious than the conquest of an empire. The desire of planting the cross in the midst of heathen nations, and of thereby bringing them from the region of the shadow of death into the light of Christian civilization, prompted the expeditions for discovery and conquest. Prescott, notwithstanding his bigotry, admits that the French and the Spaniards sought above all things the salvation of souls. The Dutch came to America to make money, while the Puritans, not being able to domineer in England, passed over to America in hopes that they might be able to exercise here a tyranny they could not exercise at home.

When we turn from the south to the French Colonies of the north, we see equal, perhaps even greater, zeal for the conversion of the Indians. Bancroft, speaking of Champlain, tells us that, full of honor and probity, of ardent devotion and burning zeal, he esteemed the salvation of his soul worth more than the conquest of an empire ; and he adds that this was natural, as the Catholic Church cherishes every member of the human race without regard to his age or skin. Such generous and Christian sentiments towards the Indian never entered into the narrow mind of the Puritans. The glory of having discovered America and of having established the first colonies, the first missions, the first colleges and schools, and the first charitable institutions in North America, belongs entirely to the Catholic Church. Mr. Bancroft bears us out in all these assertions.

Of Lord Baltimore, the founder of the Maryland colony, it was said that he was of a singularly truth-loving and generous nature. A distinguished writer, speaking of him, says that "his mildness and magnanimity were only equalled by the manly integrity of his character. In an intolerant age and country he was a model of that true liberality which springs from Christian charity. To possess truth and save his soul, he was ready to sacrifice every earthly hope."

Is it not a subject of congratulation that in contemplating the early history of America, whether we turn our eyes to the

Spanish or French colonies, or to that of Lord Baltimore in Maryland, we see noble characters, men of high aims and of the purest and most lofty intentions, men whose lives were inspired by the teachings of the Church, men who were thorough Catholics? But especially we turn to the early missionaries. What examples of zeal and heroism! It has been said of Father Brébœuf that, though his biography is not found in Butler's " Lives of the Saints," " we might search in vain through that excellent work for anything to surpass it in sublime interest. In his towering figure, iron frame and supernatural gifts he resembled St. Columbkille; in his rare meekness, kindness and practical sense he was not unlike St. Francis de Sales; while his lion heart and martyr spirit would in truth have done honor to St. Lawrence."

The zeal, meekness and heroism of Brébœuf were shared by Fathers White, Jogues, Lallemand, Baird, Dreuillettes, Rasle, and a host of others. Of Father White it has been truly said that through his whole life we see shining forth a character of crystal purity, manly, fearless and lofty. It is the union of the saint and hero. Every writer who has spoken of those early missionaries has borne testimony to their gentleness, kindness, patience, zeal and heroism, and a distinguished writer, speaking of them, says: " Their footprints must be as enduring as America itself. They hesitated not; they flinched not; for them death had no terrors. As the peaks of the Rocky Mountains rise far above other elevations in our country, so the figures of the early Jesuits in North America towered aloft in the first ages of our striking and romantic history."

Among the red men the Catholic Church made no nobler converts than the ancient warriors and chieftains of Maine. Two hundred and eighty years ago this State was the hunting grounds of the Abenaquis tribe, a branch of the great Algonquin family. The story of their conversion is a beautiful one, and will be related briefly. In 1612 Father Baird landed on Mount Desert Island and commenced a mission which he called St. Saviour's. Shortly after arriving here, on penetrating to the mainland, he heard the sound of piteous wailings

in a distant village; he hurried toward it. An Indian brave
was holding his dying child in his arms and pouring forth his
sighs and tears at the sight of the sufferings of his child,
whose death was expected at each moment. The whole
village were gathered around him in loud sympathy, uniting
their tears and sighs to those of the afflicted chieftain. Father
Baird's heart was deeply touched. He baptized the babe and
prayed for its recovery. His prayer was heard! This was
the first sacrament administered in the State of Maine. The
dusky villagers regarded Father Baird as an envoy of heaven.

But disaster was about to frown on the new mission. While
the buildings were merely in the course of erection a number
of English ships, under the bigoted and infamous Argal, sailed
past, attacked the place, killed Brother Du Thet, and carried
off all the priests and colonists. "Holy Saviour's" was now
a ruin. The broken cross alone remained above the body of
Du Thet to guard that land for Catholicity. All was silent—
"no hymn, no voice of prayer, no savages reclaimed for God
and society were gathered there." Thus, adds a writer, was
the first Abenaquis mission destroyed by the English, a nation
whose only word of peace for the Indian was the sound of
the rifle. They resolved to put Father Baird to death; but
the vessels were scattered by a storm. That bearing Father
Baird was driven to the Azores, and there, in a Catholic port,
and without a commission, the Captain found himself at the
mercy of Father Baird, who, far from seeking to avenge his
wrongs, made no appeal to the Portuguese authorities. The
vessel finally reached England, whence Father Baird returned
to France.

More than thirty years passed away before another attempt
was made to carry the Gospel to the wigwams of the Abenaquis in the forests of Maine. A warrior of that tribe had
been converted at Quebec. On returning to his kindred he
told them of the wonderful Black-gown, the Great Spirit, and
the beauties of the new faith. They heard, admired, and sent
a deputation of chiefs to Quebec to beg for a missionary. The
enterprising Father Dreuillettes responded to their call.

Before speaking of this missionary's labors among the

Abenaquis, Father Bric alluded briefly to his wintering with the Montagnais, a tribe that roamed amongst the forests on the northern boundary of Maine. Having become converted since the time of Father Lejeune, they looked upon Father Dreuillettes as a friend and father. Their conversion is, according to Parkman, the most remarkable record of success in the whole body of the Jesuit " Relations." Parkman, to substantiate this assertion, speaks of their forgiving spirit, how they stretched their beaver skins on the snow on Good Friday, knelt before the crucifix, and prayed for the forgiveness of their enemies, the Iroquois. Mr. Parkman might have added that this beautiful example of Christian charity awakened no echo amongst his Puritan ancestors in their dealings with the Catholic missionaries and the poor Indians. We might here apply the words of our Lord, Luke x, 21, " Thou hast hidden these things from the wise and prudent, and hast revealed them to little ones." Christianity in its Divine constitution and supernatural workings on the soul is something of which the proud Puritan understood nothing. The poor Indian, docile to the word of God, and assisted by His grace, had become a good and sincere Christian, showing by his actions that he was leading a supernatural life.

But to return to the Abenaquis. Father Dreuillettes set out for the mission in 1646, and soon reached the Kennebec. (Here followed a description of the Abenaquis tribe, who were naturally quite susceptible to good impressions.) The missionary's great sanctity, heroism and supernatural life convinced their minds and won their hearts to the truths of the Catholic Church, and they very soon sought baptism from the good missionary. After many instructions he called upon them, as a preliminary to their reception as catechumens, to do three things : first, to renounce intoxicating liquors ; second, to live in peace with their neighbors ; third, to give up their superstitions. To these demands they all agreed. When the Indians went to hunt, Father Dreuillettes accompanied them. The medicine men declared that they would be unsuccessful, but they returned safe and well and loaded with venison. (Here followed a description of a hunting expedition, and how the Father said Mass every morning, and recited prayers and gave instructions morning and evening.) After being there a short time he was recalled to Quebec. The Indians, who loved him sincerely, bewailed his departure. The Abenaquis in December sent for their missionary, and as they did not succeed in obtaining him, repeatedly sent deputations to Quebec. In 1650 their prayer was heard. Father Dreuillettes set out with a party of them. They suffered very much from hunger and cold, but ascribed their ultimate success to the prayers of Father Dreuillettes, as the relief which they obtained seemed truly miraculous. After twenty-four days of great hardship they reached Norridgwok, the chief Abenaquis village. He was received with great rejoicing, and was delighted to find that they had followed his instructions. He gives a most interesting description of the care with which they related to him everything they had done, especially about the baptism of their children, and their pleasure when they learned that they had followed his directions properly. Then Father Dreuillettes also bore letters, accrediting him as envoy of the Governor of Canada to the governing power in New England. The Canadian authorities wished to combine against the Iroquois, who threatened all that was Christian. The embassy, though solicited by the Puritans, failed. They had no wish or intention to help in protecting Catholic missionaries or Catholic Indians.

Amongst the Indians Father Dreuillettes found warm hearts; the good soil on which fell the word of God that came from his lips produced fruit a hundredfold. By his Indian flock he was more than revered—he was idolized. Hearing him accused in his absence by an Englishman, they indignantly exclaimed: " Know that he is now of our nation. We have adopted him into the tribe and regard him as the wisest of our chiefs. We respect him as the ambassador of Jesus Christ. Whoever attacks him attacks all the Abenaquis tribe."

Many interruptions attended the early missions in Maine. Many zealous priests labored in the fruitful field, and at length every Abenaquis was a devoted follower of the ancient faith.

Their territory being disputed ground between England and France, they were ever the faithful allies of the former. But as the power of France began to wane on the Atlantic coast they suffered dreadful persecutions at the hands of the English, especially the fanatics of Massachusetts. (Here followed a description of the ravages committed by the Puritans, destroying churches and driving out the missionaries.) The brave Indians in Maine were hunted down because they professed the faith of Columbus, but they wavered not. Under the guidance of the saintly and valiant Father Rasle, who began his labors amongst them in 1695, they stood like a rock amid the surging sea. The English made every effort to pervert the Indians; they offered them temporal advantages if they would change their creed, but the Indians remained faithful to the Church.

Father Rasle came to America in 1689, and was sent to Illinois in 1693. He wrote long descriptions of his travels, and of the habits of the western Indians. He speaks of their eloquence. (Here Father Bric remarked that western eloquence is not a thing of recent date.) In 1695 he was sent amongst the Abenaquis, where his pastoral care was only closed when his body, riddled by Yankee bullets, sank in death at the foot of his mission cross. In his letters he gives a very detailed account of the church he built, of his forty altar boys, of the piety of the Abenaquis, and of the persecutions of the English and New Englanders. His church was burned by them. In one of his journeys he fell and broke both legs, and remained a cripple ever after. On his partial recovery he returned to his mission, though the English had set a price on his head and pursued him on various occasions. They finally shot him at the foot of his cross and cut his body in pieces. They carried with them his papers and a dictionary of the Indian language which he had composed and which is now in the possession of Harvard College. The Indians, though scattered and decimated, remained faithful to the Church. They fought with Washington during the Revolution. After the English were driven out they sent a deputation, with Father Rasle's cross, to Bishop Carroll, asking for a priest. He granted their request.

History presents no people more sublimely grand than the Abenaquis in their pious attachment to Catholicity. They were the first native Americans to embrace the faith in a body, and neither the changes of time, nor cruel wars, nor the persecution of England, nor even the terrors of death have been able to shake their glorious allegiance to their God and their religion. Bishop Fenwick erected a monument where Father Rasle fell. The inscription tells that on that spot there was a house of God and a Christian village; there the pastor was slain and the flock dispersed. Bishop Fitzpatrick, of Boston, restored the mission to the Jesuits, and in 1848 Father Bapst was sent to the Abenaquis, among whom he labored for many years. During the Know-Nothing excitement of 1855 he was tarred and feathered by the descendants of those who had murdered Father Rasle. Father Bric then gave his reminiscences of Father Bapst and spoke of his great sanctity, his burning zeal, and of many miraculous events in the life of one who was the worthy successor of the old Jesuit missionaries who were so apostolic amongst the Indians after the discovery of this country.

THE EALRY REGISTERS

OF THE

Catholic Church in Pennsylvania.

[Read before the SOCIETY on May 5th, 1887, by PHILIP S. P. CONNER.]

I PROPOSE, to-night, to say something about the old registers of the Catholic Church in Pennsylvania, a sub-ject old in itself, but new, I fancy, to many, for there is scarcely anything so neglected and forgotten as are church registers—Protestant as well as Catholic. But to the point: Church or parish registers have been in use for four or five centuries,* and are usually kept under three heads, viz., mar-riage, baptism and burial.

In this country they were introduced by the first mission-aries, and Dr. Shea states, in his "Catholic Church in Colonial Days," that, two hundred years ago and more, registers existed within the Spanish missions of North America record-ing the baptisms of myriads of red Indians. But if any of this very early evangelization reached this part of our country it was soon swept away; certainly no records of it remain here within the bounds of our State, whose earliest Catholic

---

* The Rev. Dr. Middleton, O.S.A., in his introduction to St. Joseph's Registers, printed in Vol. I., p. 247, of the "Records" of this Society, states, on the authority of Cesare Cantù, that the Register of Siena begins in the year 1379. This is the oldest now known to exist (vide Cantù's "Storia degli Italiani," Tom. II., p. 659, edit. Palermo, 1858).

THE EARLY CHURCH REGISTERS OF PENNSYLVANIA.   23

registers are those begun by the missionaries of the eighteenth
century, those good men who in their turn bore the faith to
our land.

Besides being interesting and valuable as records of past
generations, these manuscripts have a special value as legal
evidence receivable in our courts.   Indeed, I am informed that
some years ago St. Joseph's register was the evidence that
decided a law-suit involving a fortune in New York; and it
was only last year that I discovered in the same register the
entry of a marriage, solemnized a century ago, which may
result in a manner similar.   Like results are not infrequent, for
it was to assure the preservation of such proof, and also that
of the orthodoxy of the parishioners, that the registers were
instituted.

You are aware that this country was discovered and chiefly
possessed by Roman Catholics, and that the first Christian
religion introduced here was that of Rome; but that ultimately
both were supplanted by the English and Protestantism.   In
fact, with the exception of Maryland and Florida, Protestants
were the first actual and permanent settlers in the region of
country now covered by New England, the Middle and
Southern seaboard States.   On this account it is that the
registers of the various Protestant sects antedate those of the
Roman Catholic Church in the parts of America just mentioned.

But when and where was the Church of Rome first per-
manently planted in the Middle States, and when might we
expect to find the beginning of its registers, the proofs of the
Church's life, of her priests' activity and of the very existence
of a faithful flock?   The Church of Rome was first established
in Maryland in the year 1634, where, surviving interruptions,
it still remains—illustrious from the past, nobly seated in the
present.   From Maryland its faith was carried into Pennsylvania and Delaware, thence to the Jerseys and New York.
So much for the foundation of the faith; now as to the beginning of the registers.   They should, and doubtless did, begin
with the beginning of each mission; but, alas! the "tooth of
time," together with indifference and neglect, have destroyed

the earliest of these records—none remain in Pennsylvania prior to 1741.

The mission to Pennsylvania, which resulted in the establishment of the Catholic Church, took place within the first third of the eighteenth century. In 1730 (or, according to the latest investigator of the subject, Mr. Martin I. J. Griffin, 1720) Father Greaton, a Jesuit, came from Maryland into Pennsylvania, in whose chief city of Philadelphia he founded St. Joseph's Church in the year 1732. In this date I follow Mr. Griffin; it is a year earlier than the one usually given, but it is corroborated, I am informed, by a letter of Father Greaton's. I am thus particular in mentioning the date of St. Joseph's foundation because it was then that the Catholics first had a fixed and permanent seat in Philadelphia, and their priests therein having a repository for their registers and other Church records, we should expect to find them still there, beginning with the beginning of the Church, viz., in 1732, but in this we are disappointed.

Instead of commencing in 1732, St. Joseph's registers do not begin until twenty-six years later, viz., 1758. All of the registers prior to this date have disappeared, absolutely all; the Goshenhoppen register, beginning in 1741, being but partially a Philadelphia list, I do not refer to it now, but will speak of it later. What has become of these old books I know not; but there is a vague tradition that they, with still older ones pertaining to Maryland, were destroyed by fire at St. Thomas' Manor, while any which may have escaped this conflagration were deliberately burned as rubbish among Father Greaton's papers at St. Joseph's after Father Barbelin's death in 1869. Thus, by accident and through ignorance, records most valuable to the genealogist and historian have been forever lost.

As for the registers which remain in Philadelphia, the oldest, as stated, begins in the year 1758. Now, besides being intrinsically valuable, this record is increased in value by the fact that it is the oldest Roman Catholic register in our city. This being the case, a further account of it may be interesting. It is a little volume of fifty leaves which measure seven and a half inches in length and six inches across, each one. With a single exception, all of these leaves are closely written over with registrations and indexes referring thereto, the entries being, as usual, in ecclesiastical Latin, proper names in some instances being given a German form, very natural to the registrar, viz., the German, Father Ferdinand Steinmeyer, *alias* Farmer. Although the lines are crowded together and the writing small, the matter is sufficiently legible except when signs and abbreviations are used—then the uninitiated would be at a loss to understand what is meant; but the mystery is not deep, and may be quickly dispelled by reference to the Key which is, or soon will be, attached to the volume.*

This old register is followed by others, bringing the records down to the year 1800, and so on to the present day. For many years all of these old books were in a very dilapidated condition—the binding broken, the leaves loose, and therefore liable to loss; but during the spring of 1886, the Rev Father Morgan entrusting them to safe hands, they were repaired and firmly rebound in strong canvas covers—a most enduring protection against damp or dry-rot—and are now carefully kept in the church fire-proof. Hence I hope that this interesting and valuable relic, viz., the manuscripts forming St. Joseph's old register, is now safe for at least another century, while I have the additional satisfaction of knowing that the preservation of its records is assured; for, owing to the efforts of this Society and the facilities liberally afforded by the Reverend Fathers at St. Joseph's, what was but a single frail manuscript is now a multitude of printed volumes endowed with the enduring life of the press.

From St. Joseph's we must turn to St. Mary's Church for old records. St. Mary's was erected in 1763, but it has no registers separate from St. Joseph's prior to 1787. After 1790 there is a sad gap of forty-eight years—a gulf in which are lost all the baptisms, with the most of the other records of the church for that space of time. This great loss is attri-

---

* The "Key" is printed in the first volume of this Society's "Records."

buted to those unfortunate contentions, now, happily, long passed away and for the most part forgotten.*

After St. Mary's records come Holy Trinity's, at Sixth and Spruce streets. Although this church was not built until 1789, its registers begin with baptisms performed in the year 1784. St. Augustine's, in North Fourth street, do not open until 1801.

Thus I have given you some slight account of the old registers yet remaining in the churches of Philadelphia; but there are others in different parts of the State whose records go back beyond the year 1800; for instance, Conewago's, in Adams County, begin in the latter part of the last century, Lancaster's in 1787,† and, first of all in point of time, that at Goshenhoppen, beginning in 1741. Since this register is now the senior one extant, it deserves a fuller notice. The mission of Goshenhoppen—but stop, perhaps I may as well tell you what Goshenhoppen is and where it is; for, although it has existed for a hundred and fifty years and more, it is unnoticed by both gazetteer and map, having no definite bounds. Goshenhoppen, Quesohopin, or Cushenhopen, as variously called, is the name applied to the region of country in the valley of the Perkiomen with its tributary streams, and, therefore, spreading indefinitely over the northwestern part of Montgomery County, with the adjoining portion of Berks; indeed, the Goshenhoppen to which I now have particular reference is in Berks County, Washington Township, and is also known as Churchville or Bally. To get to it from Philadelphia you must take the Reading Railroad to Pottstown,

---

* The following records were seen by me at St. Mary's Church, Philadelphia, in 1885, viz., Baptismal registers, from January 1st, 1787, to December 28th, 1790. From this last date to 1838 the records of this series were missing, as stated in the text; later on, in pulling down the old dwelling-house to the south of the church, some of them were found; but being at once packed away for removal and preservation, I have had no opportunity to examine them.——Marriage registers, none before 1831.——Pew lists begin December 8th, 1787.——Burial list begins January 7th, 1788.

† This register—1787 to 1804—was formerly at St. Mary's Church, Lancaster, but is now in private hands.

thence exchange for Barto, from which terminus Bally is reached by two miles of good road. The country is healthful, the plains good farming land, the hills rich in iron ore, much of which is smelted in the district and adds to its prosperity.

Here, to this pleasant, quiet land came Father Theodore Schneider in the year 1741, and here he built a house and a church, the latter still standing and now enshrining the grave of its founder, and yet holding the evidence of his pious work and journeyings in his register, written by his own hand from the 23d of August, 1741, on through many a long year, and constituting now the oldest register of the Church known in this part of our land. The book is small, convenient to carry in the pocket, and undoubtedly it was so carried from place to place, as its entries attest. Its covering is of stout canvas cloth, and, like St. Joseph's, its leaves are closely written over in Latin. It is gratifying to see fac-similes of the title-page and the first entry, bearing Father Schneider's signature, preserved in Dr. Shea's new volume, before alluded to.*

A few words more and my paper is finished. The manuscript books of which I have written this short account, and to see some of which I have traveled many miles, are invaluable as the sole existing records of the forefathers of people who may now number thousands; hence many should be actively interested in the preservation of these volumes; but through ignorance or utter indifference few of the descendants of the people noted in these registers take even the slightest interest in the matter, and so these old volumes, filled with the records of their progenitors and bearing the proofs of the toilsome journeyings and pious labors of devoted priests among rough frontiersmen and fierce Indians, are allowed to remain, year after year and generation after generation, liable to the damage arising from utter neglect and the total loss of all-consuming fire.

---

* Besides the *church* registers noted in the text, I may here mention the register of the chaplain to the military post of Fort Duquesne, under the French. This register (1753-56) was printed by Dr. Shea in 1859, and also by the Rev. A. A. Lambing, in his "Historical Researches," A. D. 1884-5.

On this account I cannot help thinking that all old church registers, after a certain limit of time, should be placed in some repository convenient to all the diocese, and safe from fire, damp and theft.   The fittest depository for the collected parish registers of a diocese is, unquestionably, the archieves of the diocese; and I would most respectfully suggest that the bishops of the various sees call in the old registers to some safe, convenient place for preservation and to facilitate transcription, when necessary.   My suggestion is not a new one; the making of transcripts was practised centuries ago by the Church; it has been revived in our day in Europe, and to it we owe the preservation of records which otherwise would now be numbered among the lost.

REV. LOUIS BARTH,

a Pioneer Missionary in Pennsylvania and an Administrator of the Diocese of Philadelphia.

[Read before the SOCIETY on May 5th, 1887, by Rev. JULES C. FOIN.]

THE following sketch of one of the most earnest and active pioneer priests of the Church in Pennsylvania is far from being as complete as it should be; yet, imperfect as it is, I hope it may prove interesting to those who revere the memory of the noble priests who, through trackless forests and in humble log-huts, brought glad tidings of great joy to the then few, scattered Catholics throughout the great State of William Penn. The name of Rev. Louis Barth is found in the early records of the Church as often, I think, as that of any of the early missionary priests, his long priestly career extending from 1790 until 1844. The hours of toil and labor, of patience and charity, of study and prayer, of counsel and advice, of preaching and administering the holy Sacraments, of trials and suffering in those years, we can form but a faint idea of; sufficient, however, to hear with pleasure something concerning such a worthy man.

Louis Barth de Walbach was born of noble parentage in Alsace, at that time a province of France. He was the second son of the noble Count Joseph de Barth and Maria Louisa de Rohmer. The title of honor conferred upon his house was that of Walbach, or De Walbach, in consequence of which we often find him alluded to as the Baron of Walbach, and the prefix is added to his name as "De" Barth. He himself, however, always signed his name in the early baptismal records

as Louis Barth or L. Barth. Although entitled to be called De
Barth, we will continue in this sketch to use his name as he
signed it. He was born at Münster on the Feast of All
Saints, Nov. 1, 1764. Early in life he showed a disposition
to embrace the clerical state and evinced a holy anxiety to
dedicate his life to the service of the sanctuary. His pious
and noble parents encouraged the evident holy vocation of
their son, and sent him to complete his collegiate course of
studies in the then celebrated college of the Premonstraten-
sians at Colley. The founder of this order was St. Norbert,
who was called by St. Bernard " the holiest and most eloquent
man of his age." From Colley the young graduate went to
the Seminary at Strasburg, where he was ordained in 1790.

The horrors of the French Revolution were about breaking
like a cloud of fire over the fair face of France, and the young
priest and nobleman, like many others, was forced into exile.
Having heard of the great need of priests in the United States,
he determined to embrace a missionary life and give to the
young Church of America the talents, labors and life which
his own country refused to accept. Right Rev. Bishop Carroll
was indeed very glad and willing to welcome the young Father
Barth to his immense diocese. Father Barth arrived at Baltimore in the fall of 1791, and began at once a most active and
successful missionary career. His first appointment was to
Bohemia Manor, in Cecil County, Maryland, as assistant to
the Rev. Father Beaston (or Beeston), where he arrived, as
we learn from an entry in a journal kept by Father Beaston
at Bohemia Manor, on December 10th, 1791. After a few
months he was sent—May 12th, 1792—to Port Tobacco, and
labored in the lower counties of Maryland for a few years,
from whence he came to Lancaster, Pa., in the year 1795.
The mission of Lancaster at that time embraced nearly the
whole of central Pennsylvania, now included in the Harrisburg diocese, which contains 10,113 square miles, in which
there were scattered here and there a few hundred Catholics.
The principal stations or missions were Lancaster, Elizabethtown, Lebanon, Sunbury, Little Britain and Elizabeth Furnace. With headquarters at Lancaster, Father Barth imme-

diately began to encourage the building of churches or chapels at the various points, notably at Elizabethtown and Lebanon, where only log chapels existed which were becoming too small for the respective congregations. Desiring the advice and counsel of the Right Rev. Bishop as regarded these important undertakings, as well as to give his people an opportunity of receiving the holy sacrament of Confirmation, Father Barth invited Bishop Carroll to pay a visit to Lancaster, which was also accepted.

In the early part of the month of July, 1798, Rt. Rev. John Carroll, the first Bishop and Father of the American Church, arrived at Father Barth's mission and encouraged the work of the young priest. In company with Father Barth the Bishop visited Elizabethtown to inspect the site of the new stone church to be erected there, and whilst here His Lordship baptized a child of Joseph and Susan Youtz, on the 10th day of July, 1798. He also administered the sacrament of Confirmation in the little log chapel, which was built on Henry Eckenroth's farm about two miles east of Elizabethtown. Mr. John Eagle, of Maytown, who made his first Holy Communion under Father Barth, was among the members confirmed on that day. Mr. Eagle was born October 4th, 1786, and died October 11th, 1881, aged ninety-five years. It is to this venerable old man that the writer is indebted for considerable information concerning the early history of the Church at Elizabethtown, of which he was a life-long member. The old church at Elizabethtown is probably one of the oldest relics of those times still standing in which the Holy Sacrifice has been regularly offered from the time Father Barth first said Holy Mass in it until the present day, and it bids well to stand another century. On the 30th day of May, 1799, Father Barth, by the instruction of the Rt. Rev. Bishop, laid the corner-stone of the old temple, and on that occasion, as was his usual custom, he preached two sermons, one in English, and the other in the German language, exhorting his hearers to continue steadfast in their allegiance to the faith of St. Peter, in whose honor the Church is dedicated, and to remain also faithful and obedient children of the Bishop of Baltimore.

These sentiments were also expressed in writing, to which the so-called trustees and other principal members affixed their names. This document, drawn up by Father Barth, is still preserved at Elizabethtown, and reads as follows :

" Diese Gemeinde nahm ihr Ursprung von Heinrich Ecken-roth: Im Yahr 1752 bestunde sie allein aus seiner Haushal-tung, jetzt aber ist die Zahl der Communicanten über die Hun-derte, Gott gebe das gleich wie wir zahlreich werden, wir auch in seiner Heiligen Furcht im wahren Glauben und in Christ-licher Liebe zunehmen mögen. Der Eckstein unser Kirche ist mit den vorgeschriebenen Kirchen-Ceremonien gelegt worden, den 30th Mai im Yahr 1799 von Rev. L. Barth Katholischer Pfarrer in Lancaster und sogleich unser Pfarrer. Die von der Gemeinde erwählte Vorsteher sind Heinrich Eckenroth, Johann Kaufmann und Andreas Gross. Da wir nicht wissen ob nicht nach unserem Abschied auch Männer aufstehen werden die wie der Heilige Paulus sagt. Acts 20–30. ' Ver-kehrte Reden reden werden, sich wieder die rechtmäsige Geïstliche Obrigkeit erheben und Hirten zu sich rufen die nicht zur Thür in den Schafstall hinein treten.' John 10-1 damit wir einer solchen Unordnung und Zerspaltung vor-kommen und gänzlich verhindern so erklären wir hier-durch ausdrücklich das es unser entschlossener Willen und fester Vorsatz ist, das kein Vorsteher oder andere Gemeinds-Glieder das Recht haben jenen Pfarrherrn der von dem Römisch-Katholischen Bishof von Baltimore geschickt und vorgesetzt wird jemals abzudanken, ihn nicht aufzunehmen oder ihn zu verhindern den Gottesdienst in dieser neue-berbauten Kirche zu halten. Unser Wille und Vorsatz ist auch das kein Priester der nicht die obengemelte Obrig-keit erkannt, ihr nicht unterthänig ist, jemals soll und kann angenommen werden und den Gottesdienst pflegen. Dieses versprechen wir alle, und verbinden uns selbst dazu mit freiwilligen Herzen weil ohne dieses wir wieder den Glauben und Einsetzungen der Römisch-Katholischen Kirche handeln thäten, dessen gehorsame und getreue Kinder wir verbleiben wollen bis in den Tod. Desentwegen unterzeichnen wir mit eigner Hand: Ludwig Barth, Pfarrer; Heinrich Eckenroth, Johann Wagner, Johann Kaufmann, Conrad Gross, Andreas Gross, George Carolus, John Lynch, Peter Felix, Stephan Felix, Ferdinand Finckele, Joseph Bernhard, Henry Kaufmann, Peter Yutz, Hermann Orendorff, Thomas Kelly, John Moyer, Dominic Egel, Johann Witmann, Charles Wede, Joseph Schitz, et alios."

At Lebanon Father Barth began to collect the few families together and infused new life and faith into their mission, which at the present writing owns one of the finest and most complete church properties in America, which is entirely free of debt, thanks to the good people and the indefatigable zeal of its present, as well as its late, beloved Pastor, A. F. Kuhlmann, a worthy successor of Father Barth, whose grand and noble work has, no doubt, gained for him an immortal crown in heaven. At Lancaster, the headquarters of Father Barth's labors, three large and beautiful churches and schools to-day attest that the seeds of faith and charity planted there by the early missionaries have not been lost. In the beginning of the present century, on account of its fast increasing population, Lancaster required the services of an assistant Pastor. Accordingly in September, 1801, we find the Rev. Anton Garnier with Father Barth for a short time; then the Rev. Michael Egan, who arrived in 1802 and left for Philadelphia early in 1803, and afterwards became the first Bishop of Philadelphia in 1810. In a letter to Father Gallitzin, dated March 1st, 1799, Bishop Carroll mentions a Rev. Egan who attended Emmittsburg and the Mountain Chapel in Maryland. Whether it was the same Father Egan who afterwards came to Lancaster I cannot determine. However, there is an old tradition around Mount St. Mary's that Father Egan, afterwards Bishop of Philadelphia, did attend that mission before the old Mountain church was built. Father Barth remained at Lancaster as its Pastor until requested to take charge of the church and temporalities of the Jesuits at Conewago. Father Barth was a secular priest, and never became a member of the Society; yet, known and beloved by the Jesuits for his prudence and amiable qualities, he was at that time made Superior or Pastor of the Conewago mission. This was during the suppression of the Society, to which he restored the mission, etc., in 1814, at the restoration of the same. In the records of the Society, kept at Georgetown, D. C., it is related of him : " Rev. Dom. Louis De Barth qui fuit e corporatione Sacerdotum Marylandiae et tempore infausto suppressione Societatis Jesu res ejus tenuit fideliterque reddidit cum faustis avibus Pius VII. Societatem restituit " Father Barth left Lancaster for Conewago, January 15th, 1804, and was followed at Lancaster by the Rev. Francis Fitzsimmons, who arrived there, according to his own statement, January 19, 1804. In the " Life of Father Gallitzin," by Miss Sarah M. Brownson, Father Barth is alluded to as coming to Lancaster about 1801, or after Father Fitzsimmons, both of which are incorrect. The departure of Father Barth from Lancaster caused considerable dissatisfaction among his people, who were very much attached to him, and quite an alarming misunderstanding or unpleasantness arose between Father Fitzsimmons and the more influential part of the congregation, which was partly caused, or at least augmented, by the fact that the Pastor could not speak German, which was not pleasing to a great part of the parish, who were headed by a certain Mr. Risdel, as we learn in one of Father Gallitzin's letters to Bishop Carroll, dated February 21st, 1804, written from Lancaster at the time. Father Fitzsimmons soon after left, and in 1805 Rev. Herman Jos. Stocker attended the Lancaster mission, who very likely requested Father Barth to pay a long visit to Lancaster in order to restore peace and harmony. At all events Father Barth, in October, 1806, returned to Lancaster, and in a short time all differences and troubles ceased. He remained until February, 1807, when he again returned to Conewago, which was still under his charge. In 1806, under Father Barth's administration, the church of St. Patrick at Carlisle, Pa., was built. He likewise laid the corner-stone of St. Patrick's Church at York, Pa., in 1810. He is also said to have built, or at least begun to build, churches at several other missions attended from Conewago at that period. His favorite work was to go on horseback to the various out-missions, and no one was better known or more beloved than Father Barth, whose coming was always hailed with delight. He was Vicar-General to Bishop Egan, and on July 29th, 1814, a few days after the death of Bishop Egan, Father Barth was appointed as administrator by Archbishop Carroll "to all the authority of the deceased until the Holy See appointed a new Bishop."

The growing discontent and troubles within the diocese at that period were happily averted by the prudence and ability of the new administrator, who was ably sustained by the Archbishop. Considerable time and trouble were expended in obtaining a new Bishop for the diocese. Father Barth was repeatedly urged to accept the mitre, and was favored by the Archbishops Marechal and Cheverus; but knowing full well the many onerous duties and cares of a Bishop, he shrank from accepting the responsibility, and refused the honor, although the Bull of investiture, as it is stated, had already arrived in Philadelphia. In consequence of the refusal of Father Barth, Rev. Henry Conwell was appointed Bishop of Philadelphia, and arrived there December 2d, 1820.

Father Barth, notwithstanding his official and various duties, had continued to look after the welfare of his beloved Conewago, which he did not care to exchange for a bishopric; and on being relieved of the administratorship, he gave his entire attention again to the humble missionary work at Conewago. Had he, however, accepted the mitre, no doubt his well-known talents and prudent management of affairs as administrator would have so continued, and the serious troubles, which soon after followed, been averted. In the arduous duties of a missionary he continued until the month of November, 1828. At the request of Archbishop Whitfield, of Baltimore, he took charge of St. John's German Catholic Church in the city of Baltimore, which is now called St. Alphonsus', and is in charge of the Redemptorist Fathers. Here he remained until August, 1838, laboring zealously and without intermission for the welfare of his people until, literally worn out, he retired from active service, and was proffered by his old friends, the Jesuit

Fathers, a home at any of their houses or colleges for the remainder of his life. He chose Georgetown College, near the city of Washington, D. C., where his brother, Gen. John Barth de Walbach, U. S. A., resided.* A comfortable room was fitted up for the aged priest in the college, near the chapel, where he continued to say Holy Mass until the close of his eventful life. For over fifty years he labored in the vineyard of his Master without the many modern conveniences of life and travel which we now enjoy. During that time he attended to various and highly important offices of trust and responsibility, besides his missionary duties. He had many trials and temptations to suffer and avoid, yet all difficulties he successfully encountered and all duties he faithfully performed, co-operating in a singular manner with the calls and inspirations of Divine Providence, and, lastly, old and feeble and poor in this world's goods, he quietly waits for the voice of his Master, who is the exceeding great reward.

On the 13th of October, 1844, after receiving the Holy Viaticum with great fervor and devotion, in presence of his brother, General Barth de Walbach, and a few friends, about five o'clock, P. M., Father Barth calmly expired. The funeral took place from the college on the 15th of October, and was attended by a great number of his friends. Solemn Requiem Mass was sung by the then Bishop of Boston, Right Rev. Benedict Fenwick, a great personal friend of Father Barth, who also pronounced the eulogy. The Deacon and Sub-deacon were Fathers Clark and Stonestreet. His grave is in the small burying ground belonging to Trinity Church, Georgetown, D. C., near the grave of Rev. Notley Young,

---

* A sketch of General Walbach is printed in the Baltimore *Metropolitan* for July, 1857 (vol. V., p. 392). But for a much more detailed account the reader is referred to J. G. Rosengarten's "German Soldiers in the Wars of the United States," pp. 55–61, where it is also stated that his father, too, came to this country at the outbreak of the French Revolution, settled at Bush Hill, near Philadelphia, where he died September 4th, 1793, and that he was buried in St. Mary's ground on South Fourth street.—ED.

where a neat tombstone marks the resting-place of the ashes of good Father Barth, whose name and deeds are certainly worthy of being remembered, at least by those who to-day are still reaping the fruits of the labors and sacrifices of his noble life.

THE CENTENARY

OF THE

Adoption of the Constitution of the United States.

[Proceedings of the Tenth Public Meeting of the AMERICAN CATHOLIC HISTOR-
ICAL SOCIETY OF PHILADELPHIA, September 15th, 1887.]

THE first centenary of the adoption of the Constitution of
the United States was celebrated in Philadelphia with
unprecedented pomp, display, and enthusiasm on the 15th,
16th, and 17th of September, 1887. Catholics took a prominent and becoming part in the event, and His Eminence James
Cardinal Gibbons, Archbishop of Baltimore, by invitation of
the Committee in charge, recited the closing prayer.

Not the least significant, if far from being the most imposing incident of the occasion, was the celebration by our Society, held, under the management of the Public Meetings Committee, in the lecture-room of the Catholic Philopatrian Literary Institute, on Thursday evening, the 15th. The meeting was successful in every respect. Though many were kept
away by reason of the reception being tendered by the Catholic Club to the Cardinal at the same time, and by the fatigue
consequent to watching the great street parade during the day,
yet the hall was filled by an appreciative audience, and all who
came remained to the close.

During the meeting the President's table was covered with
an American flag, presented to the Society by Mrs. L. Foy,

just before the evening's exercises were begun. This banner was made in 1876 by a lady then over one hundred years old, who sewed every stitch of it without the aid of glasses.

Very Rev. Ignatius F. Horstmann, D. D., Chancellor of the Archdiocese, presided and made the opening address. After alluding to the pleasure which he derived from being here in such a capacity on this occasion, and referring also to the good work done in the space of three years by the Society, of which he was proud to say that he was one of the original organizers, he went on to speak as follows:

"*Ladies and Gentlemen*—This day has witnessed the first part of the programme of the nation's celebration of the Centenary of the Constitution, which has been the secret and main spring of the prosperity and happiness of our beloved land. The marvellous progress of the country during these one hundred years has been brought visibly before our eyes. It has been a grand pageant worthy of the event it was intended to commemorate, and the thousands who took part in the same and the hundreds of thousands who were here to witness it, showed that they all realized that expression should be given to the feelings of their hearts, feelings of joy and thanksgiving for the countless blessings, personal, social, civil and religious, which have been assured to them by this, the grandest charter of liberty which thus far in the history of the world has been granted unto man. As citizens of this glorious Commonwealth, as Americans, we all rejoice this day and thank God for what He has done for us in the past and pray that this our Constitution may be perpetual, that what it has done and is doing for us, it may go on working, through the intelligence and virtue of our countrymen, for countless millions yet unborn, forming a yet more perfect union of hearts and homes, establishing justice throughout the land, insuring domestic tranquility to all its citizens, providing for the common defence against every enemy, promoting the general welfare by every honorable means and securing the blessings of liberty to all who come to our shores—yes, may this our Constitution be perpetual.

" If we have every reason as Americans to rejoice and to celebrate this hundredth anniversary of the adoption of the Constitution, which was the real birthday ot these United States, we have still stronger reasons to be glad and to thank God as American Catholics for what He has done for the Church here during the last one hundred years. Whatever that miraculous progress has been, under God, we can thank the Constitution under which we live, but especially that First Amendment thereto, made almost as soon as it was framed, which declares that ' Congress shall make no law respecting the establishment of religion or prohibiting the free exercise thereof.'

" I have spoken of the progress of the Church as miraculous, and has it not been really so ? At the close of the War of Independence statistics show that there were not more than thirty thousand Catholics in the whole country, and only twenty-five priests. There was no bishop, no Catholic school, no convent or religious community. Of course, the sacraments of Confirmation and Holy Orders had never been administered. Our first Bishop, John Carroll, of Baltimore, was appointed Superior of the American clergy by Pius VI. in 1784, but it was five years later, November 6th, 1789, that he was named Bishop of Baltimore. He went to England to be consecrated, and that happy ceremony took place on Lady Day, August 15th, 1790. With full religious liberty guaranteed, you might have thought that the spread of the true faith would have been rapid and marvellous; but such were the ignorance and bigotry and prejudice of the vast majority of the population, and so few were the zealous missionaries, who came especially from France and Belgium and Germany, that all they could hope to do for years was to save those who were already in the fold. In 1791 Bishop Carroll held his first Synod in Baltimore, introducing Church organization. In 1829 six prelates had already been consecrated and met in the First Provincial Council of Baltimore. After 1840 the tide of Catholic emigration, especially from Ireland and Germany, set in, and from that date, owing to the unheard-of development of the country, the progress of the Church has been simply marvellous. Contrast 1787 with 1887. Then the number of priests was 25, now it is 7,658; then no bishop, now 12 archbishops and 61 bishops; then a Catholic population of about 30,000, now at least 8,000,000, exceeding the membership of any six Protestant denominations in the country; then no ecclesiastical seminary, now 36. There was not a Catholic college then in the land, now there are 88; no academies then, now 593. There was no Catholic school then, now we have 2,697, with nearly 600,000 pupils. We have now 22 orders and congregations of religious men and some 45 of religious women engaged in teaching and in various charitable works. Hospitals, orphanages, retreats, asylums for almost every form of distress, have sprung up all over the land, their number being 485. I have thought it well to draw out this contrast, taken from the 'Catholic Almanac' of this year; for the figures speak more eloquently than words can—and all this progress, this wonderful prosperity of our holy religion, under God, we must ascribe to our glorious Constitution. Here you have the meaning of this public meeting of the Catholic Historical Society, and, as one of its founders, I have been asked to preside. I consider it a great honor."

Having thus concluded his address, the Rev. Doctor alluded to the enforced absence of the Hon. Michael Glennan, who had been announced to deliver an oration, but was most regretfully detained at home by business complications. He with complimentary and commendatory remarks introduced Mr. Martin I. J. Griffin, who read an exhaustive and interesting paper on "Thomas Fitzsimons, Pennsylvania's Catholic signer of the Constitution," which we print in full in this volume as a separate article.

Rev. Dr. Horstmann having at this point to leave in order to attend the reception at the Catholic Club, Very Rev. C. A. McEvoy, O.S.A., Provincial of the Augustinans, was asked and kindly consented to take the chair.

When Mr. Griffin had concluded the reading of his paper, Father McEvoy introduced S. Edwin Megargee, Esq., who

would recite a poem written specially for this occasion by Miss
Eleanor C. Donnelly, and in doing so bestowed well-merited
compliments on both author and reader. Mr. Megargee's
fine rendering was frequently applauded, as were also the
noble sentiments of the poem, which we reproduce in full.

The evening's proceedings were closed with a unanimous
vote of thanks to those who had co-operated in carrying out
the programme.

Quite a number of priests were present, among them being
Rev. Father Morgan, S.J., Rector of St. Joseph's; Rev. Fathers
Carroll, S.J., and Brady, S.J., assistants at the Church of the
Gesù; Rev. Father Lebreton, Director of the Deaf Mutes'
Catholic Mission; and Rev. Father Walsh, of Memphis, Tenn.

OUR NATION'S GLORY.

BY ELEANOR C. DONNELLY.

*An Ode composed for the Celebration of the Constitutional
Centennial by the American Catholic Historical
Society of Philadelphia.*

Unfurl the banner of the free, the glorious Stripes and Stars,
The triple hues of Liberty emblazoned on its bars,—
Shake forth its folds,—lift up its staff,—and set it firm and fair
Upon the heights where Freedom lights her fires of grateful prayer:
For, lo! the voices of the winds have borne the news abroad,
The blessed tidings of a day belov'd of man and God,
When roar of cannon, clang of bells, proclaim unto the earth
That old Columbia proudly hails her *Constitution's* birth,
And keeps, to-night, high festival, in all her halls aglow,
Because of that glad natal-day, one hundred years ago!

Fling wide the portals of the Past;—let in the light and breeze
Into the magic store-house of immortal memories!

From out the ashes and the dust of dim, historic days,
The shade of many a hero blest, in living glory, raise,—
And call from out each mould'ring vault, each sunny, grassy grave,
Those giants of a by-gone age, soldiers and sages brave,
Who nobly struggled to secure, to millions yet to be,
The sweetest boons a land can crave,—*Union* and *Liberty !*

Pater Patriae,—bid *him* rise,—illustrious *Washington*,—
Franklin and Morris,—Ingersoll,—Randolph and Madison,
Sherman and Ellsworth,—Hamilton, the Pinkneys of the South,
And last, not least, in council strong, prudent and wise of mouth,
Those loyal sons of Mother Church, those patriots true and grand,
FitzSimons of our Keystone State,—*Carroll* of Maryland!

Lo ! as they answer to the call—the roll-call of Renown,
(While round each brow *Columbia* twines her amaranthine crown),
Their spirit-voices seem to say, beyond Time's murk and mist,
" ' Mercy and truth have met ' to-day ; ' justice and peace have kissed !' "

Blessed be God! The golden seed those gallant heroes cast
Deep in our country's virgin soil, a hundred summers past,
The smallest of all seeds—the mustard-seed of Liberty,—
Hath taken root and sprouted forth, and grown into a tree,
A tree so vast, its branches spread o'er mountain, hill and plain ;
The rustle of its countless leaves make music o'er the main ;
The humblest creature of the field beneath its shade may browse,
And all the nations of the earth take refuge 'neath its boughs !

Here may the exile pitch his tent,—here may the world's oppress'd,
Far from the clank of tyrants' chains, in peace and freedom rest ;
And north and south, and east and west, by river, lake and bay,—
In the great cities of our land,—its prairies far away,
There's room for all,—there's work for all,—there's honor, wealth and
      fame
For every honest freeman who would carve himself a name !

Then glory be to God on high, who hath these marvels wrought,
Who, in the councils of the brave, hath blessed each word and thought,
And made our Nation's freedom, type of *that* Liberty
Wherewith our Saviour, Christ the Lord, hath made all people free !

High from the censers of our hearts, upon this day of days,
Let the pure incense of our prayers ascend in love and praise—
The perfumes of our grateful souls rise up before the throne
To waft their fragrance through the courts of God's Eternal Son ;
And from His Sacred glowing Heart, like heavenly dew, distil
Sweet peace on earth to ev'ry man of good and perfect will !

O ripe September! mellow month; first gem in Autumn's crown!
Bright nymph with rounded, laughing face, and tresses golden-brown,
Thy 'witching haze is on our streets,—thy fingers, pure and pale,
Around the ancient State-House spread thy fleecy, violet veil;
And, as the sunlight of thy smile illumes its hallowed halls,
We seem to see (sweet memory!), within the storied walls,
That conclave of heroic men—the immortal *Thirty-Nine*
Who gave our *Constitution* birth in the blessed *Auld Lang Syne!*

The open parchment on the desk,—the iron standish near,—
The ink yet wet upon the quill;—no trace of doubt or fear
Upon the noble faces bent in grave and earnest thought
Above the instrument whereby our Nation's life was bought,—
Who, seeing these, shall dare dispute the power of the Lord?
The statesman's pen is mightier than the warrior's blood-stained sword;
And peace may reap from battle plain her harvest's golden yield,
When Cincinnatus swings the scythe across the fertile field!

Long may the genius of our Land within her heart enshrine
The sacred scroll whereon is writ, in characters divine,
The record of her dearest rights, the glorious legacy
Bequeathed her by our valiant sires—*Union* and *Liberty!*

Fitzsimons, Carroll,—love-embalm'd,—ah! bid their ashes blest,
Like Egypt's kings in pyramids of deathless glory rest!
Crowned with the fadeless laurels of a glad and grateful land,
Cloth'd with the radiant panoply of Fame's immortal band—
Beneath the Aloes' flow'ring bloom, beneath our banner bright,
" *The Memory of the Mighty Dead!* " must be our toast to-night;
And while their virtues and their deeds, heroic and sublime,
Live, in renascent splendor, in the statesmen of our time,—
Oh! may their mantle, fluttering down, as did the Saints' of yore
Fall on *Columbia's* gallant sons now and forevermore!

THOMAS FITZSIMONS,

Pennsylvania's Catholic Signer of the Constitution.

[Read before the SOCIETY September 15th, 1887, by MARTIN I. J. GRIFFIN.]

IN the commemoration of the formulation (rather than the adoption) of the Constitution of our country, it is aptly within the lines of this Society's work not only to be AMERICAN, and thus in accord with the patriotic remembrances entwined in a recollection of the important events in our country's history, but also CATHOLIC, so as to manifest that in this Centennial, as in that of every great event in our Nation's history, Catholics take an active interest.

Of those who assembled at the State House to draft principles of government that should give to the States "a more perfect union" and to the general government greater efficiency and power, two were Catholics—Thomas FitzSimons of Pennsylvania, and Daniel Carroll of Maryland. It is of Thomas FitzSimons I will speak.

Washington said to his associates assembled to engage in the great work: " Let us raise a standard to which the wise and honest can repair. The event is in the hand of God."

What were the qualifications of those met to do this work?

James Madison, afterwards President of the United States, who preserved for posterity the debates of the Convention, gives it as his profound conviction " that there never was an assembly of men charged with a great and arduous trust, who were more pure in their motives or more exclusively or anxiously devoted to the object committed to them, than were the members of the Federal Convention of 1787 to the object of devising and proposing a constitutional system which should best supply the defects of that which it was to replace and secure the permanent liberty and happiness of their country." (Page 18, Papers of the American Historical Association, Vol. II., No. 4.)

"They were a most remarkable assemblage of men, to whom, under God, we owe our liberty, our prosperity, our high place among the nations," says McMaster in his "History of the People of the United States" (Vol. I., p. 438). "They were," said Alexander Stevens, "the ablest body of jurists, legislators and statesmen that ever assembled on the continent of America." (Ib. I., p. 18.) "It was an assemblage of demigods. It consisted of the ablest men in America." (Jefferson's Works, II., p. 260.) From such men came, as Gladstone has said, "the most wonderful work ever struck off at a given time by the brain and purpose of man."

I hope to show that Thomas FitzSimons stood in the foremost rank with the ablest of these great men, and in public services well merits our honor, as we enjoy the benefit of his services. For if "no delegation contained so many and such able men as Pennsylvania," as the historian of the American People (p. 420) says, we can show Thomas FitzSimons to have been exceeded in public services by Benjamin Franklin alone of the Pennsylvania delegation.

While, as Americans, we unite with our fellow citizens of all denominations in celebrating this great event, we can as Catholics claim our full share in the number of those who were engaged in the great work, and by Daniel Carroll and Thomas FitzSimons prove the devotion of Catholics to freedom and liberty. For, as the noble Gaston, whom it was thought to debar from just rights because he was a Catholic, said in 1835 in his speech on religious liberty before the North Carolina Legislature: "Thomas FitzSimons was one of the illustrious convention that framed the Constitution of the United States, and was for several years the representative in Congress of Philadelphia. Were these and such as these foes

o freedom and unfit for republicans? Would it be dangerous to permit such men to be sheriffs or constables in the land?"

In a short sketch of this signer of the Constitution by
Henry Flanders, in the *Pennsylvania Magazine*, Vol. II., notwithstanding his prominence a century ago, it is said that very
little is known of him; and Jas. G. Barnwell, Librarian of the
Philadelphia Library, in " Reading Notes on the Constitution"
says: "Little has been published in a collected form about
Thomas FitzSimons." Thus my task, to present as full a
record of the career of this statesman as will make it worthy
of the patriotic legislator, is the greater.

Of his papers, that would tell much of his career, few remain.
No portrait of him is known to exist. Yet he was our city's
leading merchant, active public man, foremost and representative Catholic.

Where was Thomas FitzSimons born? Col. George Meade,
whose great-grand-aunt, Catharine Meade, married Mr. Fitz-
Simons, gives me Belfast, 1741, though he cannot give the
source of his information. Miss Charity Robeson gives me
traditional information that Wicklow, Ireland, was the place,
and Mr. Maitland strengthens this by writing me: " It has
been learned that the residence of the Maitlands in Ireland
was at Tubber, County Wicklow. The probabilities are that
Thomas FitzSimons was born in that neighborhood." It was
there that Peter Maitland married Ann, sister of Thomas
FitzSimons. Mr. Flanders corrects his statement of Ireland
being the place by saying Philadelphia should be named.
Col. A. J. Dallas, U. S. A., has given me information indicating
the possibility that Limerick was the birthplace. In a letter
to Bishop Carroll, in 1806, Mr. FitzSimons speaks of Ireland
as the country of his birth. Ireland was the place, but the
locality has yet to be determined. The year was 1741. He
had three brothers—Nicholas, Andrew and John, and a sister,
Ann. All were residents of Philadelphia; but, concerning his
brothers there is an almost entire absence of any information,
even traditional, save a little concerning Andrew. In St.
Peter's (Episcopal) graveyard, Third and Pine streets, are two
graves bearing inscriptions stating that Nicholas and John

Fitzsimmons are interred there. These have been regarded as
the graves of two brothers of Thomas FitzSimons; but late
and exacting investigation destroys this supposition. Of
Andrew but little is known, save that he was in business in
1767, and that in the *Pennsylvania Evening Post*, of August
5th, 1777, Bernard Fearis (a Catholic) gave notice to "all
those having any demand upon Andrew FitzSimons, late of
this city, to present them to him in Arch street, second door
from Second, and receive their respective balances or a divi-
dend thereof." In 1788, as a letter in the possession of Mr.
Maitland shows, Andrew was then in Charleston, S. C., whence
he wrote to John in Philadelphia relative to the lands in that
section. On October 26th, 1803, Thomas FitzSimons became
administrator of the estate of John FitzSimons. The sister,
Ann, married, in Ireland, Peter Maitland, from Scotland, and
by tradition, believed to have come from the neighborhood
of the Earls of Lauderdale, whose family name was Maitland.
She died May 8th, 1808, and was buried in St. Mary's graveyard, South Fourth street. The issue of this marriage were
Peter Maitland, who died young, John Maitland, Thomas
FitzSimons Maitland, and Anne Maitland.

When did Thomas FizSimons come to America? Mr.
Flanders states, "between 1762 and 1765." I am, however,
of the opinion that he was here as early as 1760.

In the baptismal register of Old St. Joseph's (" Records
Am. Cath. His. Soc.," Vol. I, p. 253) is the record: On April
13th, 1760, Thomas Fitzsimmons was sponsor with Catharine Spengler for Thomas and Esther Allen; and on the following March 24th (1761) we find Catharine Spengler sponsor
with George Meade for John Gattringer (Cottringer); and on
November 16th, 1761, we have Mary Gattringer and Thomas
Fitzsimmons sponsors for James Nihill. Thus the Thomas
Fitzsimmons acting as sponsor is shown to be in intimate
relations with the family into which our Thomas married and
with others we afterwards find our Thomas associated with.
Several other entries of Thomas Fitzsimmons as sponsor
appear in the register.

The subscription list for the purchase of St. Mary's burial

ground was started in 1758. The eleventh name on the list is Thomas Fitzsimons, Jr., £8 5s., while near the end is that of Thomas Fitzsimons, £5 8s. The deed to Rev. Robert Harding is dated May 24th, 1763, and one of the witnesses is Thomas Fitzsimmons. In an examination of the archives of the archdiocese of Baltimore on September 5th and 6th, this year, I found a letter of Bishop Egan's of February 17th, 1811, in which he says, speaking of the title of St. Mary's Church, "the only witness to this deed is Mr. Thomas Fitzsimons. Him I consulted on this occasion, as I knew I could do with safety. I also left the deed with him to have it recorded." There are several other letters in the archives from our Thomas FitzSimons to Bishop Carroll, and other letters of Bishop Egan to Bishop Carroll speaking of the Thomas FitzSimons of whom I write. Can we doubt that he was the "witness" spoken of, and one to be trusted? Yet Mr. Maitland writes us:

"It is claimed that the person who witnessed the deed for the ground of St. Mary's Church, and to whom it was given to have it recorded, was the signer of the Constitution. This deed, as recorded, is in fact not witnessed by Thomas Fitz-Simons at all, but by Thomas Fitzsimmons (written with the small s and the two m's). There is nothing in the evidence discovered in Baltimore to show that the person who witnessed the deed, and to whom it was given for record, was identical with the signer of the Constitution." The original deed is missing.

In 1763 Thomas FitzSimons was married to Catharine, sister of George Meade. This date, sought for so long, I obtained from a letter he wrote to Archbishop Carroll in 1808, in which he speaks of having been married forty-five years.

The next record testifying to the presence and the faith of Thomas FitzSimons is obtained from the recently published volume of "Records" of our Historical Society, wherein is given the transcript from old St. Joseph's baptismal register that on September 27th, 1772, Thomas and Catharine Fitzsimons stood sponsors for *Henrietta Constantia Meade*, daughter of George and *Henrietta Meade*, born August 15th. They did the same duty on August 26th, 1774, for *George Stritch Meade*, son of the same parents, baptized the day of his birth. He died August 29th, 1774. On October 29th, 1775, Thomas FitzSimons and wife, with Garrett Meade and wife, and Thomas Straka, stood as sponsors for Robert Meade, son of George Meade. Robert died May 5th, 1796, and is buried at Christ Church. So FitzSimons and his wife were sponsors in three years and one month for three children of George Meade. This *George Meade* was born in Philadelphia. His father, Robert, is supposed to have come from Limerick.

FitzSimons was one of the founders of the Friendly Sons of St. Patrick, on September 17th, 1771, at Burns' tavern. Washington was adopted a member December 17th, 1781. FitzSimons was Vice-President when Washington, March 18th, 1782, attended the anniversary dinner.

At the last election of the Society, March 17th, 1796, Fitz-Simons was elected Vice-President, General Moylan being chosen President.

But the times were birth-hours of events that peoples and nations have been gainers by. The days were troublesome and rebellious ones for England. The bill closing the port of Boston passed Parliament in March, 1774. Paul Revere came riding " in hot haste " into Philadelphia with Boston's cry for " help." Our city's patriots met at the City Tavern, Second street above Walnut, east side, on May 20th, 1774, to consider the state of affairs. Thomas FitzSimons was there. A Committee of Correspondence was appointed, and he was named as one of the thirteen under authority to call a general meeting of the citizens ; this Committee convened such a meeting on June 18th, at the State House. Eight thousand resolutes in liberty's cause were there. Thomas FitzSimons was there.

Meanwhile, on June 1st, 1774, the day of closing of the port of Boston, " all religious denominations suspended business."

That meeting of June 18th declared the closing of Boston's port as an unconstitutional act, and pronounced its judgment that a general congress of all the Colonies ought to be convened. Subscriptions for Boston were to be collected. It appointed a Committee of Correspondence of forty-four members " to determine what is the most proper mode of collecting the sense of the Province regarding the appointment ot Deputies to correspond with sister Colonies." Thomas Fitz-Simons was one of the forty-four. The Committee met on June the 20th at the Philosophical Hall. FitzSimons was there. On June 22d the Committee met at Carpenters' Hall. FitzSimons was there also. He and James Mease, Thomas Wharton, Jr., and John Maxwell Nesbitt were appointed a committee to "carry subscription paper around Dock and Walnut Wards to obtain help for Boston."

But the people were getting animated with the principles of self-government, and so they sought to have a Committee elected by popular vote rather than by town meeting appointment. So the Committee of forty-four resigned, and a new Committee was elected. Thomas FitzSimons was of it. They called a conference of delegates from Pennsylvania to meet at Carpenters' Hall on July 15th. Thomas FitzSimons was also one of these deputies. That conference asserted America's rights. This Provincial Conference agreed: 1st. We acknowledge ourselves and the inhabitants as liege subjects of George III., to whom we owe and will bear a true and faithful allegiance. 2d. The idea of an unconstitutional independence of the parent State is utterly abhorrent to our principles. 3d. We desire that harmony with the mother country be restored. 4th. The inhabitants are entitled to the same rights as subjects in England are there. 5th. That the power assumed to bind these Colonies by statutes in all cases whatsoever is unconstitutional and therefore the source of unhappy differences. Then a list of grievances is recited. They resolved on non-importation and to break off " all trade, commerce and dealing with any colony or city or town which will refuse or neglect to adopt the resolves of Congress."

That was Pennsylvania's spirit in 1774. In the Provincial Conventions of 1775 and 1776 Mr. FitzSimons did not take part. The Conference of 1774 requested the Assembly to appoint delegates to a Continental Congress. That Congress met September 4th, 1774. Washington was a member. According to his Diary, on the afternoon of October 9th, " led by curiosity and good company," he " attended the Romish Church." Who more likely to have been the " good company " to " lead " him to our Church than Thomas FitzSimons, the only Catholic then in official prominence, and one of the conveners of the Congress Washington was attending? During the Constitutional Convention Washington again, on May 27th, 1787, "went to the Romish Church to a high Mass," and as that took place at St. Mary's, where Thomas FitzSimons had a pew, we may believe it was in his company Washington went.

The election of Mr. FitzSimons in May and his serving until July, 1774, as one of the Provincial Deputies, is the first appointment or election to office known to us to have been held by a Catholic. Though not excluded from office under Penn's government up to 1689, after the overthrow of James II., they were then " excepted " from office-holding by virtue of a positive command from England. By the test oath of 1702 they were prevented from office-holding, as the oath was one no Catholic could take. So it continued until the difficulties with England warranted a more just consideration for Catholics, though as to their religious practices they always were in Pennsylvania as free as they are to-day—to publicly worship God according to their faith.

But that Continental Congress had bigots like John Adams, and the very month that Washington with Adams visited St. Mary's church, an address was issued to the people of Great Britain, denouncing the Catholic as " a religion that has deluged your island in blood and dispersed impiety, bigotry, persecution, murder and rebellion through every part of the world."

Affairs became daily more serious ; England would coerce the unruly and rebellious. So Lexington came into the world's and humanity's history. The travel-worn courier came rushing into our streets at five o'clock on April 24th, 1775.

The Associators at once became an organized and armed force, and though they too had denounced " Popery " and also King George as its abetting ally as seeking to impose its superstitions on the good people of these colonies by the power of the Catholic Canadians, Thomas FitzSimons, knowing his country's danger, formed a company. He was assigned to the Third Battalion under Col. Cadwalader and Lieut. Col. John Nixon, who was the grandson of a Catholic from Wexford.

On June 20th the Associators were reviewed by Washington, while on his way to take command of the army at Cambridge, Mass. On June 22d the Third Battalion attended Christ Church to hear a " Sermon on the Present Situation of American Affairs," by Rev. William Smith, a hater of our faith in whose unburied skull mice have, in our own day, made their nest. " Philadelphia is wholly American—strong friends to every congressional measure. No man is hardy enough to express a doubt of the feasibility of their project." So said the fleeing Tory, Samuel Curren, the Admiralty Judge, as he left Philadelphia for England.

On August 16th, 1775, a committee of seventy-six was chosen by the freemen of Philadelphia as a Committee of Safety. One of the election tickets, headed by the names of Dr. Franklin, Thomas Mifflin, Thomas Willing, John Cadwalader and Thomas FitzSimons, is preserved in the Du Simitiere Papers (F. 960), at the Ridgway Library. " This ticket had no run at the election," is the record of Du Simitiere. By the ticket for the six months succeeding February 16th, 1776, it seems that seventeen of the committee who were members of the first committee were elected on the second committee, which was " to continue until the 16th of August and no longer." At the election held August 16th, 1775, the " Mechanicks' Ticket," except three nominees, was elected. (F. 960.) But Captain Thomas FitzSimons was busy with his command preparing for the " time which tried men's souls."

Defeat and success were alternatively Washington's. The Declaration of Independence was the defiance of the Colonies to England when the time of supplication and protest had passed. That was the day of decision. Many sturdy advocates and resolute defenders of the rights of the Colonies hesitated to take the side of the Declaration and deserted the Patriot party. It was a time of peril to all. Congress appointed June 20th, 1776, as a day of public fast. The Committee of Philadelphia, in giving notice thereof, declared, in the case of the Quakers who would, probably, " not observe the fast," that the " Committee holds liberty of conscience to be sacred, and that any difference of opinions which are not injurious to the community are to be indulged." The people were recommended " to forbear from any kind of insults to said people or any others who may from conscientious scruples or from a regard for their religious professions refuse to keep the fast." On July 3d, 1776, the Provincial Committee of New Jersey asked the Committee of Safety of Philadelphia to send troops to Monmouth Court House to check the Tories and defend the approaches to Staten Island. (Hist. Philada., p. 329.) The three battalions of Philadelphia were ordered to march. They were illy prepared. But the women of our city gathered lint and bandages. Awnings and sails were transformed into tents, clock and window weights made into bullets. Committees to care for the families of Associators were formed, and as Thomas Fitz-Simons was captain of a company in the Third, we find his friend and afterward partner, George Meade, on the Committee for the Third Battalion. This battalion did duty at Woodbridge, Elizabethtown and vicinity. Capt. FitzSimons' company served from July 10th to August 19th, and one member was not discharged until the 29th.

From a pay-roll in the possession of his grand-nephew, Mr. J. J. Maitland, I obtain the following list of members, whose accounts were paid by Pennsylvania:

Lieut. Joseph Bullock. There was a Catholic of this name in Chester County. Sergt. Young's Diary shows " he cared very little for the men " in the campaign of December to January. Gavin Hamilton, ensign ; James Hood ("kind and careful," says Young), Sergeant James Ham, Sergeant George Young, Fifer Thomas Jones (served until August 10th); Privates, Richard Guy, August 10th ; John Warner, August 10th; Peter George, Charles Forder, John McIntire, John

Smith, William Harper, Thomas Rue, George Norton, Thomas Abbott, Philip Myer, Bernard Watkinson, John Hawkins, Joseph Wetherby, David Henderson, Peter Cuthbert.

In November, 1776, a new Committee of Correspondence, one hundred and nine in number, was elected. FitzSimons was not a member of it, as from conference and committee he had now to pass to sterner duty. On November 6th George Meade & Co., of which firm Mr. FitzSimons was a member, wrote the Sup. Executive Council of Pennsylvania, presenting the request of the Canadian officers imprisoned at Bristol to be sent to Lancaster, "as they are told they can be better taken care of there than in any of the smaller towns." FitzSimons and other Associators had but a brief respite from field duty. Since the July and August campaign affairs had been growing more disastrous for the patriots.

On November 27th, 1776, the Council of Safety announced to Philadelphians: "Our enemies are advancing upon us, and the most vigorous measures alone can save this city from falling into their hands. There is no time for delay. We entreat you by the most sacred of all bonds, the love of virtue, of liberty and of your country, to forget every distinction and unite as one man in this time of extreme danger. Let us defend ourselves like men determined to be free." (F. 960, Du Simitiere Papers.)

Long Island's battle had been fought and lost; New York had been taken; Forts Washington and Lee captured, and Washington was in retreat through Jersey. His heart was in anguish and his desponding cries of "I think the game is pretty near up" and "we are near the end of the tether," best attest the deplorable state of America's struggle for liberty. But when yet did Liberty dwell with a people who had not borne sacrifice unto death for her sake? Liberty or Death had been their battle cry, and a six months' effort to sustain their Declaration was about to end in disaster. It was then indeed "the time to try men's souls." The timid or cowardly went over to Howe, for was not the struggle to end in the destruction of those found in arms? December, 1776, I think the most important period in the Revolutionary struggle and one that to my mind makes evident the hand of God guiding the patriots in council and in field and a time that gives evidence that they were, as the late Plenary Council at Baltimore declared, "but instruments in the hands of the Almighty." History is but the companion of Religion in teaching that God lives and rules the affairs of men.

Again did the Philadelphia Associators promptly respond to Washington's call for help. And when victory had come and God had sustained the patriots, Washington declared "the readiness which the militia of Pennsylvania have shown in engaging in the service of their country, at an inclement season, when my army was reduced to a handful of men and our affairs were in the most critical condition, does great honor to them."—(*Pa. Mag.*, Vol. 8, p. 256).

On December 3d., 1776, the Committee of Safety sent its members to "go around to collect all the old great coats, coats, surtouts, jackets and breeches from the inhabitants which they can spare," on account "of the exceeding great distress of our fellow countrymen now in the field for want of clothing at this cold season." (Du Simitiere Papers, F. 960)

On December 5th Captain FitzSimons with his company left Philadelphia for Trenton. They went by schooner to Bristol and marched from there to Trenton, getting to that place that night. On the 7th they retreated across the Delaware, as Howe's advance was near at hand. The next day (Sunday) the company marched a mile from shore and pitched tents. Sergeant William Young, whose diary, now in possession of the Pennsylvania Historical Society, gives the details I am repeating, says, under this date, of Captain Fitz-Simons: "Our captain is very kind to our men."

The company proceeded to make themselves comfortable by laying floors to their tents, and by Monday night "they were pleased with the works of their hands," when at night an order came that they must decamp, for Howe's army designed to cross at Dunk's Ferry. All obeyed the order, and at it "we went hurry-scurry almost head over heels," records Sergeant Young.

During the night they marched in rain and snow and "very

cold " to Neshaminy Ferry, and got there at three o'clock in the morning, "all as wet as rain could make us and cold to numbness." There they remained until Saturday, when they were marched to Bristol. Next day FitzSimons "went to town and got a discharge for the son of Sergeant Young," who was " exceedingly unwell," and also for Valentine Gellaspee.

They took up " march forward " again, and at nine o'clock on Christmas night were at Dunk's Ferry ; but on account of the ice on Jersey shore they could not land the great guns, and so crossed back again to the Pennsylvania shore amid " rain and snow and very cold," and " our men came home very wet and cold," records the Sergeant.

It was on that night, you remember, that Washington crossed at McKonkey's or Patrick Colvin's Ferry. Patrick Colvin is a new hero, whose services on that eventful night have been made known by recent Catholic historical investigation, and have been recorded by John McCormack, the Catholic historian of Trenton, in the " American Catholic Historical Researches " for January, 1887.

The next day, December 26th, was spent by FitzSimons' men in drying their clothes. They had not heard of the defeat of the Hessians at Trenton. Cadwalader's men, who were to cross at Burlington and vicinity, could not do so.

They were posted above the Neshaminy to Bristol and below it to Dunk's Ferry. In an attack on Trenton they were to cross below Burlington and attack Col. Donop from Burlington to Mt. Holly. But Cadwalader's men could not cross on account of the ice until the 27th. By that time Washington had defeated the Hessians and got back to the west bank of the Delaware, a military achievement unequaled in war annals.

In the evening of the 26th a " rumor " of the battle came to the camp of FitzSimons' men, but it was not until they crossed over at Burlington the next morning that they had the rumor confirmed that " Washington had defeated Howe's men at Trenton."

The next day, the 28th, was spent in getting baggage over to Burlington. Margaret Morris, who lived on the banks of the river, makes mention of this fact in her diary (*Pa. Mag.*, Vol. 8, p. 260). She says: "The weather clearing up this afternoon, we observed several boats with soldiers and their baggage making up to our wharf. A man who seemed to have command over the soldiers just landed civilly asked for the keys of Col. Cox's house, in which they stored their baggage and took up their quarters for the night, and were very quiet."

The next day they departed, and Margaret Morris records that "the soldiers at the next house departed, and as they passed by the door they stopped to bless and thank me for the food I had sent them." Sergeant Young mentions in his diary that "the good woman next door sent us two mince pies last night, which I took very kind." What a satisfaction to an investigator to join these two diaries in testimony more than a century after!

But FitzSimons and his men were again on the tramp and bound for Bordentown. They got here at two o'clock, and then marched to Croswick's, four miles from Trenton. They got there at sunset "very much tired," and quartered in the Quaker meeting house. There they remained until January 2d, when orders for duty were received. "Some went one way and some another." Some saw the battle of Princeton, and those of the Third Battalion who took part in it 'stood firm and to it,'" says Sergeant Young. As he does not mention the participation of his company, we may accept it as a fact that it was not ordered into active duty.

The next day the company was ordered to Burlington. On January 8th it was ordered back again and to Morristown. It arrived there on the 12th. The soldiers were very uneasy and displeased at being detained, and so most of FitzSimons' men are recorded on pay-roll only up to January 16th. On January 23d orders to march to Philadelphia were received. Sergeant Young's diary records the homeward trip as continuing with him until January 29th.

From another pay-roll of those who received bounty payable by the vote of the General Assembly, also in possession of Mr. Maitland, I get the following names of members of this company who were in this campaign: George Peter George, Charles Forder, John Hawkins, Charles Wetherby, Jr., John Smith, Edmund Edwards, Alexander Boyd, Sylvester Kintie, John McIntire, John Gray, William Tindall, Alexander Robinson, William Jones, And. Clark, Charles Riggin, Pat. Grogan, Samuel Land, Joseph Cravat, David Stinson, Jas. Swaine, Daniel McLeane, Henry Curtis, George Young, Jos. Hunter. From Sergt. Young's diary I get the following additional names: Mr. Rowe, Mr. Serrull, Fred. Williams, Jas. Hood, Edmund Allmans, John Towers. In this campaign the Third Battalion was commanded by Col. John Nixon, as Cadwalader had become Brigadier General.

On December 10th, 1776, the Assembly appointed FitzSimons an assistant to the Council of Safety, who with the Council were to exercise the powers of the Council. But at this time FitzSimons was in active duty on the Trenton campaign. He did not return until January 29th, and by that time the powers of the committee ceased and the Supreme Executive Council took charge of affairs early in March, 1777. On March 13th the Supreme Executive Council appointed a Navy Board of eleven members, "to do all matters and things relating to the Navy of the State." Thomas FitzSimons was one of the number. The Board met on the 14th, when Major Hubley by order of the Supreme Executive Council was present to administer the oath of allegiance. Ten of the Navy Board were in attendance. Nine refused to take the oath. Thomas FitzSimons was among the nine. He and Robert Ritchie were appointed to wait on the Supreme Executive Council in relation to the matter. Accordingly the next day they appeared before the Council " and presented a memorial setting forth that nine of the members had resolved not to take the oath of allegiance tendered them by Mr. Hubley, of the Supreme Executive Council." The memorial said: "We do not apprehend that the reasons on which our dissent are founded are expected, but we think it necessary to make known to your honors that we are willing and ready to take an oath of allegiance to the United States as well as the office, and that we are extremely desirous of

rendering every service in our power to this State in any
capacity in which we can be useful."—(*Col. Rec.*, Vol.
XI., p. 183.) Accompanying the memorial was a copy of the
minutes of the Navy Board with an address expressive of
"attachment to the Independence of America and their readiness to serve the State."—(See 40th Sec. of Frame of Government, for oath.)—Nothing further appears concerning the
refusal, and the Navy Board continued its duties.

On March 27th, 1777, FitzSimons and Ritchie attended the
meeting of the Supreme Executive Council and laid before it
" a state of the divers naval affairs."—(*Col. Rec.*, Vol. XI., p. 191.)
On the next day the Supreme Executive Council requested
their attendance and desired the Naval Board to recommend
commissioned officers. FitzSimons was one of the five who
attended.

Affairs were again becoming serious. On April 9th, 1777,
Thomas Wharton, Jr., President of the Supreme Executive
Council, issued an address to the people of Pennsylvania to
be ready to meet the emergencies likely soon to come upon
them.

The days of trial came when Brandywine was fought and
lost, and Philadelphia in September became the possession of
the British victor, and the seat of rebellion against his Most
Gracious Majesty became the abiding place of his warriors.
But more glorious were the defeats at Brandywine and Germantown than the entry into the captured city, and more
brilliant were the crimson marks of patriots' blood on the
frosted soil of Valley Forge than the jewels of the fair maids
of the Mischeanza to Andre and his love-lorn comrades in the
coercion of a people struggling for liberty.

On the evacuation of Philadelphia by the British in June,
1778, and the return of the Patriots, vigorous measures were
instituted against all who had aided or encouraged the British.
Amongst those arrested were Abraham Carlisle, who was
charged with having kept one of the northern redoubts for
the British, and John Roberts, of Lower Merion, was charged
with enlisting in and encouraging others to join the British
army. Both were Quakers, well advanced in years and of

good character. Petitions to save their lives were signed, and among the three hundred and eighty-seven signers in favor of Carlisle was Thomas FitzSimons. But clemency was not extended, and both were hanged on November 4th, 1778. A memorial to the Assembly in 1781 stated that though Cadwalader Dickinson was "disowned" by the Quakers for sitting on the jury in this case, Carlisle and Roberts were not "disowned" for their treason. (F. 960.)

At this time FitzSimons & Co., as the firm is in this instance only called in the "Colonial Records" (Vol. XI., p. 645), were supplying the French fleet with stores. On December 18th, 1778, he presented to the Supreme Executive Council the certificate of Gerard, the French Minister, that the ship Mary and Elizabeth was laden with biscuit and flour for the French fleet, and requesting clearance papers.

Controversies arose relative to amending the Constitution adopted in 1776. Those in favor of amending it formed, in 1779, "The Republican Society." Among the members was Thomas FitzSimons. George Meade and James White, Catholics, were also members.

During this year (1779) there was a very general distress caused by the continuance of the war, the lessening value of the continental money, and the consequent hoarding of specie and the increasing price of provisions. On March 13th, Mr. FitzSimons was elected one of the Overseers of the Poor. They met on the 25th at the Court House to attend to their duties. The distress of the people was so great and business so unsettled that on May 25th, 1779, a meeting of citizens was held in the State House yard. A Committee of Inspection to regulate prices was appointed in June. It issued a schedule of prices at which goods were to be sold or work done—flour, £12 per hundred weight; butter, 15 shillings a pound; boots from £37 to £40. Fines were imposed for making greater charges than those named on the list.

A General Committee for the city of Philadelphia, the Northern Liberties and the District of Southwark was elected on August 2d, to continue to the last day of 1779, for the purpose of "raising and supporting the value of our currency, regulating of prices, encouraging importation and preventing monopolizing." Mr. FitzSimons was elected on " The Independent and Constitutional Ticket." His name was the thirty-fifth on the list following that of Thomas Paine. It was, however, eighteenth on the list of those elected. (F. 960.)

Anthony Leckner, a Catholic, was also elected. This Committee met to consider and act on the state of affairs. Mr. FitzSimons was appointed on the Committee on " Enquiry into the State of Trade," appointed by the General Committee. This sub-committee on August 10th gave notice that "in order to enable this Committee to do justice to all persons concerned, it requested importers and retailers of wet and dry goods, and the several traders and manufacturers, to send accounts of prices they sold for or exchanged at in 1774 with list of present prices." The Committee would meet daily at the Court House to receive these reports. When Gerard, the French Ambassador, arrived, the Committee presented him with an address.

Measures were taken by the Supreme Executive Council to stop engrossing, forestalling and secreting of supplies and the preventing of extortion. A meeting of merchants was held on September 2d, 1779, to protest, for commercial reasons, against the regulations adopted. George Meade was one of the signers against fixing the prices at which sales should be made.

In July a town meeting had been held to consider the state of affairs with regard to the Continental treasury and the support of the patriot movement. It advised the stoppage of the issue of Continental money and recommended in lieu thereof for the support of the Continental treasury a house to house subscription. FitzSimons was appointed on the Committee for the Dock Ward. Nothing is known of the result of this effort. It could have had but little success, or its work would be on record.

However, while his friend, George Meade, protested against fixing the price of merchandise, Thomas FitzSimons was a member of the second Committee of Inspection regulating the prices. Were they not then business partners ?

When FitzSimons was censor in 1783-4, the censors reported " that the attempts which have been made to regulate the prices of commodities were absurd and impossible. They tended to produce the very opposite effect to that which they were designed to produce and were invasions of the rights of property."—(Report of Censors, p. 39, 1784.)

In 1780 the patriot cause was dark, gloomy and despondent. Continental money was almost valueless and distress was all-prevalent. The constant and almost unlimited issue of paper money unsettled prices. An effort to make it equal to gold or silver was made. A list was signed by all officials of the State, by lawyers, merchants and traders. Among the signers were Thomas FitzSimons, George Meade and James White.

Charleston surrendered to the British on May 28th, 1780. The news did not depress the patriots in Philadelphia. It inspired the women of our city to strive to do something for the soldiers. Committees covering the city soon collected £1500 in specie. This patriotic and humane action prompted the merchants of the city also to serve the army in the field. They organized the Bank of Pennsylvania to supply the army with provisions for two months. Each subscriber gave bond to the directors to pay their subscriptions in specie in case it was demanded to meet the bank's engagements. The subscriptions amounted to £315,000 in notes on interest; directors to borrow money on credit of bank for six months or less at six per cent. and to receive from Congress sums appropriated; all money to be used to purchase provisions and expenses of transportation.

The terms, thus detailed, to my mind strip the action of most of the patriotic or national glamor that late writers give to the combination. However, it was to serve the men in the field, and so is entitled to merit. Among the subscribers for £2000 was the firm of George Meade & Co., and at this time Thomas FitzSimons was the business associate of George Meade. The bank opened July 7th, 1780, in Front street below Walnut.

"When Congress could neither command money nor credit

for the subsistence of the army, the citizens of Philadelphia formed an association to procure a supply of necessary articles for their suffering soldiers. The advantages of this institution were great and particularly enhanced by the critical times in which it was instituted." (*Ramsey's His. Rev.*, Vol II., p. 355.)

Continental money was now valued at seventy-five to one of specie. Business was in a deplorable condition, and suffering excessive among the people. In November, 1780, a meeting of citizens was held at the State House to consider the state of affairs. It appointed a committee of thirteen to form an association of the people who would agree to pay and receive Continental money as freely as specie at a rate to be agreed on, and to expose to public odium all who refused to do so as enemies of liberty. One of the members of the committee was Thomas FitzSimons.—(*His. Phila.*, p. 409.)

In regard to all affairs pertaining to commerce Thomas FitzSimons was consulted by both State and Confederacy authorities. Alexander Hamilton bears witness to the help he obtained from Thomas FitzSimons in establishing the financial policy of the Government, and in funding the debt that was incurred in waging the Revolutionary war. Having sought his advice relative to measures for the regulation of pilots and the charge of light-houses, he received the following reply, dated November 6th, 1780: "The difficulty of making provision, by a general law, for the regulation of pilots and the superintendence of light-houses, buoys, etc., appears to me to be insurmountable, otherwise than by the appointment of commissioners in each State (say three), to reside at the principal port; to give them certain powers in the act and authority to make by-laws subject to the revision of the President of the United States, or, perhaps more properly, of the Secretary of the Treasury. By this method the complete control of the pilots would be in the United States—a thing, in my opinion, important to the revenue; and the regulations may be adapted to the circumstances of each State without interfering with each other. If you approve of the idea, and I can be serviceable in carrying it into effect, you may command me. I am, respectfully, etc."—(*Hamilton's Works*, Vol. IV., p. 82.)

I doubt not that several "Observations on the utility of funding the public debts of the United States," appearing a few years afterwards in the *American Museum*, published by his fellow-Catholic, Mathew Carey, were written by him.

On November 1st, 1781, a meeting of merchants was held at the City Tavern for the purpose of starting a bank. Among the subscribers were George Meade & Co., of which Mr. Fitz-Simons was a member, and Thomas FitzSimons, for himself, and Thomas FitzSimons for George Meade. So not only did the firm invest in the new enterprise, but each member made an investment in his personal character. (*His. Phila.*, *p. 2089.*) This was the Bank of North America. On December 31st, 1781, it was chartered by Congress. The charter named Thomas Willing as president. The directors were also named, and Thomas FitzSimons was one. Opposition was shown to Thomas Willing, as he "had been lukewarm during the war." In March, 1782, the grant of a charter from the State was sought. In the act Willing was again named as president and FitzSimons as a director. Opposition was again manifested towards Willing, but the act finally passed by a vote of 27 to 24. Thomas FitzSimons served as a director of the Bank of North America from its organization, in 1781, until 1803, when he resigned and became President of the Delaware Insurance Company.

At a meeting of the Hibernia Fire Company held at Patrick Byrnes' house, Front street below Walnut, on November 22d, 1781, Thomas FitzSimons was elected a member.

On November 22d, 1782, FitzSimons was elected a member of the Congress of the Confederacy. His counsel was availed of by Hamilton, Madison, Carroll, Gorham, Peters and others of that Congress.

On November 26th, 1782, four days after his election to the Congress, FitzSimons proposed that Commissioners of the United States, settling accounts with the States for redemption of paper money, should be empowered to take up all the outstanding old money and issue certificates to be apportioned on the States as part of the public debt; the same rule to determine the credit for redemption by the State. This proposition was considered the least objectionable by the Committee and was referred to a sub-committee made up of Rutledge, FitzSimons and Alexander Hamilton, the plan to be matured and laid before the General Committee. Hamilton suggested in its favor that " it would multiply the advocates for Federal funds for discharging the public debt and tend to cement the Union." (*Madison Papers. Debates, p. 8.*)

On January 16th, 1783, Mr. FitzSimons opposed disclosures being made as to the negotiation of Dr. Franklin with Congress relative to confiscation and to British debts.

On January 28th, when a plan of general revenue was under discussion, he urged general confidence, " as no specific plan had been preconcerted among the patrons of a general revenue." On January 30th, 1783, FitzSimons moved that the information from Virginia of its inability to give further contributions to Congress, be referred to a committee. He endorsed Mr. Gorham's animadversions on that State, and declared that Virginia for 1782 paid but " the paltry sum" of $35,000 and was, notwithstanding, endeavoring to pay no further contributions." It was referred to a committee.

On February 15th, 1783, in a debate on finances, Mr. Mercer remarked that it would be good policy to separate instead of cementing the interests of the army and the other public creditors, insinuating that the claims of the latter were not supported by justice. FitzSimons replied that it was unnecessary to make separate appropriations to one particular debt ; the mercantile interest—the chief creditors of Pennsylvania— had by their influence obtained the full and prompt concurrence of Pennsylvania in the impost, and if that influence were excluded, the State would repeal the law. He concurred with those who hoped the army would not disband unless promises should be made to do them justice.

On the clause fixing an impost for twenty-five years, Fitz-Simons voted no, as he wished it unlimited so as to bring sufficient to pay all debts.

On March 20th, 1783, Virginia sent instructions to her delegates against admitting into the Treaty of Peace with England any stipulations for restoring confiscated property. The Pennsylvania Executive Council sent a request to delegates of Pennsylvania to obtain a reasonable term for making payment of British debts. These matters were referred to a committee consisting of Osgood, Mercer and FitzSimons. During the debate Mr. FitzSimons declared, on mature reflection, that a complete general revenue was unattainable from the States and was impracticable in the hands of Congress.

His house was the scene of the social gatherings of the delegates. Questions of Congressional import were the subjects of social converse. One such meeting took place on February 20th, 1783, when the matters of revenue and the condition of the Continental army were considered by the statesmen. Until the claims of the soldiers who had battled and won independence had been satisfied, FitzSimons was not in favor of the army being disbanded. In that Congress he was an active spirit, and when Rhode Island sent Congress a letter assigning the reason for not complying with the laws of Congress relative to import duties and prize goods, Alexander Hamilton, James Madison and Thomas FitzSimons were appointed a committee to send the reply of Congress. The names of his associates alone give evidence of the most forcible character of the foremost position he occupied among the statesmen of that time, and of the standing he had in that Congress. The reply is so commercial and applies business principles and maxims so aptly, that though Bancroft (*Formation of Constitution*, Vol. I., p. 14) declares that it was written by Hamilton, yet in its commercial presentation of of views we may fairly claim that it was FitzSimons who inspired or framed, if he did not write, this portion of the reply, so very similar is it to his views. He applies principles yet worthy of the attention of our law-makers. We have him declaring that "the principal thing to be consulted for the advancement of commerce, is to promote exports. All impediments to these either by way of prohibition or by increasing prices of native commodities, decreasing by that means their sale and consumption at foreign markets, are in-

jurious." This surely is a principle of tariff legislation yet
worthy of being applied to our own times.

Thomas FitzSimons was father to " Protection to American industry " by tariff on imported goods " sufficient to afford
our workingmen a competitive chance in supplying the needs
of our people." This was said in the Congress of the Confederacy, and we will find him the advocate of protection to
American industry in the first Congress of the United States,
and acknowledged by Madison and by Webster as the first to
propose the so laying imposts as to protect American manufacturers.

But he said in reply to Rhode Island, " it is not to be inferred that the whole revenue ought to be drawn from imports ;
all extremes are to be rejected. The chief thing to be attended
to is, that the weight of the taxes fall not too heavily in the
first instance upon any particular part of the community. A
judicious distribution of all kinds of taxable property is a
first principle of taxation. The tendency of these observations is only to show that taxes on possessions, on articles of
our own growth and manufacture, are more prejudicial to trade
than duties on imports."—(*Hamilton's Works*, Vol. II., p. 221.)
Is not that principle worthy of attention to-day ?

A cessation of hostilities having been proclaimed in 1783,
Mr. FitzSimons on April 12th inquired of the Executive
Council if vessels or goods from Great Britain could be ad-
mitted to enter at the custom house.

The Constitution of our State then provided that " in order
to keep inviolate forever the freedom of the Commonwealth,
Censors should be annually chosen." Their duty was to
" inquire whether the Constitution had been preserved inviolate in every part, and whether the Legislative and Executive
branches had performed their duties as guardians of the
people, or had assumed or exercised other or greater powers
than they were by the Constitution entitled to." The knowledge and experience of Thomas FitzSimons were in this
trust given to the duty to which his fellow-citizens assigned
him.

At an election held October 14th, 1783, Thomas FitzSimons

and Samuel Miles were declared elected Censors. The Council of Censors met at the State House on November 10th. Fitz-Simons and Miles did not attend until the 13th. A protest against their being the duly elected members was presented and referred to a committee who reported that Miles received 944 votes; FitzSimons, 934; David Rittenhouse, 685; and George Bryan, 665. It appeared also that 230 votes in excess of the number of names on the voters' list had been cast. Deducting these, Miles and FitzSimons were yet in a majority. Soldiers' votes were counted, and it was charged they were used to intimidate election officers. So events in our own days, which are taken as signs of degeneracy, are but the repetition of scenes of the past. " History repeats itself." The report of the Investigating Committee of the Censors was adopted by a vote of 14 to 8, and Miles and FitzSimons entered upon the discharge of their duties. Miles resigned June 8th, 1784, and George Bryan succeeded him on June 24th.

On January 2d, 1784, Miles, FitzSimons, General Arthur St. Clair, Thos. Hartley (York), and John Arndt (Northumberland) were appointed a committee to " report those articles of the Constitution materially defective, and which absolutely require alteration or amendment." Accordingly, on January 14th, 1784, the Censors submitted to the Legislature sundry amendments and alterations which they recommended incorporating in the Constitution. One of the defects they pointed out was " the rotation in sundry offices which the Constitution established."

In the council FitzSimons favored a senate, and was opposed to a council having supreme executive power.

In 1783 the Bank of New York was founded. An unfriendliness arose between it and the Bank of North America. William Seton was cashier of the Bank of New York. On March 21st he left New York bearing a letter from Alexander Hamilton to Thomas FitzSimons, introducing him to his " acquaintance and atttention." His purpose in visiting Philadelphia, adds Hamilton, " is to procure material and information in the form of business. I am persuaded you will with pleasure facilitate his object. Personally you will be pleased with him. He will tell you of our embarrassments and prospects. I hope an incorporation of the two banks, which is evidently the interest of both, has put an end to differences in Philadelphia." But Seton found confusion at the Bank of North America, owing to the "opposition of the Bank of New York." Finances were unsettled, and bills of Robert Morris for £60,000 had just gone to protest in Holland.

In the returns of military fines from March, 1777, to April, 1783, paid to Captain Bevin's company, the name of Thomas FitzSimons appears for £13.

The partnership between George Meade and Thomas Fitz-Simons was dissolved early in 1784. In March Mr. FitzSimons was in business " on Walnut street wharf," and in January Mr. Meade announced his removal to Walnut street, next door to his dwelling house, just above the corner of Third. Then Meade & Nicholas became the firm name.

When Rev. John Carroll came to Philadelphia to administer Confirmation, which he was empowered by Rome to do on June 6th, 1784, which authorization he did not receive until November 28th of the same year, from Le Sieur Barbe Marbois, the French Consul at Philadelphia, he did not start " on a progress to administer confirmation " (Carroll to Father Plowden) until September 22d, 1785. It must have been in October when Father Carroll reached Philadelphia, and while here he " lodged at the house of Mr. FitzSimons." (*U. S. Cath. Mag.*, 1844, p. 622.) While there Rev. Charles H. Wharton, the apostate Jesuit, visited him relative to the settlement of property rights, as they were of family connection. Though they had, in 1784, issued pamphlets against each other, yet they met in a friendly manner.

On December 20th, 1785, Mr. FitzSimons was one of a committee of merchants to examine certain correspondence to William Kymner of Kingston, Jamaica. The committee certified that the correspondence was honorable and related to commercial matters. Mathew Carey & Co., publishers of the *Evening Herald*, then made a retraction for having stated otherwise.

At the election of 1785 Mr. FitzSimons was elected a member of the Pennsylvania Assembly, and during the session introduced several petitions for the repeal of the Test Laws that had been adopted relative to those who had not been active in support of the Colonies or who had been Loyalists during the Revolution. He advocated the abolition of all such Test Laws.

On March 22d, 1785, the Pennsylvania Assembly passed to second reading a bill to "protect the manufacturers" of Pennsylvania by duties on more than seventy articles. Thomas Fitz-Simons, as a foremost advocate of this measure, was but advancing protective measures he had urged in the Congress of the Confederacy. On June 2d, 1785, citizens of Philadelphia held a town meeting. After eighteen days its committee reported that Congress ought to have more power over commerce, and that "foreign manufacturers interfering with domestic industry ought to be discouraged by prohibitions or protective duties." —(*Formation of the Constitution*, Vol. I., p. 187.)

On March 25th the Assembly authorized the Supreme Executive Council to appoint five Commissioners to meet those of Maryland and Delaware on business concerning the improved inland navigation of the rivers running through these States. According to the authority thus given, the Council on April 11th, 1786, elected Mr. FitzSimons one of the Commissioners.

In the Assembly, on November 17th, 1785, on a bill to prevent vice and immorality, an amendment was offered to prohibit the erection of places for theatrical performances or for playing any such exhibitions. Thomas FitzSimons voted in the negative, and the vote was 29 in favor to 37 against. On November 21st a bill was presented for licensing and regulaing a theatre in the State of Pennsylvania. FitzSimons voted "to lay on the table," and it was so decided.

On November 29th FitzSimons voted in favor of the report on Test Laws.—(See *Penna. Gazette*, No. 2896, for report.) The report was adopted by a vote of 40 to 26. On November 30th the petition of manufacturers of bar iron for an increased duty was referred to FitzSimons, Clymer and Whitehill.

On December 3d, 1785, a petition was presented of Donaldson & Coxe, Coxe & Frazier, and John Pringle for the loan of two twelve-pound cannon for arming their sloop bound to the West Indies.   FitzSimons voted for loaning, but the motion was defeated by a vote of 30 to 31.   The voters in the negative objected to favoritism, and thought the debts of the State should be paid—"just before generous,"—and that the cannon should not go from the State while the article of the treaty with England relative to the northwestern posts was not settled.

On September 30th, 1786, at a meeting of the Friends of Equal Liberty, held in the Universal Baptist Church, Thomas FitzSimons, Robert Morris, George Clymer, William Mill and Jacob Hiltzhimer were nominated for Representatives in the Assembly.   They were elected.   In the Assembly this year FitzSimons was one of the signers of a minority report on a bill annulling the declaration of trust of the Scots Presbyterian Church.   The minority considered it as "a precedent dangerous to the religious liberties of the people."

Now came on the great event we are commemorating.   It is not within my province, nor in accord with my method, to narrate the causes that brought about an abandonment of the Confederacy form of government, under which the patriots of the Revolution sought to establish a government of the people. One event, or circumstance, or suggestion, or measure followed another until the great day of the Constitutional Convention, May 25th, 1787, came, and the delegates then in town went to the State House.   Mr. FitzSimons had been appointed delegate to the Constitutional Convention by the Assembly on December 30th, 1786, when Thomas Mifflin, Robert Morris, George Clymer, Jared Ingersoll, James Wilson and Gouverneur Morris were appointed.   By the supplementary act of March 28th, 1787, Benjamin Franklin was appointed.   Not many attended the first day, but among the few was Thomas Fitz-Simons.   It was not until July 9th that Daniel Carroll, the other Catholic member of the Convention, came.   In the Convention FitzSimons voted against universal suffrage and in favor of limiting it to freeholders, and in favor also of giving Congress power to tax exports as well as imports; also that the House of Representatives should with the Senate be necessary to ratify treaties. The Constitutional Convention finished its work on September 17th, 1787. Mr. FitzSimons was at this time also a member of the Assembly of Pennsylvania.

In the convention for the formation of the Constitution of our country, by reason of the absence of any official report of its proceedings, we are unable to trace the actions of Mr. FitzSimons in the formulation of the great charter. But from the glimpses into the assemblage afforded by the recollections and sketches of debates made by men who have gained more renown than has fallen to the lot of Mr. FitzSimons' name, and the "Journal" of the convention, we get indications of the activity and usefulness of Pennsylvania's Catholic signer.

On August 7th, 1787, when Gouverneur Morris moved to restrict the right of suffrage to freeholders, the motion was seconded by Mr. FitzSimons, and when, a month later, on September 7th, James Wilson moved that the House of Representatives should also concur with the President and the Senate in the ratification of treaties, Mr. FitzSimons seconded that motion. When, three days later, it was proposed that the Constitution, which they had nearly finished the consideration of, should be referred to the Congress of the Confederacy for its assent, Mr. FitzSimons objected, declaring that to so do would be inconsistent with the Articles of Confederation under which the Congress held authority. When, upon August 21st, the matter of taxing exports was under consideration, Mr. FitzSimons declared himself in favor of so doing, but not immediately. Power ought to be given for it to be laid when the proper time called for it. This would become the case when America became a manufacturing country.

Mr. FitzSimons served as the Pennsylvania member of the committee considering commercial measures. Daniel Carroll, his fellow Catholic, also served on that committee. He opposed permitting the legislatures of any of the States to allow vessels to enter or pay duties at any other ports than those of the State to which they were bound. He said that though to do so might be an inconvenience, he thought it would be better to require vessels bound for Philadelphia not to enter below the jurisdiction of the State.

Wilson, "the most learned civilian of the Convention," as Bancroft calls him in his "History of the Formation of the Constitution of the United States of America" (Vol. II., p. 58), was the spokesman of the Convention for Pennsylvania; and as he spoke we may assume FitzSimons voted. Before the Committee met, Gouverneur Morris and other members from Pennsylvania in the Convention urged upon the larger States in the Federal Convention the equal vote which they enjoyed in the Congress of the Confederacy; but the Virginians stifled the project. (Bancroft, *Constitution*, Vol. II., p. 7.)

In committee on May 30th, 1787, Randolph offered a resolution, which Gouverneur Morris had formulated, " that a national government ought to be established consisting of a supreme legislative, executive and judiciary." Pennsylvania voted for the resolution. Her delegates also, after three weeks' hesitation, voted that the legislature should be composed of two branches. On the question whether the members of the first branch would be chosen directly by the people or by the State Legislatures, Pennsylvania voted in favor of election by the people. "Without the confidence of the people," said James Wilson, "no government, least of all a republican government, can long subsist; nor ought the weight of the State Legislatures to be increased by making them the electors of the National Legislature (p. 17). The election by the people is not the corner-stone only, but the foundation (p. 29).

As to whether the National Executive of the Government should be one or many, Wilson and Pinkney proposed it should consist of a single person. " A long silence prevailed, broken at last by the chairman asking if he should put the question." " Unity in the Executive," said Wilson, " will be the best safeguard against tyranny." As to the mode of appointing the Executive, Wilson favored an election by the people every three years, and against the doctrine of rotation. After the Convention had decided in favor of a term of seven years, and that the Executive should not be twice eligible, "how to choose the Executive " remained the perplexing problem.

Wilson proposed that electors chosen in districts of the several States should meet and elect the Executive by ballot, but not from their own boc'y. He deprecated the intervention of the States in the choice (p. 22). His motion was supported only by the Pennsylvania and Maryland delegates, and, from sheer uncertainty what else to do, the Convention left the choice of the Executive to the National Legislature. For members of the Senate Wilson favored " an election by the people in large districts, but arranging the districts only for the accommodation of voters." He wished to " keep the States from devouring the National Government " if the legislature elected the Senate (p. 30). Yet election by legislatures was adopted, but in the Convention the State electoral system was decided on.

Concerning voting in the House of Representatives Pennsylvania demanded representation in proportion to members. And this was adopted by the votes of Massachusetts, Pennsylvania, Virginia, the two Carolinas and Georgia, and the ratio for representation was fixed at that of the " free inhabitants and three-fifths of all other persons." The appointment of Senators was fixed according to representative population, each State to have at least one, on the proposition of Wilson and Hamilton. Pennsylvania and Virginia voted against Senators being elected by the legislatures, but voted that Senators should be elected for nine years, and Delaware agreed with them.

On June 27th, 1787, the rule of suffrage in the two branches of the National Legislature was considered "and brought the convention to the verge of dissolution, so that it scarcely held together by the strength of a hair." It was decided that the House of Representatives would be in accordance with the population of the several States. And a reversal of this decision was never attempted, says Bancroft. It was then proposed that Senators should vote by States, " for," said Ellsworth, " if the great States refuse this plan, we shall be separated for ever." " If the minority will have their own will or separate the Union, let it be done," said Wilson. " I cannot consent that one-fourth shall control the power of three-fourths." But Connecticut, through Ellsworth, won the day," says Bancroft, though the motion was lost by a tie; but it was known that New Hamphire and Rhode Island, had they been present, would have voted with Connecticut. So a committee of one from each State was appointed to draw up a compromise, which reported on July 3d, 1787, that in the first branch of the first Congress there should be one member for every forty thousand inhabitants, counting all the free and three-fifths of the rest; that in the second branch each State should have an equal vote; and that, in return for this concession to the small States, the first branch should be invested with the sole power of originating taxes and appropriations. (Bancroft, *Formation*, p. 68, Vol. II.)

Wilson, of Pennsylvania, claimed the Committee had "exceeded its powers." Gouverneur Morris moved to refer the report to a committee and to have it report a ratio of representation. The committee reported in favor of the legislatures of the States regulating the representation according to the wealth and total number of inhabitants. A great deal of discussion ensued. Yates and Lansing, of New York, withdrew, and Hamilton afterwards "took but little part." Representation by numbers was adopted after several exciting sessions, and finally "without a negative."

Wilson resisted an equality of votes in the Senate. It was finally adopted and the number fixed at two from each State.

Seven years was fixed as the time of citizenship prior to eligibility to the House of Representatives. Wilson wished less so as to encourage immigration, and stated that "almost all the general officers of the Pennsylvania line and three of her deputies to this convention, Robert Morris, FitzSimons and himself, were not natives." But seven years was adopted. Pennsylvania voted against nine years of citizenship before one could be elected a Senator. It was thought too long.

The Constitution was signed September 17th, 1787, in Philadelphia, "the home of the Union" and the "citadel of the love of one indivisible country."—(Bancroft, *Format. of Const.*, Vol. II., pp. 238–241.)

The same day the following communication was sent to the

Pennsylvania Assembly, as is shown by the proceedings of the Assembly as recorded by Thomas Lloyd (a Catholic); the letter being read, on motion and by special order the same was read a second time:

"PHILADELPHIA, September 17th, 1787.

SIR:—The Convention having decided on the form of a Constitution to be recommended to the consideration of the United States, we take the earliest moment to communicate this important intelligence to the Assembly of the Commonwealth of Pennsylvania, and to request you to inform the honorable House that we shall be ready to report to them at such time and place as they may direct.

With respect, we have the honor to be, sir,

Your most obedient and humble servants,

B. Franklin,	Robert Morris,
Thomas Mifflin,	Jared Ingersoll,
George Clymer,	Thomas FitzSimons,
Gouverneur Morris,	James Wilson.

To the Honorable the Speaker of the House of Assembly."

Whereupon, on motion of Mr. FitzSimons, it was ordered that 11 o'clock to-morrow morning be assigned for reading the said report.

The next morning, at 11 o'clock, Franklin, "fulfilling his last grand public service, was ushered into the hall of the Assembly" (of Pennsylvania), followed by his seven colleagues of the Convention which had formed the Constitution.

The Assembly's report reads:

"The honorable delegates representing this State in the late Federal Convention were introduced, when his Excellency, B. Franklin, addressed the Speaker:

"'SIR:—I have the very great satisfaction of delivering to you and to this honorable House the results of our deliberations in the late Convention. We hope and believe that the measures recommended by that body will produce happy effects in this Commonwealth as well as to every other of the United States.'

"His Excellency then presented the Constitution agreed to in convention for the government of the United States.

"After the reading of the document, his Excellency, the President of this State, now addressed the chair:

"'Sir :—Your delegates in convention conceive it their duty to submit, in a more particular manner, to the consideration of this House, that part of the Constitution just now read which confers on Congress exclusive legislation over such district as may become the seat of government of the United States. Perhaps it would be advisable to pass a law granting the jurisdiction over any place in Pennsylvania not exceeding ten miles square ; which, with the consent of the inhabitants, the Congress might choose for their residence. We think, sir, that such a measure might possibly tend to fix their choice within the bounds of this Commonwealth, and thereby essentially benefit the citizens of Pennsylvania.'"

Adjourned. No action was taken for ten days.

On September 29th (the last day but one of the session), Clymer proposed to refer the act of the Federal Convention to a convention of the State. Pleas for delay were made, to which Mr. FitzSimons replied thus :

"I think too highly of the good sense of this House to suppose it necessary to say anything to prove to them that their agreement to calling a convention is not unfederal, as every member must have fully considered the point before this time; now I do not think a single gentleman supposes that it would be unfederal. Though the member from Westmoreland has taken some pains to persuade us that Pennsylvania has been hitherto a federal State, and that we are about to depart from that conduct, and to run before even prosperity itself, I think it greatly to the honor of Pennsylvania that she deserves the gentleman's commendation, by having always stood foremost in support of federal measures; and I think it will redound still more to her honor to enter foremost into this new system of confederation, seeing the old is so dissolved or rotten as to be incapable of answering any good purpose whatsoever. Has the gentleman ever looked at the new Constitution ? If he has, he will see it is not an alteration of an article in the old, but that it departs in every principle from the other. It presupposes, sir, that no confederation exists;

or if it does exist, it exists to no purpose, as it can answer no useful purpose; it cannot provide for the common defense, nor promote the general welfare. Therefore, arguments that are intended to reconcile one with the other, or make the latter an appendage to the former, are but a mere waste of words. Does the gentleman suppose that the Convention thought themselves acting under any provision made in the Confederation for altering its articles? No, sir, they had no such idea. They were obliged, in the first instance, to begin with the destruction of its greatest principle, equal representation. They found the Confederation without vigor, and so decayed that it was impossible to graft a useful article upon it; nor was the mode, sir, prescribed by that Confederation, which requires alterations to originate with Congress. They found at an early period that no good purpose could be effected by making such alterations as were provided by the first articles of Union. They also saw that what alterations were necessary could not be ratified by the legislatures, as they were incompetent to ordaining a form of government. They knew this belonged to the people only, and that the people only would be adequate to carry it into effect. What have Congress and the Legislatures to do with the proposed Constitution? Nothing, sir—they are but the mere vehicles to convey the information to the people. The Convention, sir, never supposed it was necessary to report to Congress, much less to abide their determination; they thought it decent to make the compliment to them of sending the result of their deliberations—concluding the knowledge of that would be more extensively spread through this means—not that I would infer there is the least doubt of the most hearty concurrence of that body. But should they decline, and the State of Pennsylvania neglect calling a convention, as I said before, the authority is with the people, and they will do it themselves; but there is a propriety in the legislatures providing the mode by which it may be conducted in a decent and orderly manner.

"The member from Westmoreland agrees that a convention ought to take place. He goes further, and declares that it must and will take place, but assigns no reason why it should

not early take place. He must know that any time after the
election will be proper, because at that time the people, being
collected together, have full opportunity to learn each other's
sentiments on this subject. Taking measures for calling a
convention is a very different thing from deciding on the plan
of government. The sentiments of the people, so far as they
have been collected, have been unanimously favorable to its
adoption, and its early adoption, if their representatives think
it a good one; if we set the example now, there is a great
prospect of its being generally come into; but if we delay, ill
consequences may arise. And I should suppose, if no better
arguments are offered for the delay than what has been advanced by the gentleman on the other side of the House, that
we will not agree to it. As to the time for election, that has
been all along conceded, and gentlemen will propose such
time as they think proper "* (pp. 131–132).

Mr. Findley replied " in favor of delay," and in answer to
Mr. FitzSimons said that every member had not read the
Constitution " with the view of considering it in this House ";
that he thought it "unwise to throw away the dirty water
before we get the clean, and before I go into my new house I
wait till it is finished and furnished."

The question in favor of a convention was adopted by 43 to
19, but the date was not set. FitzSimons voted in its favor.

Robert Whitehall, on behalf of the minority, asked a post-
ponement until the afternoon. It was granted.

The House then adjourned until 4 P. M. On reassembling
the nineteen members were absent. The sergeant-at-arms was
sent after them. They were found, but refused to return. The
speaker " wished to know what the members would choose
to do." Mr. Wynkoop said, " if there was no way of compelling those who deserted from duty to perform it, then God be
merciful to us." "The following morning a number of citizens, whose leader is said to have been Commodore John

* Proceedings and Debates of the General Assembly of Pennsylvania.
Taken in Short-Hand by Thomas Lloyd. Volume the First. Phil-
adelphia : Printed by Daniel Humphreys, in Spruce street, near the
Drawbridge, 1787.

Barry, forcibly entered the lodgings of James McCalmont, a member from Franklin county, and Jacob Miley, a member from Dauphin county, who were among the seceders, and whom they dragged to the State House and thrust into the chamber where the Assembly was in session without a quorum."

There were then forty-six members present. McCalmont "informed the House that he had been forcibly brought into the Assembly room contrary to his wishes by a number of citizens whom he did not know, and begged he might be dismissed."

Mr. FitzSimons said he "would be glad to know if any member of the House was guilty of forcing the gentleman from the determination of absenting himself; if there was, he thought it necessary that the House mark such conduct with their disapprobation. But we are to consider, sir, that the member is now here, and that the business of the State cannot be accomplished if any one is suffered to withdraw; from which consideration I conclude it will be extremely improper for any member to leave the House until the laws and other unfinished business are complete. He hoped the member would not be dismissed; for he thought no one man ought to be allowed to break up the Assembly of Pennsylvania, which could be done agreeably to the Constitution only by the time expiring for which it was chosen. * * * *
He was a friend to good order and decorum, but he believed McCalmont's complaint was not to be redressed by the House. The member is now here and we may determine that he shall stay, not only on constitutional grounds, but from the law of nature, that will not permit anybody to destroy our existence prematurely."

McCalmont made for the door. FitzSimons addressed him, but so as not to be heard (by Lloyd). Others called out to stop him; citizens at the door barred his departure, and he returned. FitzSimons said McCalmont "told him he had occasion to go out, and was willing to go with the sergeant"; so FitzSimons hoped it might be complied with. The Speaker put the question. The House refused.

A messenger that day arrived from New York. He had

been sent by William Bingham, representative in Congress, which was then in session in that city. He brought a copy of a resolution of Congress recommending conventions of the States to consider the new Constitution.

After the proceedings above detailed the Assembly voted that an election should be held on the first Tuesday in November, and Philadelphia should be the place of meeting of the State Convention to consider the proposed Constitution, and November 21st the time. The Pennsylvania Assembly, within twenty hours of the passage of the recommendation by Congress, resolved to call a convention. But the friends of the Constitution had to use force to secure a quorum of the Assembly so it could do so. "The announcement was hailed by three cheers and the ringing of church bells."

Seceding members issued an address protesting against the action of the Federal Convention and Assembly; that the Pennsylvania delegates were all from Philadelphia, and represented the landed interest, and had exceeded their authority.

The minority opposed the "aristocratic influence," and feared that the upholders of the Constitution would "become the seed of a a permanent national party," which would override the States. They wanted a bill of rights which, among other needs, should "secure liberty of conscience in all matters of religion."

The election was held November 6th, 1787. The city delegates (Republicans) received 1215 votes (the highest number). The Constitutionalists, headed by Franklin, but from 132 to 255 votes each. The Republicans were George Latimer, Benjamin Rush, Hilary Baker, Thomas McKean and James Wilson. Both Wilson and McKean favored the Constitution.—(See Lloyd's report of their speeches, the only ones reported.) The Constitutionalists were Benjamin Franklin, David Rittenhouse, Charles Pettit, John Steinmetz and James Irvine.

That night a mob attacked the house of Major Boyd, in which the anti-Constitutional members of the Executive Council and of the Assembly were sleeping.

The Convention met from November 21st to December

12th, when the ratification of Pennsylvania by a vote of 46 to 23 was given to the Constitution of the United States.

The change made by the new and supreme law is well set forth in the words of James Wilson in the Convention of Pennsylvania considering the Constitution: "When we had battled all the menaces of foreign power, we neglected to establish among ourselves a government that would ensure domestic vigor and stability. What was the consequence? The commencement of peace was the commencement of every disgrace and distress that could befall a people in a peaceful state. Devoid of national power, we could not prohibit the extravagance of our importations, nor could we derive a revenue from their excess. Devoid of national importance, we could not procure, for our exports, a tolerable sale at foreign markets. Devoid of national credit, we saw our public securities melt in the hands of the holders, like snow before the sun. Devoid of national dignity, we could not, in some instances, perform our treaties, on our parts; and, in other instances, we could neither obtain nor compel the performance of them on the part of others. Devoid of national energy, we could not carry into execution our own resolution, decisions or laws."—(Debates of the Convention of Penna., p. 37.)

Next day the members of the convention and of the Supreme Executive Council, with the officers of the State and city, and others, went in procession from the State House to the old court house, corner of Second and Market streets, where the ratification of the instrument was formally proclaimed. A salute of twelve guns was fired, and bells were rung. The convention then returned to the State House, where two copies of the ratification of the Constitution were signed. At three o'clock the convention met again, and, with members of the Supreme Executive Council and Congress, went to dinner at Eppley's tavern. "The remainder of the day was spent in mutual congratulations upon the happy prospect of enjoying once more order, justice and good government in the United States."

When Pennsylvania had ratified the Constitution the opposition did not cease. The anti-Federalists met at Harrisburg in September, 1788, and nominated Blair McClenachan and Charles Pettit for Congress. Others friendly to the Constitution met at the State House on October 25th, and named FitzSimons, George Clymer, Henry Hill, Hilary Baker, William Bingham, and John M. Nesbitt as suitable men from whom two could be selected as nominees. The convention met at Lancaster, and selected FitzSimons and George Clymer at the election held November, 1788. FitzSimons received 2478; Clymer, 2468; McClenachan, 575; and Pettit, 687 votes. Mr. FitzSimons was re-elected to the second and third Congresses.

FitzSimons, as we have seen, was a member of the Pennsylvania Assembly in 1787, and at the same time he was a member of the Constitutional Convention. He was present in the Assembly during September, 1787. On the bill for the " Better Regulation of Juries," he favored the reduction of the fine for non-attendance from £6 to £3. He was a member of the committee reporting the bill. He did not think it proper " that executive officers should be left at liberty to impose penalties or punishment in a Republic." The reduction was not, however, agreed to. A clause was reported in favor of paying jurymen 5s. a day. FitzSimons said he " was not much acquainted with the subject nor very solicitous about it. He had little to do with courts, and therefore he could not say how they were attended. But he had made inquiries of gentlemen well informed, and they had told him the present system was burdensome and disagreeable, without any equivalent. Philadelphia had paid more than £1500 annually on this account, and the effect in the dispatch of public business was not altogether as great as had been represented, nor had it other good effects. On the contrary, there were bad ones arising for the city. Many of the lower people, he was informed, sought employment in this way, and were anxious to serve on juries for the pay by which that desirable routine of citizens was prevented in a great measure. Every man in society pays something to that society for which compensation cannot be made. The service of jurors is of this nature, and the reward for each is reciprocal. It is that kind of reward more suitable to the inhabitants of a republic and agreeable to the people of Pennsylvania above all others. The practice in many courts is to collect, but not to pay jurors." The clause stopping payment to jurors was adopted.

On the question of issuing license to auctioneers he wanted the collection uniform in all counties or exemption for Philadelphia. It had paid £6000 or £8000. "Nor can the people of Philadelphia longer suffer themselves to be taxed so partially."

Dr. Logan, in reply, did not consider the license so oppressive as FitzSimons had represented. "It had affected principally those numerous foreigners who came among us and particularly disposed of their property by vendue. The citizens of Philadelphia bore but a small part of the expense."

When the bill to incorporate the Episcopal Church of St. John, at York, was introduced, FitzSimons proposed several amendments to the charter, and to endow the school of the church. In answer to the objection of Mr. Clymer against " erecting a public school for the instruction of any particular society," FitzSimons replied: " We all know that the public schools erected by the Legislature are in fact under the direction of persons of a particular persuasion, though such is not expressed in the law, and though there may be objections to attaching them to a particular church by express language, there is none to the fact. That while the College at Carlisle and the University in Philadelphia were under the direction of a particular society, and he knew no ill consequences to arise therefrom, as they did not exclude children of another form from receiving an education, he had some doubts of the propriety of adding the clause to the charter. The clauses were put into his hands by members from that county." The bill passed.

On September 14th, 1787, FitzSimons presented the annual report of the Pennsylvania Hospital, and was then appointed on a committee to visit the institution. The same day a bill for the erection of parts of Westmoreland and Washington counties into a new county being under consideration, he acknowledged himself totally "ignorant of that country," but "though ignorant of the country he had heard with satisfaction that its capital, Pittsburgh, was considerable in extent, and possesses a great number of inhabitants, and from the advantages it enjoys from nature likely to increase and become a place of some consequence. The great convenience of having courts of justice there, already the port was visited by all whose business leads them to the western country, is apparent. The county town, with the gaol, was to be on the west side of the river, " and there is not a soul to commit, for there is not a soul lives on that side of the river." FitzSimons thought the bill premature and would answer no good purpose either to the State or the people who ask it. "I am rather against the measure than for it."

On September 15th, 1788, a bill to enable the erection of a floating bridge across the Neshaminy being under consideration, FitzSimons " thought useful improvements worthy of the particular patronage of the Legislature, and permanent bridges were extremely useful ; and those who hazard their money in such structures ought to have it in their power to reimburse themselves in a moderate manner. But he saw no necessity of erecting another bridge so near one already there, in sight of the other, and so as he wished justice to be done he wished Mr. Besonet to be reimbursed for his expense and trouble before he voted to erect the bridge. In reply to the charge of monopoly, FitzSimons said that he detested monopolies as much as any member, but did not consider this one, as no one was compelled to cross it. The bill was defeated.

On September 19th, 1788, FitzSimons voted for the division of Bedford county.

On September 20th FitSimons presented and read the amount of taxes for 1787 up to September 6th. " Thinking an inquiry into the management of the treasury necessary, he moved the appointment of a committee of seven to inspect into the public treasury and to report to the House." He was named by the House as chairman. On the 27th the committee reported "that in consequence of the delinquencies of many counties in paying taxes, a review of our tax laws is necessary."

In June, 1788, a meeting of the friends of the Constitution was held at Eppley's tavern to arrange for the celebration of the adoption of the Constitution when nine States should have ratified it.   On June 21st New Hampshire gave the ninth en-dorsement.   The commemoration of the adoption was cele-brated on July 4th, by which time Virginia had added her ratification.   A parade of the trades of the city took place. The procession started from Third and South streets, and marched up Third to Callowhill and thence to Fourth, thence to Market, and out to Union Green at Bush Hill, where the day was spent in speech-making and the drinking of American porter, beer and cider, and festivities.   In the procession Mr. FitzSimons, representing the French Alliance, rode the horse of Count Rochambeau.   He carried a flag of white silk having three *fleur-de-lis* and thirteen stars in union, and overhead the words " Sixth of February, 1778," in gold letters.

That Franklin was not one of those originally named as dele-gates seems to have been charged to the enmity of Dr. Rush. This the latter resented as unjust, and accordingly wrote to Mr. FitzSimons, who was in New York attending the sessions of the first Congress.   Mr. FitzSimons replied as follows:

NEW YORK, 29th July, 1789.

DEAR SIR :—I am happy to have it in my power to contribute in any degree to remove an impression, which by your letter of 27th seems to have given you great uneasiness. I am the better able to do it because your predictions have been so perfectly verified.   I have frequently reflected on the circumstances with pleasure since the thing happened.

I remember your lamenting to me several times that Doct. Franklin had not been elected one of the delegates to the convention, and that toward the close of the sessions of Assembly, previous to the meeting of that body, you pressed me strongly to propose it ; his name had been among the first nominations, and it was then generally understood his health rendered him unable to attend, and as that suggestion was sup-posed to come from his friends, I was unwilling to bring him again into view for the appointment.   The reasons you gave, however, made some impression upon me, and I inquired of a particular friend of the Doct. whether the appointment would be acceptable.   From the answer I was satisfied it would, and on the succeeding day I proposed it to our friends in the house, who very readily concurred in and supported the measure.

I have very frequently since that time mentioned how fortunate it was that the appointment was made. The Doctor's punctual attendance proved that it was agreeable to him, and I always believed that his name recommended the Constitution. These were the effects that you predicted; they struck me at the time, and induced me to interest myself more in the measure than I otherwise should have done, as I was, perhaps, less acquainted with Doct. Franklin than any other of the members. I am very sorry to hear his latter days are attended with so much pain. I very much respect his general character and consider him as one of the innumerable instances in which eminent services have been treated with ingratitude. With that regard, I am, dear sir,

Yr. mt. obt. servt.,

THOMAS FITZSIMONS.

Doct. Rush.

[Rush MSS., Ridgway Library.]

On September 13th, 1788, the Legislature passed "an act to incorporate the members of the Religious Society of Roman Catholics belonging to the Congregation of St. Mary's in the city of Philadelphia." The incorporators (and thus the first trustees) were Rev. Robert Molyneux, Rev. Francis Beeston, Rev. Lawrence Graessl, pastors, and George Meade, Thomas FitzSimons, James Byrne, Paul Esling, John Cottringer, Jas. Eck, Mark Willcox and John Carrell.

Mr. FitzSimons was elected a member of the First Congress, which met in 1789 in accordance with the requirements of the Constitution which we are now commemorating. He was named a member of the Committee on Ways and Means. On February 9th, 1789, he requested the Supreme Executive Council of Pennsylvania to appoint a committee, to confer with his committee respecting the provision necessary to be made for payment of pensions. On April 8th he was appointed on the committee to draft an act "for regulating the collecting of imposts and tonnage." On May 25th he was appointed on the committee to fix the compensation to be paid the President, Vice President, Senators and Members of the House of Representatives. On July 14th he was appointed chairman of a committee to prepare a bill for the government of the North-West Territory, on the Ohio, and reported on the 16th. On July 21st Mr. FitzSimons wrote to President Mifflin of

Pennsylvania relative to certain requirements of the Continential Loan Office. He said: "If my agency in that or any other business which concerns the State can be useful, you may command my services.—(*Pa. Archives*, Vol. XI., p. 595.)

In August, 1789, the question of fixing the capital of our country came before Congress. It was first proposed, on September 7th, to name "the east bank of the Susquehannah, in Pennsylvania," but an amendment was offered naming "the north bank of the Potomac, in Maryland." The vote stood 21 to 21, with FitzSimons voting against the Potomac. Wilmington, Del., was proposed, but defeated by a vote of 19 in favor of and 32 against, with FitzSimons in the negative. To establish it on "the Potomac, Susquehannah or Delaware" was lost by a vote of 23 to 28, with FitzSimons in the negative.

To "the banks of either side of the Delaware not more than eight miles above or below the Falls of Delaware" was tried; it got but four votes, with FitzSimmons among the forty-six nays. To insert "banks of Susquehannah" instead of "east bank" of the same river, received twenty-six votes to twenty-five nays, with FitzSimons among the nays. To insert after Pennsylvania the words "or Maryland," was lost by twenty-five to twenty-six, with FitzSimons voting nay. Efforts were made to insert "Philadelphia." The vote for our city was twenty-two in favor to twenty-nine against; but FitzSimons, we may think it strange, is among the nays. So the "banks of the Susquehannah in Pennsylvania" was adopted by a majority of one vote. Thomas FitzSimons is thus shown to have favored the east bank of the Susquehannah. Then it was resolved that a committee of three should be appointed by Washington, to select the most eligible location on the banks of the Susquehanna, in Pennsylvania. The vote was twenty-eight to twenty-one; FitzSimmons voting in the affirmative. But we know the capital was not established as the first Congress decreed. On September 8th the Georgetown inhabitants petitioned Congress offering "to put themselves and their fortunes under the exclusive jurisdiction of Congress in case that place should be selected as the seat of government." On September 21st came the offer from the Assembly of Pennsylvania offering Philadelphia. From one point to another the question continued until it was laid over for the action of the next Congress.

On May 27th, 1790, FitzSimons was appointed chairman of the committee of Congress to provide for a settlement of accounts between the United States and the various States.

On December 24th, 1790, he was appointed chairman of the committee of Congress to ascertain " how far the owners of ships shall be liable to freighters of goods shipped on board." On December 27th he was also appointed chairman of a commitee to prepare a bill to enable the Collector of the Port of Philadelphia to land goods at other places than this city when navigation is obstructed by ice. On the 30th such a bill was presented by this committee and became a law on January 5th, 1791.

On February 15th, 1791, President Washington sent Congress a message notifying it that he had come to an understanding with the Court of London in relation to points of commerce between the two nations on principles of reciprocal advantages. This message was referred to a committee of which Mr. FitzSimons was a member. Five days previously he had been appointed one of a committee of three to draft an act as a supplement to the act re-establishing a treasury department. On October 28th, 1791, he was appointed on a committee to bring in a bill for registering ships and regulating those in constant service.

On February 8th, 1791, Washington notified Congress that an article of expense in the department of Foreign Affairs had been incurred for which no provision had been made by law; he sent the letter to the Secretary of State " so that you may do therein what you shall find to be right." It was in relation to a claim of John Brown Cutting, and to Thomas FitzSimons as chairman of a committee was referred the duty of ascertaining what was right.

In considering the act to collect import duties it is of special interest to us of this protective community to know that Madison and Webster "regarded it as important historical evidence that Thomas FitzSimons was the first to suggest, as the clear duty of Congress, the so laying of imposts as to encourage manufacturers." This, says Flanders, "should be the delight of every true-born Pennsylvanian to know." An examination of the records of Congress will sustain this declaration by the abundant evidence of the efforts of Mr. FitzSimons to impose protective duties. Thus on unwrought steel, for every 112 lbs., FitzSimons proposed a duty of 66 cents. In opposition to this it was urged that it would be oppressive of the agricultural interests. So strong were the denial of this on Mr. FitzSimons' part and the facts he brought to sustain his position, that the duty was fixed at 56 cents. On cable and cordage he strove to impose 100 cents. He got seventy-five; but on tarred cordage he succeeded in getting 90 cents. On nails and spikes he got one cent per lb., "so as to protect their manufacture." After the several duties had been settled by the committee of the whole of the first Congress Mr. FitzSimons was a member of the committee appointed to draft an Act in accordance with the resolves of the committee.

In the Congress in 1789, the question of taxing imports came up. The debate reflects the sentiments of some eminent men. Hon. Roger Sherman, of Connecticut, proposed a tax of fifteen cents per gallon on West India rum. Mr. Lawrence, of New York, argued that so high a duty would lead to smuggling, and consequent loss of revenue. Mr. FitzSimons, of Pennsylvania, thought there was no object from which they could collect revenue more to be subjected to a higher duty than ardent spirits of every kind, and if they could lay the duty so high as to lessen the consumption in any degree, the better, for it is not an article of necessity, but of luxury, and a luxury of the most pernicious kind."—(*Liquor Problem, by Dr. Dorchester*, p. 163.)

One has but to examine *The Congressional Directory* of the first Congress containing a synopsis of the debates, as reported by his fellow-Catholic of Philadelphia, Thomas Lloyd, to discover FitzSimons' strenuous advocacy of protection, and his knowledge of finances, commerce and measures for the regulation of navigation.

He favored a duty upon ale, beer and porter imported, as

their manufacture deserved encouragement, for if the people were to be improved by what entered into their diet it would be prudent for the National Legislature to encourage the manufacture of malt liquors. In committee he proposed six cents a gallon, but James Madison's motion for eight cents was adopted, but in Congress ten cents was moved by FitzSimons, and adopted.

On candles imported, FizSimons moved for an impost of two cents a pound. He said: " I have no doubt but that in a few years we shall be able to furnish sufficient to supply the continent. Pennsylvania lays an impost on candles from Ireland and England; and the necessity of encouraging those manufactures which the State Legislatures deemed proper, exist, in a considerable degree. It will be politic for the United States to continue such duties till their object was accomplished."

So we might go through the record and develope at length his views on protection to American industry. He was the earliest advocate of that principle, though it is important to note that he " thought there was a clear distinction between taxing manufactures and raw material well known to every enlightened country."

On February 27th, 1793, the Secretary of the Treasury complained to Congress of inaccuracies in printing the statements he sent that body. FitzSimons was chairman of the committee to which the complaint was referred. The committee discovered that the printer, solicitous for the rapid dispatch of the public business, had of late omitted to send proofs to the department. Experience even now justifies the belief that the proofs were not returned in due time, and thus the printer was incommoded and no doubt under the restrictions which prevented him from charging time on the work, and so " the intention of the House to have the business speedily executed " was a commendable one. At any rate, FitzSimons stood by the printer and reported that no new regulation was necessary. So we may hope the Treasury department was taught that a printer had to have a fair chance to do work that Congress had in hand.

So I might give many more extracts from the proceedings of Congress from 1789 to 1794. Enough has been given to show the activity and general usefulness of Mr. FitzSimons, especially in matters relating to the public revenue, commerce and finances. A study of his life in a historical aspect is best presented by the evidence of his worth and usefulness. His works live after him and influence not this generation and country alone, but all mankind, for as our nation's birth, struggles, progress and trials have concerned and influenced all people, so the work of those who did valiant duty or legislated wisely for our country's advancement is worthy of remembrance.

The first Congress under the new Constitution met March 4th, 1789, at New York. On July 4th it passed the first act imposing duties on imports. This was the second law which the new Congress passed.

After the Revolution, England endeavored commercially to master the new nation and to crush it so that the people would be glad to return to her authority. "They mean," said John Adams, while Minister to England, "Americans should have neither ships nor sailors to annoy her trade." " Patience will do no good ; nothing but reciprocal prohibition and imposts will have any effect." (Bancroft's *Form. Const.*, Vol. I., p. 206.) This, too, after Adams had told George III. that they were a people having "the same language, a similar religion and kindred blood." The King replied : " The moment I see a disposition to give this country the preference, that moment I shall say, let the circumstances of language, of religion and of blood have their natural and full weight."—(*Ibid.*, p 201.)

On March 24th, 1789, the Pennsylvania Assembly resolved that a convention should be called to revise the Constitution of the State. Mr. FitzSimons and his fellow Catholic, Mark Wilcox, of Delaware county, voted in favor of the convention.

The Supreme Executive Council of Pennsylvania refused to promulgate this action. The revision project had been brought about by the efforts of " The Republican Society," started in 1779, which urged the revision of the Constitution of 1776. Associated with FitzSimons in that Society were such men of distinction as Benjamin Rush, John Nixon, Robert Morris, Thomas Mifflin, Francis Hopkinson and John Cadwalader. The Constitutional Convention was held, and on September 2d, 1790, a new Constitution of the State was adopted.

The College Academy and Charitable School of Philadelphia was, by the friends of American liberty, considered as being conducted by officials inimical to the cause of independence. Whether justly charged or not, the charter of the College was annulled by the Assembly in 1779 and a new charter granted to the University of Pennsylvania. Under this charter the Rev. Ferdinand Farmer was chosen as a trustee representing one of "the six principal religious denominations." He acted as such. He was the first Catholic priest to hold even such an office in our State. In 1789 the charter was restored to the College of Philadelphia, and at the second meeting of the corporators, held March 11th, 1789, Thomas FitzSimons was elected a trustee. He served until the union of the college and the university in 1791.

After the Constitution was sent to the States for ratification, then came the great controversy as to its merits and its value to promote the welfare of the people and to serve the purposes of good government. Mr. FitzSimons took a very active part in securing the ratification by Pennsylvania, as we have seen. He was in correspondence with the leading men concerning its ratification by the other States. The following letters from Cyrus Griffin, the President of the Congress of the Confederacy, show how he was kept informed:

"NEW YORK, 16th June, 1788.

"I am not a little happy that the important business of the proposed Constitution is going on so well in Virginia. Governor Randolph's recantation, though embarrassing enough with respect to himself, may produce some pleasing consequences.

"New Hampshire will certainly adopt the system. About two-thirds of this State are at present in opposition, but the Federal members expect to convert a great number—and, from good authority, I am told that Governor Clinton thinks it absolutely necessary that New York should adopt the measure also. Governor Collins and some of the leading men of Rhode Island are advocates for the plan now. From the appearance of things, taken together, we have good reason to conclude that the Union will be complete."—(Bancroft's *Hist. Format. Const.*, Vol. II., p. 470.)

" NEW YORK, 15th Feb., 1788.

" Colonel R. H. Lee and Mr. John Page, men of influence in Virginia, are relinquishing their opposition; but what to us is very extraordinary and unexpected, we are told that Mr. George Mason has declared himself so great an enemy to the Constitution that he will heartily join Mr. Henry and others in promoting a southern confederacy."—(*Hist. Format. Const.*, Vol. II., p. 461.)

Mr. FitzSimons was in 1790 an advocate of the election to the Governorship of Pennsylvania of Gen. Arthur St. Clair. He was foremost in promoting his nomination, and to the suggestion that St. Clair might not be elected, he wrote that soldier this noble sentence : " I conceive it to be a duty to contend for what is right, be the issue as it may." St. Clair was defeated, and Gen. Mifflin was elected.

While in the first Congress, the failure of the Expedition against the Indians of the North-West under St. Clair provoked much unfavorable comment upon that commander. Gen. St. Clair asked Washington to appoint a court of inquiry, to ascertain the cause of the failure. He declined. It was proposed in Congress to request Washington to do so. Fitz-Simons suggested " the impropriety of requesting the President to institute a court of inquiry, as the reasons and propriety of such courts are better and more fully known to the President than to the members of the House." Accordingly FitzSimons moved the appointment of a special committee. That committee of seven, with FitzSimons as chairman, unanimously reported that the failure could in no respect be attributed to St. Clair. The report went over until the next session, when communications from the Secretary of War and others were refered to the committee, which again reaffirmed its previous reports.

After the election of Washington to the Presidency, under the Constitution we are now testifying our loyalty to, various religious denominations and other organized bodies presented addresses to the Father of our Country, testifying their admiration for his character, and grateful recognition of his services to his country. On behalf of the Catholics of the country, an address was presented, signed by Rev. John Carroll, for the clergy, and by Charles Carroll of Carrollton, Daniel Carroll, Thomas FitzSimons, and Dominic Lynch of New York on behalf of the laity.

"ADDRESS OF THE ROMAN CATHOLICS OF AMERICA TO GEORGE WASHINGTON.

" Sir :—We have been long impatient to testify our joy and unbounded confidence on your being called by a unanimous vote to the first station of a country, in which that unanimity could not have been obtained without the previous merit of unexampled services, of eminent wisdom, and unblemished virtue. Our congratulations have not reached you sooner, because our scattered situation prevented the communication and collecting of those sentiments which warmed every breast. But delay has furnished us with the opportunity, not only of presaging the happiness to be expected under your administration, but of bearing testimony to that which we experience. It is your peculiar talent, in war and in peace, to afford security to those who commit their protection into your hands. In war you shield them from the ravages of armed hostility; in peace you establish public tranquility by the justice and moderation not less than by the vigor of your government. By example as well as by vigilance, you extend the influence of laws on the manners of our fellow-citizens. You encourage respect for religion, and inculcate, by words and actions, that principle on which the welfare of nations so much depends— that a superintending Providence governs the events of the world, and watches over the conduct of men. Your exalted maxims and unwearied attention to the moral and physical improvement of your country have produced already the happiest effects. Under your administration America is animated with zeal for the attainment and encouragement of useful literature; she improves agriculture, extends her commerce, acquires with foreign nations a dignity unknown to her before. From these happy events, in which none can feel a warmer interest than ourselves, we derive additional pleasure by the recollection that you, Sir, have been the principal instrument to effect so rapid a change in our political situation. This prospect of national prosperity is peculiarly pleasing to us on another account; because whilst our country preserves her freedom and independence, we shall have a well-founded title to claim from her justice the equal rights of citzenship, as the price of our blood spilt under your eyes, and of our common exertions for her defense under your auspicious conduct— rights rendered more dear to us by the remembrance of former hardships. When we pray for the preservation of them where they have been granted, and expect the full extension of them from those States which restrict them,—when we solicit the protection of heaven over our common country, we neither omit nor can omit to recommend your preservation to the singular care of Divine Providence, because we conceive that no human means are so available to promote the welfare of the United States as the prolongation of your health and life, in which are included the energy of your example, the wisdom of your counsels, and the persuasive eloquence of your virtues.

In behalf of the Roman Catholic Clergy,

J. CARROLL.

In behalf of the Roman Catholic Laity,
CHARLES CARROLL, of Carrollton,
DANIEL CARROLL,
THOMAS FITZSIMONS,
DOMINIC LYNCH."

To that Address Washington made this reply:

"*Gentlemen* :—While I now receive with much satisfaction your congratulations on my being called, by an unanimous vote, to the first station of my country, I cannot but duly notice your politeness in offering an apology for the unavoidable delay. As that delay has given you an opportunity of realizing instead of anticipating the benefits of the general government, you will do me the justice to believe that your testimony of the increase of the public prosperity enhances the pleasure which I would otherwise have experienced from your affectionate address.

"I feel that my conduct in war and in peace has met with more general approbation than could reasonably have been expected, and I find myself disposed to consider that fortunate circumstance in a great degree resulting from the able support and extraordinary candor of my fellow-citizens of all denominations.

"The prospect of national prosperity now before us is truly animating and ought to excite the exertions of all good men · to establish and secure the happiness of their country in the permanent duration of its freedom and independence. America, under the smiles of a Divine Providence, the protection of a good government, and the cultivation of manners and morals, cannot fail of attaining an uncommon degree of eminence in literature, commerce, agriculture, improvements at home, and respectability abroad.

"As mankind become more liberal they will be more apt to allow that all those who conduct themselves as worthy members of the community are equally entitled to the protection of civil government. I hope ever to see America among the foremost nations in examples of justice and liberty. And I presume that your fellow-citizens will not forget the patriotic part which you took in the accomplishment of their Revolution and the establishment of their Government, or the important assistance which they received from a nation in which the Catholic faith is professed.

"I thank you, gentlemen, for your kind concern for me. While my life and my health shall continue, in whatever situation I may be, it shall be my constant endeavor to justify the favorable sentiments which you are pleased to express of my conduct. And may the members of your society in America, animated alone by the pure spirit of Christianity, and still conducting themselves as the faithful subjects of our free government, enjoy every temporal and spiritual felicity.

G. WASHINGTON."

The funding system proposed by Hamilton was adopted in July, 1790. FitzSimons voted for it. It provided for the settlement and payment of the debts of the Revolution. There were two points of prominent interest, whether the State debts should be assumed by the nation, and whether the evidences of debt (called then public securities) should be "funded" for the benefit of the holders at the nominal value, or at some depreciated value. They had long been in circulation, and were sometimes as low as at one-eighth of the sum for which they were issued. These securities had gathered in the hands of those who expected payment if the Constitution took effect; and this was among the causes of the deep interest which the conventional meeting excited. When "the funding system," on Hamilton's report, engaged the attention of Congress, "speculation" might be called a public distemper. At one time the securities rose above their nominal value. Fortunes were won and lost in a single hour. "No one who can remember those days needs to be reminded of the intense excitement which prevailed among speculators; nor of the sullen dissatisfaction manifested by individuals of the opposition."—(Familiar Letters on Public Characters and Public Events from the Peace of 1783 to the Peace of 1815. Boston: Russell, Odiorne & Metcalf, 1834. Page 41. Letter XI., March 1, 1833.)

In Congress, on December 9th, 1790, FitzSimons opposed ordering three newspapers for the members. They were ordered, however, by a vote of 22 to 15. On December 16th he favored a military law for all between eighteen and forty-five years.—(Annals of Congress, pp. 1805, 1813.)

In Porcupine's Works (Vol. II., p. 158) we find Washington's speech to Congress, November 19th, 1794, referring to the Whisky Insurrection in Western Pennsylvania: "It is well known that Congress did not hesitate to examine the complaints which were presented, and to relieve them, as far as justice dictated or general convenience would permit. But the impression which this moderation made on the discontented did not correspond with what it deserved. The arts of delusion were no longer confined to the efforts of designing individuals. The very forbearance to press prosecutions was misinterpreted into a fear of urging the execution of the laws ; and associations of men began to denounce threats against the officers employed.   From a belief that by a more formal concert their operation might be defeated, certain self-created societies assumed the tone of condemnation."

• The Senate, in answering the speech, said the resistance to the laws had been increased by the proceedings of certain self-created societies relating to the laws and administration of the government, but the House of Representatives, according to Cobbett (Porcupine), " had a majority on the French or Democratic side."   These self-created societies were local organizations of citizens in Western Pennsylvania (*ibid.*, p. 174).

The answer of the House of Representatives, as reported by the committee, took no notice of that part of the speech which alluded to the Democratic societies ; an amendment was, therefore, proposed by Mr. FitzSimons in the following words :

" As part of this subject, we cannot withhold our reprobation of the self-created societies which have arisen up in some parts of the Union, misrepresenting the conduct of the government, and disturbing the operation of the laws, and which, by deceiving and inflaming the ignorant and the weak, may naturally be supposed to have stimulated and urged the insurrection.   These are institutions not strictly unlawful, yet they are not less fatal to good order and true liberty, and reprehensible in the degree that our system of government approaches to perfect political freedom " (*ibid.*, p. 175).

It produced a very long and acrimonious debate, during which all the ingenuity of both parties was amply displayed.

FitzSimons does not appear to have taken part in the debate. Amendment was voted down.   Democratic societies protested against the action of the President of the Senate.

FitzSimons was a Federalist of the party of Washington, and so an opponent of the French Republican principles then active in opposition to English influence.   At the election of 1794 John Swanwick was elected.   This was a " stinging change for the aristocracy," wrote Madison to Jefferson, on

November 16th, 1794; and on December 4th, that the election of Swanwick, in preference to FitzSimons, "was of material consequence." This closed FitzSimons' political career. Hon. John Swanwick, his successor, was not a Catholic, though he was a pew-holder in St. Mary's, and the friend and associate of Fathers Farmer and Molyneux. He on the death of Father Farmer gave expression to his grief and of his appreciation of his dead friend in verses which will be found in his book of poems. I have also a poetical tribute of his to the memory of Mrs. Garrett Cottringer.

By the treaty of peace of 1783 England was to give up certain posts on the western frontier. This was not done because, as England alleged, merchants and others had grievances relating to debts, estates and property in the several States which the States were not discharging. The holding of the western posts, which was a continuance of the war, had no connection with this debt (due English creditors), and no proportion to it; for the profits of the fur trade, thus secured to great Britain, in each single year very far exceeded the whole debt of which the collection was postponed.—(Bancroft's *Format. of Const.*, Vol. I., p. 206.)

Congress resolved that the States ought to repeal acts repugnant to the Treaty of Peace, " as well as to prevent their continuing to be regarded as violations of the treaty so as to avoid the disagreeable necessity there might otherwise be of raising and discussing questions touching their validity and obligation." Nothing was done, however. In 1794 a new treaty with Great Britain was made by Jay. It was provided therein that commissioners were to be appointed to ascertain the losses and damages of the British merchants. Thomas Mc-Donald and Henry Pye Rich were the British Commissioners, and Thomas FitzSimons and James Innes, of Virginia, the American. By lot they selected John Guillemard, whose name had been put in by the British Commissioners. Mr. Innes died and Mr. Samuel Sitgreaves was named in his place. (*Porcupine's Works*, Vol. XII., p. 70.)

When the Naturalization Bill of 1795 was under considera-tion, it was proposed to prevent titled foreigners from becoming citizens until they had explicitly renounced their titles in open court. FitzSimons was one of the thirty-two Federalists voting against the amendment. Fifty-eight were in in its favor.

In 1796 FitzSimons subscribed for £3959 11s. 9d. of the South Carolina Debt Loan, authorized December 29th, 1795.

On March 4th, 1797, Washington retired from the Presidency. The leading citizens of our city tendered him a dinner on the afternoon of that day. It took place at Rickett's Circus, where now the *Public Ledger* office is located. The guests assembled at Oellers' Hotel, on Chestnut above Sixth, where is now the *German Democrat* office. Oellers was a German Catholic and the grandfather of Mr. Oellers, now cashier of the Philadelphia *Record*. At the dinner thus given to Washington the most distinguished citizens were not only, of course, present, but it is evidence of dignity among the distinguished that Thomas FitzSimons and Thomas Willing were the presiding officers. There were 240 guests present. "The circus was floored over for dancing, and otherwise suitably prepared; and a settee, with a canopy over it, arranged in an elevated position for Mr. and Mrs. Washington. He did not confine himself to this, but moved about the circus, conversing freely with the company, which consisted of distinguished members of Congress, all foreign ministers, and invited strangers. An opening was made through the wall of the hotel from the circus, and the company passed through this into the hotel for supper. This hotel was shortly after destroyed by fire; and the circus has long since given place to other buildings."—(Familiar Letters on Public Characters and Public Events—from the Peace of 1783 to the Peace of 1815: Boston, Russell, Odiorne & Metcalf, 1834. Letter XXI., March 30th, 1833, pp. 85–86.)

In 1797 " a great disturbance took place in Trinity Church, Philadelphia. An unworthy clergyman (Rev. J. Nepomucen Gœtz) undertook to supplant the lawful pastor of that congregation. He, unhappily, succeeded by popular intrigue."—·(Archbishop Marechal, in Pastoral Letter to the Catholics of Norfolk, Va., 1819, p. 53.—*Note*.) Mr. FitzSimons appears to have been one of those endeavoring to make peace between the malcontents and Bishop Carroll. On September 5th, 1797, the Bishop wrote to Mr. FitzSimons, stating the conditions without which "he could not again receive these deluded Catholics into the Church."

Not until 1802, January 29th, did the trustees acknowledge "ourselves subject to the Episcopal authority of the Bishop of Baltimore."—(*Ibid.*, pp. 56–59.)

On April 10th, 1798, Mr. FitzSimons was elected a trustee of St. Mary's Church. He served, however, but one year.

General Maitland, having abandoned San Domingo to Touissaint L' Ouverture, went to England and from thence came to the United States to make a contract for beef and pork for the British navy, on the awards which would be granted by the commissioners for the settlement of debts. FitzSimons published a letter announcing that the awards had not been made and were uncertain as to time and amount.—(The *Aurora*, April 30th, 1799.) At this time it was stated by the *Aurora* of the same date that a tailor on Spruce street was making uniforms for Touissaint L'Ouverture.

These were indeed perilous times, not only for American seamen but also for merchants in the shipping trade. Recall the ravages on our commerce by the French, Spaniards and Barbary ships of war, and how uncertain became the ventures of our merchants. Many left no other legacies to their families than their claim on a foreign government or on our own. And nigh on to a century has passed and these claims are not yet paid. Of the Philadelphia merchants Thomas FitzSimons was the foremost, and being the President of the Chamber of Commerce, he addressed on October 10th, 1801, a memorial to James Madison, then Secretary of State, for presentation to Jefferson, in protest against the seizures by Spanish vessels.—(*Am. State Papers*, Vol. IV., p. 428.)

On January 4th, 1802, the sufferers by French spoliation met and formed a committee to memorialize Congress. A claim for $20,000 made by FitzSimons is now before the Court of Claims recently authorized by Congress to consider the French spoliation claims. FitzSimons was a member of the committee. They declared that in 1792–3–4 they sent merchandise to the West Indies, which was sold to colonial officers of the French Republic or taken by force. The amount claimed is $2,000,000.—(*His. Phila.*, 512.)

In 1805 Mr. FitzSimons failed, owing to the obligations assumed to sustain Robert Morris and others.

Though but very few of Mr. FitzSimons' papers now remain, yet the following certificate, in possession of Mr. John J. Maitland, shows where they were:

" Marshal Smith, whose family resided occasionally in Pittsburgh, lodged all his papers with Harvey Hurst in this city, amongst which were the whole papers of Mr. FitzSimons' estate.   He, Mr. Smith, afterwards removed said papers to Mr. Stœver in Dock street ; it is believed that a son-in-law of Mr. Smith, who is an officer in the army, had possession of many of them, I believe by the name of Goldsborough, or some such name ; this officer was in Cincinnati or Louisville some time ago, and is believed to be in the West still.

" WILLIAM PRIMROSE.

" Philadelphia, November 9th, 1839."

He was a son-in-law of John Smith, Marshal.

About 1844 many, if not all, of these papers were with Mr. Stœver, a merchant in Decatur street.   They were examined by John and Joseph Maitland, and an abstract of their contents was made.   This abstract yet exists.   It shows the papers to have been business documents, principally relating to lands and commercial transactions, and being about one hundred in number.   One (No. 38) is a statement of Mr. FitzSimons in relation to matters between himself and Robert Morris and John Nicholson, of his having in 1796 endorsed Morris' notes in favor of Nicholson for £14,000.   In these transactions he had no interest directly or indirectly, never having received one dollar for them, " nor is it possible that I ever can." £5700 sterling with the damage was paid by him on their return protested.   In March, 1798, the remaining £8300 sterling were likewise returned protested; suit was commenced against him as indorser in September, and judgment was obtained. After some negotiation the bill holders made the following proposition: That if T. F. would assume the payment of $5000 due to one of them by a connection of R. M.'s, and give certain securities specified for the whole debt, time would be given for payment. This and immediate execution were the alternatives. It was reluctantly acceded to, and property more than sufficient was assigned in consequence—notes for the amount and the property as collateral security. For the $5000 no consideration was ever received. The person owing it became a bankrupt, but no property came to the hands of T. F. or could be claimed by him, he having never received any assignment or conveyance of the debt. Indeed, at the time it was imposed upon him it was not worth one dollar. The bill holders have received on account of their debt $45,000, besides the one-half of the $5000. They claim a further sum exceeding the amount T. F. thinks due, and although solicited by him for two years to arbitrate, they refused to do it. They hold as security for balance due a lien on a valuable estate in Ontario county, New York. If these facts can be brought before a Court of Equity it will be shown that of the £14,000 sterling $4000 only were paid, and that he has already paid about $75,000. " I have in truth over and above the value of these bills paid R. Morris more than $150,000." The nature of the lien on the Ontario property stands thus: " I made to these bill holders an absolute deed of the estate, which was regularly recorded in the county. Afterwards the estate was sold under the judgment to the Holland Land Company, in the same manner as the trust property you are now contesting. By paying its proportion of the judgment Mr. Cooper made to me a deed for it, and I made a deed to the Bank of North America, subject to the payment of any balance that might be due to the bill holders, on which footing it now stands. The Bank of North America has executed a defeasance to me, reciting the deed to them as collateral security," &c.

The above is a copy of a letter to his counsel in New York. This and like documents prove the aid Thomas Fitz-Simons rendered to the " Financier of the Revolution," and show how Morris' failure brought to bankruptcy Thomas Fitz-Simons. I have seen the evidence of Robert Morris sending by Mr. Cottringer notes for many thousands of dollars to be signed by FitzSimons for accommodation. When Morris failed he assigned land to FitzSimons, in the endeavor to secure his friend as far as possible; but the latter never derived any benefit from them—he failed and died a bankrupt. After his failure he removed to 220 Mulberry (now Arch) street, and in February, 1806, wrote to Bishop Carroll that though "unpleasant things had occurred," he was "comfortably situated."

In 1806 a meeting of merchants relative to ravages on commerce, chiefly by England, was held. Mr. FitzSimons was appointed chairman.

On June 20th, 1810, Mrs. Catharine FitzSimons, wife of Thomas FitzSimons, died of consumption, aged seventy years. Her burial is not recorded in St. Mary's burial register until June 27th. An obituary notice in the *Portfolio* of November, 1810, says: "She was the daughter of Robert Meade, Esq., of the County of Limerick, who settled in this city in 1742." Mrs. FitzSimons had been ill for many years, as appears from her husband's correspondence with Archbishop Carroll. On February 19th, 1806, he said, "She is as well as she has been for a long time." He looked for her death in November, 1808, for on the 5th he wrote:

"You may therefore judge what my situation is, with this connection of forty-five years. Whenever that separation shall take place I am left without a reed to lean on. I entered very early into life, and my companions were generally much older than myself, so scarcely any remained. I have to be thankful for better health than most men of my age. I have the pleasure of knowing that I can yet be useful without laying myself under obligations to any one, and the more consoling hope of a meeting hereafter that is even denied us here."

After the death of his wife, Mr. FitzSimons' housekeeper was Maria O'Brien, daughter of Michael Morgan O'Brien, who had been consul to Paris. Mr. FitzSimons, in his letters to Archbishop Carroll, speaks in words of praise of Miss O'Brien. She became Mrs. Clymer.

In November, 1807, Daniel Clark, delegate from the newly acquired Louisiana, came to Philadelphia, and was given a banquet, at which FitzSimons presided. Clark was the father of Mrs. Myra Gaines Clark, of New Orleans suit fame.

In the archives of the Archdiocese of Baltimore there are letters of Mr. FitzSimons to Bishop Carroll, dated November 19th, 1804; February 15th, 1807; November 5th, 1808, and perhaps of other dates, from which we do not extract. We present the following:

"PHILA., Feb. 19th, 1806.

REVEREND FATHER :— I know not how to offer a sufficient apology for so long delaying to answer your affectionate and kindly letter. I find it more difficult because in truth it was most acceptable. Mrs. F. and myself were apprehensive that something on our part had occasioned your very long silence, nor will I conceal from you that a little jealousy existed as though we had been neglected. Forgive the surmise, and make allowances for our feelings. Whatever they might have been, your affectionate letter dissipated them all, and operated a salutary reproof. The period which has elapsed since we last parted has not been a pleasant one. Many unpleasant things have occurred, but they are now passed, and I know your kindness will be gratified to know that we are comfortably situated. I am now, thank God, as well as I might expect, and Mrs. F. as well as she has been for a long time. Your friends at St. Mary's acquit themselves most highly. Mr. Egan is everything you could wish except his want of a little more spirit and health. Modest and unassuming, he is hardly fit to deal with the set of people he has to manage. He is subject to a complaint that his duties render dangerous, a pulmonary one. It will really be necessary soon to procure him an assistant, but do not let it be one of his or my countrymen.

THOS. FITZSIMONS."

From a letter of February 11th, 1811, we make the following extract:

"I sometimes hear mention of your paying us a visit here. If it should take place I really believe you would be very much gratified with the improvement that has taken place in the situation of your congregation. Good sense, unassuming conduct, a strict regard to the duties of their functions, with a moderate degree of popularity, has procured to the gentlemen

of St. Mary's that respect which enables them to control to no
small degree the insubordinate tendencies which the times
have produced. They have enlarged their church without the
labors which commonly attend the same, and will beside increase their revenue. Need I say how agreeable your company
would be in Arch street. If I cannot have that privilege at
present, I hope with the assistance of your prayers we may
meet in a better place. " The following August he died.

On January 31st, 1809, the "friends of Constitution, Union
and Commerce" met at the State House to denounce the famous
Embargo Act of Congress. Its friends the Democrats had
met on January 23d. The Democrats, considering themselves
as "friends of the Constitution, Union and Commerce," resolved
to attend the meeting on the 31st to "express their approbation of the late measures of the Government." When the
meeting assembled many sailors were present who prevented
the Democrats from breaking up the meeting or making
disturbance. Commodore Truxton presided. The resolution
declared the Embargo Law " unjust, oppressive and as a means
of coercion weak and inefficient."

A committee to memorialize Congress was appointed. Commodore Truxton and Thomas FitzSimons headed the committee. The *Aurora* denounced the meeting as an English mob.
After the Federalists retired from the State House yard the
Democrats took possession, organized a meeting and passed
resolutions denouncing those just passed by the Federalists.
Col. Timothy Pickering was especially denounced. A week
later he was burned in effigy in front of the town hall in Second
street, Northern Liberties. This induced the Federalists to
tender a complimentary dinner to Col. Pickering. It took
place at the Mansion House, Third street above Spruce. In the
three large rooms of that hotel 250 friends took part. Thomas
FitzSimons presided in the first room, Commodore Truxton
in the second, and George Latimer in the third. Bishop White
was present. The Federalists rejoiced when on March 1st the
Embargo Act was repealed.

On February 2d, 1809, Mr. FitzSimons was elected President of the Chamber of Commerce.

Among the MSS. of Dr. Rush, preserved in the Ridgway Branch of the Philadelphia Library, is one dated June 26th, 1809, to William Vaughan, of London, introducing Mr. James Rush, son of Dr. Benjamin Rush, and directing to give him credit for £100 at any time. Another (without date) reads:

MY GOOD SIR:—A worthy friend, Mr. Carrell, is taken ill, at his store in Front street, nearly opposite Mordecai Lewis's. I beg and entreat that you will send somebody to him as soon as possible.

God preserve you.

THOS. FITZSIMONS.

To Dr. Rush.

This was Mr. John Carrell, a Catholic.

On January 23d, 1811, a meeting was held at the Coffee House of those in favor of the rechartering of the Bank of the United States. Thomas FitzSimons, Stephen Girard, William Day, Emanuel Eyre and Robert Waln were appointed a committee to memorialize Congress in favor of the rechartering. In February the Democrats held a meeting and sent an opposing memorial. The bank was not rechartered.

In 1785 Mr. FitzSimons lived on Walnut street between Second and Third. In 1791–2–3 at No. 91 Spruce street. His store was No. 3 Walnut street. In 1794–5 he lived at No. 243 Chestnut street, north side, opposite "Morris' Folly." In 1800 on Fourth street between Spruce and Pine. In 1801 to 1805, at No. 243 Chestnut street. After 1805 he lived at No. 220 Mulberry or Arch street until his death, August 26th, 1811.

But the last scene in life's eventful history was approaching. In fourteen months after the death of his wife death came too to Thomas FitzSimons, also in the 70th year of his age. He died on Monday, August 26th, at his residence on Arch street, and was buried the next morning, the 27th, as the funeral notice in the papers of that date notify "the friends" and "the members of the Chamber of Commerce" to attend "this morning at ten o'clock." His merchant associates met at the Coffee House and proceeded therefrom to the house on Arch street and attended the funeral of their late President.

During his illness Bishop Egan often called to see him and

no doubt prepared him for death. Bishop Egan wrote to Archbishop Carroll, on June 5th, 1811, less than three months prior to Mr. FitzSimons' death, saying : " Mr. FitzSimons is seriously indisposed. I often visit him and have spoken to him on the subject that ought to interest him the most. He thanks me and promises he will when he gets better. I fear, however, he has not long to live, and shall endeavor all I can, with God's assistance, to dispose him to make serious preparations for the other world."

The following obituary tribute to his memory appeared in the *Daily Advertiser* and also in the *U. S. Gazette* of August 29th, 1811 : " On Monday, 26th, in the 70th year of his age, Thomas FitzSimons, Esq. He was justly considered one of the most enlightened and intelligent merchants in the United States, and his opinions upon all questions connected with commerce were always regarded with respect, and even homage, by the mercantile part of the community. He filled many important stations, both in the General and State Governments, with great reputation during the Revolutionary War. In private life he was eminently useful. Hundreds in various occupations owe their establishment in business to his advice and good offices. His friendships were steady, ardent and disinterested. He possessed an uncommon firmness of mind upon all occasions except one, and that was when his friends solicited favors from him. From his inability to resist the importunities of distress he suffered a reversal of fortune in the evening of his life. Even in this situation his mind retained its native goodness, and hence it may be truly said, after many and great losses he died in the esteem, affection and gratitude of all classes of his fellow-citizens."

Notice of the death also appeared in the *Mercantile Advertiser* and Washington *Intelligencer.*

Can we, after three-quarters of a century, portray his character and services more accurately, even though the hand of friendship and perhaps of gratitude may have penned these lines.

He was buried in St. Mary's graveyard. The entry of the interment was not made until January 31st, 1812, when the name, without record of age or cause of death, alone was entered, followed by the mention of " $12 " as the burial fee paid.

In a draft of an affidavit of Mrs. Ann Maitland, wife of Thomas FitzSimons Maitland, she said " Thomas FitzSimons was buried in the ground belonging to the Maitland brothers, St. Mary's Church." Also that a grave-stone with his name on it was then or a short time before over the grave.*

But that stone has disappeared.

Thomas FitzSimons made a will some time previous to his death by which he devised and bequeathed all his real and personal estate to his wife for life, the remainder in fee to his sister, Mrs. Ann Maitland, and appointing George Clymer his Executor. Thomas Ketland and John Vaughan witnessed this instrument. Mrs. FitzSimons died before the testator. The will was mislaid at the Register's office before (as it is believed) it was proven. Decedent left no lineal heirs, and Mrs. Ann Maitland, as next collateral heir, was entitled to inherit. She died, leaving three children—John, Thomas and Mary Ann Maitland. A Mr. Thomas Reynolds took out letters of administration to the estate of Thomas FitzSimons, and subsequently John Maitland became administrator *de bonis non.*

.* Mr. John J. Maitland has had, since this paper was read, a memorial tomb erected, containing the names of all interred beneath, including those of Thomas FitzSimons and his wife.

ADDENDUM.

THOMAS FITZSIMONS AND ROBERT MORRIS.

AS the financial ruin of Thomas FitzSimons was due to his "accommodation" of Robert Morris, "the Financier of the Revolution," who became a large operator in lands, it may be well to give evidence of this fact from the written statement of Robert Morris himself.

After Morris' failure he made an account of his transactions by which it appears that, in 1790, he bought a tract of one million acres in the Genesee district, and the next year sold it in England at a handsome profit. This set him to speculating in land. So in 1791 he bought, in the State of New York, four millions of acres. Tract No. 1, as he described it, "commenced at that point on the Pennsylvania line where Gorham & Phelps' western boundry intersected the same, and from thence running westerly twelve miles to a point from which the first meridian, running into Lake Ontario, forms the western boundary of the said tract, Lake Ontario the northern boundary, Gorham & Phelps' west line and the Genesee river the eastern boundary, and the Pennsylvania line the southern boundary." This was computed to have 500,000 acres, but on survey had 765,641. A portion of this tract, called Mount Morris, had 10,240 acres. One-half was given to his son Thomas in 1793, and the other half, on January 25th, 1798, was conveyed to Thomas FitzSimons "in part security of the debt I owe him." On February 14th, 1798, 110,641 acres of this No. 1 tract were conveyed to Thomas FitzSimons, Jos. Higbee and Robert Morris, Jr., to secure the payment of sundry debts enumerated in the deed, "being debts arising from disinterested loans of money or names, or attended with circumstances that rendered them of superior claim upon my justice or integrity." This trust deed gave the right of redemption "by paying the debts."

Mr. Morris, in a further enumeration of his properties, says: "My Springettsbury estate* was in the first instance assigned to Thomas FitzSimons, Esq., in the hope that it would secure to him a part of his heavy claim on me; but on account of circumstances attending this estate, the assignment to him became secondary to one made to the directors of the Bank of North America. Public sales have been made of parts of this estate, but I am uninformed whether the whole has been sold. When the claim of the bank is satisfied, any remainder or surplus goes, I suppose, in part payment to Mr. FitzSimons, but I have seen no accounts."

"Morrisville," in Bucks County, was mortgaged to the Insurance Company of North America. It was sold by the sheriff for less than the mortgage, "but the purchasers agreed to make resales and to apply any surplus to the final discharge of the mortgages, and any remainder to be paid to Thomas FitzSimons in part of my debt to him."

In 1796 Morris bought 500,000 acres in Wythe, Russell and Greenbriar counties, Virginia. "These lands were conveyed to Mr. FitzSimons in security."

In 1797 "I purchased of William Cooper and General Lee 44,300 acres lying in Hardy and Shenandoah counties, Virginia. This tract I conveyed to Thomas FitzSimons, Esq., in part security for the debt due him."

"In 1794 Thomas FitzSimons and myself purchased sundry tracts of land of James Montford, and afterwards other tracts; so that I now hold two-thirds in 361,235 acres and in 31,450 acres, and half in 94,000 acres, all lying in the State of Georgia; my interest therein being conveyed or assigned to the said Thomas FitzSimons, in part security of the claim he has on me, in which is included part of the bonds given for this land."

"The ferry and seventeen acres of land on the Jersey side near to Trenton, opposite to Morrisville, was conveyed to Thomas FitzSimons, Esq., in part payment or security of the debt due to him." This ferry was bought from Patrick Colvin,

---

* Count de Barth had lived here. See p. 36, *note*.—ED.

whom we have named as ferrying Washington's army on the night of the battle of Trenton. Morris acknowledged himself indebted to Patrick Colvin (deceased) for $4666.67, which he detained from the payment for the ferry, "because he was under covenant to make me a perfect title; his wife refused to sign the deeds, and since his death has claimed dower."

"In February, 1794, I purchased an undivided third part of two tracts containing about 500 acres, including a lead mine, then called Bryan's Lead Mine, now called the French Broad Lead Mine, lying near the French Broad river in Jefferson county, territory of the United States, south of the Ohio. This estate I conveyed to Thomas FitzSimons, Esq., in part security of his claims on me. It hath also been attached and sold by the sheriff."

"My household furniture was conveyed and delivered to Thomas FitzSimons, Esq., in 1797, and afterwards sold by public auction. What is now in Mrs. Morris' use has been lent her by Mr. FitzSimons principally."

In reporting the "Accounts Open on the Books of Robert Morris," he said "Thomas FitzSimons' ac't for Georgia stands. This account stands charged with a balance, being his portion of bonds unpaid at the date when that balance was struck, and which will be acquitted by the payment of said bonds, and, as probably he has paid, or will pay, my part as well as his own, this account will in the end show an increase to his claims to me."

But here is an entry which proves the aid FitzSimons gave to Morris:

"*Thomas FitzSimons, Esq.*: The balance of this account as it stands is $156,386.58. And as this has arisen almost entirely out of the loan of his name for my accommodation, I have endeavored to secure the debt to him by various securities that have been already mentioned in sundry parts of this report: which securities I hope will prove effectual, and if any surplus arises it is to be accounted for to my assignees."

CATHOLIC CHOIRS

AND

Choir Music in Philadelphia.

[Prepared by MICHAEL H. CROSS, and read before the SOCIETY by FRANCIS X.
REUSS, October 26th, 1887.]

A SKETCH of the music in some of the older Catholic
churches in this diocese, while not of interest to many of
the present generation, cannot fail to be so to some yet living
of that which has passed away.

In this paper it is proposed to speak of the choirs, and musical administration thereof, of St. Augustine's, St. Mary's, St.
Joseph's, and St. John's. While the writer is fully aware of
the many interesting performances which other choirs have
given, he does not think that the limits of a paper such as this
is intended to be, would admit of their being recorded.

The music sung in the choirs at the beginning of this century was of the most primitive, simple and uninteresting kind.
If it were to be sung again in these times, it would not fail to
attract the attention and receive the censure of five-sixths of
almost any congregation obliged to listen to it. We all know
that Catholics do not go to church to hear the music—indeed
Catholic congregations are remarkably insensible to it—but I
cannot believe that the early Catholic music of the century
would be endured now.

The first selection of music in use was that published by
John Aiken in 1791. It was composed of Masses, Hymns,
Litanies, the Vesper psalms, &c. There are among them

many English hymns, the words of which are to-day sung in all Protestant churches ; I might mention " Children of the Heavenly King," " Jesus, Saviour of my Soul," " Come, Holy Spirit "—not a translation of the " Veni Creator "—" Soldiers of Christ, arise," " Vital spark of heavenly flame," &c. The organ accompaniment, as arranged in the book, is simply beneath criticism, and many of the selections are open to the same remark. It does not appear to the writer, from any data that he has been able to obtain, that even the Gregorian notes received any attention. Most of the music was evidently sung in two parts, and even the solo parts were sung by the choir in unison. This was the rule. The exceptions were, of course, that when anyone was present who could sing, he or she did sing the solos.

This was the condition of Catholic choir music when Mr. B. Carr took charge at St. Augustine's church, when it was opened in June, 1801. He was an accomplished musician and a gentleman. He had had the advantage of a solid musical education in England prior to making this country his home, and was in every way fitted for the position in which he was placed. His influence on musical matters was of the most valuable kind, and indeed it might not be inappropriate to say that he was the father of music in Philadelphia. He at once directed his efforts towards forming a good choir, and he did so with immediate success. He wrote much music for the church, to supersede that which he found in use, and in 1806 published a collection of church music which at that time must have been invaluable. The compositions in it were largely from a book published some years before by Samuel Webbe, Sr., in London.* This Samuel Webbe was one of England's greatest glee composers, cotemporary with, and the peer of Callcott, Mornington, Danby, J. S. Smith, and others. Mr. Carr's book contains a beautiful Mass and "Te Deum" of his own. The writer distinctly remembers hearing them sung in the old church of St. Augustine.

The organ was built by Charles Taws. He was probably

---

* There are copies of all these works in our Society's library.—ED.

the first organ builder in the city.   The instruments of that day were certainly very mediocre.

Mr. Carr at this time, 1807, had of course some musical confrères.   I might mention Mr. Raynor Taylor, organist of St Peter's; Mr. George Schetkey, violoncellist; Mr. John Hommann, father of Mr. Charles Hommann, and others. Some of these men were professionally engaged at the Chestnut Street Theatre.

In 1810, June 10th, a grand sacred concert was given at St Augustine's.*   It consisted of selections from oratorios, solos, &c.   It was under Mr. Carr's direction.   He had the assistance of all the orchestra players at that time in the city.   The trombones were supplied from Bethlehem.   Miss Eliza Taws, who had been a member of the choir from an early date, was the soprano.   Mr. Benjamin Cross, a pupil of Mr. Carr, made his first public appearance as a singer at this performance.   He sang an aria for the bass voice, by Hasse, a German composer who wrote a vast amount of music, such as operas, oratorios, cantatas, &c., nearly all of which are now forgotten   In all his endeavors at St Augustine's Mr. Carr appears to have had the judicious aid of the pastor, Rev. Dr. Matthew Carr, who evidently understood how to assist without interfering.   These performances at the church were from time to time repeated, Mr. Carr introducing such music as proved interesting, and meeting with Dr. Carr's approval.   Mr. Carr had collected quite an extensive musical library, which contained a great deal of choice sacred music, among the rest a selection in six volumes, now very rare, published in London by C. J. Latrobe. Much of the music which was in this library has come into the writer's possession.   From the choir associations many private musical coteries were formed, at which it was the aim to improve musical taste and introduce new music.

It does not appear, however, that any four part Masses were introduced by Mr. Carr.   Those sung were either for soprano, tenor and bass, or two sopranos and bass.   At the death of the Rev. Dr. Carr, in 1820, the Rev. Dr. Michael Hurley suc-

* A copy of the programme is in the Library A. C. H. S.—Ed.

ceeded to the pastorate. He was also an ardent admirer of music, a fine singer, and always took the greatest interest in abetting Mr. Carr in every way.

Catholic music was greatly enriched at this time by the publications of Vincent Novello in London, where he was the organist of the Portuguese Chapel. He was the founder of the house of Novello, Ewer & Co. of the present day. He introduced to the public all the great Masses of Hadyn, Mozart, Beethoven, Hummel, Schubert and others. His two collections, of twelve books each, for the morning and evening services, were a mine of wealth of good music. We all know how extensively his work has been republished in this country.

Mr. Carr held the position of organist until his death on the 24th of May, 1831. He was buried on May 26th at St. Peter's. The choir erected a tablet to his memory. He was quite a voluminous composer, having written a great amount of sacred music, ballads, piano-forte music, etc. The writer has a very interesting volume of his manuscripts.

At the death of Mr. Carr, Mr. Benjamin Cross succeeded to the position of organist. He retained the position until 1838, when he went to St. Mary's. During the time he was at St. Augustine's he followed as nearly as possible in Mr. Carr's footsteps. He introduced a beautiful Mass by Mazzinghi, written in 1823 for the consecration of an Augustinian abbey in England. It was constantly sung for many years. Zimmer's Mass was also introduced, as well as one or two others.

There was published in Baltimore about this time, by Jacob Walter, a valuable collection of sacred music. It contained a Mass by De Monti which became very popular.

Mr. Cross was succeeded by Mr. Dos Santos, who was the organist until the church was burned in 1844. In the same year, immediately after the destruction of the church, a chapel was built on Crown street. It was opened October 27th, 1844. Mrs. John R. Welsh, a daughter of Benjamin Cross, played the organ and took charge of the choir. She was assisted by her husband and one or two other singers. Mrs. Welsh was succeeded by Henry Corrie, a son of the Henry Corrie who built the first organ in St. John's church. He remained until the new church, which was being rebuilt, was finished. It was opened on Christmas Day, 1847. Mr. Benjamin Cross was appointed organist. The choir was in the second gallery of the church, at the Fourth street end. The organ, built in Baltimore, which was placed in the church in 1850, was located in the tower. Its effect was thereby ruined, and in the course of a few years it was rebuilt, moved down to the first gallery and placed in its present case, which was expressly designed for it by the builder. The service on the opening day was merely with organ accompaniment. The choir which was at that time organized consisted of: sopranos, Mrs. John Brown, Mrs. Welsh, Miss Mary Downs, Miss Durang; altos, Miss McManus, Miss J. Meyers, Miss Keller; tenors, Mr. Charles Ryan, Mr. Moore, Mr. Brown; bassos, Mr. H. Fleming (afterwards an Augustinian father), Mr. Fox and Mr. Smythe. On January 1st, 1848, the choir sang Zimmer's Mass, with "Venite Adoremus" by Cross, at the morning service; and in the afternoon the Gregorian Vespers, "Venite Adoremus" by Webbe, as well as his "Magnificat" in A, and his "Alma." A great feature of the service on Christmas Day was the rendition of Handel's "Let the Bright Seraphim" by Mrs. Eliza Brown. Four part Masses were sung during this administration of the choir. On November 5th, 1848, the new church was consecrated. The music was under the direction of Mr. B. Cross and led by him. A four part Mass by C. Mieneke, of Baltimore, was sung with orchestral accompaniment. The choir was assisted by Mr. and Mrs. J. R. Welsh, Mrs. Stephens and others. Mr. Welsh sang, at the close of the service, "Sound the Trumpet in Zion."

Mr. B. Cross was succeeded in 1849 by his son, Mr. B. Carr Cross, who again was succeeded very shortly afterwards by Mr. Henry Thunder, an accomplished musician and organist. He was brought from Baltimore, where he had until then been playing, through the influence of Very Rev. Dr. Moriarty. Mr. Thunder had charge of the music until 1875, when he went to New York to become the organist of St. Stephen's. He returned in 1879 and remained until his death. During all the time that he was organist he filled the position ably, and

always in a spirit in accordance with its dignity. He introduced Kalliwoda's beautiful Mass, as well as Gounod's "St.
Cecilia," together with much new and interesting music. It
affords the writer the greatest pleasure to bear witness to his
skill and erudite taste as an organist. Certainly as an *ex tempore* player he had no superior in the city. He was succeeded
by his son, who is the present incumbent,* and on whose
shoulders the mantle of the father appears to have fallen.

During Mr. Thunder's absence in New York, his place was
filled by Mr. William A. Newland, who is the oldest Catholic
organist living in Philadelphia, and whose faithful, conscientious services, in the many churches in which he has been
organist, bear ample witness to his unswerving discharge of
duty and to his love for the cause. The writer is indebted to
him for data which his ripe experience and recollections so
eminently enable him to give.

In closing this sketch of St. Augustine's, a few remarks as
to the kind of music and selections sung at the present day in
Catholic choirs generally may not be out of place. Until the
time of the Rt. Rev. Bishop Kenrick, a great many English
hymns, etc., were sung; it did not matter at what service, it
was a universal custom. A return to Latin hymns, etc., was
the means of correcting many of the abuses and *absurd*, not
to say irreverent, selections which were used. But a new
abuse crept in. All kinds of adaptations of Latin words to
unsuitable, undevotional, trashy music, operatic and other,
were made. In fact, the writer has heard "Tantum Ergo,"
"O Salutaris," and other most sacred hymns sung to music
only fit for the theatre. Sometimes selections have been sung
without any adaptation of Latin words at all, but with the
original words, French, Italian, or whatever they might have
been. The good Masses of former years have been superseded by trashy Italian or still worse home-made ones.
Strange selections in English, to say the least, have been
made at funerals. The idea of singing "Love's Last Greet-

---

* Mr. Henry G. Thunder, Jr., left St. Augustine's late in the Autumn
of 1887, to become organist of the new St. James' church, in West Philadelphia.—ED.

ing," or "We Miss Thee Every Hour," and more of that stripe, certainly calls for some censorship in regard to such things.

At St. Peter's church the music of the St. Cecilia Society is sung.* This is an organization which has for its object the restoration of the music of the Church to its original purity and dignity. It was founded in one of the western cities, has Pontifical approval, and is doing noble work. Its influence and authority are sadly needed in Philadelphia. The only objection which can in any way be made against it is, that it excludes all the great Masses on account of the repetition of the words they contain. In their place it uses the old Masses of Palestrina and others. I have nothing to say against these Masses, they are great, but by excluding the others which are equally great, this noble society retards its own usefulness, for many organists are not willing to abandon the noblest music ever written. Yet if some check to such abuses could be instituted, it would be of untold value. The endless wealth of beautiful music written for the Catholic Church is unknown to all who pervert her liturgy in this dreadful way. Let us hope that the time will come when such things will cease to be.

At the beginning of the present century the organist at St. Mary's was John Rudolph, a German. We have no data of interest regarding the choir at this time. We presume that John Aiken's book, published in 1791, formed the staple of Catholic music, and poor it was indeed. In 1806 Mr. John Huncker, father of our townsman of the same name, was elected. He appears to have had difficulty with one John Azam, who had evidently been, and still aspired to be, leader. In this connection we may exclaim, or remark, how often the wrong people want to be leaders. This is the case to-day in some choirs, and one-half of the trouble in them arises from this cause. If the organist should happen to be competent, he finds it a little difficult to tolerate the leader's mistakes. It appears to us that with many leaders, confidence, not know-

---

* A modification has taken place here since this paper was written.—ED.

ledge, is the one thing necessary. 'Mr. Huneker, however, would not submit to interference under the name of leading, and was given entire charge of the choir. He held the post for many years, when, being stricken with sickness, he was obliged to resign. Mr. John Janke, Sr., officiated during his illness, and finally succeeded him, remaining until 1835. Mr. Newland, whose name is so prominently identified with so many choirs, followed him and remained until 1837, when Mr. Benjamin Cross took charge. The organ was the old one built by Taws in 1806 or 1807.

The appearance of the church at this time is vividly remembered. The ceiling was arched, painted a dark blue, and had gilt stars on it. The organ stood in a gallery built for it. It was, of course, like all the organs of that day. The church was at this time remodeled and painted. The frescoing and picture on the ceiling were done by Monachesi.

A large new organ was built by Henry Erben, of New York, and placed in the gallery. It was considered at that time the finest in the city.

The choir, during Mr. Cross's term, was composed of a paid quartette, consisting of Miss Strahan, afterwards Mrs. Stephens, soprano; Miss Margaret A. Cross, alto; Dr. F. Crowly, tenor; and Mr. Garrett Ruth, bass. There were other voices which formed a chorus. Mr. Cross introduced two Masses of Mozart, the first and seventh, Zimmer's second Mass in B flat, Novello's two part Mass in E major, Mr. Charles Hommann's beautiful Mass in E flat for two sopranos and bass; Zingarelli's " Laudate Pueri Dominum," which was sung first in Philadelphia by Plumber, an operatic tenor of long ago, and Gardini's " Tibi Omnes Angeli." All of this music, except Mozart's First Mass, and, indeed, in many choirs that also, has been given the go-by.

Mr. Cross remained until about 1845. Mr. Dos Santos succeeded him. It was at this time that Haydn's third Mass was first done in Philadelphia, and in this church, under the direction of .L. Meignen, Esq., a musician well known in Philadelphia at that time. He was the leader of the Musical Fund Society, teacher of singing and harmony, etc. He died a few years since, leaving in manuscript a Mass for organ, orchestra, solo voices and chorus, and a lengthy and comprehensive work on composition.   The latter is in possession of the Misses Drexel.   Haydn's Mass was done with orchestra. The solo singers were the Misses Lejambre, Miss Pintard, Mr. Armstrong and others.   It was a glorious performance, and marked an epoch in church music in Philadelphia.   Mr. Dos Santos, I believe, remained at St. Mary's until his death, which took place a few years ago.

Dr. Meignen's Mass was sung with great effect at St. Mary's and St. Augustine's.   It has never, we believe, been published.

Since the death of Mr. Dos Santos, St. Mary's choir has had several organists, and, we believe, leaders, but with the death of Mr. Dos Santos all that had become historic connected with its choir ceased.   The changes of the last few years are, without doubt, recorded, and will be written at some future date.

The earliest account we have regarding the choir of St. Joseph's church dates from the opening of the new church in 1839, when Mr. Dos. Santos was organist.*

Before this date the music at St. Joseph's must have been very primitive in its character and performance, no doubt much in the same style as that at St. Mary's and Holy Trinity.

Mr. Dos Santos had also been organist at the old church.† When the new church was built it was desired that the choir should attend during the Month of May services, that is, every evening.   Mr. Dos Santos found this impracticable, and resigned his position.   He was followed by Mr. Le Brun,

---

*Almost continuously from the time the old church was enlarged in 1821, by Bishop Conwell, until it was demolished in 1838, Tobias M. Durney was the organist, and his two brothers, John and Paul, sang in the choir.   During a brief interruption, about 1835, a Miss Lebreton was organist.—ED.

† It must have been for a very short time indeed.   See preceding note. —ED.

who was an amateur.   He was the well-known architect of Philadelphia.   He remained until 1842.

Mr. W. A. Newland followed, and remained until 1844.   He was succeeded by Pedro A. Dannas, a Spaniard, who was at that time engaged in Philadelphia, in music publishing, teaching, etc.   Dannas and Ashe in 1846 published a fine quarto edition of Haydn's Third Mass, which about this time was first sung in the city.   While he was at St. Joseph's its choir became quite well known.

In 1852 Mr. Newland was again organist, and remained in the position until 1868, when Mrs. Aledo, the present incumbent, was selected.

St. Joseph's choir has had as members many excellent singers, both male and female.   The organ has never been very good, although we believe it has lately been remodeled and is now quite effective.   The choir duties at this church have always demanded a great deal of attention from its members.   It has had much gratuitous service rendered by many singers.

St. Joseph's church is dear to Philadelphia Catholics.   It has had a succession of saintly and illustrious men as pastors, and the choir has always been faithful in carrying out their wishes in regard to the music.

Of St. John's church Mr. B. Carr Cross was the first organist.   He was appointed in 1832, and held the position until 1844, when he was succeeded by Mr. William A. Newland. We would like to be able to give the names of the members of the first choir of St. John's, and we have tried in every way to obtain data, but regret to say that we have only had partial success.   From what we can learn, however, we may mention a few names, such as Miss Mary Warren, afterwards Mrs. B. C. Cross; Miss Williams, Mr. Beyer, Mr. and Mrs. Gubert, Mrs. Dr. Roper, Mr. F. M. Drexel, Mr. Lankenau, Mr. C. Janke, Mr. F. X. Kelly, Mr. and Mrs. J. R. Welsh, Miss De Becquer.   Of course these ladies and gentlemen were not all members of the first choir.   As years rolled by and changes took place, they were connected with the choir, and gave their services to the church.   In the early years the singers were to a great extent volunteers.

During Mr. B. Carr Cross's term, Mozart's Twelfth Mass was first sung in Philadelphia.   It was an important musical event.   The choir was largely augmented for the occasion by all the available local talent in the city.   The orchestra score of the Mass does not call for what is termed a " full orchestra."   There are no flute or clarionet parts in the original. They have been added, of course, in late years, and the Twelfth Mass has been made to sound just as Mozart intended it should *not* sound.   There is an organ part by Mozart designed to be used with the orchestral parts.   This has been superseded by Novello's accompaniment.   The first organ in St. John's was built by Mr. George Corrie, father of another Mr. George Corrie, later known as an organist and professor of music.   This organ was replaced after many years by one of J. C. B. Stanbridge's instruments.

Mr. T. E. Gubert was well known as a leading amateur vocalist.   He was a tenor singer, and an active member of all the leading musical organizations.   His daughter, Miss Louisa Gubert,—many remember her,—made, it might be said, her *debut* in St. John's choir.   This was during Mr. Newland's term.

Haydn's Mass No. 1, Eykens' Mass, and other interesting compositions were introduced by Mr. Newland.

At this time the Rev. F. X. Gartland, pastor of the church, made an effort to have the Vesper service done as it is in the Gradual, i. e., with the proper psalms, antiphons and hymns of the day.   This was a feature, and made the service a very beautiful one.   After the Rev. Mr. Gartland was made Bishop of Savannah this reform fell into disuse, and the Vesper service became again what it is in every Catholic choir in the diocese to-day, a sort of miscellaneous afternoon concert—so far as the music is concerned, I mean, of course.

Mr. Newland was succeeded in 1852 by Mr. Michael Cross, who was organist until 1856.   During his term Haydn's Masses Nos. 2, 6 and 16 were first sung in the city, together with much other music new to choirs.

In 1856 Mr. John Janke succeeded Mr. Cross. He in turn was followed by Mrs. Harron, who held the position until 1869, when Mr. Newland again was organist. In 1872 Mr. Guhlmann occupied the position, and Mr. Barili about this time became the leader of the choir.

Mr. Barili was in every way capable for the position, and he formed a choir of solo voices, mainly his own pupils, and a chorus. He was a zealous worker, and made the music at St. John's very effective and satisfactory. Miss McCartney will be remembered with pleasure as one of his very best singers. At Mr. Barili's death Mr. Carl Wittig, the present incumbent, assumed charge of the choir. He had become organist during the early years of Barili's leadership. Mr. Wittig has lately produced a Mass of his own, which has, we believe, been accorded much praise.

This brings our sketch of the choirs to a close. Of course we could have made it much more lengthy, but have thought it best not to do so. It is mainly the early data of the choirs under notice which we try to give with some little detail, events of the last few years being too fresh to have as yet any historic value.

ADDENDUM.

CHARLES TAWS.

THE same evening on which Mr. Cross's paper was read, Mr. Reuss announced the presentation to the Society, by Miss Henrietta M. Bradshaw, of a piano made in Philadelphia in 1794 by Charles Taws. The instrument had been shown in the industrial parade in connection with the celebration of the centenary of the United States Constitution. In a note enclosed with the history of the manufacturer, Miss Bradshaw says the article may have passed through many hands before her family obtained possession of it ; she knows nothing more about it. But she gives the following account of the manufacturer and his family :

" Charles Taws, the first manufacturer of pianos in Philadelphia, settled here in the year 1785, his place of business being on Walnut street below Third. He built many of the organs in the Catholic and Episcopalian churches. St. Peter's congregation, Third and Pine streets, had one which was in their possession quite recently. Mr. Taws had the honor of visiting at the house of George Washington, and selected pianos for his family. He was a Scotchman by birth. Most of his life, however, was spent in Philadelphia. He was a staunch Catholic, and from the beginning of his residence here was a member of St. Mary's congregation, holding a pew there from 1785 until his death in 1836, when he had reached the advanced age of 95 years. His son, Joseph, was one of the earliest organists at Holy Trinity church, at Sixth and Spruce streets, and several other children were quite prominent as singers in the other Catholic churches."

CATHOLICITY

IN

Southeastern (Lee County) Iowa.

[Prepared by REV. JOHN F. KEMPKER and read before the SOCIETY on Thursday, November 29th, 1887, by EDWARD J. ALEDO.]

THE county of Lee in Iowa is attractive on account of its geographical advantage and beauty of landscape; but it no less enhances our admiration when we study the beginning and growth of our holy Church within its borders.   This portion of the State eminently merits the appellation which, it is said, the Indian name of Iowa signifies, namely, *the beautiful land.*

Here we have rich woodlands alternating with fertile prairies, bordered on the east by the majestic Mississippi, south by the beautiful Des Moines, north by the prosaic Skunk river; and the enchanting sceneries presented to the wondering eye are made yet more pleasing by variety in beholding the Lower or Des Moines Rapids in the Mississippi river, the cascades in the Des Moines river, the romantic views of Devil creek, the sunny slopes of Le Molièse creek, the shady maple groves of the Sugar creeks, the rocky cliffs of the stone quarries, the garden plaques of the sand prairies, or the sporting and meadow lands of Green Bay.   These advantages have endowed the place with that beauty which we seek for in a home site, that invited the *Illini* to build their wigwams on the Des Moines banks two centuries ago, made it a highway for the tribes journeying east and west with their Indian trail leading from the head of the rapids to the present site of Kansas City, marked it as a favorite resort for the Saukie and Musquaukie villages at the present locations of Fort Madison, Montrose and Keokuk, and caused it to be an early point of destination for the pioneers of fifty years ago when they sought the agriculturists' lot in the West.

In point of religion this county claims the first foot-fall of the missionary in this region, when Père Marquette left his frail canoe in the limpid waters of the Mesi Sepo, the grand river, on the 25th of June, 1673, and with M. Jolliet followed the trail of the unknown people to their village on the hill-sides of the *Moinguena*, our present Des Moines river, bearing to them the sign of redemption and the gospel of peace; and although no definite monument or record marks the spot of the historic site, the claim of Lee county seems so well established by the narrative in Père Marquette's journal and the markings on his map that it can hardly be controverted.

We are *Ilini*, said they to the missioner, the signification of the word being "*men*"; and we believe them to possess the nobility of manhood when we hear them greet their visitors with the peaceful welcome: "How beautiful is the sun, O, Frenchman, when thou comest to visit us! All our town awaits thee, and thou shalt enter all our cabins in peace."

It had been the ardent desire of the saintly priest to convert these tribes on the great river to Christianity; he now preached to them the saving truths of his holy Church, for he was able to address these Indians in their own language, the knowledge of which he acquired from Indians of the tribe at Michilimackinac; he visited the three villages and their wigwams, and it is ceatain that he tarried at least until the afternoon of the 26th of June; it is, however, probable, that his sojourn was extended for several days, as the words of his narrative also would indicate: "Sur la fin de Juin," at the close of June.

It must remain a matter of conjecture whether the zealous priest celebrated the holy Mass at this time; but we know that he, with his companions, offered up daily devotions in their novenas to the Blessed Virgin for a successful accomplishment of his object—the exploration of the great river, and bearing the knowledge of God to its people.

The inhabitants of Lee county in our day cannot read the intensely interesting and valuable narrative of Père Marquette without acknowledging a debt of gratitude to the learned historian, Dr. Shea, for his work, "Discovery and Exploration of the Mississippi River."

The Ilini begged for the return of the missionary, and seemed well disposed to receive the grace of conversion; but their successors in the possession of the land a century later, the Sacs and Foxes, were foes of the Cross, nor is it known that a priest again visited these shores until after 1833. Whether Father Hennepin tarried here, or any other missioner found his way to this part of Iowa, can only remain a matter of surmise; nor can any record be found to show that the Jesuit Father, F. C. Van Quickenborne, or the zealous young priest, J. A. Lutz, made any visit in Lee county, although both these pioneer priests, in the years from 1828 to 1832, made some journeys up stream as far as Prairie du Chien, to bring the consolations of religion to scattered settlements of Catholics on the banks of the river.

Iowa remained in possession of the Indians until June 1st, 1833, and although they did not remove from their abundant hunting grounds on that day, they conveyed title with right of possession to the United States Government for a tract sixty miles in width along the western bank of the river, which was designated as the *Black Hawk Purchase;* nevertheless, previous to this time various settlements had been made in Lee county, which, although not sanctioned by law, seem to have continued without disturbance; among which may be mentioned the log cabin of Dr. Muir at Keokuk in 1820; the house and trading post of Le Molièse, at what now is Sandusky, in 1821; the house and trading post of Maurice Blondeau, a mile farther north, in the same year; of Louis Tesson Honori at Montrose in 1796, besides a number of others who came at this time and some years later; and however certain it is that many of these were not Catholics, it is equally certain that some were descendants of Catholics, and continued in the profession and practice of their faith. At the bier of Dr. Muir, who died in 1832 at Keokuk, lighted candles formed part of the funeral ceremonies, and in 1834 Father Lefevre speaks of many Catholics at the foot of the rapids, in the " New Purchase," and among the " Half Indians."

The first priest who performed missionary duties among the early settlers of Lee county was the zealous and pious Father P. P. Lefevre, later distinguished as the first Bishop of Detroit, but at that time resident priest of St. Paul's church, Ralls county, Missouri, having for his mission territory all the northeast of Missouri, the southeast of Iowa, and a large contiguous portion of Illinois, who attended to the spiritual wants of the Lee county people as best he could, from 1834 till the summer of 1837. But as my dull pen can only imperfectly portray to you a picture of his busy life and merits gained in this place, permit me to cull pertinent passages from his most interesting letters of these times, the possession of which I owe to the courtesy of the Very Rev. Mr. Van der Sanden, in the archives of St. Louis.

In a report written to Rt. Rev. Bishop Rosati, on the 3d of July, 1834, he speaks of one of his missionary trips, and arranging with his congregation, he says : ". . . . . . I told them . . . . that now I was going to visit the scattering Catholics on the side of Illinois and beyond the limits of the State of Missouri. This visit took me about three months, during which I never would pass more than three nights at the same place. I went from Atlas (a town near Quincy) to the head of the rapids, forty and fifty miles backwards and forwards in the interior of the country . . . . . then I returned to this side of the Mississippi (that was the Iowa side) among the Half Indians, and in the new purchase where the Catholics are increasing very fast . . . . . . At the head of the rapids, about fifty miles above Quincy, there is still greater prospect for a church, because the Catholics there are still more numerous, and very zealous towards building a church *in Commerce* (that was the present site of Nauvoo). . . . . . People also seem to move to it from every part of the Union. If St. Cyr, or any other priest, were stationed at

Quincy or the head of the rapids, he would find there a wide extensive field for the cause of God. Besides many other Catholics scattered through the country, he would find there four little congregations in a circuit, as it were, of 40 or 50 miles at most. Those congregations would be small, but daily increasing. There is one at Quincy, one at the head of the rapids, another on the forks of Crooked creek, a fourth at the foot of the rapids among the Half Indians (that is in our county), where there are several French and American families living. From there he could even sometimes go to Sangammon county. On the other hand it would be very consoling for the missionary: it would be placing the spiritual and temporal comforts within the reach of both, and also that of the priest stationed at Galena. Then, at least, we could see sometimes one or another. We could ask for consolation in affliction, counsel in doubts, without being exposed so much to die without the consolation of receiving the last Sacraments, as Mr. McMahon of afflicting memory . . . . . ."

How touching is this appeal for more assistance in the vineyard of the Lord!

So few in number were the priests in our early days that one of them, the Very Rev. S. Mazzuchelli, O. P., was obliged to make a journey of nearly 500 miles for his annual confession, while Father McMahon succumbed to cholera in 1833 at Galena, far away from any neighbor priest, and his successor shared the same fate in 1834. We are not surprised, therefore, that Father Lefevre should again ask for assistance in a letter of October 6th, 1836, in which he also remembers his Half Indians in Lee county and the dwellers on the rapids.

In the following spring, under date of March 9th, 1837, he makes a report of his missions, saying: ". . . . . . In the missions I have hitherto attended there are fourteen stations," among which he enumerates "two in the Wisconsin Territory (that is our Lee county), viz.," and having enumerated those in Missouri and Illinois, he proceeds: " In the Wisconsin Territory, 1st, at Keokuk, in the Half Indian tract between the river Des Moines and the Mississippi; 2d, on the Skunk river ten miles west from Fort Madison . . . . . . Last

winter I was called to the sick, ... once to the Des
Moines river, and once into the Wisconsin Territory, 150
miles north from Ralls county . . . . . ."—where he found
snow 18 inches deep, made 12 miles over the ice of the Mississippi, and was threatened with loss of life in a freshet from
a sudden thaw.

Our present State was Michigan Territory in 1834, became
Wisconsin Territory in 1836, and received the name of Iowa
Territory in 1838.

Father Lefevre's description "west" of Fort Madison,
should undoubtedly read "north," as that is the direction of
Skunk river from Fort Madison, and several Catholics settled
there in 1834, and some later, near what now is St. Augusta,
in Des Moines county.

Thus for three years was Lee county placed under the spiritual guidance and tender solicitude of a most zealous and famous
priest, when in 1837, on the 15th day of August, Father Augustus Brickwedde assumed charge of his appointment to Quincy,
and upon him devolved the attendance of the Wisconsin Territory.   He was a most exemplary priest, who came from h's
native Fuerstenau in Hannover to confirm in the faith his
many brethren in the western wilds of America, quite a number of whom also made settlements in Lee county in the years
from 1834 to 1842, principally choosing their homesteads on
the present sites of Fort Madison, West Point, St. Paul and
Pleasant Ridge.   Father Brickwedde visited these localities
from 1838 to 1841, but it seems that he limited his visits to
once in the year, and then made them with a view to the
Easter duties of the people.   It does not appear that he made
any visits to Keokuk or Montrose, and it is probable that these
places were considered to be subject to the jurisdiction of
English-speaking priests, as Father Hunter was at this time
in Quincy ond visited the present Warsaw and Nauvoo.

Father Brickwedde made his first visit to Fort Madison in
May, 1838, celebrating High Mass in the house of J. H. Dinz-
man (a log cabin), and from there proceeded to the settlement
named "Sugar Creek," now St. Paul, where he held the
divine service in a newly-completed log barn of J. H. Kempker

on the 13th day of May, 1838, and on this occasion baptized
the infants Herman Henry Hellmann, Gerhard H. Dingmann,
Bernard Hellmann; on April 16th, 1839, he held his missionary visit at West Point, and there baptized Gerhard Henry
Grover, Gerhard Henry Hellmann, and on the following day,
at the same place, Mary Elizabeth Rump and Barbara Ritt.
At this time an episcopal invitation to a synod for April 21st
was one of his engagements; however, in making this last
named visit to Lee county, the steamboat which carried him
ran aground in the rapids, delaying the passengers eight days;
and he writes the apology to his Rt. Rev. Ordinary in English,
whereby we see that he did not neglect to acquaint himself
with the language of the country. In presenting the report
for Lee county for the year 1838, he gives the number of
souls as 58, Germans; baptisms, 4; paschal communions,
34; marriages, 2; and deaths, 3; and for the following year,
1839, the number of souls amounts to 62.

For the year 1840 he made his visit to West Point in the
beginning of May, and on the 11th baptized Anna Mary
Thebacher, Anna Theresa Ritt, and Joseph Stucky, and at Fort
Madison, May 13th, John Henry Dingmann.

His last visit was to West Point, occurring July 18th, 1841,
when he baptized Gerhard Henry Dingmann, Bernard Schlie-
mer and Hermann Dingmann.

We can speak of this missionary priest only in terms of
highest praise, and what he has done in consoling the struggling pioneers in Lee county was no doubt the cause of in-
ducing many others to come as neighbors of those good
people.

In the summer of 1840 another priest came to take charge
of Lee county, where he remained for eleven years. This
was the Dominican Father J. J. Alleman, who had received
permission from his superiors in St. Joseph's monastery, Ohio,
to follow his desire of attending the straggling Catholics in the
west, and passing through Illinois he came to the Mississippi
river in this year, and extended his visits to every German
family or settlement that he could hear of, not only in Iowa,
but also on the eastern shore of the river. However, the

principal field of his exertions, from 1842 till 1849, was this county. In the autumn of 1840 he collected the families at Fort Madison, about twelve or sixteen in number, and encouraged them to build a small church of brick, 16 x 18 feet in size, the building which still exists on the present church site. This humble structure for a number of years formed his church, his school and his abode. He was absent much of the time in attending other stations; yet, when in Fort Madison, he frequently assembled the children and conducted school with them himself, until 1846, when Mr. Stephen Schulte was secured as the first Catholic school-teacher in this town.

The church was dedicated in honor of St. Joseph, and the congregation numbered among its first members the families of John Abel, John H. Dingmann, Henry, John K. and Joseph Schwartz, Joseph Hellmann, Henry Tieken, Bernard Tieken, Liborius Nelle and Henry Becker, to whom others were added so rapidly that in 1847 Father Alleman directed a more suitable church to be built, which was erected on the same ground, about 30 x 50 feet in dimensions. In 1850 the number was more than 100 families and still rapidly increasing, so that when shortly afterwards Father Alexander Hattenberger was appointed as the resident pastor he soon found it necessary to add a large extension to the church, and was able to further the improvements still more by the building of a school, the purchase of two large bells and construction of a tower; and in his tour in Europe, in 1857, he secured the Stations and some other paintings of no little merit. He was an energetic and zealous priest who came from Alsace with Father Crétin in 1847, was ordained in Chicago January 5th, 1850, and under his wise guidance St. Joseph's church gained a strength which it has never lost. After his removal to another parish in 1861, Father Michels and some other priests attended the parish for a brief period, when in 1864 Father J. B. Weikmann became the pastor. The congregation had attained the number of nearly 400 families, and this priest at once made preparations for the building of a large new church, to be located in the central part of the city, with the intention of closing the old church. For some years past the parish schools had been placed under the direction of the Sisters of Notre Dame, but the school buildings were inadequate. The first step of the pastor now was to erect a substantial school-house on the new site, in which the sisters continued their school with marked success. In 1866 the foundation for the church was laid, 64 by 130 feet in size, to be constructed of brick and in Gothic style. But at this time a difference of opinion prevailed amongst some in regard to closing the old church, and when the pastor obtained a removal to another parish Rev. James Orth succeeded him, and in three years brought the building of the church to a successful completion   Then Rev. Aloysius Meis was appointed the pastor, during whose incumbency the church was named in honor of the Blessed Virgin Mary. He attended faithfully to his large trust, built a handsome parochial residence, added a convent home for the sisters to his school property, provided for beautiful and appropriate church furniture and costly vestments, and enriched his church with a peal of weighty bells, a large organ, and heating apparatus. At his death, on the 15th of July, this year, the entire congregation grieved in losing a good priest and a zealous pastor.

In August Rev. P. Kern received the appointment as pastor.

When the time came for closing the old church, the attempt was resisted by the pioneer settlers in the neighborhood of its hallowed walls; and upon their earnest protestations Bishop Hennessy sent them another pastor in the person of the Rev. Edward Gaule, who reorganized St. Joseph's parish with about seventy families in a most commendable manner. It was now found that the greater number of the parishioners entertained a predilection for the language of "Vaterland," and the Rev. I. J. Grieser, from Suavia, was sent as the incumbent, who attended the congregation until 1879, during which time he built a parochial school, 40 x 45 feet, and introduced the Dominican sisters as teachers. Upon his transfer your humble servant received the appointment, and for three years endeavored to the best of his abilities to guard the spiritual and temporal welfare of this church ;—it is almost the place of my nativity, the first good, noble-harted pioneer priest of this church baptized me in the summer of 1848, and the place and its people have my unbounded esteem.

Then Father John Gosker was for a brief period the pastor, who in the autumn of 1884 was succeeded by Rev. Louis de Cailly. Soon after his arrival he commenced the building of a new church, 50 x 110 feet in size, very beautifully designed on a Gothic plan and finished in a very neat and pleasing manner. It was dedicated December 21st, 1886, by Bishop Cosgrove.

Time will not permit to consider further the growth of the Church in the city of Fort Madison, but what has here been said will be sufficient to indicate that the Church has prospered, and that the ardent labors of the priests, as well as the generous sacrifices of the people in this place, have borne their good fruits.

Other cities merit our attention in no less degree, as we may see by the following quotation from a recent daily paper in Keokuk:

" The congregation of St. Peter's is one of the largest and most cultivated in the State. It is composed largely of educated and refined people. Its influence in life for good has reached supremacy. This has all been brought about from the most humble beginning. The present pastor of St. Peter's, Rev. Father O'Reilly, is well known and beloved by the congregation and the people of this community. He is noted for his kindly and benevolent disposition, his piety and zeal in the work of the Church. He is of a modest and retiring nature, and only those who know him best can appreciate his true worth as a man and pastor. He is endowed with a fine . mind, which he has studiously cultivated and stored with knowledge. As a scholar and teacher he ranks high among those who have acquired learning in all its branches. Yet it is not our province to eulogize this truly good man."

From 1837 to 1840 it is not apparent that any priests ever visited Keokuk. When Father Alleman assumed charge of Lee county, he made Keokuk one of his stations, which he attended regularly and administered faithfully to the spiritual wants of the people, but could make no effort for material progress. During this time of his charge, however, there was one exception, and that was in the month of August, 1844, when Rt. Rev. Dr. Loras, Bishop of Dubuque, sent Keokuk a resident pastor in the person of Rev. Lucien Galtier, whom he transferred from St. Peter's river, where he had built the pioneer St. Paul's church, and named the village which later became the capital and metropolis of Minnesota.

At Keokuk this most exemplary priest engaged H. V. Gildea to build the church, which he superintended in person. The site was on Second and Blondeau streets, on the brow of the hill overlooking the rapids, with a magnificent view of Illinois and Missouri; the building material was stone and logs; the size 20 x 30 feet, and 12 feet high. The stones for the foundation, rudely formed, were taken from the building site. T. Fanning, from Dubuque, owned a timber claim a few miles up the stream, and gave unlimited privilege of taking the logs. Thither the priest wended his way, and with the aid of two or three French settlers, hewed the timber and rafted it to the building site. In the fatigue of the first day's labor it was found that no one had provided a hamper for appeasing the hunger, but fishing in the river proved to be good. The roof of the church was made of clap-boards, and within one month the building was completed, and dedicated in honor of St. John the Evangelist. There were at this time only very few Catholics in Keokuk, and the Bishop, much in need of priests, recalled Father Galtier with an appointment to Prairie du Chien. The congregation continued to make gradual progress under the spiritual guidance of Father Alleman until the year 1848, when Rev. J. B. Villars was appointed pastor. He remained in Keokuk until 1862, and during the first few years of his pastorate St. John's church was several times enlarged with an addition of frame-work. So rapid was the increase of members that sufficient space was not acquired by these improvements. In 1853 the Bishop bought a handsome and valuable block of 12 lots in the central portion of the city, to be used for the future improvements of the church, and in the same year the Ladies of the Visitation, six in number, arrived and commenced the building of a convent and academy on the present site of the Sisters of Charity convent. In order to promote the growth of the Church at an equal pace with the growth of the city, Father Villars now began to think of erecting a grand church on the *sisters' property;* and whether it happened on this account, or by some oversight or misplaced confidence, at all events the Bishop's most excellent church property in the heart of the city was lost, and when in 1856 he sent to Keokuk the sum of $2600 for the safe keeping of the site and redemption of tax titles, it was already lost beyond recovery. Therefore he sent to this city a most excellent young priest, in whom he placed entire confidence, instructed him to do something in Keokuk to gain a foothold and to build a church. Father William Emonds at once took his place as co-laborer of Father Villars, and although building sites were held at a high price, succeeded in securing a church property on Exchange street, between Ninth and Tenth streets, on which he completed a brick church in 1857, 34 x 70 feet in size, for which the corner-stone was laid April 20th, 1856.

Quite a storm of disapprobation was raised against Father Emonds for his independence of action ; but when the Bishop came and saw the work so successfully accomplished, he was highly pleased, accepted the church, and dedicated it in honor of St. Peter the Apostle. As Father Emonds was of German nationality, and that element had already grown numerous in the congregation, the understanding was that St. Peter's Church was to be for their exclusive use and benefit, whilst all others were to continue with old St. John's. The wish of Bishop Loras, however, was that there should be only *one* congregation, and as all had contributed with equal generosity in building this new church, the priest made a virtue of necessity and declared the church to be for the use of all.

Some of the Germans were very much hurt, but in 1867 rallied once more and built their beautiful little *St. Mary's church*, on Fourteenth and Johnson streets, of which Father Clement Johannes became the first pastor, who was succeeded in turn by Fathers Joseph Weikmann, J. P. Maly, Joseph Knæpple, J. Orth (four years), John F. Kempker (over two years), and the present incumbent, Rev. Charles Hundt. They are an excellent little congregation, and most commendable for their devotion and perseverance.

Father Emonds, upon the completion of the church, took a tour to Europe, to recuperate broken down health and invite some German seminarians to Iowa. He was succeeded in St. Peter's church by Rev. J. G. Réffé, a priest of most angelic and amiable disposition, and no less known for his nobility of character than for his scholarly attainments.

The church, though scarcely completed, proved to be too small, and he set about enlarging it with the " **T** " form addition and basement rooms, in which shape it continues to exist to the present day, and has served the prosperous, good and faithful congregation for 27 long years. At the close of 1858, before he had time to liquidate all the debts, Father Réffé was superseded by Rev. Louis de Cailly, a nephew of Bishop Loras, who remained as pastor until 1868. During these years the congregation continued to remain very prosperous, and gained prominence as one of the best and most refined congregations in the diocese. The old St. John's church was abandoned, and part of the building moved on the new church grounds to be used as a school-room. An ardent desire was frequently expressed for better schools, and Father de Cailly had a building erected on the south side of the church, at a cost of about $6000 or $7000, with the intention of introducing the Christian Brothers. But these designs were frustrated, the building was converted into a parochial residence. In 1868 Father de Cailly took his letters dismissorial from the diocese, and was succeeded by Rev. A. Trevis as pastor, who remained until 1875. During his time he had for assistant, nearly one year, the Rev. George W. Heer, who is still remembered by the parishioners with unabating devotedness. The congregation frequently clamored for the construction of a more appropriate church edifice, but Father Trevis never had the courage to undertake the necessary improvement.

In 1875 the Rev. Thomas O'Reilly succeeded to the pastorate, who, though frequently delicate in health, has continued to administer the affairs of the congregation with fidelity and devotion. He is a man conspicuous for indomitable will power and eminent in good example, and for the past twelve years has guided his church on the up hill path to progress with an unerring hand. He is a friend of Christian education and has labored assiduously to elevate his schools to a laudable degree of perfection. To the sick he attends with unwearying devotion and tenderness, whilst the pious sodalities and church societies are in a flourishing condition under his protection.

But the main work of his pastorate was the construction of St. Peter's church, on Bank and Ninth streets, a prominent elevation on which the grand structure may be seen for miles in every direction, bearing aloft in the skies, in gilded lustre, the sign of salvation. On the 12th of June, 1881, Father B. Spalding, of Peoria, laid the corner-stone, assisted by the pastor and neighboring clergy. The structure was planned in the Gothic style and of the best construction, and the cost was originally underestimated. This brought about a struggle for the congregation; but if the task was great they were equal to it, and their devotion, self-denial, willing sacrifice and faithful interest merit the highest praise. The pastor proved himself a good leader, but without the faithful flock he must succumb. An incident worthy of remark was the neighborly hand of the non-Catholics. In five years $51,000 were accumulated and expended on the building; but the result was a noble monument of Christian art, without one cent of debt.

The edifice measures 60 x 140 feet, with 84 feet to the gable and 183 feet to the cross on the tower. The windows are of beautiful stained-glass design, nestled between the prominent buttresses in due proportion. The large window in the tower front, with many niches, pilasters and interchanges, give the entrance an inviting appearance, whilst the lofty octagon sanctuary, with cosy vestries adjoining, gives this portion of the building a most convenient and desirable finish. The commodious corner turrets on the front are subservient to beauty, strength and comfort in reaching the first and second galleries by a winding staircase. The interior of the church is lofty, enhanced by the subdued light, and enchanting the devout visitor with the beauty of richly groined ceilings, graceful pilasters, chaste fresco paintings and beautiful proportions.

On September 27th, 1885, the church was solemnly dedicated in honor of St. Peter, by Father M. Flavin, of Davenport, assisted by the pastor and many of the neighboring clergy and a vast concourse of people. The event of the day was a most eloquent oration from Bishop Hennessy, who appeared at 10.30 o'clock, and for one and a half hours held his intelligent and select audience in breathless attention, electrifying them with the grandest sublimity of thought, clearness and beauty of diction, and irresistibly fascinating force of logic. In the evening a large audience assembled to listen to a strong and eloquent sermon by Father Tallon, an eminent young man given by St. Peter's congregation to the priesthood.

The members of St. Peter's congregation are noted for promptness in attending the divine service, for fervor in receiving the holy Sacraments; for self-sacrifice, temperance, devotion, faithful adherence to Church discipline, obedience and many works of piety. As they are honored at home, so are they regarded with respect by the outside world. Although grown to great strength even at an early day, the congregation has not increased in proportionate degree in late years. Their numerical strength is now estimated at about 1700 souls.

But time is limited, and I have already trespassed on your patience, and can therefore add nothing more of the *res gestæ* of West Point, where the church was built in 1842, which has grown to be a most exemplary country parish; or of St. James', the little log church on Sugar creek, which later became the village of St. Paul, or of Montrose and its mission station, or of St. Francis de Sales', or of Charleston in the Half Breed tract, or of Farmington and its little frame church, or of Primrose, or Franklin, or the little Brown Shanty church on the canal near the site of Maurice Blondeau's house; to say nothing of the sisters, the schools, societies, priests, students, buildings, cemeteries, the languages, tornadoes, little war parties and charitable encouragements which the church has witnessed in beautiful Lee county in the past fifty years.

SKETCHES

OF

CATHOLICITY IN TEXAS.

[Prepared by VERY REV. C. JAILLET, V. G., and read before the SOCIETY by FRANCIS X. REUSS, January 17th, 1888.]

IT would be an agreeable task for me to give you and all the gentlemen of our Society a complete though brief sketch of our Catholic missions in Texas since their establishment, as I am requested to do in your last communication. But these questions have been treated by Catholic historians as well as could be desired, with the few materials at hand. It would be but a tedious repetition, and, at the same time, too much presumption on my part, to attempt to describe what they have done already. The lapse of time assigned to me is also too short, considering my numerous other occupations, to set in order and with accuracy the different data relating to Catholic missions, from the time the first Spanish missionaries started them even until the present time. Should it be possible for me to write a history of the Catholic Church in Texas, I would like to divide it into three different epochs: the first, beginning with the arrival of the first Spanish Franciscans and Jesuits, who evangelized the wild inhabitants of the boundless prairies extending from El Paso to the mouth of the Rio Grande and from Mexico to Nagadoches, and ending at the time the late Right Rev. Dr. Odin was appointed the first Vicar-Apostolic of Texas. The second period should extend from March, 1842, to December, 1874, when the Lone Star State was divided into three different dioceses. The last period would embrace the last thirteen years. But I am unable to cope with such a gigantic task for lack of time, and, alas! also, for lack of material. God alone knows the many trials and acts of heroic abnegation of those saintly pioneers, who, like Father Margil and Right Rev. Dr. Odin, have been called to the ungrateful labor of planting the precious and · heavenly seed among the savage aborigenes, and also among the hardy but pure first settlers of such an immense State.

Other writers, more fitted than myself for such work, will one day, I hope, collect here and there the few scattered vestiges from monuments left by these holy men, unknown to the world, but rich in merit before God, and trace through three centuries the slow but steady progress of our Holy Faith in this our State, and be called to a glorious destiny in times to come.

I will content myself at present with giving you a brief, but, as far as possible, an accurate account of the missions of southern Texas, improperly called the " Vicariate Apostolic of Brownsville."

It is the first time that I have seen a vicariate called after the name of a city. Everywhere else vicariates are supposed to be a territorial division, having no fixed see. Thus we have the vicariates of North Minnesota, Dakota, Wyoming, etc. Why is it, then, that this vicariate of southern Texas is called Vicariaté Apostolic of Brownsville ? Perhaps because the Propaganda had not been well informed at the time of the division of Texas into three dioceses, and had taken Browns-ville to be a district as well as a city, while there is no terri-torial division known under that name. Perhaps, also, when the said division was made, the name of San Antonio being given as the name of a new see, the fact was overlooked that the southern division being destined to be a vicariate only, a more proper appelation should have been presented to the authorities of the Church. For the time being, ours is the Vicariate-Apostolic of Brownsville.

Previous to the year 1842 Texas was nominally under the jurisdiction of Durango, and, perhaps, of Monterey, for the southwestern part. Some years ago I was delegated by Right Rev. Bishop Dubuis, who since has returned to France, in order to ascertain the exact state of affairs, and I came to know that, according to an old document from Rome, the Bishop of Durango was invested by the Holy Father with jurisdiction over Texas *usque ad terminos notos* towards the north. I think also that the limits between Durango and Monterey (if, however, the latter had any jurisdiction in Texas) were at least in Texas no more accurately specified. The old Mexican priests at El Paso, San Antonio and Laredo belonged to Durango, while the other missions were under the care of religious orders. The last priests who, to my knowledge, belonged to the Mexican jurisdiction were Father Barrajo, of San Elizario, Father Garza, of San Antonio, and Father Garcia, of Laredo. The population here in those old times was very small, Texas being then the camping and hunting-ground of Comanches, Lipans, Apaches and other wild tribes of Indians.

A new era began for the Church with the appointment of Rt. Rev. Dr. Odin as first Vicar-Apostolic of Texas. So few were his clergy that he could count them on his fingers. Their field of action was an immense one. One of them had for his mission a larger area than the whole State of Pennsylvania; it extended from Galveston to the Red river, a distance of about 400 miles. Another had the whole western part, with headquarters at Castroville and San Antonio. Another was stationed at Houston. Those were trying times, and the Church of Texas was truly an apostolic mission. But let it be said to the honor of our dear ancestors and fathers in the holy ministry that they were equal to the task. The names of the saintly Odin and his zealous successor, Bishop C. M. Dubuis, and those of fathers Chambodur, Padey, Timon and several others, will always be held in great reverence by the Catholics of Texas. With the new administration several missions were opened and scattered over distant places. Victoria mission was opened, and its missionary priest, Father Giraudon, had at least ten counties to visit, which to-day form six large missions, Victoria, Befugio, San Patricio, Aransas, Lamar and Corpus Christi. Rev. Father Padey, who died a year ago in Lyons, had charge of Lavaca and Brushy missions, comprising at least six counties. Rev. Father Anstaet's extended over eight counties, mainly settled by Germans, where now actually ten different missions, with as many priests, are to be found.

Another German priest, Father Miller, had under his charge the Brazoria and Velasco missions, comprising all the country between the mission of Galveston and that of Victoria. All the missions northwest of San Antonio were turned over to Father Mentzell, with a residence at Fredericksburg. That mission is sub-divided to-day into six missions, with as many priests. Eagle Pass mission, limited south by the Rio Grande, but unlimited in other directions, was entrusted to Father Domenech, the witty historian-priest of old-fashioned Texas. Brownsville mission, extending 200 miles northwest and 150 north, was assigned to the Oblate Fathers, viz., Fathers Telmont, Sauterin and Gaudet. Their worthy successors have labored with untiring zeal and energy among the hard Mexican missions of the frontier. Afterwards, but still before the late war, new missions were established at Austin, with Father Mackin, and Bandera, with Father Prozieski. The Spanish missions, near San Antonio, were assigned to Father Bouchur. Corpus Christi's first church was built in 1854, by Rev. Bernard O'Reilly, now dead several years. Frelsburg and Colorado county missions were given in charge to Fathers Gury and Tarillon. Father Faure, a popular Texan priest, now retired in France, was stationed at Lavaca. The Mexican priest at Laredo was succeeded by Fr. Giraudon, the present pastor. The Rev. Father Sauchon, already twenty-seven years a priest, was then his assistant. These were zealous priests, who also have left lasting proofs of their piety and labors. The present Bishop Neraz, with another priest, had charge of the whole border of Louisiana, than which a harder, poorer, and more unhealthy mission could not be found in the whole Republic. To give you an instance of the hardships of such missions, in one year the missionary priest did not receive $80 from all sources into his exchequer. His fare from the beginning of the year to the end was corn-bread, black coffee and bacon. Other missions were established at New Braunsfeld and Panna Maria, under the care of the Benedictine Fathers and Resurrectionists. San Patricio, an old Irish settlement, received a priest; so did the mission of Refugio. Another new mission was founded at Roma, on the Rio Grande, its first incumbent being Father Planchet, who died in Monterey, enjoying the esteem and confidence of the highest class of citizens there. A temporary mission was established at Washington, Texas, under Father Gounard, who died in Corpus Christi twenty years ago, a victim of his charity and zeal in attending his unfortunate congregation decimated with yellow fever.

These were the principal changes that had taken place during the period. Rt. Rev. Dr. Odin was the first Vicar Apostolic of Texas. At the same time he was appointed Archbishop of the metropolis of the South. Right Rev. C. M. Dubuis was chosen as his successor, and well did he deserve the honor, for he was a most zealous, disinterested and energetic missionary. Endowed with an iron constitution, he could stand hardships unknown to others. I have known him for years, and have accompanied him on several of his diocesan visitations along the frontier. He used to sleep very little. Ordinarily we were up at four in the morning, and on the saddle for days and days, with nothing but scanty food and his indomitable energy to support him, and notwithstanding such a hard life always cheerful and fond of jokes. Under his administration the first foundations were secured; many convents and academies were started at Dallas, Houston, Victoria, Corpus Christi, Laredo and many other places. Hospitals, too, were started at Galveston and San Antonio. Large churches also were erected at Dallas, Houston, San Antonio, Laredo, Brownsville, Halletsville, D'hanis, and a great number of churches were built in many of the missions. New missions were started at Clarksville under Father Thomas Buffard, at Corricuna, Fayetteville, High Hill, Jefferson, Texarkana, Palestine, Denison, Sherman, Waco, in the present diocese of Galveston; at Medina, Fort Davis, Graytown, Indianola, now destroyed entirely by a cyclone, in the diocese of San Antonio; San Diego, in the vicariate of Corpus Christi. The task Bishop Dubuis was given to perform was astounding. This diocese extended over 250,000 square miles; and though constantly traveling by land and sea, on railroads (which were few twenty years ago), and more frequently on horseback, by day and by night, he could not visit his immense diocese in less than two years; and let it be known that of him, as well as of Bishop England, it might be said he was a " steam bishop," sometimes confirming in three or four different settlements, widely distant, on the same day. I will by and by speak of the difficulties of the ministry attending such journeys. All I can say now is that if our old Right Rev. Bishop is crippled with rheumatism and other diseases, it was on account, no doubt, of his hard life as missionary priest first, and as missionary bishop after. It is wonderful how he was able to stand it so long. It was hard for a priest to undertake several days' journey with him. May God grant him relief in his ailment while on earth and some days of much needed rest.

Since 1874 Texas has been divided into three districts: Galveston and San Antonio as dioceses, and the southern part of the State as the vicariate apostolic of Brownsville. Bishop Dubuis was assigned his former see of Galveston, and the limits of his diocese were on the south and west the Colorado river and New Mexico, with the Red river on the north. Galveston is still the principal diocese of Texas, for it comprises about the half of the State. A new bishop was appointed for San Antonio, and this new diocese comprises the central part of the State; it extends from the Colorado, on the north, to the Nueces, on the southwest; it is limited by Paso county in Texas, which belongs ecclesiastically to Arizona. Right Rev. Dr. Pellicer was its first bishop, who, thanks to his courteous and amiable disposition, has left a cherished name, beloved by both clergy and laity.

The new southern ecclesiastical division is the smallest of the three; it contains but the eighth part of the State. In the northern States it would be a tolerably good-sized diocese, but here it is the baby of the three; not only in extension, but also in resources. Its limits in 1874 were the Nueces river on the north, and the Rio Grande on the south. This former division was a little amended afterwards, at the request of Right Rev. D. Manucy. Now it is limited on the northwest side by the two little creeks called Las Hermanas and San Roque, thence by the Nueces as far down as Live Oak county. Further below it comprises the following counties, to wit: Live Oak, San Patricio, Bee, Refugio, Goliad and Aransas, all situated north of the Nueces river. The other limits are the same as before. The first vicar apostolic of southern Texas was Right Rev. Dominic Manucy, consecrated in the cathedral of New Orleans on the 8th of December, 1874, as Bishop of Dulmen (*quondam in part. inf.*) and as Vicar Apostolic of Brownsville (see above explanations). He remained ten years in Texas, until 1884, when he was appointed to the See of Mobile, left vacant by the death of Right Rev. Bishop Quinlan. But at the same time he retained the administration of this Vicariate. His health being impaired, and finding also financial difficulties he thought he could not overcome, he resigned the same year the see of Mobile, intending to come back to his old vicariate. But it was too late. He was completely worn out, and died in Mobile on the 4th of December, 1885. Since then the vicariate has remained without a vicar apostolic.

At the time Rt. Rev. Dr. Manucy left Texas for Mobile, I was appointed by him as Vicar General and Administrator *ex officio sed non in titulo*. After his death I was reappointed as administrator by the late Most Rev. Archbishop Leray, and a few weeks after, in February, 1885, my appointment was confirmed by Cardinal Simeoni, under the title of Administrator *sede vacante*. Some time in May, 1887, Right Rev. J. C. Neraz, Bishop of San Antonio, was appointed also Admin-

istrator of Brownsville; but having already an immense diocese to visit, delegated me as vicar general to administer the
vicariate. So I am the vicar general for the second time.

Let me show you the premises, now that we are so well
acquainted.

The vicariate, called " of Brownsville," comprises the fourteen most southern counties of Texas, with part of three
others, namely: Cameron, Hidalgo, Starr, Zapata, Webb,
part of Demmit, part of La Salle, part of McMullen, Encinal,
Duval, Nueces, San Patricio, Aransas, Refugio, Goliad, Bee
and Live Oak. Its area must be over 25,000 square miles,
and the total population over 65,000 inhabitants, out of whom
40,000 are Mexicans. Out of the 25,000 remaining Americans about one-tenth of them are Catholics. Therefore our
vicariate is mainly Spanish. It is divided into ten missions,
as follows :

1st. The mission of Brownsville, comprising Cameron county
and half of Hidalgo. There are, in that mission, seven
Oblate Fathers, in charge of Brownsville, and about 200
ranches scattered over an area 40 miles wide by 150 long, and
containing a Catholic population of 18,000 souls, 500 of whom
are Americans. Brownsville itself has about 5000 Catholics.
Rev. Father Parisot, an old though still a vigorous pioneer, is
there at the head of the mission, and it is to be hoped that he
will soon be called to the helm to pilot the boat, than whom
none has been better and so long and so efficiently acquainted
with it. In that city stands a beautiful brick church, nicely
decorated and adorned; it is the jewel of the frontier, and
therein services in both English and Spanish are held constantly. The same clergy have under their care a half dozen
chapels, scattered along the Rio Grande, regularly visited and
attended, besides over 200 settlements scattered over their
immense missions, which are also yearly or semi-yearly visited.
It was not very long ago that I forwarded to you some copies
of a newspaper that was edited monthly by the Rev. Oblate
Fathers. They contain precious information about the missions of Texas in general, and of Brownsville in particular.
I refer you to them for more developments.

2d. The mission of Roma, which at present is entrusted to Rev. Father J. M. Clos, who is assisted by Rev. Fathers Gaye and Piat, was established before the civil war, its first pastor being Father Planchet, whom I have mentioned before, and who went over to Monterey about twenty years ago. After he left the mission was turned over to the Oblates. They have done wonderful work among untold difficulties. They only last year built a nice convent, where the poor people of the frontier can easily find a good Catholic education. They have built, also last year, two new chapels. From Brownsville up to Roma the Oblates are placed as the vanguard trying, not without success, to check the evil influences aiming at the destruction öf faith and spreading of immorality.

3d. A few years ago a new mission was formed at Rio Grande city, below Roma, which comprises half of both Hidalgo and Starr counties, while Roma comprises half of Starr and the whole of Zapata county. Two priests are in charge of Rio Grande City mission: Rev. L. Pitoye, assisted by Father Desaules. The former succeeded a year ago in building a convent, where, as at Roma, a Christian education is given to the poor people of the frontier. They receive pupils from both Texas and Mexico, for you know that since "our sister republic" is under a liberal (!) government, religious communities cannot exist there legally. Such is the verdict of liberty! There a priest needs a permit to baptize an infant, and if the child dies suddenly, of course he must wait for the permit in order to be baptized! Madame Roland, going to the scaffold, is said to have exclaimed: "O Liberty, how many crimes are committed in thy name!" I would say in my turn, when I look at Mexico: "O Liberty, how many absurdities those monkeys calling themselves Liberals are loaded with under thy nose." In Mexico they were thoroughly liberal (I do not mean the people, with whom I have been a friend for twenty years, and who are victimized by their unscrupulous government). They have robbed the Church of her land; now they threaten to rob her of her churches and ornaments. An Indian can go there half-naked, but a priest cannot wear his cassock without being fined. I

know of a case in Laredo (Mexico) of a priest who was fined
$25 because, on Palm Sunday, he was bad enough to bless
the palms at the entrance of his church, though it was inside.
That's a sample of Mexican liberty.   These Mexican authorities are worthy brothers of the French *sans culottes* and com-
munists.   This little digression may help you to understand
what demoralization is going on with a people so timid and
weak, though good-hearted, as the Mexicans are; and it will
help you to understand the difficulties our devoted priests are
meeting constantly in their arduous labors.   Add to these the
incessant Protestant propagandism which, if it makes but few
converts to its decayed cause, helps infidelity in mocking and
slandering religion.

4th. The mission of Laredo is an older mission than the
two foregoing.   There was already an old church built there
before Texas became a State of the Union.   When Father
Giraudon went there under Bishop Odin, there was not a
twentieth part of the population married by the Church.   To-
day they have a flourishing convent with sixteen sisters of the
Ursuline order.   The church here is 110 feet long by over 50
feet wide, built of good solid rock, with a high spire seen for
many miles around.   The population of Laredo (Texas) is
about 7000, out of which 6000 are Catholics, or at least claim
to be so.   On the Mexican side of the Rio Grande there is
another town as populous as the one on this side.   Besides
the town there is a population of 3000 or 4000 souls out in
Webb and Encinal counties, which are visited from Laredo.

5th. I come now to my beloved mission of San Diego,
though I am no longer in charge of it.   It was the first one
I had when ordained priest, and I was the first priest they ever
had there.   Therefore we are good friends and old acquain-
tances.

When I first came there I was a very small fish.   I was
sent *sine pera*, though with boots.   I had to supply myself with
ornaments wherever I could.   I took an old missal from
Corpus Christi, stole a little chalice from San Patricio, but
afterwards tried to square my accounts.   Then I borrowed a
saddle and a horse, and thus equipped made my solemn entry

into the little town which had been assigned to me as headquarters. But here began the trouble. I could not speak twenty words of Spanish, and did not know to what house to go. I was sent by Bishop Dubuis with *carte blanche* about my residence; after some inquiry I struck upon a good-hearted Mexican, who lent me his house, that is to say, a thatched little rock dwelling-house, ten yards long by three wide, with a little bed at each corner. That was my cathedral, presbytery and school for six months. But in order to make the story short, I must say now that the priest has four lots, a church 70 x 30, a house with five rooms. Besides, he has three new chapels, built by my zealous successor, the energetic Father J. P. Bard, whose mission extends over Duval county and three-quarters of Nueces, with a population of 6000 or 7000 Catholics.

6th. The mission of Corpus Christi was visited in early times by Fathers Giraudon and Prendergast. The first church, a rickety building, was built by Rev. Father Bernard O'Reilly in 1854 or 1855. Now there is a beautiful church, frame building, costing, with improvements, $18,000—100 feet long by 54 feet wide and about 25 feet high in the centre. It was built under the late Bishop Manucy. A new convent, costing $15,000, was built two years ago. The Catholic population of Corpus Christi is 1500, two-thirds of whom are Mexicans and one-third Irish-Americans and other nationalities.

Besides these missions there are four exclusively American missions, north of the Nueces river. San Patricio, with two chapels, one of which is at Garrettville; Aransas and Papalate, with two chapels; Lamar, with a concrete brick church; Refugio, with a church and convent, besides a very large and old church, built by the Spaniards at La Bahia before Texan independence.

I have given a short narration of the Church in Texas. Excuse the shortcomings of this communication; but, as you can see, I have written *currente calamo*, for I am very busy.

FATHER LOUIS DELLA VAGNA,

CAPUCHIN,

Pastor of St. Mary's Church, Toronto,

1856-1857.

[Written by H. F. McINTOSH, and read before the SOCIETY by EDWARD J. ALEDO, February 17th, 1888.]

IN the month of June of last year, while tearing down the walls of the old church of St. Mary, Bathurst street, Toronto, the workmen came upon a stone slab, bearing the following inscription :

BENEATH ARE DEPOSITED THE REMAINS
OF
THE VERY REVEREND

FATHER LOUIS DELLA VAGNA

OF THE ORDER OF CAPUCHINS,

A NATIVE OF GENOA—HE LOVED POVERTY, OBEDIENCE, CHASTITY.

HE LED A MORTIFIED LIFE, AND WAS A STRICT OBSERVER OF THE RULE OF

ST. FRANCIS.

HE DIED ON THE 17TH OF MARCH, 1857.
Jesus and Mary receive his soul.

As the excavations proceeded, the stone was removed, and beneath was found the iron coffin in which the corpse had been interred. When the slide had been removed the face was seen to be in precisely the state in which it had been buried. Intelligence of this discovery soon spread throughout the city, and multitudes flocked to view the remains. Early in the day His Grace, Archbishop Lynch, accompanied by His Lordship, Bishop O'Mahony, Very Rev. Father Rooney, V. G. (the present pastor of St. Mary's), and Very Rev. Father Laurent, V G., of St. Michael's Cathedral, visited the chapel in which the coffin had temporarily been placed, and reverently looked upon the face of the priest, who, just thirty years before, had been laid to rest beneath the church over which he had during one short year of his life exercised pastoral control.   Drs. Wallace and McConnell made an examination of the body and found it to be in a remarkably good state of preservation, there being little, if any, decomposition. It has since been re-interred in the vault prepared for it beneath the sanctuary of the new church, never again, perhaps, to be exhumed until it shall come forth at the last day. Among others, the writer of this paper was privileged to look upon the face of the dead monk, and, having regard to the circumstances of his life, an attempt to record which he has here made, he shall ever esteem it one of the greatest privileges God has permitted to him.

The priest whose body had thus been brought to light was at one time pastor of the church of St. Mary. Many old residents of Toronto remember him well. Although his sojourn amongst them was of brief duration, his character and his work were such as to leave an indelible impression upon all who had come in contact with him. But those who were in man's estate then, and still survive, are old and "full of years," and the children of that day are the men and women of this; so that should no effort be made to preserve the memory of so remarkable a man as Father Louis della Vagna undoubtedly was, there is some danger of the dictum quoted by Mgr. Seton being found still to contain an atom of truth, *i. e.:* "There is no antidote against the opium of time,

which temporally considereth all things . . . . . Grave-
stones tell truth scarce forty years." Recognizing, therefore,
the necessity of doing something towards preserving to future
generations the memory of this holy Franciscan friar, I immediately set about collecting all the information possible
having the least reference to him, and when asked to prepare
a paper for the American Catholic Historical Society of Philadelphia, on a subject of my own choosing, I determined to
put together what I have been able to glean concerning this
man. That his memory is worth preserving, the facts will
show. In the words of the Bishop of London, Ont., who was
his immediate successor in the pastorate of St. Mary's church,
" his memory has remained amongst his people like a sweet
fragrance, like the good odor of Christ unto God."

Fortunately I have met with a brief biographical sketch of
Father Louis, written about the time of his death, and to
this I am principally indebted for facts relating to his life
previous to coming to Toronto. It is, however, extremely
rare, and I have not been able to discover a second copy. The
one I have was found by the merest accident in a woodshed
in the city of Ottawa and has been kindly loaned to me by a
friend for the purposes of this paper. According to this
authority, which was, no doubt, inspired by Mgr. de Charbonnel, Father Louis della Vagna was born in the year of
our Lord 1801, in the city of Genoa, the chief commercial
city of Italy and famous as the birthplace of Christopher
Columbus. Although dating back to the days of the Roman
Empire, when it was famous as a harbor, and carried on an
extensive trade in the products of the Ligurian coast, it was
not until the middle of the thirteenth century that Genoa rose
to the zenith of its power and wealth. Then the genius and
enterprise of its merchants advanced it to the position of one
of the greatest and most prosperous commercial cities of the
world. It carried on a large Levantine trade even before
Venice, with which city, as with Pisa, it maintained a fierce
and energetic rivalry. From its beautiful harbor there sailed
forth over the unknown seas, in quest of riches and adventure,
the ships of the Genoese merchants, and their prestige as

traders and navigators may be imagined when it is remembered that in those days Genoa had almost monopolized the trade with the Black Sea; had a lucrative trade with India, and held many rich possessions in the East. The city had, after the breaking up of the empire of Karl the Great in the ninth century, constituted itself a republic, presided over by Doges, and the realization of this political independence, coupled with their success in commercial and maritime enterprises, had the effect of giving to the merchants of Genoa that lofty spirit and proud, passionate air of independence, which, it may be said, is their characteristic even to this day. To one of these old merchant families Louis della Vagna belonged, and from his earliest years it was the design of his family that he should, when arrived at a suitable age, enter, as had his father before him, into commercial pursuits. But Genoa, at the time of Father Louis' childhood, had, from its former lofty position as one of the first maritime cities of the world, dwindled down to a place of minor importance. Situated on the Mediterranean Sea, with a fine harbor, one of the most beautiful, as well as one of the safest in the world, with an industrious and indefatigable population, it still, indeed, maintained a certain rank in commerce, but as to political standing or national aspirations its prestige had long since departed. Its former glory had become but as a memory, and there was left to the ancient maritime republic, amid the relics of its past greatness, only the missionary zeal of its ecclesiastical sons and the devotion and self-sacrifice of its religious orders. In these modern times the Genoese could not glory in their martial prowess; but the apostolic zeal and piety of their monks, and, above all, their solicitude in the education of youth, still emitted a shining light, which shone far beyond the environs of the Gulf of Genoa.

In the midst of this truly religious city, says his biographer, the young Louis, from his earliest infancy, exhibited traits of the most ardent of temperaments. His boyish aspirations were vehement; and despite of his semi-conventual education, his ambitions leaned rather to the distinctions of the world than the humility of the cloister. It was the lofty spirit he inherited from his fathers that thus stirred him.   His family, as has already been said, was a noble one.   Even were he not of the proud, passionate sons of Italy, there was that within him which could not brook control—which prompted resistance.   His was that strong spirit, based upon a foundation of deep thought, which, when entangled in the meshes of the world, turns from it with disgust, and fixes its glance on the haven that is alone the true destination of man.   It may readily be imagined that a youth of this character should meet with difficulties in early life, which, as in the case of almost all those men who, having betaken themselves to the cloister, have afterwards become distinguished in their order, gradually inclined him to give up the allurements of the world.

As soon as his tender age would permit, Louis was sent to the primary schools of Genoa, in order to learn the rudiments of a sound education.   These schools were under the control of that eminent society of men, devoted solely to the education of youth, known as the Brothers of the Christian Schools. Under their skilful instruction and vigilance for the welfare of their pupils' souls, young Louis advanced in knowledge and in virtue.   Even at this early period he was remarkable for his studiousness and industry, and it soon became evident that he was gifted with unusual talents, being specially distinguished by the facility with which he acquired foreign languages.   He seems even at this early age to have had a predilection for the English language, perhaps, as in the case of another great servant of God (Father Dominic, the Passionist, who labored with such great success in England, contemporary with the subject of this sketch), unsuspectingly inspired by the Holy Ghost thus to prepare himself for his future labors amongst English-speaking peoples.   Be that as it may, it is certain he must have applied himself with singular diligence to the acquirement of the English tongue, as we find him at a subsequent period using it with the skill and capacity of a master.   This fact is the more striking, since, of all European languages, English is the most unmusical to Italian ears.

It was to his early association, in the city of Genoa also,

that the youth was indebted for that spirit of charity which he exhibited in after life in a most heroic degree. Genoa " the proud," " *la superba*," in the midst of its splendid palaces of black and white marble, did not, like Dives in the parable, neglect the poorer members of the Church. The whole place in young Louis' day teemed with hospitals, asylums and other benevolent institutions, and one of these, in which Father Louis spent the greater part of his leisure hours, was under the charge of the Ladies of the Third Order of St. Francis. The number of indigent persons daily relieved by them, at this one convent alone, did not fall far short of 2000. It was no wonder, then, that a scion of such a city should be ever ready to relieve the distressed, for in so doing he was engaged in the practice of that virtue which had been engraven upon his heart in the walks of his youth—a virtue, moreover, which was increased and developed as he advanced in years, and as he traveled in Ireland and the west of England amongst the poor and distressed.

The religious education of his early years, the sound principles which he had imbibed in season, and the sacred influence of the external evidences of the Catholic religion, by which he was surrounded from his cradle—all these tended to keep him free from the deeper vices of the world, and, as age advanced, to turn his thoughts into the channels of a religious life.

At length, the time having arrived when, according to the designs of his family, Louis della Vagna should enter upon the trials and duties of life, he was placed by his father in a counting-room on the Exchange, where, by his intelligence, ability and probity, he demonstrated the superiority of the judicious moral and religious training to which he had been subjected, over any merely secular system, such as that towards which it is characteristic of this age to tend. For the space of five years he remained at this employment, at first at the ordinary routine of office work, but latterly entrusted with the foreign correspondence, a promotion which his energy and application had earned for him. In this position he first realized the utility and advantage of his linguistic studies, more especially of his knowledge of English, a language which was then (as, indeed, it is even now) little known or studied in Italy or the adjoining countries. Owing to this fortunate promotion also, he was enabled to acquire a power of expression in that language, without which he might never have extended the influence of his character beyond the precincts of his native city.

Having attained his majority, with an excellent reputation for diligence and discernment—in any walk of life an indispensable requisite to success—he became principal of an extensive banking institution. This of itself proves him to have been no ordinary man, and had it been his vocation to remain in the world, it is not too much to assume that his career would have been one of great distinction to himself and of illustrious service to his native city. He threw himself with all the ardor of his being into the duties and responsibilities of his office, so much so that the passion for wealth and fame took complete possession of his soul. He fell off from the religious fervor of his youth, and almost entirely abandoned the practice of his religion. But this state of things was not to last long. God had designs upon him, other than those of earthly distinction, and in the service ef other peoples than his own. In subsequent years often did the good man lament his blindness during these four years. Many a time did he shed bitter tears of repentance over his former indifference, which he had come to regard as a most flagrant crime. His love of Our Lord, and compassion for the sufferings which He endured because of the sins and ingratitude of men, caused Father Louis, as in the case of God's saints, to look upon himself as the " chief of sinners." Although he lived to be fifty-six years of age, he never ceased to lament this temporary backsliding, and the recollection of it gave a tinge of melancholy to all his meditations to the day of his death.

Being at length aroused by the operations of Divine Grace, he suddenly announced his intention of quitting the world. In the seclusion of the cloister he designed, or rather God designed for him, that he should make reparation for his folly; and therefore divesting himself of all his riches, and placing his banking concerns in the hands of his brother, he entered the Convent of St. Francis of Assisium, and subjected himself to the severe rules and heroic austerities of the Franciscan order. This was in the year 1825, the year of the Grand Jubilee, he being then in his twenty-fourth year.

The order to which Louis della Vagna had thus attached himself was established by St. Francis of Assisium in 1221, in Poggi Bonzi, a town in the grand duchy of Tuscany, and in a place called Cannerio, in the valley of Spoleto. After a succession of years, certain relaxations in the original rules were introduced; but great dissatisfaction being felt by many of the members on this account, a reformation was carried out by Matteo Di Bassi, of Urbino, in 1525. The new branch thus established was called the Capuchin Friars. The members of this order in Genoa maintained the ancient rule with much of its pristine vigor and severity, and it is easy to see, therefore, that, in entering it, Louis della Vagna was in reality crucifying himself with his Divine Master. He was committing himself to the practice of austerities second only to those of La Trappe. But, as previously he had devoted himself to worldly pursuits with that vigor and energy characteristic of his nature, so now he threw himself with his whole soul into the spirit of the founder of his order. At first he was sorely tempted and tried by the recollection of the worldly ease and splendor to which he had been accustomed, but perseverance and prayer at length freed him from these assaults, and left him in possession of that " peace which passeth understanding," and which is ever the blest reward of the true disciple of St. Francis. Like Mary, " he had," in the words of our Lord, " chosen that best part, which should never be taken from him." Year after year, whilst he continued to reside in Italy, he associated the spirit of prayer with the highest degree of activity. In imitation of St. Francis, he spent all the time at his command in according spiritual consolation to the sick, in exhorting sinners to conversion and repentance, and in setting the poor and lowly an example of poverty for the sake of Christ. Though blest with a benign gift of heavenly contemplation in return for the victory he had gained over the flesh, he was, nevertheless, amongst those to whose wants he ministered, a man of simplicity and sweetness. Having been ordained priest, he continued for twenty-five years to fast and pray, and to fulfil the ordinary requirements of his state under the reformed rule, until he was chosen by his superior to perform another function, one in which the Franciscan Friars have been always eminently successful. After having preached with much profit in the various departments of southern France, he was nominated to the mission of the northwestern coasts of Europe.

In the year 1850 he bade farewell to his native city, which he was destined never to see again, and sailing across the Gulf of Genoa reached Lyons, where he remained a short time only, and then proceeded in the direction of Paris. He was then 49 years of age, in the prime and vigor of manhood. His constitution, however, not naturally robust, was being gradually undermined by the rigorous vigils and penances to which he had long subjected himself. He reached Paris in the year 1851, and remained for some time in one of the houses of his order making preparations for the arduous duties of the mission upon which he was about to enter. During his sojourn in that city he met for the first time Mgr. Armand François Marie de Charbonnel, who had the year previous been nominated Bishop of Toronto by His Holiness Pius IX. Bishop de Charbonnel was at this time on his way to Rome on the business of his consecration, and taking advantage of the interviews which he then had with Father Louis, to whom he was greatly attracted, he expatiated with all the earnestness and eloquence at his command upon the vast field for missionary enterprise which the soil of Upper Canada presented. He besought Father Louis to join him in the evangelization of the new country, and he was the more pressing in his solicitations, since Father Louis was so well versed in the knowledge of the English tongue. But the holy friar, though his heart burned within him at the prospect of so rich a harvest of souls as the earnestness of the bishop convinced him the diocese of Toronto presented, was too well grounded in the virtue of humility to be persuaded that he possessed the gifts or qualifications which could render him a valuable acquisition to his lordship, nor could he think of moving to the right or to the left unless in perfect obedience to his superiors. But, undeterred by these obstacles, Bishop de Charbonnel extracted from Father Louis a promise to the effect that, should permission be obtained for him at any future period to depart for Canada, he would do so. At the same time the zealous missionary made no secret of his desire to undertake such a journey, and to co-operate with the bishop in the work of saving souls. Having completed such preparations in Paris as he deemed necessary, he crossed the Channel in 1851 and proceeded to Liverpool, and from thence on his mission to the people of Wales. Regarding details of his six years' labor on the missions in England, Ireland and Wales, we have not much information, but we know that in company with several members of his order he founded the monastery of Pantasaph. For two years subsequent to this he performed a series of most fatiguing missions, giving himself no rest nor relaxation. In Liverpool he preached regularly in one of the principal churches for a period of several months, and the crowds that flocked to hear him, together with his remarkable success in bringing people to the sacraments, afford a striking evidence of the power which he wielded over the hearts of men. From Liverpool he extended his labors over other parts of England, and we find him, later on, repeating his successes in the metropolis of the world, that modern Babylon of sin and misery—the city of London. In 1854 he visited Ireland and gave missions in Dublin and Cork, accomplishing, as elsewhere, an incalculable amount of good. Returning to his monastery at Pantasaph, he was met with instructions from his superior to hold himself in readiness for the Bombay missions, the ranks of the Franciscan missionaries in the countries of the East having been greatly thinned by the ravages of fever. Providence, however, had not so ordained; he was to fall a victim to another destroyer than the scorching sun of the Indies. Preparations for his voyage to the East were completed, and he was awaiting marching orders when, in the midst of his work, he was stricken down by the

hand of disease, brought on by his excessive labors in the
United Kingdom. In the meantime the orders he had been
awaiting arrived, but his sickness continuing, another was
substituted for him, much to the good friar's chagrin. The
affection which he had conceived for Bishop de Charbonnel
was enthusiastic, and the desire to join him in the missions
of Canada strong, but to a missionary of Father Louis' zeal
and fervor it was a severe trial to be deprived of the privilege
of co-operating, even by a decree of stern necessity, with that
glorious cordon of saints who were at that moment planting
the standard of the Cross, like the apostles of old, in the
deserts of India, or sealing the faith of Jesus Christ with
their blood in the vast provinces of the Chinese Empire.
But the good priest, recognizing God's hand in this, to him,
severe trial, submitted without a murmur. What to him,
however, was a heavy cross, proved to be to Canada a great
gain.

In the autumn of the year 1855 he resumed his missionary
labors in England with undiminished success, and in the
spring of 1856 crossed over again into Ireland. On the Sunday
preceding the 17th of March he arrived at All Hallows College, Dublin, that *alma mater* of so many Irish missionaries
scattered throughout the whole world. Here he was received
with the same respect as would have been St. Francis of
Assisium himself, or St. Anthony of Padua, and the influence
which he exerted over the young Levites of that institution,
during his brief sojourn amongst them, was of a beneficent
and lasting character. His ascetic appearance and great
sanctity, of which his face was but a feeble reflection, made a
great impression upon all who looked upon him. Among the
inmates of All Hallows at that time was Father Mulligan,
whom he was destined to meet not long afterwards in Toronto.
Father Mulligan himself labored for nearly thirty years in
the diocese of Toronto in various capacities, but latterly as
Dean of St. Catherine's, which office he resigned only a year
or two ago owing to ill-health. He is now in Ireland. Father
Mulligan relates that when he saw Father Louis for the first
time at All Hallows, he appeared, notwithstanding the labor-

ious nature of his missionary journeyings, and the severe illness from which he had but recently recovered, to be in a good state of health and likely for many years to continue his labors.

In the meantime Bishop de Charbonnel was renewing his exertions to secure him for the missions in his diocese. Being repeatedly baulked in his endeavors, and finding many difficulties in the way of such a consummation, he at length determined to make application through the Propaganda. The representations he made to that Congregation were of such an urgent and reasonable character that the Propaganda was induced to interest itself in the matter, and finally, through the influence of the Sacred College, Father Louis was ordered to Upper Canada in the beginning of the month of April, 1856. With his characteristic promptitude and obedience he immediately set out for his destination, and such was his diligence that before the month was out he had arrived in Toronto. On the feast of the Ascension he made his first appearance in public at St. Paul's church, Power street, now under the pastoral care of His Lordship, Bishop O'Mahony. He accompanied Mgr. de Charbonnel thither, and sat at his right hand during the celebration of High Mass, and it is related by residents, who were present in the old church (St. Paul's is the oldest Catholic church in Toronto) on that day, that the devout and recollected demeanor of Father Louis had an effect upon the assembled congregation such as is not likely soon to be forgotten. At the conclusion of the Holy Sacrifice the bishop delivered an impressive sermon, a report of which I find in the *Toronto Mirror* of that date. During the course of his sermon the bishop said: " I have the happiness to announce to you the arrival amongst us of a holy monk, the Rev. Louis della Vagna, who comes all the way from Italy, burning with zeal for the salvation of souls. I have known him for nearly eight years; I have sought him for you for the last six; but obstacles continually presented themselves. At length, through the kindness of the Pope and the Propaganda, he is here." On the Sunday following he was inducted into the pastoral charge of St. Mary's church, which was to be the scene of his labors for the rest of his mortal life. "From that day," says the biographer to whom reference has already several times been made, "until the day of his death, he administered the Sacraments and the spiritual consolations of religion with unremitting care and attention. He was literally day and night with his flock. All day long he sought after and promoted their welfare. He visited the sick, comforted the afflicted, and performed deeds of which, till a further manifestation of Divine Providence, we forbear to speak. Youth, laboring under the ills incident to a residence in miasmatic places, almost deprived of the light of heaven, being moved to repentance, knelt at the feet of the holy friar, and went away with the sweet consolations of religion. It was remarkable, too, that they thought no more of death or material darkness, but seeing, believed. The poor man lying on his sick bed, clasped the hand of the good missionary, was enveloped in his warm embrace, and receiving from him the consolations of the Holy Eucharist, was rejoiced, as Father Louis, who knew nothing about medicine, told him that his illness was but temporary, and that he would in a few days be numbered amongst the workmen of the world—a fact which was verified in less time than that mentioned. To recount his prayers, his exhortations, his multiform duties, while pastor of St. Mary's, is impossible. Suffice it to say that while all the day long he worked and preached, it may be said that all the night long he prayed and wept for the faults of his people, and with the deepest humility, while living the life of a saint, he accounted himself the lowliest Christian amongst them."

To these words of a contemporary I now add such testimony as I have been able to glean from people still living, who either resided in St. Mary's parish during Father Louis' time, or came into contact with him in one capacity or another at St. Michael's palace or elsewhere. Notwithstanding the severity of our Canadian winters, the good monk continued to adhere to the strict rule of his order. He fulfilled, after the example of St. Francis, the canonical hours. He rarely slept more than barely sufficed to sustain nature, and frequently during the silent hours of the night would he rise from his hard couch to pray and intercede for his charge. His bed consisted of a rough wooden box, at the bottom of which were laid a few shavings. This box was one in which a statue of the Blessed Virgin had been packed. The statue, which he had himself brought from France, is now in St. Paul's church, but how it came to be transferred thither from St. Mary's I have not been able to ascertain. The room in which this uninviting bed was placed was uncomfortable and inconvenient in the extreme, and utterly devoid of anything approaching ornament. Here, when not engaged in his active pastoral duties, he lived like a recluse, and he would permit no one to enter his retreat. It was only after his death that the facts related came fully to light. As to his food, it was of the coarsest and plainest kind, and was always prepared with his own hands. He kept no servant or housekeeper until within two months of his death, when he was commanded to do so by his bishop. The only assistance he had until then was that of an elderly lady who lived in close proximity to the church, and who, taking compassion on him, would sometimes insist on performing various little offices for him. On one occasion, observing how coarse and uninviting his food was, she prepared a little toast, and taking it to him begged him to eat it. He took it, but no sooner was her back turned than, approaching the small fire he had made in order to cook his food, he burned the toast until it was as black and hard as a coal, and was in the act of eating it in this state when she returned. He rarely ate more than one fair meal in the day, and meat scarcely ever passed his lips. He observed the holy season of Lent by what is known as the "black fast." He washed his own clothes, and anything in the way of repairs about his house or church he executed with his own hands. The Stations of the Cross used in the church for many years after his death were made by him, so that it is evident he must have possessed some skill as a handicraftsman. From his vow of holy poverty nothing could induce him to swerve. So firmly did he adhere to it that he would only receive contributions in money from his people when commanded to do so, and when speaking to the congregation concerning the customary dues, he would point to the unadorned walls of the church, and telling them that his vow of poverty prevented him from possessing more than was sufficient for the necessaries of life, would add : " But all that you can spare is required for beautifying the House of the Lord." " The virtue of humility," it is recorded, " he practised in the highest degree of perfection." We have already seen how, when, years before, Bishop de Charbonnel first urged upon him to come to Canada, he disclaimed the possession of any talents likely to be of great service to this country. His whole career, in fact, was one of continual self-denial. In conversation he never presumed to press his opinions upon others, and he always preferred to defer to the will of another rather than have his own way. " His garments, his plain and simple demeanor, the subdued tone of his actions, the love which he entertained for the company of the poor and simple, were all so many evidences of a humility which was deeply seated within his breast." Nor was the virtue of obedience less firmly engrafted in his soul. In all his actions he bowed to the slightest will of his superiors. I have been informed by a worthy priest, who had many opportunities of observing him, that he carried this virtue to such an extent, that the winter was far advanced before he permitted himself the comfort of a fire in his house, simply because he had not asked or received permission to do so. It was the month of February before he went to Father Soulerin, C. S. B., Superior of St. Michael's College, and, in the absence of the bishop, administrator of the diocese, to ask if he might have a fire in his house. Father Soulerin, of course, at once commanded him, under obedience, to do so. But this was not all. All the winter through he went about the streets clothed in his coarse habit, and with nothing on his feet but sandals. It does not require a very protracted experience of a Canadian winter to appreciate the heroic self-abnegation of the man who could submit himself to an ordeal of this nature.

As a preacher, though not what might be called eloquent, he was wonderfully persuasive, and his words went to the hearts of his hearers. The wonderful saintliness of the man became evident as the words came from his lips. When speaking of Our Lord, or of the Blessed Virgin, or of heaven, the angels, or the saints, he would seem to be consumed with the fire of Divine love; his whole body would become animated; and his face become as if in an ecstacy. He was gifted also with a spirit of deep contemplation, and at all times and in all places he wore an abstracted countenance, as if continually wrapt in meditation. He cherished a particular devotion to St. Francis, and on the occasion of his feast, which falls in October, he had a celebration on a grand scale. He had also a great love for St. Anthony of Padua. But his special characteristic, and that which he possessed in common with the greatest of saints, was love for the Holy Mother of God. In her he had the greatest confidence, and he was accustomed to say that he had never asked anything of her in vain.

From Father Louis' conversation, I am informed by a well-known religious who knew him intimately, it was easy to gather that he had been in close fellowship with very holy persons. There was that about him which betokened a deep insight into the spiritual life; and to his profound human learning he added that which is of a far higher order, i. e.: a mind well disciplined in the "Science of the Saints."

In this manner was spent the short year of Father Louis' pastorate of St. Mary's church. His life was a continual round of labors, often of the most exacting character, and of severe acts of mortification. He was never idle, and he was heard once to remark that if he lost a moment of time he would consider himself a thief. His time, he said, was God's, and as such, he had no right to squander it. Thoroughly and well did he carry out this, the guiding rule of his life, and when death came to him it found him literally in harness.

On Friday, March 13th, 1857, he celebrated the holy sacrifice of the Mass, but, feeling unwell from the effects of the dampness of a newly-plastered wall in the room in which he rested, he was forced to retire for the day. On the day following (Saturday) he grew worse, and towards evening it became evident that his condition was critical. The physician who was called in pronounced his illness to be a severe attack of inflammation of the lungs, brought on, no doubt, by exposure to the severe weather of a Canadian winter. He was immediately removed to St. Michael's Palace, where every possible care and attention was bestowed upon him by the good Sisters of St. Joseph. Notwithstanding their exertions, however, he gradually sank, and on the evening of the 17th of March, the feast of St. Patrick, the glorious Apostle of Ireland, he calmly resigned his soul into the hands of his Creator. The last rites of the Church had been administered to him by Rev. Father Mulligan, who was the only person present when he expired. He seems to have had a presentiment of his death, and was heard several times to predict it. Shortly before this, a well-known physician, a Catholic, had died, and at the Requiem Mass said for the repose of his soul a sermon was preached by Rev. Father Lawrence. When Father Lawrence was about to go into the pulpit for this purpose he was accosted by Father Louis, who had been assisting at the service, with these words : " You are going to preach this man's panegyric now. You will preach my funeral sermon shortly, and *it will be the next one that you will preach*," a prediction which was fulfilled to the letter.

On Wednesday his body was laid out and exposed in the Cathedral, where his parishioners and the people at large were permitted to cast a last look upon him, and to pay that tribute of respect which Catholics never fail to render to the remains of their clergy. St. Michael's Cathedral has been the scene of many remarkable events, but, it is quite safe to say, the scene presented during the two days the body of Father Louis remained within its walls was quite unique in its history. Throughout the whole of Wednesday and Thursday the church was crowded by persons of both sexes and of all ages, who pressed forward with the greatest eagerness that they might touch if only the hem of the holy friar's garment or the bier on which he lay. And so great was the desire of the people to have some memento of one whom they so dearly loved, that, as I am assured by eye-witnesses, the coarse rough

garment in which he was clothed was literally torn from him.
Many had the pieces of his habit thus secured made into
scapulars, with which they were afterwards invested, and, it
seems natural to infer, which they cherished for many years.

Though Father Louis, when not engaged in the active
duties of his pastoral office, lived like a recluse, yet his people
had seen enough of him to know that he was an unusually
holy man. Notwithstanding all his efforts to conceal from
them the rigid austerities which he practised, they had more
than a suspicion of them. But it was not until after his death
that they came fully to know and to realize the extent of his
mortifications. When preparing his body for burial it was
found that he had worn a hair shirt, and, in addition to this,
there was found about his waist, next to his skin, a girdle made
of twisted wire, the wire every here and there being bent in-
wards and cut off as if with a pair of pliers, and the barbs
thus formed protruded into the flesh. Of these barbs there
were thirty-seven in all, and this ingenious instrument of
torture must have been his constant and loving companion for
many years, as the skin about the holes thus formed had
grown quite hard. A lady, to whom I am indebted for many
interesting details concerning Father Louis, had this wire
girdle in her possession for many years, and prized it highly
as a relic, but it was unfortunately lost on occasion of the house
which she occupied being burned down.

After the body had been exposed to the veneration of the
people for two days, it was temporarily placed in one of the
crypts of the Cathedral. Here it remained for only a month,
when, on Thursday, the 16th of April, it was transferred to St.
Mary's church and placed in the spot where it was found
thirty years afterwards. The funeral cortege left the Cathedral at half-past nine o'clock, and passing at slow and solemn
pace through Church and Queen streets, arrived at St. Mary's
at eleven o'clock. The Rev. J. M. Bruyere (since created a
Monsignore, and who, at the age of eighty years, died only a
few days ago in the city of London, of which diocese he was
vicar-general) celebrated Solemn Mass for the dead; Rev.
Father Lee of Brock being deacon and Rev. Father Mulligan

of the Cathedral sub-deacon. The sermon was preached by Rev. Father Walsh (now Bishop of London), and his concluding words are worthy of reproduction here. "You have this day," he said, "given a splendid proof of the chain of affections and sympathies that links priest and people in the Catholic Church; you have demonstrated that the genius of Christianity reigns amongst you and guides your actions; for Christianity has torn down the wall of separation which formerly divided nations and peoples, making of them but one nation and one people. Your late pastor was a Genoese; he was reared beneath the bright skies of Italy; but he was a Christian priest, and as such you have honored him; thus showing that in our Church there is neither Jew nor Gentile, Greek nor barbarian; thus proving that we are all brothers, as being the children of the Holy Church whose spouse is Christ. We may conclude in the words of the prayer recited in the Mass of this day: 'O God, who hast united various nations in the confession of Thy Name, grant that they who are born again by the waters of baptism, may have the same faith in their hearts and the same piety in their actions.'"

I might fittingly conclude with these beautiful and appropriate words of the Bishop of London, but it still remains for me to add a few words about Father Louis' personal appearance. He is described as being rather below the medium height, and of slight, almost attenuated frame. He was never of robust build, but his constant mortifications doubtless made great inroads upon his constitution and hastened his death. But though small of body, he had a clear eye and a quick, penetrating glance, which, it is said, seemed almost to go through one. His complexion was dark, and he wore his beard long, after the manner of the Capuchins. He was always conspicuously neat and tidy. I have said nothing about the miracles which he is said to have wrought, and which can, I believe, be well authenticated, as it is not my province to deal with such matters. Further, it would not be proper to anticipate the judgment of the ecclesiastical authorities, who will, no doubt, take such steps as are necessary to preserve what evidence exists on this point, with a view to the introduction of his cause before the proper tribunal at Rome.

Thus lived Father Louis della Vagna, and thus he died, literally "a stranger in a strange land." Yet not a stranger, because, bearing in mind the words quoted above, as a member of the great Catholic family, he was at home amongst his children of the same faith to whom he had ministered. If he was taken away at the very time when the people of St. Mary's were becoming alive to the possession of "the jewel, set in its rich casing of ascetic brilliants," which Providence had placed in their midst, yet, to quote once more the words of the Bishop of London, "his memory has remained amongst them like a sweet fragrance, 'like the good odor of Christ unto God.'"

THE ORIGIN

OF THE

Flathead Mission of the Rocky Mountains.

[Written by MAJOR EDMOND MALLET, LL.B, and read before the SOCIETY by
FRANCIS X. REUSS, on April 5th, 1888.*]

The Flathead Indians—La Vérendrye, the discoverer of the Rocky
Mountains, meets them at the headwaters of the Missouri—Lewis
and Clark's expeditionary corps encamps with them in the Bitter
Root valley—Patrick Gass' account of them—The fur companies
establish posts in their midst—Religious influence of the Canadian
and Iroquois *voyageurs* and hunters in the Indian country—Visit of
four Indians from the Upper Columbia to Saint Louis—Bishop
Rosati's account of their visit—Protestant accounts two years afterwards create great excitement in missionary circles—Establishment
of a Methodist Mission in Oregon—Presbyterian Missions on the
Upper Columbia—Iroquois—Flatheads visit Saint Louis and ask for
Catholic Missionaries—A deputation *en route* for St. Louis is massacred by the Sioux—The Abbé Blanchet establishes the first Catholic
mission in Oregon—Still another deputation reaches Saint Louis from
the Flatheads—Bishop Rosati promises a missionary—Fr. Barbelin
offers himself for the Rocky Mountain Mission—Fr. De Smet appointed to visit the Indians—He establishes a mission in the Bitter
Root valley—Fr. De Smet, Apostle of the Flatheads.

SOME time ago I had the honor of reading before the
United States Catholic Historical Society of New York

---

* This paper, soon after it was read, was printed in the Washington
Church News, and from that journal the greater part of it was copied
into the *United States Catholic Historical Magazine,* of New York, for
January, 1888, which was not actually published until the middle of May
following.—ED.

a paper on the origin of the Oregon mission,* in which I deplored my inability, for want of time, to enter upon the consideration of the kindred subject of the origin of the Flathead mission of the Rocky Mountains.   The gracious invitation of your Society to read a paper at this meeting has given me an opportunity of making a special study of the subject, and of presenting it to your indulgent appreciation. The task which I imposed upon myself has proved much more difficult than appeared to me at first sight— for I have undertaken to make an original study of the subject, and yet I have boldly, perhaps rashly, undertaken the duty in the interest of researches into the Catholic history of our country.

I.

From time immemorial the Flathead tribe of the Salish nation of Indians has inhabited the Bitter Root valley in the Rocky Mountains.   Its earlier history is enveloped in the obscurity of past ages.

The first white men who saw these Indians were the Chevalier La Vérendrye and his party of Canadian explorers, who discovered the Rocky Mountains in January, 1783, whilst searching for "the great river of the west," by which they hoped to penetrate to the Pacific Ocean.   The Indians were then on their winter hunt for buffaloes on the eastern slope of the mountains, evidently between the headwaters of the Missouri river and its tributary the Yellowstone.   The fall of Canada and of the Illinois country into the power of England, and the cession of Louisiana by Napoleon I. to the American Republic, arrested the onward march of the intrepid Canadian and French pioneers toward the setting sun : it had been reserved to noble representatives of the young American Republic to make alliances of friendship with the tribes of the inmost recesses of the Rocky Mountains, and to follow the

---

* Published in *New York Freeman's Journal*, February 27th, 1886 ; *Proceedings First Annual Meeting U. S. Catholic Historical Society*, 1886 ; *Catholic Sentinel*, Portland, Oreg., 1886 ; and *U. S. Catholic Historical Magazine*, 1887, Vol. I., No. 1.

course of the great Columbia river to the confines of the western sea.

Pending the negotiations which resulted in the transfer by France of the Northwest to the United States, under the title of the Louisiana Purchase, President Jefferson organized an exploring expedition " to trace the Missouri to its source, to cross the highlands, and follow the best water communication which offered itself from thence to the Pacific Ocean."[*] Captain Meriwether Lewis was given command of the expedition, with First Lieutenant William Clark as his associate. Fourteen soldiers of the United States army, nine young men from Kentucky and two Canadian *voyageurs*, all of whom were enlisted for this special service, composed the body of the expeditionary party.   Later it was increased to thirty-two persons, including five Canadian hunters, guides and interpreters, an Indian woman (the wife of one of the interpreters), her young child and a negro servant belonging to Lieutenant Clark.   The expedition left the Mississippi, above St. Louis, Mo., on May 14, 1804, and after wintering at the Mandan villages on the Upper Missouri,—sixty-six years after La Vérendrye visited this Indian tribe at the same place,—reached a village of Shoshones, or Snake Indians, in the Rocky Mountains, on August 13, 1805.

Having left the headwaters of the Jefferson fork of the Missouri and obtained horses at the Shoshone village, located on the headwaters of the Salmon, a tributary of the Snake or Lewis river, which flows into the Columbia, the expedition moved in a northwesterly direction to cross the Bitter Root mountains.   On September 4th they found a party of 430 Flatheads encamped on the Bitter Root river, a tributary of the Flathead. This stream is now known as the St. Mary's river, it having been so named by Father Peter John De Smet, S. J., the Apostle of the Flatheads. As the journals kept by the Lewis and Clark expedition contain the first detailed account ever written as to these Indians, I shall take the liberty of presenting a few extracts from the one which was first given

---

* Letter of Thomas Jefferson to Paul Allen, August 18, 1813, in Lewis and Clark, *History of the Expedition*, &c., Phila., 1814: i., xi.

to the public in book form. Sergeant Patrick Gass—who, by
the way was a Catholic, and who lived long enough to be
known as the last survivor of the expedition,* in his journal
thus mentions the first view the expeditionary corps had of
the Flatheads:

"Wednesday, 4th, ... We kept down the valley about
five miles, and came to the Tussapa band of the Flathead
nation of Indians or a part of them. We found them encamped
on the creek, and we encamped with them.

"Thursday, 5th. This was a fine morning with a great
white frost. The Indian dogs are so hungry and ravenous,
that they eat four or five pair of mockasons last night. We
remained here all day, and recruited our horses to forty and
three colts; and made four or five of this nation chiefs. They
are a very friendly people; have plenty of robes and skins for
covering, and a large stock of horses, some of them very good;
but they have nothing to eat but berries, roots and such
articles of food. This band is on its way over to the Missouri
or Yellowstone river to hunt buffaloes. They are the whitest
Indians I ever saw.

    *   *   *   *   *

* Patrick Gass was of Irish parentage, and was born June 12, 1771, at
Falling Springs, Cumberland county, near the present city of Chambersburg, Franklin Co., Pa. When a young man he worked as a carpenter,
and built a house for James Buchanan, the father of President Buchanan,
whom he always called "Little Jimmy." He saw Gen. Washington in
1794 at Carlisle. In 1803 he was a soldier, stationed at Kaskaskia, and
responded to the call for volunteers for the Lewis and Clark expedition
to Oregon. After the death of Sergeant Floyd, who was buried at
Floyd's Bluff, Iowa, he was promoted sergeant, and was instructed to
keep a journal of the expedition, which journal he prepared for the press,
with the assistance of an Irish school-master, named David McKeehan,
the year after his return from the Pacific Coast. In 1859 his biography
was published by the editor of a country newspaper in a volume entitled, *The Life and Times of Patrick Gass, now sole survivor of the
Overland Expedition to the Pacific under Lewis and Clark, in 1804-5-6;
also a soldier in the War with Geeat Britain, from 1812 to 1815, and
a participant in the Battle of Lundy's Lane, &c.—By J. G. Jacobs.*
Portrait, 12mo., pp. 280. *Wellsburg,* Va.: 1859.

" Monday, 9th, ... At two o'clock we again went forward, and crossed over the Flathead river, about 100 yards wide, and which we called Clark's river. . . .

*　　　*　　　*　　　*　　　*

" Tuesday, 10th, ... At night our hunters came in and had killed five deer. With one of the hunters, three of the Flathead Indians came to our camp. They informed us that the rest of their band was on the Columbia river, about five or six days' journey distant, with pack horses; that two of the Snake nation had stolen some of their horses, and that they were in pursuit of them. We gave them some presents, and one stayed to go over the mountains with us; the other two continued their pursuit."*

The above observations certainly refer to the tribe now known as the Flatheads; but Sergeant Gass, in subsequent pages of his journal, speaks of other bands of Indians under the general appellation of " Flatheads," who were really Nez Percés, Umatillas, Walla Wallas, &c., belonging to a different nation.

The only other observations which Sergeant Gass makes concerning the " Flatheads "—and these appear to apply more particularly to the Nez Percés and other tribes of the Upper Columbia, with whom he confounds them throughout his journal—is the following—he makes a comparison, on the return trip, of the conduct of the women of the Lower Columbia with the conduct of those of the Rocky Mountain region :

" . . . . To the honor of the Flatheads, who live on the west side of the Rocky Mountains and extend some distance down the Columbia, we must mention them as exceptions, as they do not exhibit those loose feelings of carnal desire, nor appear addicted to the common customs of prostitution, and they are the only nation on the whole route where anything like chastity is regarded."†

* Gass, *A Journal of the Voyages and Travels of a Corps of Discovery;* Pittsburgh, 1807, 132–34.

† Gass, *A Journal,* 189, 190.

The account of the Indians given in Capt. Lewis' "Journal," which was published several years after the volume from which I have quoted, is more detailed, and therefore more satisfactory; but want of time and space will not allow me to make citations. He distinguishes between the Flatheads and their neighbors, the Nez Percés, but calls the Flathead tribe the *Ootlashoots*, and their nation, whose correct name is Salish (and which is composed of the Flathead, the Pend d'Oreille, the Cœur d'Alêne, the Chaudière or Colville, the Spokane and the Pisquouse tribes), *Tushepaws*.*

The next accounts of the Flatheads are given in the histories of the expedition fitted out by John Jacob Astor to establish the Pacific Fur Company at the mouth of the Columbia, in 1811–13.† Gabriel Franchère, the first to publish a narrative of these expeditions,—there were two, one by sea from New York, and another overland from St. Louis,—having been mostly employed on the Lower Columbia, does not mention the Flatheads. Indeed, Ross Cox, "the little Irishman," as he was called by his companions, is the only one who gives authentic additional information concerning the interesting tribe whose history I am examining.

The North-West Company, which was waging a disastrous opposition to the Honorable Hudson's Bay Company in the Canadian Northwest, on learning of the departure of the Astor overland expedition, determined to oppose, also, the Pacific

---

* The Lewis and Clark corps did not see the Flatheads on the return journey over the Rocky Mountains in 1806. They, however, learned that they were called *Shalles*, a band of the Tushepahs, by the Nez Percés, or Pierced Noses. They were shown an old road, much beaten by the frequent visits of the Ootlashoots, from the valley of Clark's river to the fishery on the Salmon river, and later they observed a road which led to "a fine extensive valley on Clark's river, where the Shalees or Ootlashoots occasionally reside." Lewis and Clark, *History of the Expedition*, ii., 324, 329.

† Franchère, *Relation*, Montreal, 1820; the same, Eng., *Narrative*, N. Y., 1854; Cox, *Adventures on the Columbia*, N. Y., 1832; Irving, *Astoria*, Phil., 1836; Ross, *Adventures of the first settlers on the Oregon*, Lond., 1849. For a biography and portrait of the Catholic traveler, Gabriel Franchère, see Tassé, *Les Canadiens de l' Ouest*, Montreal, 1878; also the *Catholic Family Annual* for 1887.

Fur Company. Scarcely had the expedition by sea arrived at the mouth of the Columbia, and founded Astoria, when a party of North-Westers appeared beyond the Rocky Mountains and founded a post, named Fort Spokane, on the Upper Columbia. From this point the North-West Company sent adventurous agents to establish posts in the very midst of the various tribes ; among those established was one in the midst of the Flatheads, by a clerk of the company named Finan McDonald. The Pacific Fur Company, to oppose McDonald, immediately sent two of its clerks—Russell Farnham and Ross Cox—with a party of twelve men, mostly Canadians, to the same place. Farnham's post was established on November 10th, 1812, and was abandoned in May, 1813. Cox thus speaks of his visit to the Flatheads on this occasion :

" On the 10th we came to a small village of the Flathead nation, chiefly consisting of old men, women and children. We were quite charmed with their frank and hospitable reception, and their superiority in cleanliness over any of the tribes we had hitherto seen. Their lodges were conical, but very spacious, and were formed by a number of buffalo and moose skins thrown over long poles, in such a manner as to keep them quite dry. The fire was placed in the centre, and the ground all around it was covered with mats and clean skins free from the vermin we felt so annoying at the lower parts of the Columbia. They had a quantity of dried buffalo, of which we purchased a good deal ; and, as they gave us to understand that the great body of their tribe were in the mountains hunting, we determined to stop here, and accordingly set about constructing a log house. . . .

" While the house was being built many of the tribe arrived, from whom we purchased a number of beaver skins. Their hunt had been rather unsuccessful, and attended with disastrous results ; for they informed us that after killing buffalo sufficient for the winter, they were surprised by their old enemies the Blackfeet Indians (whose lands lie on the east side of the Rocky Mountains), who killed several of their warriors and took many prisoners. They appeared much dejected at their misfortunes, and one of the chiefs seemed deeply to

lament the loss of his wife, who had been captured with some
other women by the enemy.   Part of the tribe pitched their
tents some distance above us, at the North-West establishment.
They were passionately fond of tobacco, and while they remained with us never ceased smoking.   Having bought all
their skins, and given them credit for some articles until the
spring, the greater part of them set off to make their winter's
hunt, which their recent misfortunes had protracted to a very
late period.   When the house was finished, I got a good canoe
built of cedar planks, in which I embarked with six men, and
taking leave of Farnham on the 18th of December, descended
the Flathead river on my return to Spokane."*

The war of 1812 proved disastrous to the Pacific Fur Company.   On October 16th, 1813, the company having been
dissolved, its establishments, with the stock on hand, were
transferred to the rival association.   Cox now joined the victorious North-West Company, and was a second time sent to
the Flatheads, where he remained from December 24th, 1813,
to April 4th, 1814.   He devotes a whole chapter of his book
to his observations among the Flatheads during the winter.
Whilst he again shows that these Indians possessed many good
natural qualities, he also demonstrates, notably by suggestions
of hideous and revolting treatment of female prisoners captured
from their traditional enemies, the Blackfeet, that they were at
that time, like all savages, a barbarous and—would I were not
compelled to say it—a brutal people !   Happily for them, and
for the name of humanity, there were already in their midst,
and at the posts which they frequented, men whom the successors of Laval had marked with the sign of the Cross, and
who, like St. John the Baptist, the patron of their nation, were
as a voice in the wilderness crying, " Make straight the way
of the Lord."

II.

The French Canadians were the pioneers of Christianity
and of civilization in the great West.   In the Oregon country

---

* Cox, *Adventures*, 102, 103.

they were the first, with their brethren the Christian Iroquois and Nippissings, to impress their religion upon the benighted Columbian tribes, and also the first to establish permanent agricultural colonies in their midst. They were in every expedition of discovery—in every commercial enterprise. Of the Astor party which went to Oregon on the ship *Tonquin*, they numbered eighteen out of thirty-three persons, and of the overland party, under Hunt, forty out of sixty. They were greatly in the majority in every party of the North-West Company, and the same is true of the Hudson's Bay Company, after it had absorbed its rival organization, in 1821. At this period, and up to the time of the great American emigration, the French was the language of the country among the whites; and the Chinook jargon, which the Canadians formed, was the language used with the Indians. They married the native women, and their solicitude for the religious and moral welfare of their wives and children prompted them to petition for missionaries of their faith. The Oregon mission, founded by the saintly Archbishop Blanchet, had its origin in these petitions; it was also the influence of their respect for religion which produced the Flathead mission of the Rocky Mountains. In their isolation and miseries in the great Fur Land, they never entirely forgot the Christian teaching of their pious mothers, who prayed and wept for them on the banks of the St. Lawrence during their long years of absence. The votive offerings in the old church of St. Anne on the head of the island of Montreal, the crosses at the foot of dangerous rapids on the Ottawa, the Winnipeg, the Saskatchewan, the Athabaska and the Columbia, which missionaries and travelers observed in their voyages through the continent, show that some, at least, of these intrepid hunters, traders and canoemen remained true to the noble traditions of their race.

That the Canadians carried their religion with them into the wilderness will best appear by a few extracts drawn from the early histories of travel in the Indian country. I give them not only to illustrate the influence of the Canadians in that country, but also to delineate the manners and customs of those days in the broad expanse beyond the Rocky Mountains.

Franchère, when returning overland to Canada from Astoria, in 1814, lost two of his companions, named Olivier Roy, *dit* Lapensée, and André Belanger, who were drowned in the Athabaska by the wreck of a canoe in one of the rapids. He thus describes the obsequies of one of them : " Toward evening, in ascending the river . . . . . we found the body of Lapensée. We interred it as decently as we could, and planted at his grave a cross, on which I inscribed, with the point of my knife, his name and the manner and date of his death. . . . The rapid and the point of land where the accident I have described took place, will bear, and bears already, probably, the name of Lapensée."*

Cox thus describes the burial, in the same year, of one of his companions, named Jean-Baptiste Lamoureux, who was killed on the Columbia in an attack by the Indians on a party of the North-West Company :

" We put ashore at a low, sandy point covered with willows and cotton wood, for the purpose of breakfasting and interring the body of L'Amoureux. The men were immediately set to work to dig a grave, into which were lowered the remains of the unfortunate Canadian. A few short prayers were said in French ; and after the earth was thrown in, to a level with the surface, it was covered over with dry sand, in such a manner as to keep the natives in ignorance of the occurrence."†

Captain Bonneville, of the United States Army, engaged in a commercial enterprise, visited the Upper Columbia in 1832, and he recorded the fact in his journal that before missionaries of any denomination had visited the country, the Indians had made progress in Christian observances. These facts have been transmitted to us by Washington Irving :

" Fort Wallah Wallah is surrounded by the tribe of the same name, as well as by the Skynes and the Nez Percés ; who bring to it the furs and peltries collected in their hunting

---

* Franchère, *Narrative*, 306.
† Cox, *Adventures*, 162.

expeditions. The Wallah Wallahs are a degenerate, worn-out tribe. The Nez Percés are the most numerous and tractable of the three tribes just mentioned. Mr. Pambrune * informed Captain Bonneville that he had been at same pains to introduce the Christian religion, in the Roman Catholic form, among them, where it had evidently taken root, but had become altered and modified to suit their peculiar habits of thought and motives of action; retaining, however, the principal points of faith and its entire precepts of morality. The same gentleman had given them a code of laws, to which they conformed with scrupulous fidelity. Polygamy, which once prevailed among them to a great extent, was now rarely indulged. All the crimes denounced by the Christian faith met with a severe punishment among them.

"There certainly appears," continues Irving, "to be a peculiar susceptibility of moral and religious improvement among this tribe, and they would seem to be one of the very, very few that have benefited in morals and manners by an intercouse with white men. The parties which visited them about twenty years previously, in the expedition fitted out by Mr. Astor, complained of their selfishness, their extortion and their thievish propensities. The very reverse of those qualities prevailed among them during the prolonged sojourn of Captain Bonneville."†

Mr. Townsend, a naturalist, who accompanied the trading party with which Rev. Jason Lee, the leader of the first Methodist missionary party to the Columbia, traveled, relates the circumstances of a Canadian's death, and the ceremonies observed in his burial, at the traders' rendezvous on Green river, north of Great Salt Lake, Utah:

"In the evening, a fatal accident happened to a Canadian belonging to Mr. McKay's party. He was running his horse in company with another, when the animals were met in full career by a third rider, and horses and men were thrown with great force to the ground. The Canadian was taken up com-

---

* Pierre Chrysologue Pambrune. For a biography of him see Tassé, *Les Canadiens de l' Ouest*, ii., 299–320.

† Irving, *Adventures of Captain Bonneville*, N. Y., 1860, 300.

pletely senseless and brought to Mr. McKay's lodge, where we were all taking supper. I perceived at once that there was little chance of his life being saved. He had received an injury of the head which had evidently caused concussion of the brain. He was bled copiously and various local remedies were applied, but without success; the poor man died early next morning.

"He was about forty years of age, healthy, active and shrewd, and very much valued by Mr. McKay as a leader in his absence, and as an interpreter among the Indians of the Columbia.

"At noon the body was interred. It was wrapped in a piece of coarse linen, over which was sewed a buffalo robe. The spot selected was about a hundred yards south of the fort, and the funeral was attended by the greater part of the men of both camps. Mr. Lee officiated in performing the ordinary church ceremony, after which a hymn for the repose of the soul of the departed was sung by the Canadians present. The grave is surrounded by a neat palisade of willows, with a black cross erected at the head, on which is carved the name 'Casseau.' "*

Rev. Samuel Parker, a Presbyterian minister, who visited the Rocky Mountains in 1835–36, under the direction of the American Board of Commissioners for Foreign Missions, relates a sad occurrence which corroborates the testimony of Captain Bonneville, and illustrates the Christian simplicity of the Indians. I forbear giving expression to the feeling of indignation, mingled with sadness, which the account of the writer's manifest lack of Christian feeling inspires.

" . . . . The night of our arrival (in the Nez Percés' country) a little girl, of about six or seven years of age, died. The morning of the twelfth they buried her. Everything relating to the ceremony was conducted with great propriety. The grave was dug only about two feet deep. They have no spades, and a sharpened stick was used to loosen the earth,

---

* Townsend, *Narrative of a Journal across the Rocky Mountains,* Amer. Ed., 1839, 92.

and this was removed with the hands; and with their hands they fill up the grave after the body is deposited in it. A mat is laid on the grave, then the body wrapped in its blanket with the child's drinking-cup and spoon, made of horn; then a mat of rushes is spread over the hole and filled up, as above described. In this instance they had prepared a cross to set up at the grave, most probably having been told to do so by some Iroquois Indians, a few of whom, not in the capacity of teachers, but as trappers in the employ of the fur companies, I saw west of the mountains. One grave in the same village had a cross standing over it, which was the only relic of the kind I saw, together with this just named, during my travels in the country. But as I viewed a cross of wood made by men's hands, of no avail to benefit either the dead or the living, and far more likely to operate as a salve to a guilty conscience, or a stepping-stone to idolatry, than to be understood in its spiritual sense to refer to a crucifixion of our sins, I took this, which the Indians had prepared, and broke it to pieces. I then told them we place a stone at the head and foot of the grave, only to mark the place, and without a murmur they cheerfully acquiesced and adopted our custom."*

Rev. Mr. Spalding, another Presbyterian minister, when traveling to the Nez Percés' country in 1836 to select the site of his station, was witness of an edifying scene, an account of which he recorded in his journal and afterward repeated to his society in Boston. I reproduce it:

"October 10, 1836. Marched about fifty-two miles and camped on a considerable stream running into Lewis river. Were greatly affected at night at witnessing the Nez Percés at prayer. They were assembled in a circle on their knees, with an old man, to all appearance, very earnest in prayer. I learned through the interpreter something of the prayer. It appeared to be the Lord's Prayer, with, perhaps, some additions. I inquired of myself, is it not possible that some of these poor benighted heathens are even now numbered in the sheepfold of Christ? and while waiting the dilatory motions

---

* Parker, *Journal of an Exploring Tour*, 1838, 275, 276.

of the Christian church may have been led by an unseen hand to the Lamb of God."*

Rev. Mr. Demers, Mgr. Blanchet's associate, who visited Fort Okanagan in 1840, in a report to his superiors eulogizes a worthy Canadian whom he found in that place. After describing the post, he says:

" . . . . The population there is, however, yearning for God's word. I had the pleasure of meeting there a zealous Christian of the name of Robillard, who had taught the Indians their prayers. This unexpected help saved me much labor in this mission."†

Fr. De Smet, who visited the Flat-Bows,—evidently the band since called Kootenais, of the Pend d'Oreilles tribe,—for the first time in 1845, pays a tribute of praise to another devoted Catholic instructor. He says:

" . . . . Since my arrival among the Indians, the feast of the glorious Assumption of the Blessed Virgin Mary has ever been to me a day of great consolation. I had time to prepare for the celebration of this solemn festival. Thanks be to the instructions and counsels of a brave Canadian, Mr. Berland, who for a long time has resided among them in the quality of trader, I found the little tribe of Arcs-à-plats docile, and in the best disposition to embrace the faith. They had already been instructed in the principal mysteries of religion. They sang canticles in the French and Indian tongues. They number about ninety families. I celebrated the first Mass ever offered in their land, after which ten adults, already advanced in age, and ninety children received baptism . . . . They ardently desire to be taught agriculture, the advantages of which I have explained, and promised to procure the necessary seed and implements of husbandry."‡

It is thus seen that humble Catholic Canadians and Iroquois had instructed the poor Indians of the Upper Columbia in

---

* *Missionary Herald*, 1837, xxxiii., 427.

† *Rapport sur less Missions du diocèse de Québec*, iii., 48.

‡ De Smet, *Oregon Missions* and *Travels in the Rocky Mountains*, 1847, 120.

the elementary principles of Christianity before the advent of missionaries of any denomination into their country, and inspired them with an ardent desire to receive among them those who, being specially sent, could teach them with the plentitude of Apostolic authority.

III.

In the autumn of the year 1831, four Indians from the Upper Columbia country arrived in the city of St. Louis, presumably with one of the fur-trading parties from the Rocky Mountains. The old French town of St. Louis had at that time a population of about 6000 inhabitants, and was the principal frontier city of the West. The appearance of strange Indians on the streets at that place, in those days, was of such common occurrence that our Columbians attracted no special attention, and it was only a long time afterward that they became an object of interest. It would require many ponderous volumes to reproduce all the fanciful stories that have since been written about them and the purpose of their visit to the Mississippi Valley.

The first published statement of the Indians' visit is contained in a letter from Rt. Rev. Joseph Rosati, Bishop of St. Louis, to the editor of the *Annales de l'Association de la Propagation de la Foi*, dated December 31st, 1831. This account, published within a few months after the occurrence to which it relates, is entitled to the greatest weight in establishing the facts in the case. I give a literal translation of so much of the letter as bears upon the subject :

"Some three months ago, four Indians, who live at the other side of the Rocky Mountains, near the Columbia river, arrived in St. Louis. After visiting General Clarke, who, in his celebrated travels, had seen the nation to which they belong and had been well received by them, they came to see our church, and appeared to be exceedingly well pleased with it. Unfortunately there was no one who understood their language. Some time afterward two of them fell dangerously

ill.   I was then absent from St. Louis.   Two of our priests visited them, and the poor Indians seemed delighted with their visit.   They made signs of the cross and other signs which appeared to have some relation to baptism.   This sacrament was administered to them ; they gave expression of their satisfaction.   A little cross was presented to them ; they took it with eagerness, kissed it repeatedly, and it could be taken from them only after their death.   It was truly distressing that they could not be spoken to.   Their remains were carried to the church for the funeral, which was conducted with all the Catholic ceremonies.   The other two attended and acted with great propriety.   They have returned to their country.

" We have since learned from a Canadian, who has crossed the country which they inhabit, that they belong to the nation of *Têtes-Plates* [*Flat-Heads*], which, as with another called the *Pieds-Noirs* [*Black-Feet*], have received some notions of the Catholic religion from two Indians who had been to Canada, and who had related what they had seen, giving a striking description of the beautiful ceremonies of the Catholic worship, and telling them that it was also the religion of the whites ; they have retained what they could of it, and they have learned to make the sign of the cross and to pray. These nations have not yet been corrupted by intercouse with others ; their manners and customs are simple, and they are very numerous.   We have conceived the liveliest desire not to let pass such a good occasion.   Mr. Condamine has offered himself to go to them next spring with another.   In the meantime we shall obtain information on what we have been told, and on the means of travel. . . . ."*

---

* *Annales de L'Association de la Propagation de la Foi,* Lyons, 1832, v., 599, 600.   Compare with *Annales de la Propagation de la Foi,* 1840, xii., 275 ; The same ; Eng., *Annals of the Propagation of the Faith,* Lond., 1839–40, i., 377 ; Verhaegen, in *The Indian Missions under the care of the Missouri Province of the Society of Jesus,* Phila., 1841, 7 ; De Smet, in the same, 25 ; De Smet, *Letters and Sketches, with a Narrative of a Year's Residence among the Indian Tribes of the Rocky Mountains,* Phila., 1843, 16, 91, 173 ; De Smet, *Origin, Progress and Prospects of the Catholic Mission to the Rocky Mountains,* Phila., 1843, 2 ; Shea, *History of the Catholic Missions among the Indian Tribes of the*

The register of burials of the cathedral at St. Louis shows that one of the Indians, Narcissus Keepeellelé, or Pipe Bard, of the Nez Percés tribe of the Chopoweck nation, called Flatheads, aged about forty-four years, who came from the Columbia river beyond the Rocky Mountains, was buried in the Catholic cemetery on October 31st, 1831, Rev. Edmond Saulnier officiating; and that the other, Paul, "Indian of the nation of Flatheads," was buried in the same cemetery on November 17th, 1831, Rev. Benedict Roux officiating.*

From the authorities cited, the following facts are established: 1st, that the visit of the Indians was in 1831; 2d, that one of them, at least, was a Chupunnish, or Nez Percés; and 3d, that if the original purpose of these Indians' visit

---

United States, N. Y., 1855, 458, 467; Blanchet, *Historical Notes and Reminiscences of Early Times in Oregon*, Portland, 1883, 29, 30; Van Rensselaer, "Sketch of the Catholic Church in Montana," *in American Catholic Quarterly Review*, 1887, xii., 493.

Fr. Grassi, of the Rocky Mountain missions, in a lecture delivered a few years ago before the Cercle Catholique of Quebec, gave an entirely new version of the circumstances which induced the Flatheads to send to St. Louis for Catholic missionaries. As the newspaper account of this lecture, which I have before me, may not be entirely reliable, I think it prudent not to state his argument.

*   Le trente et un d'Octobre mil huit cent trente et un, Je
Narcisse   sousigné ai inhumé dans le Cimitière de cette Paroisse le
Keepéellelé corps de Keepéellelé ou Pipe Bard du Nè Percé de la tribu
Sauvage   de Chopoweck Nation appellée tète plate agé d'environs
tète platte quarante quartre ans administré du St. Bapêtme venant
            de la rivière Columbia audela des Rocky Mountains.

EDM. SAULNIER,
PR.

Paul   Le dix Sept de Novembre mil huit cent trente et un, Je,
Sauvage   sousigné ai inhume dans le Cimitière de cette Paroisse le
de la nation corps de Paul Sauvage de la nation des têtes plattes venant
des têtes   de la rivière Columbia audela des Rocky Mountains, ad-
plattes.   ministré du St. Baptême et de l'exrtême onction.

ROUX,
PR.

I am indebted to Very Rev. H. Van der Sanden, Chancellor of the archdiocese of St. Louis, for an official copy of the above certificates from the Registry of Sepultures kept in the cathedral.

was to obtain missionaries, they were missionaries of the Catholic faith—about whom they had heard through the Canadians and Iroquois—that they desired.

Rev. Matthew Condamine, who offered his service to evangelize these Indians, was at that time a member of Bishop Rosati's household at the cathedral, and had special charge of a mission at *Vide Poche*, since known as Carondelet, and now a suburb of St. Louis. He was never to see the Rocky Mountains: it was reserved for another to carry the Cathoic Faith to the Upper Columbia.

Nearly two years after the departure of the two companions of the Indians, whose mortal remains were deposited in the Catholic cemetery of Saint Louis, a sensational account of the visit of the Flatheads, furnished to Mr. G. P. Disosway by Mr. William Walker, the exploring agent of the Wyandotts, appeared in the columns of the *Christian Advocate and Journal*, of New York, the principal organ of the Methodist Episcopal Church. The substance of the account was that a deputation of Flathead chiefs, who had been sent by the council of their nation, had come to Saint Louis from the Columbia river to inquire concerning the true God, about whom they had heard from an adventurer, who was providentially present at one of their idolatrous feasts, and who told them that their mode of worshiping the Great Spirit was displeasing to Him, and that the white men away toward the rising sun had a Book that taught them how to worship God acceptably. General Clark explained the Christian doctrine to them, but, alas! they did not all live to bear home the tidings. Change of climate and mode of life produced diseases, and two of them finished their pilgrimage to Saint Louis. The other two, it was understood, reached their home in safety.*

---

* Holdich, *Life of Willbur Fisk, D. D.*, 1856, 276. Compare with Lee and Frost, *Ten Years in Oregon*, 1844, 110–12; Hines, *Oregon, its History*, 1851 ; Catlin, *Illustration of the manners, customs and conditions of the N. A. Indians*, 10th ed., Lond., 1866, 108, 109; Gray, *History of Oregon*, 1870, 106; Spalding, *Early labors of the missionaries of the A. B. C. F. M. in Oregon* (Senate Ex. Doc. No. 37, 41st Cong. 3d Sess.), 1871, 8; Eells, *History of Indian Missions on the Pacific Coast*, 1882, 18;

On reading this article, Willbur Fisk, D. D., President of the Wesleyan University in Connecticut, sent forth a ringing appeal for missionaries to answer to the Macedonian cry of the Flatheads. The excitement produced by this appeal, and its echo through the press and pulpit, became phenomenal. In a short time the contributions to the missionary societies were more than doubled, and at last their managers were obliged to assign the care of the proposed Flathead mission to the branch societies in Connecticut, to prevent the subject from absorbing the whole of the missionary efforts of the people of that denomination.

In the year 1834, Rev. Jason Lee, of Stanstead, Canada, with his newhew, Rev. Daniel Lee, and three laymen, started from Saint Louis to found a mission under the auspices of the American Methodist Episcopal Church among the Flatheads; but instead of stopping in the Rocky Mountain region, the party proceeded down the Columbia and established their mission in the midst of the French Canadian colony on the Willamette. The reason for this departure from the original plan is related by the historians of the mission, and is interesting in this connection:

" In treating of the occasion in which the Oregon mission originated, it was shown that the supposed claim of the Flathead Indians on the first missionary efforts made in the country were unfounded; and subsequent inquiries had furnished reasons to the missionaries that could not justify even the attempt to commence their mission among them. 1st. The means of subsistence in a region so remote, and so difficult of access, were, to say the least, very doubtful. It is

---

Barrows, *Oregon*, 1884, 103–113; Bancroft, *History of Oregon*, 1886, 54, 55.

After a careful examination of all the authorities, Catholic, Protestant and Secularist, cited in this study, and of numerous notes, based on the testimony of old Flatheads and Nez Percés Indians, reputed wise men among their people, in my possession, I am disposed to conclude that the Indians who visited Saint Louis in 1831 were not Flatheads of the Salish nation, but Nez Percés of the Sahaptin nation! and that their visit was induced by worldly considerations rather than by a desire to inquire or learn of God or religion.

not a small matter to transport all necessary implements and
tools to build houses and raise our provisions six hundred
miles.   2d. The smallness of their number.   Their perpetual wars with the Blackfeet Indians had prevented their
increase, and they were, for their safety, confederated with the
Nez Percés.   3d. Their vicinity to the Blackfeet, as well
the white man's enemy as theirs, and who would fall upon
the abettors of their foes with signal revenge.   4th. A
larger field of usefulness was contemplated as the object of
the mission than the benefiting of a single tribe.   The wants
of the whole country, present and prospective, so far as they
could be, were taken into account, and the hope of meeting
these wants, in the progress of their work, led to the choice of
the Walamet location, as a starting point, a place to stand on,
and the centre of a wide circle of benevolent action."*

In the year 1835, Rev. Samuel Parker, as a missionary, and
Marcus Whitman, M.D., as physician, were sent to the Oregon
country to examine into the condition of the Indians with the
view of establishing missions under the auspices of the
American Board of Commissioners for Foreign Missions.
The Flatheads, hearing that missionaries were crossing the
Laramie plains, Insula, one of the most influential chiefs, with
a party, started to meet them *en route*, but having been
attacked by a war party of Crows, they missed them.   They,
however, overtook them at the rendezvous on Green river,
where a number of other Indians were gathered.   Rev. Mr.
Parker and Dr. Whitman assembled the Flathead and Nez
Percés chiefs, and laid the object of their appointment before
them.   Having received encouragement, especially from the
Nez Percés, the envoys held a conference, and it was determined that Rev. Mr. Parker should continue his tour of exploration, whilst Dr. Whitman should return to the States to
recommend the sending of missionaries immediately.†

Late in the same year Ignace La Mousse, called " Le
Vieux Ignace," an Iroquois from the Caughnawaga mission

---

* Lee and Frost, *Ten Years in Oregon*, 127.

† *Missionary Herald*, 1836, xxxii. 71 ; Parker, *Journal of an Exploring Tour*, 77, 78.

at Saut St. Louis, near Montreal, who had settled with the Flatheads eighteen years before, started for Canada with his two sons to have them baptized, but having learned that there were priests at Saint Louis of Missouri, he changed his course toward the banks of the Mississippi. The two boys, one of them aged only ten years, were instructed and baptized by the Jesuit Fathers at their college and received the Christian names of Charles and Francis Xavier. After going to confession, and receiving a promise from Bishop Rosati that, according to his request, missionaries would be sent to his people as soon as possible, Ignace and his sons returned to their home at the headwaters of the Flathead river.*

In 1836 the American Board of Commissioners for Foreign Missions sent a party, consisting of Rev. H. H. Spalding, missionary, and Dr. Whitman, physician and catechist, with their wives as assistant missionaries, and Mr. W. H. Gray as mechanic, to establish a mission among the Nez Percés and Flatheads. The Nez Percés kept their engagement, made with Dr. Whitman the preceding year, to meet them *en route* to conduct them to their country; but the Flatheads appear to have changed their minds, for they did not meet them; at least no mention is made of them by the missionary party in their reports of their travéls in the Indian country. The missionaries were much tempted to go to Puget Sound, among

---

* *Annales de la Propagation de la Foi*, 1836, ix., 103; The same, 1840, xii., 275. Bishop Rosati's statement that the Iroquois father was killed by the Sioux on his return to the Rocky Mountains is erroneous; it was on another journey to Saint Louis that he was killed, as will appear in subsequent pages of this study.

All the Catholic writers who have heretofore written on the visit of " Le Vieux Ignace " to Saint Louis, give the year 1834 as the date. A letter of Fr. Theodore de Theux, mentioned in the September, 1836, number of the *Annales*, gives the date as the eve of the feast of St. Francis Xavier preceding, and the following transcript from the Baptismal Record kept in the Saint Louis University, kindly furnished me by Very Rev. H. Moeller, its president, establishes 1835 as the correct date. Unfortunately the original record is not signed:

" 1835. 2 Decembris Carolus & Franciscus Xavierius filii legitimi Ignatii, Partus Indiani ex Tribu vulgo Flatheads solemniter baptizati fuerunt."

the real Flatheads, to establish their mission, but they finally established themselves on the Upper Columbia—Rev. Mr. Spalding and wife among the Nez Percés, at Lapwai, and Dr. Whitman and wife among the Cayuses, also of the Sahaptin nation, at Waülatpu.

The story of the Flatheads having induced the missionary movement to the Oregon country, the Presbyterian missionaries of the Upper Columbia were desirous of taking this tribe under their care, and they accordingly sent Mr. Gray back to the States, in 1837, for assistants to enable him to found a station amongst them.* Instead of taking the usual southerly route, he followed that leading through the Bitter Root valley, in order that he might visit the Flatheads in their own country. The Indians appear to have given him no encouragement, for three of them, with another Indian of a neighboring tribe, under the leadership of "Le Vieux Ignace," the Iroquois, started with him and his party for St. Louis, according to Gray himself, "to urge their claims for teachers to come among them."† This, without tergiversation, means "to renew their petitions for Catholic missionaries." But the valiant Iroquois and his Indian companions never reached their destination, as they were all killed by the Sioux on the Platte River!‡ "Thus perished," says a judicious writer, referring

---

* Bancroft, *Hist. of Oregon*, i., 137.

† Gray, *Hist. of Oregon*, 173.

‡ Gray's account of the killing of the Flathead party which traveled with him is as follows: "The party reached Ash Hollow, where they were attacked by about three hundred Sioux warriors, and after fighting for three hours killed some fifteen of them, when the Sioux, by means of a French trader then among them, obtained a parley with Gray and his traveling companions—two young men who had started to go to the States with him. While the Frenchman was in conversation with Gray, the treacherous Sioux made a rush upon the three Flatheads, one Snake and one Iroquois Indian belonging to the party, and killed them. The Frenchman then turned to Gray and told him and his companions they were prisoners. . . ."—Gray, *Hist. of Oregon*, 173.

The Flathead tradition on the massacre of their brethren is as follows: "Three Flatheads, a Nez Percés and an Iroquois Indian, whose son named François La Mousse is still living in the Bitter Root valley, among the Flatheads, started again for St. Louis, but by a misunder-

to old Ignatius, " he who might justly be called the Apostle
of the Flatheads, and through them of many of the Indian
tribes of the Rocky Mountains.*"

In the following year Very Rev. Francis Norbertus Blanchet, Vicar-General to the Bishop of Quebec, with Rev.
Modestus Demers, his associate, crossed the Rocky Mountains through the Athabaska pass, and descended the Columbia river to Fort Vancouver, where they established the first
Catholic mission in the Oregon country. When passing Fort
Colville, on November 6th, 1838, a large number of Colvilles,
Pend d'Oreilles, Spokanes and Pisquouses of the Salish nation,
of which the Flatheads are the principal tribe, flocked to see
the " French Chiefs," of whose coming they had been advised by an express which had come to the fort a week before.
The Abbé Blanchet assembled the Indians several times during his stay of three days at the fort, instructing them in the
elements of religion and coufirming them in their good dispo-
sitions. At Fort Walla Walla the Cayuse and Walla Walla
tribes also assembled to see the Catholic missionaries. The
Sacrifice of the Mass was offered up in their presence, after
which the Indians made a formal call on the Abbé Blanchet.

Strange as it may seem, in the summer of 1839 the Flatheads had not heard of the arrival of the Canadian missionaries, who, it is true, had passed a considerable distance to the

---

standing they were all killed by the Sioux not far from Fort Laramie.
When the delegation reached Fort Laramie, a Protestant minister—so
the report runs—whom they met there, joined them. They met with a
scouting party of Sioux, who, inquiring from the white man, the minister,
what tribes the Indians belonged to, and hearing from him that they
were Snake Indians, they determined to kill them. The minister thinking that the Sioux were at enmity with the Flatheads and friendly with
the Snake Indians, or he himself having been mistaken about them, was
the cause of their death. The Iroquois being dressed like a white man,
the Sioux told him to get out of the way, that they would not kill him.
The brave Iroquois answered that he would not abandon his friends,
and if they would not let his companions go free he was willing to share
their fate and die with them. They were thus all killed." *Historical
Notes on St. Mary's Mission in the Bitter Root Valley.* MS., 2-4.

* Van Rensselaer, "Sketch of the Catholic Church in Montana,"
in *Amer. Cath. Qr. Rev.*, xii., 494.

north and west of their country. Constant in their devotion to the Christian principles received from their fathers, and persevering in their purpose to obtain missionaries of their faith for their adopted country, two other Iroquois, named Pierre and "Le Jeune Ignace," determined to undertake the dangerous journey to St. Louis, to prevail upon the bishop, if possible, to send the missionaries promised to their chief, who had nobly laid down his life for the Faith and for his compatriots. The devotion of the Indians touched the paternal heart of the good bishop, and he gave them a positive promise that a missionary would visit them in the following spring. In a letter to the Father-General of the Society of Jesus in Rome, dated October 20th, 1839, Bishop Rosati relates the facts connected with the visit of the Indians, and of his determination to establish a mission in their country. After reviewing the several efforts made by the Flatheads, or rather the Iroquois, to obtain missionaries, he concludes:

" Finally a third deputation has arrived at St. Louis, after a long journey of three months. It is composed of two Christian Iroquois; these Indians, who know how to speak French, have edified us by their truly exemplary conduct, and interested us by their conversation. The fathers of the college have heard their confessions, and to-day they approached the Holy Table at my Mass, in the Cathedral church. I afterward administered the sacrament of Confirmation to them, and in an address which preceded and followed the ceremony I rejoiced with them in their happiness, and gave them hopes of soon having a priest.

" They will depart to-morrow : one of them will carry the good news promptly to the Flatheads ; the other will spend the winter at the mouth of Bear river, and in the spring he will continue his journey with the missionary whom we will send them. Of the twenty-four Iroquois who formerly emigrated from Canada, only four are still living. Not only have they planted the Faith in those wild countries, but they have besides defended it against the encroachments of the Protestant ministers. When these pretended missionaries presented themselves among them, our good Catholics refused to receive

them : ' These are not the priests about whom we have spoken
to you,' they would say to the Flatheads, ' these are not the
long, black-robed priests who have no wives, who say Mass,
who carry the crucifix with them !'   For the love of God, my
Very Rev. Father, do not abandon these souls !"*

IV.

In the year 1835 the Second Provincial Council of Baltimore confided the Indian missions of the country to the
Society of Jesus, and the Fathers of the province of Missouri
at once prepared to establish missions among the tribes west
of the Mississippi.   After making a tour to the Atlantic
cities to obtain funds for the purpose, Rev. Charles Felix Van
Quickenborne, S. J., superior, started westward from Saint
Louis, and founded a mission among the Kickapoos, near the
present Fort Leavenworth, in Kansas.   This was in 1836, and
in his travels the missionary found at the confluence of the
Kansas and Missouri rivers twelve families who had recently
come from the Rocky Mountains with the intention of settling
near the missions, in order that they might have their marriages blessed by the Church and find facilities for saving their
souls.   Three of the men were Canadians, and they informed
Fr. Van Quickenborne that the Flatheads had been instructed
by a Canadian doctor, and that they observed many Christian
usages, such as the sanctification of the Lord's Day, abstinence, and the fasts prescribed by the Church, and they desired
a priest to instruct them in religion.   With these Indians,
they said, were a large number of Catholic Algonquins and
Iroquois, who had come from Canada ; they had married
Flathead women, and they now wished to have their marriages
blessed and their children baptized.   The good missionary,
relating these facts to another Father of his Order, in Europe,
referred to the annual trips of a steam vessel from Saint Louis
to the headwaters of the Missouri, and added that he regarded it a duty to send some one to encourage the Indians

---

* *Annales de la Prop.*, xii., 275–77.

in their good, commendable desires until something more could be done for them. " I most willingly offer to go myself on this holy expedition," he said with generous enthusiasm.*

At about this time another worthy son of Loyola, then a young priest, whose name is now a household word, synonymous with virtue and charity, in this goodly city of Philadelphia, offered his services to carry the standard of the Cross to the faithful Iroquois and the devoted Flatheads in the Rocky Mountains. I knew him ; he was my friend ; and I utter his name with reverence—Felix Joseph Barbelin,—" Father " Barbelin, as we all affectionately called him.

Like the Rev. Mr. Condamine and the Rev. Fr. Van Quickenborne, who in their charity ardently desired to carry the Gospel to the Flatheads, Father Barbelin was never to see these Indians in their mountain home. In a letter to his brother in France, written in the year 1864, Father Barbelin, recurring to events of by-gone days, said, in his characteristic French way of expressing himself:

" Twenty-seven or twenty-eight years ago I offered myself for the Indians of the Rocky Mountains, but our Rev. Father Provincial told me that he had other Indians, and he sent me to Philadelphia to help Fr. Ryder, who had charge of St. Joseph's."† Fortunate Indians of Philadelphia, to have had such a missionary !

In the year 1837 Rev. Peter John De Smet, S. J., who five years before had withdrawn from the American Mission to return to his home in French Flanders on account of ill health, returned to the United States ; and in the following year he established a mission among the Pottawatomies, then located on the Missouri river, near the present city of Omaha. He was preparing to advance his missionary work farther west, into the country of the Sioux, when the Iroquois, Pierre and " Le Jeune Ignace," appeared in Saint Louis to again press the claims of the Flatheads for missionaries. The bishop, unable to longer delay complying with their petition, after

---

* *Annales de la Prop.*, x., 144, 145.

† Donnelly, *A Memoir of Father Felix Joseph Barbelin, S. J.*, Phila., 1886, 359.

consulting with the vice-provincial of the Society of Jesus, appointed Fr. De Smet to visit the Flathead country to ascertain the true condition of affairs in that region, and to lay the foundations for a mission, if in his judgment such an enterprise could be undertaken with any degree of success.

It had been designed by the superior of the Jesuits to send two Fathers on the tour of exploration to the Rocky Mountains; but so poor was the diocese of Saint Louis and the Missouri Province of the Society of Jesus at that time that the necessary amount of $1000 for an outfit could not be secured, even through the medium of a loan. It was accordingly determined to send Fr. De Smet without a companion.*

Fr. De Smet undertook his tour of exploration in the spring, starting from Saint Louis on April 5th, and from Westport, near Kansas City, on April 30, 1840. Here he joined the annual expedition of the American Fur Company to the rendezvous on Green river, which arrived at that place June 30th. An escort of Flathead warriors was there awaiting him. On Sunday, July 5th, the day before his departure for the Flathead camp, Fr. De Smet celebrated the holy sacrifice of the Mass *sub dio*, on an altar placed on an elevation in the prairie, around which boughs and garlands of wild flowers had been planted in the form of a large semi-circle. The missionary addressed the motley crowd of attendants in French and English, and also spoke to the Flatheads and Snakes through interpreters. The Canadians sang a portion of the Mass in Latin, and canticles in French, whilst the Indians chanted hymns in their native tongues, and for a long time afterward the place where the edifying ceremony was held was known as *La prairie de la Messe*.† On the following day Fr. De Smet bade adieu to his companions of the plains, and with his Indian escort and a dozen Canadian hunters, who followed him to have an opportunity of going to their religious duties, started northward through the mountains in the direction of the headwaters of the Henry fork of the Snake or Lewis

---

* *Indian Missions*, 8.

† De Smet, Letter to Fr. Barbelin, in *Indian Missions*, 23; also in his *Letters and Sketches*, 15.

river. After journeying eight days through mountain defiles
and rugged valleys, infested by bands of warlike Blackfeet
and Crows, the party arrived safely in the camp of the Flatheads and Pend d'Oreilles in the beautiful valley called Pierre's
Hole, situated north of the group of peaks known as the
Trois Tétons.

"Immediately the whole village was in commotion," related
Fr. De Smet to his friend Fr. Barbelin, in a letter describing
his reception; "men, women and children all came to meet
me and shake hands, and I was conducted in triumph to the
lodge of the great chief, Tjolizhitzay (the Big-face). He has
the appearance of an old patriarch. Surrounded by the principal chiefs of the two tribes and the most renowned warriors,
he thus addressed me : 'This day Kyleeyou (the Great Spirit)
has accomplished our wishes, and our hearts are swelled with
joy. Our desire to be instructed was so great that three times
had we deputed our people to the Great Black-gown in St.
Louis to obtain a father. Now, father, speak, and we will
comply with all you will tell us. Show us the road we have
to follow to come to the place where the Great Spirit resides.'
Then he resigned his authority to me, but I replied that he
mistook the object of my coming among them; that I had
no other object in view but their spiritual welfare, that with
respect to temporal affairs they should remain as they were,
till circumstances should allow them to settle in a permanent
spot. Afterwards we deliberated on the hours proper for their
spiritual exercises and instructions. One of the chiefs brought
me a bell with which I might give the signal.

"The same evening about 2000 persons were assembled
before my lodge to recite night prayers in common. I told
them the result of my conference with the chiefs; of the plan
of instructions which I intended to pursue, and with what disposition they ought to assist at them, etc. Night prayers
having been said, a solemn canticle of praise, of their own
composition, was sung by these children of the mountains, to
the Author of their being. It would be impossible for me to
describe the emotions I felt at this moment. I wept for joy,
and admired the marvelous ways of that kind Providence

who, in His infinite mercy, had deigned to depute me to this poor people, to announce to them the glad tidings of salvation."*

Two months were spent by Father De Smet in the camp, living, like the Indians, on the products of the chase. During this time he prepared six hundred persons for baptism and instructed two thousand. After describing the every-day life of the Indians during his stay, he exclaims: "Who would not think that this could only be found in a well-ordered religious community, and yet it is among Indians in the defiles and valleys of the Rocky Mountains!"

On the eve of the new year, Father De Smet was back at the University of St. Louis, having returned through the Blackfeet, Crow and Sioux country, instead of by the more southern route.

Immediately after his return, a special appeal was made for the necessary funds to establish a permanent mission in the Flathead country, and through the exertions of zealous Fathers of the Society of Jesus, among whom Father Barbelin was conspicuous, a sufficient amount was realized to send a well-appointed missionary party. It consisted of Father De Smet, Father Nicholas Point, a Breton; Father Gregory Mengarin, a Roman; Brother Joseph Specht, an Alsacian; and Brother Charles Huet and Brother William Claessens, Belgians, all members of the Society of Jesus. They left St. Louis by steamer on April 30th, 1841, and after seven days' journey on the bosom of the Missouri arrived at Westport, where they remained until May 10th, awaiting the formation of a party of emigrants which was to travel overland to California. All preparations having been made, the caravan took up its march across the country to the Platte river, whose banks were followed for more than two months.

The Flatheads had promised Father De Smet to send a delegation to meet him at the foot of the Wind River Mountains on July 1st, but it was not until after the middle of the month that the caravan reached the height of lands between

---

* De Smet, Letter to Fr. Barbelin, in *Indian Missions*, 24, 25.

the Sweet Water and Green rivers—the first a tributary of the Platte, which flows eastward into the Missouri, and the latter a tributary of the Colorado of the West, which flows southward into the Gulf of California. The caravan crossed the divide at the South Pass, and John Gray, a noted mountain-man, was sent to a hunters' camp, some distance away, to inform the Indian and Metis hunters of the arrival of the missionaries. The camp of ten lodges was already on the march toward Green river, when Father De Smet sent a second messenger to the hunters to request Gabriel Prud 'homme, a Canadian Metis, who had been adopted by the Flatheads, and Charles Lamousse, the eldest of the two Iroquois youths who were baptized in St. Louis, to meet the Fathers before reaching the rendezvous. On the following day the caravan arrived at Green river, and soon afterward the hunters also arrived. Here it was learned that the Indian escort had waited for the Fathers until July 16th, when it had been compelled to go on a hunt, their provisions having become completely exhausted.

The missionaries had a wagon and four carts with them, but their horses were so jaded that it was necessary to procure new ones before undertaking the journey through the mountainous region separating them from the Jefferson fork of the Missouri, where the Flatheads were encamped. It was accordingly determined that Gabriel and another horseman should go to the place where the Flatheads were hunting, four hundred miles away, for fresh horses, while François Saxa, or Lamousse, would accompany Father De Smet to Fort Hall, a post of the Hudson Bay Company, situated on the Snake or Lewis river, to purchase supplies for the journey.

After traveling several days through the Bear river valley and the plains watered by the Portneuf, Father De Smet arrived at Fort Hall on the 15th or 16th of August. At about the time that the caravan reached the fort, Gabriel arrived with a small delegation of Flatheads under an old chief named Wistelpo, with horses to conduct the missionary party to the Indian camp. On August 19th, leave was taken of the emigrants, and the missionaries wended their way up the Snake river and across the mountains to a large plain through which passes the Beaver Head river, one of the sources of the Missouri in the Rocky Mountains. Here, on August 30th, they were met by a larger delegation of Flatheads, under chief Ensyla,* who came to escort them to the camp on the Beaver Head, the tribe being on the march toward the plains, on the eastern slope of the mountains, on their summer hunt for buffaloes. Great was the joy of the Fathers and of the Indians at being at last united! After a few days spent in happy intercourse, the missionaries, with an escort of a few lodges of Flatheads, started for the Rocky Mountains, whilst the Indians, promising to join the Fathers in the autumn at one of two places agreed upon for the mission in the Bitter Root valley, went on their hunt in the plains between the Yellow Stone and the Missouri.†

Father De Smet with his party now ascended the slope of the mountains, recrossed the divide through Deer Lodge pass, and descended into the prairie below. They now followed Hell Gate river—to which the Fathers gave the name of St. Ignatius—and on September 24th they arrived at the stream upon whose banks they were to found their first mission. This was the Bitter Root river—a tributary of the Flathead or Clark river, which flows in a northwesterly direction until it falls into the great Columbia of Oregon. Several days were spent in following the stream toward its source, until the place designated by the Indians was reached. Here, on October 3d, 1841, the feast of the Holy Rosary, Father De Smet, with his heroic band of missionaries, in the presence of a few Canadians, Iroquois and Flatheads, planted a cross on the river bank, and after chanting the " Vexilla Regis" took solemn possession of the surrounding country in the name of the Christian religion, and laid the foundation of the first Catholic church in Montana, and in the Upper Columbia country. To

---

* This, evidently, is the Flathead chief heretofore mentioned as "Insula" in connection with Rev. Mr. Parker's conference with the Indians, at the rendezvous on Green river in 1835, as related on page 193 of this volume.—ED.

† *Historical Notes on St. Mary's Mission in the Bitter Root Valley.* MS., 8, 9.

the river, the highest peak overlooking the valley, and the
mission, was given the name of St. Mary.* Thus, ten years
after the visit of the four Columbian Indians to St. Louis of
Missouri, was established the Flathead mission of the Rocky
Mountains.

V.

Nearly fifty years have passed since Fr. De Smet and his
noble band of Jesuit missionaries planted the standard of the
Christian religion in the wilderness under the protection of
Mary, the Mother of Christ. What wondrous changes have
taken place in the intervening time! From that one lonely
mission have sprung a dozen others, not only among the
several tribes of the Salish nation, but also among the fierce
Blackfeet and Crows, the traditional enemies of the Flatheads!
Then, the place is no longer a boundless waste, for the iron
horse now passes with lightning speed through the Bitter
Root valley, stopping at intervals to receive passengers at the
station of De Smet. But the great Black-robe is no longer
there! his mortal remains sleep on the banks of the Mississippi, and his monument, as Evangelizer and Pacificator of the
Indians, stands in his native city in far-off Belgium. All has
changed, save the fame of the founders of the mission which
proclaims him the Apostle of the Rocky Mountains.

---

* De Smet, *Origin, Progress and Prospects of the Catholic Mission*, 5.
Historical Notes on St. Mary's Mission, MS., 10.

HISTORY OF THE CHURCH

OF

Our Lady of Perpetual Succor in Boston.

[Written for the AMERICAN CATHOLIC HISTORICAL SOCIETY OF PHILADEL-
PHIA, BY REV. CHARLES W. CURRIER, C. SS. R.]

A BEAUTIFUL church in Romanesque style, dedicated to
Our Lady of Perpetual Help, and in charge of the Redemptorist Fathers, has of late years been erected in the city of
Boston, in that portion of it known as Roxbury. The present
paper presents to the reader a brief history of said church and
the adjoining building, the dwelling of the Redemptorists.

Roxbury, Massachusetts, was settled as early as 1630, under
the lead of William Pynchon. It was the sixth town incorporated in Massachusetts, and until 1793 formed a part of the
county of Suffolk. It lay to the west of Boston, and was
bounded on the north by Muddy river (now Brookline) and
Newton; Dedham lay on the west, and Dorchester on the
south. Its name is derived from its rocky and uneven surface, and was originally spelled Rocksbury or Rocksborough.
One of its principal features is the conglomerate or pudding-
stone with which it abounds. Roxbury was united to the
city of Boston in 1868.

"Roxbury," says Drake, "is a mother of towns, as many
as fifteen prosperous New England communities, including the
flourishing cities of Springfield and Worcester, having been
founded or largely settled by her citizens. She can fairly

claim to be the banner town of the Revolutionary war, furnishing to it three companies of minute-men at Lexington, one of which was the first that was raised for the defence of American liberty, and having also given birth to three of the generals of the Revolutionary army. She played a promnent part in the siege of Boston, and was greatly injured both by friend and foe. No less than ten of the governors of Massachusetts have been natives or residents of Roxbury."*

The old house on Tremont street, now in possession of the Redemptorists, one of the oldest historic mansions in Roxbury, was built about the year 1723 by Col. Francis Brinley, upon the estate of eighty acres formerly Palsgrave Alcock's. It was styled by its owner Datchet House, having been modelled after the family-seat of the Brinley's at Datchet, in England. Col. Francis Brinley, a native of London, came to Newport, Rhode Island, in 1710, at the invitation of his grandfather, Francis Brinley. He died November 27th, 1765, and is buried at King's Chapel, in Boston. Rev. William Gordon, minister of the third church in Roxbury in 1772, and chaplain to the Provincial Congress of Massachusetts, resided at this house until the parsonage at Jamaica Plains had been prepared for him. He is the author of a work on the "History of the Rise, Progress and Establishment of the Independence of the United States of America." He died in England in 1807. In 1773 the old house came into possession of Robert Pierpont, merchant, member of the Boston Committee of Correspondence and Commissary of Prisoners during the war of the Revolution.†

A niece of Mr. Robert Pierpont, who, it appears, owned, conjointly with her uncle, "Pierpont Castle," as the old mansion is said to have been called, married Captain Gustavus Fellowes. She visited Europe and was presented at the Court of St. James, where she was called the beautiful American.

The mansion was remarkable for the magnificence of its structure. Tradition speaks of an apartment in it hung with blue damask, known as the blue chamber. A descendant

---

* Francis S. Drake, in the "Memorial History of Boston."
† Drake's Roxbury.

of Captain Fellowes, Emily Pierpont de Lesdernier, speaks
thus of it:

"It was situated in the midst of a large domain of park
and wooded hills, and presented a picture of grandeur and
stateliness not common in the New World. There were
colonnades and a vestibule whose massive mahogany doors,
studded with silver, opened into a wide hall, where tessellated
floors sparkled under the light of a lofty dome of richly-
painted glass. Underneath the dome two cherubs, carved in
wood, extended their wings, and so formed the centre, from
which an immense chandelier of cut-glass depended. Upon
the floor beneath the dome there stood a marble column, and
around it ran a divan formed of cushions covered with satin
of Damascus, of gorgeous coloring. Large mirrors with
ebony frames filled the spaces between the stair-cases, at
either side of the hall of entrance. All the paneling and
woodwork consisted of elaborate carving done abroad, and
made to fit every part of the mansion where such ornamenta-
tion was required. Exquisite combinations of painted birds
and friuits and flowers abounded everywhere, in rich contrast
with the delicate blue tint that prevailed upon the lofty walls.

"The state rooms were covered with Persian carpets, and
hung with tapestries of gold and silver, arranged after some
graceful artistic foreign fashion."*

The "Memorial History of Boston" calls this description
rather extravagant. The writer may have, perhaps, allowed
some liberty to imagination, although, in the preface of her
work, she says that her book has the merit of truth. She
also says that "traditions of the princely grandeur of the
ancient home have often been recalled at family reunions."
Views of the place in Lossing's "Field-Book of the War of
1812," and in Drake's "Town of Roxbury," hardly represent
this magnificence.

During the siege of Boston, in 1776, General Ward, who
commanded the right wing of the American army under
Washington, had his headquarters in the Brinley house, at

---

* Fannie St. John, by Emily P. de Lesdernier.

Roxbury.* At a short distance from it, on Parker Hill, were encampedd the Connecticut regiments of Spencer, Huntingdon and Parsons. In the room to the right of the hall, the reception-room, were held the councils of officers at which Washington presided, and where the details of the occupation of Dorchester Heights were arranged. At a council of war held there, March 16th, 1776, it was determined that if Boston were not evacuated the next day, Nork's Hill, in South Boston, should be fortified.† The evacuation of Boston by the British soon followed. It is said that Washington was entertained at a banquet in this house after the battle of Bunker Hill.

Brinley Place passed into the hands of General Henry Dearborn in 1809. General Dearborn was born in Hampton, New Hampshire, in 1751. He served in the war of the Revolution and in that of 1812, and was Collector of the Port of Boston and Secretary of War under Jefferson. In 1821 the West Point cadets, two hundred and fifty in number, marched from West Point to Boston to visit General Dearborn; they encamped on the hill opposite Brinley Place, and a day or two after their arrival partook of a sumptuous repast in the garden to the rear of the building. General Dearborn died in 1829, and was buried on the little hill to the left of the mansion, in front of where the church now stands. The body was afterwards removed. Dearborn, when Collector of the Port, was accustomed to entertain many and distinguished guests in this house. His son, General H. A. T. Dearborn, born in 1783, continued to reside here until his removal to Hawthorne cottage in Bartlett street. He died in 1851.‡

After the events of August 11th, 1834, when the Ursuline convent on Mount Benedict, Charlestown, Massachusetts, was burned down by a cowardly mob, thus attaching a stain to the history of Massachusetts that time cannot efface, the homeless sisters, having been first the guests of the Sisters of Charity in Boston, took refuge at Brinley Place. Even here

---

* Memorial History, p. 116.
† Drake's Roxbury.   ‡ Drake.

the poor sisters were not left in peace, and threats were made of burning this refuge of defenceless women. There was not a little excitement among the better classes of citizens of Roxbury, who organized a volunteer patrol to protect them. Messrs. Jno. J. Clarke, Ebenezer Seaves and other citizens distinguished themselves by their efforts to defend the sisters. General Bradley patrolled the premises with gun in hand, and Captain Spooner's military company were also on guard. It is said that several of the men who aided in the burning of the convent were singularly punished by God. The man who took the chalice from the convent committed suicide a few days after the event. Two others were hanged for a subsequent burning of a dwelling in Boston. Seven were drowned within two years after the event, and three of the suspected incendiaries were blown up by powder within the three following years. Drake, in his " Town of Roxbury," says that the Ursuline sisters remained a year at the Brinley Place in Roxbury. A young consumptive, Sister St. Mary, expired in this house eleven days after their arrival.

Subsequently the place became the property of Mr. Samuel S. Lewis, when he was agent for the Cunard steamers. The commanders of the steamers, mostly officers of the English navy, and many of the passengers, were frequently guests at the house at this time, among others Charles Dickens on his first visit to this country. In 1860 the house was occupied as a summer boarding-house by Mrs. Sheppard.*

Mr. Bumstead having become owner of the old property, a sub-cellar was accidently discovered that had not been known since Col. Brinley's time. It had been the wine cellar, and still contained several empty casks. According to an anecdote, the Colonel once gave a thrashing in this place to two negroes for stealing his wine. Mr. Bumstead's daughter having married Mr. Wells, of New York, it became the latter's property. For some time it formed a pleasure resort, and, with the adjoining grounds, was called " The Franklin Gardens." It had suffered many changes at the hands of its

---

* Lossing's Field-Book.

various owners, and almost every vestige of its former magnificence had been lost.

The first step toward bringing the Redemptorist Fathers to Roxbury was taken by Rev. James Healy, then pastor of St. James' church, now Bishop of Portland. The mission given in his church, in May, 1869, was attended with such great success that he proposed to Rev. W. Wayrich, superior of the mission, the matter of selecting this place for a mission church. Archbishop Williams approved of the idea, and Father Wayrich entered upon the work with great zeal.

Finally, on the 25th of September, 1869, the estate was purchased from Mr. Wells by Rev. Joseph Helmpraecht, Provincial of the Redemptorists. This Father celebrated his silver jubilee Mass in the house on Christmas Day, 1870.

The Redemptorist Fathers began to dwell in the old mansion in 1871. The first Father, Rev. A. Kreis, arrived there on January 14th of that year. He had a few days before been preceded by Brothers Denis and Seraphicus, and was soon followed by Fathers William O'Connor, Joseph Wissel, Timothy Enright, Louis Cook, Frank Muller and Brother Christopher. The first superior of the house was Father Wissel.

Meanwhile a wooden church had been erected on the east side of the building, forming a rectangle with it. The church was blessed on January 29th, 1871, by Rev. Joseph Wissel, and dedicated to Our Lady of Perpetual Succor. It was, not including the space occupied by the altar, 100 feet long and 48 feet wide.

Two months later a new member was added to the community in the person of Rev. William Gross, now Archbishop of Oregon City.

On May 28th, the Feast of Pentecost, the picture of Our Lady of Perpetual Succor was solemnly enthroned over the high altar. It was carried in procession from the house to the church amidst an immense concourse of people. The effect produced on the multitude was marvellous; so much so that even a few were seen to shed tears. Father Wissel preached on the occasion. About this time Our Blessed Lady began that long, uninterrupted chain of extraordinary favors granted to her clients that have continued down to the present time.

Of the many extraordinary cures that were wrought, we will relate that of Louisa Julia Kohles. It happened on May 29th, 1871. This child had been ill from her birth, and was much troubled with a great shortness of breath, somewhat resembling asthma. When she was a year and a half old the disease settled in her leg. This member was operated on, and pieces of bone were extracted. The opening of the leg relieved the shortness of breath, but otherwise the child's sufferings were great. During the triduum celebrated in the church in honor of Our Lady of Perpetual Help, Mrs. Kohles began a novena for the cure of her child. On the evening of the first day of the novena she heard Father O'Connor relate that a certain soldier had performed his devotions, during a novena, prostrate on the ground; this impressed her, and she proposed to her family to do the same? Accordingly, on the second morning, they said the prayers at home, all lying prostrate. What was their astonishment when little Louisa was seen doing the same. After the prayers the child arose, stood erect, though she could not stand before, and cried out: Mamma, mamma! She pushed her mother away when she ran to take her up, and sat on the floor again and laughed. The night following she suffered more than ever, so that she appeared to be dying. In the morning, when her mother had undressed the leg, before she had time to look at the wound, the little one had tossed away the poultice that was prepared; she escaped from her mother and began to run around the table for about an hour. When the leg was examined it was found to be perfectly healed; the projecting bone had disappeared, and nothing remained of the ailment save the scars that exist to the present day as they were on the morning of the cure. When a short time after she visited the church with her mother, who knelt in prayer before a statue of the *Mater Dolorosa*, the little one, looking at the statue of Our Lord on His Mother's knee, exclaimed: "Face like papa, foot like mine." And indeed the place of the wound on Our Lord's foot resembled very much the scar on her own.

Louisa Kohler is now a young lady of eighteen, and has enjoyed good health since the day she received it from Our Lady of Perpetual Help.

On July 11th, 1871, Rev. William Gross succeeded Father Wissel as superior of the house. Father Kreis was sent to New York, and Father Rathke appointed to take his place in Boston. In the same month a triduum was celebrated in honor of St. Alphonsus, who had in the same year been proclaimed Doctor of the Church.

In January, 1872, a mission was given in the church of Our Lady of Perpetual Help, and in the following month the Anchor of Eternity of the Holy Family was erected. The year after, June 1st, 1873, the same confraternity was also established for women.

In 1873 an extrordinary event occurred: Rev. William Gross was appointed Bishop of Savannah, Georgia. Father Petsch was appointed to succeed him. The Feast of Corpus Christi was this year celebrated with extraordinary splendor; the Blessed Sacrament was carried in procession through the garden, and it is supposed that about 8000 persons were present.

On the 22d of October the relics of the holy martyr St. Nazarius arrived, nearly a month after the community had begun to occupy the additional building that had been added to the old mansion. On December 28th the relics of the holy martyr were solemnly placed under the high altar. Solemn High Mass was celebrated by Rev. Father Fulton, S. J., in presence of the Most Rev. Archbishop.

The church had now become a centre of attraction for the entire city of Boston: Pious adorers were to be seen in it at all hours of the day, and the confessionals were thronged. The community had also greatly increased; it consisted of Fathers Leopold Petsch, Joseph Wissel, Augustine Freitag, Francis X. Schnüttgen, Timothy Enright, Henry Kuper, Matthew Bohn, William O'Connor, F. Lamy, Lawrence Werner, and six brothers.

On June 8th, 1875, the first stone was laid for the new church; it was to be indeed a church built upon a rock, for

the foundation was laid upon the solid rock. The corner-
stone was solemnly blessed and laid by His Grace Archbishop
Williams, on May 28th of the year following. Right Rev.
Bishop Healy, of Portland, Maine, preached a beautiful sermon on the occasion. This was a day never to be forgotten
by those who then formed the community. The festivities
were at an end, and the numerous guests belonging both to
the secular and regular clergy had departed. The shades of
night-fall were welcomed by the members of the community,
exhausted by the fatigues of the day. All, with few exceptions, had retired to rest, when suddenly, at half-past eleven
o'clock, the terrible cry of fire broke upon the air. The
irregular tolling of the community bell and the smothering
smoke aroused the community from their first sleep. The
house was on fire, and the flames were already darting from
the library and adjoining staircases. After some time the
little church bell announced the appalling tidings to the neighbors. The Blessed Sacrament and the sacred vessels were
safely brought to a neighbor's house. The firemen soon
arrived on the spot. The Catholics worked more to save the
church than if their own property had been in danger. Crowds
of those who could not work knelt in the garden, on the
opposite side of the street, and on the rocks across the way,
and prayed aloud: "O God, save the little church. Blessed
Mother of Perpetual Help, save the Fathers." Others said
the Rosary together. How the fire originated no one could
tell; it raged until half-past two in the morning. The church
was saved from its wild fury, but two-thirds of the house became a victim to it. At seven o'clock in the morning one of
the Jesuit Fathers was at the church, inviting the community
to take up their abode with them for as long a time as they
should wish. Fathers McInerney, Bausch, Loewekamp and
Rebhan were the guests of the hospitable Jesuit Fathers for
five days, while the rest of the community lodged for a time
in the remaining part of the building and in the church. The
sympathy and charity of the people was very great. The
Fathers noticed especially the devoted affection of the poor
people.

When the confusion occasioned by the calamity had subsided, the Fathers began to turn their attention to the necessary repairs.   Part of the old house that had been left standing was cut away, the church was moved to the spot where the burnt building had stood, and some additions were made to the house.

When the new year opened, the community consisted of Father Retsch, the rector, and Fathers Freitag, Kuper, Oates, Miller, Stuhl, McInerney, Bausch, Rebhan, Sigl, and seven brothers.   On the 26th of July Rev. William Loewekamp became rector of the community.

On April 7th, 1878, the new church, having been completed, was solemnly blessed by Most Rev. J. J. Williams, Archbishop of Boston.   His Excellency, Governor Rice, was present on the occasion, besides a great number of distinguished clergymen and nearly twenty-five hundred people.   Rev. Father Fitton, of East Boston, preached on the occasion.   The evening sermon was delivered by Rev. Robert Fulton, S. J.

In the month of September following, on the 8th, the first Mass was celebrated on the new marble altar of Our Lady of Perpetual Help by Rev. Father Dold, who had furnished the design thereof.   On the 24th of November, the same Father preached for the first time from the new marble pulpit he had himself designed, and the different parts of which he had collected from twenty-four different workers in marble of the city of Boston.   It was said to be the first marble pulpit ever built in this country.

On July 16th, 1879, about four o'clock in the afternoon, a terrible tornado swept over the city.   Several windows of the Church of Our Lady of Perpetual Help were broken, all the confessionals on the Gospel side were flooded, whilst penitents called for absolution as if they were on the point of death.   The lightning struck in several places in the neighborhood, a great many vessels were wrecked in the harbor, and many corpses were washed ashore next morning.

On October 13th the relics of St. Nazarius were privately transferred from the basement to the altar of St. Alphonsus in the church, and in March of the following year marble steps were added to the pulpit. They were a present of Father Dold's sister.

In the summer of 1880 Rev. Father Loewekamp was succeeded as rector of the community by Rev. Joseph Henning. On June 17th Rev. Father Frawley, C. SS. R., of Brookline, sang his first Solemn High Mass in the Church of Our Lady of Perpetual Help, in presence of his many relatives and friends·

Thus far the ruthless hand of death had spared the members of the Boston community, but finally the grim monarch crossed the threshold of this abode of quiet, and claimed as its victim the Rev. Leopold Petsch. Father Petsch was born at Moeren, in Bohemia, on August 23d, 1821, and entered into the Congregation of the Most Holy Redeemer at Eggenburg, in Austria, in 1842. He was professed in the year following. In 1848 he was sent to America. He labored zealously during his life for the salvation of souls at Baltimore, Buffalo, Rochester, New York, Annapolis and Pittsburgh. Several times he filled the office of superior. In 1873 he succeeded Bishop Gross as superior of the house of Boston. The blessing of God was with his labors in this community. His principal activity he displayed in the confessional. He labored zealously up to June 16th, 1882. For some time he complained of a dizziness, and as the evil increased the best physicians were consulted, who pronounced his condition serious. The immediate cause of his death was a fatty degeneration of the heart. With the greatest resignation and inward joy he looked forward to his dissolution. On the 19th the last sacraments were administered to him by Rev. Father Henning. He spoke very rarely. To several questions as to what he wished, he replied: " I want God." On the evening of the same day the community was summoned to his room, and the Litany for the Dying was recited. Finally, on the next day, June 20th, at ten minutes past one o'clock, the soul of Father Petsch winged its flight to the world beyond the grave. The community was present, as also Dr. McNulty and, by special permission, Messrs. O'Grady and McCarthy. The following day the body was removed to the church, where Mass was celebrated for the deceased. The obsequies

took place on June 22d.   The Archbishop, five Jesuit Fathers
and thirteen secular priests were present.   His Grace gave the
absolution.   Among those present was Rev. Augustine
Freitag, whose name has several times been mentioned in this
history.   He was himself an invalid, and obliged to lean on
his cane.   Only a few days separated him from the grave, for
he died on July 26th of the same year, in the city of New
York.   The sermon at the funeral of Father Petsch was
preached by Rev. Father O'Connor, S. J.   The body was laid
to rest in the garden ; a simple slab marks the spot where his
ashes await the resurrection.   Father Petsch, says a contemporary article in a Catholic paper, the *Volks-Zeitung* belonged to those souls who, as much as possible, hide themselves from men in order to live and labor only in God and
for God.

The predecessor of Father Petsch, as superior of the house
of Boston, Right Rev. W. Gross, arrived in July on a visit.
He was gladly received and honored by his old friends of the
Mission Church, as the Church of Our Lady of Perpetual
Help was called.

In April, 1883, the Mission Church obtained parochial
rights, and became a parish church.   In the same year His
Holiness, Leo XIII., granted to those persons who would
pray twelve times, at the seven altars of the Mission Church
during the month of May, the same indulgences they would
gain by visiting the altars of St. Peter's Basilica, in Rome.

In May, 1884, a meeting was convoked at the Boston
Music Hall, in which an audience, composed of all creeds and
classes, assembled, to protest against the spoliation of the
property of the Propaganda by the Italian government.
Fathers Henning, Schmidt and McGivern were present.

Our Blessed Lady of Perpetual Succor had, from the beginning of the foundation, continued to pour down her favors on
her devout clients.   Up to the year 1884 no less than three
hundred and thirty-one well authenticated miraculous cures
had been wrought in favor of persons from Boston and of
others from very remote localities, even as distant as West
Virginia and Texas.   One of the most remarkable cures was

that of Grace Mary Hanley, effected on August 18th, 1883.
We will give the history of this miracle in the lady's own
words :

" When a little over four years of age, I went to spend the
summer with my aunt, in the country. I was very strong
and healthy, until one day we were allowed to play driving
in an unused carriage, which stood in a carriage-shed adjoining the house. By the side of the carriage-house stood a
large, rough rock to prevent the wheel from rubbing off the
paint. Wishing to get out, and climbing down backward, as
children do, when they began to jolt the carriage, my hands
lost their hold and I fell, striking the lower part of my back
on the rock, between which and the wheel I was tightly
wedged. Grandma, who had come to spend the day, hearing
my cries, ran to my assistance, and had some difficulty in
releasing me from my painful position. They examined my
back, but found not even a scratch upon it, though I could
neither sit nor lie down, standing being the least painful position. After violent crying, I fell asleep in grandma's arms,
but during the night awoke screaming with fearful pain.
The next morning mamma took me to the doctor, who, after
examining my back, pronounced my suffering growing pains.
Every week this pain grew worse, and seemed to be in the
side rather than the back, which puzzled the physicians. For
one year I suffered intense agony, as the physicians could do
nothing to relieve me. At the close of the year papa called
in Dr. Cheever, chief surgeon in the city hospital. After a
thorough examination, he said one of the small bones in the
spinal column was cracked, that being the cause of the intense pain. He ordered a pair of steel and leather corsets to
be put on, which I wore for one month. My grandmother
came to see me one day, and advised mamma to bring me to
Dr. Buckminster Brown, a noted specialist in all bone diseases, who then resided on Bowdoin street. He ordered me
to be put to bed, without a pillow under my head, with weights
of sand hanging from the head and foot of the bed, and
pillows of the same on each side, so that I could not move my
body at all. I never lifted my head, even to take my meals.

At this time mamma began to make novenas, assisted by papa, the children, grandma, grandpa, uncles and aunts. When one was finished we commenced another. At the end of a year the doctor permitted me to get up, although he said I was the first of his patients who was able to get up under a year and a half, in the condition I was when he first took charge of me, and mamma attributed this improvement to the novenas we made, assisted by the Sisters of Charity and the Good Shepherd. The doctor told mamma to expect the formation of an abcess, as it generally followed the decay of an old bone. In about a year after this a dreadful abcess formed, causing intense suffering. In the meantime mamma taught me reading and writing, and dear Father Cooper instructed me for my first Holy Communion, which I received on the 8th of December, at the age of nine years. I remained under the care of Dr. Brown until the age of twelve, wearing the heavy corsets continually. One morning in November I went with papa and mamma to Mass, at which we received Holy Communion. On our way home from church I was scarcely able to walk, and gradually lost the use of my lower limbs; and at Christmas I could not even stand. The pain of my back returned with renewed force. Dr. Brown was very much discouraged, and ordered leeches to be applied, and when they failed, blisters and powerful liniments; but all to no avail. He then advised mamma to begin again the old treatment of putting me to bed, as a last resort. I remained lying on my back for over six months. About the 1st of September we heard of Dr. Bradford, a specialist in all bone diseases, like Dr. Brown, but using a different treatment. He took my case in hand, with Dr. Brown's consent, and began by placing me in a 'plaster of Paris' jacket, which, when hardened, caused so much pain that he, with an assistant, was obliged to saw it off. He then ordered a wheel-chair. In March he advised me to go to St. Margaret's Hospital, under the care of the 'Episcopal Sisters.' I remained there three months. While I was at the hospital they applied electricity, ice-bags, etc., to my back, but every application made it worse. About this time I had been troubled with fearful headaches, which grew worse every day, and for which the doctors could do nothing. Dr. Bradford managed to get me up on crutches, and had a very heavy pair of corsets made, which I wore day and night, and a steel frame, into which I was strapped every night, was also made to prevent me from turning on my side. Rev. Father O'Brien brought me Holy Communion several times while I was at the hospital. When I was able to use the crutches fairly well, the doctor advised me to go home. I never found any relief for my pain, either in the head or spine. During this period we continued our novenas, and when one was finished without any result, I always thought the next one would cure me. In July Dr. Bradford paid me a visit, and felt discouraged when he saw how helpless I was without the crutches. He said the headache came from my spine, and he could do nothing to relieve me. He left, advising me to sit on the piazza and get all the fresh air I could. One day in August, Rev. Father Rathke called and advised me to make a novena in the church, before Our Blessed Lady's altar. The next morning papa carried me in his arms down stairs and into the buggy. This caused me great pain. In the church, before the altar, assisted by papa, grandma, Aunt Ella, my brothers and sisters, I began another novena. Rev. Father Delargy also knelt with us, and said the Rosary. From the moment I began this novena I felt sure I was going to be cured. Rev. Father Henning gave me great encouragement before I went home. The third day of the novena I woke up without a headache, which did not happen for the last three years. This, in itself, mamma said, was a miracle. My back seemed to grow worse, though the violent pains in my head were entirely gone. The wide space which had opened on the top of my head was closed. The ninth day I felt my back much worse. When we arrived in church Rev. Father Delargy gave me Holy Communion. While making my thanksgiving, after receiving, a very strange feeling came over me, everything seemed to grow dark; I thought, perhaps, I was going to faint; this had not passed off when another feeling, I never can describe it, passed through me from head to foot, like a thrill (and something like electricity). My

Aunt Ella, seeing me looking pale, came with my crutches, and I looked up and said: 'O, I do not want them; I can walk.' She said: 'If you can walk, Grace, walk over to the altar.' I got up, passed my aunt, who still held the crutches, and walked to the altar, where I knelt to thank our dear Lord and His Blessed Mother. Papa and grandma were spellbound, as they did not hear me speak, but only saw me get up and walk. I walked down the aisle, out into the street, by my papa's side, and I did not stop until I reached my mother's room, up one flight of stairs. The corsets, without which I could not before sit up, were taken off; the pain was gone from my back, and my head was as well as that of any one. I did not even feel tired, thanks to our Blessed Lord and our Dear Lady of Perpetual Help." Thus far Miss Grace Hanley wrote herself. The miracle was soon noised abroad; it was published in several papers throughout the country, and attracted a great deal of attention. Crowds followed the young lady day after day, on her way to church, attracted by curiosity. Great numbers of people, belonging to all conditions and all creeds, visited her house to behold with their own eyes the subject of the miracle, and assure themselves of the reality of the prodigy. Miss Hanley has continued to enjoy good health to the present day, and is ever filled with gratitude towards her Heavenly Deliverer.

On September 23d of the same year Rev. Father Daly, C. SS. R., sang his first Mass in the church of Our Lady of Perpetual Help, and administered the Holy Communion to his father.

In December, 1884, the Redemptorist community at Boston was startled by the intelligence that three of its members, Fathers O'Brien, McGivern and Delargy, had been attacked by Orangemen while giving missions in the Island of Newfoundland. These Fathers were finally obliged to invoke the protection of the United States government, and consequently, through the interference of the American consul in Newfoundland, a British gun-boat, the Tenedos, was dispatched from St. Johns to Bay Roberts, to their assistance. This had the desired effect, and further trouble was averted, so that the Fathers could continue their missionary labors.

On February 1st, 1885, Rt. Rev. C. Seghers, Bishop of Vancouver's Island, preached in the church for the benefit of his missions. On March 15th, of the same year, Father Cunningham, C. SS. R., of Roxbury, celebrated his first Mass in the Church of Our Lady of Perpetual Help, and Father McNamara, of Brookline, celebrated his on the 17th of the same month. Things passed on quietly from this date without any important event until November 8th, when the sad news of the death of an absent member of the community reached Boston. Father John O'Brien, who was engaged in giving a mission in the city of Philadelphia, had been suddenly cut off in the flower of his age. He was in his thirty-sixth year at the time of his death. He was born in Ireland, but came to this country when quite young. Having, in course of time, entered the Congregation of the Most Holy Redeemer, he was ordained in 1880, and was stationed in Boston almost from the time of his ordination. Having concluded a mission in Philadelphia, he obtained leave from his superiors to pay a visit to Ilchester, his "alma mater." Inflammatory rheumatism, that struck to his heart, snatched him suddenly out of life a short time after his arrival, to the great grief of his friends and brethren in religion. His remains were conveyed to Boston, and his obsequies took place in the church of Our Lady of Perpetual Succor. Many clergymen were present. Father Lucking, C. SS. R., preached the sermon. His body was temporarily interred in the lot of the Most Reverend Archbishop in Calvary Cemetery. Father O'Brien was an active and talented priest, dearly beloved by all who knew him. He had been preceded to the grave only a few days before by Father McGivern, who was then stationed at St. Alphonsus' church, New York, and died in Philadelphia at St. Teresa's church while engaged in a mission. Both these Fathers had been the objects of the fury of the Orangemen in Newfoundland.

Another first Mass was celebrated in this church on April 4th, 1886, by Rev. Father Sheehan, C. SS. R., in presence of his father and his numerous friends. On September 5th, Rev. Father Henning preached on the necessity of Catholic schools. On the next day a collection was begun for the purpose of erecting a school in the parish. On the 19th of the same month a collection was taken up for the sufferers from the earthquake in Charleston, S. C. On September 21st Rev. Father Kerns celebrated his silver jubilee.

The year 1886 had taken its departure and 1887 had been ushered in, when death's dark shadow once more crossed the threshold of the Redemptorist house of Boston. Father John McNamara, C. SS. R., a young priest of the Redemptorists' house of Quebec, who was staying at Boston, passed away from this valley of tears on January 30th. He was a native of Brookline, Massachusetts. He was buried at Calvary cemetery.

On the 11th of June the Rector, Rev. Jos. Henning, celebrated the twenty-fifth anniversary of his ordination, on the occasion of which the people showed their love and veneration. The good Father did not remain long in Boston after this celebration, for the new appointments of superiors having arrived from Rome in the same month, he was transferred to the house of the Redemptorists in Toronto, where he now fills the office of superior. His successor in Boston was Rev. Augustine J. McInerney, who still occupies the post of Rector. He entered upon his office on June 21st, 1887.

On August 19th the ground was broken for the schoolhouse to be erected in the rear of the existing buildings.

Thus far we have followed the history of Brinley Place from its days of terrestrial grandeur to those of spiritual greatness. If its first occupants could arise from the dead, how astonished they would be to behold the change ! The beautiful hills and green fields are now covered with houses and cut up by streets ; the waters that washed the base of Roxbury hills have disappeared, and the city of Boston has reared its edifices where the cattle were wont to graze.

The splendid old mansion of the Brinleys, Pierponts and Dearborns has almost entirely disappeared, and in its place stands a modest structure occupied by a few unpretending followers of St. Alphonsus de Liguori. There, where once fashion and beauty reigned, the poor may be seen from morning till night, seeking relief for their ills both of body and soul. The hill beside the Dearborn mansion has been leveled, and on the rocky surface of its site one of Boston's most superb edifices rears its head. The church is built in the Romanesque style, and surmounted by a cupola. The exterior length is 215 feet and its width across the transept 115, while the body of the church is 78 feet wide, and is divided into nave and two aisles. Over the intersection of the nave and transept rises an octagonal dome to a height of 110 feet. This dome is supported by four clusters of four columns each, all of polished granite, and the capitals of freestone, richly carved with symbolic figures. The sanctuary is very large, and closes with a semi-circular apse, in which the high altar is placed. The chapel of Our Lady of Perpetual Help is built out semi-circular on the westerly transept, which opens to the same with a large arch supported by two polished granite columns. The church can seat about 2000 persons and contain about 4000.

A large school is being erected. The corner-stone was laid by Most Rev. Archbishop Williams on Sunday, April 8th, 1888, and Father Henning, the former rector, preached on the occasion. The building is progressing rapidly, and will be completed in a few months.

LIST OF BAPTISMS

REGISTERED AT

ST. JOSEPH'S CHURCH, PHILADELPHIA.

———

(SECOND SERIES.)

———

FROM JANUARY 1, 1776, TO OCTOBER 21, 1781.

———

[COPIED FROM THE ORIGINAL RECORDS BY FRANCIS X. REUSS, LIBRA-
RIAN OF THE AMERICAN CATHOLIC HISTORICAL SOCIETY OF
PHILADELPHIA. WITH SOME PREFATORY REMARKS AND BRACK-
ETED NOTES BY REV. DR. MIDDLETON, O. S. A., PRESIDENT OF
THE SOCIETY.]

———

IN the first volume of the " Records of the American Catholic Historical Society of Philadelphia " were published the
baptisms for eighteen years, registered at St. Joseph's church,
Philadelphia, from August 29th, 1758, the earliest recorded,
down to December 31st, 1775. Their number amounted to
eighteen hundred and sixty-five. This constituted the first
series of the registers.

In this present volume the publication of the baptismal registers has been continued for the six years from January 1st,
1776, and has been carried down as far as October 21st, 1781.

The number of baptisms given in this second series amounts to eight hundred and ninety.

It may here be observed that all the baptisms printed in this series are entered in the registers at St. Joseph's church in the handwriting of the Rev. Ferdinand Farmer, and, with three exceptions, were apparently conferred by him. The exceptions are two baptisms on February 11th, 1780, where the name of Rev. Robert Molyneux, S. J., is recorded as the minister of the sacrament, and on October 10th, 1778, where the Rev. Father Valerian Durand, O. S. F., is named as having baptized Elizabeth Scantlen at Chester, Pennsylvania.

The places mentioned in the registers where baptisms were conferred were in widely-separated districts. Father Farmer's wonderful activity led him nearly everywhere through New Jersey and southeastern Pennsylvania, and in southern New York. The various localities named in the records are Philadelphia and Kensington, in Philadelphia county; Goshen, in Lancaster county; Pikesland and Whiteland, in Chester county; Goshenhoppen, in Berks county; Haycock and the vicinity of Bristol, in Bucks county, and Concord, in Delaware county. These all are in Pennsylvania. In New Jersey are Pompton and Ringwood, in Passaic county; Change Water, in Warren county; Long Pond, in Sussex county; Mount Hope, in Morris county; Gloucester, in Camden county; Deerfield, Woodstown, Salem and Pilesgrove, in Salem county, and Greenwich and Cohansey, in Cumberland county. Baptism was administered also at Charlottenburg, Pottsgrove and in Hunterdon and Burlington counties, besides in the vicinity of Fishkill, in Dutchess county, New York.

In the first volume of these Records the writer, in his endeavors to locate the various places where baptisms had been conferred, supposed, on grounds drawn from the registers themselves, that Geiger's, a name so frequently met with in reference to the missionary visits of Father Farmer, was somewhere near Philadelphia or Salem, N. J. This supposition of his has now been transferred to the domain of positive certainty, through the researches of John Gilmary Shea, the untiring historian of the American Catholic Church. In his history—"The Catholic Church in Colonial Days," etc. (New York, 1886)—at page 395, Vol. I., he gives a picture of the house of Matthew and Adam Geiger, still standing, in Salem county, N. J., "where Mass was celebrated from 1744."

The reader is directed to the introduction to the first series of the baptismal registers given in the first volume of these "Records" for 1884–86, at page 246. Little else can, at present, at least, be added to what there may be found.

FR. THOMAS C. MIDDLETON, O. S. A.
Villanova College, Pa., October 25th, 1888.

NOTE.—The insertion of (P.) after a name in the following registers indicates that the person was a Protestant.

REGISTER OF BAPTISMS FOR 1776.

Graff, Catharine, of Anthony and Barbara Graff, born January 1st, baptized January 1st, sponsors George and Mary Spengler.

Boudrot, Stephen, of Michael and Anna Boudrot, born January 2d, baptized January 2d, sponsors John Aiken and Mary Vincent.

Ghilkar, Elizabeth, of George and Prudence Ghilkar, born December 3, 1775, baptized January 7th, sponsors Michael and Mary Galagher.

Bremich, Adam, of Leonard and Margaret Bremich, born January 8th, baptized January 9th, sponsors Adam and Margaret Bremich.

Buckley, Michael, of James and Mary Buckley, born October 12th, 1775, baptized January 14th, sponsors William Malone and Judith Kenedy.

Daniel, Esther, of Isaac and Esther Daniel, seventeen years of age, baptized January 15th, sponsors Archibald Shaw and Mary Recans.

Nunck, John, of Henry and Mary (P.) Nunck, born December 13th, 1775, baptized January 21st, sponsors John Nadler and Catharine Nadler.

Morris, Philip, of Philip and Elizabeth Morris, born August 15th, 1774, baptized January 21st, sponsors John and Catharine Smith.

Hollingsworth, Margaret, of James and Anna (Dealy) Hollingsworth, born January 21st, baptized January 21st, sponsor Barbara Schultz.

McKenley, Elizabeth, of John and Mary McKenley, born November, 1774, baptized January 22d, sponsor Barbara Keil, in vicinity of Philadelphia.

Masterson, Mathias, of Mathias and Martha Masterson, born November 9th, 1774, baptized January 22d.

Tissotau, John, of Leonard Nicholas and Magdalen Tissotau, sixteen years of age, baptized January 23d, sponsors Herman Carpé and Catharine Boudrot.

Lean, Mary, of Lawrence and Judith Lean, born June 10th, 1775, baptized January 23d, sponsor Mary Nagler.

Willson, Barbara, of William and Rosa Willson, born January 15th, baptized January 28th, sponsor Elizabeth Sudric.

Warner, William, of Hugh and Margaret Warner, born January 29th, baptized January 29th, sponsors James Byrne, Jr., and Margaret Deacon.

Carpé, Julia, of Herman Carpé and Margaret Lebeauve, born January 29th, baptized January 30th, sponsors Jacques Clement Hierce and Margaret LeBlanc.

Raubin, Charlotta, of John and Anna Raubin, born January 30th, baptized January 30th, sponsors Anthony Toussaint and Magdalen Vincent.

Bonaventure, Francis, born October, 1775, baptized February 3d, sponsors Bonaventure and Venanda Dartoit.

Lechler, Mary Elizabeth, of Anthony and Catharine Lechler, born January 31st, baptized February 4th, sponsors George Ernest Lechler and Christina Horn (for her mother).

Schneider, John Adam, of Henry and Barbara Schneider, born February 2d, baptized February 10th, sponsors Adam and Anna Mary Göck.

Will, George, of Philip and Elizabeth Will, born February 6th, baptized February 11th, sponsors George Freind and Catherine Freind.

O'Hearn, Mary, of Lawrence and Abby O'Hearn, born January, 1776, baptized February 11th, sponsor Patrick Grogan, and witness Margaret Grogan.

Carson, James, of James (P.) and Mary Carson, born February 12th, baptized February 14th, sponsor William Dolton.

Schilling, Mary Margaret, of Philip and Eva Schilling, born February 8th, baptized February 18th, sponsor Tobias Rudolph, and witness Mary Margaret Rudolph.

Kelly, William and Margaret, twins, of James and Elizabeth Kelly, born May 28th, 1775, baptized February 19th, sponsors James and Elizabeth Conway.

Lewis, Joseph, of Emmanuel and Margaret Lewis, born September 14th, 1775, baptized February 20th, sponsors Joseph and Catharine Eck.

Zängerle, Mary Magdalen, of Ignatius and Anna Elizabeth Zängerle, born February 18th, baptized February 20th, sponsors George Ernest Lechler and Mary Magdalen, his wife.

Horn, Mary Catharine, of Henry and Justina Horn, born February 17th, baptized February 20th, sponsors George Ernest and Mary Magdalen Lechler.

Welsh, John, of James and Lydia Welsh, born January 4th, 1775, baptized February 23d, sponsor Johanna Nicols.

Rice, Andrew, of James and Esther Rice, born December 26th, 1775, baptized February 25th, sponsors Philip and Grace McDead.

Merchant, Mary, of James and Eleanor Merchant, born February 11th, baptized February 26th, sponsors Paul and Margaret Cuningham.

Ryan, John, of Michael and Elizabeth Ryan, born February 17th, 1771, baptized March 1st, sponsor Simon Leblanc.

Ryan, Mary, same parents, born October 17th, 1772, baptized March 1st sponsor Catharine Boudrot.

Ryan, Alice, same parents, born March 19th, 1774, baptized March 1st, sponsor Catharine Boudrot.

Haug, John, of John and Catharine Haug, born February 21st, baptized March 3d, sponsors Christopher and Catharine Viel.

Gordon, John, of William (P.) and Barbara Gordon, born February 25th, baptized March 3d, sponsors Thomas Carraher and Mary Springer.

Connor, Catharine, of Michael and Mary Connor, born February 28th, baptized March 4th, sponsors Matthew Cotringer and Elizabeth White.

Hardnet, Anna, of James and Johanna Hardnet, born January 28th, baptized March 9th, sponsor Elizabeth Campbell.

Hoffman, Elizabeth, of Adam and Catharine Hoffman, born March 6th, baptized March 13th, sponsors' Adam Lechler and Elizabeth Hoffman.

Garby, Mary, of Bartholomew and Eleanor (Williams) Garby, born March 11th, baptized March 14th, sponsor Mary Scantlen.

Lamy, Grace, of James and Hannah Lamy, born October 15th, 1775, baptized March 17th, sponsors Frederic Scheimer and Anna Tims, at Pikesland [Chester county, Pa.].

Makenna, John, of John and Sarah Makenna, born January 29th, baptized March 17th, sponsors James Weissenburger and Margaret Kean, *ibid.*

Weissenburger, Margaret, of Christian and Hannah Weissenburger, born October 7th, 1775, baptized March 17th, sponsors James Weissenburger and Margaret Walter, *ibid.*

Landry, Mary, of Anthony and Barbara (Leblanc) Landry, born January 24th, baptized March 19th, sponsors Simon Leblanc and Margaret Bourg.

Magill, Johanna, of Peter and Barbara Magill, born January 25th, baptized March 24th, sponsors James and Johanna Magill.

Spängler, Mary Catharine, of George and Mary Spängler, born March 22d, baptized March 26th, sponsors Anthony Graff and Catharine Spängler.

Daugherty, Margaret, of James and Catharine Daugherty, born March 24th, baptized March 26th, sponsor Rosanna Dwyer.

Mason, William, of Thomas and Priscilla Mason, born November 22d, 1775, baptized March 27th, sponsor Rosanna Davern.

Malhollin, Patrick, of Patrick and Margaret Malhollin, born March 29th, baptized March 29th, sponsors Owen Mullen and Mary McMullen.

Bauman, John, of Benedict Charles and Magdalen Bauman, born March 17th, baptized March 29th, sponsor John Heiser, and witness his wife Mary Agnes.

Geiger, Mathias, of Henry and Barbara Geiger, born December 3d, 1775, baptized March 31st, sponsors Simon and Mary Geiger, at Pilesgrove [Salem county, N. J.].

Lort, John, of Isaac and Anna Lort, born April 4th, baptized April 4th, sponsors James and Anna Gallagher.

Orkart, Catharine, of Onias and Catharine Orkart, born March 1st, baptized April 4th, sponsor Catharine Dardis.

Sullivan, Philip, of Jeremiah and Catharine Sullivan, born April 3d, baptized April 7th, sponsors James Castela and Catharine Boudrot.

Spier, Barbara, of Matthew and Mary Spier, born February 26th, baptized April 9th, sponsors John and Barbara Heitz.

Mayer, Anna Sophia, of Jodocus and Gertrude Mayer, born April 4th, baptized April 11th, sponsors Peter Hegner, Jr., and Elizabeth Hegner.

Schmid, John George, of Nicholas and Eva Schmid, born March 25th, baptized April 14th, sponsors George Freind and Catharine Keil.

Shea, Arthur, of John and Anna Shea, born April 11th, baptized April 14th, sponsors Jeremiah Sullivan and Alice Castela.

Rowan, John, of John and ———— Rowan, born 1773, baptized April 15th, sponsors John Connolly and Margaret Corcran.

Mullen, Joseph, of James and Anna Mullen, born March 22d, baptized April 17th, sponsors Patrick and Mary Byrne.

Monchère, Bridget, of Thomas and ———— Monchère, born January 11th, baptized April 18th, sponsor Margaret Dirksin.

Maher, Mary, of Patrick and Catharine Maher, born March 29th, baptized April 20th, sponsors Michael Green and Margaret Glass.

Ryan, Michael, of Michael and Hannah Ryan, born April 16th, baptized April 21st, sponsors Moses and Elizabeth Boosee.

Kean, Henry, of William and Eleanor Kean, born December 17th, 1775, baptized April 26th, sponsors Joseph and Anna Elizabeth Wingart, in Morris county [N. J.].

Kelly, William, of Luke and Margaret Kelly, born June 13th, 1770, baptized April 28th, sponsors James Maruny and Johanna McDonald, at Charlottenburg [N. J.].

Larkins, Eva, of John and Anna Larkins, born March 20th, baptized May 1st, sponsor Eva Fichter, at Longpond [N. J.]

Cobole, David, of John and Catharine Cobole, born April 27th, baptized May 1st, sponsors David Fichter and Anna Mary Callin, *ibid.*

Rüger, Anna Eva, of John and Elizabeth Rüger, born April 12th, baptized May 1st, sponsors Nicholas and Anna Eva Jungfleisch, *ibid.*

Burns, Anna Catharine, of Laghlin and Margaret Burns, born April 20th, baptized May 2d, sponsors Bartholomew Cobole and Anna Catharine Cobole, *ibid.*

Dealy, Mary, of James and Esther Dealy, born August 9th, 1772, baptized May 5th, sponsors Thomas and Magdalen Price, at Mount Hope [N. J.].

Schäffer, John William, of George and Jeannette Schäffer, born August 9th, 1775, baptized May 5th, sponsors Richard and Mary Murphy, *ibid.*

Renschmid, Anna Margaret, of Bernard and Mary Dorothy Renschmid, born April 9th, baptized May 5th, sponsors Francis Zech and Margaret Engelhard, *ibid.*

Whetcock, Charles, of Richard and Mary (Brown) Whetcock, born February 18th, baptized May 5th, sponsors Caspar Engelhard and Grace Brown, *ibid.*

Welsh, Mary, of Thomas and Catharine Welsh, born December 21st, 1775, baptized May 5th, sponsors Hugh Quigg and Anna Catharine Demuth, *ibid.*

Holtzhäser, Caspar, of Sebastian and Joanna Holtzhäser, born April 2d, baptized May 5th, sponsors Caspar and Margaret Engelhard, *ibid.*

Hiffernan, Joanna, of John and Teresa (P.) Hiffernan, born January ——, baptized May 12th, sponsors Henry Grey and Anna Hudson, at Philadelphia.

Hohms, Emmanuel, of Emmanuel and Mary Magdalen Hohms, born May 7th, baptized May 12th, sponsors Emmanuel and Charlotte Bryer.

Broadfield, Mary, adult, baptized May 15th, sponsor Sarah Tims.

Higgins, Catharine, of Cornelius and Elizabeth Higgins, born May 9th, baptized May 19th, sponsors William Dean and Eleanor Green.

Cooper, John, of Thomas and Judith Cooper, born May 16th, baptized May 19th, sponsors John Macoy and Susanna Tricks.

Steiner, James, of Adam and Catharine Steiner, born April 11th, baptized May 26th, sponsors James and Catharine Nagel.

Macky, Mary, of John and Elizabeth Macky, born June 30th, 1772, baptized May 26th, sponsors Thomas Whealan and Catharine Shaw.

Boosee, Isaac, of Moses and Elizabeth Boosee, born May 23d, baptized May 26th, sponsors Michael Ryan and Barbara Graff.

Betagh, John, of Thomas and Josepha Betagh, born May 26th, baptized May 27th, sponsors John Aitkin and Alice Baxter.

Ghillmore, Hannah Dent, wife of James Ghillmore, baptized May 27th, sponsor Bridget McNamara.

Smith, Catharine, of Daniel and Mary Smith, born May 31st, baptized

June 2d, sponsors Augustine Power and Margaret Agnew, witness Archibald Burns.

Laller, John, of Henry and Alice Laller, born May 25th, baptized June 5th, sponsors William Doyle and Elizabeth White.

Brothers, John, of William and Eleanor Brothers, born May 22d, 1775, baptized June 7th, sponsors Paul Cuningham and Elizabeth Farguson.

McFall, Anna, of Patrick and Catharine McFall, born May 17th, baptized June 9th, sponsors Hugh and Margaret Magill.

Grey, John, of ———— and Martha Grey, born March 30th, baptized June 11th, sponsor Mary Hart.

Cully, Anna, of ———— and Mary Cully, born March 30th, baptized June 11th, sponsor Mary Hart.

Sissel, John and Mary, twins, of Frederic and Mary Sissel, born June 9th, baptized June 11th, sponsors, for John, James Gillmor, for Mary, Mary Clark.

Fitzgerald, Thomas, of Thomas and Mary Fitzgerald, born June 9th, baptized June 12th, sponsors John Barret and Anna Gallagher.

Mignio, Mary, of Charles and Pelagia Mignio, born June 13th, baptized June 13th, sponsors Charles Mignio, Jr., and Mary Sheney.

Gabin, Mary, of James and Catharine Gabin, born June 3d, baptized June 14th, sponsor Sarah Tims.

Bolton, Mary, of ———— and Catharine Bolton, born January 10th, baptized June 16th, sponsors Thomas Morrey and Mary Carty.

Albrecht, James, of James and Anna Mary Albrecht, born June 10th, baptized June 16th, sponsors Joseph and Magdalen Springer.

Haas, John Adam, of Peter and Elizabeth Haas, born June 12th, baptized June 16th, sponsors John Adam Poth and Martha, his wife.

Egan, John, of William and Eleanor Egan, born August 19th, 1775, baptized June 18th, sponsors Patrick Kearns and Margaret Scot, in Burlington county [N. J.].

Käffer, Anna, of John and Regina Käffer, born June 19th, baptized June 21st, sponsors John Späth and Anna Theusen.

Welte, Tobias, of Bernard and Mary Welte, born June 2d, baptized June 23d, sponsor Tobias Rudolf, and witness Margaret, his wife.

Condon, John, of Michael and Elizabeth Condon, born June 13th, baptized June 23d, sponsor Edward Macoy, and witness Alice Fraser.

O'Neil, Elizabeth, of Barnabas and Barbara O'Neil, born May 12th, baptized June 24th, sponsors Joseph Cromley and Martha Lebeau.

Prügel, Eleanor, of Henry and Margaret Prügel, born December 24th, 1775, baptized June 24th, sponsors Thomas and Eleanor Green.

Clark, James, of Raphael and Mary Clark, born June 13th, baptized June 24th, sponsors James Gillmor and Margaret Class.

Cateca, Sarah, a young girl, baptized June 24th, sponsor Joanna Levan.

Jameson, Francis, of Richard and Martha Jameson, born June 20th, baptized June 25th, sponsor Mary Selby.

Foy, Mary, of Henry and Sarah Foy, born May 12th, baptized June 30th, sponsors John Gans and Catharine, his wife, at Pikesland [Chester county, Pa.].

McGuire, Eleanor, of Bartholomew and Catherine McGuire, born June 9th, baptized July 7th, sponsors Henry Schneider and Elizabeth Bauman.

Duchemin, Mary Barbara, of Daniel and Susanna Duchemin, born January 7th, baptized July 9th, sponsor Sarah Tims.

Lee, William, of Thomas and Mary Lee, born May 1st, baptized July 9th, sponsors Philip and Elizabeth Morris.

Hollaran, James, of Morgan and Catharine Hollaran, born July 8th, baptized July 9th, sponsors Robert Welsh and Joanna Harden.

Treim, Catharine, of James and Elizabeth Treim, born July 9th, baptized July 14th, sponsors Francis Jung and Catherine, his wife.

——, James, adult, slave of John Barry, baptized July 16th, sponsor Hannah, slave of N. White.

Sigfrid, Christian Joseph, of Joseph and Elizabeth Sigfrid, born June 4th, baptized July 17th, sponsors Christian Schumacher and Anna Mary, his wife.

Currey, Elizabeth, of Walter and Bridget Currey, born June 28th, baptized July 21st, sponsors John Shelleman and Susanna Doyle.

More, Thomas, of Thomas and Mary More, born May 27th, baptized July 21st, sponsor the priest and Anna Macra.

Hayle, Eleanor, of Caspar and Elizabeth Hayle, born July 21st, baptized July 22d, sponsors Matthew Poor and Catharine Miller in the vicinity of Philadelphia.

Jung, Mary Magdalen, of Francis and Catharine Jung, born July 19th, baptized July 24th, sponsors Peter Regimenter and Mary Magdalen, his wife, *ibid.*

Montgomery, James, born November, 18th, 1771, John, born March 22d, 1774, and William, born May 2d, of John Montgomery, a baptized Moor, and Bridget Maloy, his wife ; sponsors Peter and Mary Magdalen Regimenter, *ibid.*

Dun, James, of Richard and Rachel Dun, born October 16th, 1775, baptized July 25th, sponsors John and Anna Galagher.

Bastian, John, of Joseph and Catharine Bastian, born July 12th, baptized July 28th, sponsors James Treim and Catharine Tscharté.

More, Anna Mary, of George (P.) and Sarah More, born June 18th, baptized July 28th, sponsors James and Anna Mary Albrecht.

Lawla, James, of James and Mary Lawla, born June 17th, baptized July 29th, sponsor Anna Morgan.

Cammerloch, Joseph, of John Frederic and Anna Mary Cammerloch, born August 1st, baptized August 4th; sponsors Joseph Rübel and Catharine Stahl, Sr.

Doyle, John George, of James and Christina Doyle, born May 28th, baptized August 4th, sponsors Anselm and Elizabeth Schreiner.

Pahl, Elizabeth, of Lawrence and Anna Pahl, born August 4th, baptized August 5th, sponsors James and Elizabeth Klein.

Welsh, Andrew, of Richard and Catharine Welsh, born July 31st, baptized August 5th, sponsors John Shelleman and Margaret Malowny.

Cullen, Margaret, of Jeremiah and Hannah Cullen, born July 20th, baptized August 11th, sponsors Gerald Savage and Margaret Martin.

Huston, Charles, of Charles and Anna (P.) Huston, born May 22d, baptized August 14th, sponsors Michael Clark and Eleanor Connely.

Martin, Mary Jessop, wife of Thomas Martin, baptized August 22d, sponsor Susanna Shaw, in the vicinity of Bristol [Bucks county, Pa.].

Martin, Richard, born December, 1770, baptized August 22d, of Thomas and Mary Martin, sponsors Daniel Shaw, John Maconigl and James Robinson, *ibid*.

Martin, Anna, born August 18th, 1773, baptized August 22d, of Thomas and Mary Martin, sponsors Daniel Shaw, John Maconigl and James Robinson, *ibid*.

Martin, Lawrence, born November 10th, 1775, baptized August 22d, of Thomas and Mary Martin, sponsors Daniel Shaw, John Maconigl and James Robinson, *ibid*.

Maservey, Catharine Barbara, of Thomas and Mary Maservey, born August 2d, baptized August 25th, sponsors Bonaventure Dartoit and Barbara Schultz.

Gans, Elizabeth, of Balthasar and Sarah Gans, born June 16th, baptized September 1st, sponsors John Gans and Anna Mary Weissenburger, at Pikesland [Chester county, Pa.].

Reily, John, of Patrick and Catharine (Regan) Reily, born July 11th, baptized September 1st, sponsors Henry Murphy and Elizabeth Gans, *ibid*.

Schindler, Andrew, of Henry (P.) and Mary Catharine Schindler, born December 29th, 1775, baptized September 1st, sponsors Christian and Catharine Weissenburger, *ibid*.

Macalgen, Anna, of Michael and Mary Macalgan, born April 3d, baptized September 2d, sponsors James Carrol and Mary Groanan, in Chester county [Pa.].

Miller, Anna, of Martin and Anna Miller, born July 31st, baptized September 2d, sponsors Thomas and Margaret Quigley, *ibid*.

Plain, Joseph, of James (P.) and Catharine Plain, born August 23d, baptized September 6th, sponsor Mary Dodd.

Reinolds, James, of Nathaniel and Eleanor Reinolds, born February 2d,

1773, baptized September 15th, sponsors Dominic Laurence and Anna Burns.

Finney, Joseph, of John and Mary Finney, born August 30th, baptized September 19th, sponsors John Field and Honora Downey.

Forest, Moses, of James and Margaret Forest, born September 20th, baptized September 24th, sponsors James Mullen and Anna Kean.

O'Neal, John, of Henry and Anna O'Neal, born August 18th, baptized September 28th, sponsors Henry and Sarah Tims.

Warrel, Elizabeth, of Francis and Elizabeth Warrel, born September 19th, baptized September 29th, sponsors Christopher Herberger and Elizabeth Essling.

Conway, Mary, of James and Elizabeth Conway, born September 11th, baptized October 6th, sponsors John and Anna Hackett and Bridget Cooper.

McKue, Luke, of James and Anna McKue, born October 3d, baptized October 6th, sponsors Jonathan Baxter and Sybilla O'Shoghnocy.

——, Catharine, six months old, a black slave of Catharine Tolly, baptized October 7th, sponsor Mary Wood (for Catharine Tolly).

Coffey, Catharine, of George and Catharine Coffey, born October 1st, baptized October 13th, sponsors Nicholas and Anna Wochman.

Ells, Catharine, of John and Anna Elizabeth Ells, born September 27th, baptized October 16th, sponsor Catharine Callin, witnesses Peter Strobel and Catharine Butz, while traveling in New Jersey.

Call, John William, of John Nicholas and Anna Margaret Call, born July 7th, baptized October 17th, sponsor Conrad Phillips, for John William Schäffer, at Change Water [Warren county, N. J.].

Wattcock, Mary, of Richard and Mary Wattcock, born September 12th, 1768, baptized October 20th, sponsors John Burk and Margaret Kelly, at Mount Hope [N. J.].

Dealy, Esther, of James and Esther Dealy, born August 18th, baptized October 20th, sponsors Edward Darmoty and Catharine Welsh, *ibid*.

Wattcock, Richard, of Richard and Mary Wattcock, born September 20th, 1773, baptized October 20th, sponsors John and Margaret Viché, *ibid*.

Krämer, James, of William and Patience Krämer, born January 18th, baptized October 20th, sponsors James and Grace Brown, *ibid*.

Welsh, Mary, of William and Elizabeth Welsh, born April 2d, baptized October 20th, sponsors Caspar and Margaret Engelhard, *ibid*.

Powr, Lucy, of Thomas and Susanna Powr, born June 28th, baptized October 20th, sponsors Francis Dealy and Margaret Engelhard, *ibid*.

Hayman, Anna Mary Gertrude and John George, twins, of John and Susanna Hayman, born July 7th and July 8th, baptized October

20th, sponsors John Antler and Gertrude Sig for the former, John George Sig and Anna Catharine Demuth for the latter, *ibid.*

Philipps, Robert, of John and Mary Philipps, born August 19th, baptized October 21st, sponsors Caspar and Margaret Engelhard, *ibid.*

Stuart, Sarah Brewer, wife of John Stuart, baptized October 22d, sponsor Catharine Robertson, at Charlottenburg [N. J.].

Stuart, John, of John and Sarah Stuart, born September 9th, baptized October 22d, sponsors Joseph Wingart and Anna Mentzenbach, *ibid.*

Wingart, Julianna, of Joseph and Elizabeth Wingart, born July 19th, ceremony supplied October 23d, witnesses Daniel Cobole and Anna Mary Rieder, *ibid.*

Marian, Joseph, of Hubert and Anna Mary Marian, born October 22d, baptized October 23d, sponsors Joseph Wingart and Catharine Schott, *ibid.*

Schop, David, of Philip and Mary Eva Schop, born June 27th, baptized October 24th, sponsors David Fichter and Mary Lobisa Schop, *ibid.*

Lawless, Margaret, of Mary and Martin Lawless, born October 17th, 1775, baptized October 26th, sponsors John and Elizabeth Rüger, at Longpond [N. J.].

May, Magdalen, of Anthony and Margaret May, born June 13th, baptized October 26th, sponsors Nicholas Call and Magdalen May, *ibid.*

Haycock, Mary, of Thomas (P.) and Sarah Haycock, born September 2d, 1771, baptized October 26th, sponsors David Fichter and Mary Dentz, *ibid.*

Monk, William, of John and Margaret Monk, born September 16th, baptized October 27th, sponsors James Fichter (for W. Harrison) and Eva Fichter, *ibid.*

Boone, David, of John and Anna Boone, born May 25th, baptized October 27th, sponsors David and Joanna Fichter, *ibid.*

Cole, Margaret, of Henry and Elizabeth Cole, born March 28th, baptized privately October 27th, witnesses William Lary and Mary Clark, *ibid.*

Riddle, Mary Ann, of Thomas and Fanny Riddle, born May 14th, baptized October 27th, sponsors John and Mary Ann Cobole.

Lafarty, Mary, of John and Margaret Lafarty, born March 10th, baptized October 27th, sponsors James Dogherty and Margaret Burns, *ibid.*

Grey, Andrew, of John and Anna Grey, born May 23d, baptized October 27th, sponsor Daniel McShafery and witness Mary Burk, *ibid.*

Freemund, Catharine, of John and Margaret Freemund, born October 29th, baptized conditionally November 4th, sponsors Joseph and Catharine Egg, in Philadelphia.

McKan, John, of Charles and Catharine McKan, born November 5th, baptized November 5th, sponsor Daniel Hays and witness Mary Mathes.

Castela, Bridget, of Richard and Alice Castela, born November 3d, baptized November 10th, sponsors John and Eleanor McConigel.

O'Hara, James, of Bryan and Mary O'Hara, born October 30th, baptized November 10th, sponsors Dennis Dougherty and Barbara Groff.

Stoop, Hannah, of Andrew and Elizabeth (McGora) Stoop, born October 26th, baptized November 11th, sponsor Mary Hart. .

O'Neill, Sarah Turner, wife of Constantine O'Neill, baptized November 16th, sponsor Frederick Scheimer, at Pikesland [Chester county, Pa.].

O'Neill, John, of Constantine and Sarah O'Neill, born September 1st, baptized November 16th, sponsors Daniel and Elizabeth Scheimer, *ibid.*

Bender, John, of Frederic and Catharine (P.) Bender, born September 4th, baptized November 17th, sponsors John and Catharine Gans, *ibid.*

Cullen, Thomas, of Thomas and Sabina Cullen, born November 7th, baptized November 18th, sponsor Michael Connor (for Morgan Connor), at Pottsgrove.

Stuart, Margaret, of James and Mary Stuart, born November 20th, baptized November 22d, sponsors Thomas and Phœbe Stuart, at Philadelphia.

Göck, John, of Mathias and Charlotte Göck, born August 29th, baptized November 24th, sponsors Simon Geiger and Mary Geiger, at Pilesgrove [Salem county, N. J.].

Magill, Stephen, of John and Catharine Magill, about seven months old, baptized November 24th, sponsors Henry Geiger and Susanna Thurnbach, *ibid.*

Lester, Conrad, of Daniel and Catharine Lester, born October 13th, baptized December 1st, sponsors Michael and Joanna Robeson.

Beaufort, Anthony, of Caspar and Anna Beaufort, born November 6th, baptized December 2d, sponsors Anthony and Mary Lechler.

Loan, Eleanor, of Henry and Catharine Loan, born September 22d, baptized December 7th, sponsors Charles Tolly and Christina Horn.

Hanley, Thomas, of Thomas and Rachel Hanley, born November 23d, baptized December 8th, sponsors Dennis and Margaret Dougherty.

L'Hercule, Margaret, of John and Josephine L'Hercule, born December 8th, baptized December 8th, sponsors Peter Leblanc and Margaret Landry.

Roberts, Mary, of Thomas and Mary Roberts, born August 17th, baptized December 8th, sponsors John Walton and Mary Badford.

Clare, Mary Magdalen, of John and Anna Margaret (Görtz) Clare, born December 2d, baptized December 10th, sponsors George Ernest and Mary Magdalen Lechler.

More, Amy Mary, of Samuel and Elizabeth (Corbet) More, born November 25th, baptized December 19th, sponsor Mary Fowloo.

Seibert, Mary Anna, of Sebastian and Mary Elizabeth Seibert, born December 4th, baptized December 22d, sponsor Salome Schwartz.

Jacobs, Anna Mary, of William (P.) and Catharine Jacobs, born November 26th, baptized December 23d, sponsors John and Margaret Ridiger.

Connoly, Mary, of William and Elizabeth Connoly, born August 22d, 1773, baptized December 23d, sponsors William Hussy and Susanna Madole.

Nadler, Philip James, of John and Magdalen Nadler, born December 26th, baptized December 29th, sponsors Philip and Elizabeth Will.

Whole number of baptisms—two hundred and three.

REGISTER OF BAPTISMS FOR 1777.

Miller, Mary, of John and Susanna Miller, born December 19th, 1776, baptized January 1st, sponsor John Christy.

Morris, Elias, of Stephen and Sarah Morris, born October 19th, 1776, baptized Jauuary 4th, sponsor Mary Hart.

Ryan, James, of Bryan and Margaret Ryan, born September 30th, 1776, baptized January 6th, sponsor Catharine Beal, witness Henry Beal.

Rodgers, William, of Francis and Mary Rodgers, born January 8th, 1769, baptized January 8th, sponsor Rebecca Cornely.

Hans, James, of Christopher and Catharine Hans, born December 18th, 1776, baptized January 8th.

Jonston, Anna, of —— and Mary Jonston, about two years old, baptized January 13th, sponsor Sarah Tool and witness Alexander Alexander.

Clark, Thomas, of Michael and Mary Clark, born December 19th, 1776, baptized January 13th, sponsors Patrick and Elizabeth Rice.

Kneul, Catharine Frances, of Balthasar and Christina Kneul, born January 12th, baptized January 19th, sponsor Catharine Frances Wagner.

Clifton, Elizabeth, of Benjamin and Martha Clifton, born January 23d, baptized privately January 23d.

Brown, John, of John and Elizabeth (Kelly) Brown, born January 14th, baptized January 25th, sponsor Wallburga Bremich.

Zeiss, John, of George and Eva Zeiss, born January 2d, baptized January 26th, sponsors Francis Wolf and his wife, Anna Margaret.

Dugan, Thomas, of John and Mary Dugan, born January 23d, baptized January 26th, sponsors James and Anna Welsh.

Jonston, Mary, of Peter and Sarah Jonston, born August, 1776, baptized January 27th, sponsor Mary Jonston.

Savoy, Elizabeth, of Peter and Mary (L'Hercule) Savoy, born January 27th, baptized January 27th, sponsors Peter Denuye du Pommant and Clara L'Hercule.

McMahan, Jeremiah, of Jeremiah and Susanna McMahan, born January 10th, baptized January 29th, witness John Huntson and sponsor Catharine Cook.

Sipplee, Andrew, of Andrew (P.) and Alice Sipplee, born November 25th, 1776, baptized January 30th, sponsor Alice Fitzgerald.

Cuningham, Margaret, of Paul and Margaret Cuningham, born December 7th, 1776, baptized February 2d, sponsors Daniel Whealan and Mary Byrne.

Welsh, Margaret, of Henry and Mary (Glass) Welsh, born February 2d, 1775, baptized February 2d, sponsors Michael McChristal and Susanna Doyle.

Burk, Sarah, aged twenty-three years, baptized February 3d, sponsor Margaret Roage.

Meaz, Sarah, of George and Mary Gertrude Meaz, born about August, 1775, baptized February 9th, sponsor Mary Gertrude Tscharté.

Landy, John, of James and Elizabeth Landy, born January 20th, baptized February 9th, sponsors Peter and Phœbe Duffy.

Blanchard, Peter, of Peter and Mary Blanchard, born February 10th, baptized February 11th, sponsors Peter Lairette and Anna Lebeaume.

Dougherty, Martin, of Dennis and Margaret Dougherty, born February 12th, baptized February 13th, sponsors Joseph Kauffman and Mary, wife of Patrick Byrne.

McJilton, William, adult, baptized February 15th, sponsor Barnabas Cox.

Kelly, Mary, of James and Margaret (Dewetter) Kelly, born Decemher 15th, 1776, baptized February 16th, sponsor Catharine Donoly.

Landry, Charles, of Joseph and Sarah Landry, born February 14th, baptized February 16th, sponsors Placidus and Margaret Landry.

Humann, Joseph, of John and Mary Humann, born February 16th, baptized February 20th, sponsors Cassian and Anna Mary Huber.

Connor, John, of Michael and Mary Connor, born February 19th, baptized March 5th, sponsor John Cotringer (for Morgan Connor) and Catharine Cotringer.

Sylvester, Mary Magdalen, of Simon and Elizabeth (Christman) Sylvester, born January 29th, baptized March 8th, sponsor Mary Magdalen Christman.

FitzPatrick, Mary Ann, of John and Honora FitzPatrick, born March 6th, baptized March 9th, sponsors Edward McCoy and Eleanor Welsh.

Motley, Mary, of Walter and Mary Motley, born April 7th, 1776, baptized March 9th, sponsors Philip Dwyer and Johanna Motley (for Rosanna Dwyer).

Welsh, Mary Ann, of Miles and Ann Welsh, born February 23d, baptized March 17th, sponsor Barnabas Magill, in Chester county [Pa.].

Burk, Barbara, of Patrick and Ruth Burk, born September 5th, 1769, baptized March 20th, sponsor Johanna Fegan.

Burk, Thomas, same parents, born August 29th, 1771, baptized March 20th, same sponsor.

Bartley, Margaret, of Joseph (P.) and Margaret Bartley, born November 25th, 1776, baptized March 22d, sponsor Johanna Fegan.

——, Joseph, of Nicholas and Flora, negroes, born October, 1776, baptized March 23d, sponsors Francis and Anna.

Asky, Archibald, of parents unknown, born April 3d, 1773, baptized April 3d, sponsors Leonard and Mary Anna Lasher.

McCurtin, Mary, of Thomas and Deborah McCurtin, born August 12th, 1776, baptized April 4th, sponsors Michael Green and Anna Deleany.

Mitchel, Thomas, of Thomas and Rosanna Mitchel, born January 27th, baptized April 6th, sponsors Patrick Punch and Anna McMahan.

Göck, Henry, of Lawrence and Christina Göck, born November 16th, 1776, baptized April 9th, sponsors Henry Geiger and Hannah Huber, at Pilesgrove [Salem county N. J.].

Miller, Susanna, of Mathias and Anna Mary Miller, born December 25th, 1776, baptized April 9th, sponsors Simon Geiger and Susanna Benner, *ibid*.

McMullen, James, of Cornelius and Rebecca (P.) McMullen, born September 7th, 1776, baptized privately April 10th, *ibid*.

Morson, Elizabeth, of ——— Morson, born 1775, baptized privately April 12th.

Stafford, James, of James and Margaret Stafford, born March 25th, baptized April 13th, sponsors James Gillmore and Mary Galagher.

Magill, Mary, of James and Mary (P.) Magill, born July, 1764, baptized April 17th, sponsor Margaret Francis.

Magill, Rachel, same parents, born January, 1770, baptized April 17th, sponsor Catharine Haug.

Magill, Theresa, same parents, born March, 1773, baptized April 17th, sponsor Johanna Nickols.

Magill, Elizabeth, same parents, born March, 1773, baptized April 17th, sponsor Mary Casey.

Joyce, Peter, of Dominic and Jeannette Joyce, born April 9th, baptized April 20th, sponsor John Telez and witness Mary Sibbald.

Viel, Susanna, of Peter and Lucretia Viel, born April 13th, baptized April 20th, sponsors Christopher Herberger and Susanna Viel.

More, George, of David and Eva More, born April 16th, baptized April

27th, sponsors Udalric Freind (for George Freind) and Catharine Freind.

Stalter, Nicholas, of Nicholas and Elizabeth Stalter, born March 7th, baptized May 4th, sponsors Nicholas and Anna Eva Jungfleisch, at Longpond [N. J.].

Cahel, Sarah, of Thomas and Eleanor Cahel, born January 28th, baptized May 4th, sponsors David and Johanna Fichter, *ibid.*

Call, Anna Catharine, of Nicholas, Jr., and Anna Mary Call, ceremony supplied May 5th, sponsor Anna Catharine Waibl, at Ringwood [Passaic county, N. J.].

Card, John, of Peter and Sarah (P.) Card, born May 20th, 1775, baptized May 5th, sponsors Anthony and Margaret May, *ibid.*

Card, Stephen, same parents, born January ——, baptized May 5th, sponsors Henry Call and Mary Catharine Rüger, *ibid.*

Strickland, Anna, of William and Amy (P.) Strickland, born March 11th, baptized May 5th, sponsors Anthony and Margaret May, *ibid.*

May, Charles, of James and Magdalen May, born January 29th, baptized May 5th, sponsors Charles Waibl and Anna Mary Cobole, *ibid.*

Gordon, Joseph, of Hugh and Margaret Gordon, born December 20th, 1776, baptized May 7th, sponsor Joseph Stecher, at Charlottenburg [N. J.].

Stecher, Lawrence Martin, of Joseph and Anna Stecher, born January 16th, baptized May 8th, sponsor Martin Bachman, *ibid.*

Bachman, Ferdinand, of Martin and Anna Barbara Bachman, born May 2d, ceremonies supplied May 8th, sponsors John Cobole and Anna Eva Jungfleisch, *ibid.*

Zech, Mary Anna, of Francis Anthony and Anna Catharine Zech, born November 27th, ceremony supplied May 8th, sponsors Joseph Wingart and Mary Anna Cobole, *ibid.*

Jones, Mary Ann, of Peter and Mary Jones, born May 13th, baptized May 20th, sponsors Francis Robutin and Anna Lebeaume.

Gans, George, of John and Catharine Gans, born March 18th, baptized May 25th, sponsor Catharine Weissenburger, at Pikesland [Chester county, Pa.].

Schneider, Margaret, of Burchard and Catharine Schneider, born March 31st, 1776, baptized May 25th, sponsors Jacob Weissenburger and Anna Mary Gans, *ibid.*

Dugan, Mary, of James and Sarah Dugan, born November 24th, 1776, baptized May 25th, sponsor Catharine Gans, *ibid.*

Magee, John, of John and Joanna (Haley) Magee, born March 29th, baptized June 1st, sponsors George Graff and Margaret Sauerwald.

Mealy, Mary, of Jeremiah and Elizabeth Mealy, born April 15th, 1776, baptized June 2d, sponsors Thomas Villar and Mary Rodt.

Schmeil, Mary Gertrude, of Joseph and Mary Magdalen Schmeil, born

March 12th, 1776, baptized June 8th, sponsors Peter Christman and Mary Zängerle.

Ferree, Eleanor, of Joseph and Eleanor Ferree, born May 29th, baptized June 15th, sponsors Joseph Feinauer and Anna Mary Spengler.

Kean, Hugh, of Hugh and Elizabeth Kean, born June 3d, baptized June 18th, sponsors Nicholas Walter and Mary McDonald.

Talbot, James, of James and Honora Talbot, born May 26th, baptized June 21st, sponsor Catharine Davis.

Raubin, John, of John and Anna Raubin, born June 26th, baptized June 27th, sponsors Peter L'Airette and Catharine Freind.

Kitzinger, Margaret, of Philip and Ottilia Kitzinger, born June 24th, baptized June 29th, sponsors Sebastian and Margaret Vanié.

Curren, Thomas, of William and Margaret Curren, born June 28th, baptized July 6th, sponsor Thomas Mulry and witness Catharine Hayd.

Buch, John Joseph, of Joseph and Hannah Buch, born June 17th, baptized July 8th, sponsors Adam Buch (for Joseph Springer) and Magdalen Springer.

Graff, Anthony, of Anthony and Barbara Graff, born July 12th, baptized July 14th, sponsors Joseph Kaufman and Catharine Spengler.

Dorsey, George, of Michael and Catharine Dorsey, born October 5th, 1776, baptized July 17th, sponsor Mary Erwin.

Hanecker, Anthony, of John and Mary Hanecker, born July 11th, baptized July 20th, sponsors Anthony and Catharine Lechler.

Rübel, George, of Francis and Regina Rübel, born July 26th, baptized August 1st, sponsors Adam and Catharine Rübel.

McKenly, Susanna, of Thomas and Euphemia McKenly, born July 19th, baptized August 2d, the priest being sponsor.

Henesy, James, of John and Margaret Henesy, born July 25th, baptized August 3d, sponsors Patrick Byrne and Margaret White.

Morton, Sarah, of Lawrence and Jemima (Campbell) Morton, born July 7th, baptized August 4th, sponsor Walburga Bremich.

Scott, John, of Charles and Catharine Scott, born July 12th, baptized August 9th, sponsors John Halahan and Johanna Fitzgerald.

Benner, John, of Henry and Mary Benner, born August 3d, baptized August 10th, sponsors John and Eva Poth.

Byrne, Henry Lawrence, of Patrick and Mary Byrne, born August 9th, baptized August 10th, sponsor Catharine Flahavan.

Lynch, John, of John and ——— Lynch, born August 7th, baptized August 12th, sponsors Alfred Clifton and Mary Barret.

Powr, John, of Joseph and Amy Powr, born June 8th, baptized August 13th, sponsor Timothy Carrol.

Morris, Edward, of Philip and Elizabeth Morris, born March 19th, baptized August 13th, sponsors John Faran and Mary Watts.

McElwayne, Andrew, of William and Mary McElwayne, born August

13th, baptized August 14th, sponsors James Dougherty and Mary Currey.

Harty, William, of Jóhn and Catharine Harty, born August 10th, baptized August 19th, sponsors James Welsh and Rebecca Cornely.

Boutin, John Baptist, of John Charles and Pelagia Boutin, born August, 1776, baptized August 24th, sponsor Josephine Gallerm.

Hoffman, Adam, of Adam and Catharine Hoffman, born August 21st, baptized August 31st, sponsors Adam and Catharine Lechler.

McGovran, Frederick, of Bridget McGovran, servant at Lauterbach's, born March 20th, 1776, baptized August 31st, sponsor John Manderfield.

Blum, Barbara, of Anthony and Barbara Blum, born August 25th, baptized August 31st, sponsors Prudence La Jeunesse and Mary Magdalen Davernac.

Weidtner, Elizabeth, of Samuel and Mary Weidtner, born July 6th, baptized privately September 2d.

Buttler, Anna Mary Sophia, of Edward and Anna Buttler, born August 27th. baptized September 2d, sponsor Anna Mary Sophia Cameloch.

Martin, Sarah, of Henry and Margaret Martin, born March 10th, baptized September 2d, sponsors Thomas Dugan and Mary Dealy.

O'Squillian, Joseph, of Francis and Anna O'Squillian, born December 21st, 1776, baptized September 3d, sponsors Bartholomew Tool and Mary Reilly.

West, Frances, of John and Bridget West, born August 20th, baptized September ——, witness Edward Reemer and sponsor Johanna Griffin.

Bray, John, of John and Judith Bray, born September 12th, baptized September 12th, sponsors Anthony Graff and Catharine Cook.

Gilkar, Catharine, of George and Prudence Gilkar, born August 20th, baptized September 14th, sponsors John Aitken and Anna Ducray.

Pay, John, of William and Elizabeth Pay, born September 4th, baptized September 21st, sponsors John Heffernan and Catharine Huston.

Connor, Margaret, of Simon and Mary Connor, born September 10th, baptized September 23d, sponsors John Morris and Mary Evan.

Philipps, Sarah, of —— and Mary Philipps, born May 1st, 1768, baptized September 24th, sponsor Barbara Schultz.

Songfield, Elizabeth, of Frederic and Anna Songfield, six months old, baptized September 30th, sponsor Mary Johnson.

Dougherty, Edward, of Felix and Johanna Dougherty, born September 26th, baptized October 2d, sponsors Catharine Barnfield and witness her husband, William.

Piercy, Catharine, of John and Margaret (Haly) Piercy, born September 20th, baptized October 2d, sponsor Mary Loyd.

Greswold, Anna, of Joseph and Mary Greswold, born October 1st, baptized October 3d, sponsor Anna Hill.

McDonald, Mary, of George and Elizabeth McDonald, born August 5th, 1776, baptized October 3d, sponsors John Ryan and Catharine Jackson.

Ghibens, Adam, of Henry and Elizabeth Ghibens, born August 21st, baptized October 5th, sponsors Adam and Catharine Rübel.

Halfpenny, Catharine, of Thomas and Margaret Halfpenny, born September 26th, baptized October 6th, sponsors Thomas O'Hara and Anna Allen.

McKenley, Elizabeth, of John and Mary McKenley, born September 19th, baptized October 7th, sponsor Anna Barbara Berger.

Patterson, Catharine, of John and Catharine (Rice) Patterson, born September 28th, baptized October 8th, sponsor Margaret Sauerwald.

Bauer, Catharine, of Francis and Elizabeth Bauer, born September 29th, baptized October 12th, sponsors Adam Poth, Jr., and Catharine Poth.

Hammel, Crispin, of James and Margaret Hammel, born October 9th, baptized October 12th, sponsors Edward Faran and Mary Gordon.

Smith, Elizabeth, of James and Anna Smith, born August 17th, baptized October 12th, sponsors James Welsh, Jr., and Johanna Burn.

Metzger, Mary Elizabeth, of John and Cecilia Metzger, born October 11th, baptized October 18th, sponsors George Ernest and Mary Magdalen Lechler.

Dunfield, James, of Edward and Esther Dunfield, born September 12th, baptized October 18th, sponsors Richard Welsh and Mary Wessels.

Ross, Hugh, of Hugh and Anna (P.) Ross, born October 9th, baptized October 19th, sponsor Catharine Dougherty.

Brimigeom, George, of John and Margaret Brimigeom, born October 14th, baptized October 19th, sponsors James and Elizabeth Conway.

Web, Anna, of John and Martha Web, born October 11th, baptized October 19th, witness Timothy Burrington and sponsor Mary Masters.

Tagart, John, of Archibald and Mary Tagart, born August 8th, 1776, baptized October 23d, sponsor Hannah Curren and witness Mary Lipper.

Schneider, John, of Henry and Catharine Schneider, born October 20th, baptized October 26th, sponsors John and Regina Schneider.

Boosee, John, of Moses and Elizabeth Boosee, born October 25th, baptized October 26th, sponsors John Keeth and Barbara Graff.

Welsh, James, of James and Anna Welsh, born October 20th, baptized October 26th, sponsors John Aitkin and Catharine Malowny.

Krombell, Mary Margaret, of Philip and Margaret Krombell, born October 31st, baptized November 2d, sponsor Tobias Rudolph and witness his wife, Mary Margaret.

Conrad, Mathias, of Mathias and Catharine Conrad, born November

1st, baptized November 4th, sponsor John Wagner and witness Barbara Steinmetz.

Rübel, Anna Catharine, of Adam and Catharine Rübel, born October 31st, baptized November 4th, sponsors Joseph Rübel and Anna Catharine Stahl.

Fitzgerald, James, of Richard and Margaret Fitzgerald, born April 2d, baptized November 13th, sponsors John Campbell and Margaret Giles, witness Peter Flaharty.

McGrath, Michael, of John and Mary McGrath, born November 5th, baptized November 14th, sponsors James and Bridget O'Brian.

Mahany, Edward, of Edward and Catharine Mahany, born November 10th, baptized November 15th, sponsors Alfred Clifton and Mary Dugan, witness Eleanor Donaho.

McHuin, Anna, of James and Anna McHuin, born September 24th, baptized November 18th, sponsors James and Mary Gorman.

McDonald, Sarah, of Alexander and Honora McDonald, born November 8th, baptized November 24th, sponsors Jeremiah Mealy and Mary Murphy.

Faran, Mary, of John and Mary Faran, born November 20th, baptized November 30th, sponsors Thomas McKeavres and Mary Martin.

——, Sarah, of Potina, a slave of Thomas Badge, about nine months old, baptized December 1st, sponsor Mary Badge.

Scheifeltgen, Mary Ann, of Andrew and Catharine Scheifeltgen, born June 11th, baptized December 5th, sponsor Mary Anna Lascher.

Fegan, Edward, of Edward and Margery Fegan, born November 15th, baptized December 8th, sponsors Fortunatus Adienn and Elizabeth Sline.

Boudrot, Joseph, of Michael and Anna Boudrot, born December 7th, baptized December 8th, sponsors Thomas Betagh and Christina Veit.

Talbert, John, of James and Catharine Talbert, born November 18th, baptized December 11th, sponsors John Manderfeld and Walburga Bremich.

Caroll, Mary Anna, of James and Mary Caroll, born July 23d, baptized December 13th, sponsor Catharine Dougherty.

Hagenmiller, John George, of Melchior and Frederika Hagenmiller, born December 14th, baptized December 15th, sponsors John George and Elizabeth Bauer, in vicinity of Philadelphia.

Feinauer, John, of Joseph and Anna Mary Feinauer, born December 17th, baptized December 21st, sponsors John and Christina Staler.

Viel, Susanna, of Paul and Mary Viel, born December 13th, baptized December 25th, sponsors Nicholas Veil and Catharine Veil, Sr.

Gantly, Mary, of Patrick and Catharine Gantly, born December 5th, baptized December 25th, sponsor James Hieran.

Owen, William, of John and Alice Owen, born November 1st, baptized
December 26th, sponsor Catharine Hanbury.

Lechler, Anna, of Anthony and Catharine Lechler, born December 18th,
baptized December 27th, sponsors George Ernest and Mary Magdalen Lechler.

Horn, George Henry, of Henry and Christina Horn, born December
11th, baptized December 27th, sponsors George Ernest and Mary
Magdalen Lechler.

Whole number of baptisms—one hundred and forty-eight.

_____

REGISTER OF BAPTISMS FOR 1778.

Carpé, Joseph, of Herman and Margaret Carpé, born December 31st,
1777, baptized January 1st, sponsors Walter and Mary Fitzgerald.

McFarlin, Mary, of —— and Catharine McFarlin, born November,
1777, baptized January 4th, sponsor Elizabeth Townsend.

Erwin, Letitia, of Abraham and Hannah Erwin, born December 30th,
1777, baptized January 4th, sponsor Catharine Boudrot.

Rowin, Mary, of John and Catharine Rowin, born May, 1770, baptized
January 8th, sponsors Peter and Elizabeth Galagher.

Colbert, Elizabeth, of John and Dorothy Colbert, born December 19th,
1777, baptized January 10th, sponsor Mary Albrecht, near Philadelphia, Pa.

Kelly, Thomas (O'Reily), of Thomas and Mary Kelly, born January
9th, baptized January 12th, sponsor Dennis McElway.

Hines, Thomas, of Edward and Elizabeth Hines, born December 21st,
1777, baptized January 12th, sponsors Thomas Ellis and Elizabeth
Piercy.

Curran, Hugh, of Thomas and Anna Curran, born November 22d, 1777,
baptized January 17th, sponsor John Curran and witness Grace
Linsey.

——, John, of Betty, slave of John Tolly, born September 11th, 1777,
baptized January 19th, sponsor Abraham Readin.

Speir, Mathias, of Mathias and Mary Speir, born November 2d, 1777,
baptized January 19th, sponsors John Heitz and Margaret Gruber.

Reily, Michael, of Patrick and Catharine Reily, born September 30th,
1777, baptized January 20th, sponsors Patrick Sheahy and Johanna
McElway.

Merchant, William, of James and Eleanor (Cready) Merchant, born December 3d, 1777, baptized January 25th, sponsors Michael Rollins
and Anna Byrne, and witness Michael Derny.

Blake, Elizabeth, of Michael and Anna Blake, born September 9th,

1777, ceremonies supplied January 28th, sponsor Mary Albrecht, in vicinity of Philadelphia.

Betagh, Mary, of Thomas and Margaret Betagh, born January 28th, baptized January 30th, sponsors John Diamond and Christina Veit.

Graig, John, of Peter and Johanna Mary (Vessels) Graig, born December 21st, 1777, baptized February 1st, sponsors Peter Eck and Elizabeth Götz, in vicinity of Philadelphia.

Welsh, Anna, of John and Catharine Welsh, born January 31st, baptized February 1st, sponsors Edmund Gnash and Mary Heart, *ibid.*

Welsh, Thomas, same parents, born January 31st, baptized February 1st, sponsor William Ross, *ibid.*

Späth, Anna Margaret, of John and Margaret Späth, born January 1st, baptized February 2d, sponsor Anna Theusen.

Cæsar, of Thomas and Letitia, slave of Thomas Leak, three years old, baptized February 4th, sponsor Catharine Gordon.

William, same parents, two weeks old, baptized February 4th, the same sponsor.

Rogers, John Herman, of Francis and Mary Rogers, born January 18th, baptized February 5th, sponsor Mary Vans and witness John Herman Puley.

Potié, John George, of Louis and Catharine Potié, born December 15th, 1777, baptized February 8th, sponsors Elizabeth Släuch and witnesses George Shear and Margaret Young.

Pranger, Barbara, of William and Catharine Pranger, born February 9th, baptized conditionally February 15th, sponsors Anthony Bastian and Barbara Krumholtz.

Briar, Paul, of Emmanuel and Mary Briar, born February 8th, baptized February 15th, sponsors Paul and Christina Essling.

Günther, John, of John George and Frances Günther, born February 16th, baptized February 18th, sponsors John Wagner and Catharine, his wife.

Benner, Henry, of Martin and Christina Benner, born February 8th, baptized February 22d, sponsors Henry and Mary Benner.

Devenac, Mary, of Joseph and Magdalen Devenac, born February 21st, baptized February 22d, sponsors John Peter Defelon and Mary Vincent.

Smith, Michael, of Michael and Rosa Smith, born November 13th, baptized March 7th, sponsor Margaret Corcran.

Boyde, Richard, of Patrick and Anna Boyde, born February 16th, baptized March 8th, sponsor Edward Cavenogh and witness his wife, Elizabeth.

Berg, Mary Gertrude, of Ernest and Mary Gertrude Berg, born March 6th, baptized March 10th, sponsors Christopher and Mary Dorothy Tscharté, in vicinity of Philadelphia.

Hoffman, Anna Margaret, of John and Christina Hoffman, born February 17th, baptized March 10th, sponsor Walburga Bremich, *ibid.*

Wilhelm, John, of John Adam and Anna Wilhelm, born February 21st, baptized March 15th, sponsors John and Christina Stahler.

Broadley, John, of Thomas and Mary Broadley, born December 1st, 1777, baptized March 19th, sponsors Patrick Ladwith and Anna Kelly.

Schreiner, Anna, of Anselm and Elizabeth Schreiner, born March 15th, baptized March 22d, sponsors Joseph and Anna Eck.

Ridiger, Catharine, of John and Margaret Ridiger, born March 19th, baptized March 22d, sponsors Peter Hegner, Jr., and Catharine Vanié.

Hardnet, Honora, of James and Johanna Hardnet, born March 9th, baptized March 29th, sponsors Edward Macoy and Anna Maher.

Waltrich, John Henry, of Peter and Catharine Waltrich, born November 14, 1777, baptized April 3d, sponsors Henry and Catharine Schneider.

Bartley, Catharine, of James and Eleanor Bartley, born December 26th, 1777, baptized April 5th, sponsors Edward Dunfee and Esther Dunfee, in vicinity of Philadelphia.

Campbel, Joseph, of John and Catharine Campbell, born April 8th, baptized April 14th, sponsors Joseph Whiteaker and Winifred Austin.

Spangler, George, of George and Anna Mary Spangler, born April 4th, baptized April 16th, sponsors Anthony Graff and Catharine Spängler.

Lester, Margaret, of Daniel and Catharine Lester, born April 5th, baptized April 16th, sponsors Thomas and Margaret Betagh.

Biron, Henrietta, of William and Wilhelmina Biron,. born February 9th, baptized April 20th, sponsors John Dun and Mary Ryan.

Barret, Richard, of John and Bridget Barret, born April 14th, baptized April 23d, sponsors Richard Barret and Mary Byrne.

Yarock, Anna Mary, of Matthew and Allinavia Yarock, born April 8th, baptized April 25th, sponsors Hugh O'Brian and Mary Badge.

Champain, Stephen, of Stephen and Mary (Benoit) Champain, born April 24th, baptized April 25th, sponsors Gregory Trahan and Margaret Bourg.

Tumy, William, of Dennis and Anna Tumy, born April 23d, baptized April 26th, sponsors James Hays and Mary Martin.

Doyle, Joseph, of John and Esther Doyle, born December 3d, 1777, baptized May 4th, sponsor Mary Madgalen Lechler.

Duffy, Elizabeth, of Peter and Phœbe Duffy, born May 2d, baptized May 4th, sponsors James Gillmor and Margaret Readin.

Morgan, John, of John and Anna Morgan, born April 30th, baptized May 4th, sponsor Francis Connor.

Ross, Margaret, of Thomas and Elizabeth (Hansley) Ross, born May 1st, baptized May 5th, sponsor Judith Power.

Hohl, John, of Peter and Catharine (Miller) Hohl, born May 2d, baptized May 5th, sponsors John Rudolph and Mary Bodevin, in vicinity of Philadelphia.

Flammins, Margaret, of George and Julia Flammins, born February 23d, baptized May 13th, sponsor Margaret Sauerwald.

Gerard, Thomas, of William and Eleanor Gerard, born February 4th, baptized May 24th, sponsors Thomas O'Dwyer and Mary Small.

Murphy, Elizabeth, of Daniel and Julia Murphy, born May 8th, baptized May 24th, sponsors Jeremiah Macarty and Christina Schuman.

Delamar, William, of Thomas and Mary Delamar, born March 1st, baptized May 25th, sponsors Alexander Lishman and Mary McMullen.

Fudge, William, of James and Anna Fudge, born October 23d, 1777, baptized May 26th, sponsor Barbara Schultz.

Barret, Edward, of James and Mary Barret, born February —, baptized May 27th, sponsors John O'Neil and Margaret Groghan.

Wilkison, Hannah, thirteen years old, baptized May 29th, sponsor Deborah Blanchard.

Dawson, Anna, of James and Mary (Philips) Dawson, born May 12th, baptized June 1st, sponsor Mary Hart.

Maudsley, John, of John Cavendish and Eleanor Maudsley, born January 30th, baptized June 1st, sponsor Clement Maudsley and witness Dennis Dowlan.

Lederman, Mary Catharine, of John and Catharine Lederman, born May 18th, baptized June 7th, sponsors Joseph and Elizabeth Becker.

Rittisheim, John, of John and Catharine Rittisheim, born December 28th, 1775, baptized June 9th, sponsor Lawrence Connor, at Kensington.

Rittisheim, Anna Catharine, same parents, born March 7th, baptized June 9th, sponsor Julianna Abt, *ibid.*

Byrne, Mary Ann, of Raymond and Anna Byrne, born June 12th, baptized June 14th, sponsors Timothy Carrol and Mary Byrne.

Shaw, Anna, of Daniel and Susanna Shaw, born March 7th, baptized June 21st, sponsors John McOnigl and Eleanor, his wife.

Regimenter, Catharine, of Peter and Magdalen Regimenter, born June 27th, baptized July 1st, sponsors Joseph and Catharine Eck, near Philadelphia.

Whealin, John (Park), of Edward and Catharine Whealin, born June 2d, baptized July 15th, sponsors John Park and Mary Anna Riole.

Wall, Joseph, of Patrick and Anna Wall, born April 2d, 1777, baptized July 19th, sponsors Barnabas Mullen and Margaret Corcran.

Bayerle, George, of Dieterich and Sabina Bayerle, born March 16th, 1777, baptized July 19th, sponsor George Abt and witness Magdalen Wibiro.

Buckley, Mary, of James and Mary Buckley, born June 28th, baptized July 27th, sponsors John Callanan and Mary Buttler.

Alexander, Joanna, of John and Catharine Alexander, born October, 1776, baptized August 4th, sponsor Sarah Aman.

Alexander, Mary, same parents, born July 31st, baptized August 4th, sponsor Susanna McDowl.

Oelers, Catharine .Elizabeth, of James and Catharine Oelers, born August 5th, baptized August 5th, sponsors the priest and Christina Horn.

Mignion, Lawrence, of Charles and Pelagia Mignion, born August 11th, baptized August 11th, sponsors the priest and Margaret Landry.

Becker, Mary, of Bartholomew and Elizabeth Becker, born August 5th, baptized August 15th, sponsors Lawrence and Magdalen Schöne.

Hueber, Sarah, of Michael and Anna Hueber, born June 18th, baptized August 16th, sponsor Salome Schwaitz.

Tims, Mary, of Henry and Anna Tims, born April 31st, baptized August 23d, sponsors James Hicky and Eleanor Hollys, at Pikesland [Chester county, Pa.].

Welsh, Eleanor, of Miles and Anna Welsh, born July 23d, baptized August 24th, sponsors Daniel FitzPatrick and Anna Tims, at Whiteland [Chester county, Pa.].

Glimpson, Mary, of William and Sarah Glimpson, born July 9th, baptized August 24th, sponsors Francis Sohl and Anna Welsh, *ibid*.

Campbel, Margaret, of John and Anna Campbell, born August 31st, 1777, baptized August 24th, sponsor Miles Welsh, *ibid*.

Lamy, Mary, of James and Hannah Lamy, born March 30th, baptized August 25th, sponsors Daniel FitzPatrick and Anna Tims, at Goshen [Pa.].

Schütz, Magdalen, of Jodocus and Sarah Schütz, born February 28th, 1776, baptized September 7th, sponsor Magdalen Schütz, in Salem county.

Schütz, Joseph, of Joseph and Louisa Schütz, born June 23d, 1777, baptized September 7th, sponsor Magdalen Schütz, *ibid*.

Geiger, John, of Henry and Barbara Geiger, born February 8th, baptized September 8th, sponsors John and Catharine Bucher, *ibid*.

Kessler, Helen, of Andrew and Catharine Kessler, born August 11th, 1777, baptized September 9th, sponsors George Sigfrid and Catharine Kessler, Jr., at Gloucester [N. J.].

Moore, John, of Michael and Bridget Moore, born September 5th, baptized September 12th, sponsors Henry Lynch and Mary Brannon.

Galagher, William, of Andrew and Johanna Galagher, born August 1st, baptized September 14th, sponsor Elizabeth Clark and witness Edward Hevington.

Currey, Mary, of Walter and Bridget Currey, born September 10th, baptized September 20th, sponsors Joseph and Mary Feinauer.

Prigl, Mary, of Henry and Margaret Prigl, born September 11th, baptized September 20th, sponsor Elizabeth Dimond.

Sig, Helen, of John George and Gertrude Sig, born November 4th, 1777, baptized September 27th, sponsors Francis Zech and Magdalen Welker (for Helen Menzebach), at Mount Hope [N. J.].

Power, Anna Mary, of Thomas and Susanna Power, born June 24th, baptized September 27th, sponsors Edward Darmoty and Mary Grinder, *ibid.*

Weber, Margaret, of James and Anna Catharine Weber, born July 24th, baptized September 27th, sponsor Margaret Engelhard, *ibid.*

Fichter, Philip, of David and Johanna Fichter, born September 11th, 1777, baptized September 27th, sponsors Louis Herman (for Philip Schup) and Catharine Zech, *ibid.*

Holzheber, Peter Joseph, of Sebastian and Johanna Holzheber, born May 2d, baptized September 27th, sponsors Peter Joseph and Mary Grips, *ibid.*

Schup, Anna Mary, of Philip and Mary Eva Schup, born March 27th, baptized September 29th, sponsors Jacob Fichter and Anna Mary Mentzebach, at Charlottenburg [N. J.].

Marian, Henry, of Hubert and Mary Marian, born July 18th, baptized September 30th, sponsors Martin Bachman and Barbara Welker, *ibid.*

Cobole, Catharine, of Daniel and Mary Anna Cobole, born September 29th, 1777, ceremony supplied September 30th, sponsors Francis Zech and Catharine Coblin, *ibid.*

Seeholtzer, Mary Barbara, of Martin and Elizabeth Seeholtzer, born July 28th, ceremony supplied September 30th, sponsors Daniel Cobole and Barbara Welker, *ibid.*

Schley, James, of Conrad and Anna Schley, born June 28th, baptized October 2d, sponsor James Fichter and witness Catharine Ward at Longpond [N. J.].

Burns, Eleanor, of Laghlin and Margaret Burns, born August 29th, baptized October 3d, sponsors (I think) John Cobole and wife, *ibid.*

Robertson, Mary, of Dominic and Mary Catharine Robertson, born August 1st, 1777, baptized October 3d, sponsors James Dogherty and Anna Mary Mentzebach, *ibid.*

Cobole, Henry, of Bartholomew and Mary Anna Cobole, born January 19th, baptized October 4th, sponsors John Cobole and Catharine Cobole (for Mary Anna Cobole, Sr.), *ibid.*

Corbit, William, of John and Mary Anna Corbit, born July 3d, 1773, baptized October 4th, sponsor William Fitzgerald, *ibid.*

Fitzgerald, Bridget, of William and Margaret Fitzgerald, born November 1st, 1777, baptized October 4th, sponsors James Ward and Leah Mace, *ibid.*

Sanderson, James, of Thomas and Margaret Sanderson, born July 15th, baptized October 4th, sponsors John McLaughlin and Eleanor Cahel, *ibid.*

Marsolé, John Francis, of Peter and Dorcas Marsolé, born January 8th, baptized October 4th, sponsors John and Johanna Swiney, *ibid.*

Dentz, Sarah, of Charles and Mary Ann Dentz, born September 24th, baptized October 4th, sponsors Charles and Susanna Waibl, *ibid.*

McKormick, Catharine, of Edward and Charity McKormick, born May 26th, 1777, baptized October 4th, sponsor Catharine Gobole, *ibid.*

May, John, of James and Magdalen May, born June 20th, baptized October 4th, sponsors John Cobole and Julianna May, *ibid.*

Brady, Mary, of Adam and Eva Brady, born December 24th, 1777, baptized October 4th, sponsors Thomas and Eleanor Cahel, *ibid.*

Lafarty, Sarah, of John and Margaret Lafarty, born March 21st, baptized October 4th, sponsors William Fitzgerald and Johanna Swiney, *ibid.*

Call, John Henry, of Henry and Catharine Call, born April 21st, baptized October 4th, sponsors Henry Reitenauer and Catharine Waibl, *ibid.*

Dentz, Mary Anna, of Charles and Mary Anna Dentz, born May 17th, 1777, ceremonies supplied October 4th, sponsor Catharine Cobole, *ibid.*

Cobole, Charles, of John and Catharine Cobole, born April 30th, ceremonies supplied October 4th, sponsors Charles and Susanna Waibl, *ibid.*

Schaga, Anna Elizabeth, of John George and Jeannette (P.) Schaga, born September 2d, baptized October 6th, sponsors James Welker and Gertrude Sig, at Mount Hope [Morris county, N. J.].

———, Alice, slave of William Schäfer, baptized October 6th, sponsor the same, in Hunterdon county.

Scantlen, Elizabeth, of John and Bridget Scantlan, baptized October 10th by Rev. Father Valerian Durand, O. S. F., at Chester, Pa.

Gleicher, Barbara, of Francis and Gertrude Gleicher, born October 7th, baptized October 12th, sponsor Barbara Stäling.

Ghillmor, Mary and Elizabeth, twins, of James and Hannah Ghillmor, born October 17th, baptized October 17th, sponsor for both Elizabeth Boosee.

Lort, Isaac, of Isaac and Anna Lort, born October 22d, baptized October 23d, sponsors Joseph and Mary Greswold.

Murphy, Margaret, of Daniel and Catharine Murphy, born April 20th, baptized October 24th, sponsor Francis Lewis.

Weiler, Elizabeth, of Francis and Mary Weiler, born October 24th, baptized October 25th, sponsors John and Margaret Ridiger.

Schilling, John Philip, of Philip and Eva Schilling, born October 29th, baptized October 29th, sponsor Tobias and witness Margaret Rudolph.

Rodt, George, of Thomas and Mary Rodt, born September 28th, baptized October 30th, sponsor Mary Brown (I think).

Abt, John George, of Henry and Elizabeth Abt, born September 13th, baptized November 1st, sponsors John George Abt and Catharine Keil.

Cammerloch, Anna Mary, of Frederic (P.) and Anna Mary Cammerloch, born October 30th, baptized November 1st, sponsor Anna Mary Albrecht.

Dorgan, Daniel, of Timothy and Catharine Dorgan, born July 18th, baptized November 2d, sponsors Christopher Schultz and Mary Hare.

Stout, Mary Elizabeth, of John and Margaret Stout, born October 14th, baptized November 8th, sponsors George Ernest and Magdalen Lechler.

Morrison, Edward, of Philip and Elizabeth Morrison, born August 25th, baptized November 8th, sponsor Catharine Schmid.

Kauffman, James, of Joseph and Barbara Kauffman, born November 13th, baptized November 13th, sponsor the priest, in Philadelphia county.

Miller, Martin, of Martin and Anna Miller, born October 21st, baptized November 15th, sponsors Frederick Scheimer and Catharine Scheimer, at Pikesland [Pa.].

Geiger, Matthew, of Simon and Anna Mary Geiger, born September 27th, baptized November 22d, sponsors Matthew and Anna Mary Miller, in Cohansey [N. J.].

McHughin, Mary, of John and Martha McHughin, born February 28th, 1776, baptized November 23d, sponsors Edward Coleman and Catharine Bucher, at Pilesgrove [Salem county, N. J.].

Ghibens, Adam, of Henry and Mary (Nunck) Ghibens, born October 31st, baptized December 1st, sponsors Adam and Catharine Rübel.

Rowel, Sarah, of Thomas and Johanna Rowel, baptized December 2d, sponsor John Honecker.

Welte, Mary Margaret, of Bernard and Mary Welte, born December 1st, baptized December 13th, sponsor Tobias and witness Margaret Rudolf.

Seibert, Sophia, of Sebastian and Elizabeth Seibert, born December 13th, baptized December 14th, sponsor Mary Salome Schwartz.

Rogers, John, of John and Mary (Brian) Rogers, born November 10th, baptized December 14th, sponsor Bridget Flin.

Roadman, Elizabeth, of Michael and Johanna Roadman, born April 15th, 1770, baptized December 16th, witness Mary Henry.

Dealy, Mary, of Daniel and Mary Dealy, born October 21st, baptized December 18th, sponsors James Proffy and Anna Hackett.

McDaniel, John, of John and Elizabeth McDaniel, born December 11th, baptized December 20th, sponsor John Manderfelt and witness Mary Flaharty.

Donahy, William, of Cormick and Elizabeth Donahy, born October 31st, baptized December 20th, sponsor Mary Rennet.

Stuart, Mary, of James and Anna Mary Stuart, born November 2d, baptized December 20th, sponsor Elizabeth Pfäfferley.

Scot, Dorothy, of John and Margaret Scot, born February 6th, 1776, baptized December 25th, sponsor Terence Donahan.

Galagher, John, of Peter and Elizabeth Galagher, born December 12th, baptized December 28th, sponsors John and Johanna Mary Leavan. Whole number of baptisms—one hundred and forty-six.

REGISTER OF BAPTISMS FOR 1779.

Grier, Anthony, of Charles and Catharine Grier, born January 3d, baptized January 5th, sponsors Thomas Villar and Catharine Magee.

Nadler, Elizabeth, of John and Magdalen Nadler, born January 3d, baptized January 10th, sponsors Henry Schreiner and Elizabeth Götz.

Mahony, John, of William and Catharine Mahony, born November 9th, 1778, baptized January 10th, sponsors Andrew Birge and Mary Smith.

Connor, Mary, of Michael and Mary Connor, born January 3d, baptized January 10th, sponsors Thomas and Catharine FitzSimons.

Coffey, Mary, of John and Lydia Coffey, born January 15th, baptized January 16th, sponsor Pelagia Mignot.

——— Francis, born January 18th, baptized January 18th, sponsor Christina Essling.

Hault, Adam, of Samuel (P.) and Catharine (Göck) Hault, born January 13th, baptized January 18th, sponsors Adam Mayer and Mary Göck.

Ott, Joseph, of James (P.) and Appollonia Ott, born January 18th, baptized January 22d, sponsors Joseph Becker and Elizabeth Becker.

Motley, Walter, of Walter and Mary Motley, born December 6th, 1777, baptized January 25th, sponsors Timothy McNamra and Anna Campbel.

Rübel, Francis, of Francis and Anna Regina Rübel, born January 23d, baptized January 26th, sponsors John and Barbara Heitz.

Runy, William, of William and Margaret Runy, born June 29th, 1778, baptized January 30th, sponsor William Dixon.

Dixon, George, of William and Mary Dixon, born January 3d, baptized January 30th, sponsor Henry Beal.

Bauer, John, of John and Elizabeth Bauer, born January 19th, baptized January 30th, sponsors John Sedou and Eleanor Wright.

Ryan, Mary, of Owen and Mary Ryan, born January 25th, baptized February 2d, sponsors Thomas Haley and Johanna Robeson.

Greswold, Anna, of Joseph and Anna Greswold, born February 3d, baptized February 7th, sponsor Anna Hill.

Roan, Anna, of Daniel and Mary Roan, born February 4th, baptized February 14th, sponsors Edward Coghran and Julia Murphy.

Wall, Hannah, of Galloway and —— Wall, slave, born June 11th, 1778, baptized February 14th, sponsor Hannah White, slave.

——, Eva Magdalen, born January 15th, baptized February 14th, sponsors John and Eva Poth.

Barry, Anna, of Thomas and Anna Barry, born February 15th, baptized February 15th, sponsor John Barry and witness Sarah, his wife.

Murphy, Elizabeth, of William and Mary Murphy, born May 5th, 1777, baptized February 19th, sponsors James Hardnet and Mary Corcran.

Schmid, Peter, of Nicholas and Eva Schmid, born January 20th, baptized February 21st, sponsors Peter Bremich and Catharine Keil.

Macy, Julia, of Nicholas and Ositha Macy, born February 22d, baptized February 25th, sponsors James Veilon and Julia Marc.

Williams, Elizabeth, of Joseph and Eleanor Williams, born February 4th, baptized March 1st, sponsors Richard Barry and Mary Henry.

Boyé, Mary, of Peter and Magdalen (Trahan) Boyé, born March 3d, baptized March 5th, sponsors Francis Deherlé and Mary Vincent.

Hutchinson, Margaret, of N. and Margaret Hutchinson, born March 4th, baptized March 9th, sponsors Edward Tool and Eleanor McCullogh.

Raubin, Peter Louis, of John and Anna (Vincent) Raubin, born March 12th, baptized March 13th, sponsors Peter L'Airette and Catharine Freind.

L'Hercule, Nicholas, of John and Josephine (D'Aroit) L'Hercule, born March 15th, baptized March 15th, sponsors Nicholas Mazy and Modesta Landry.

Griffin, John, of James and Elizabeth Griffin, born March 20th, baptized March 21st, sponsors Frederic Scheimer and Mary Magdalen Sohl, at Pikesland [Chester county, Pa.].

Hayle, Anna Dorothy, of Caspar and Elizabeth Hayle, born March 20th, baptized March 25th, sponsors John and Hannah Dorothy Zorne.

Martin, Eleanor, of Patrick and Mary Martin, born March 21st, baptized March 28th, sponsors Patrick Crawfordson and Eleanor Welsh.

Flin, John, of John and Bridget Flin, born February 21st, baptized March 29th, sponsors William and Catharine Banfield.

Byron, Mary, of Walter and Margaret Byron, born March 21st, baptized April 4th, sponsors Mathew McHugh and Elizabeth Carrol.

Albrecht, Frederic, of James and Anna Mary Albrecht, born April 4th, baptized April 5th, sponsors the child's father (for Frederick Cammerloch) and Sophia Cammerloch.

Roberts, James, of Henry and Margaret Roberts, born January 1st, bap-

tized April 9th, sponsor Margaret Bremich, witnesses Richard
Wilson and Mary Johnson.

Trépanié, Anna Margaret, of Augustine and Anna (Davis) Trépanié, born
April 15th, baptized April 15th, sponsors Bruce Trépanié and
Magdalen Vincent.

Kelly, John, of James and Anna Mary Kelly, born March 29th, baptized
April 18th, sponsors John Dewetter and Catharine Donnoly.

Sheal, Benjamin, of John and Anna Sheal, born December 19th, 1776,
baptized April 22d, sponsors Francis and Catharine Zech, at Mount
Hope [N. J.].

Sheal, Sarah, of same parents, born February 25th, baptized April 22d,
sponsors Caspar and Margaret Engelhart, *ibid.*

Robertson, John, of Dominic and Catharine Robertson, born March 28th,
baptized April 25th, sponsors John and Catharine Cobole, at Long
Pond [N. J.].

Theusen, Henry, of —— and Mary (P.) Theusen, born December 14th,
1778, baptized April 25th, sponsors Anthony and Margaret May, *ibid.*

May, Conrad, of Anthony and Margaret May, born March 23d, baptized
April 25th, sponsors Conrad Waibel and Julianna May, *ibid.*

Riddles, Margaret, of Thomas and Frances Riddles, born December 2d,
1778, baptized April 25th, sponsors James Daugherty and Margaret
Burns, *ibid.*

Wider, Anna Catharine, of Joseph and Margaret Wider, born October
18th, 1778, baptized May 2d, sponsors Francis and Catharine Zech,
at Mount Hope [N. J.].

Zech, John James, of Francis and Catharine Zech, born January 13th,
baptized May 2d, sponsors James Welker and Eva Jungfleisch, *ibid.*

Grips, Elizabath, of Peter Joseph and Mary Grips, born January 17th,
baptized May 2d, sponsors John and Honora Türk, *ibid.*

Schäffer, Anna Eva, of William and Susanna Schäffer, born October 13th,
1778, baptized May 5th, sponsors James Ruppel and Anna Catharine Horn.

Franklin, Thomas, of Francis (P.) and Mary Franklin, born January 3d,
baptized May 6th, sponsor Bridget Jinnins.

Doyle, James, of John and Esther Doyle, born May 2d, baptized May
7th, sponsor Susanna Doyle.

Loan, Catharine, of Henry and Catharine Loan, born September 8th,
1778, baptized May 9th, sponsors John Hany and Mary Shiney.

Stättenfeld, Elizabeth, of James and Christina Stättenfeld, born March
30th, baptized May 11th, sponsor Catharine Freind.

Swiney, Edmund, of James and Catharine Swiney, born December
28th, 1778, baptized May 12th, sponsor Denis Kelly.

Douett, Sarah, of William and Sarah Douett, born May 15th, baptized
May 15th, sponsor Mary Roanan.

Lary, Catharine, of Cornelius and Margaret Lary, born May 12th, baptized
May 17th, sponsors Edmund McDonald and Bridget Donaho.

Schönfeld, John, of John Christian and Mary Anna Schönfeld, born
1775, baptized May 24th, sponsor John Miller.

Schönfeld, Michael, of John Christian and Mary Anna Schönfeld, born
1777, baptized May 24th, sponsor John Miller.

Vogel, James, of Adam (P.) and Margaret Vogel, born November 30th,
1772, baptized May 27th, sponsors Anthony Graff and Mary Waas,
in Gloucester county [N. J.].

Vogel, Adam, of Adam (P.) and Margaret Vogel, born July 7th, 1776,
baptized May 27th, sponsors Anthony Graff and Mary Waas, *ibid*.

Boosee, Margaret Apollonia, of Henry (P.) and Margaret Boosee, born
April 3d, baptized May 30th, sponsors Francis and Apollonia Sohl,
at Pikesland [Pa.].

O'Neil, Henry, of Constantine and Sarah O'Neil, born January 24th,
baptized June 1st, sponsors John Kauffman and Barbara Kauffman.

Briar, Paul, of Emmanuel and Magdalen Briar, born June 1st, baptized
June 3d, sponsors Paul and Christina Essling.

Vosser, Valentine, of Valentine (P.) and Susanna (Bener) Vosser, born
January 21st, baptized June 6th, sponsors Christian and Susanna
Thurnbach, in Cumberland county [N. J.].

Thurnbach, Mathias, of Christian and Susanna Thurnbach, born November 27th, 1778, baptized June 6th, sponsors Matthew Göck and Eva
Lehman, *ibid*.

Miller, Joseph, of Matthew and Anna Mary Miller, born March 6th, baptized June 6th, sponsors Matthew and Charlotta Göck, *ibid*.

Caspar, Mary Anna, of Lawrence and Margaret Caspar, born January
28th, baptized June 6th, sponsors Mathias and Anna Mary Miller,
ibid.

Göck, Mathias, of Mathias and Charlotta Göck, born March 27th, baptized June 6th, sponsors Matthew and Anna Mary Miller, *ibid*,

McHuin, John, of John and Martha McHuin, born May 6th, baptized
June 7th, sponsors Miles Dougherty and Eleanor (Narret) McCarty,
in Salem county [N. J.].

Magill, Thomas, of Patrick and Elizabeth Magill, born October 21st,
1778, baptized June 7th, sponsors John and Martha McHuin,
ibid.

Narret, John, of James (P.) and Eleanor Narret, born December 23d,
1778, baptized June 7th, sponsors Philip McHugh and Hannah
Hart, *ibid*.

Albou, Anna, of Edmund and Honora Albou, born June 5th, baptized
June 13th, sponsors William and Anna Sanderson.

McClasky, Elizabeth Gregory, wife of James McClasky, baptized June
18th, sponsor Eleanor Connelly.

McClasky, James, of James and Elizabeth McClasky, born May 25th, baptized June 18th, sponsors George and Eleanor Connelly.

Brewer, George, of Jonathan (P.) and Margaret Brewer, born May 25th, baptized June 19th, witness George and sponsor Catharine Atkinson.

Landy, Mary, of James and Elizabeth Landy, born June 13th, baptized June 20th, sponsor Henry Dubbin and witness Mrs. Peter Duffy.

Klemmer, John, of John and Anna Mary Klemmer, born December 23d, 1776, baptized June 22d, sponsor Joseph Haag, in Burlington county [N. J.].

Scot, Mary, of John and Margaret Scot, born May 29th, baptized June 23d, sponsors Patrick Kearns and Catharine Hogan, *ibid*.

Hoy, George, of John and Catharine Hoy, born July 26th, 1776, baptized June 24th, sponsors John Scot and Catharine Hogan, *ibid*.

Welsh, John, of James and Anna Welsh, born June 25th, baptized June 29th, sponsors Stephen and Catharine Barden.

Dauber, Peter, of Sebastian and Mary Magdalen Dauber, born June 1st, baptized July 5th, sponsors Peter and Mary Magdalen Regimenter, in vicinity of Philadelphia.

Willcox, Mary, of John and Rebecca Willcox, born March 17th, 1775, baptized July 11th, sponsor Joseph Colgan (for Patrick Byrne) and Mary Byrne.

Willcox, John, of same parents, born November 19th, 1777, baptized July 11th, sponsors James Byrne and Elizabeth White.

Buttler, Lawrence, of Michael and Priscilla Buttler, born December 18th, 1776, baptized July 14th, sponsors Patrick O'Neal and Susanna Maginnis.

Barry, Sarah, wife of John Barry, baptized July 21st, sponsor Anna Barry.

Lalor, Henry, of Henry and Alice Lalor, born July 19th, baptized July 25th, sponsors John and Johanna Levins.

Cuny, John, of James and Mary Cuny, born June 29th, baptized August 1st, sponsors Barnabas Cox and Eleanor Karker, at Pikesland [Chester county, Pa.].

Dun, Catharine, of —— and Sarah (McKee) Dun, born December 25th, 1774, baptized August 1st, sponsors Edward Burns and Mary McDonald, *ibid*.

Bryan, John, of John and Mary Bryan, born January 5th, baptized August 1st, sponsors Mark Welsh and Anna Campbel, *ibid*.

McCanna, Anna, of John and Sarah McCanna, born May 16th, baptized August 1st, sponsors Jeremiah Nocé and Margaret Kean, *ibid*.

Kraus, John, of John and Elizabeth Kraus, born February 24th, baptized August 1st, sponsors Francis and Apollonia Sohl, *ibid*.

McMahan, Jeremiah, of Jeremiah and Susanna McMahan, born February 24th, baptized August 6th, sponsor Margaret Connel.

Shaw, Jeremiah, of Dennis and Anna Shaw, born April ——, baptized August 8th, sponsors Patrick and Martha Welsh.

Tracy, William, of Matthew and Mary Tracy, born August 4th, baptized August 8th, sponsors James Welsh, Jr. and Mary, his wife.

Foy, Margaret, of Matthew and Anna Foy, born July 22d, baptized August 10th, sponsor Mary (Vance) McFarlin.

Viel, Susanna, of Peter and Lucretia Viel, born August 5th, baptized August 15th, sponsor Henry Herberger and witness Susanna, his wife.

Byrne, James, of Patrick and Mary Byrne, born August 8th, baptized August 15th, sponsors James and Anna Gallagher.

McGovran, Thomas, of Paul and Mary McGovran, born August 15th, baptized August 16th, sponsors Barnabas Scully and Catharine Macan.

——, Judith, slave of Captain John Barry, adult, baptized August 19th, sponsor Anna, the preist's servant.

Bucher, Joseph, of John and Anna Catharine Bucher, baptized August 21st, sponsors the priest and Mary Harlan, in Salem county [N. J.].

Göck, Lawrence, of Lawrence and Christina Göck, born August 1st, baptized August 22d, sponsors Lawrence and Margaret Caspar, at Cohanzy [N. J.].

Greissler, Philip Joseph, of Elias and —— Greissler, born August 18th, baptized August 27th, sponsors Philip and Eva Schilling.

Landry, Joseph, of Joseph and Sarah Landry, born August 27th, baptized August 29th, sponsors Peter David and Margaret Bourg.

Speir, John and Mary, twins, of Matthew and Mary Speir, born August 29th, baptized August 30th, sponsor Barbara, wife of John Heitz.

Baxter, Robert, of John and Eleanor Baxter, born August 29th, baptized August 30th, sponsors John and Elizabeth Carrol.

Carrol, Daniel, of Daniel and Mary Carrol, born August 23d, baptized August 30th, sponsor Susanna Glansey.

FitzPatrick, Elizabeth, of John and Honora FitzPatrick, born August 28th, baptized August 30th, sponsors Michael Diamond and Mary Shannon.

Pranger, William, of William and Catharine Pranger, born August 31st, baptized privately August 31st.

Pryor, Anna, adult, baptized September 1st, witness John O'Connor.

Opperman, Elizabeth, of Adam and Elizabeth Opperman, born August 22d, baptized September 5th, sponsors Sebastian and Cunegunda Hoffman.

Price, Joseph, of Joseph and Mary Price, born September 2d, baptized September 5th, sponsors Anthony Graff and Margaret Sauerwald.

Clark, Anna, of Michael, Jr., and Elizabeth Clark, born August 28th, baptized September 5th, sponsors Matthew and Anna McHugh.

Bauman, Catharine, of Charles and Mary Bauman, born September 8th, baptized September 9th, sponsor Catharine Freind.

Regimenter, Anthony, of Peter and Magdalen Regimenter, born September 9th, baptized September 12th, sponsors Anthony and Barbara Graff.

Bauer, John, of Francis and Elizabeth Bauer, born September 8th, baptized September 16th, sponsors John and Eva Poth.

Kelly, Eleanor, of Edward and Margaret Kelly, born March 21st, 1775, baptized September 20th, sponsors Francis and Apollonia Sohl, at Pikesland [Pa.].

Field, Mary, of Paul and Mary Field, born September 20th, baptized September 23d, sponsors Stephen and Catharine (Viel) Barden.

Wall, William, of James and Rachel Wall, born June 14th, baptized September 23d, sponsor John Connor and witness Mary Down.

Dougherty, Joseph, of Dennis and Margaret Dougherty, born September 25th, baptized September 28th, sponsors Joseph Kaufman and Mary Dougherty.

Bayerle, Anna Mary, of Dietrich (P.) and Sabina Bayerle, born July 18th, baptized September 29th, sponsor Anna Mary Abt.

Rudder, Mary, of George and Hannah (Bennet) Rudder, born September 18th, baptized October 12th, sponsors William McGloghlin and Judith Wright.

Cook, George, of George and Catharine (Emot) Cook, born July ——, baptized October 12th, sponsor Mary Heart.

Cavenogh, Mary, of James and Elizabeth Cavenogh, born September 15th, baptized October 12th, sponsors James, Jr., and Mary Welsh.

Carpé, John Baptist, of Herman and Margaret Carpé, born October 14th, baptized October 15th, sponsors Joseph and Elizabeth Labeauve.

Göck, David, of David and Margaret (P.) Göck, born March 14th, baptized October 17th, sponsors Lawrence and Christina Göck, at Cohanzey [N. J.].

Rodgers, Alexander, of Alexander and Amy Rodgers, born October 18th, baptized October 21st, sponsors Lawrence Coock and Hannah Deleany.

Schneider, John Henry, of Henry, Jr., and Catharine Schneider, born September 26th, baptized October 23d, sponsors John Henry Waltrich and Catharine Schneider.

——, Catharine, slave of James Oelers, sixteeen months old, baptized October 23d, sponsor James Oelers.

Buckley, Rosanna, of William and Eleanor Buckley, born August 3d, baptixed privately October 28th.

Berg, John, of Ernest and Gertrude Berg, born October 24th, baptized October 31st, sponsor John Tscharté.

Günther, John George, of George and Frances Günther, born October 29th, baptized October 31st, sponsors John and Catharine Wagner.

Henderson, Dorothy, of ——— and Mary Henderson, a few weeks old, baptized conditionally October 31st, sponsor Catharine Beal.

Wharton, Charles, of Charles and Elizabeth Wharton, born September 3d, 1778, baptized November 2d, sponsors James Hardnet and Johanna Hardnet.

Garoutte, Margaret, of Michael and Sophia Garoutte, born July 24th, baptized November 3d, sponsors Stephen Tissonau and Margaret L'Hercule.

Lewis, Peter, of Emanuel and Margaret Lewis, born November 13th, baptized November 14th, sponsors Joseph and Catharine Eck.

Shortel, Mary, of Thomas and Johanna Shortel, born May 28d, baptized November 14th, sponsors Richard Barret and Mary Fitzgerald.

Kelly, Mary and Eleanor, twins, of Patrick and Rose Kelly, born November 14th, baptized November 17th, sponsors for Mary, James Smith and Mary McGuire; for Eleanor, Dominic Lawrence and Eleanor Smith.

Conrad, John Michael, of Matthew and Catharine Conrad, born November 13th, baptized November 21st, sponsors John Wagner and Barbara Steinmetz.

Byrne, John, of Raymond and Anna Byrne, born November 12th, baptized November 21st, sponsors Patrick and Mary Byrne.

Barret, William, of John and Bridget Barret, born November 20th, baptized November 25th, sponsors Patrick Byrne and Anna Mullen.

Benner, Joseph, of Henry and Mary Benner, born November 22d, baptized November 25th, sponsors Joseph and Catharine Poth.

Fitzgerald, Catharine, of Edward and Catharine Fitzgerald, born November 30th, baptized December 4th, sponsors Adam Mayer and Margaret Sauerwald.

Gallagher, Thomas, of James and Anna Gallagher, born November 27th, baptized December 5th, sponsors Mark and Mary Willcox.

Beaufort, John Baptist, of Caspar and Anna Beaufort, born November 19th, baptized December 9th, sponsors John Cortez and Johanna Favier.

Buch, Adam, of Joseph and Hannah Buch, born November 29th, baptized December 9th, sponsor Magdalen Springer.

Durand, Valentine, of James and Catharine Durand, born November 14th, baptized December 10th, sponsors Valentine and Clara Schierling.

Schreiner, Anna, of Anselm and Elizabeth Schreiner, born December 4th, baptized December 12th, sponsors Joseph and Catharine Eck.

Ebair, Elizabeth, of Francis and Mary Ebair, born December 1st, baptized December 12th, sponsors Claude Rouse and Johanna Kayser.

Murphy, Johanna, of Daniel and Julia Murphy, born December 10th, baptized December 30th, sponsors James Murphy and Mary Coock.

Whole number of baptisms—one hundred and forty-eight.

REGISTER OF BAPTISMS FOR 1780.

Lechler, Mary Magdalen, of Adam and Catharine Lechler, born January 7th, baptized January 9th, sponsors George Ernest and Mary Magdalen Lechler.

Henry, Elizabeth, of Philip and Mary Henry, born November 30th, 1779, baptized January 23d, sponsors John McEninge and Mary Cunningham.

Forester, Thomas, of Gerald and Diana Forester, born January 27th, baptized February 7th, sponsors William French and Elizabeth Carrol.

——, Sarah, slave of James Oellers, adult, baptized February 11th, sponsor James Oellers.

Oellers, Helena, of James and Catharine Oellers, born February 11th, baptized February 11th, by Rev. Robert Mollineux, sponsor Father Farmer.

Hold, Mary Magdalen, of Peter and Catharine Hold, born February 16th, baptized February 20th, sponsors George Ernest and Mary Magdalen Lechler.

Boudrot, Elizabeth, of Michael and Anna Boudrot, born February 14th, baptized February 22d, sponsors Edmund Nugent and Elizabeth Seibert.

Maxvill, Letitia, of Alexander and Anna Maxvill, born September, 1772, baptized February 23d, sponsors James and Anna Welsh.

Ryan, Sarah, of Philip and Anna Ryan, born February 25th, baptized February 25th, sponsor Johanna Robeson.

Macra, Patrick, of Charles and Sarah Macra, born January 26th, baptized February 27th, sponsors John Murray and Eleanor Walker.

Gallagher, Bridget, of John and Anna Gallagher, born February 24th, baptized March 6th, sponsor Thomas Carrol, and witness Deborah, his wife.

Feinauer, Charles, of Joseph and Anna Mary Feinauer, born March 2d, baptized May 9th, sponsors Charles Benedict Bauman and Mary Schneider.

Krumbel, Mary Justina, of Philip and Magdalen Krumbel, born March 3d, baptized March 9th, sponsor Mary Justina Horn.

Barret, James, of James and Mary Barret, born February 11th, baptized March 14th, sponsors Kenedy Hogan and Margaret Archbold.

Horn, George Ernest, of Henry and Christina Horn, born March 11th, baptized March 14th, sponsors George Ernest and Magdalen Lechler.

Willhelm, Mary Salome, of Adam and Anna Willhelm, born March 3d, baptized March 10th, sponsors John and Salome Staler.

Bastian, Adam and Peter, twins, of William and Magdalen Bastian, born March 19th, baptized March 21st, sponsors for Adam, Adam and Margaret Bremich; for Peter, Peter and Catharine Bremich.

Farrel, Cecilia, of John and Mary Farrel, born March 19th, baptized March 27th, sponsors John Faran and Bridget Donaho.

Bremich, Sarah, of Peter and Catharine Bremich, born March 30th, baptized April 2d, sponsors Anthony and Sarah Aman.

Stanley, Mary, of Michael and Martha Stanley, born March 15th, baptized April 2d, sponsor Catharine Mullen, and witness Hugh Tool.

Ford, Edward, of Thomas and Bridget Ford, born December 25th, 1779, baptized April 5th, sponsor Martha Clifton.

Korn, John Caspar, of Caspar and Anna Mary Korn, born January 18th, baptized April 9th, sponsors Adam and Elizabeth Opperman.

Maxvill, Alexander, of Alexander (P.) and Anna Maxvill, born March 18th, 1777, baptized April 10th, sponsors Charles Smith and Anna Welsh.

Maxvill, Eleanor, same parents, born March 3d, 1779, baptized April 10th, sponsors James Welsh and Mary Friel.

Connoly, Rebecca Susanna, of —— and Lydia Connoly, born February —, baptized April 12th, sponsor Margaret Sauerwald.

Frederick, Samuel, of Abraham and Elizabeth (Griskam) Frederick, born January 9th, baptized April 13th, sponsor Catharine Boudrot.

Diamond, John, of Michael and Eleanor Diamond, born April 21st, baptized April 22d, sponsors Bartholomew Tool and Honora FitzPatrick.

Boyd, Mary, of Patrick and Anna Boyd, born April 1st, baptized April 23d, sponsors Joseph Becker and Elizabeth Pierce.

Guerry, Frances (Fanny), of Cato and Margaret Guerry, slaves of Thomas Barry, born December, 1779, baptized April 23d, sponsors Thomas Barry and Catharine Boudrot.

——, Louis, of Chloe, a slave of Mr. Price, born March 6th, baptized April 24th, sponsor John Louis Farrié.

Yokeum, Anna, wife of George Yokeum, baptized April 26th, sponsors Jeremiah Sullivan and Barbara Schultz.

O'Neal, Mark, of Constantine and Sarah O'Neal, born February 3d, baptized April 29th, sponsors John Kauffman and Mary Kauffman, in Philadelphia county [Pa.].

Dümler, Elizabeth, of Philip and Sarah Dümler, born December 12th, 1779, baptized April 30th, sponsor Apollonia Sohl, at Pikesland [Chester county, Pa.].

Eimold, Peter, of Peter and Mary Eimold, born November 8th, 1779, baptized April 30th, sponsor James Weisseburger, *ibid*.

Cox, Francis, of Barnabas and Magdalen Cox, born April 26th, baptized April 30th, sponsors James Weisseburger and Anna Mary Weisseburger, *ibid*.

Whright, William, of Randle and Margaret Whright, baptized April 30th, sponsors James Cuny and Elizabeth Scheimer, *ibid.*

Welsh, Anna, of Miles and Anna Welsh, born April 30th, baptized May 1st, sponsor Elizabeth Scheimer, in Chester county [Pa.].

McCalagan, Sarah, of Michael and Mary McCalagan, born March 19th, baptized May 2d, sponsors Daniel FitzPatrick and Mary Cusick, *ibid.*

Human, Mary Catharine, of John and Mary Anna Human, born May 1st, baptized May 4th, sponsors Peter Viel, Jr., and Catharine Viel.

Connor, Eleanor, of Lawrence and Margaret Connor, born April 20th, baptized May 7th, sponsors Thomas and Eleanor Green.

Dugan, John, of Paul and Mary Dugan, born May 8th, baptized May 15th, sponsors John McDaniel and Catharine Jinkins, witnesses Richard Jinkins and Catharine Stuart.

Kitzinger, Catharine, of Philip and Ottilia Kitzinger, born May 13th, baptized May 15th, sponsors Joseph Honecker and Catharine Vanié.

Adams, William, of John (P.) and Grace Adams, born May 9th, baptized May 15th, sponsors John Kelly and Sarah Kearney.

Willcox, Eleanor, of Mark and Mary Willcox, born May 15th, baptized May 19th, sponsors James Gallagher and Deborah Sutton, at Concord [Delaware county, Pa.].

Mayer, John, of George and Regina Mayer, born March 20th, baptized May 21st, sponsors Lawrence and Christina Göck, at Cohanzy [N. J.].

Holtzhäfer, Margaret, of Sebastian and Johanna (P.) Holtzhäfer, born April 25th, baptized June 4th, sponsors Caspar and Margaret Engelhard, at Mount Hope [N. J.].

Schup, Henry, of Philip and Mary Eva Schup, born May 12th, baptized June 4th, sponsors David and Johanna Fichter, in vicinity of Charlottenburg [N. J.].

Hason, Rosanna, of Felix and Margaret Hason, born May 24th, 1778, baptized June 4th, sponsor the child's mother (for Mary Mentzebach), *ibid.*

Call, John William, of Nicholas and Anna Mary Call, born July 16th, 1779, ceremonies supplied June 9th, sponsors John Henry and Catharine Call, at Ringwood [Passaic county, N. J.].

May, Mary Catharine, of James and Magdalen May, born October 24th, 1779, ceremonies supplied, June 9th, sponsors Conrad Waibl and Catharine May, *ibid.*

Cahel, Catharine, of Thomas and Eleanor Cahel, born October 1st, 1779, baptized June 10th, sponsors Dominic and Catharine Robertson, at Longpond [N. J.].

Swiney, Mary, of John and Johanna Swiney, born October 19th, 1779, baptized June 10th, sponsors John and Mary Ward, *ibid.*

Macan, Mary, of William and Barbara Macan, born May 27th, 1779, baptized June 10th, sponsors Henry Call and Anna Mary Mentze-bach, *ibid*.

Marselé, James, of Peter and Dorcas Marselé, born May 16th, baptized June 10th, sponsors James and Magdalen May, *ibid*.

Hason, William, of Felix and Margaret Hason, born April 27th, baptized June 6th, sponsor John Burns, near Charlottenburg [N. J.].

FitzPatrick, Mary, of John and Bridget FitzPatrick, born June 16th, baptized June 20th, sponsors Edward McDonagh and Anna Barry.

Schneider, Mary Teresa, of Ignatius and Catharine Schneider, born June 29th, baptized July 2d, sponsor Peter Field and witness Lucretia, his wife.

Meade, George, of George and Henrietta Constance (P.) Meade, born June 4th, baptized July 2d, sponsors Thomas Meade (of Montser-rat), Thomas Russel, Madam De Miralles and Elizabeth Ferguson.

Boyd, Elizabeth, of John and Judy (Lynch) Boyd, born June ———, baptized July 3d, sponsor Anna Maddocks (Tritt).

Runion, Thomas, of Daniel and Catharine Runion, born June 22d, baptized July 3d, sponsors Philip McHugh and Anna Collins.

Blanchard, Mary Ross, wife of Peter Blanchard, baptized July 7th, the priest was sponsor, the consent of the parties was renewed.

Stuart, James, of James and Eva Stuart, born July 9th, baptized July 13th, sponsors Adam Poth, Jr , and Catharine Freind.

Lechler, George Ernest, of Anthony and Catharine Lechler, born July 11th, baptized July 13th, sponsors George Ernest and Mary Magdalen Lechler.

Röhr, Anthony, of Martin and Anna Mary Röhr, born July 18th, baptized July 23d, sponsors Joseph Schorp and Margaret Hoffman, at Cushenhopen [Goshenhoppen, Berks county, Pa.].

Strong, Mary Barbara, of William and Mary Elizabeth Strong, born June 25th, baptized July 23d, sponsors Peter and Barbara Käffer, at Cushenhopen [Goshenhoppen, Pa.].

Welsh, Abigail, of David and Phœbe Welsh, born July 24th, baptized August 2d, sponsors Martin Pendergrast and Catharine Ryan, *ibid*.

Sincox, Sarah, of Joseph and Catharine Sincox, born December 13th, 1779, baptized August 6th, sponsors William Gogan and Margaret Corcran, *ibid*.

Halfpenny, Johanna Mary, of Thomas and Margaret Halfpenny, born August 8th, baptized August 13th, sponsors Edmund Nugent and Johanna Levins, *ibid*.

Ryan, Thomas, of Edward and Elizabeth Ryan, born March 31st, 1779, baptized August 13th, sponsors John McDonald and Anna Savage, *ibid*.

Robeson, Sarah, of Alexander and Margaret Robeson, born August 6th, baptized August 13th, sponsors John Shaw and Anna Boyd, and witness Anna Smith, *ibid*.

Mullen, Anna, of Owen and Jerusha (P.) Mullen, born February 6th, baptized August 16th, sponsor the priest, *ibid.*

Coleman, Anna, of Edward and Anna Coleman, born November 30th, 1777, baptized August 22d, sponsors Henry Thurnbach and Hannah Huber, Jr., in Salem county [N. J.].

O'Brian, Daniel, of Jeremiah and Mary O'Brian, born August 24th, 1777, baptized August 22, sponsors Manes Dougherty and Susanna Thurnbach, *ibid.*

Geiger, Simon, of Henry and Barbara Geiger, born August 15th, baptized August 22d, sponsor Simon Geiger, at Pilesgrove [Salem county, N. J.].

Cusick, John, of Michael and Mary Cusick, born June 23d, baptized September 4th, sponsors James Hickey and Mary Calagan, in Chester county [Pa.].

Curtin, Elizabeth, of Joseph and —— Curtin, born December, 1769, baptized September 4th, sponsors ———— and Anna Cavenough, *ibid.*

Bird, Catharine, of Samuel and Anna Bird, born September 2d, baptized September 11th, sponsor Anna Hudson.

Knowles, Richard, of William and Jane Knowles, baptized privately September 14th.

Robins, Sarah, of Thomas (P.) and Sarah Robins, born August ——, baptized September 16th, sponsor Margaret White.

Ryan, Lydia, of John and Margaret Ryan, born September 15th, baptized September 27th, sponsor David Kaples, witness Lydia Ryan.

Bimpel, John, of Paul and Deborah Bimpel, born May 11th, baptized September 18th, sponsor Andrew Sullivan.

Mitchel, James, of Philip James and Anna Mitchel, born September 24th, 1776, baptized September 23d, sponsor Anna Shaw.

Harris, Elizabeth, of John and Ruth Harris, born July 29th, 1779, baptized privately September 28th, witness David Hiliard, sponsor Margaret Dyer.

Biron, Anna, of Walter and Margaret Biron, born September 3d, baptized October 3d, sponsors Augustine Power and Margaret McClosky.

Abt, Catharine, of Henry and Elizabeth Abt, born September 21st, baptized October 8th, sponsors John George and Catharine Abt.

Boosee, John, of Moses and Elizabeth Boosee, born October 3d, baptized October 8th, sponsors John Tracy and Barbara Graff.

Pranger, Mary Elizabeth, of William and Anna Catharine Pranger, born October 8th, baptized October 11th, sponsors Joseph Bastian and Elizabeth Tcharté.

Donnum, Anna, of Joseph (P.) and Anna Donnum, born February 12th, baptized October 17th, sponsor the mother (by mistake), in Salem county [N. J.].

L'Hercule, Isaias, of Francis and Pelagia (Douzet) L'Hercule, born October 20th, baptized October 20th, sponsor Margaret Landry, witness Joseph Melanzon.

Swaine, Anna, of Silas and Elizabeth Swaine, born September 15th, baptized October 21st, sponsors James Mullen and Anna Kelly.

Würth, George, of Joseph and Barbara Würth, born October 13th, baptized October 22d, sponsors Anthony and Barbara Graff.

Mayer, Joseph, of Joseph (P.) and Gertrude Mayer, born October 17th, baptized October 22d, sponsors Sebastian and Catharine Vanić, in vicinty of Philadelphia.

Gallagher, Eleanor, of Peter and Elizabeth Gallagher, born October 19th, baptized October 22d, sponsors James and Anna Gallagher.

——, James, infant of unknown parentage, baptized privately October 24th, while in a dying condition, in vicinity of Philadelphia.

Addison, Thomas, of Thomas and Lucia (Kennedy) Addison, born May 24th, baptized privately October 24th, sponsor Hannah Edward, *ibid.*

McKeaver, Hannah, of Michael and Deborah (Britton) McKeaver, born July, 1779, baptized November 5th, sponsors Daniel FitzPatrick and Mary McDonald, at Pikesland [Chester county, Pa.].

Strubel, Mary, of Peter and Magdalen Strubel, born November 4th, baptized November 12th, sponsors John and Mary Honecker.

Nadler, Dorothy, of John and Magdalen Nadler, born November 5th, baptized November 12th, sponsors John Tscharté and Mary Dorothy Treim.

Burns, Archibald, of Archibald and Johanna Burns, born October 27th, baptized November 12th, sponsor Anna Macanarny.

Gorman, Elizabeth, of Lawrence and Elizabeth Gorman, born November 3d, baptized November 13th, sponsor Peter Gill.

Kelly, Mary, of Thomas and Mary Kelly, born November 3d, baptized November 18th, sponsor Mary Heart.

Foster, John, a dying infant, baptized November 21st, sponsor —— Sullivan.

Carrel, Thomas, of Thomas and Deborah Carrel, born November 15th, baptized November 23d, sponsors Hugh Fieldon and Anna Gallagher, a widow.

Pinion, Peter, of Peter and Mary (Bourg) Pinion, born November 23d, baptized November 24th, sponsors Armand Douzet and Margaret Carpé.

Schneider, Thomas, of John and Magdalen Schneider, born November 17th, baptized November 26th, sponsors Adam and Margaret Bremich.

Abt, Mary Magdalen, of John George and Catharine Abt, born November 27th, baptized December 9th, sponsors Francis Abt and Magdalen Cappl, at Kensington [near Philadelphia, Pa.].

Roage, Elizabeth, of John and Margaret Roage, born November 6th, baptized December 10th, sponsors George Kientz and Anna Philipps.

Gillmor, Hannah, of James and Hannah Gillmor, born November 26th, baptized December 10th, sponsors Michael Derny and Rosanna Bryer.

L'Hercule, Mary Ursula, of John and Josephine L'Hercule, born December 11th, baptized December 11th, sponsors William Metea and Ositha Macy.

Greenvillan, John, of Anna, slave of Elias Hand, born February, 1779, baptized December 17th.

Rouse, Felicitas, of Claude and Felicitas Rouse, born December 19th, baptized December 19th, sponsors Louis and Louisa Busson.

Prügl, Mary, of Henry and Margaret Prügl, born December 25th, baptized December 31st, sponsors Francis and Mary Rogé.

Blanchard, John, of Peter and Mary Blanchard, born December 18th, baptized December 31st, sponsors Denis Macarthy and Mary O'Hara.

Whole number of baptisms—one hundred and fourteen.

REGISTER OF BAPTISMS FOR 1781.

Corcran, Mary Ann, of Patrick and Mary Corcran, born January 30th, 1780, baptized January 5th, sponsor Catharine Boudrot.

Edwards, Sarah, of Charles and Sophia Edwards, born September 1st, 1780, baptized January 7th, sponsors Augustine and Eleanor Power.

Gleicher, Eustace, of Francis Xavier and Ursula Gleicher, born December 21st, 1780, baptized January 8th, witness Eustace Laurens, sponsor Margaret Wolf.

Macoy, Lawrence, of Edward and Mary Macoy, born December 29th, 1780, baptized January 9th, sponsor Patrick Murphy, witness Margaret Karagan.

Durand, Nicholas Joseph, of James and Catharine Durand, born January 4th, baptized January 11th, sponsors Nicholas Säring and Elizabeth Becker.

Beauprés, Elizabeth, of Francis and Margaret Beauprés, born January 13th, baptized January 13th, sponsor, Mary Magdalen Le Blanc, witness Sebastian Jollain.

Bryar, Eva, of Emmanuel and Mary Bryar, born January 10th, baptized January 14th, sponsors Joseph Becker and Eva Essling.

Schilling, Eva Christina, of Philip and Eva Schilling, born January 15th, baptized January 21st, sponsors Paul and Christina Essling.

Diamond, John, of John and Mary Diamond, born January 11th, baptized January 21st, sponsors Nicholas Bernard and Margaret Brewer.

Buch, John James, of Joseph and Hannah Buch, born January 6th, baptized January 21st, sponsor Barbara Gordon.

McCagan, Susanna, of James and Jane McCagan, born December 24th, 1780, baptized January 21st, sponsor Walter Byron, and witness Margaret Ager.

Warner, Mary, of |Hugh and Margaret Warner, born June 5th, 1777, baptized January 22d, sponsors John and Rebecca Cornély.

Warner, Richard, same parents, born November 15th, 1779, baptized January 23d, sponsor Helen Denny.

Morelly, Judith, of Francis and Elizabeth Morelly, born January 6th, baptized January 29th, sponsors Francis Smith and Margaret Magill.

Eckel, Peter, of Peter and Anna Mary Eckel, born February 4th, baptized February 4th, sponsors Peter and Catharine Bremich.

Foster, Michael, of James and Elizabeth Foster, born January 28th, baptized February 6th, sponsors Michael and Mary Ann Anderle.

McClasky, Patrick, of Patrick and Mary McClasky, born January 31st, baptized February 11th, sponsor Henry Herberger, and witness Susanna, his wife.

Stuart, James, of John and Mary Stuart, born October 5th, 1780, baptized February 11th, sponsor Phœbe Stuart.

Veit, George Ernest, of Christian and Barbara Veit, born January 20th, baptized February 11th, sponsors George Ernest and Mary Magdalen Lechler.

Buspin, Anna, of Samuel and Sarah Buspin, born December 22d, 1779, baptized February 18th.

Sculley, Samuel, of John and Elizabeth Sculley, born November 21st, 1780, baptized February 22d, sponsors John and Margaret Scot, in Burlington county [N. J.].

Viel, John George, of Paul and Mary Viel, born February 18th, baptized February 25th, witnesses John George and Mary Magdalen Yokel.

Rose, William, of Hugh and Mary Rose, born May 13th, 1780, baptized February 25th, sponsors Francis and Elizabeth Bauer.

Doe, Mary, of William and Martha Doe, born January 15th, baptized February 27th, sponsors Charles Ross and Mary Johanna Sosett.

Rübel, Peter, of Francis and Hannah Rübel, born February 7th, baptized March 15th, sponsors Peter and Catharine Bremich.

Will, Catharine, of Philip and Elizabeth Will, born March 13th, baptized March 18th, sponsors Anthony and Sarah Aman.

Cammeloch, Johanna Catharine, of John Frederic and Anna Mary Sophia Cammeloch, born March 19th, baptized March 19th, sponsor Catharine Wagner.

Halder, John Nicholas, of James and Anna Christina Halder, born December 26th, 1780, baptized March 25th, sponsor Mary Rodt, witnesses Nicholas and Christina Weber.

Geiger, Anna Mary, of Simon and Mary Geiger, born March 13th, baptized April 3d, sponsor the mother (for Hannah Huber), in Salem county [N. J.].

Huin, Margaret, of William and Margaret Huin, born July 1st, 1779, baptized privately April 4th, in Gloucester county [N. J.].

Huin, Thomas, of same parents, born November 6th, 1780, baptized privately April 4th, *ibid.*

Lort, Joseph, of Isaac and Anna Lort, born April 4th, baptized April 8th, sponsors Bartholomew Tool and Mary Henry.

McCurtin, John, of Thomas and Deborah McCurtin, born June 30th, 1780, baptized April 10th, sponsor Margaret Lenard.

Denny, Esther, of William and Helen Denny, born April 19th, baptized April 20th, sponsors Roger Flahavan, Sr., and Margaret Connel.

Goff, William, of Archibald and Anna Goff, born 1779, baptized April 21st, sponsors John Planey and Mary Jolly.

Tschabio, Peter, of Athanasius and Catharine Tschabio, born January 22d, baptized May 6th, sponsor Peter Sailer, and witness Catharine, his wife, at Pikesland [Chester county, Pa.].

Schmidt, Elizabeth, of Francis and Jane Schmidt, born February 12th, baptized May 6th, sponsors Sarah Thimler (Sohl), *ibid.*

Perry, John, of William (P.) and Bridget Perry, born January 25th, baptized May 6th, sponsor Apollonia Sohl, *ibid.*

McCarty, Mary, of Nicholas, Jr, and Elizabeth McCarty, born October 6th, 1780, baptized May 15th, sponsors Simon Höny and Mary McCarty, at Haycock [Bucks county, Pa.].

Sary, William, of Lawrence and Mary (Robin) Sary, born September 9th, 1778, baptized May 17th, sponsors Nicholas and Anna Eva Jungfleisch, at Change Water [Warren county, N. J.].

Robin, Margaret, of ——— and Mary Robin, born February 5th, baptized May 17th, sponsors Joseph and Margaret Wider. *ibid.*

O'Neal, Anna, of Peter and Sarah (Kelly) O'Neal, born August 13th, 1780, baptized May 20th, sponsors John and Johanna Swiney, at Long-pond [N. J.].

Riddle, Catharine, of Thomas and (P.) Frances Riddle, born April 3d, baptized May 20th, sponsors Henry and Mary Burns, *ibid.*

Burns, Hannah, of Laghlin and Margaret Burns, born January 15th, baptized May 20th, sponsors Thomas and Eleanor Cahel, *ibid.*

Fitzgerald, William, of William and Margaret Fitzgerald, born March 22d, baptized May 20th, sponsors William Macan and Mary Catharine Call, *ibid.*

Call, Mary Elizabeth, of Henry and Mary Catharine Call, born July 30th, 1780, baptized May 22d, sponsors Eugene (son of William) Pfältzer and Anna Mary Call, at Ringwood [Passaic county, N. J.].

Poiress, Anna Mary, of ———, and Margaret Poiress, born October 5th, baptized May 22d, sponsors Nicholas Call and Anna Marry Reitenauer, *ibid.*

Thomer, Christopher, of Christopher and Elizabeth (P.) Thomer, born December 14th, 1775, baptized ———, sponsors Dominic Robertson, in vincinity of Longpond [Sussex county, N. J.].

Marian, Anna Mary, of Hubert and Mary Marian, born April 8th, baptized May 24th, sponsors John Aussom and Helen Menzebach, at Charlottenburg [N. J.].

Aussom, John Stephen, born December 25th, 1765; Eva Clarissa, born March 31st, 1769; Joseph, born February 28th, 1773; children of John and Elizabeth Aussom, baptized conditionally May 24th, sponsor Joseph Wingart, at Pompton [N. J.].

Osterhout, Catharine, of —— and Elizabeth Osterhout, born March 12th, 1774, baptized conditionally May 24th, sponsor Joseph Wingart, *ibid.*

Osterhout, Elizabeth, adult, baptized May 24th, sponsor Elizabeth Aussom, *ibid.*

———, Peter, a negro boy about seven years old, baptized May 24th, sponsor Joseph Wingart, *ibid.*

Fichter, James, of David and Johanna Fichter, born November 15th, 1780, baptized May 27th, sponsors James Fichter and Eva Brady, at Mount Hope [N. J.].

Grips, Francis Anthony, of Peter Joseph and Mary Grips, born November 27th, 1780, baptized May 27th, sponsors Francis Anthony Zech and Margaret Engelhart, *ibid.*

Sig, Christopher, of George (P.) and Gertrude Sig, born December 5th, 1780, baptized May 26th, sponsor Francis Anthony Zech (for Christopher Thomer) and Anna Catharine Zech, *ibid.*

Willson, Hannah, of Henry (P.) and Margaret Willson, born April 28th, baptized May 29th, sponsors Henry Miller and Elizabeth Schäffer, at Change Water [Warren county, N. J.].

Sary, Mary Robins, wife of Lawrence Sary, baptized May 29th, sponsor Anna Eva Jungfleisch, *ibid.*

Friend, Salome, of George and Catharine Friend, born May 27th, baptized June 3d, sponsors Tobias Rudolf and Salome Friend.

Doyle, Leah French, wife of Hugh Doyle, baptized June 7th, sponsor Eleanor Connoly.

French, Rachel, uterine sister of the last named (Mrs. Doyle), baptized at the same time, and having the same sponsor.

Collwell, Elizabeth, of Alexander and Mary Collwell, born January 6th, 1779, baptized June 7th, sponsors Patrick Byrne and Mary Clark.

L'Hercule, John Baptist, of Maturin and Margaret L'Hercule, born June 12th, baptized June 12th, sponsors John François and Felicitas Rose.

Nihil, Mary, of Lawrence and Anna (P.) Nihil, born May 27th, baptized June 14th, sponsors John Aitkin and Brdget Barret.

Miller, James, of Mathias and Anna Mary Miller, born May 6th, baptized June 17th, sponsors Lawrence and Christina Göck, at Deerfield [Salem county, N. J.].

Coleman, Hannah, of Edward and Catharine Coleman, born January 20th, baptized June 19th, sponsors Henry Thurnbach and Çatharine Bucher, in Salem county [N. J.].

Norret, Margaret, of James (P.) and Eleanor Norret, born October 31st, 1780, baptized June 19th, sponsors John McHugh and Eleanor Connor, *ibid.*

Magill, James, of Patrick and Elizabeth Magill, born May 9th, baptized June 19th, sponsors Simon Geiger and Susanna Benner, *ibid.*

Fitzgerald, Isabella, of Nicholas and Jane Fitzgerald, born November 13th, 1780, baptized June 24th, sponsors David Groty and Margaret Pearson.

Pepin, Victor, of Andrew and Judith (Dona) Pepin, born August 3d, 1780, baptized June 25th, sponsors Joseph Traversie and Charlotte Pepin.

Fitzgerald, John, of Lawrence and Deborah Fitzgerald, born May 26th, baptized June 25th, sponsors Henry Calaghan and Jane Dwyer.

Kelly, Margaret, of James and Margaret Kelly, born June 19th, baptized July 1st, sponsors Adam and Margaret Bremich.

Duffy, James, of James and Sarah Duffy, born June 23d, baptized July 1st, sponsors Dennis Glancy and Catharine Green.

Tréspanié, Maria Modesta, of Augustine and Anna (David) Tréspanié, born July 1st, baptized July 2d, sponsors John Louis and Modesta Landry.

Harby, Elizabeth, adult, baptized July 3d, sponsor Mary Macanarney.

Henderson, John, of David (P.) and Mary Henderson, born March 11th, baptized conditionally July 3d, sponsor the priest.

Clark, Amelia, of James and Catharine Clark, born December, 1780, baptized July 7th, sponsor Margaret Regan.

Muny, Jane Connert, wife of Hugh Muny, baptized July 7th, sponsor Anna Fitzgerald.

Muny, Neal, of Hugh and Jane Muny, born December 16th, baptized July 7th, sponsors Michael and Margaret Sauerwald.

McDonald, Sarah, of James and Margaret McDonald, born June 16th, baptized privately July 8th.

Lallor, John, of Thomas and Sarah Lallor, born June 5th, baptized July 11th, sponsor George Fitzgerald.

Klem, William, of John and Anna Mary Klem, born September 17th, 1778, baptized July 17th, sponsors John and Catharine Hoy, in Burlington county [N. J.].

Graff, Anna, of Anthony and Barbara Graff, born July 19th, baptized July 20th, sponsors Moses and Elizabeth Boosee.

O'Connor, Anna Christina, of John and Anna O'Connor, born July 19th, baptized July 22d, sponsor Joseph Westmor, and witness Mary Connor.

Schneider, Anna Catharine, of Henry, Jr., and Catharine Schneider, born July 22d, baptized July 24th, sponsors George Graff and Catharine Waltrich.

——, James, of Chloe, negro slave of Mr. Price, born July 17th, baptized July 25th, sponsor Johanna Grey.

Cuny, James, of James and Mary Cuny, born April 7th, baptized July 29th, sponsors Francis and Apollonia Sohl, at Pikesland [Chester county, Pa.].

Dugan, Elizabeth, of James and Sarah Dugan, born May 13th, 1779, baptized July 29th, sponsor Frederick Scheimer, *ibid.*

Dugan, James, same parents, born November 7th, 1780, baptized July 29th, sponsors Daniel FitzPatrick and Mary Weisseburger, *ibid.*

Eyenson, Mary, of John and Anna Eyenson, born June 3d, 1780, baptized July 29th, sponsors James Weisseburger and Mary Walter, *ibid.*

Yokel, John, of George and Mary Yokel, born August 4th, baptized August 5th, sponsor John Manderfelt.

Smith, Catharine, of Nicholas and Eva Smith, born July 25th, baptized August 9th, sponsors Peter and Catharine Bremich.

Küster, Thomas, of William and Catharine (Hönig) (P.) Küster, born July 20th, baptized August 11th, sponsor Barbara Carlin.

Mackey, Mary, of William and Elizabeth (Darney) (P.) Mackey, born May 7th, baptized August 18th, sponsors John and Anna Bucher, at Woodstown [Salem county N. J.].

Berg, John George, of Ernest and Gertrude Berg, born August 22d, baptized August 26th, sponsor Christopher Tscharté, and witness Mary Dorothy, his wife.

Cuny, Elizabeth, of John and Mary Cuny, born December 26th, 1779, baptized August 26th, witness Thomas Maybury, and sponsor Eleanor Walker.

Douglass, Charles, of William and Catharine Douglass, born March 17th, 1776, baptized privately August 26th.

Berchot, William, of William and Elizabeth (Mayer) Berchot, born February 15th, 1769, baptized August 30th, sponsors Ignatius Boisset and Charlotte Pepin.

Cole, Levina [Lavinia?], adult, baptized August 31st, sponsor Catharine Boudrot.

McDonald, Edmund, of Edmund and Margaret McDonald, born September 2d, baptized September 9th, sponsors Raymond Byrne and Johanna Mary Levins.

Raubin, Joseph Louis, of John and Anna Raubin, born September 11th, baptized September 11th, sponsors Joseph Traversy and Magdalen Carboulet.

Schindler, Elizabeth, of Henry (P.) and Mary Catharine Schindler, born

November 14th, 1779, baptized September 16th, sponsors Jacob and Catharine Weissenburger, at Pikesland [Pa.].

Gans, Catharine, of Balthasar and Salome (P.) Gans, born February 26th, baptized September 16th, sponsors Peter Eimold and Elizabeth Rute, at Pikesland [Chester county, Pa.].

Wider, Anna Eva, of Joseph and Margaret Wider, born August 24th, baptized· September 25th, sponsors Nicholas and Anna Eva Jung-fleisch, at Greenwich [Cumberland county, N. J.].

Bachman, Joseph, of Martin and Anna Barbara Bachman, born June 14th, baptized September 28th, sponsors the priest and Anna Mary Menzebach, at Mount Hope, N. J.

Robertson, Catharine, of Dominic and Mary Catharine Robertson, born June 8th, baptized October 1st, sponsors William and Catharine Mullen, at Longpond [N. J.].

Strickland, William, of William and Amata Strickland, born May 4th, baptized October 2d, sponsors William and Catharine Mullen, at Ringwood [Passaic county, N. J.].

McLaghlin, Andrew James, of Patrick and Mary McLaghlin, born November 20th, 1776, baptized October 4th, sponsor James Doyle, while traveling in New York.

[A note by Father Farmer says that: "The following children and infants were baptized conditionally by me while near Fishkill, New York :"]

Monty, John, of Francis and Josephine (Berjevin) Monty, baptized October 5th, sponsors Amatus Boiteau and Mary Louisa Taupié, near Fishkill [N. Y.].

Monty, Louisa, same parents, baptized October 5th, sponsors Harduin Merlet and Josephine Couturié, *ibid.*

Merlet, Adrian, of Harduin and Elizabeth (McKenly) Merlet, born August 31st, 1778, baptized October 5th, sponsors the priest and Amatus Marnay, *ibid.*

Merlet, Mary Magdalen, same parents, born April 23d, 1780, baptized October 5th, sponsors Lawrence Olivié and Charlotte Guibord, *ibid.*

Ferriole, Catharine, of Alexander and Mary (Mayotte) Ferriole, born February 5th, 1779, baptized October 6th, sponsors Louis Marnay and Mary Ferriole, *ibid.*

Bouvet, Amatus, of Louis and Josephine (Gallerson) Bouvet, born December 24th, 1776, baptized October 6th, sponsors Louis Marnay and Mary Mayotte, *ibid.*

La Fleur, Mary, of Joseph and Mary (Diligau) La Fleur, born ——— 5th, 1780, baptized October 6th, sponsors Louis Marnay and Charlotte Chartier, *ibid.*

Pollin, Peter, of Anthony and Theodista (Goddard) Pollin, born March 15th, 1778, baptized October 6th, the priest being sponsor, *ibid.*

Pollin, Mary Angelica, same parents, born December 26th, 1780, baptized October 6th, sponsors John Goulé and Charlotte Chartier, *ibid.*

Chartier, Charlotte, of Nicholas Constantine and Charlotte Chartier, born February 3d, 1779, baptized October 6th, sponsors Anthony Pollin and Mary Ferriole, *ibid.*

Chartier, Genevieve, same parents, born August 8th, 1781, baptized October 6th, sponsors John Goulé and Genevieve Bouché, *ibid.*

Ferriole, Louis Philip, of Alexander and Mary (Mayotte) Ferriole, born November 9th, 1780, baptized October 7th, sponsors Louis Philip Profanier and Mary Ferriole, *ibid.*

Varley, Catharine, of Michael and Josephine (Raymond) Varley, born November 5th, 1780, baptized October 7th, sponsors Joseph Laurent and Mary Boileau, *ibid.*

Guilmet, Mary Frances, of Francis and Mary Frances (Chandron) Guilmet, born April 16th, 1779, baptized October 7th, sponsors Peter Charland and Mary Robinet, *ibid.*

May, William, of James and Magdalen May, born September 26th, baptized October 10th, sponsors William and Catharine Mullen, at Ringwood [N. J.].

Zech, John Bernard, of Francis Anthony and Anna Catharine Zech, born September 19th, baptized October 14th, sponsors John and Anna Mary Grinter, at Mount Hope [N. J.].

Sheal, John, of John and Anna Sheal, born August 20th, baptized October 14th, sponsors Peter Joseph and Mary Grips, *ibid.*

Davenac, Elizabeth, of Joseph and Margaret Davenac, born October 15th, baptized October 21st, sponsors Joseph Honecker and Catharine Vanié.

Haycock, Amos, of Daniel and Catharine Haycock, born April 26th, 1774, baptized October 11th, sponsor Hubert Marian, at Pompton [Passaic county, N. Y.].

Haycock, Abigail, same parents, born April, 1779, baptized October 11th, sponsors John Aussom and Anna Elizabeth Wingart, *ibid.*

Haycock, Elizabeth, same parents, born February, 1781, baptized October 11th, sponsor Elizabeth Aussom, *ibid.*

Whole number of baptisms—one hundred and thirty-two.

Whole number from January 1st, 1776, to October 21st, 1781—eight hundred and ninety-one.

FATHER FARMER'S

MARRIAGE REGISTER,

1758—1786.

PRESERVED AT ST. JOSEPH'S CHURCH, PHILAD'A.

[Copied from the original records, and translated and prepared for publication, by FRANCIS T. FUREY, Corresponding Secretary of the AMERICAN CATHOLIC HISTORICAL SOCIETY OF PHILADELPHIA.]

THE two precious volumes of Father Farmer's registers contain, besides the record of baptisms, that also of marriages throughout his extensive mission, during the entire term of his residence in Philadelphia, covering a period of twenty-eight years. This register is now made public for the first time. In his first volume he gives a separate list of marriages of Acadians; but these we have incorporated with the general list, in regular chronological order. They may, however, for the most part, be easily distinguished; for in other cases in which French names occur, it is generally stated where the parties came from.

The lists in the first volume include all the marriages down to the close of the year 1768, and are introduced by the following statement :

"Sequentes ego Ferdinandus Farmer, Soc. Jesu Missionarius, interrogovi, eorumque mutuo consensu habito, solemniter per verba de presenti matrimonio conjunxi.

There is a similar statement at the beginning of the registers in the second volume, opening with the year 1769; but in it there is an interpolation that furnishes strong proof of this register being an original record, and not merely a copy. The introduction in this instance reads thus:

" Sequentes ego Ferdinandus Farmer (Soc. Jesu, *usque ad dissolutionem ejusdem*), presbyter et missionarius, interrogavi, eorumque mutuo consensu habito, solemniter per verba de præsenti matrimonio conjunxi."

The words we have italicised are an interpolation: they were not written at the same time as the others. This conclusion flows naturally from their position above the line to which they belong, the place to insert them being indicated by a caret mark. The color of the ink, too, is slightly different from that of the words accompanying them, not being quite so black. Thus it is plain that they refer to an event happening after the registers were written; for, as the dissolution of the Society of Jesus did not take place until July, 1773, Father Farmer could not have alluded to it in January, 1769. The presumption of the registers being an original record is thus brought within the range of fact.

Father Farmer did not himself officiate in all the instances mentioned in the following pages; but the exceptions are always indicated by mentioning the names of the other priests who did, for instance, Fathers Harding and Geisler.

In the spelling of proper names the original has been faithfully followed in every instance. Thus variations of what is evidently the same name are accounted for.

When no place is mentioned the marriage is supposed to have been celebrated in Philadelphia. The insertion of (P.) after a name indicates that the person was a Protestant.

The following records are of incalculable service to the genealogist:

MARRIAGES FOR THE YEAR 1758.

Harakaum—Trostler: September 5th, in the Philadelphia chapel, Joseph Harakaum to Mary Magdalen Trostler, widow.

Dilier—Gras: September 25th, James Dilier to Helen Gras (P.).

Bennoit—Charmel: October 3d, Hubert Bennoit to Barbara Charmel.

Metzger—Kneuler: October 30th, John Metzger to Cecilia Kneuler.

MARRIAGES FOR THE YEAR 1759.

Hoffman—Bieler : January 1st, John Hoffman to Christina Bieler (P.).

Walliser—Schütz: Februay 5th, Michael Walliser to Anna Maria, daughter of John and Anna Schütz.

Treitz—Reibold : February 6th, Peter Treitz to Margaret Reibold (P.), widow.

Waas—Braun : April 17th, Sebastian Waas to Anna Maria Braun.

Murphy—Arnold : May 2d, in Cushenhopen chapel, Philip Murphy to Margaret, daughter of George and Catharine Arnold, after dispensation from publication of the banns ; witnesses Paul Miller, Catharine Spengler and Gertrude Hegner, all of Philadelphia ; the nuptial blessing was given afterwards at Mass.

Halder—Veith: May 25th, in the Philadelphia chapel, Francis Joseph Halder, widower, from the New Jersey mission, to Anna Margaret, daughter of George and Christina Veith.

Hueber—Bertle : October 3d, in Adam Geiger's house, in New Jersey, Michael, son of John James Hueber, of the same mission, to Hannah Bertle (P.).

_____

MARRIAGES FOR THE YEAR 1760.

Galater—Partié : January 10th, in the Philadelphia chapel, Michael Galater, widower, to Elizabeth Catharine Partié, widow.

Thurnbach—Geiger : April 23d, in Adam Geiger's house, in New Jersey, Christian Thurnbach to Susanna Catharine, daughter of Matthew Geiger, both of the New Jersey mission ; witnesses Adam Geiger and John Martin Halder, also of New Jersey.

Sexton—Buch: February 14th, John Sexton to Catharine, daughter of Adam and Elizabeth Buch ; after dispensation from the banns.

Poth—Faust: May 26th, in the Philadelphia chapel, Adam Poth, widower, to Mary, widow of Herman Faust.

Coleman—Deleany : June 11th, at Adam Geiger's, Edward Coleman to Ann Deleany, widow, both of the same mission.

Graff—Waltrich : July 14th, in the Philadelphia chapel, Anthony Graff to Barbara Waltrich.

Göck—Gras : July 15th, Adam Göck, widower, to Mary Gras.

Newkom—Abl : August 24th, Henry Newkom to Anna Mary Abl.

Magill—Ketz ; October 2d, in Patrick Magill's house, John, son of the said Patrick and Margery Magill, to Catharine Ketz (P.), both from the neighborhood of the New Jersey mission ; witnesses Adam Geiger and others.

Haug—Friderich: November 25th, in the Philadelphia chapel, Anthony Haug to Mary Friderich ; the nuptial blessing given at Mass.

MARRIAGES FOR THE YEAR 1761.

Babin—Vincent: January 7th, Charles Babin to Frances Vincent.

Guétry—Melançon: January 22d, Simon Yetry (Guétry) to Magdalen Melançon.

Reicher—Bimpl: January 26th, James Reicher to Margaret, widow of Balthasar Bimpl; witnesses Peter Weissenburger and Catharine Spengler; the banns had been published only twice.

Viel—Walter: January 27th, Rudolph Viel, a widower, to Susanna Walter ; the third publication of the banns dispensed with for a good reason ; witnesses to the marriage Paul Essling and Christopher Viel ; the nuptial blessing given at Mass.

Feinauer—Willhelm : March 29th, Joseph Feinauer to Anna Mary Willhelm ; witnesses Anthony Ottman and Catharine Spengler ; the nuptial blessing given on April 13th following.

Ribau—Benoit: May 11th, Joseph Ribau to Margaret Benoit.

Schoch—Jacobi: May 14th, in Adam Geiger's house, the seat of the New Jersey mission, William Schoch (Luth.) to Catharine Jacobi ; the banns had been published twice in Philadelphia, where the young man lived, it is presumed, and once in the New Jersey mission, to which the bride belonged; witnesses of the marriage John Adam Geiger, Francis Halder, and other Catholics of the same mission.

Le Blanc—Landry : June 10th, Charles Le Blanc to Anna Landry.

Daniel—Doiron: June 29th, Eustache Daniel to Margaret Doiron.

Birt—Selié: July 2d, Jonathan Birt, an English Protestant, to Mary Blanche Ebair, widow of N. Selié, an Acadian ; witnesses (strangers) Joseph Wright and Elizabeth Townsen.

Sauerwald—Werl: September 1st, Michael Sauerwald to Margaret Werl; witnesses Paul Essling and Anna Angela Schwartzman ; the nuptial blessing imparted aftewards at Mass.

Buttler—Arnold : October 4th, William Buttler to Catharine, widow of George Arnold, shoemaker; witnesses William Foster and Margaret, his wife, and Catharine Spangler.

Bimpel—Scheltle : October 5th, after dispensation from the banns, James (or Jacob) Bimpel to Mary, widow of Joseph Scheltle ; witnesses George Haug and Catharine Spengler.

Viel—Weitinger: October 6th, Nicholas Viel to Sophia Weitinger; witnesses Charles Smith and Rudolph Viel; the nuptial blessing was afterwards given at Mass.

Diezy—Vincent: October 20th, Joseph Diezy, widower, to Mary Vincent, widow, both Acadians ; witnesses Alexis Dibautau and Oliver Dibautau, also Acadians.

Blanchart—Le Blanc : October 20th, Oliver Francis Blanchart to Euphrosine Le Blanc, widow, both Acadians; witnesses the same as last named.

Krafft—Zeit: November 1st, James (or Jacob) Krafft (P.), widower, to Anna Mary Zeit, widow; witnesses Adam Mayer, Christopher Viel and Catharine Haydin; one of the three publications of the banns had been forgotten.

Gliche—Landry: November 3d, Louis Gliche, a Canadian, to Magdalen Landry, an Acadian-; witnesses Charles Le Blanc and John Baptist Sencere.

Arnold—Schmid: November 23d, Henry Arnold to Agnes Schmid ; witnesses Lancelot Harrison, Michael Sauerwald and George Mertz; the nuptial blessing was given alterwards at Mass.

Doiron—Blanchart: November 25th, Paul Doiron to Mary Blanchart ; witnesses Alexis Dibautau, Francis Blanchart and Joseph Labau.

MARRIAGES FOR THE YEAR 1762.

Walter—Erter: January 7th, John Walter, widower, to Elizabeth Erter; witnesses Paul Essling and Michael Sauerwald; the nuptial blessing was given afterwards at Mass

Ridiger—Vanié: January 12th, Matthew Anthony Ridiger, of Philadelphia, to Mary Vanié, of the New Jersey mission.

Kientz—Ridiger: at the same time and place, Andrew Kientz to Mary Eva Ridiger; witnesses at both marriages, Sebastian Vanié, John Ridiger and Joseph Kientz; the nuptial blessing was given afterwards at Mass.

Brian—Kohl: January 31st, Anthony Brian, a Frenchman, to Catharine Kohl (P.) ; witnesses Anthony Gabriel, Caspar Kriechler (P.), Catharine Willhelm (P.), and Catharine Kriechler (P.).

Buttler—Arnold: February 2d, Edmund Buttler to Barbara, daughter of George and Catharine Arnold; witnesses Philip Murphy and Catharine Spengler.

Dibotau—Le Blanc: February 17th, after dispensation from banns, Alexis Dibotau, widower, to Catharine Le Blanc, widow; witnesses Daniel Le Blanc, Paul Bourg and Joseph Dibotau.

Dibotau—O'Koin: April 19th, Joseph Dibotau, widower, to Mary Josepha O'Koin, widow; dispensation from publication of the banns had been obtained; witnesses to the marriage, Alexis Dibotau, Francis Savoy and John Douzar.

Landry—Le Prince: May 26th, Peter Landry, widower, to Magdalen Le Prince, widow of Peter O'Koin; witnesses Peter Landry, Jr., Oliver O'Koin and Joseph O'Koin.

Bifar—Kost: June 1st, Sebastian Bifar, widower, to Rosina, daughter of

Henry Kost; witnesses William Makey, Conrad Moch, a stranger, and Frederick Holtzhauser.

Glutié—Ebair: June 2d, Louis Glutié, a Canadian, to Magdalen Dupuis, widow of Anthony Ebair; witnesses John Baptist Sencere and Paul Le Blanc.

Caron—Dibotau: on the same day, Ignatius Caron, a Canadian, to Anna Maria, daughter of Oliver Dibotau; witnesses John Baptist Bijou, Joseph Diezy, Stephen Mayer and Eustache Favron.

Jäger—Spring: June 29th, Matthew Jäger to Mary Spring (P.); witnesses John Miller, Anthony Brehmen and Catharine Brehmen.

Böhm—Gruber: the same day and place, Joseph Böhm to Mary Catharine Gruber (P.); witnesses Stephen Foratch and Conrad Schneider.

Schwartzman—Miller: September 14th, Andrew Schwartzman to Charlotte Miller; witnesses Joseph Eck, Mark Hanecker and Barbara Steling; afterwards the nuptial blessing was given at Mass.

Kessler—Sigfrid: the same day and place, Andrew Kessler to Catharine Sigfrid; witnesses Michael Galater, Joseph Würth, and John Stauter.

O'Koin—D'Aigle: October 9th, Oliver O'Koin, widower, to Margaret D'Aigle, widow; witnesses Alexander Rodohal, Oliver Dibotau and Peter Babin.

Würth—Steling: November 21st, Joseph Würth to Barbara Steling; witnesses John Gatringer, Catharine Spengler and Andrew Steling; the nuptial blessing was given at Mass on the 22d.

MARRIAGES FOR THE YEAR 1763.

Mayer—Hegner: January 4th, after dispensation from the banns, Joseph Meyer (P.) to Catharine, step-daughter of Peter Hegner; witnesses Peter Hegner and Tobias Rudolph.

Heitz—Rübl: January 6th, John Heits to Barbara, widow of George Rübl; witnesses Adam Meyer, Joseph Rübl and Catharine Meyer.

Krämer—Bub: January 11th, Henry Krämer to Catharine Bub; witnesses Francis Senner and Adam Meyer; the nuptial blessing was given afterwards at Mass.

Conrad—Geiger: January 11th, Nicholas Conrad to Elizabeth Geiger; witnesses Charles Conrad and George Conrad.

Le Blanc—Vincent: January 27th, Marin Le Blanc to Isabella Vincent, both Acadians; witnesses Charles Le Blanc and Joseph Vincent.

Bishau—Chiroir: February 3d, John Baptist Bishau to Anatolia, daughter of Peter Chiroir; witnesses Joseph Dibotau and Oliver O'Koin.

Raphael—Votremere: the same day and place, Joseph Raphael, a

Frenchman, to Helena Votremere ; witnesses Charles Moienau and Joseph Ribau.

Babin—Linou : the same day and place, Simon Babin, widower, to Anastasia Le Blanc, widow of John Linou ; witnesses Francis Savoy and Peter Babin.

Le Blanc—Dendon : February 10th, Alexis, son of Charles Le Blanc, to Anna, daughter of Claude Dendon ; witnesses Peter Savoy, Charles Le Blanc, Jr., and Joseph Diezy.

Manio—Gallerm : the same day and place, Charles Manio, widower, to Pelagia, daughter of John Baptist Gallerm ; witnesses Joseph Ribau, Zachary Babin and Joseph Raphael.

Le Core—Dechamps : February 14th, René Le Core to Blanche, daughter of Joseph Dechamps ; witnesses Halin d'Aigre and Joseph Ribaud ; the nuptial blessing was given afterwards at Mass.

Geiger—Hopkins : April 5th, Adam Geiger, widower, to Catharine Margaret Hopkins, widow ; witnesses Adam Göck and George Laub.

Miller—Krafft : the same day and place, by Father Robert Harding, John Miller (P.) to Mary Ann, widow of James (or Jacob) Krafft.

———— —Gallerm . April 11th, Lawrence ———— to Mary Josepha, widow of N. Gallerm.

Mayer—Lechler : May 16th, John Mayer, widower, to Elizabeth, daughter of George Ernest Lechler ; witnesses George Mertz and Anthony Lechler ; the nuptial blessing given later at Mass.

Bucher—Becker : May 23d, John Bucher to Anna Catharine Becker ; witnesses Francis Senner, Joseph Böhm and Christian Bub ; the nuptial blessing was given at Mass on the 26th.

Schütz—Eglis : June 20th, John Schütz to Mary Eva Eglis ; witnesses Michael Walliser, Christian Schütz and Valentine Korn.

Hauff—Amsperger : June 27th, Valentine Hauff to Magdalen Amsperger ; witnesses John Schütz and Paul Bishoff.

Bodar—Kost : August 7th, Anthony Bodar, an Acadain, to Barbara Kost ; witnesses Firmian Bodoin and Stephen Swerber.

Jocobi—Bischoff : August 17th, in New Jersey, Philip Jacobi to Margaret Bischoff (P.) ; witnesses Catharine Schoch and Barbara Kneul.

Nagel—Sier : August 28th, George Nagel to Anna Mary Sier ; witnesses Firmian Bodoin and George Mertz.

Seitz—Schreiner : August 29th, George Seitz to Eva Schreiner ; witnesses Francis Wolf and Anselm Schreiner.

Ridiger—Schmid : October 10th, John Ridiger to Anna Angela Schmid ; witnesses Matthew Anthony Ridiger and Andrew Kientz.

Siffert—Schütz : November 9th, Joseph Siffert to Catharine Schütz ; no witnesses but the priest.

MARRIAGES FOR THE YEAR 1764.

Vincent—Babin : February 28th, Peter Vincent to Mary Magdalen, daughter of Baptiste Babin ; witnesses John Baptist Sincere, Joseph Vincent and Paul Blanchart.

Leckner—Darms: March 25th, Mathias Leckner to Barbara Darms; witnesses Francis Moltz, James Ryan and Barbara Kneul.

Schütz—Schorp, April 24th, Christian Schütz to Elizabeth Schorp; witnesses Michael Walliser, John Schütz and Andrew Schwartzman.

Kneul—Umes : April 30th, Balthasar Kneul to Christina Elizabeth Umes ; witnesses George Ernest Lechler, John Lederman and John Feltz.

Doiron—Bourg: May 17th, Paul Doiron, widower, to Mary Bourg, both Acadains ; witnesses Paul Bourg, the bride's father, Oliver Dibotau and Oliver Dibotau, Jr.

Halder—Feinshman : June 14th, by Father Robert Harding, after dispensation from banns, Martin Halder to Catharine Feinshman.

Häffner—Hauck : June 21st, by the same, John Häffner to Eva Hauck.

Veit—Hauck : the same day and place, by the same, Christian Veit to Barbara Hauck.

Ruffener—Kuhn : July 1st, at Cushenhopen, Christian Ruffener to Ottilia Kuhn, both of that vicinity, opposite the church ; subsequently the nuptial blessing was given at Mass.

Dibotau—Boirié: July 19th, Charles Dibotau, widower, to Magdalen Doiron, widow of Joseph Boirié; witnesses Oliver Dibotau, Paul Doiron and John Boirié.

Walter—Dihin : July 22d, Francis Walter to Catharine Dihin ; witnesses Anthony Graff and John Sauerwald ; the nuptial blessing was given at Mass on the 23d.

Duliere—Godot: July 23d, Peter Duliere, widower, to Clara Boudrot, widow of Joseph Godot ; witnesses Oliver Dibotau, John Boirié and Joseph Boudrot.

Sauerwald—Wegfort: October 2d, John Sauerwald to Magdalen Wegfort; witnesses Michael Sauerwald, Mark Wegfort, the bride's father, and Christian Bub.

Cire—Vincent: October 24th, Francis Cire to Anna, daughter of Peter and Genevieve Vincent; witnesses John Boirié, Joseph Boudrot and Peter Vincent.

Blanchard—Dibotau : October 25th, Paul Blanchard to Cecilia, daughter of Charles and Anna Dibotau; witnesses Oliver Blanchard, John Poirié and Peter Vincent.

MARRIAGES FOR THE YEAR 1765.

Gerard—Henrich: January 7th, Matthias Gerard to Sophia, widow of Nicholas Henrich; witnesses John Orth, John Henrich and George Lechler.

Heiser—Welsch: January 8th, after dispensation from the banns, John Heiser to Agnes Welsch, widow; witnesses George Nagel, Charles Ewald and John Truckenmiller.

· Boyd—Davadge: April 8th, Patrick Boyd to Ann Davadge.

Späth—Sun: April 14th, John Späth to Margaret Sun.

Ridiger—Vainé: April 15th, John Ridiger, widower, to Margaret, daughter of Sebastian and Margaret Vainé; witnesses Matthew Ridiger and the bride's father.

Wider—Gril: April 28th, at Ringwood, Joseph Wider to Margaret, daughter of Francis and Anna Emily Gril; subsequently the nuptial blessing was given at Mass.

Caspar—Halder: May 8th, in Adam Geiger's house, Lawrence Caspar to Margaret, daughter of John Martin and N. Halder; witnesses the bride's father and sister, Adam Geiger and others; the nuptial blessing was given afterwards at Mass.

Kneul—Berk: May 22d, George Kneul to Catharine Berk, *alias* Frauenfelder; witnesses John Feltz and Balthasar Kneul.

Grünewald—Schmid: June 18th, in Philip Schmid's house, John Grünewald to Barbara, daughter of Philip Schmid; witnesses the bride's father and brothers, also Henry Fredder and others.

Jocobs—Schmid: July 28th, William Jacobs (P.) to Catharine Schmid; witnesses Christian Schütz and his wife, Mary Elizabeth.

Korn—Weber: August 20th, Caspar, son of Valentine and Barbara Korn, to Anna Mary, daughter of Stephen and Anna Mary Weber; witnesses the bridegroom's father, William Miller and Christain Fidler.

Sullivan—Sly: November 11th, at Ringwood, Denis Sullivan to Catharine Sly.

Forage—Wahl: November 18th, Stephen Forage to Anna Mary Wahl.

Magill—Grimes: November 27th, in Adam Geiger's house, Peter Magill to Barbara Grimes; witnesses James (or Jacob) Magill, his wife, and others.

O'Koin—Blanchart: December 26th, Simon O'Koin, widower, to Cecilia Dibotau, widow of Paul Blanchart, an Acadian; witnesses Charles Dibotau, Oliver Dibotau and John Poirié.

MARRIAGES FOR THE YEAR 1766.

Kientz—Lochbaum: February 11th, Andrew Kientz, widower, to Eva Clara Lochbaum; witnesses Christian Bub, Lawrence Göck and Joseph Kientz.

Collins—Eck: March 4th, in James Eck's house, John Collins to Isabella, daughter of the aforesaid James Eck and his wife, Anna.

Escher—Sigfrid: March 31st, John Conrad Escher to Mary Felicia Sigfrid.

Stolls—Dewetter: April 6th, Charles Stolls to Margaret, daughter of John and Anna Mary Dewetter; witnesses the bride's father, etc.

Labauve—Broc: April 7th, Joseph Labauve, widower, to Margaret Le Vache, widow of Simon Broc, Acadians; witnesses John Poirié and Paul Bourg.

Finey—Miller: April 10th, John Finey to Mary Miller (Ottilia Freymiller).

Welsch—Kauffman: April 21st, at Ringwood, Conrad Welsch to Elizabeth Kauffman; subsequently the nuptial blessing was given at Mass.

Gotrau—Bourg: May 12th, John, son of Charles and Mary (Le Blanc) Gotrau, to Anna, daughter of Paul and Judith (Ebair) Bourg; witnesses Daniel Le Blanc, John Poiriet and James Lecomte.

Depuis—Dibotau: September 16th, Peter, son of Germain and Angelica (Le Blanc) Depuis, to Agatha, daughter of Basil and Anna (Le Prince) Dibotau; witnesses Jacques Lecomte, Bruno Trahan and Paul Bourg.

Haug—Arnold: July 22d, John Haug to Catharine Arnold; witnesses George Haug and George Mayer.

Maistertsheim—Galathar: August 17th, Emanuel Maistertsheim, widower, to Catharine Galathar; witnesses Valentine Hauff, Henry Orich and George Weber.

Dunn—Wigmor: September 16th, after dispensation from the banns, William Dunn to Bridget Wigmor.

Senner—Hardin: November 11th, after dispensation, Francis Senner, widower, to Mary Hardin; witnesses John Gatringer and Christian Bub.

Madden—Lynch: December 24th, John Madden to Elizabeth Lynch.

MARRIAGES FOR THE YEAR 1767.

Macarty—Kohl: January 20th, at Haycock, Nicholas, son of Edward and Catharine Macarty, to Albertina, daughter of George and Barbara Kohl; witnesses Joseph Kohl, Anna Macarty, widow, and several others; subsequently the nuptial blessing was given at Mass.

Stephan—Christman : January 19th, by Father Robert Harding, Mathias Stephan to Catharine Christman.

Lynch—Prefontain : February 1st, John Lynch to Elizabeth Prefontain.

Treim—Götz : February 8th, James Treim to Elizabeth Götz, a widow.

Henessy—Boulter : March 1st, after dispensation, John Henessy to Mary Boulter.

Fruhwirth—Griesmayer : March 2d, John George Fruhwirth to Mary Catharine Griesmayer; witnesses Adam Geiger and Christian Benner; the nuptial blessing was given subsequently at Mass.

Trahan—Ebair : the same day and place, Bruno Trahan, widower, to Catharine Josepha Ebair, widow; witnesses Simon O'Koin and Peter Savoy.

Eck—Schmid : March 3d, James (or Jacob) Eck, widower, to Elizabeth Schmid; witnesses Anna Angela Schwartzman and Barbara Schmid.

Swerber—Veit : April 26th, William Swerber, widower, to Ottilia, widow of Henry Veit; witnesses Stephen Swerber and Firmian Bodoin.

Göck—Geiger : April 28th, in Adam Geiger's house, in New Jersey, Lawrence, son of Adam and N. Göck, to Christina, daughter of Adam and Agnes Geiger; witnesses Henry Geiger, Simon Geiger and David Göck; subsequently the nuptial blessing was given at Mass.

Jungfleisch—Welcker : June 18th, at Ringwood, Nicholas Jungfleisch to Mary Eva, daughter of Peter and Mary Barbara Welcker; witnesses Peter Welcker, Joseph Wingart and others; the nuptial blessing was given subsequently at Mass.

Seeholtzer—Morlo : June 19th, *ibid.*, Martin Seeholtzer to Susanna Morlo ; witnesses Nicholas Stalter, John Mayer and others; subsequently the nuptial blessing was given at Mass.

Ohms—Essling : July 2d, Emanuel Ohms to Magdalen, daughter of George and Magdalen Essling; witnesses Rudolph Essling and John Willhelm; subsequently the nuptial blessing was given at Mass.

Benner—Reichman : July 14th, after two publications of the banns (one having been forgotten), Martin, son of Mathias and Johanna Benner, to Anna Christina, daughter of John and Anna Mary Reichman; witnesses John Willhelm and Christian Bub.

Gräs—Bartram ; August 20th, John George Gräs, widower, to Elizabeth Bartram, widow; witnesses Michael Bremich and John Feltz.

McMahan—Dedy : September 20th, at Pikesland, Barnabas McMahan to Johanna Dedy ; witnesses Patrick McFall and Daniel Dagherty.

Otto—Whitehead : October 25th, after dispensation, James (or Jacob) Otto to Mary Whitehead, widow; witnesses Charles Schmid and Adam Göck.

Hirt—Eberl: November 8th, Francis Joseph Hirt, widower, to Mary Barbara Eberl, widow.

Bremigeon—Bryan: November 24th, William Bremigeon to Catharine Bryan.

MARRIAGES FOR THE YEAR 1768.

Huber—Röttler : January 26th, John Huber to Mary Elizabeth Röttler ; the banns were published later.

Coffee—Haug : February 2d, George Coffee to Catharine Haug ; witnesses John Heffner and William Nunan.

Griffin—Sohl : February 21st, James Griffin to Elizabeth, daughter of Francis and Apollonia Sohl ; witnesses Thomas Griffin, Bartholomew Tool and Frederick Scheimer.

Griffin—Grogan : the same time and place, Thomas Griffin to Johanna Grogan ; the banns to be pulished after Easter.

Springer—Koch : April 26th, Joseph Springer to Magdalen Koch (Bronner) ; witnesses John Aronts and John Willhelm ; the blessing given later at Mass.

McCanna—Cane : May 29th, at Pikesland, John McCanna to Sara Cane ; witnesses the bride's mother, Eleanor Cane and others.

Kehl—Beck : June 28th, Sebastian Kehl to Catharine Beck (P.) ; witnesses John Benner, James (or Jacob) Schäffer and George Zeis.

Häffner—Lechler : July 5th, Peter, son of George and Catharine Häffner, to Eva, daughter of George Ernest and Mary Magdalen Lechler.

Lechler—Faust : the same time and place, Henry, son of the same George and Mary Magdalen Lechler, to Catharine, daughter of John and Catharine Faust ; witnesses Charles Schmid, James (or Jacob) Klein and Andrew Gerstenberger.

Hedings—Scherhammer : July 15th, John Hedings to Mary Magdalen Scherhammer ; witnesses George Ernest Lechler, James (or Jacob) Klein and Anthony Graff.

Lariol—Cire : October 12th, John Lariol, a Frenchman, to Anna Vincent, widow of Francis Cire ; witnesses Peter Vincent and Eustache Daniel.

Cobole—Welcker : October 24th, at Charlottenburg, Daniel Cobole to Mary Ann, daughter of Peter and Mary Barbara Welcker ; witnesses Martin Bachman, Christian Butz and Nicholas Jungfleisch ; the nuptial blessing was given subsequently at Mass.

May—Heuser : October 26th, at Ringwood, John May, widower, to Elizabeth Heuser (P.), widow ; witnesses James (or Jacob) Walter and John Mayer.

Engelhart—Hayl : November 3d, Andrew Engelhart, widower, to

Catharine Hayl, widow; witnesses Adam Poth and Bartholomew
Becker.

Champin—Benoit: the same day and place, Stephen Champin, a Frenchman, to Mary Benoit, an Acadian; witnesses Peter Savoy and
Joseph Ribau.

Kauffman—Buttler: November 22d, after dispensation, Joseph Kauffman, widower, to Barbara, widow of Edward Buttler; witnesses
John Gatringer and Denis Dagherty.

Welte—Schnitzer: November 27th, Bernard Welte to Mary Schnitzer
(P.); witnesses Christian Schneider and Michael Sauerwald.

MARRIAGES FOR THE YEAR 1769.

Hayle—Bodov'n: January 8th, Caspar Hayle to Elizabeth, widow of
Jeremiah Bodovin; witnesses Jacob Klein, Anthony Graff and
Andrew Schwartzman.

Probst—Berner: February 16th, after dispensation from the banns,
Henry Probst, widower, to Mary Barbara Berner (P.), widow; witnesses Paul Kofer and Nicholas Wochman.

Hauff—Schab: August 13th, Michael Hauff, widower, to Mary Magdalen Schab, widow; witnesses Henry Probst, Nicholas Wochman
and others.

Theusen—Probst: August 21st, by Rev. Luke Geisler, John Theusen to
Elizabeth Probst; witnesses, Henry Probst, Nicholas Wochman,
and Paul Coper; the nuptial blessing was given subsequently at
Mass.

Bray—Cotter: September 14th, without publication of banns, John Bray
to Judith Cotter.

Ryan—Arnold: September 22d, without publication of banns, Denis
Ryan to Agnes, widow of Henry Arnold.

Newnan [Noonan?]—McGuire: October 3d, in Thomas McGuire's
house, after dispensation from banns, William Newnan, widower,
to Eleanor, daughter of Thomas and Margaret McGuire; witnesses
Patrick Travers and the bride's parents and sister; the nuptial
blessing given subsequently at Mass.

Coneley—Quinup: October 8th, Thomas Coneley to Mary Quinup.

Polumbo—Ogle: October 12th, after dispensation from banns, Gaspar
Polumbo to Susan Ogle.

McCann—Bell: December 2d, after dispensation, Gabriel McCann to
Mary Bell.

Landry—Le Blanc: December 27th, Anthony, son of Peter and Josepha
(Le Blanc) Landry, to Barbara, daughter of Daniel and Margaret
Le Blanc, Acadians; witnesses Daniel Le Blanc and Peter Savoy.

MARRIAGES FOR THE YEAR 1770.

Hahn—Durstroff: February 13th, Joseph Hahn, widower, to Christina Durstroff, widow; witnesses Christopher Tscharté and Sebastian Kehl.

Honecker—Lechler: April 21st, after dispensation from banns, Mark Honecker, widower, to Christina, daughter of George Ernest and Mary Magdalen Lechler; witnesses the bride's father and Anthony Groff.

Lechler—Honecker: April 22d, Anthony, son of George Ernest and Mary Magdalen Lechler, to Cath arine, daughter of Mark and Anna Honecker; witnesses Mark Honecker and Anthony Groff.

Wibirau—Glaser: May 27th, Martin Wibirau, widower, to Regina Glaser; witnesses John Wagner and Sebastian Seibert.

Bremich—Jung: May 29th, Mathias, son of Michael and Walburga Bremich, to Margaret Elizabeth, daughter of John and Catharine Jung (Prs.); witnesses John Sauerwald and John Häffner.

Kamber—Schwerber: July 9th, Valentine Kamber to Ottilia, widow of William Schwerber; witnesses Christopher Viel and Francis Senner.

Faran—Kohl: September 22d, Thomas Faran to Mary Dorothy Kohl; witness John Kohl.

Schultz—Kneul: September 23d, after dispensation from banns, Christopher Schultz, widower, to Barbara Kneul; witnesses Mathias Miller and Adam Meyer.

Hanley—Kagan: the same day and place, Thomas Hanley to Rachel Kagan; witnesses John Cornéli and Rebecca, his wife.

L'Hercule—Douzet: October 18th, Francis, son of Francis Lecueil (L'Hercule) and Margaret Gouchy (Gouzy), his wife, to Pelagia, daughter of Claude and Margaret (Pelrin) Douzet; witnesses Peter Savoy and Peter Vincent.

Robert—Williams: November 4th, Joseph Robert to Anna Williams; witnesses Margaret Lucar, Margaret Nehil and Daniel Ghillan.

More—Freind: the same day and place, David More to Eva, daughter of Stephen and Salome Freind; witnesses the bride's father, Thomas McCullogh and Catharine Miller.

Dorff—Holtzhauser: November 8th, after dispensation from the banns, William Dorff, widower, to Christiana Holtzhauser (P.), widow; witnesses Francis Senner and Philip Shilling.

MARRIAGES FOR THE YEAR 1771.

Schnaller—Kaumann: January 6th, Nicholas Schnaller to Anna Mary Kaumann; witnesses Francis Abt and Henry Orich.

Jung—Stephan: April 7th, Francis Jung to Catharine, widow of Mathias Stephan; witnesses Anthony Blum, John Wagner and Mary Elizabeth Christman.

Stauter—Miller: June 24th, John Stauter, widower, to Helena Miller; witnesses John Miller and Christopher Schultz.

Göck—Leipart: July 9th, Mathias Göck to Charlotte Leipart; witnesses Adam Göck and Andrew Leipart.

Savoy—Lerquieul: July 31st, Peter Savoy, widower, to Mary, daughter of Francis and Margaret (Gouché) Lerquieul [L'Hercule]; witnesses Peter Vincent and Peter O'Koin.

Stiller—Lik: November 26th, John Stiller to Mary Lik; witnesses Nicholas Viel, Gabriel Macan and John Lipp.

MARRIAGES FOR THE YEAR 1772.

Wurtzer—Bremich: January 1st, John George Wurtzer to Mary Eva Bremich; witnesses Matthew Bremich and Anthony Bremich.

Coil—Maddin: January 19th, after dispensation from banns, John Coil to Ann Maddin; witnesses Hugh Kearney, Thomas Fleming, Mary Fleming and Mary Maddin.

Viel—Bifar: April 29th, after dispensation, Paul, son of Rudolph and Magdalen Viel, to Mary, daughter of Sebastian and Barbara Bifar; witness Rudolph Viel.

Chesson—Brown: May 11th, after dispensation, Thomas Chesson to Lucy Brown, widow; witnesses James Galagher and Ann Ball.

Horn—Honegger: May 21st, after dispensation, Henry Horn to Justina, widow of Mark Honegger; witnesses George Ernest Lechler and Christian Hauck.

Wingart—Marian: May 28th, at Charlottenburg, Joseph Wingart to Anna Elizabeth, daughter of Hubert and Anna Julianna Marian; witnesses Nicholas Jungfleisch and Jacob Demuth.

Ells—Welker: June 2d, at Ringwood, John Henry Ells to Anna Elizabeth, daughter of Gottlieb and Mary Magdalen Welker; witnesses Thomas Kauffman and John James Welker.

Mayer—Bensh: June 29th, after publication of the banns in New Jersey,

Joseph Mayer, widower, to Jane Bensh ; witnesses Johanna Morris and John Steling.

Kitzinger—Vanié: July 12th, George Philip Kitzinger to Judith, daughter of Sebastian and Margaret Vanié ; witnesses Sebastian Vanié and John Ridiger.

Gruber—Feltz: July 26th, Anthony Gruber, widower, to Mary Margaret, widow of John Feltz ; witnesses Joseph Rübel and Christopher Schultz.

Noble—Roenun [Ronayne?] : August 5th, after dispensation, Edward Noble to Mary Roenun ; witnesses Mary Macan and Margaret Bennet.

Regimenter—Mayer : August 23d, Peter Regimenter to Mary Magdalen, daughter of Adam and Catharine Mayer ; witnesses Peter Eck, John Lipp and John Steling.

Dreux—Bijau : September 3d, Augustin Dreux to Margaret Bijau ; witnesses Louis Guerin and George Bauman.

Lipp—Laub : September 12th, John Lipp to Philippina Laub ; witnesses Nicholas Essling and Charles Viel.

Reniger—Bald : September 15th, Reinhard Reniger to Elizabeth Bald ; witnesses John Kessler, Catharine Jackus and Charlotte Theusen.

Welsh—Kenedy: September 19th, after dispensation, John Welsh to Catharine Kenedy, widow ; witnesses Thomas Badge and Timothy Carrol.

Martin—Klein : September 24th, after dispensation, Anthony Martin, widower, to Anna, daughter of James and Elizabeth Klein ; witnesses the bride's father and Anthony Graff.

De La Beaume—David : the same day and place, John Joseph De La Beaume, a young Frenchman, to Anne David, an Acadian maiden ; witnesses Joseph Ribau, John La Riole and Margaret Le Blanc.

Boudrot—Blanchart : October 10th, Michael Boudrot to Anne Blanchart, both Acadians ; witnesses Peter Blanchart and John Steling.

MARRIAGES FOR THE YEAR 1773.

Rauch—Demich : January 3d, Martin Rauch, widower, to Anna Catharine Demich ; witnesses George Ernest Lechler and Henry Schneider.

Ott—Reutter : January 18th, James Ott to Apollonia Reutter ; witness Margarget Späth.

Doyle—Clansey: January 22d, after dispensation, Patterson Doyle to Susan, daughter of David and Margaret Clansey ; witnesses William Craig, Patrick Jackson and Margaret Vealun [Whelan?].

Greswold—Fletcher : February 1st, after dispensation, Joseph Greswold to Mary Fletcher ; witnesses Alfred Clifton and Isaac Laud ; nuptial blessing given afterwards at Mass.

Burns—Archdeacon : March 9th, Archibald Burns to Jane Archdeacon.

Bremich—Vealan [Whelan ?] : April 13th, Leonard, son of Michael and Walburga Bremich, to Margaret, daughter of ———— and Johanna Vealan ; witnesses John Fagan and John Arthur O'Neil.

Pola—Studd : the same day and place, after dispensation, Peter Pola to Anna Studd ; witness Henry Herberg.

May—Waibl : May 21st, at Longpond Ironworks, after dispensation, James May to Magdalen Waibl ; witnesses the bridegroom's father and the bride's mother ; subsequently the nuptial blessing was given at Mass.

O'Neil—Goff : June 17th, after dispensation, Arthur John O'Neil, widower, to Margaret Goff.

Gillan—O'Haughon [Hagan or Hogan ?] : July 8th, after dispensation, Daniel Gillan to Catharine O'Haughon, widow, witnesses Patrick Loughan and Margaret Lee.

O'Connely—Reily : July 22d, Brian O'Connely, widower, to Margaret Reily, widow ; witnesses Christopher O'Brian and Mary Colton.

Bastian—Krumholtz : July 27th, John William Bastian, widower, to Mary Magdalen, daughter of Charles and Catharine Krumholtz ; witnesses Charles Krumholtz, Nicholas Kappel and Francis Senner.

Logan—Talbert : July 30th, after dispensation, John Logan to Ann Talbert, widow ; witnesses Andrew Sanford and Mary Shannon.

Dougherty—Matson : September 6th, by Rev. Luke Geissler, Philip Dougherty to Hannah Matson ; witnesses Adam Meyer and Anthony Schneider.

Klemm—Haag : September 12th, John Klemm to Anna Mary, daughter of Joseph and Ursula Haag ; witnesses Christopher Viel and Catharine, his wife.

Murrey—Egan : September 15th, Patrick Murrey, widower, to Catharine Egan ; witnesses William Clover and George Macum.

Cavenogh—Hartman ; October 5th, Edmund Cavenogh to Elizabeth Hartman : witnesses James Welsh and John Furlong.

More—Conner : October 25th, at Ringwood, Richard More to Martha Conner ; witnesses Edmund Welsh and others.

Kreiss—Kientz : November 21st, Martin Kreiss to Catharine Kientz ; witnesses Philip James Michel and John Hardy.

Dealy—Christ : November 22d, Daniel Dealy to Elizabeth Christ ; witnesses James Brown and Ann Rebecca Bready.

Zängerte—Christman : November 23d, Ignatius Zängerte to Elizabeth Christman, widow ; witnesses Caspar Geyer, Christopher Ott and George Ernest Lechler.

Telez—Welsh : November 24th, after dispensation, John Telez to Margaret Welsh, widow ; witness Dominick Joyce.

Castela—Swaine : December 3d, after dispensation, Richard Castela to Alice Swaine ; witnesses ———— Kelly, Lawrence Cook's wife, and others.

Ohlmar—Swerez : December 27th, Frederick Ohlmar (P.), widower, to Catharine Swerez, widow ; witnesses William Willmar and Nicholas Capple.

MARRIAGES FOR THE YEAR 1774.

Herman—Schuman : January 2d, Francis Louis Herman to Catharine, widow of Henry Schuman ; witnesses John Martin Holder, Gabriel Herman and Elizabeth Holder.

Tobin—Richman : January 9th, John Tobin to Margaret Richman ; witnesses George Brown, Martin Benner and Elizabeth Benner.

Connor—Cottringer : the same day and place, after dispensation, Michael Connor to Mary, daughter of John and Catharine Cottringer ; witnesses Thomas FitzSimons and Catharine, his wife, and the bride's father.

FitzPatrick—Lee : February 12th, after dispensation, Daniel FitzPatrick to Catharine Lee ; witnesses Lawrence Dugan and Amelia Price.

Call—Pfältzer : April 26th, at Ringwood, John Nicholas Call to Ann Mary Pfältzer ; witnesses John James May and John Anthony May ; the nuptial blessing was given later at Mass.

Cobole—Walter : April 28th, at Longpond, Bartholomew Cobole to Mary Ann Walter ; witnesses John Cobole and Daniel Cobole ; the nuptial blessing was given afterwards at Mass.

Abt—Uder : June 2d, Henry, son of Francis and Julianna Abt, to Mary Elizabeth Uder (P.) ; witnesses Caspar Schiessler and George Bruner.

McClone—Brown : June 18th, after dispensation, Andrew McClone, widower, to Margaret Brown ; witnesses John Dugan, Moses Boosee and Anthony Groff.

Francis—Casey : June 28th, after dispensation, Robert Francis, widower, to Margaret Casey, widow ; witnesses Catharine Field and Margaret Bourg.

Groghan—Mallaby : July 6th, after dispensation, Denis Groghan to Margaret Mallaby ; witnesses ———— Flin and Elizabeth Pierce.

Wallace—O'Neal : July 13th, after dispensation, John Wallace to Ann O'Neal, who said they had been brought up Catholics ; witnesses Patrick Buttler and Sarah Barr.

Netzelnoder—Kientz: July 17th, Michael Netzelnoder, widower, to Catharine, widow of Michael Kientz; witnesses John Kientz, Joseph Rubel and Anna Mary, his wife.

Schütz—Folk: after dispensation, at Pilesgrove, Salem county, Joseph Schütz to Lobisa Folk; witnesses Henry Geiger, Mary Geiger and others.

Gallagher—Brannin: August 4th, after dispensation, Michael Gallagher to Mary Brannin (Brennan); witnesses Patrick Loghan, Christopher Schultz and Barbara Schultz.

Potier—Schäffer: August 9th, Louis Potier to Catharine Schäffer; witnesses Christopher Schläuch, Alfred Clifton and Mary Hogan.

Weiler—Ridiger: October 2d, Francis Weiler, widower, to Mary Ann, widow of Matthew Anthony Ridiger; witnesses Martin Greiss and Philip Kitzinger.

Berg—Miller: October 3d, Ernest Berg to Elizabeth Miller; witnesses John Schäffer, Joseph Hahn and George Freind.

McGary—Lewis: the same day and place, John McGary to Isabella Lewis (P.), widow; witnesses Bartholomew Bailey and Eunice, his wife.

Swiney—Watts: October 18th, near Ringwood, Bergen county, New Jersey, after dispensation, John Swiney to Johanna Watts; witnesses John Glub and Richard Lemasney.

Robertson—Mentzenbach: October 20th, at Charlottenburg, New Jersey, Dominick Robertson to Mary Catharine, daughter of Nicholas and Helena Mentzenbach; witnesses Humphrey Booth and Peter Welker; the nuptial blessing was given afterwards at Mass.

Welsh—Brown: the same day and place, Thomas Welsh to Catharine Brown; witnesses Hugh Quig and William Graty.

Bender—Parmer: the same day and place, Mathias Bender to Abigail Parmer; witnesses the bride's parents.

Dirk—Alleton: October 24th, at Mount Hope, New Jersey, after dispensation, John Dirk to Hannah Alleton; witnesses Anthony Schumers, Peter Welker and Anna Catharine Zech.

Smith—Keil: November 8th, Nicholas Smith to Eva, daughter of Henry and Barbara Keil; witnesses George Haas and Adam Bremich.

O'Neil—Campbel: November 18th, after dispensation, Henry O'Neil to Ann, widow of Philip Campbel; witnesses Arthur John O'Neil, Joseph Hunter and Hugh Fargurson.

McMahon—Calahan: November 24th, after dispensation, Bernard McMahon to Ann Calahan, widow; witnesses Andrew Minahan, Ann Kelly and Ann Minahan.

Buckley—Campbel: December 20th, after dispensation, James Buckley to Mary Campbel, widow; witnesses Archibald Burns and John Burns.

MARRIAGES FOR THE YEAR 1775.

Connor—Deany: January 1st, William Conner, widower, to Sarah Deany; witnesses James Sullivan, John Nagle, and Alice, his wife.

Bryer—Buch: January 2d, Emmanuel Bryer to Charlotte Buch; witnesses Christopher Schultz and Emanuel Hohms.

McDaniel—Matson: January 24th, after dispensation, Edmund Mc-Daniel to Mary Matson; witnesses James Matson and Michael Ryan.

Rümmel—Treiber: January 31st, George Rümmel to Anna Barbara Treiber; witnesses John Hirt and John Westermayer.

Clark—Butler: the same day and place, after dispensation, Michael Clark, widower, to Mary Butler; witnesses James Byrne and Patrick Byrne.

Lipp—Sigfrid: March 23d, after dispensation, John Lipp, widower, to Mary, daughter of Andrew and Catharine Sigfrid; witnesses Andrew Kessler and Catharine Spengler.

Spängler (Laub)—Schöner: April 17th, after dispensation, George Spängler, *alias* Laub, to Mary Schöner; witnesses Catharine Spängler, Joseph Kauffman and Anthony Graff.

Hoffman—Killmann: April 24th, Adam, son of Sebastian and Cunegunda Hoffman, to Anna Margaret Killman; witnesses the bridegroom's father, George Freind and Nicholas Schmid; nuptial blessing given subsequently at Mass.

Robert (Raubin)—Lariole: May 3d, after dispensation, John Robert (Raubin) to Anna Vincent, widow of John Lariole; witnesses Peter Vincent, Peter Porié and Dorothy Caput.

May—Waibl: May 28th, at Longpond, Bergen county, John Anthony May to Margaret Waibl; witnesses John May, John James May and Susanna Waibl; the nuptial blessing given afterwards at Mass.

Nunck—Birkenbine: June 11th, Henry Nunck to Mary Birkenbine; witnesses Michael Netzelnoder and Catharine, his wife.

Pahl—Martin: July 2d, after dispensation, Lawrence Pahl to Anna Klein, widow of Anthony Martin; witnesses Jacob Klein and George Ernest Lechler.

Sullivan—Casey: July 3d, after dispensation, Jeremiah Sullivan to Catharine, widow of Denis Casey; witnesses Alfred Clifton and Catharine Shaw.

Lester—Weaver: July 23d, after dispensation, Daniel Lester to Catharine, daughter of Conrad and Magdalen Weaver; witnesses Thomas Houghton, Charles Tolly and Elizabeth FitzPatrick.

Poirié—Babin: August 15th, Peter Poirié, a Canadian, to Anna, widow

of Simon Babin; witnesses Anthony Guera (Guerin), John Raubin
and Aimé Elbeau.

Betagh—Blanchard: August 27th, after dispensation, Thomas Betagh to
Margaret Blanchard; witnesses John Aitken and Anna Boudrot.

Prouschier—Harty: September 3d, James Prouschier, a Canadian, to
Ann Harty, widow; witnesses Charles Delié and Daniel Eustace.

Condron—FitzPatrick: September 5th, after dispensation, Michael Condon
(Condron) to Elizabeth FitzPatrick; witnesses Archibald Burns and
Daniel Shaw.

O'Daniel—Bryan: September 7th, after dispensation, Michael O'Daniel to
Eleanor Bryan; witnesses Henry Worthworth, Francis Sloan and
Barbara O'Neal.

Speir—Warenton: September 25th, Mathias Speir to Mary Warenton,
both Protestents; witnesses John Heitz, John Henry Stout and
John Speir.   •

Gallagher—Shannon: October 30th, after dispensation, Andrew Gallagher
to Johanna Shannon; witnesses James Gallagher and Patrick Tonry.

Veyrent—Burau de Civrac: November 6th, after dispensation, Noel Barnabas Veyrent, son of Joseph and Clara (Brachet) Veirent, to Mary
Anna Bruillhet, widow of Henry Burau de Civrac; witnesses William Constant, Francis Foussard, John Macé and Joseph Ribau.*

Anderson—Copps: November 25th, after dispensation, Thomas Anderson
to Susan Copps; witness Angus McDonald.

Keyser—Lush: November 28th, after dispensation, Henry Keyser to Mary
Lush; witness Anthony Lechler.

Broadley—Macarty: November 30th, Thomas Broadley to Mary Macarty; witnesses Patrick McGrill, James Jonston and Daniel Mullen.

MARRIAGES FOR THE YEAR 1776.

Bremich—Esser: January 1st, Adam, son of Michael and Wallburga
Bremich, to Margaret Esser; witnesses James Klein, Peter Bremich
and Regina Schneider.

Shea—Montgomery: February 4th, after dispensation, John Shea to
Ann Montgomery; witnesses Denis McElway, Belle (his wife), and
Laura Deragh.

------

* To this record by Father Farmer are attached the signatures of the
four witnesses in two lines opposite the word " temoins " at the left and
a bracket at the right; and to the right of the bracket are the autograph
signatures of the contracting parties. The first named witness charac-
terizes himself as "jéune" (junior), and the last spells his name " Ribaud."

Stuart—Kinseler: the same day, James Stuart to Mary Kinseler; witnesses John Brown, Thomas Stewart and Patrick Buttler.

Preston—Ryan: February 13th, after dispenstation, Manasses Preston to Ann Ryan; witnesses Thomas Ryan, Thomas Slatery and Prudence Willcox.

Nadler—Götz: February 20th, John, son of Michael and Catharine Nadler, to Magdalen, daughter of Andrew (P.) and Elizabeth Götz; witnesses James Treim and William Bastian.

Garby—Williams: March 15th, Bartholomew Garby to Eleanor Williams; witnesses Samuel Rains and Mary Barry.

McGrath—Lynch: March 20th, after dispensation, John McGrath to Mary Lynch; witnesses James Kearns and Peter Lynch.

Cavenogh—Toy: March 23d, after dispensation, Timothy Cavenogh, widower, to Hannah Toy, widow; witnesses John Viel and Simon Le Blanc.

Roulin—Doutoya: April 8th, after dispensation, Charles Roulin de Mombos, a young Frenchman, to Elizabeth Doutoya, a young lady from the island of San Domingo; witnesses Julien Achard, Comte de Bonvoulier and others.

Welsh—Haas: May 13th, after dispensation, Richard Welsh to Catharine Haas; witnesses John Shelleman and Charles Sheny.

Schneider—Waltrich: May 19th, Henry, son of Henry and Ann Elizabeth Schneider, to Anna Catharine, daughter of Peter and Catharine Waltrich; witnesses Henry Schneider and Peter Bremich.

Roach—Moore: June 5th, after dispensation, John Roach to Margaret Moore; witnesses John Smith and Catharine, his wife.

Joyce—Sibbald: June 22d, after dispensation, Dominick Joyce to Johanna (Jenny) Sibbald (P.); witnesses the bride's father and mother and two sisters.

Welsh—Mellarkey: July 4th, after dispensation, James Welsh, widower, to Honora Mellarkey; witnesses Denis Dougherty and Edward Cavenogh.

Le Pillaire—Schönenberg: July 28th, Jacques Le Pillaire, a young Frenchman, to Elizabeth Schönenberg; witnesses Peter Poiré, Peter Dugalvette and Prudence La Jennesse.

Reily—Regan: September 1st, at Pikesland, Patrick Reily to Catharine Regan; a large number of witnesses present (see register of baptims for this date).

Frymund—Schön: September 8th, John Frymund to Anna Margaret Schön; witnesses John Tissaire and James Pillaire.

Rübel—Stahl: September 10th, Adam, son of Joseph and Anna Mary Rübel, to Catharine, daughter of ——— and Catharine Stahl; witnesses Peter Bremich and Adam Lechler.

Rübel—Stahl: at the same time, Francis Joseph Rübel to Regina Stahl (brother and sister of the preceding couple); the same witnesses.

Brady—Fichter: October 27th, at Longpond, Adam Brady to Eva, widow of Philip Fichter; witnesses Thomas Cahel, Eleanor, his wife and others.

Fichter—Brady: at the same time, David Fichter to Johanna Brady; witnesses the same as above, and the whole congregation.

Halbou—Smith: November 3d, Edmund (Amatus) Halbou to Honora Smith, widow; witnesses Peter Poiret, Prudence Lejeuness, Anthony Guera, Louis Prunette and Peter L'Airêt.

Doyle—Eyenson: November 3d, John Doyle to Esther Eyenson; witnesses James Rob and John Henry.

Benner—Poth: November 10th, Henry, son of Mathias and Johanna Benner, to Mary, daughter of John and Eva Poth; witnesses Adam Lechler, Christopher Herberger and the bride's father.

Mayer—Wegfort: November 22d, Adam Mayer, widower, to Apollonia Wegfort, widow; witnesses John Sauerwald and Barbara Graff.

Winters—Steel: December 16th, Timothy Winters to Catharine Steel; witnesses Philip Will and Elizabeth Tisdale.

MARRIAGES FOR THE YEAR 1777.

Lean—O'Brian: January 6th, Lawrence Lean, widower, to Judith O'Brian; witnesses Brian Ryan and his wife.

Sissel—Hook: January 28th, Sidrach (Shedrich) Sissel to Mary Hook; witnesses Raphael Clark and Mary, his wife.

Fudge—Fitzgerald: February 9th, James Fudge to Ann Fitzgerald; witnesses Thomas Mulree, Walter Motley and Johanna Motley.

Scantlen—Lard: the same day, Daniel Scantlen to Mary Lard; witnesses Lawrence Cook, Catharine Cook and Mary Scantlen, the bridegroom's mother.

Dowling—Hughins: February 11th, Thomas Dowling to Catharine Hughins; witnesses Charles Graham, Catharine Graham and Mary Macra.

Barret—Hogan: March 31st, James, son of Edward and Alice Barret, to Mary, daughter of Patrick and Elizabeth Hogan; witnesses Michael Maddon and Mary Johnson.

Barret—Byrne: April 11th, John Barret to Bridget Byrne; witnesses James and Patrick Byrne.

Günther—Wagner: April 20th, John George Günther to Catharine Frances, daughter of John and Catharine Wagner; witnesses John Wagner and Ernest Berg.

McCauley—Shea: April 25th, Timothy McCauley to Mary Shea, widow; witnesses John Haney and his wife.

Call—Rüger: May 6th, at Ringwood, George Henry Call to Mary Catharine Rüger, both of that place; witnesses Nicholas Call, Jr., John Rüger, the bride's father and others.

Grips—Krauskopf: May 12th, at Mount Hope, Peter Joseph Grips to Mary Krauskopf; witnesses James Welker and James Demuth.

Meighan—Tate: on the same occasion, William Meighan to Elizabeth Tate; witnesses Thomas Poor and Edmund Darmoty.

Glissan—Till: May 29th, James Glissan to Susan Till; witnesses Richard Hornett, John Riddle, Mary Mill and Susan Anderson.

Maxeiner—Wagner: June 29th, Adam Maxeiner to Mary Wagner; witnesses Nicholas Wochman, George Reinhart and Charles Miller.

Pranger—Bastian: July 6th, William Pranger to Anna Catharine Bastian; witnesses William Bastian and William Hautzel.

Drommond—Edgar: July 19th, Thomas Drommond to Sarah Edgar; witnesses Michael Green and Stephen Cronin.

Barrey—Karrick (Minan): August 5th, Richard Barrey to Ann Karrick (the widow Minan); witnesses John Rudolf and James McHuin.

Foreman—Macky: August 23d, Edward Foreman, widower, to Mary Macky, widow; witnesses Michael Fowloo and Mary, his wife.

Ferguson—Hill: September 28th, John Ferguson to Bridget Hill, widow; witnesses William Hussy and Susan Dwyer.

Burley—McDaniel: November 2d, William Burley to Catharine McDaniel; witnesses the bride's father and ———— Babe.

Leemang—Lock: November 7th, James Leemang to Elizabeth Lock; witnesses Thomas Farran, Dorothy, his wife, and Eleanor McCullogh.

Sullivan—Stormont: December 13th, Thomas Sullivan, a soldier of the forty-ninth regiment, to Sarah Stormont; witnesses Daniel McCarthy and Elizabeth Mealy.

Welsh—Dowlan: December 23d, James Welsh, Jr., to Mary Dowlan; witnesses Johanna Balden and John Manderfield.

Dunfee—Jonston: December 30th, Edward Dunfee to Johanna Jonston, widow; witnesses Anthony Broadley and William Allen.

———

MARRIAGES FOR THE YEAR 1778.

Donaho—Strong: January 10th, William Donaho to Elizabeth Strong, widow; witnesses James Taylor, James Kenedy and Elizabeth Taylor.

Murphy—Knight: January 11th, Henry Murphy to Martha Knight, widow; witnesses Denis McElway, Isabella, his wife, and Johanna McElway.

Ryan—Burk: January 18th, Owen Ryan to Mary Burk; witnesses Nicholas Agan, Nicholas Currey and Matthew Tracy.

Oelers—Haffner : February 7th, James Oelers to Catharine Haffner ; witnesses Henry Horn and Christina, his wife.

Ruppert—Kellerman : February 20th, Michael Ruppert, of Aschaffenburg, to Catharine, widow of Michael Kellerman, both of the Hessian regiment of *chasseurs* ; witnesses John Farber, Ignatius Limbeck, and Anna Maria Farber, all of the same regiment.

Diamond—Tisdall : March 1st, John Diamond to Elizabeth Tisdall, widow ; witnesses John Edmundston and John Manderfield.

Burkart—Schaff : March 3d, Francis Burkart, widower, to Anna Mary Schaff, widow ; witnesses Cassian Huber and James Nagel.

Rollo—Allen : March 12th, Robert Rollo, a substitute in the ———— regiment, to Ann Allen ; witnesses Patrick Byrne, Roger Flahavan, Patrick Rice and others.

Boyé—Trahan : April 12th, after dispensation, Peter Boyé, of the parish of Bonpierre, in the province of Angoumois, France, to Magdalen, daughter of Bruno and Magdalen (Vincent) Trahan ; witnesses the bride's father, Peter Poriet and John Baptist Fougerit.

Bauer—Reinhart : May 1st, John George Bauer to Elizabeth Reinhart ; (they had already been married in Germany, but without due observance of the decrees of the Council of Trent) ; witnesses Adam Mayer and John Manderfeld.

Schneider—Viel : May 5th, Ignatius Schneider, of Vienna in Austria, and of the seventeenth regiment, to Catharine, daughter of Christopher and Catharine Viel ; witnesses Hector Miller and Elizabeth Catharine, his wife.

Talbert—Mahany : May 14th, James Talbert to Honora Mahany ; witnesses John FitzPatrick and Mary Simpson.

Hohl—Miller : May 28th, Peter Hohl to Catharine Miller ; witnesses Caspar Hayle, Elizabeth, his wife, and Mary Bodevin.

Dun—McBride : the same day, John Dun to Elizabeth McBride ; witnesses Patrick Donegan and Michael Sauerwald.

Fear—English : June 17th, William Fear to Margaret, daughter of Thomas and Catharine English ; witnesses, the bride's parents and James Altenreith.

McGinnis—Maddin : July 5th, after dispensation, Patrick McGinnis to Susan Maddin, widow ; witnesses Owen Ryan, Denis Glansy and Mary Ryan.

Mahan—Fox : August 7th, Patrick Mahan to Elizabeth Fox, widow ; witnesses John Manderfeld and Catharine Boudrot.

Opperman—Hoffman : August 16th, Adam Opperman to Elizabeth, daughter of Sebastian and Cunegunda Hoffman ; witnesses the bride's father and George Ernest Lechler.

Miller—Rauch : August 27th, Peter Miller (P.) to Catharine, widow of Martin Rauch ; witnesses Anthony Graff and James Klein.

Cusigh—Toy: October 16th, Michael Cusigh to Mary Toy; witnesses Timothy Cavenogh and George Graff.

Otto—Nickel: November 8th, Francis Otto to Ann Elizabeth, widow of Peter Nickel; witnesses Nicholas Wochman, Philip Heinrichs and Mary Magdalen Lechler.

Macoy—Geiger: November 23d, at Pilesgrove, Edward Macoy to Mary, daughter of Adam and Agnes Geiger; witnesses Henry Geiger, Lawrence Geiger and Catharine Bucher.

Schwager—Ohlmar: December 16th, John Schwager to Catharine, widow of Frederick Ohlmar; witnesses William Caffeeroth and Margaret Lapp.

Herberger—Miltenberger: December 31st, after dispensation, Henry Herberger to Susanna Miltenberger; witnesses George Miltenberger and Christopher Herberger.

MARRIAGES FOR THE YEAR 1779.

Capless—Reutemeyer: January 10th, after dispensation, David Capless to Elizabeth, widow of Dieterich Reutemeyer; witnesses John Human, Anna Mary, his wife, and Mary Bimpel.

Connoley—Käffer: February 2d, after dispensation, Brian Connoley, widower, to Rachel (Regina) Käffer, widow; witnesses Thomas Haly and Ann Sanderson.

Proffy—Poor: February 5th, after dispensation, James Proffy to Honora Poor, widow; witnesses Lawrence Cook and Catharine, his wife.

Sigfrid—Middleton: February 8th, Andrew Sigfrid to Bridget Middleton; witnesses Joseph Schumacher and Catharine Kessler.

Zängerle—Wibiro: February 16th, Ignatius Zängerle, widower, to Regina Wibiro, widow; witnesses George Ernest Lechler and John Wagner.

Kelly—Fitzgerald: March 3d, after dispensation, Thomas Kelly to Mary Fitzgerald; witnesses Thomas Boyd and Margaret Shaw.

Orlandy—Eustace: March 11th, after dispensation, Paul Orlandy to Mary, daughter of Daniel and Margaret (Doiron) Eustace; witnesses, Joseph Ribau, Peter Cousin, Anthony Vitaly and Francis Raubitin.

Glä—Lauer: March 21st, at Pikesland, Ernest Glä to Christina Lauer; witnesses Francis Sohl, Frederick Scheimer and others.

Bremich—Keil: April 5th, after dispensation, Peter Bremich to Catharine Keil; witnesses Adam Bremich, John Field, James Klein and Nicholas Schmid.

Forester—Hull: April 15th, after dispensation, Gerard Forester to Diana

Hull; witnesses the bride's mother and sisters, and Timothy Carrol and wife.

Willcox—Flahavan: April 18th, after dispensation, Mark Willcox to Mary Flahavan: witnesses Roger Flahavan, James Byrne and others.

Decharlé—Vincent: May 10th, Francis Decharlé, a Canadian, to Mary, daughter of Peter and Genevieve (Boudrot) Vincent; witnesses the bride's father, Armand Douzet and Bruce Tréspanié.

Baxter (L'Hercule)—Trahan: June 14th, after dispensation, Mathias Baxter (Maturin L'Hercule), son of Francis and Margaret L'Hercule, to Margaret, daughter of Bruno and Margaret Trahan; witnesses Herman Carpé, Joseph Davenac and Margaret Carpé.

Gandolph—Dunn: June 30th, after dispensation, Dominick Gandolph to Margaret Dunn; witnesses Peter Cusin, Thomas Agan and Benedict Fallewolt.

Kelly—Dewetter: July 15th, after dispensation, James Kelly to Margaret, daughter of John and Mary Dewetter; witnesses the bride's father, Catharine Donnoly and Mary Anderle.

O'Conner—Pryor: September 2d, after dispensation, John O'Conner, widower, to Ann Pryor; witnesses Louis Sprogell and Mary York.

McGonaughy—Bryan: September 15th, after dispensation, Patrick McGonaughy to Bridget Bryan; witnesses Margaret Sudric and Mary Macanarney.

Wall—Gilberth: September 23d, after dispensation, James Wall to Rachel Gilberth; witnesses John Connor, John Down and Mary, his wife.

Douruse—Serren: November 17th, after dispensation, John Claude Douruse to Felicitas, daughter of Andrew and Lucy Serren; witnesses Peter Savoy and John L'Hercule.

Tisonau—L'Hercule: November 24th, after dispensation, Stephen Tisonau, of Bordeaux, France, to Clara, daughter of Francis and Margaret L'Hercule; witnesses Peter Savoy and John Marques Cavett.

Taylor—Steel: November 25th, after dispensation, Mathias Taylor, widower, to Mary Steel; witnesses William Willson and William Hunter.

Pinion—Bourg: December 29th, after dispensation, Peter Pinion, of the diocese of Bordeaux, France, to Mary, daughter of Belonius and Frances Bourg; witnesses John Marquis Cadet, Joseph Boudrot, Francis Decharlé and Gregory Trahan.

MARRIAGES FOR THE YEAR 1780.

White—Brooks: January 16th, after dispensation, Joseph White to Margaret Brooks; witnesses George Brett and James Linum.

Schneider—Rauch: January 25th, after dispensation, John, son of Henry and Barbara Schneider, to Mary Magdalen Rauch; witnesses Henry Schneider, Jr., Peter Miller and James Eckfeld.

Krumholz—Korn : January 27th, after dispensation, Charles Krumholz, widower, to Barbara Corn, widow; witnesses Sebastian Hoffman and Adam Opperman.

Abt—Cappel: February 1st, John George, son of Francis and Julianna Abt, to Catharine, daughter of Nicholas and Magdalen Cappel; witnesses Nicholas Cappel and Israel Ruh ; blessing given afterwards at Mass.

La Plane—Vincent : February 2d, after dispensation, Benedict La Plane to Mary Magdalen, daughter of Peter and Genevieve Vincent; witnesses Honoré Plann, Andrew Rosigniole and John Raubin.

Field—Veit : February 6th, after dispensation, John Field to Christina Veit ; witnesses William Rogers and Sarah Tricket.

Peccare—Haly : February 7th, after dispensation, Vincent Peccare, widower, to Catharine Haly ; witnesses Mathias L'Hercule and Joseph Davenac.

Cortez—Waas : February 14th, after dispensation, John Cortez, of Genoa, Italy, to Margaret Waas ; witnesses Peter Poiriet, Benedict La Plan, Bartholomew Salvy, John Cadet and Andrew Rosignole.

Laborde—Strong: February 27th, Francis Laborde, a Frenchman, to Mary Strong, widow ; witnesses Conrad Hingel and Catharine Rübel.

König—Brown: April 4th, John George König, widower, to Catharine Brown, widow; witnesses John Grey and Adam Mayer.

Rübel—Zörne : April 10th, Francis Rübel, widower, to Ann Dorothy, daughter of John Martin and Dorothy Zörne; witnesses John Viel, Mary Bodevin and the bride's father.

Diamond—Bernard : April 13th, after dispensation, John Diamond, widower, to Mary, daughter of Nicholas and N. Bernard ; witnesses the bride's father and mother.

Jockel—Bodevin : April 25th, after dispensation, John George Jockel to Mary Bodevin ; witnesses James Klein, Joseph Backer and Caspar Hayle; the blessing given afterwards at Mass.

Bauman—Stahler : May 7th, Charles Bauman, widower, to Salome, daughter of John and Christina Stahler ; witnesses Daniel McCurtin and John Heisser.

Rudolph—Brand : June 29th, after dispensation, John, son of Tobias and N. Rudolph, to Anna (P.), daughter of John and N. Brand ; witnesses Tobias Rudolph and Stephen Forage.

McClosky—Henesy : July 13th, after dispensation, Patrick McClosky to Margaret Henesy, widow ; witnesses William Willson, Margaret White and Sarah Robin.

Lamb—Dillan : August 3d, Christopher Lamb to Mary Dillan ; witnesses William Wall and Ann Amot.

Meyer—Schneider: October 5th, after dispensation, George, son of John and N. Meyer, to Regina, daughter of Henry and Barbara Schneider; witnesses Henry Schneider, Henry Schneider, Jr., John Schneider and Anthony Schneider.

Conway—Kelly: October 28th, after dispensation, John Conway, widower, to Ann Kelly, widow; witnesses John Dewetter and Catharine Boudrot.

Skillen—Cannon: November 10th, after dispensation, William Skillen, widower, to Elizabeth Cannon, widow; witnesses Robert Mordock and Johanna Burns.

Terradou—Janssivre: November 14th, after dispensation, John Terradou, a Frenchman, to Alti [?] Janssivre, widow; witnesses Matthew Gery, Francis Culprong and Elizabeth Dartoit.

Connor—Groves: November 5th, after dispensation, Michael Connor to Mary Groves; witnesses Francis Harrison and Catharine Baur.

McCurtin—Martin: November 26th, Daniel McCurtin to Margaret Martin; witnesses Jane Levins, John Watts and others.

Wall—Emmit: November 30th, after dispensation, William Wall to Ann Emmit; witnesses Peter Gill and Susanna Darmot.

Metea—L'Hercule (Baxter): December 9th, after dispensation, William Metea, a Frenchman, to Margaret L'Hercule (Baxter); witnesses Peter Savoy and Francis Gotié.

MARRIAGES FOR THE YEAR 1781.

Davenac—Ridiger: January 7th, Joseph Davenac, widower, to Margaret, widow of John Ridiger; witnesses Philip Kitzinger and Herman Carpé.

Poth—Freind: January 7th, after dispensation, Adam, son of John and Eva Poth, to Catharine, daughter of Stephen and Salome Freind; witnesses Adam Poth, Sr., and the bridegroom's father and mother.

Wasserling—Armbrust: January 14th, John Wasserling to Ann Elizabeth, widow of John Armbrust; witnesses George Ernest Lechler and Philip Krombel.

Antony—Brown: January 16th, Francis Antony to Mary Brown; witnesses John Murphy, Elizabeth Lynn and Francis Purvine.

Bastian—Tscharté: January 24th, Joseph, son of William and Anna Catharine Bastian, to Mary Elizabeth, daughter of Christopher and Mary Dorothy Tscharté; witnesses the bridegroom's father, John Tscharté and Mary Dorothy Tscharté

McSwaine—Lean: January 29th, Hugh McSwaine, widower, to Jane Lean, widow; witnesses John Conway and Anna, his wife.

Rogé—Philipps: January 31st, after dispensation, Simon Rogé, a native of France, to Ann Philipps; witnesses Dominick Crogniolo and Eleanor Green.

McCarty—O'Hara: February 4th, after dispensation, Denis McCarty to Mary, daughter of Brian and Mary O'Hara; witnesses the bride's parents, John O'Hara and James Cotringer.

Shiney—Benson: February 10th, after dispensation, Lawrence Shiney, widower, to Catharine Benson (P.), widow; witnesses James Klein, Andrew Summers, Ann Paul and Elizabeth Leech.

Tracy—Murray: February 10th, after dispensation, John Tracy, widower, to Mary Murray; witnesses Mary Murray and Joseph Harrison.

Purvine—Hammel: February 12th, Francis Purvine to Catharine Hammel; witnesses John Fritz, James Cock and Francis Greiss.

Pollock—Farrel: May 10th, after dispensation, Thomas Pollock (P.) to Margaret, daughter of Patrick and Alice Farrel; witnesses Patrick Byrne, Jane Gallagher and others.

Mullen—Waibel: May 22d, near Ringwood, New Jersey, William Mullen to Anna Catharine, daughter of Charles and Susanna Waibel; witnesses the bride's father and mother and Dominick Robertson.

Davis—Campbell: June 5th, William Davis to Sarah Campbell; witnesses Henry O'Neal, the bride's mother and sister and others.

Ross—Kidney: July 2d, after dispensation, Charles Ross to Mary Kidney; witnesses Francis Smid and John Cornély.

Muny—Connert: July 7th, Hugh Muny to Jane Connert; witnesses John McGowen, Sarah Shaw, Michael Sauerwald and his wife.

Crowley—Waas: July 24th, Samuel Crowley to Mary Waas; witnesses John Bason and Susan Maginnis.

Schäffer—Götz: August 16th, John Schäffer to Elizabeth Götz; witnesses James Treim and Mary Dorothy Treim.

La Haye—Dervis: September 7th, after dispensation, Francis La Haye, a Frenchman, to Johanna (Jeannette) Dervis, also from France; witnesses Andrew Rous and William Metea.

Chartier—Robinet: October 6th, near Fishkill, marriage contract renewed between a son of Joseph and Mary Ursula (Eubair) Chartier and Mary, daughter of James and Mary Frances (Chandron) Robinet; witnesses the same as at their previous marriage, Philip Smidt and Alexander Bicat.

Guilmet—Chandron: October 7th, at the same place, consent renewed between Francis Guilmet and Mary Frances Chandron; witnesses Louis Marnay, Peter Charland, Mary Robinet and others.

Buda—Poth: November 15th, after dispensation, Peter Buda to Catharine, daughter of John and Eva Poth; witnesses Adam Lechler and George Lechler.

Champneys—Downey: November 22d, after dispensation, James

Champneys to Hannah Downey; witnesses Timothy Carrol and Richard Tibbit.

Warren—Karragan: November 23d, after dispensation, Christopher Warren to Margaret Karragan; witnesses James Reed, James Willcans and the bride's father, Owen Karragan.

Griesser—Gordon: November 29th, Anthony Griesser to Rachel Gordon; witnesses Adam Bremich and Nicholas Serring.

Sähring—Beverhoud: December 2d, Nicholas Sähring to Catharine Beverhoud, widow; witnesses Adam Bremich and Margaret, his wife.

MARRIAGES FOR THE YEAR 1782.

Becker—Klein: January 8th, Francis Bartholomew, son of Bartholomew and Elizabeth Becker, to Teresa, daughter of James and Elizabeth Klein; witnesses the bridegroom's father, the bride's father, Joseph Becker, Thomas Cahel and Nicholas Essling.

De Sylva—Myers: March 12th, after dispensation, Anthony De Sylva to Margaret Myers; witnesses Emanuel Brier, Charles De Costa and Frederick Essling.

Mayer—Frick: April 4th, Adam Mayer, widower, to Catharine Frick; witnesses Adam Bremich and Barbara Schultz.

Powr—Park: April 7th, John Powr to Eleanor Park; witnesses Michael Green and Lawrence Fitzgerald.

Hönig—Cabe: April 8th, Anthony Hönig to Sarah Cabe; witnesses Simon Hönig and Anna Mary Molsberger.

Bifar—Williams: April 14th, William Bifar to Catharine Williams; witnesses William Gogin, James Litshinham and Patrick McDowl.

Marian—Mentzebach: April 30th, at Charlottenburg, New Jersey, Anthony Marian to Anna Mary Mentzebach; witnesses Martin Bachman, Francis Zech and others; the blessing was given at Mass.

Sähring—Meyer: August 2d, after dispensation, Nicholas Sähring, widower, to Eva Meyer; witnesses Henry Horn and Christina, his wife.

Dixon—Braun: August 4th, William Dixon to Mary Braun; witnesses Joseph Hirt, John More and others.

Ruppel—Schäffer: October 24th, in Hunterdon county, New Jersey, John George Ruppel to Elizabeth Schäffer; witnesses Jacob Ruppel, Jr., William Schäffer and Mary Ruppel.

Lechler—Leimbach: November 19th, after dispensation, George Ernest Lechler, widower, to Salome Leimbach, widow; witnesses Valentine Schierling and Margaret Sauerwald.

Perrée—Buttler: November 24th, Nicholas Perrée, from Grandville in

Normandy [France], to Ann, daughter of Thomas and Bridget (Bennis) Buttler, a native of Limerick, Ireland ; witnesses the Abbé Bandol, Chaplain to His Excellency the Minister of France, Joseph Mercier and Charles Carré.*

Eppert—Anderle : November 28th, John Eppert to Mary Ann, widow of Michael Anderle.

Thevenot—Pepin : December 23d, Francis Thevenot, from Gray, in Franche Comté, to Mary Josepha, daughter of Andrew and Judith Pepin ; witnesses Joseph Ribaud and Th. Cronier.†

————

MARRIAGES FOR THE YEAR 1783.

Honecker—Viel : January 2d, Joseph Honecker to Catharine, daughter of Rudolph and Susanna Viel ; witnesses Peter Viel, John Honecker and Peter Viel, Jr.

Schreinemacher—Besançon : January 21st, Francis Schreinemacher (while lying dangerously ill) to Catharine Besançon, widow ; witnesses George Ernest Lechler and Peter Kappus.

Bonifaud—Schierling : February 10th, John Bonifaud, from the diocese of Besançon, France, to Christina, daughter of Valentine and Clara Schierling ; witnesses John Lefèvre and Pierre Mercier.‡

Neth—Kessler : February 17th, Sebastian Neth to Catharine Kessler ; witnesses James Kessler, Nicholas Sähring and others.

Robeson—Le Bretton : March 15th, William Robeson to Susanna Le Bretton, a native of France ; witnesses Oliver Daniel and Mary Daniel.

Heart—Johnson : April 15th, Daniel Heart to Elizabeth Johnson (P.) ; witnesses Joseph Bœhm and Ann Morrow.

Burne—Christie ; March 27th, after dispensation, Anthony Burne to Mary Christie ; witnesses Anthony Graff, John Carroll and others.

Schad—Lederman : April 22d, after dispensation, Peter Schad, widower, to Catharine, widow of John Lederman ; witnesses Joseph Becker and Elizabeth Becker.

———————————

* Attached to this entry in the records are the autograph signatures of both the contracting parties and the witnesses. For a fac-similie of that of the Abbé Bandol, see Dr. Shea's " Life and Times of Archbishop Carrol " (page 198), just published.

† Here also are attached the autograph signatures of the contracting parties and the witnesses.

‡ Witnesses and contracting parties wrote their own names here too.

Narbone—Lawton : May 1st, after dispensation, John Narbone, a native of France, to Elizabeth Lawton ; witnesses Henry Herberger and Susanna, his wife.

McCurtin—O'Hara : May 6th, Daniel McCurtin, widower, to Margaret O'Hara ; witnesses Catharine Hay, Margaret Scott and Mary Klem.

Buchman—Bodar: May 11th, Adam Buchman, widower, to Barbara Bodar, widow ; witnesses Anselm Schreiner and Ann Buchman.

Plumondon—Délugau: May 21st, near Pompton, consent renewed of Joseph Plumondon and Mary Délugau, Canadians ; witnesses Joseph Dencoss and Denis Lebell.

Waibl—May : May 26th, at Ringwood, Conrad, son of Charles and Susanna Waibl, to Julianna May ; witnesses the bridegroom's father and mother and the bride's brothers.

Lacy—Lyons : June 11th, Lawrence Lacy, widower, to Dorothy Lyons, widow ; witnesses, Cornelius Brown and Elizabeth, his wife.

Hickman—Livingston : June 12th, Selby Hickman to Ann Livingston, widow ; witnesses Father Robert Mollineux and R. D. Hasset.

Fitzgerald—Carrel : June 22d, Edward Fitzgerald to Deborah Carrel, widow ; witnesses Michael Ryan and Hugh Fieldon.

Durand—Potter (Häffner) : June 22d, James Durand, widower, to Eva Potter (Häffner), widow ; witnesses Adam Bremich and John Durand.

Norbeck—Gettman : July 8th, Daniel Norbeck to Margaret Gettman ; witnesses the bridegroom's father and mother.*

Taaffe—McClosky: July 30th, John Taaffe, widower, to Margaret McCloskey, widow ; witnesses Nicholas Richardson, John Foran, Margaret White and Sarah Roabins.

Picque—La Haye : August 2d, Ambrose Picque to Johanna La Haye, widow ; witnesses Louis Juquet, Anthony Guerin, John Francis Vallet and Peter Arons.

Barret—McCoy : August 15th, after dispensation, Tobias Barret to Mary McCoy ; witnesses Luke Peal and Catharine Boudrot.

Schneider—Crämer: August 20th, Peter Schneider, widower, to Christina Crämer, widow ; witnesses William Hautzer and William Pranger.

Krupp—Cullom : August 25th, after dispensation, John Krupp to Susan Cullom ; witnesses John Günther and William Jung.

Dachin Du Bois—Benardau : August 27th, Basil Dachin Du Bois, a native of Franche Comté, to Elizabeth Claudina Benardau, from the island of San Domingo ; witnesses Nicholas Bernard and Catharine Boudrot.

---

* Father Farmer here makes the following note : " Matrimonium hoc censeo nullum ob impedimentum vis et metus injusti ex parte juvenis. Sed fuit renovatum."

Welsh—Wagner : September 14th, Patrick Welsh to Ann Wagner, widow; witnesses Joseph Hirt and Clara Imfeld.

Rübel—Kneul : September 16th, Adam Rübel, Jr., to Catharine Kneul ; witnesses Balthasar Kneul and Joseph Rijbel.

Schäffler—Schreinemacher : September 20th, Bernard Schäffler to Catharine Schreinemacher, widow; witnesses John Gross and John Mayer.

Hooper—Treacy : September 29th, Thomas Hooper to Mary Treacy, widow; witnesses John Zörne, William Hooper and Elizabeth Dixon.

Ryan—Gordon : October 5th, after dispensation, John Ryan,·widower, to Barbara Gordon, widow; witnesses James Ryan, Joseph Harrison and Frances Frinck.

Kean—Stott : October 7th, after dispensation, Roger Kean to Jane Stott; witnesses —————— Quinlan and others.

Balthasar—Delié : October 9th, Ignatius Balthasar to Mary Delié, widow; witnesses John Baptist Montsenis, John Smith and Elizabeth Smith.

Bischoff—Krauskopf : * October 20th, at Mount Hope, in Morris county, New Jersey, Adam Bischoff to Margaret Krauskopf; witnesses Simon Hönig and Catharine Sig.

Dünnel—Seeholtzer : October 24th, at Charlottenburg, N. J., Peter Dünnel to Elizabeth Seeholtzer ; witnesses John Schmidt and Catharine Wittiger.

Provendié—Freole ; November 2d, near Fishkill, consent renewed between Louis Philip Ferdinand Provendié and Mary Margaret Freole ; witnesses William Lusignan and Alexander Freol.

Marnay—Boileau : November 3d, *ibid.*, consent renewed between Louis Marnay, Jr., and Genevieve Boileau ; witnesses John Goulette and Clement Gosselin.

Constantinau—Chartier : the same day and place, consent renewed between Nicholas Constantinau and Charlotte Chartier; witnesses Louis Marnay and Aimé Boileau.

Herzog—Bastian : November 23d, Valentine Herzog, widower, to Catharine Bastian; witnesses Michael Fux, Margaret Veit, William Smith and Elizabeth Bastian.

Douin de la Combe—Bonifaud : November 23d, after dispensation, John Anselm Douin de la Combe to Christina, widow of John Bonifaud ; witnesses Valentine Schierling and Clara, his wife, the bride's parents.

---

* This and the following records are entered in a different part of the book from the preceding, and in prefacing them Father Farmer styles himself Missionary Apostolic. The preface here reads :

"Sequentes ego Ferdinandus Farmer, Sacerdos et Missionarius Apost., interrogavi, eorumque mutuo consensu habito, per verba de præsenti solemniter matrimonio conjunxi."

MARRIAGES FOR THE YEAR 1784.

Nelson—Nardon: January 5th, after dispensation, Lawrence Nelson, widower, to Elizabeth Nardon, widow; witnesses Patrick Lavi, Bridget Brian and Charlotte Pepin.

Le Beau—Weiler: February 17th, Philip Le Beau to Mary Ann Weiler, widow; witnesses Sebastian Vanié and Louis Luké.

Nickols—Swanwick: March 18th, after dispensation, James B. Nickols to Mary Swanwick; witnesses John Swanwick and Gerard [Garret] Gatringer.

Sarmento—Craig: April 1st, after dispensation, Francis Caverlier Sarmento, a native of Portugal, to Catharine Craig; witnesses Joseph and Virginia De Lugo, Julianna Sitgraves and Elizabeth Miller.

Blum—Kitzinger: April ——, Anthony Blum, widower, to Ottilia Kitzinger, widow; witnesses Sebastian Vanié and James Albrecht.

Makelway—Curtin: April ——, Denis Makelway, widower, to Margaret Curtin, widow; witnesses George Fitzgerald and Robert Stephens.

Fux—Lawrence: April ——, Michael Fux to Margaret Lawrence; witnesses Thomas Oldin, John Fux and John Haug.

Wagner—Dewetter: April 25th, Christopher, son of John and Catharine Wagner, to Catharine (Margaret), daughter of John and Anna Mary Dewetter; witnesses James Kelly and Adam Bremich.

Dun—Puy: May 22d, after dispensation, William Dun to Honora Puy: witnesses Edmund Connor and Luke Pea.

Waas—Vogel (Bird): May 31st, Francis Xavier Waas to Christina Vogel (Bird); witnesses Sebastian Waas and Adam Vogel.

Lechler—Steiner: June 29th, George Ernest, son of George Ernest and Magdalen Lechler, to Elizabeth, daughter of Adam and Catharine Steiner; witnesses the bridegroom's father and the bride's father.

Sarazen—Mangen: July 8th, after dispensation, Bartholomew Sarazen to Mary Mangen; witnesses Bartholomew Terrasson and Peter Dominick Robert.

Buisson—Perreaut De La Previère; July 9th, after publication of the banns in both English and French, Joseph, son of Arnold Buisson, a native of Bayonne, France, and his wife, Mary Heart, to Jane, daughter of John Baptist Perreaut De La Previère and his wife, Jeanne Roussière De La Previère, from the diocese of Nantes, France; witnesses Nicholas Bernard, David Henderson and William Oliphant.

Steinbach—Boudrot (Buttler): July 19th, after dispensation, John Steinbach to Anna Boudrot (Buttler), widow; witnesses Peter Blanchard and John Christoffel.

Essling—Lawrton : July 20th, Rudolph Essling to Sarah Lawrton ; witnesses Frederick Essling, Mary, his wife, and Christina Essling.

Lucar Des Peintreaux—Sebin : August 10th, John Baptist Charles Lucar Des Peintreaux, a native of the parish of St. Ouen de Pontaudemers, diocese of Lisieux, Normandy, France, to Anna Emily Sebin, a native of Pont Leveque, in the same diocese ; witnesses Catharine Boudrot and Anna Bijou.

Reynolds—Beech : August 16th, after dispensation, Nicholos Reynolds to Elizabeth Beech ; witnesses John Web, Sarah Web, Mary Web, Abraham Jones and Catharine Oellers.

Bouschle—Stevenson : August 18th, after dispensation, Peter Bouschle to Abigail Stevenson, widow ; witnesses John Pollard, John Tuston, Margaret Stilly and Elizabeth De Haven.

Bauer—Eckel : August 29th, Peter Bauer to Mary, widow of Peter Eckel ; witnesses John Klein, George Graff and Catharine Rixin.

Huber—Stealy : September 8th, Anthony Huber to Mary Stealy ; witnesses Peter Bremich and Peter Gary.

Smith—McDermot : September 14th, without publication of banns, Michael Smith to Mary McDermot ; witnesses Edward Freel and Mary Smith.

Vico—Ramirez : September 23d, Anthony Joseph Vico to Anna Ramirez, widow ; witnesses Anthony Remon, Joseph Perpegas, Maurice De Devio and Michael Gasky.

Fitzgerald—O'Neal : September 26th, without publication of banns, James Fitzgerald to Sarah O'Neal, widow ; witnesses George Bennet and Elizabeth, his wife.

Lederman—Cross : November 15th, after dispensation, Michael Lederman to Mary Cross ; witnesses Peter Schad and Joseph Becker.

Derblin—Rixin : November 16th, Nicholas Derblin to Catharine Rixin ; witnesses Francis Otto, Anthony Stahl and John Klein.

Essling—Schneider : November 17th, after dispensation, Nicholas, son of Paul and Christina Essling, to Catharine, daughter of Henry and Barbara Schneider ; witnesses Paul Essling, Henry Schneider and Anthony Schneider.

Greims—Robeson : December 13th, Patrick Greims, widower, to Mary Robeson, widow ; witnesses John Hoy and Nathaniel Brown.

MARRIAGES FOR THE YEAR 1785.

Pottel Le Febure—Frecourt : January 1st, after dispensation, Louis Pottel Le Febure to Mary Louisa Frecourt ; witnesses Gaspard Cenas and F. C. Farget.*

---

* The autograph signatures are attached. The bridegroom writes Pottin Lefébure and the bride Frecour.

Moriarty—Mistar : January 5th, after dispensation, Denis Moriarty to Elizabeth Mistar ; witnesses William and Martha Roage.

Brassar—Barnevllle : January 6th, Louis Brassar, a native of the parish of Ste. Eugénie, Nismes, France, to Mary Elizabeth Barneville. *

Betagh—Seibert: January 18th, after dispensation, Alexander Betagh to Mary, daughter of Sebastian and Elizabeth Seibert; witnesses Thomas Betagh and Peter Anthony Seibert.

McMahan—Hoy: February 7th, John McMahan to Margaret Hoy; witnesses John Hoy, James Fennel and Edward Flaharty.

Jonston—Duffin : February 8th, after dispensation, John Jonston to Mary Duffin ; witnesses Barnabas Duffin, Edward McGuire and Hugh Swiney.

Burelle—Bird : February 22d, without publication of the banns, John Burelle, a native of France, to Patience Hannah Bird ; witnesses Luke Pea and Catharine Boudrot.

McDonald—Fitzpatrick : March 26th, after dispensation from the banns, Charles McDonald·to Ann Fitzpatrick ; witnesses John Weinman, John Johnson and Thomas McKormick.

Beavens—Wochman : March 29th, Kinsey Beavens to Barbara Wochman ; witnesses Nicholas Wochman, Henry Probst and John Roach.

Clark—Atkinson : March 29th, without publication of the banns, Andrew Clark, widower, to Elizabeth Atkinson, widow ; witnesses Luke Pea and Catharine Boudrot.

Miller—Poth : March 29th, Christian Miller to Eva Poth ; witnesses Joseph Poth, Daniel Brewer, Elizabeth Prosches and Susan Finey.

Klein—Sauerwald : April 7th, John Klein to Mary Magdalen Sauerwald ; witnesses William Heiser, Anthony Schneider and George Graff; the nuptial blessing was given afterwards at Mass.

Cotringer—Cullen : May 26th, after dispensation, Garret (Gerard) Cotringer to Bridget Cullen ; witnesses James Cotringer, Joseph Cullen and others.

Heiser—McDaniel : June 9th, after dispensation, William Heiser to Margaret McDaniel ; witnesses James Klein, James Stahl, and others.

Mackensey—Fogarty : June 12th, after dispensation, Jackson Mackensey to Mary Fogarty ; witnesses Jeremiah Lallor, Thomas and Catharine Hurley.

Vanié—Köck : June 23d, near Philadelphia, Sebastian Vanié, widower, to Mary Köck, widow ; witnesses Mathias Köck, Joseph Davenac and Anthony Blum.

---

* Here are written the autograph signatures of the newly-married pair (the bridegroom written Brassa) and of J. Goss, Busque, Baizere, and another, very hard to decipher, as witnesses.

Bast—Jung : June 26th, Christian Bast, widower, to Anna Mary Jung, widow ; witnesses Adam Mayer and Mary Ann Norbeck.

Collins—Malone : June 26th, Bartholomew Collins to Mary Malone witnesses William Robeson and Ann Hunter.

Walnut (Noie)—Raphoon : June 28th, after dispensation, Jeremiah Walnut (Noie) to Mary Raphoon : witnesses the bride's father, mother and brother, and Jeremiah Dartoit.

Ryan—Green : July 11th, after dispensation, Timothy Ryan to Ann Green, widow ; witnesses, Michael Dowling, John Foster and Hannah Reilly.

Petri—Morris : August 11th, Bernard Petri to Mary Morris ; witnesses Catharine Brädes and Mazy [Mary ?] Patoles.

Finn—Abraham : August 18th, after dispensation, William Finn to Mary Abraham ; witnesses Henry Abraham, Thomas Keanan and Mary Kervy.

Schneider—Feinauer : September 8th, Anthony Schneider to Mary Feinauer ; witnesses Adam Rischart and Joseph Graff.

Jones—Waas : September 11th, Thomas Jones, widower, to Elizabeth Waas ; witnesses Thomas Hill and Mary, his wife.

Jansen (Jacque)—Thomas : September 15th, John Jansen (Jacque) to Rebecca Thomas, both free negroes ; witnesses Absalom Davis and Phœbe Bowers.

Hays—Maginnis : September 18th, after dispensation, Lawrence Hays to Susan Maddin, widow of ——— Maginnis ; witnesses Michael Macra and Patrick Grogan.

Fux—Will : September 20th, George Fux to Sarah Will ; witnesses John Fux and wife, Anthony Aman and wife, Michael Fux and Adam Fux.

Myers—Rust : October 6th, George Myers to Sophia Rust ; witnesses James Essling and Mathias Grabel.

Flanagan—Grey : October 24th, near Mount Hope Furnace, in Morris county, New Jersey, Thomas Flanagan to Ann Grey, widow ; witnesses Henry Hager and Christina Emick.

Donovan—Devan : November 10th, after dispensation, William Donovan to Mary Devan ; witnesses John Rice and John Quin.

Ducomb—Ribaud : November 14th, after dispensation, Vincent Ducomb to Rose Ribaud ; witnesses Joseph Ribaud, Francis Ferre and John Jainton.*

Craig—Waas : November 27th, William Craig to Martha, daughter of Sebastian and Anna Mary Waas ; witnesses Ignatius Waas, Jeremiah Cronin and Samuel Crowley.

Dickhoud—Bucher : December 6th, Francis William Dickhoud to Catharine, widow of John Bucher ; witnesses Bartholomew Becker, Joseph Becker and James Huston.

---

* Autograph signatures, of witnesses only, are given here also.

Schmidt—Nagel: December 8th, George Schmidt to Barbara Nagel; witnesses John Human, Adam Mayer and Catharine, his wife, and Conrad Cooper.

McCarty—McIntire: December 13th, after dispensation, Charles McCarty to Mary McIntire, widow; witnesses John Welsh and wife, and Elizabeth Carrol.

Hoffman—Abt: December 26th, James Hoffman to Eva Abt: witnesses Henry and George Abt.

Casey—Hughs: December 29th, after dispensation, William Casey, widower, to Mary Hughs; witnesses John Scott, Johanna Macarty and Alice O'Brian.

MARRIAGES FOR THE YEAR 1786.

Zeiss—Kelly: January 5th, George Zeiss, widower, to Margaret Kelly, widow; witnesses Charles Syng, John Gräff and Adam Bremich.

Car—Waas: January 28th, John Car to Mary Waas; witnesses Samuel Crowley, Noble Groan and Daniel McCurdy.

Röhr—Sweres (Uhlmar): February 29th, after dispensation, Martin Röhr to Catharine Sweres (Uhlmar); witnesses Charles Rauchbarth (Robert) and George Smith.

Cummings (Commyns)—Williams: February 9th, after dispensation, Paul Cummings (Commyns), a young man from Spain, to Catharine Ann Williams, widow; witnesses Manuel Maravir and Elizabeth Price.

Cronan Buttler: February 16th, after dispensation, Denis Cronan to Judith Buttler; witnesses Garret (Gerard) Barry and Sarah Sickel.

Gillis—Lefarty: February 19th, John Gillis to Catharine Lefarty; witnesses Michael Macra, Jane Macaulay, Margaret Nesbit and Susan Macauly.

Cambron—Mignot: February 23d, Peter Cambron to Pelagia Mignot, widow; witnesses Joseph Davenac, Francis Bangi and John Baptist Denerié.

Plattenberger—Bloom: February 27th, John Plattenberger (P.) to Elizabeth Bloom; witnesses David Tittemary, Anthony Blum and Thomas Cromley.

Eck—Dugan: April 17th, after dispensation, John Peter Eck to Catharine Dugan; witnesses Christopher Herberger and Rachel Frasure.

Burrell—McHuin: April 18th, John Burrell to Mary McHuin; witnesses Peirce Veal and Mary Veit.

Strack—Premaurer: May 1st at Hancock, Bucks county, Pa., John W i l

liam Strack, widower, to Gertrude Premaurer, widow; witnesses
Nicholas Macarty and James Hönig.

Essling—Bush: May 31st, James Essling to Margaret Bush; witnesses
George Mayer and Mathias Grabel.

Ferguson—Witteer: June 4th, after dispensation, Archibald Ferguson to
'Mary Witteer; witnesses Joseph Würth and Barbara, his wife, and
others.

Blum—Schreiner: June 8th, Peter Blum to Margaret Schreiner; witnesses Peter Field and Peter Cavill.

Herberger—Burk: June 11th, after dispensation, Christopher Herberger,
widower, to Susan Burk; witnesses Joseph Würth, Barbara, his wife
and Archibald Ferguson and wife.

Barron—Senner: June 15th, after dispensation, James Barron to Mary
Senner; witnesses Thomas Pearce and Thomas Carroll.

Kräuscher—Treim: July 16th, John Kräuscher to Mary Dorothy Treim;
witnesses Joseph Egg and Peter Treim.

Miller—Huber: August 2d, Simon Miller to Hannah Huber, both from
the West Jersey mission; witnesses Adam Caspar, Christina Caspar
and Anna Mary Miller.*

---

* Thus ends Father Farmer's marriage register, and immediately following the last entry, on the same page, is a record of his death, written
by the hand of a fellow preist at St. Joseph's, most probably Father
Robert Mollineux.   This record reads as follows :

" Hoc anno obiit piæ momoriæ R. Pater Ferdinandus Farmer *alias*
Steinmyer 17° die Augusti.   Requiescat in pace.   Amen."

FATHER SCHNEIDER'S

GOSHENHOPPEN REGISTERS,

1741—1764.

[Transcribed for the SOCIETY, and translated and prepared for publication, by FRANCIS T. FUREY.]

THE contents of the oldest Catholic Church register of the original thirteen English colonies now known to be in existence are here given to the public. A brief mention of the book has already been made in this volume: Mr. Philip S. P. Connor describes its form and appearance in a paper which he read last year before our Society.* Dr. Shea, too, in his " Catholic Church in Colonial Days," refers to it and gives fac-simile reproductions of its title-page and first entry.†

Only a small portion of the book is really Father Schneider's work, by far the geater part of it being taken up with the registers of his successor, Father John Baptist De Ritter, the publication of which is reserved for a future occasion.

It will be noticed with much regret that Father Schneider's registers are far from being a complete record of his missionary labors in America. There is, unfortunately, a very wide gap, beginning with the middle of the year 1747 and extending to 1758; and even then only the list of marriages is resumed. We are, therefore, left without any authentic account of the missionary's journeyings during the years that

---

* See page 27.   † See Shea, pp. 393, 402.

were probably the most interesting period of his labors, that of the hostile Indian incursions and massacres in Berks county.

The editor had originally intended to give, along with these registers, geographical and historical annotations; but his investigations have been rewarded with so vast and rich a mass of valuable material that he has been persuaded to utilize it in a separate historical essay covering the territory and time of Father Schneider's mission in this country. This work is now nearly completed. It is put in the form of a paper, which he intends to read before the American Catholic Historical Society some time in the early part of next year. Until then the uninitiated are left to guess at the location and present name of many of the places mentioned by our pioneer missionary, whose parish embraced all the territory in Pennsylvania north of the Schuykill and the Neshaminy rivers, and had the whole colony of New Jersey as an annexed mission.

We now proceed to give a translation and adaptation of the registers under their separate headings:

I. BAPTISMS.

BAPTISMS FOR THE YEAR 1741.

Kohl, Albertina, of George and Barbara Kohl, born May 6th, baptized August 23d, in John Utzman's house in Falkner's Swamp; sponsors John Utzman and Albertina (Luth.), his wife.

Magudiens, Catharine and Mary, of Patrick and ——— Magudiens (Irish), baptized December 23d, in their parents' house, in the Swedish settlement; sponsor Judith Coners, widow.

Utzman, George, of John and Albertina (Luth.) Utzman, baptized December 26th; sponsor George Kuhn.

Lery, George Henry, of Derby Lery (Irish) and Anna Margaret ———, baptized December 28th, in the house of Henry Michel, who served as sponsor.

————

BAPTISMS FOR THE YEAR 1742.

Comins, Timothy, of Michael and ——— Comins (Irish), baptized January 13th, in parents' house, in the Swedish colony; sponsors John Larkin and Judith Coners, widow.

Crossby, Thomas, of Farrel and —— Crossby (Irish), baptized the same day, at the same place; sponsor Michael Magdanel.

Mayer, Joseph Caspar, of Caspar and ——— Mayer, baptized January 22d; sponsor Joseph Kuhn.

Lang, Eva Mary, of James (Calv.) and Apollonia Lang, baptized February 28th; sponsors George Kuhn and his sister, Eva Mary.

Frantz, Mary Apollonia, of James and —— Frantz, baptized March 4th, in Wendelin Helffer's house, in Bethlehem country; sponsors Simon Becker and Wendelin Helffer's wife.

Friderich, George Reinold, of Philip (commonly called the stone-breaker) and —— Friderich, baptized March 9th, near Germantown; sponsors John George Schwartzmann and his wife.

Kuhn, Anna Barbara, of Henry and Margaret Kuhn, baptized March 28th, in John Kuhn's house; sponsors John Kuhn and Anna Barbara, his wife.

Kill, Philip, of George and —— (P.) Kill, baptized April 18th (Easter Sunday), in John Kuhn's house; sponsor Eva Maria Kuhn.

Canceler, Sara, of John and —— Canceler (Irish), baptized April 20th, in Henry Guibson's house; sponsors Ambrose Rilay and Judith, his wife.

Pawlitz, Michael, of Jacob and ——— (P.) Pawlitz, baptized May 17th, in parents' house in Allemängel.

Meyer, John, (posthumous child) of John (P.) and Mary (P.) Meyer, baptized the same day at the same place; sponsor John Meyer (P.).

Onan, Denis, of Denis and Rebecca Onan, baptized May 27th, in Christian Haug's house in Dinekum; sponsor Wendelin Helffer.

Maguin, Margaret, of Henry and Mary Maguin; sponsor Mary Apollonia Helffer.

Blayny, John, of Edmund and Ann Blayny; sponsor Patrick Karmick.

McCardy, Nicholas, of Edward and Catharine McCardy; sponsor Edmund Gueréti.

McCardy, Edward, of the same parents; sponsor Lawrence Mair.

Dörm, John, of John and Catharine Dörm; sponsor Denis Onan.

(All of the above were Catholics, beginning with Onan, Denis.)

Spengler, Mary Eva, of Peter (P.) and Mary Eva Spengler, baptized July 25th, in John Kuhn's house; sponsor George Kuhn.

Bricker, Ann Elizabeth, of John and Barbara (P.) Bricker, baptized August 15th, in Jacob Pawlitz's house; sponsors James (P.) and Anna (P.) Lantz.

MaKarmick, Elias, of Patrick and —— MaKarmick, baptized August 29th, in Christian Haug's house; sponsors Lawrence Mair and Ann Blayny.

Schwartz, George James, of John (puddler) and Agnes Schwartz, baptized September 26th, in John Kuhn's house; sponsor James Danckel.

[Here Father Schneider makes an entry to the effect that in the latter part of August three persons, whose names were not recorded, were baptized at the New Forge, near Jotter's Mill.]

————, John and David, children of a widow whose husband was a Protestant, baptized October 17th, in the house of William Hall (Irish), near North Wales Meeting House.

Haug, Simon, of Christian and —— Haug, baptized October 28th, in parents' house; sponsors Thomas McCardy and his wife.

Helffer, Mary Apollonia, of Wendelin and Mary Apollonia Helffer, baptized in the same place; sponsors John Utzman and Anna Barbara Lorentz.

Gust, Rosina, of Henry and Mary Magdalen Gust, baptized November 7th, in the chapel in Philadelphia; sponsor George Esselin.

Arnold, George, of George and —— Arnold, baptized November 8th, in parents' house, in Germantown; sponsor Catharine Spengler, wife of George Spengler, who stood *quasi* god-father.

Molitor, Anna Martha, of John and —— (P.) Molitor, baptized the same day and in the same place; sponsor Anna Martha, wife of John Schmidt, who stood as *quasi* god-father.

Lechler, John, of George Ernest (weaver) and —— (P.) Lechler, baptized December 12th, in Mark Schiffer's house, in Oley.

Doeri, John, of James and —— Doeri, baptized December 13th, in Falkner's Swamp; sponsor John Utzman.

Keffer, John Peter, of Matthew and —— Keffer, baptized December 19th, in parents' house, at Maxetani; sponsor Ursula Luckenbihl.

Reppert, Mary Apollonia, of Stephen and —— Reppert, baptized December 25th, the Feast of the Nativity, in John Kuhn's house; sponsor Mary Apollonia Lang.

————

BAPTISMS FOR THE YEAR 1743.

Melchior, George, of Nicholas (P.) and —— Melchior, baptized February 13th, in Cushenhopen; sponsor John George Gauckler.

Johnson, John, of Patrick and —— Johnson, baptized February 14th, near New Furnace.

Calver, Patrick, of Philip and —— Calver, baptized February 27th, in Henry Guibson's house.

Becker, Elizabeth Mary, of Simon and Elizabeth (P.) Becker, baptized March 16th, in Wendelin Helffer's house; sponsors Maurice Lorentz and Eva Mary Immel.

Minime, Anna and Martha, of John and —— Minime, baptized March 17th, near Dörm Furnace; sponsor Edward Garden.

Leehoffer, Johanna Catharine Albertina, of Ursula Leehoffer and ——

———, baptized March 22d, in the house of John Utzman, who stood sponsor.

Maurer, John, of John (Calv.) and M. Catharine (Calv.) Maurer, baptized April 4th, in the same house and with the same sponsor.

———, James, of a certain married negress, baptized April 17th, in James Hoffman's house, in Philadelphia ; sponsors James Hoffman and his wife.

Pulton, Charles, of Charles and Ruth Pulton (English), baptized May 28th, in parents' house, near Durham Road.

Dörm, Anna, of John and Catharine Dörm, baptized May 29th, the Feast of the Most Holy Trinity, in Thomas Garden's house, at Haycock ; sponsors Patrick Cardy and Catharine, wife of Edward Cardy.

Mair, David, of Lawrence and Mary Mair, baptized May 30th, in Maurice Lorentz's house.

Meyer, Catharine, of John (P.) and Mary Meyer, baptized the same day at the same place ; sponsors, for both Catharine Seibert, and for David Patrick MacKarmick.

Rilay, M. Margaret, of Ambrose and Judith Rilay, baptized June 19th, in parents' house, near New Furnace ; sponsors Frank Gibson and Margaret, his wife.

Ridgens, Samuel, of John and Mary Ridgens, baptized May 29th, in Thomas Garden's house ; sponsors Edward Cardy and his wife, Catharine.

———, ———, of Patrick and ——— ——— (an Irish married couple), baptized July 2d, in Handlon's house, in Frankford ; sponsor Cornelius ———.

Fick, Mary Susanna, of Jodoc[?] (P.) and Anna Regina (P.) Fick, baptized July 17th, in Jaacob Pawlitz's house ; sponsor Godfrey Bezel.

Blany, Catharine, of Edmund and Anna Blany, baptized July 31st, in the house of Thomas Cardy, who stood sponsor.

Lorentz, John Wendelin, of Maurice and Barbara Lorentz, baptized August 1st, in parents' house ; sponsors John Wendelin Helffer and A. M. Meyer.

Fitzcharroll, John and Gerald, of Patrick and Elizabeth Fitzcharroll, baptized in the same place ; sponsors Lawrence Mair for John, Wendelin Helffer for Gerald, and A. M. Meyer for both.

MacKarmick, Martha, of Patrick and Johanna MacKarmick, baptized August 2d, in parents' house ; sponsor Frank McAgane.

O'Nayl, Thomas, of John and Catharine O'Nàyl, baptized on the same occassion ; sponsor John McClaughlen.

Schüssler, John George, of Henry (Calv.) and Catharine Schüssler, baptized at the same place ; sponsor James Frantz.

Stockschlager, John Adam, of John and A. Martha Stockschlager, baptized August 4th, in parents' house ; sponsor John Adam Bender.

Kohl, M. Apollonia, of John George and —— —— (P.) Kohl, baptized August 14th, in George Gauckler's house; sponsors Wendel Helffer and Mary Apollonia, his wife.

Canceler, Elizabeth, of John and Mary Canceler, baptized August 24th, in Mark Schiffer's house, in Oley; sponsor John Mulcastor and Margaret, wife of Francis Gibson.

Reiss, David, of Valentine and Elizabeth (P.) Reiss; sponsor ——————, commonly known as "the old widow."

Bender, John Peter, of Adam and Margaret (P.) Bender, baptized September 18th, in parents' house; sponsors John Stockschleger and A. Martha, his wife.

Alter, John Martin, of John Martin and Catharine Alter, baptized October 5th, near the Glass Works; sponsor Joseph Walter.

Schwartzmann, Andrew, of John and Anna Maria Schwartzmann, baptized October 6th, in parents' house, near Germantown; sponsors Andrew Engelhard and Walburga, his wife.

Laydon, James, of Maurice and Margaret (Linnert) Laydon, baptized October 16th, in John Mulcastor's house; sponsors Frank Gibson and Margaret, his wife.

Mayer, Peter James, of Caspar and —————— Mayer, baptized December 26th, in John Utzman's house; sponsor James Doeri.

Onan, Mary, of Denis and Rebecca Onan, baptized December 28th, in parents' house; sponsor Ann Blainy.

Rilay, Thomas, of Hugh and —————— Rilay, baptized in Thomas Cardy's house; sponsor Edmund Blany.

BAPTISMS FOR THE YEAR 1744.

Savage, Henry, of Henry and —————— Savage, baptized January 1st, in the chapel in Philadelphia; sponsor Catharine Spengler.

——————, Eva Helena, of a certain English married couple, baptized January 8th, in John Kuhn's house; sponsor M. Eva Schmidt.

Stagle, Melon, of Matthew and Anna Stagle, baptized March 18th, in Maurice Lorentz's house, in New Jersey; sponsor Patrick Mac-Karmick.

Ridgens, John, of John and Mary Ridgens; sponsors James Lorentz and Catharine Seibert.

Riley, John, of Charles and Sarah Riley, baptized March 27th, in Henry Gibson's house; sponsors Frank Gibson and Margaret, his wife.

Cawlvert, William, of Patrick and Margaret Cawlvert; sponsors Philip Cawlvert and Margaret Gibson.

Utzman, Margaret Apollonia, of John and Albertina (Luth.) Utzman,.

baptized March 28th in parents' house; sponsors Wendel Helffer and Apollonia, his wife.

Bischof, Paul, of Peter and Charlotta Bischof, baptized April 1st, in the chapel in Philadelphia; sponsors Paul Müller and Elizabeth Gatringer.

Müller, Charlotte Elizabeth, of Paul and M. Magdalen Müller, baptized April 2d, in the same place; sponsors Peter Bischoff and Elizabeth Gatringer.

Staab, Eva Catharine, of John Adam and Catharine Staab, baptized April 15th, in parents' house, in Allemängel; sponsors George Kuhn and Sara Catharine Bewerts.

Koch, Henry, of John Adam and A. Maria (Con.) Koch, baptized April 17th, at Cedar Creek; sponsors Henry Kuhn and Marg. his wife.

Kuhn, Margaret, of Henry and Margaret Kuhn, baptized April 22d, in John Kuhn's house; sponsors John Eckenroth and Margaret, his wife.

Schmidt, A. Barbara, of Philip and Eva Mary Schmidt; sponsors John Kuhn and Anna Barbara, his wife.

Wentzel, Simon, of John William and Catharine (P.) Wentzel, baptized April 25th, at the Glass Works; sponsors Simon Griesmeyer and Susan, his wife.

————, Margaret Elizabeth, an adult, baptized April 30th, in the chapel in Philadelphia; sponsor Elizabeth Gatringer.

————, Christina, an adult Negress, slave (or servant) of Dr. Brown, in whose house she was baptized; sponsors the same Dr. Brown and his wife.

Griesmeyer, Anna Mary, of Simon and Susanna Griesmeyer; sponsors Caspar Alter and A. M., his wife.

Madin, Margaret, of Patrick and Sarah Madin, baptized May (April) 9th, in Michael Comins' house, at Branson's Iron Works; sponsors William Sands and Frances Langford.

Maxfield, Margaret, of James and Catharine Maxfield; sponsor Patrick Madin.

Konlen, Patrick, of Denis and Honora Konlen; sponsor Susan Hickey.

Comins, Thomas, of Michael and Anna Comins; sponsor Thomas Connor.

Mair, Helena, of Lawrence and Mary Mair, baptized May 19th, in Jacob Frantz's house, in New Jersey; sponsors John Murphay and A. M. Meyer.

Buttler, William, of James and Mary Buttler; sponsors James Toy and Catharine Morgan.

Sauter, Simon, of Philip and Christina Sauter, baptized June 6th, in Matthew Geiger's house, in New Jersey; sponsors Simon Griesmeyer and A. M. Beitelmann.

Geiger, John Henry, of Matthew and A. Mary Geiger; sponsors William Wentzel and M. Eva Halter.

Bucher, Elizabeth, of Peter and A. Barbara Bucher, baptized June 17th, in Jacob Pawlitz's house, in Allemängel; sponsors Jacob Pawlitz and M. Elizabeth Seissloff.

Lechler, Martin, of George Ernest and M. Magdalen (P.) Lechler, baptized July 24th, in parents' house, in Oley; sponsors Martin Reisel and Catharine Riffel.

Eckenroth, Margaret, of John and Margaret Eckenroth, baptized July 25th, in the priest's house; sponsors Wendel Helffer and Apollonia, his wife.

Connely, Peter, of Bernard and Brigid Connely, baptized July 27th, in Thomas Cardy's house; sponsors Edward Cardy and Catharine Harvy.

Frantz, Elizabeth, of Jacob and Eva M. Frantz, baptized July 29th, in parents' house; sponsors Adam Sommer and Elizabeth Reiffenberger.

Kelsey, Anna, of Bartholomew and ——— Kelsey, baptized July 30th, in parents' house, at Bonbrook; sponsor Nicholas Power.

Chateau, A. Barbara and Catharine, of Nicholas (Calv.) and M. Eva Chateau, baptized August 7th, in John Molitor's house, near Germantown; sponsors A. Barbara Fridrich for the former, and Catharine Riffel for the latter.

Groskopff, A. Margaret, of James and Anna Mary (Calv.) Groskopff; sponsor John Molitor.

Normand, Richard, of John and Johanna Normand, baptized August 19th, in James Darnay's house, near Branson's Iron Works; sponsors James Darnay and Rose, his wife.

Shay, John, of Edward and Eleanor Shay, in Michael Comins' house; sponsors Michael Comins and Sarah, his wife.

Arnold, —— ——, of George and Margaret Arnold, baptized September 2d, in George Arnold's house in Philadelphia; sponsor Catharine Spengler.

Fues, Margaret, of John and Dorothea Fues, baptized September 20th, in George Ernest Lechler's house, in Oley; sponsors Martin Reisel and Margaret Gibson.

BAPTISMS FOR THE YEAR 1745.

Ruffener, Jo. M. Eva, of Simon and M. Barbara Ruffener, baptized February 4th, near Croner's Mill; sponsor M. Eva Lorentz.

McCardy, Thomas, of Patrick and Ann (P.) McCardy, baptized February 17th, at Haycock; sponsors Matthew Handlon and Ann Blany.

Dörm, Margaret, of John (P.) and Catharine Dörm ; sponsors Denis Onan and Ann Blany.

Gibson, Henry, of Frank and Margaret Gibson, baptized March 31st, in Charles Riles's house; sponsors Charles Riles and his wife.

Johnson, Edward, of Patrick and ——— Johnson, baptized April 16th ; sponsors John Utzman and Albertina, his wife.

Morgan, Ann, of Francis and Catharine Morgan, baptized April 20th, sponsors John McCray and A. M. Meyer.

Sommer, John Adam, of Adam and ——— Sommer, baptized April 20th, sponsor James Frantz.

Minimay, John, of John and Mary Minimay, baptized April 22d.

Canceler, George Ernest, of John and Mary Canceler, baptized May 23d ; sponsors George Ernest Lechler and his wife.

Reppert, Daniel, of Stephen and ——— Reppert, baptized May 26th ; sponsors James Lang and Apollonia, his wife.

Halter, Andrew, of Caspar and Anna Eva Halter, baptized June 2d, in Philadelphia; sponsors Martin Gassner and his wife.

Noulen, Ann, of Denis and Honora Noulen, baptized June 16th ; sponsors Thomas Donahew and Rose Darnay.

Normand, Joseph, of John and Johanna Normand, baptized June 19th, sponsor James Darnay.

Grismeyer, M. Agnes, of Simon and Susanna Grismeyer, baptized July 9th ; sponsors Caspar and Christina Alter.

Alter, A. Margaret, of Martin and Catharine Alter ; sponsors Christopher Stumpff and Margaret Schæffer.

Doeri, George Peter, of James and ——— Doeri, baptized August 12th ; sponsors George Kuhn and Catharine, his wife.

Pulton, Barbara, of Charles and Ruth Pulton ; sponsor Catharine Harvay.

———, Isaac, of a certain Sarah, who said her husband was a Catholic; sponsor Charles Pulton.

Riles, Elizabeth, of Charles and Sarah Riles ; sponsor Michael Comins.

Staab, George Adam, of Adam and Catharine Staab ; sponsors Adam Koch and Anna Mary, his wife.

Koch, Frederick, of Adam and Anna Mary Koch ; sponsor Henry Kuhn.

Væth, Elizabeth, of Adam and Magdalen (Brückner) Væth ; sponsors John Peter Högener and Elizabeth, his wife.

Molitor, Elizabeth, of John and ——— Molitor ; sponsor Adam Spæth.

Riffel, Anna Barbara, of Matthew and Christina Riffel ; sponsors John Kuhn and Anna Barbara, his wife.

Wolflinger, ———, of Bernard and ——— Wolflinger.

Kuhn, M. Ottilia, of Henry and Margaret Kuhn ; sponsor Ottilia Meyer.

Schmidt, Catharine, of Philip and Eva Mary Schmidt; sponsors George and Catharine Kuhn.

BAPTISMS FOR THE YEAR 1746.

Krafft, John George and Michael, twins, of Anna Catharine, widow of
Frederick Krafft, baptized February 20th; sponsors John George
Gauckler and Michael Reiser (Luth.).

Kohl, George Bernard, of George and ————— Kohl, baptized March
9th.

Connely, Mary, of Bernard and ————— Connely, baptized March 16th;
sponsor Ann, wife of Edmund Blany.

Castelah, Mary, of Pierce and Sarah Castelah, baptized March 23d;
sponsors Thomas Catugn and Mary, wife of Patrick Johnson.

Madin, Elizabeth, of Patrick and Sarah Madin; sponsors James Ryan
and Eleanor Püsert.

Flaharty, Margaret, of Patrick and Frances Flaharty; sponsors Charles
Riles and A. M. Utzmann.

Kuhn, George James, of George and Catharine Kuhn, baptized March
31st; sponsors Jacob Riffel and Ottilia Meyer.

Ridgens, Margaret, of John and Mary Ridgens, baptized April 11th;
sponsor Edward Morpheu.

Meyer, John James, of John and Anna Mary Meyer, baptized April 13th;
sponsor Jacob Lorentz.

Onan, Rebecca, of Denis and Rebecca Onan, baptized April 14th; sponsors Matthew Handlon and Ann, wife of Edmund Blany.

Stockschleger, M. Apollonia, of John and A. Martha Stockschleger, baptized April 17th; sponsors John Wendelin Helffer and Apollonia,
his wife.

Steyerwald, M. Catharine, of Theobald and A. Marg. Steyerwald, baptized April 20th; sponsor Adam Koch.

Keffer, A. Dorothy, of Matthew and A. M. Kefter; sponsors John Fues
and Dorothy, his wife.

Helffer, John Maurice, of John Wendelin and Apollonia Helffer, baptized
May 11th; sponsors Maurice Lorentz and John Stockschleger.

Kerck, Mary, of John and Bridget Kerck, baptized June 15th; sponsors
Thomas Donahew and Eleanor Shehea.

Ulrich, John Francis, of John and Barbara Ulrich; sponsor Frank Gibson.

Lechler, Anthony, of George Ernest and M. Magdalen Lechler, baptized
June 16th; sponsor the priest.

Cognway, Margaret, of John and Mary Cognway, baptized June
29th; sponsors John McCray and Catharine, wife of Francis Morgan.

Stasy, Matthew, of Matthew and Ann Stasy, sponsors John McClaughlen
and Gaudentia, his wife.

Mair, John, of Lawrence and ———— Mair; sponsor Edward Morpheu.

Spies, Anna Magdalen, of Wolffgang and Catharine Spies, baptized July 14th; sponsor A. Mary Bechtl.

Lorentz, Joseph, of Maurice and Barbara Lorentz, baptized July 17th; sponsors John Wendelin Helffer and Apollonia, his wife.

Fuss, A. Catharine, of John and Dorothy Fuss, baptized July 20th; sponsors Adam Staab and Catharine, his wife.

Wentzel, Theodore, of William and Catharine Wentzel, baptized August 5th, in Matthew Geiger's house; sponsor the priest.

Villar, John George, of Anthony and M. Eva Villar, baptized September 14th, in Philadelphia; sponsors John George Ulrich and Anna Catharine ————.

Shaw, Johanna, of ———— and ———— Shaw, baptized September 21st.

Reppert, James, of Stephen and ———— Reppert, baptized September 28th; sponsors James Lang (P.) and Apollonia, his wife.

Schwager, Wolffgang Adam, of Peter and Anna Magdalen Schwager; sponsors Adam Væth (the bridge builder) and Magdalen, his wife.

Sommer, John Henry, of Adam and ———— Sommer, baptized September 29th, in the priest's house; sponsor John Henry Pisbing.

Gassner, Edward Daniel, of Caspar and Elizabeth Gassner, baptized October 5th, in Philadelphia; sponsor Edward ————.

Darsey, Daniel and Johanna, of Charles and Elizabeth Darsey, baptized October 6th, in Matthew Geiger's house; sponsor James Lestrange.

Guill, Peter, of Patrick and ———— Guill; sponsor Daniel Sulivan.

Sauter, Philip, of Philip and Christina Sauter; sponsors John Martin Alter and Eva, wife of Caspar Alter.

Bewerts, Henry, of John and M. Ottilia Bewerts, baptized October 19th, in Adam Staab's house; sponsors Henry Kuhn and Margaret, his wife.

Eckroth, Catharine, of John and Margaret Eckroth, baptized November 17th, in parents' house; sponsors George Kuhn and Catharine, his wife.

Smith, Philip, af Patrick and Elizabeth Smith, baptized November 30th, at Haycock; sponsors Edmund Morphey and Catharine Harvey.

———

BAPTISMS FOR THE YEAR 1747.

Noulen, Denis, of Denis and Honora Noulen, baptized January 8th; sponsor Edward Hogan.

Hogan, Mary, of Edward and Sarah Hogan; sponsor Denis Noulen.

Cardy, John, of Patrick and Ann Cardy, baptized January 18th, at Haycock.

Handlon, John, of Matthew and Rachel Handlon ; sponsors Edward Morpheu and Catharine Harvey.

Ruffener, Adam, of Simon and M. Barbara Ruffener, baptized April 17th, in the preist's house ; sponsors Adam Brückner and Magdalen, his wife.

Kuhn, Anna Catharine, of Henry and Margaret Kuhn, baptized April 13th, in parents' house ; sponsors Adam Staab and A. Catharine, his wife.

Minimay, William, of John and ———— Minimay, baptized April 25th, in Thomas Cardy's house ; sponsors Edward Cardy and Rebecca Onan.

Smith, David, of Patrick and Elizabeth Smith ; sponsors Thomas Cardy and Ann, his wife.

Frantz, Simon, of Jacob and Eva M. Frantz, baptized April 26th ; sponsors Simon Becker and ———— Immel.

Morgan, M. Elizabeth, of Frank and Catharine Morgan ; sponsors David Conaugh and A. M. Meyer.

Pulton, Ruth, of Charles and Ruth Pulton, baptized April 28th.

Alter, Simon, of Caspar and Eva Alter, baptized May 4th; sponsors Simon Griesmeyer and Barbara Bachmann.

Geiger, Simon, of Matthew and A. M. Geiger ; sponsors Martin Alter and Christina, his sister.

————, Rachel ; sponsor Simon Griesmeyer.

Utzman, Sarah, of John and Albertina Utzman, baptized May 17th, sponsors Frank Gibson and Mary Johnson.

Maxfield, Isabella, of Catharine, widow of James Maxfield; sponsors James Bryan and A. M. Utzman.

Keragan, Thomas, of Manasses [Manus ?] and Johanna (Crames) Keragan ; sponsor Thomas Bissit.

[Thus abruptly ends Father Schneider's register of baptisms. Closely following, on the same page, but in a far different hand and much smaller characters, more difficult to read, are recorded three baptisms, dated November 18th, 1764 (which will be found placed in their proper chronological order in this list); and on the next page are two others, of the Bock (Buck) family, one dated October 16th, 1763, and the other of the year 1764, but without mention of month or day. Closely following the last of these is a single line of an unfinished record, which reads, "1740, 10 Julii Ann. Margaretha fil." Then, with two blank pages intervening, there is a whole page of entries of the Hookey family, which look as if they might have been copied in Father De Ritter's time from memoranda that had been hept privately by some interested person. The spelling of the surname may seem peculiar to modern eyes acquainted

with the present generation of the family; but it is the same as was used
by Father De Ritter thirty years later than the birth of these children.

There are a few other records of the year 1764, preceding the death of
Father Schneider, which occurred on July 10th of that year; and in these
instances Father Farmer came from Philadelphia to officiate. The few
scattered registers referred to above are given below in regular chronological order.]

Hucki, Elizabeth, of Nicholas and Catharine (Kleyss) Hucki, born September 29th, 1751, baptized October 17th following in Edward
Carty's house ; sponsors Anthony Grüsser and Elizabeth, his wife.

Hucki, Catharine, of the same parents, born January 12th, 1753, baptized February 18th following, in the same place; sponsors George
Kohl and Barbara, his wife.

Hucki, Anthony,* of the same parents, born April ——, 1755, baptized
on the 17th of the same month, *ibid.*; sponsors Anthony Grüsser and
Elizabeth Kleyss, his wife.

Hucki, Nicholas, of the same parents, born about the end of March or
beginning of April, 1757, baptized in the same place on April 17th
of the same year ; sponsors Joseph Kohl and Barbara Henrich.

Hucki, John George,† of the same parents, born May 6th, 1759, baptized
in the same place June 17th following; sponsors George Kohl and
Barbara Kohl.

Bock, Leonard, of Nicholas and Apollonia Bock, baptized October 10th,
1763, sponsors Leonard Beutelman and Salome Fricker.

Bock, Joseph, of the same parents, baptized —— ——, 1764, sponsor
Joseph Kohl.

Schmidt, John George, of Philip and Ursula (Zip) Schmidt, born Novem-
ber 23d, 1763, baptized [privately ?] when eleven weeks old, by Henry
Fredder, the schoolmaster, at Couissahopen; Chrism given by P.
Frambachs [ceremonies supplied by Father Farmer?] ; sponsors
George Zip and Eva Zip.

Ristel, Bernard, of Matthew and Christina (Danner) Ristel, born in Macunshi, May 22d, 1764, baptized June 30th following, at Goshenhoppen, by Father Farmer ; sponsors Melchior Ziegler and Catharine,
his wife.

Röhr, John Martin, of Martin and Anna Mary Röhr, born this year, baptized in the parents' house the same month as the last named infant
by Father Ferdinand Farmer, Father Theodore [Schneider] being
then in his last illness ; sponsors John Grett and Elizabeth, his
wife.

Lorentz, Henry, of Maurice and Mary Lorentz, baptized November 18th ;
sponsors Henry Fredder and Anna Mary, his wife.

---

* Ancestor of the Drexel family of Philadelphia.
† Ancestor of the present Hookey family of Philadelphia.

Norbudy, John Daniel, of Henry and Mary Norbudy; sponsors Henry Hein and Magdalen, his wife.

Hoffman, Margaret, of Michael and Catharine Hoffman; sponsors Martin and Catharine Moulier.

[The last three entries, which are recorded on the same page with the last of Father Schneider's own records, are so indistinctly written that some of the words can only be guessed at. They are the last in date recorded at Goshenhoppen prior to Father De Ritter's arrival in the Summer of 1765, after which time the registers were kept regularly.]

— .—

II. MARRIAGES.

Laub— ———: December 8th, 1741, in the chapel in Philadelphia, John Michael Laub to Regina ———, widow; witnesses John Schmidt and several others, Protestants as well as Catholics.

Dubon—Krebs: March 7th [1742], *ibid.*, Lawrence Dubon, widower, to Anna Mary Walburger (Luth.), widow of Jacob Krebs, in the presence of several witnesses.

Magdanel—Welsh : March 9th, *ibid.*, after dispensation and in presence of witnesses, Edmund Magdanel to Sarah Welsh, both Irish.

Rilay— ———.— : April 19th, after publication of the banns in the city and in the country, in Henry Guibson's house, in presence of many witnesses, Catholics and non-Catholics, Ambrose Rilay to Judith (O'Nayl) ———, widow.

Schwartz—Fischer : July 12th, in George Zimmermann's house, John Schwartz, puddler, to Agnes Fischer (P.); witnesses George Zimmermann and wife.

Müller—Gärtner : Christmas day, in John Kuhn's house, John Henry Müller (P.) to Anna Margaret Gärtner(P.),in the presence of witnesses.

Högner— ———: March 8th [1743], in the Philadelphia chapel, Peter Högner, widower, to Elizabeth ——— (P.), widow; in presence of several witnesses.

Staab—Bewerts : April 4th, in John Utzman's house in Falkner's swamp, John Adam Staab to Catharine Bewerts ; several witnesses were present.

Gibson—Brodbeck : April 5th, in Henry Gibson's house on the Schuylkill, Frank, son of the said Henry Gibson, to Margaret Brodbeck, a German ; witnesses the bridegroom's father and mother and another married couple of the neighborhood.

Müller—Walltrich : April 11th, in the Philadelphia chapel, Paul Müller to Mary Magdalen Walltrich ; witnesses the bride's parents and several others.

Beck—Stengler: April 12th, *ibid.*, John Beck to Barbara Stengler, both Lutherans; witnesses Catharine Spengler and several Protestants.

Schmidt—Kuhn: April 26th, in John Kuhn's house, Philip Schmidt to Eva Kuhn; witnesses the bride's parents and several others.

Grosskopf—Stumpf: September 5th, in the Philadelphia chapel, Jacob Grosskopf to Anna Mary Stumpf; witnesses a number of Protestants, relatives of the bride's father, who had recently come here with her.

Smith—Sanders: November 8th, in the priest's house, John Smith to Margaret Sanders; witnesses some English people who came with the young couple, Peter Schwager and Valentine Wildt.

Cardy [McCarty]—Sanderson: February 14th [1744], at Haycock, Patrick Cardy to Ann Sanderson (P.); witnesses the bridegroom's parents, brothers and sisters.

Schwager—Schwitz: February 28th, in the priest's house, John Peter Schwager, widower, to Anna Magdalen Schwitz (Luth.); witnesses Valentine Wild and several Protestants.

Morgan—Seibert: May 19th, in Jacob Frantz's house in New Jersey, Francis Morgan, an Irishman, to Catharine Seibert; witnesses Jacob Frantz and his wife, and others.

Fernandez—Leonard: September 24th, in Charles Riles's house, John Fernandez, an Italian, to Margaret Leonard, an Irish girl; witnesses Charles Riles, James Darnay and others.

Kuhn—Riffel: November 27th, in John Kuhn's house, John George Kuhn to Catharine Riffel; witnesses the bridegroom's parents and brothers, and others.

Reisel—Bewerts: December 16th, in Jacob Pawlitz's house in Allemængel, Martin Reisel to Sarah Catharine Bewerts; witnesses the bride's parents and others.

Hopkins—Roosberry: January 6th, 1745, in Henry Gibson's house, James Hopkins to Mary Roosberry; witnesses Henry Gibson and Frank Gibson.

Jacks—Herp: December 26th, in Jacob Keller's house, Michael Jacks to Catharine Herp (Luth.); witnesses Jacob Keller and Nicholas Schappert.

Schappert—Stockschleger: April 17th, 1746, Nicholas Schappert to Mary Clara Stockschleger; witnesses the bride's father and Wendel Helffer.

Hecht—Fridrich: January 1st, 1747, William Hecht to Barbara Fridrich; witnesses several Catholics and some others.

Riffel——————: January 8th, Jacob Riffel to Mary Catharine ——————; witnesses Maurice Lorentz and his wife.

[Here there is a wide gap of eleven years in the marriage registry. Why this record is resumed at all, while that of baptisms is not, will, most probably, ever remain a mystery. The entries of marriages for the six years beginning with 1758 are in the same handwriting as those we have already given. They are as follows :]

Ehrman—Sigfrid : January 30th, 1758, in George Sigfrid's house in the Oley hills, John Ehrman to Eva Sigfrid ; witnesses George Sigfrid, the bride's father, John Michael and Andrew, her brothers, and others.

Ledermann—Becker : February 6th, in Philadelphia, John Ledermann to Catharine Becker.

Kientz—Geidlinger : at the same time and place, Michael Kientz to Catharine Geidlinger.

Riedacker—Brunner : April 19th, 1759, in the chapel [at Goshenhoppen], Jacob Riedacker (Luth.) to Anna Mary Brunner ; witnesses Maurice Lorentz and Nicholas Frantz.

Fricker—Kohl : April 16th, 1760, in the chapel [at Goshenhoppen], John Fricker, widower, to Salome Kohl ; witnesses Michael Kohl, Maurice Lorenz and others.

Kohl—Becher : in George Kohl's house, Michael Kohl to Elizabeth Becher ; witnesses the bridegroom's father, the bride's father and others.

Zipp—Schreik : June 26th, 1761, in the chapel [at Goshenhoppen], Joseph Zipp to Apollonia Schreik ; witnesses Maurice Lorenz and John Wendel Lorenz.

Müller—Grünewald : April 19th, in Edward Cardy's [McCarty] house, Michael Müller to Elizabeth Grünewald ; witnesses the bride's father and others.

Bock—Kohl : April 21st, in George Kohl's house, Nicholas Bock to Apollonia Kohl ; witnesses the bride's parents and others.

Lorentz—Reppert : May 12th, in the chapel [at Goshenhoppen], Maurice Lorentz to Mary Apollonia Reppert ; witnesses Nicholas Cardy, Wendel Lorentz and others.

Reppert—Peter : June 30th, *ibid.*, Melchior Reppert to Barbara Peter ; witnesses Mathias Reichart, Joseph Lorentz and others.

Eimold—Meck : April 22d, 1762, *ibid.*, Peter Eimold to Marian Meck ; witnesses Maurice Lorentz and Joseph Lorentz.

Egg— —— : October 26th, *ibid.*, John Egg, Sr., widower, to Mary Magdalen ——— ; witnesses Francis Hartman and Maurice Lorentz.

Keffer—Hartmann : November 7th, in Christopher Henrich's house, Peter Keffer to Barbara Hartmann ; witnesses Joseph Lorentz and Wendel Lorentz.

Sigfrid—Zweyer : November 8th, in Zweyer's house in the Oley Hills, Andrew Sigfrid to Mary Agatha Zweyer ; witnesses Jacoh Kuhn and Paul Huck.

Stahl—Kolb : December 13th, *ibid.*, Michael Stahl to Margaret Kolb ; witnesses Paul Huck and Anthony Zinck.

Shaw—Carroll : December 20th, in John Faller's house, Denis Shaw to Ann Carroll ; witnesses Philip McDeed and his wife.

Huck—Zweyer : April 11th, 1763, in Zweyer's house, Paul Huck to Julianna Zweyer ; witnesses the bride's parents and others.

Lorentz—Kauffmann : June 7th, in the chapel [at Goshenhoppen], Wendel Lorentz to M. Eva Kauffmann ; witnesses Maurice Lorentz, Joseph Lorentz and others.

Zweyer—Stahl : June 13th, in Zweyer's house, Stephen Zweyer to Anna Mary Stahl ; witnesses the bridegrom's parents and others.

Leibig—Kraus : August 2d, in the chapel [at Goshenhoppen], John Leibig to Gertrude Kraus ; witnesses George Demand and John Bischoff.

Bewerts—Eckroth : August 14th, in Philip Schmid's house in Magunshi, Conrad Bewerts to Anna Margaret Eckroth.

[Thus ends Father Schneider's marriage register ; and before the arrival of Father De Ritter only one more marriage is recorded in the book, namely, the following :]

Grünewald—Schmidt : June 18th, 1765, in Macunshi, by Father Farmer, John Grünewald to Barbara Schmidt ; witnesses Henry Fredder, Christian Henrich and Mathias Riffel.

III. BURIALS.

[Of these only three are recorded before Father De Ritter came to Goshenhoppen, and none of them are dated ; they are :]

Kuhn, Margaret, daughter of Henry and —— Kuhn, died July 19th, from being burnt while her parents were away attending a religious service at Magunshi, buried July 21st, near her father's house at Cedron Creek.

Maguin, Mary, wife of Henry Maguin, buried May 27th at Dinekum [Tinicum].

Bisping, Henry, commonly called "the old Hollander," died December 13th, after having been fortified with the last rites, buried December 15th, near the church used in common by the Calvinists and the Lutherans, above Goshenhopen.

DEPARTMENT OF GENEALOGIES.

IN response to the circular of the Genealogical Committee published in the first volume of these " Records," the following genealogies have been furnished the AMERICAN CATHOLIC HISTORICAL SOCIETY, and several others are in course of preparation for subsequent publication or filing in the Society's archives. The Committee has lost by death since its last report the valuable services of Mr. Thompson Westcott; and Mr. Edward J. Aledo has been appointed to the vacancy thus created.

CHARLES H. A. ESLING,

Chairman of Committee.

NOVEMBER 20th, 1888.

ESLING.·

PRELIMINARY NOTE.

The name of ESLING is a primitive in family nomenclature, and in its various spellings of Esling, Asling, Isling, etc., can be traced back to very remote antiquity. Frequently the penultimate S is doubled, sometimes this second S is changed into T, thus Estling or Esterling, though probably the inserted T instead of indicating a harsher form denotes a derivative of totally different root coming from Oester or East, signifying much the same thing as our English Easter, and indicating one who comes from the East, whereas the softer form has, as will be shown, quite a different signification. It is noteworthy that in England the T is more frequently inserted than in Germany. Ferguson in his " Teutonic Name System applied to the Family Names of France, England and Germany," published by Williams & Howgate, London, 1864, says, on page 119, that the particles *as, os, es,* etc., are Norse words signfying much the same as the Greek *Theos,* or the Latin *Deus,* and applicable to the Norsemen's god, Odin, the counterpart of the Jupiter of the classic mythology or the Jehovah of Hebrew theology. The termination *ling* is well known to be simply a diminutive; thus combining the two and allowing for different aspirations of the initial vowel, we have ESLING, the very example quoted by the author, and which may be translated a little god or the son of a god, to wit: a decendant of Odin. The Saxon word *Ing* also means a meadow, and sometimes a home, from which is probably derived our modern word *Ingle*, meaning a hearth or fireside, while in Icelandic dialect *ling* means a heath.

A somewhat different rendition is given of the word Esslingen, the name of the well-known Imperial Free City of Suabia, Wurtemburg, which name is said to be a derivation of the compound German words *Eisen*, iron, and *Klingen*, to clink, *i. e.*, by striking, hence the compound, to work in iron. May we not be permitted to accommodate this with the previous interpretation, and then by translating it back to German get Es ein-Klinger, God, a blow striker; *i. e.*, Odin, the thunderer. (*See Webster's Dictionary*, edition of 1861, page 1424.)*

Esslingen is an imperial city of Suabia, stuated on the river Neckar, about nine miles from Stuttgart. It was founded in the eighth century. Its antiquity is proved by the fact that Charlemagne mentions it under the name of *Cella Ezzelinga* in a patent of collection, which he accorded to Volrad, Abbot of the Church of St. Denys, at Esslingen, in which he allows him to collect not only at Esslingen, but also at Germund, to relieve the necessities of certain convents. For an interesting account of the city, see Moreis' *Dictionnaire Historique*. This account comes down, however, only to the eighteenth century, and subsequent authors must be consulted for the city's later history.† The arms of the city as given in Helmer's *Wappens Buch*, Vol. II., plates of cities, page 16, are an Eagle *Sable* displayed on a shield *Or*. In the same work, published at Nuremberg, edition of 1700, and which seems to be a standard authority on German Heraldry, certainly a very copious one, under the head of *Schlessingische*, that is, *of or belonging to Silesia*, is the coat of arms marked "DIE ESSLINGER," that is, THE ESLINGS, the German termination being the nominative plural of the patronymic Esling, meaning and referring to the entire family, Esslinger and Esling being the same name generically, the later generations dropping the termination *er*.

---

* "The name of this God is spelt *Odin* when referred to as the object of Scandinavian worship; *Woden* when applied directly to the deity of the Saxons."—*Bulwer's Harold*, note to chapter II.

† "For a full and amusing account of Meister Heinrich von Esslingen, *i. e.*, 'Master Henry, of the city of Esslingen,' a famous troubadour and satirist, who, about the year 1280, conducted a school of minnesingers in that town from which he took his name, see *Didot, Nouvelle Biographie Universelle*, edited by Dr. Hofer; 46 volumes, Paris, 1852–1866; and also Larousse, Vol. VII., page 955. He was particularly severe in satirizing Rudolph of Hapsburg, on his accession to the imperial throne. His poems preserved in *MS*. in the imperial library (Paris ?) marked No. 7566, have a curious colored portrait as a frontispiece."

" Arms, *or*, a tortoise in pale, *vert*, the shield surmounted by a mantle and helmet full-faced. Crest, from a ducal coronet, *or*, two wings addossed of the first, charged over both with a tortoise, paleways *vert*."

This would clearly indicate that the family bearing these arms was of ducal rank in Silesia, and knighted prior to the year 1605, the date of the publication of the *Wappens Buch*. But this is not all. That this family was one of prominence may be inferred from the fact that Marc de Wilson, Sieur de la Colombiere, chevalier de l'ordre de St. Michel, etc., etc., in his celebrated work, *La Science Héroique*, Paris, 1644, page 342, and plate No. 44, in treating of the typical signification of animals in heraldic emblazonment selects this shield: DIE ESSLINGER, from among all the arms of continental Europe, as the best exemplification of THE TORTOISE, and thus quaintly comments upon it :

" DIE ESLINGER, en Silesie, d' *or*, a une tortue de Sable Montant. La Tortue est le Symbole de parrasse, et quelquesuns anssi luy ont fait representer la garde de Virginité, pource qu'étant tardive & n'abandonnant jamais sa maison, cela signifie qu'elle qui est curieuse de se la conserver, doit peu souvent parôitre en public, d'où est venu ce beau mot de Boëze: *Casta pudicitiam servat domus*. Les poètes ont feint que la tortue porte toujours sa maison sur le dos, pource que Jupiter ayant comie aux nopeces de Thetis tous les animaux, ils y comparûrent tous excepté la Tortue, ce quay de grand Dieu indigné en voulut savoir la cause, qui fut pour toute raison qui'il n'y avoit meilleur logis que chez soi elle se tenait contente et ne le vouloit abandonner, ce qui obligea Jupiter à la condamner à porter toujours sa maison sur soy."*

Two things are to be noted here, first, that the date of the publication of *La Science Héroique*, 1644, confirms what has been said about these arms having been granted prior to 1605, the date of the earliest edition of Helmer's work, and secondly, while Helmers gives the color of the tortoise *vert*, Wilson makes it *sable*. The commentator, however, does not

---

[* The following is a translation of the *words* of the author, but it would be scarcely possible to repeat in English the quaint *spirit* of the old French text :

" DIE ESSLINGER. In Silesia, *or*, a tortoise *Sable* mounting. The tortoise is the emblem of sloth, and some have likewise represented it as the typical guardian of virginity ; because being sluggish and never leaving its house, it signifies that whoever is anxious to preserve this gift, ought to appear but seldom in public ; whence comes the beautiful sentiment of Boetius : *A chaste house preserveth purity*.

" The poets have pretended that the tortoise always bears its house on its back, because Jupiter having invited all the animals to the wedding of Thetis, they all came but this one, whereat this great deity being justly indignant, inquired the cause, and received for his only answer, that the tortoise being unable to find any better lodging than its own home, was quite content to stay there, and declined to leave it, whereupon Jupiter declared it should never go out of it, and at once fastened the house to the reptile's back."]

seem to have remembered the fact that, at least from the days of Æsop, the tortoise has also been regarded as the exemplar of that patient virtue so well expressed in the canting motto of the Onslow family of England: *Festina Lente.*

"The tortoise is a long-lived animal and cannot be destroyed without some difficulty, ... and its shell is invulnerable to every attack of the most formidable foe; this may imply its proper use in armory." (Book of Family Crests, volume I, page 161, London, Reeves & Turner, 1882).

The name was probably introduced into modern Europe by the Ostermen or Saxons; this would account for its being common in Saxony or southern Germany. Thence it was probably borne by the Saxon invaders into Britain and perpetuated in ENGLAND, where it undoubtedly has a very ancient foothold. Another theory is, that it may have been brought by the Norsemen, under Rollo, into France, thence spreading from Normandy into western France, the Rhineland and southern Germany, and finally carried over into England by the Norman conquerors under William I.

It is said to be very common in Lincolnshire and along the east coast of England, and where it is spelt *Asling*, it is *authoritatively* supposed to be only a corrupted form of *Esling*. It is also perpetuated in "Islington," a suburb of London, probably nothing more than a contraction of Islings'town. Miss Strickland, in her "Queens of England," mentions that Adelicia of Louvaine, Queen consort of Henry I. and niece of Pope Calixtus II., gave her manor of ESSLINGHAM for a hospital; the termination *ham* signifies home, *i. e.*, Esling's home or village. The Earl of Ravensworth of Ravensworth Castle, Gateshead, Durham, before his succession to the Earldom, at the death of his father, Thomas Henry Liddell, in March, 1878, took his title as heir of Ravensworth from Esslington Park, and was known in the baronage as Lord Esslington. He authorizes the statement under date of May 22d, 1878, that Esslington Park, one of the Earl of Ravensworth's seats located in Northumberland, about forty miles from Newcastle-on-Tyne, has held that name from time long anterior to its possession by his family, well nigh immemorial, and as corroborative of this statement the following passage from Ferguson's work already referred to may be added: "All founders of the Anglo-Saxon kingdom claim a descent from Odin, but it was only in the Northumbrian branch that the name was common. This word *as* is nearly peculiar to the royal god-born race of Northumberland, and occurs rarely in the south of England." Of course, this remark might be equally applied to all family names beginning with the same particle, such as Ascot, Oscott, Osburn, etc., etc., but then the name ESLING possesses this peculiarty, in that, even at this late time, it is still as essentially German as English, never having lost its originally Teutonic character, and practical retention at home, by its adoption and adaptation in England;

which thing cannot be strictly said concerning the others here mentioned, which have a peculiarly English savor.

Coming down to the times subsequent to the Norman conquest, we find the name firmly established in England ; among the list of the English nobility and gentry who accompanied Richard I. Coeur-de-Lion to the crusades, which list of names is given in Wiffen's translation of Tasso's "JERUSALEM DELIVERED," published by Appleton & Co., New York, 1861, and was gathered from various old rolls and documents therein mentioned, appears the name of RAFFE DE ESLYNGE, and the compiler of that list declares that of the Norman Crusaders mentioned therein he has selected only such as from the evidence of old charters he knows to have possessed English fiefs.

Burke, in his armorial, under the various spellings of the name of ES-LING, gives no less than eight different coats of arms of the various branches of the family bearing it in England. Edmonstone in his Heraldry, Vol. I., page 32, index to the Ordinary of Arms, and in the Alphabet of arms, Vol. II., Berry's *Enclycopedia Hearaldrica*, Ordinary of Arms, page 12, and again in Vol. III., repeats several of these with slight variations. The most common and apparently correct of all being " ESLINGE *Azure*, a bend cotised, *argent*, between six boars' heads of the second couped ;" to one of these a crest is added " a demi talbot *gules* in the dexter paw a battle axe ; " yet between these coats of arms, even when a T is inserted in the name, there is always sufficient similarity to indicate throughout a common family stock, *azure* and *argent* being the predominant colors, and the boar's head and bend the prevailing emblazonment, though sometimes *or* and *gules* are substituted as colors, and in one instance *sable*. " ESLINGTON," however, seems to prefer " swans " and " crosses."

IN FRANCE, the name is not indigenous. The French word *Eslingue*, from the verb *Eslinguer*, meant, in ancient French military language, a soldier whose weapon was a sling. Wherever the name does appear, however, in that country, it obviously is derived, not from that verb, but is simply the old German form transplanted to French territory. John Evelyn in his quaint Diary, Vol. I., page 64, writing under date Paris, March, 1644, says he went : " Thence to Essone, a house of Mons'r. Essling, who is a great vertuoso ; there are many good payntings in it, but nothing so observable as his gardens, fountaines, fish pooles especially yt in a triangular forme, the water cast out by a multitude of heads about it ; there is a noble cascade and pretty bathes with all accommodations, under a marble table is a fountaine of serpents twisting about a globe." This is the earliest mention of the name in that country which the complier of this paper has yet found. The prevalence of the name in modern France, as a title of nobility, is due entirely to General Massena's having gained his great victory at the village of Essling, near Vienna, in Austria. Napoleon, as was his manner of rewarding his victorious marshals, created him Duke of Rivoli and Prince of Essling. The title still continues in Massena's descendants, and is to be found on many statues throughout France, and on the keystone of the *Arc de Triomphe de l'Étoile*, at Paris, and is also the designation of one of the new Boulevards of the same city, "Avenue d'Essling." The old Princess of Essling, Duchess of Rivoli, who was mistress of the wardrobes to the Empress Eugenie, accompanied her in her flight from the Tuilleries at the overthrow of the second Empire, and it may scarcely be necessary to add that the collection of the Prince of Essling in the Philadelphia Academy of the Fine Arts was the gift of Massena to that institution. It is obvious, however, that there is no blood connection between the family name and the French title.

IN ITALY, however, the case is different; here the name following Charlemagne's Latinized spelling has been unpleasantly perpetuated in the person of EZZELINO, THE TYRANT OF PADUA, who, though himself a native of Italy, having been born in the Marquisate of Treviso, was of German extraction; his father was Ezzelin, surnamed *the Monk*, who in turn was the son of Ezzelin, surnamed *the Stammerer*, and grandson of Alberic, who followed the German Emperor Otho III., and established himself in northern Italy. Moeris' *Dictionnaire Historique*, etc.

Ezzelin I., a German knight, established himself about 1036 in Italy, where the Emperor Conrad II. gave him, in recompense for his services, several fiefs and castles, including those of Onara and Romano. This last named was situated on a fortified rock, in an almost impregnable position, and from the castle the family took their name, styling themselves, when by their conquests they had grown rich and powerful, *Gli Ezzelini da Romano*. See Larousse, *Dictionnaire Universelle*, page 1236. Also *Verci, Storia degli Ezzelini*, Bassano, 1779, 3 volumes, and Venice, 1844.

IN AMERICA also the the name and family has sprung *directly* from the German stock, and, I may add, is pre-eminently CATHOLIC; and in its simple form of spelling is very rare thoroughout the United States. The following genealogy, probably including almost every descendant of the original ancestor bearing the name in this country.

The Rev. P. A. Jordan, S. J., in his gossipy History of St. Joseph's Church, Philadelphia, and published in those private annals of the Jesuits known as the Woodstock Letters, in Vol. II., No. 3, September, 1873, says: "Until 1800 the Catholics of Philadelphia, with the exception of a few families, the Hayes, Careys, *Eslings*, Meades, Barry's, FitzSimmons, Moylans, O'Brians, Powels, and Keefes were not only poor, but exceedingly humble as to their social standing."

The loss of the records of St. Joseph's Church prior to Rev. Ferdinand Farmer's Register, begining in 1758, may account for any omissions which occur in the *data* of the earlier generations, between 1740 and 1758.

All the works of reference mentioned in this note can be found in the Philadelphia Library or in that of the Pennsylvania Historical Society.

FIRST GENERATION.

JOHAN* GEORGE ESLING, a native of the Palatinate on the Rhine, or thereabouts, born *circa* 1692, sailed from Rotterdam, *via* Deal, in the ship *Loyal Judith*,† Captain Lovell Paynter, arrived at Philadelphia and qualified at the court house, November 25, 1740.‡ He settled first at Germantown, afterwards at Philadelphia, where, according to tradition, he resided on a farm, near what is now Seventh and Market streets. He was a Roman Catholic, and it is said he used to walk all the way from Germantown to St. Joseph's church, Philadelphia, to hear Mass on Sundays and holydays of obligation. His wife's name was Mary Magdalen'————. The date of his death is unknown. He is said to have been buried in a section of what is now Washington Square, Philadelphia, which was, at that time, reserved as a burial place for Catholics. There is no further date nor tradition concerning him.

SECOND GENERATION.

EXTINCT LINES.

The children of Johan George and Mary Magdalen Esling were :

I. PETER, born ————? married Maria Elizabeth ————? died ————?

II. JOHAN PAUL, treated under head of second generation surviving line, as he is the *stirps* or direct ancestor of the subsequent generations.

III. NICHOLAS, born ————? married Maria Johanna ————? died————?

IV. Eve, born ————? married Philip Schilling, died ————?

V. MARY MAGDALEN, born ————? married Emmanuel Ohms, July 2, 1767. This marriage seems to have been quite an event in the Esling family. The record in Father Farmer's handwriting is as follows :

"*1767, Philadelphiæ, Julii 2, præmissis 3 denuntiationibus, Emanuel Ohms, juvenem, et Mariam Magdalenam filiam Georgii et Magdalenæ Essling, conjugum, ambos Catholicos, præsentibus testibus Rudolpho Esling et Johanna Wilhelm, Catholicis. Postea eis in celebratione Missæ benedixi.*"

Not only were they married with a nuptial Mass, as this record proves, but it was also one of the earliest celebrated in the colony, which ceremony, from its infrequency, always gives a spiritual brilliancy to such an occasion ; but family tradition has also perpetuated the primitive splen-

---

* The prefix JOHAN seems to have been a *Lieblingenamen* among the older Germans and is practically dropped in usage.
† A companion ship to the " Charming Nancy."
‡ See Rupp's list of German settlers in Pennsylvania, page 143.

dor of the wedding feast which followed, and which, with the rustic simplicity and merriment of those days, was held under the wide-spreading
branches of a great tree which stood in front of the farm-house of the
bride's father on Seventh Street near High (now Market Street).

All the branches of Johan George Esling's children, with the single
exception of Paul, the second son, appear to have run out after the third
generation; therefore for the sake of convenience, and in order to more
easily trace the order of descent from him, the second and third generations
have been divided into two lines, the extinct and surviving, and the extinct branches treated first, then he being constituted the *stirps* or stock
of the surviving lines, he has been placed at the head of that generation instead of being considered in his regular place among his father's
issue. It ought to be added that the descent and *seniority* of Peter Esling
from Johan George is only suppositive, but founded on *very sufficient*
reasons. The descent of Nicholas Esling from Johan George is also *unsupported by proof*, but is *not reasonably doubtful*. Of the three remaining
children, Paul, Eve and Mary Magdalen, there is no question, as their
descent is established by Father Farmer's Register at St. Joseph's Church.

THIRD GENERATION.

Extinct Lines.

The issue of Peter and Mary Elizabeth Esling as far as known were:
I. John, born July 20, 1759, baptized July 29, 1759, at St. Joseph's
Church, Philadelphia, by Rev. Ferdinand Farmer; sponsors John and
Anna Maria Grosser; married November 26, 1782, by license, to Bar-
bara Keeler, at St. Michael's Zion and Lutheran Church, Philadelphia.
II. Anna Christina, born January 1, 1762, baptized January 3,
eo anno, by Rev. Ferdinand Farmer; sponsors Paul and Anna Christina
Esling, *married (suppositively)* June 14, 1778, to Francis Ward, at
Gloria Dei, Old Swedes' Church, Philadelphia.
III. Helena, born December 7, 1763, baptized January 1, 1764, by
Rev. Ferdinand Farmer; sponsors John Sauerwald and Helen Villars.
IV. James, born April 26, 1765, baptized May 26, 1765, by Rev. Ferdinand Farmer; sponsors James Rice and Mary Magdalen Esling; married May 31, 1786, at St. Joseph's Church, by Rev. Ferdinand Farmer,
to Margaret Bush. In the published lists of those who died in Philadelphia in 1793 from yellow-fever, and were buried in the *Catholic* cemeteries, appears the name of Margaret Estling; she is supposed to have
been James Esling's widow. In the burial register of the "New Chapell,"

Saint Mary's, appear the following entries: "March 22, 1789, for the burial of James Eslin's child, paid five shillings."

"July 11, 1790, James Eslin buried poor." *

V. MARGARET, born November 24, 1767, baptized December 6, *eo anno*, by Rev. Ferdinand Farmer; sponsors Henry Lechler and Margaretta Holls; married ———— GRABEL. Margaret is the only one of Peter Esling's descendants of whom any subsequent clue can be found; she lived to an advanced age and was familiarly known as "Aunt Peggy Grabel." She is said to have died a Protestant. All this is the *tradition* concerning her; there is nothing of record but her birth and baptism.

VI. JOHAN GEORGE, born January 20, 1770, baptized January 30, *eo anno*, by Rev. Ferdinand Farmer; sponsor Anna Mary Grosser.

VII. LAURENCE, born January 1, 1774, baptized January 6, *eo anno*, by Rev. Ferdinand Farmer; sponsor Anna Mary Grosser.

———

The issue of NICHOLAS and MARY JOANNA ESLING as far as can be traced were:

I. PAUL, born July 30, 1759, baptized August 4, *eo an.*, at St. Joseph's by Rev. Ferdinand Farmer; sponsors Paul and Christina Esling.

Beyond this single record nothing is known of this branch, which is supposed to have run out.†

———

* It will be observed that in St. Mary's Registry James Esling is set down as having been buried " poor "; this requires explanation. The burials at St. Mary's are recorded under three headings, " Paid," " Free " and " Poor." The first is self explanatory; the second applies to those who, from being owners of lots or pewholders, were entitled to the privilege of free burial; the third, of course, refers to charity funerals. That James Esling should have fallen under the latter classification may not be improbable, for there is a tradition that his father, Peter Esling, lost his means, though there is nothing positively known of this branch of the family beyond what is here given. It does seem strange, however, that while James' child was paid for at the then rather extravagant rate of five shillings, the father should within fourteen months afterwards have been buried "poor"; and also that there was no one of his apparently numerous, and, as we know from records, certainly at that time *wealthy* collateral relatives to remove such a stigma from him. A similar entry appears in the same register under date of August 9th, 1791: "George Esling's child, buried poor." This may have been the child of Johan George, son of Peter; if not, all clue to its idenity is lost, as from the date it could not have been a child of either the original Johan George or any of the subsequent Georges hereinafter mentioned; but the entire disappearance of Peter Esling's line, both from records and from family tradition, is altogether a most singular circumstance.

† The issue of Philip and Eve Esling Schilling, all baptized at St. Joseph's by Rev. Ferdinand Farmer, were:

A—Peter, born January 14, 1759.
B—John Michael, born February 8, 1760.
C—Anna Catharine, born February, 1762.

While treating of this generation the following records are given without the compiler being able to identify or trace the names mentioned.

Among the marriages at Gloria Dei, Old Swedes Church, besides the one already given *ante*, are found the following :

" 1772, July 5 ; Mary Esling and Ellick Frey."

" 1778, May 29 ; Hannah Esling and Andrew Dwyer."

" 1778, June 14 ; Christina Esling and Francis Ward," already traced *ante*.

" 1790, April 7 ; Sarah Esling and Jacob Schroudy." (See *postea* title " Rudolph Esling.")

In the administration records of the City of Philadelphia, it appears that Hannah Esling took out letters of administration on the estate of her deceased husband, Philip Esling, under date 1799, security being entered in £100.   The entry is No. 122, Administration Book H, page 368. "ANDREW ESLING, 229 Cedar St.," City Directory, 1814, of whom nothing is known.

SECOND GENERATION.

DIRECT SURVIVING LINE.

JOHN PAUL ESLING, second (?) son of Johan George and Mary Magdalen Esling, born *circa* 1725, a native of the Palatinate on the Rhine or thereabouts, is believed to have accompanied his father to America

D—John Philip 1st, born April 15, 1763.
E—Mary Catharine, born May 9, 1764.
F—John Philip 2d, born April 25, 1770.
G—Stephen, born August 26, 1772.
H—John Theodore, born November 6, 1773.
I—Mary Margaret, born February 8, 1776.
J—John Philip 3d, born October 29, 1778.
K—Eva Christina, born January 15, 1781.

The sponsors to the last named were Paul and Anna Christina Esling. The issue of Emmanuel and Mary Magdalen Esling Qhms, as far as known, were :

A. JAMES, born November 20, 1768, baptized November 22, by Rev. Robert Harding; sponsors Simon and Mary Magdalen Haug. [The name is here written *Holmes* in the register.]

B. MARY, born November 3, 1772, baptized by Rev. Ferdinand Farmer November 5 ; sponsors Francis Varrel and Catharine Keasey (Casey ?). [The name is here written Holmes in the register.]

Ohms is undoubtedly the original spelling, the anglicization of which is probably *Holmes*. There are three other entries in the registry in which Emmanuel and Mary Magdalen Ohms acted as sponsors, to wit : (A) Mary Lariole, daughter of John and Anna (*aliunde* La Viole), baptized December 30, 1769.   (B) Emmanuel Joseph Roderigo, son of ———— and Joseph Roderigo, August 26, 1771. (C) Matthew, son of Francis and Elizabeth Varrel baptized October 10, 1773. And in each case the name is spelt Ohms.

in 1740. He was one of the original subscribers to St. Mary's in 1758 ; his contribution for the purchase of the ground was £3 ; that for the erection of the church in 1763 was £7. One of its incorporators in 1788 ; a pew holder all his life, his pew being No. 54, middle aisle ; that is, if there was a middle aisle in the church before its enlargement in 1810, but if not, then it was on the south side, 19th from the sanctuary. One of the original trustees from 1788 consecutively, by annual re-election, to 1798 ; also one of the original trustees of the Holy Trinity German Catholic school-house property in 1788. See Deed Book, J. W., No. 8, page 660. He was also one of the list of subscribers to T. Lloyd's publication, " *The Unerring Authority of the Catholic Church*," prob-ably the first Catholic book published in the United States, Philadelphia, 1789. He was a tanner, and learned his trade with Nagle, of German-town ; but in consequence of large beds of clay having been discovered on his lands, he established his sons in the brickmaking business and created an extensive reputation in that industry.*

He owned considerable real estate throughout the city, and resided in a large old mansion on the west side of Fifth street, between Chestnut and Market streets, which property he purchased in 1785.†

---

* By an amusing misprint in one of the early city Directories, the word brickmaker after his name is made to read " breeches-maker."

† [The property in question was purchased from James Anthony Mor-ris, gentleman, of Burlington, N. J. The deed is recorded in Deed Book " D," 13, page 385. He seems to have lived here before he purchased the premises. The house stood back some distance from the street line, which was occupied by a second or smaller house, belonging to the same premises, but which was rented out by the Eslings. This latter house served as a barrier between the Esling mansion and the street, the intervening and surrounding space being occupied by a garden. The small tenement house opened, of course, on the street, but the entrance to the Esling residence was up a side passage-way on the south of the lot, which led to the entrance gate facing on the south side of the house. Most persons, for convenience, entered by this side door, although the main entrance, opening directly into the parlor, was on the east front. The south entrance led into the kitchen, which, in turn, led into a middle or dining-room, from which, by an ascent of two steps, a passage was gained into the parlor. The house was only two stories high, and the staircase rose from the middle room to the bed-chambers above. Back of the house, on the west front, the garden space continued for a short distance leading across to the stable and outbuildings, including a wood-shed, beneath which was a flat stone, upon which the fuel was usually split, until, as is related, young Mr. Morris, most probably Isaac, whose property adjoined on the south, having one morning observed some one so engaged, walked over and begged that the family in future desist from making such use of the stone, *because his father was buried beneath it*. To the north, or back of this, was the residence of the Cresson family, and to the west lay the property of Hon. Patrick Robinson, for whom there is reason to suppose the Esling house was originally built. The house was marked as No. 8 in the old Directories, and was just below the cor-ner of Minor street, which was the site of Pepper's famous brewery. It

Paul Esling was married August 4th, 1746, to Anna Christina Bitten-bender. She was a Lutheran, and the ceremony was performed at Ger-mantown, by the·Rev. Henry Muhlenberg, and the marriage is recorded in the Registry of St Michael's and Zion's Lutheran Churches, the register styling him a Catholic. She is said to have been the daughter of the burgomaster of the city of Darmstadt. Two of her brothers preceded her to America, and settled near Easton, Pa. She was seized with an intense desire to follow them, and despite her father's oppostion did so. Shortly after her arrival in this country, her brothers were killed by the Indians in the great massacre of the settlers, which took place in what is now Northampton county. After her marriage, she became a Catholic and acquired such a reputation for piety that tradition claims she was favored with a vision of the Blessed Virgin. It is said that she was praying for one of her sons, who was somewhat wayward, when Our Lady suddenly appeared before her, saying : " Fear not, he will be saved,'' and then vanished.   There is still preserved in the family her large volume of the Lives of the Saints, printed in German text, dated 1750 ; the edition being dedicated to the Empress Maria Theresa, of Austria. Christina Esling died, of yellow fever, as is supposed, in the latter part of 1793.

Paul Esling died September ———, 1798, and was buried " free " (which term has been explained *ante*) in St. Mary's churchyard, on the 21st of that month.

His will is recorded as No. 37, in Will Book Y. A. D., 1798.

THIRD GENERATION.

SURVIVING LINE.

The children of Paul and Anna Christina Esling, as far as known,. were :

I. NICHOLAS, born, ———.

Among the list of the inhabitants of the Province of Pennsylvania be-

---

was not torn down until about 1853, and this description of it was furnished by one who was a frequent visitor to it. Thompson Westcott, in a description of the square published in the Philadelphia *Ledger*, about the beginning of October, 1887, curiously enough makes no allusion to any of the private residences above mentioned.

For the subsequent history of this property, which is very interesting,. see Deed Book S. H. F., No. 11, page 78 ; Sheriff's Deed Book O, page 203 ; Deed Book L. T. C., No. 5, page 110 ; Deed Book T. H., No. 98, page 241 ; Also Esling *vs.* Williams, 10 Barr, Penna. State Reports,. page 126 ; and Esling *vs.* Zantzinger, 1 Harris, 13 Penna. State Reports, page 50.

For other properties owned by him, see Sheriff's Deed Book B, No. 3, page 421, O. C. P.; and Deed Book D, 40, page 240.   Also Deed Book G. W. R., No. 16, page 638.

tween the years 1776 and 1786 who took the oath of allegiance to the newly created State government after the Declaration of Independence, appears, under date December 27, 1781, the name of *"Nicholas Esling, lately deserted from the British lines at New York."* He was also a member of the FRIENDLY SOCIETY about 1795. He was one of the earliest pewholders of St. Mary's Roman Catholic Church, his pew being part of No. 3, south gallery, and trustee of the church from 1798, consecutively till 1803. He was also one of the original pewholders of St. Augustine's Church, 1800. His name also appears on the list of subscribers to Thomas Lloyd's publication, " The Unerring Authority of the Catholic Church," reprinted in Philadelphia, 1789. On May 26th, 1800, Patrick Henehan, trustee of St. Mary's Church, bought, at public sale, two lots on Thirteenth street, between Pine and Spruce, for a burying ground. Nicholas Esling loaned $1000 to purchase the ground and to pay a claim of Mr. Peacam. The house and lot next to St. Mary's Church was mortgaged to Mr. Esling as security. (See minutes for St. Mary's trustees.) This mortgage was satisfied of Record Mortgage Book E. F., No. 2, page 276. He was very wealthy and owned, besides the family mansion and grounds on Fifth street, considerable real estate of his own acquisition. (See Deed Book S. W. R., 16, page 638.) His brickyards occupied what is now the entire square between Walnut and Locust, Sixteenth and Seventeenth streets. This property he purchased in 1801, and it remained in the hands of his heirs until 1828, when they sold it to Charles Wharton. (See Deed Book G.W.R., No. 21, pages 414 and 416.) In " Robert Morris's Report of his Debts," etc., No. 147, Ledger C., folio 86 (Printed List, page 49), is this entry: " NICHOLAS ESLING. This account is for Bricks, at his credit, $120.00."

Nicholas Esling was married at St. Joseph's by Rev. Ferdinand Farmer, September 24, 1784, to Catherine, daughter of Henry and Barbara Snyder.*

She survived her husband and carried on his business. She furnished the bricks for the enlargement of "St. Mary's Chapple " 1808; bill $224.27½. (See original documents, A. C. H. S.) Her name appears as one of the signers to the call to support the compromise ticket offered by the " Bishop's Party " during the Hogan troubles at St. Mary's. In consequence of the sudden and terrible death of her son Samuel (see *postea*) she became melancholy during the latter years of her life. She died intestate in 1842. She is set down in city Directories as " widow of Nicholas Esling " and " Mrs. Esling, gentlewoman, 8 South Fifth street." Nicholas Esling died December, 1803. His will is recorded as No. 105, Will Book No. 1, 1803, page 158.

---

* The somewhat amusing will of Henry Snyder, who was a prominent Catholic, can be seen in Will Book W, page 213, will No. 126, and for the lists of his children see Deed Book G. W. R., No. 1, page 633, and St. Joseph's Church Registers of Baptisms and Marriages.

II. MARY EVE, born March 25, 1759, and baptized at St. Joseph's by Rev. Ferdinand Farmer, April 5, 1759; sponsors Philip and Eve Schilling, the latter being her father's sister. Her baptismal name was appropiate to the day of her birth, the festival of *The Annunciation*, but for some inexplicable reason she always signed herself *Anna* Eve, or simply Eve. She was of an exceedingly lively and lovable disposition, and with her two elder sisters, mentioned hereafter, was accounted quite a beauty. When the British troops took possession of Philadelphia in the autumn of 1777, the soldiers were billeted upon the inhabitants, each family being obliged to quarter a certain number of officers or men; but when the commander-in-chief, Sir William Howe, whose headquarters were on Market street, near Sixth street, close to Paul Esling's house on Fifth street,* was consulted as to how many men should be billeted upon the family, he replied, "*not a man shall be quartered in the house with those three pretty Esling girls.*" The family, however, were obliged to furnish their quota of provisions, and among the family relics long preserved by Eve Esling's grandchildren was a large iron pot from which, according to tradition, both the Hessian and American soldiers were fed. One day during the winter of 1777–78, the period of the British occupation, the supply of flour for the family gave out, and there was no means of procuring any in the city, Eve volunteered to solve the difficulty by declaring that if her brother Nicholas would catch her a horse *she* would go to Germantown after some. The horses of the British troopers were then roaming loose about the neighboring commons, so Nicholas, possessing himself of one by "French leave," led it up to the house, and Eve, throwing the flour bag across the animal's back, prepared for her adventurous and risky journey. To the repeated inquiries of the family as to how she was going to pass the British lines, she laughingly replied that she would manage the matter, and they, knowing, and probably having full confidence in her dare-devil spirit, allowed her to depart. Now it had so happened that in looking out of the window early that same morning she had observed General Howe passing, and with quick ingenuity seized upon that slight circumstance as the foundation of her plan. Riding leisurely along, she soon approached the pickets, and was, of course, challenged by the guard. "Where are you going?" "To Germantown after flour." "But you cannot pass without an order." "Oh, that's all right," said Eve, carelessly, "*I've seen General Howe.*" Whether it was that her pretty "face was her fortune," or that her glistening eye, like that of Coleridge's Ancient Mariner, held the sentry spellbound, and instinctively taught him that she was not to be trifled with,

---

* Paul Esling purchased this property only in 1785, but appears to have lived there before he became its owner. The house referred to as Howe's Headquarters was the same afterwards occupied by Washington as President of the United States. It belonged to Mrs. William Masters, afterwards Mrs. Richard Penn.

we know not; but certain it is that, unlike the thick-headed Scotch sentinel told of in one of Punch's jokes, the Briton or Hessian on guard at the outposts of Philadelphia never once thought of demanding that she should *show him the verbal orders*, but allowed her at once to pass. So she made her six miles journey through the British lines to Germantown, and returned triumphantly with her bag of flour; and lived for nearly four score years afterwards to tell the tale "with unaffected glee" to all her latest descendants.

Her husband, Michael Waltman, was said to have been of noble lineage. His father, Emmanuel Waltman, was an Alsatian by birth and had been head forester to the Dukes of Saxe Coburg-Gotha,* hence, possibly, the origin of the name, which, after the German fashion, most generally bespoke the occupation of the individual; thus Waldmann would signify, in the original German, a woodman, from *wald*, a wood or forest, and *mann*, a man. While in the discharge of his official duties his personal attractions succeeded in winning for him the affections of the Princess Margaret von Gotha, a younger daughter of that ducal house. They were secretly married and then fled to America, where they settled in Virginia, near what is now the town of Berlin, in the present county of Louden, where some of their decendants still reside, and where both Emmanuel and Margaret Waltman lie buried in the Lutheran cemetery. One of their sons, Michael, migrated thence to Pennsylvania, and became the husband of Eve Esling; he was in comparatively humble circumstances, but is said to have been very fine looking and much esteemed by his wife's family. His father, Emmanuel Waltman, was a Luthern, and so intensely hostile to Catholicity that when his son Michael became a convert to that Church, he threatened to shoot him if he ever approached the paternal roof, and is said to have kept a rifle always at hand for that purpose. He did not, however, disinherit him, as he is mentioned in his father's will, which is on record in Louden county. These data, except when otherwise noted, are all traditional, but there are records extant of deeds to Michael Waltman's heirs as far back as 1790, in the town of Montgomery, Harrison county, Virginia.

Mr. and Mrs. Waltman lived, after their marriage, first on Front street, near Pine. Among their immediate neighbors were: Captain Stephen Decatur, afterwards the celebrated Commodore Decatur, and Captain, afterwards Comodore, Truxton; and it is said that Mrs. Waltman used to excite the jealousy of some of her female neighbors by the attention which her good looks and effective manners won for her from Captain Truxton.

Her husband and she resided in this locality until the breaking out of the yellow fever in 1793, when they removed, as a matter of sanitary precaution, to their farm house, situated at what is now Locust street,

---

* The same family as H. R. H. Albert, the Prince Consort of Queen-Victoria of England.

just above Eleventh street, on the north side, which at that time was far out into the country, with a creek running across Eleventh street, spanned by a bridge ; and so open were the intervening fields that she used to stand in her doorway on Sundays and see the congregation coming out of the " New Chapell " of St. Mary's, on Fourth street, near Spruce street, which by that time was " new " no longer except in a comparative sense. A queer little old house it was, as the author of this paper remembers it, having originally stood upon a hillock with three steps up to the ascent ; but after the grading of the city it was deposed from its lofty position, with two or three steps leading *down* to the front door below the level of the pavement ; the door itself being a " Dutch door," that is, after the fashion of old time country houses, being divided breadthways through the middle. The house itself was of frame front and a brick rear ; the latter portion being at this time, 1888, still standing and adjoining the large academy property which some of the members of the American Catholic Historical Society desired lately to purchase for the use and occupation of that body. The frame work of the house was made at and transported from Valley Forge. A charming old-time body, too, was she, who for many years a widow dwelt therein, as the writer distinctly remembers both the house and its occupant, he having been sometimes taken there by his mother or grandparents when he was not more than four or five years old ; and he remembers to this day, as one who glances at a time-faded picture, seeing the old lady standing once of a beautiful summer evening, a quaint figure, framed, as it were, in the quaint old doorway. She was fond of keeping up many of the old German customs, and always had cakes or something good for the children ; and it has been said that old Mrs. Waltman's Christmas dinner-board, no matter how many delicacies it boasted, never failed to display among them the Teutonic conventionality a roast goose and sour kraut.

She subsequently purchased from the estate of David Holahan the property on the southeast corner of Eleventh and Locust streets. (See Deed Book J. C., No. 27, page 63.)

This David Holahan's widow, formerly Hannah Dale, took for her second husband William Waltman, the only son of Michael and Eve Waltman, who, as far as can be discovered, left no issue. Mrs. Eve Waltman was a pewholder of St. Mary's, but lost her pew because she declined to recognize the "Hoganite" trustees, the powers that rightfully were. Contrary to the advice of Mr. Jacob Holahan, who, though himself an anti-Hoganite, recognized their authority *de facto*, she declined paying her pew rent, and in this she was sustained by Charles Johnson, a prominent pewholder of the "Bishop's Party." On account of some legal quibble he told her nothing was legally due. She took his advice. When, some time afterwards, she determined upon paying it, she went before the Board of Trustees to do so, they looked sheepishly, one at the other. Finally one of them, who afterwards became a member of the Philadelphia Judiciary, spoke up and said : " Madam, your pew is sold." She replied: "My pew sold? Gentlemen, you might as well have come and sold my house over my head."

She had survived her husband many years, and lived herself, hale and hearty, to the good old age of ninety-two years, and died in 1849. She had in all ten children, seven sons and three daughters. Most of her sons and one daughter died young. Of the one already mentioned as having married, William, there is a fine portrait extant, depicting him in his boyhood, and a very charming face it is. Another one of her sons, being in failing health, had gone to England for the benefit to be derived from the voyage, but returned home in a dying condition. As soon as his ship arrived at the wharf word was sent to her, and she hastened to see him. On the way she met him being borne on a couch. As she approached he was rapidly sinking. The bearers happened to be near St. Joseph's church, and they carried him in. He had scarcely time to recognize his mother and receive the last Sacraments, and then died at the very gates of the Sanctuary.

It is said that Mrs. Waltman had a Teutonic aversion for the Irish, yet by a singular fatality, and strongly against her will, her two daughters who lived to womanhood both married Irishmen. One of them, Catharine, married Dr. James Greene, who was for many years the oldest surgeon in the United States Navy, and who was stationed some forty years ago at the Philadelphia Naval Asylum, and at the city of St. Louis, after making several professional voyages. At this wedding Mr. and Mrs. Jacob Way Holahan were the witnesses of honor. Dr. Greene died June 9, 1871, and is buried in St. John's churchyard, Thirteenth street above Chestnut, of which church he was a pewholder of long standing. His wife died January, 1880, and is buried beside him. Their issue was one son, Dr. Francis V. Greene, also of the U. S. Navy, and still residing (1888) in Philadelphia. He had two children, one son, James Montgomery Greene, unmarried, and a daughter, Laura, married December 22, 1887, to Mr. Arthur Sylvester. Of the three daughters of Dr. James Greene, Mary, Margaret and Catharine Ella, all well known in Protestant as well as in Catholic society in Philadelphia, the last named alone married, her husband being Mr. De Becquer, of Cuba, and died some years ago. Her issue were two daughters, Agnes, unmarried, and Stella, betrothed to Count Filipo Marini, of Naples, Italy, both now residing with their aunt, in Rome, and one son, Rupert, who, after graduating from college in Europe, returned to the United States, and died after a sudden illness in his twenty-third year, unmarried, December 15, 1887, at Trinidad, Cuba, whither he had just gone on a short business visit. He was buried there. Mrs. Greene was Mrs. Waltman's younger daughter; the elder, Mary Ann, married Mr. Patrick O'Reilly, and was one of the pioneers of Catholicity in the city of Cincinnati. She died April 4th, 1875, and from an obituary notice in one of the Cincinnati papers, *The Enquirer*, the following account of her has been taken:

"THE SUNSET OF LIFE.

" DEATH OF THE OLDEST CATHOLIC IN CINCINNATI.

" Mrs. Mary Ann O'Reilly, the oldest Catholic in this city, died at her home on East Pearl street, yesterday morning, at seven o'clock. She will be remembered by the older inhabitants as the relict of Patrick O'Reilly, who was many years ago a prominent citizen of Cincinnati. Mrs. O'Reilly was in the 85th year of her age, which, besides being the oldest Catholic of the city, made her about the oldest female resident. There was much in her life that was strange, if not romantic. Her girlhood was spent in Philadelphia, where she married at the age of twenty-two. In her youth she was recognized as a great beauty, and even now, as she lies still and cold in death's embrace, at the close of a long and good life, the faded traces of a ripe and mellow loveliness enshroud her features. We saw a portrait of her, painted when she was in the prime of her womanhood, and we were struck with the marvelous wealth of beauty which makes it up. It reminded the writer of portraits which he had seen of some of England's celebrated court beauties. To look at the portrait without being acquainted with its history one would be inclined to think he was gazing upon some poet's ideal.

" Her husband preceded her to Cincinnati by a year, at the end of which time—during 1815—she followed him, and since then has never lived elsewhere. Her husband, immediately upon his arrival in this city, erected a sugar refinery on Arch street near Ludlow, but soon after quit the business and connected himself with the Perry Brothers in brewing malt liquors, which we believe he followed until his death, in 1836. The widow never married again, but lived a faithful relict, cherishing a fond remembrance of him who had been her lover, her husband and the father of her children. With her great womanly beauty she could have married again before the grass had grown green upon her dead husband's grave. Suitors she had by the score, all anxious to take the place made vacant by her husband's death, and among them was Governor Brown, Chief Executive of the State.

" Her early experience in this city as a devotee of the Catholic Church was a strange one. When she first came on here from her Eastern home she was grieved to find that there was no church of her faith at this place, and not even a congregation or a priest. Six persons, including herself, were in the habit of meeting in a small room ten by twelve feet, situated in a house which, at that time, stood on Flat-iron Square, and there to worship in a manner after their belief and opportunities.

" That may be said to have been the nucleus of the Roman Catholic Church in Cincinnati, which to day consists of forty places of worship, and a membership of seventy-five thousand persons. Of these six original Catholics who, sixty years ago, met for worship in the little room on

Flat-iron Square, the deceased was the last. She had lived in the little stone house which stands away back from the street, on the north side west of the alley, midway between Pearl and Lawrence streets, ever since the year 1839. Three children out of ten that were born to her survive their mother.

"Mrs. Catharine Sheppard of Brown county, the first born, is now sixty years of age, though like her mother is still a handsome, hale lady, looking twenty years younger than what she really is. Mrs. Christie is living in New Orleans, and Miss Margaret O'Reilly lived with her mother in the old homestead, a faithful, loving daughter and a great comfort to the aged parent in her declining years. We had the painful duty only a few weeks ago to record the death of the only surviving son, William O'Reilly, who for many years had been a favorite engineer of the City Fire Department, with headquarters at the Ten's engine-house. His death made a great void in the home of the aged mother and devoted daughter, leaving them alone and lonely. Captain Frank O'Reilly, another son, was killed in front of Fort Donelson while at his post on board Comodore Foot's flag ship, the St. Louis. Still another son, Charles, contracted a fatal disease while serving as a private in the Union army, came home and shortly afterwards died. All three lie neath the sod in Spring Grove, where that which is earthly of their mother will join them to-morrow. The funeral services will be conducted by Father Driscoll from St. Xavier's Church, to-morrow morning at 9 o'clock, by the celebration of Requiem High Mass. Inasmuch as deceased is a pioneer of the Church, there will doubtless be an immense turnout of Catholic citizens to pay a tribute of respect to the venerable remains."

III. FREDERICK, born May 8, 1761, baptized at St. Josephs by Rev. F. Farmer May 17, 1781. Among the list of inhabitants of the Province of Pennsylvania who took the oath of allegiance to the State Government after the Declaration of Independence, appears under date of "Oct. 12, 1784, Frederick Esling, son of Paul Esling, of Philadelphia, a native, come to the age of 21 years." (See list of same published by Thompson Westcott.) "Frederick Esling ran away from the ship General Green, of the Pennsylvania Navy, August 22, 1799." "This ship was in commission only about six months; great difficulty was experienced in manning her, the men running away." (For the full history of this ship, with a list of her officers and men, see Pennsylvania Archives, vol. 1, pages 237 and 300–304.) He bought, February 27, 1799, a property on Spruce street between Thirteenth and Juniper, where he lived. (See Deed Book "D, 74," page 299, and Administration Book "H," page 61, No. 243.) Of his marriage there can be found no record, but his wife survived him, as she is set down in the City Directory after his death as "Mary Esling, widow, Juniper Lane." He is believed to have had issue, one son and one daughter, of whom there is no record. He died intestate in 1800.

IV. MARY MAGDALEN[2] born —— ——, baptized —— ——.   The only matter of record proving the existence of this daughter is the 9th item of her father's will, which reads : " I bequeath to my daughter, Mary Hawke's children, Frederick, Elizabeth and Ann, ten pounds Pennsylvania currency each."   But wherein the records fail, tradition, to a certain extent, supplies.   It is said that she was engaged to be married to Thomas Carroll ; the wedding day was fixed, and the guests had actually assembled to witness the ceremony; the wedding entertainment was spread, and expense had not been spared ; among the rare, and for those days luxurious, adornments of the ample board, were a number of candelabra containing a curious kind of candle made by a then well-known artificer, Peter Field.*   These candles were decorated, and by an ingenious process were made to explode in a shower of beautiful but harmless pyrotechnics.   Everything was in readiness for the ceremony to begin, the bridal party had entered.   Suddenly the candles flamed up, to the astonishment and applause of the company, but when the excitement had subsided the bride had disappeared.   Taking advantage of the confusion, she had slipped away from the company, and all arrayed as she was in her bridal costume, had leaped the rear fence of her father's garden, and met on the outside one whom she prized higher than her intended husband, Carroll, a waiting lover, who bore what was under the circumstances the very appropriate name of Hauck, since he had not only swooped down in such an unceremonious manner on the company, but had also captured her whom we may poetically designate as the dove, though practically her conduct bespoke more of the cunning of the serpent.   But Mr. Hauck having first found, took care to hold fast bound, for the eloping lovers were married, where or by whom no record has been found to tell; but that such marriage took place is evident from the following entries in St. Joseph's Register :

"31 July, 1792, baptized by Rev. Lawrence Græssl, Anna Christina, born 24 of October, 1790, of Frederick and Magdalen Hauck, C. C., L. C." (that is, both Catholics, and lawfully married).   Godmother, Christina Esling.

2. "June 16, 1793, baptized by Rev. Christopher Vin. Keating, Frederick, born —— ——, 1793, of Frederick Hauck and Mary, his wife; witness Frederick Esting and Mary Rust," evidently intended for *Esling* and *Rush*.

The compiler has been unable to find the baptismal record of Elizabeth, the third grandchild mentioned in Paul Esling's will.   If the tradition be true, about nine years must have elapsed between the marriage and the date of the birth of the first mentioned child.   This statement will be understood when the date of the marriage of the next mentioned daughter of Paul Esling is given, for the jilted Carroll married her.   It is also

---

* Peter Field is frequently mentioned in the old City Directories and Catholic Church records.

said that Paul Esling never recognized the eloping daughter after the momentous night. There must, however, have been some kind of a recognition, or at least a sympathetic feeling, or he would not have mentioned her children in his will; but it will also be observed that their shares are much smaller than those of his other grandchildren. Moreover, Christina Esling, their grandmother, standing sponsor *alone* for one of these grandchildren, and that baptism taking place so long after the child's birth, has a tendency to confirm the tradition.

V. ANNA ELIZABETH, born April 17, 1763, baptized at St. Joseph's by Rev. F. Farmer April 26, 1763; sponsors Frederick Grosser and Mary Elizabeth Grosser. The same difficulty which occurs about her sister Eve's name is repeated with regard to this child. She was baptized *Anna* Elizabeth, while in fact she was always known in the family as *Mary* Elizabeth. She was twice married, her first husband being the same Thomas Carroll who had been engaged to her sister, Mary Magdalen. Thomas Carroll was not a Catholic, it would seem. The marriage is recorded in the Register of St. Michael's and Zion Lutheran Church thus: "Aug. 26, 1783, by license, Thomas Carroll (cordwainer) and Elizabeth Esling. The issue of this first marriage, as far as known, was one son. Paul, born March 17, 1785, baptized at St. Joseph's by Rev. F. Farmer; sponsors Paul and Anna Christina Esling."

She appears to have had no other children by this husband, who shortly after died, for on July 2, 1787, she took out letters of administration on his estate. (Administration Book I. 192.) Elizabeth Esling again married, her second husband being apparently, from the records, a well-to-do Irish widower; for in St. Joseph's Register appears the following entry: "Married May 13, 1790, by Rev. Francis Beeston, *cum licentia Præsidis* (by license of the Governor), Patrick Kelly and Elizabeth Carroll, widow; witnesses present, John Kelly and Edward Lodier." The issue of this marriage was also one child, a daughter, named Catharine, whose baptismal record cannot be found. Elizabeth Esling became again a widow, her second husband dying towards the end of the year 1795. His will is recorded, Will Book X, 365, No. 220. In it he tells a great deal about himself and his family affairs. She survived him but three months; her own will being recorded in Book X, page 403, No. 257. She left a contingent legacy to the poor of St. Mary's parish, which bequest seems to have been defeated. Her son Paul seems to have died under age, and about the same time as his grandfather, Paul Esling, who had made him one of the legatees of his will; for in St. Mary's Register under date of September, 1798, appears this entry: "Paul Carroll, a boy," buried "free," which would indicate that his family were pewholders of standing in the church. Her daughter, Catharine, was married at St. Joseph's April 16, 1807, by Rev. J. Rosseter, to James Johnston; the witnesses being Eve Waltman and Martha Holahan.

VI. RUDOLPH, born —— ——, baptized —— ——; married July 20, 1784, at St. Joseph's, by Rev. F. Farmer, to Sarah Lawton; witnesses, Frederick Esling and Mary, his wife, and Anna Christina Esling.

He lived only four years after his marriage, for on August 20, 1788, he was buried "free" in St. Mary's grave yard. (See fourth generation.)

The Sarah Esling married on April 7, 1790, at Gloria Dei, Old Swedes Church, to Jacob Schroudy, is believed to have been Rudolph Esling's widow.

VII. CATHARINE, born September 12, 1765, baptized at St. Joseph's by Rev. F. Farmer, September 20, 1765; sponsors Frederick and Elizabeth Grosser. She *is supposed* to have been married to a Mr. Rush, about 1797, and to have died about a year after, having issue one daughter, Sarah, mentioned in Paul Esling's will. This daughter is said to have married Lemuel Lauer, but no records have been found concerning her.

FOURTH GENERATION.

The issue of Nicholas[1] and Catherine Snyder Esling was as follows:

I. NICHOLAS,[2] born September 17, 1786, baptized at St. Joseph's by Rev. —— —— ; sponsors Paul and Anna Christina Esling.

Nicholas[2] Esling was a prominent member of the Whig party.* He was City Commissioner for the Fifth District of Philadelphia in 1813; "Assistant" to the Committee for the Defence of the City, and auxiliary superintendent for the erection of the fortifications, 1814; Health Officer of the Port of Philadelphia January 31, 1817, 1818, 1819; Harbor-Master March 21, 1836, 1837, 1838, 1839. In the unfortunate controversy between Bishop Egan and the trustees of St. Mary's church with the Harolds in 1812, he was one of the pew-owners who signed the circular

---

* A good story is told of him in his political career. During one of the exciting political campaigns which distinguished those days, when, after "the era of good feeling," the heated contests of Clay and Jackson broke out, Nicholas Esling was acting as Whig supervisor of elections in a certain up-town district. The district was supposed to have polled a large Democratic majority, but what was the astonishment when the count, upsetting all previous calculations, showed a tremendous Whig success. As there was of course a Democratic supervisor always present to prevent any unfair play, no reason could be given for a result which preached so loudly the logic of facts. In vain did the minority search the room for missing ballots, even the cinders being analyzed to discover burnt papers, but nothing could be found; so in their anger and disappointment the Democracy ever after declared that "*Nick Esling must have swallowed the ballots.*" They evidently assumed that the savor of success had seasoned into a palatable relish what would otherwise have been a hard dish for a sound Whig stomach to digest, *i. e.*, Democratic votes.

defending the trustees. His pew was No. 12, south aisle, and on March 22, 1828, he assigned over for "valuable consideraton," all his right, title and interest in the same to his mother, Catharine Esling. (See Church Records.) He was also a prominent member of the "Bishop's party" during the Hogan troubles at St. Mary's church. At the election of 1822 he was one of the candidates of that party for trustees of the church, and although that ticket was defeated, his name appears as a signer attached to several of the circulars issued from that side during the melancholy controversy. He married, about 1807, Catharine, daughter of Jeremiah and Elizabeth Hornketh.* After his marriage he resided on Buttonwood street, No. 57, just below Eighth street, at the northwest corner of what is now Loraine, formerly Lawrence street. He died in 1845, having dropped dead while sitting down to dinner. His wife survived him, living with her daughters on Filbert street, between Ninth and Tenth streets (modern number 927). She was originally a Protestant, but became a Catholic before her death, which occurred July 19, 1854, from cholera, aged 68 years. Nicholas Esling and his wife both died intestate, he having in his lifetime made assignments of all his property. (See Deed Book D., page 434, O. D. C. Also Deed Books G. W. R., 16, page 638 ; G. W. R., 21, page 414, and G. W. R., 25, page 584.)

II. GEORGE,[2] born July 18, 1791, baptized at St. Joseph's by Rev. Lawrence Græssl, July 24, *eo anno.;* sponsors Paul and Christina Esling. This child is erroneously set down as the son of Nicholas and *Mary* Esling. No further record; but in the Burial Register of St. Mary's, under date August 29, 1791, appears this entry of interment : "Nicholas Esling's child, paid 10 shillings," which was most probably this son.

III. ANNA CHRISTINA,[2] born February 24, 1793, baptized at St. Joseph's by Rev. Lawrence Græssl March 3, *eo anno.;* sponsors Paul and Ann Christina Esling. She was a great business woman, and largely managed the affairs of her family. On June 18, 1839, she purchased the house 927 Filbert street, where she resided with her mother and sisters, and an old family colored servant, Julia Hill, for many years. (Deed Book G. S., No. 6, page 12, and F. T. W., No. 170, page 261.) She was also the plaintiff of record in the leading legal cases of *Esling vs.* Williams, reported in 10 Barr, Pennsylvania State Reports, page 126, and *Esling vs. Zantzinger,* 13 Pennsylvania State Report, 1 Harris, page 50. These concerned the old Esling property on Fifth street, which she and her sisters finally sold on June 20, 1853. She was for many years a prominent member of St. Mary's church ; she and her three sisters occupying the old pew, No. 12, south aisle. She died September, 1871. Her will is recorded October 19, 1871. (Will Book 72, page 514.)

---

* Jeremiah Hornketh was a brickmaker. He died October, 1812. His will is recorded, Will Book 4, No. 101, page 187. See also Deed Books E. F., No. 9, page 512, and Book D., 55, page 42, and E. F., 33, page 412.

IV. SAMUEL RICKARDS, born January 5, 1795, baptized at St. Joseph's by Rev. Christopher V. Keating, January 17, *eo an.;* sponsors Paul Esling and Barbara Snyder. Married Elizabeth Riccles, and had issue. (See fifth generation.) He was killed by the giving way of an overcrowded shed or platform, at a great barbecue held by the Democrats, in honor of the inauguration of General Jackson to the Presidency, at the celebrated old Lebanon Garden kept by John Pascal, March 4, 1829. It was this event which caused his mother to become melancholy during the latter years of her life.

V. MARIA, born January 13, 1797, baptized at St. Joseph's by Rev. Leonard Neale February 3, *eo an.;* sponsors Paul Esling and Barbara Snyder. Married in 18— to John Vincent Myers of Pittsburg.*

VI. CATHARINE[2], born October 4, 1798, baptized at St. Joseph's by Rev. Leonard Neale, November 14, *eo an.;* sponsors Joseph Snyder and Barbara, his wife. Married April 18, 1833, by Right Rev. Francis Patrick Kenrick to Abraham Baker. He died at Williamsport, Pa., June 28, 1834, leaving issue by this marriage, one son, George, who died by drowning, unmarried. Catharine Esling Baker died January 25, 1884. (See Deed Book F. T. W., No. 193, page 191; also Will Book 114, page 226, No. 194.) Among its provisions is a legacy of $500 to Julia Hill, the old family colored servant. Abraham Baker's sister, Catharine Anna,

---

* Her issue were (A) one son, Henry W., married to Emily, daughter of Joseph Snyder, of Philadelphia, and died without issue.
  (B) KATHARINE K.,[1] married to John Fenlon.
  (C) SUSAN S., a nun of the Order of the Sisters of Mercy; her name in religion, Sister Gonzaga.
  (D) MARGARET C., unmarried.
  (E) ELIZABETH A.,[2] married to Henry A. Shoemaker.

---

[1] The issue of John and Katharine Fenlon are:
  (A) John M. Fenlon.
  (B) Katharine M. Fenlon, married to Celestine J. Blair, of Pittsburg, whose children are Francis A. Blair, Mary Grace Blair, Manuelita M. Blair, Eleanor M. Blair and Louisa K. Blair.
  (C) Henry Esling Fenlon.
  (D) Paul B. Fenlon.
  (E) Phillip G. Fenlon.
  (F) Rosalie C. Fenlon.
  (G) Grace M. Fenlon.
[2] The issue of Henry A. and Elizabeth A. Shoemaker are:
  (A) Gertrude F. Shoemaker; dead.
  (B) William Esling Shoemaker.
  (C) Maude N. Shoemaker.
  (D) Philip N. Shoemaker.
  (E) Bessie A. Shoemaker.
  (F) Edward Shoemaker.
  (G) Mildred A. Shoemaker.
  (H) Hilda C. Shoemaker.

married Jacob Way Holahan, and their daughter, Mary Anna, also married into the Esling family. (See *postea*, page 358.)

VII. LOUISA, born May 2, 1800, baptized at St. Josephs by Rev. Matthew Carr, May 25, *eo an.;* sponsors Joseph and Barbara Snyder. She died unmarried January 15, 1882. Buried in Old Cathedral cemetery. (See Will Book 104, page 592, No. 159.)

VIII. MARGARETTA, born November 24, 1801, of Nicholas and Catharine *Smith;* baptized at St. Joseph's by Rev. Michael Lacey; sponsor Barbara *Smith*. The name *Smith* twice repeated in this record is a manifest misnomer for *Snyder*. In the first place it is intended for Mrs. Esling's middle, or maiden name. No further record.

IX. SUSAN, born December 2, 1802; baptized at St. Joseph's by Rev. John Rosseter December 12, *eo an.;* unmarried. Still living, 1888.*

The issue of Rudolph and Sarah Lawton Esling, was

I. PAUL, born August 23, 1785, and baptized August 28, by Rev. F. Farmer; sponsors Paul and Christina Esling, his grandparents. He is supposed to have been the "grandson, Paul Esling," mentioned in the sixth item of the will of Paul Esling, Sr., who left him $450.

FIFTH GENERATION.

The issue of Nicholas[2] and Catharine Hornketh Esling were

I. ELIZABETH, born January 19, 1808, baptized at St. Joseph's by Rev. Michael Egan, February 7, *eo an.* She died August 14, 1814, from fright, at seeing her father placed in a perilous position at a fire in the vicinity of the family residence.

II. CATHARINE[3], born March 6, 1809, baptized at St. Joseph's by Right Rev. Michael Egan, Bishop of Philadelphia, May 7, *eo an.;* sponsors Ann Esling and Rev. William Vincent Harold. She died unmarried July 31, 1841.

III. ANNA MARIA, born July 16, 1811, baptized at St. Joseph's by Rev. J. Harold, August 25, *eo an.;* sponsors Susan and Joseph Snyder. She died August 21, 1825.

---

* At a dinner given some years ago by the Hon. Benjamin Harris Brewster to the distinguished actor, Joseph Jefferson, of *Rip Van Winkle* fame, the name of Esling was casually introduced. Mr. Jefferson, after making some inquiries, recalled with evident pleasure the fact that he had at one time been a neighbor and frequent visitor at the house of "the three Misses Esling, who lived on Filbert street," as the sisters, Ann, Louisa and Susan (III. VII. IX.), were often designated.

IV. JOSEPH JEREMIAH, born May 9, 1813, baptized at St. Joseph's by Right Rev. Michael Egan, Bishop of Philadelphia, September 5, 1813; sponsors Joseph and Barbara Snyder. Immediately after the death of Abraham Baker, at Williamsport, Mrs. Baker's brother, Nicholas Esling, accompanied by his daughter, Louisa, started for Jersey Shore, Mr. Baker's home on the Susquehanna, to spend the summer. Young Joseph Esling, who was just come of age, had desired to take a trip to what was " The Great West " of those days, and had previously arrived at Jersey Shore. The summer was a very hot one, and it was Joseph's filial attentions to his father during the prostrating heats of July and August that first attracted the favorable notice of Mrs. Holahan, Mr. Baker's sister, to her future son-in-law. In the fall he escorted his aunt back to Philadelphia. He had been brought up by his aunts and was a general favorite.

He was educated as a machinist. In the list of members of the Franklin Institute of Philadelphia appears the following entry : " *2315, October, 1844. J. J. Esling, Machinist, 51 Filbert St.*" He gave up this business about the time of his marriage and engaged in the coal trade. His coal and wood yards were at Broad and Spruce streets, and at Lombard street wharf on the Schuylkill; his offices on Walnut street between Third and Fourth streets. He was married November 30, 1843, to Mary Anna, eldest living daughter of Jacob and Catharine Holahan. The wedding ceremony took place at St. John's Roman Catholic Church, Thirteenth street above Chestnut street, Philadelphia; the Right Rev. Francis Patrick Kenrick, D. D., Bishop of Philadelphia, officiating. The witnesses were Hart Carr, George M. Holahan, Mary Baker and Mary Quinn.*

His wife was the great-granddaughter of Cornelius Holahan, the first Catholic settler of Delaware, who emigrated from Ireland about 1740. (See " Records," Vol. I.) In the other lines of her paternal ancestry she was of English and German descent, her earliest known American ancestor having come to America with Governor John Winthrop in 1630. (See Vol. I. Records American Catholic Historical Society, page 145, *et seq*.) In the maternal line she was descended from the Bakers and Millefelts, who figured historically in our local history during the Revolutionary war. She was educated at the schools of Miss Dean and Miss Jane Campbell, and went to old Father Varin, at Holy Trinity Church, to study French out of Wanostrocht's, or Noel & Chapsal's Grammar, but completed her studies at the then celebrated school of William Ashton, and graduated head of her class at the age of 13 years ; proficient in all the then highest accomplishments of a young lady's finished education. Besides the scientific branches of astronomy and natural philosophy, she excelled in the use of the guitar, and the specimens of her embroidery in silk, still preserved, are considered by connoisseurs

---

* Afterwards Mrs. Jerome Eagle.

as rivalling the work of the celebrated Kensington schools of London. She was an excellent horsewoman, and a most graceful elocutionist, and took the palm for oratory in a public competition when she first entered Mr. Ashton's school, from his then most finished post-graduate, Miss Sophie Ashmead, now the mother of Mr. Ashmead Bartlett, the husband of Lady Burdett Coutts, of England. Mrs. Esling was a lady of staunch faith and sincerest piety, and a marvellous cheerfulness of patience under long years of trial and suffering. She was universally beloved for her many social graces and dignity of character, as well as for her brilliant qualities of intellect and winning charms of soul. She was for many years active in religious works; was one of the earliest members of the Archconfraternity of The Most Holy and Immaculate Heart of Mary, after its introduction from *Notre Dame des Victoires*, Paris, into the United States, where it was at once established in St. Mary's church, Philadelphia, she having been enrolled by Very Rev. Charles I. H. Carter, pastor of that church, November 2, 1844, and was all her life a most earnest member. She was also one of the original members and first secretary of the Confraternity of the Christian Mothers, established in this city at the convent of Notre Dame, about 1870. She was also affiliated by patent with the Passionist Order, to whose members she invariably accorded hospitality on account of their having no monastic house of their own in Philadelphia. She would never permit her child to attend a Sunday-school, but gave him his religious instructions at her own knee. She was born in Philadelphia, July 21, 1820, and died, after a lingering and painful illness of seven years' duration, June 3, 1882. Her funeral ceremonies took place at St. Mary's church, June 7, and she was buried at St. Charles's cemetery, Kellyville, Delaware county, Pennsylvania.* The funeral sermon was delivered by Rev. Ignatius F. Horst-

---

* The following account of the funeral is appended :

"The obsequies of Mrs. Mary A. Esling, which took place on Wednesday last, were attended by a large number of clergymen, a delegation of the Sisters of Charity from St. Joseph's Asylum, and four Sisters of St. Francis from St. Mary's Hospital, who had nursed her in her long illness, walked immediately behind the coffin, upon which was laid a simple wreath of crimson roses, and a large palm-branch. The celebrant of the Mass was Rev. J. Ignatius Otis, of Manayunk ; Rev. Dr. Horstmann and Rev. Joseph C. Kelly, of St. Mary's, acting as deacon and sub-deacon. As the body was borne into the church the choir sang " *Rest in the Lord*." The music of the Mass was Ohnewald's Requiem ; at the offertory the "Quis Est Homo," from Rossini's Stabat Mater ; at the absolution Handel's " *Angels Ever Bright and Fair*," and Mrs. Hemans' beautiful hymn, "*Ave Sanctissima ! 'Tis Nightfall on the Sea*," which had been a great favorite with Mrs. Esling during life. The sermon was by Rev. Dr. Horstmann. The pall-bearers were Very Rev. J. B. A. Brouillet, Vicar-General of the Diocese of Nesqually, W. T.; Gen. Thomas Kilby Smith, Mr. Leandro De La Cuesta, Dr. Francis V. Greene, U. S. N.; Messrs. Walter George Smith, Augustus Thouron, Bernard L. and Ernest Douredoure. As the funeral cortege, on its way from the church to the

mann, D. D., who, taking for the keynote of his discourse the text, "To-day for me, to-morrow for Thee," spoke of the uncertainty of death, and most impressively of the necessity of being always prepared for it. After some general remarks of that nature, he touched upon the character of the deceased, and told the following anecdote, which, as its simplicity and quaint anachronisms, full, however, of telling effect, might indicate, was taken from the French, and from which he drew the personal moral which concludes it :

" Our Divine Lord once had a servant who asked him for leave to go to the marriage feast of one of his nieces. Our Lord said to him : ' Yes, you may go, but only stay as long as is necessary ;' behave like a good Christian, and tell no lies on your return.' The servant returned after eight days. Our Lord said to him : ' You have been very long away, tell me why ?' ' O, my Lord ! if you knew how good it was to be there, the table cloth was always laid, there was nothing but drinking, singing, and dancing from morning to night, and during the whole time they never once spoke of you.' ' Never once spoke of me ?' ' Not at all.' Six months later the servant asked our Divine Lord for leave to go to the marriage of another of his nieces, for he had several. Our Lord said to him : ' Yes, you may go, but only stay as long as is necessary ; be-have like a good Christian, and tell no lies on your return.' The servant started at dawn, and this time returned before evening. ' You did not stay long,' said our Lord.' ' O, my Lord,' replied the servant, ' it is not well there, the country is desolated with fevers and plagues ; nothing is to be seen but the sick, the dead and the dying, and everywhere the peo-ple are crying out : My God, my God, Jesus, Jesus.' ' Ah ! you see that they speak of me now,' said our Lord."

It was not so with Mrs. Esling. She served God with equal fidelity in joy as well as in sorrow, in pleasure as well as in pain.

Joseph J. Esling died, fortified by the last Sacraments of Holy Church, February 5, 1874. Issue one son, treated under head of sixth generation.

V. GEORGE JACKSON, born January 27, 1815, baptized at St. Joseph's by Rev. Terrence McGirr, September 24, 1818 ; sponsor Catharine Esling.

He was by profession a captain in the Merchant Marine, trading prin-cipally to Rio Janeiro. He was married October 26, 1840, to Miss Cath-arine Harbeson Waterman, born in Philadelphia, April 12, 1812, but of Irish descent. She was quite a celebrated poetess, and is said to have been the originator of the expression, "the poetry of motion," as applied to the dancing of the famous Fanny Esler. In 1850 she published a vol-

---

cemetery, passed the convent of Notre Dame, on Rittenhouse Square, to the community of which she had been much devoted, the children of the schools placed upon the coffin a wreath of immortelles, which had been laid upon the coffin of Sister Mary Euphrasia, a much-beloved nun, who had died some years before ; and the choir Sisters chanted the *Miserere* and *De Profundis*."

ume of verses entitled, " The Broken Bracelet and Other Poems." Several of her poems are addressed to her husband during his absence at sea. One of her hymns, " *Come unto Me when Shadows darkly Gather*," is a great favorite with Protestant clergymen of different denom nations. Nearly all the Biographical Dictionaries in referring to her position as an authoress quote the following passages by Mrs. Sarah J. Hale, published in " The Womens' Record ": " As a contributor to the periodicals of the day Miss Waterman obtained great and deserved celebrity . . . . . Mrs. Esling's poems are the expression of a true woman's soul. She excels in portraying feeling, and in expressing the warm and tender emotion of one to whom home has ever been the lodestone of the soul ; in pathos and delicacy she has few equals." Four years of her married life were passed with her husband at Rio. She is now residing in Philadelphia.

George J. Esling died September (25, 28 ?), 1883, leaving issue. See sixth generation.

VI. NICHOLAS³ HENRY, born October 4, 1817 (church register), September ——, 1817 (private record), baptized at St. Joseph's by Rev. Terrence McGirr, September 24, 1818 ; sponsor Ann Esling.

He was, by profession, a sea captain, and for many years commanded the barque, "White Wing," sailing between Philadelphia and Rio Janeiro. He was also commander of the historic Cuban privateer "Hornet." He married Leonora Shougard. He died suddenly in the bath at his residence in New York, August 20, 1874. His wife died December, 1878. Issue, see sixth generation.

VII. LOUISA² HENRIETTA, born July 1, 1819 (church register), July 19 (private record), baptized at St. Joseph's by Rev. Terrence McGirr, October 12, 1819 ; sponsor Louisa Esling ; unmarried (still living, 1888).

VIII. JOHN VINCENT, born September 6, 1821 (church register), September 16 (private record), baptized at St. Joseph's by Rev. Samuel Cooper, January 30, 1826 ; sponsors John V. Myers (who acted by his proxy, Joseph Jeremiah Esling) and Susan Esling.

John V. Esling, like his two preceding brothers, adopted the profession of seamanship, and while returning from sea on one of his preliminary voyages as a student of navigation, died July 13, 1839, some say off the capes of Delaware ; another, and probably the more correct account, asserts that he died at Maracaibo and was buried in the Island of Sico, on the bar at Maracaibo. He was unmarried.

IX. WILLIAM VINCENT, born March 29, 1823, died May ——, 1824.

X. LEMUEL THEODORE, born April 27, 1825, baptized at St. Joseph's by Rev. Samuel Cooper, January 30, 1826 ; sponsors John V. Myers (who acted by his proxy, Joseph Jeremiah Esling) and Susan Esling.

L. Theodore Esling, as he was always known, was, like his father, a prominent member of the Whig Party. He for a long time held a position in the sheriff's office, custom house and other municipal offices at Philadelphia, and was several times an earnest, but unsuccessful aspirant for the nomination to the sheriffalty of the city. The famous yacht, which for several years was the champion racer of the Delaware, was named after him. For her record see *Sunday News*, Philadelphia, February 20, 1887.

He married Jane Catharine Siddons, who survived him. He died April 7, 1868. For his issue, see sixth generation.

X. HENRY CLAY, born November 15, 1828 (church register), November 4 (private record), baptized at St. Joseph's by Rev. John Hughes, March 20, 1830; sponsors Joseph J. Esling and Maria Cross.

He married June 28, 1863, Sarah Weaver, who was a Protestant, but became a Catholic; she surviving him. He died March 1, 1881 (1880, private record), buried in Cathedral Cemetery, Philadelphia. Issue, one son; see sixth generation.

XI. SUSAN, born ———, baptized ———, unmarried; died suddenly in the main building of the Centennial Exhibition, November 9, 1876.

The issue of Samuel Rickards and Elizabeth Riccles Esling as far as known, was:

I. JAMES, born January 19, 1825, baptized at St. Joseph's by Rev. William Vincent Harold, December 21, 1825; sponsor Margaret Campbell. Died in infancy.

II. WILLIAM HENRY, born April 19, 1827, baptized ———, married Elizabeth ———, alive as late as 1849.*

III. SAMUEL,[2] no record found, supposed to have died before coming of age.

SIXTH GENERATION.

The issue of Joseph Jeremiah and Mary Anna Holahan Esling, was one son.

I. CHARLES HENRY AUGUSTINE, born January 21, 1845, baptized at St. John's church by very Rev. Edward J. Sourin, Vicar-General of the diocese of Philadelphia, on Tuesday in Passion week, March 11, 1845; sponsors the officiating priest and Madame Anita Knight,† confirmed by

---

*See Deed Book G. W. C., 31, page 211. See also Deed Book A. W. M., No. 81, page 430.

† Madame Anita Knight was well known to the Catholics of Philadelphia of one or two generations back. She was a French lady, of accom-

Right Rev. John N. Neumann, D. D., bishop of Philadelphia, in St. Mary's church, May 28, 1854. The name of "Augustine" was assumed in Confirmation. Educated at the Dame School of Mrs. Maria Noronah,* and entered preparatory department of St. Joseph's Jesuit College, Philadelphia, October 3, 1854. Graduating class, Collegiate department, July 3, 1863.† Entered law office of Hon. William Morris Meredith (his last

---

plished manners and deep piety, and was for several years president of the Blessed Virgin's Sodality, attached to St. John's church, Thirteenth street. Her maiden name was Gilleman. Her father was French consul at Havana, Cuba, and dying there left her quite alone, her sister, Madame Andrè, being absent. She married Mr. Knight, of Boston, who was engaged in business in Havana. He was a widower with several children, two of them daughters, Annie and Mary; the latter married Mr. Beylle, a French Catholic gentleman and a brother of the Misses Beylle, so well known to the old parishioners of St. Mary's church, Philadelphia. Mr. Knight was connected with the Sweetsers, Hoppers and other prominent Boston families. He died in Havana a few years after his second marriage, whereupon his widow, with her two children, John and Caroline, took up her residence in Philadelphia with her stepdaughter, Miss Annie Knight, who subsequently married an Irish gentleman of this city. Mrs. Knight remained here until the completion of her children's education, when about 1855 she returned to France, where she died about 1863. A Requiem Mass was celebrated for her in St. John's Church, Philadelphia. Of her two children, John, who had graduated at Mount St. Mary's College, Emmittsburg, Maryland, subsequently entered L'Ecole Polytechnique, Paris, became a civil engineer, married the daughter of a senator of France, and has since died. Caroline married the Count Villeneuve Flayausse, of the French army, and died shortly afterwards, leaving two children surviving her.

   * Of the small class of little boys who for two or three years attended this then well-known Dame school, several are now men of note in the social, professional and business circles of Philadelphia. Among them may be mentioned, Rev. Jesse Y. Burke, the present secretary of the Board of Trustees of the University of Pennsylvania; Rev. Henry C. Graeff, late rector of St. Jude's Protestant Episcopal Church, Philadelphia, now of Christ Church, Williamsport, Pennsylvania; Beauveau Borie, of the firm of Borie Brothers, bankers; Professor James Chase; Charles Beale, founder of Arden Park, North Carolina; Dr. Neville Tyson, Norristown; Dr. George McClellan, and others; and it is a curious coincidence that two of them should have been representatives at European courts; Mr. Esling at the Vatican and Mr. Wharton Barker at St. Petersburgh, where he was created by the Czar a Knight of the Order of St. Alexander Nevski.

   † The class, *as a body*, did not graduate. The college, then at Filbert and Juniper streets, being in financial difficulties, was suddenly closed by order of the Rev. Father Sopranis, who had been sent over from Rome as official visitor of the Jesuit Institutions in the United States. Of its four members pursuing the full regular curriculum, and who were about entering on their "Junior" or "Rhetoric" year, Mr. William L. Hirst, Jr., and Mr. Charles Lacy Philips graduated each with the first honors of his class, the former at Georgetown University, D. C., the latter at St. John's College, Fordham, New York. Mr. Esling finished his studies privately at the old college on Willing's alley until the date given,

student), September, 1866; admitted to Philadelphia Bar June 19, 1869;
received degree of L. L. B. University of Pennsylvania, June 15, 1882;
appointed official representative of the Primate and laity of the United
States to the Vatican at the Golden Episcopal Jubilee of his Holiness
Pius, IX., 1877; created an honorary member of the Passionist Order by
patent, dated from the monastery of Sts. John and Paul on the Cælian
Hill, Rome, June 3, 1877. Founder and first vice-president of the De
Sales Institute (Catholic Club), of Philadelphia, 1870. One of the organizers and first vice-president of the American Catholic Historical So-
cietiy of Philadelphia, 1884; Chairman of its genealogical committee.
Co-founder and first president of the "Pegasus" (Poets' club), of Philadelphia, 1885. Compiler of Esling, Holahan, Baker and Way genealogies. Member of the Pennsylvania Historical Society, Penn Club and
University Club, of Philadelphia, and New England Society of Pennsylvania. He has for several years contributed largely to Catholic and
secular literature in both prose and poetry, and is the author of several
historical monograms; unmarried.

The issue of George Jackson and Catharine Harbeson Waterman Esling were

I. GEORGE W ———, born November 17, 1841. Married Mary E.
Downing. He was an engineer by profession, and died by an accident
while engaged in building the tunnel of the Baltimore and Ohio Railroad, at Fairmount Park, Philadelphia, October 12, 1885. Issue. See
seventh generation.

II. ROBERT, born October 31, 1843. Married Emma Ross. Still living (1888). Issue. See seventh generation.

III. MARY ELLA, born June 4, 1847. Died October 22, 1847.

IV. CATHARINE H., born June 8, 1850. Unmarried. Still living (1888).

V. THOMAS MANUEL, born May 22, 1854. Married Clara Myers.
Died April 5, 1883. Issue. See seventh generation.

The issue of Nicholas Henry and Leonora Shougard Esling were

I. CATHARINE ELIZABETH, born March 18, 1843. Married July 23,
1863, to Octavius A. Law, of the Philadelphia Bar, who died in 1888,
leaving issue. Mrs. Law is still living (1888).

---

and Mr. Henry W. Sayen went immediately into business. Another
member of this class was Augustine Stuhl, afterwards superior of the
Redemptorist House at Ilchester, Md.

II. JOHN DEVEREAUX, born October 26, 1846. Unmarried and still living (1888).

III. NICHOLAS B———, born February 21, 1849. Married Sarah Miller. Died September 15, 1876, leaving issue. See seventh generation.

The issue of Lemuel Theodore and Jane Catharine Siddons Esling were

I. HELEN ANN, born November 5, 1854. Died December 19, 1854.

II. LEMUEL THEODORE[2], born November 3, 1855. Unmarried. He was editor and proprietor of the Newark *Delaware Ledger*. Died December 29, 1880. Buried in Mount Moriah cemetery, Philadelphia.

III. MATILDA HERON, born August 21, 1857. Died October 5, 1857.

IV. PAUL SIDDONS, born December 7, 1858. Died January 13, 1859.

V. HOWELL ROBERTS, born March 25, 1860. Died March 11, 1862.

VI. MARY DAY, born October 21, 1863. Married ——— ———, 1888, to George Henry Davidson, of Birmingham, England.

VII. JOHN SIDDONS, born February 13, 1865 (Registration office record). February 25, 1866 (Private record). Died July 15, 1866.

VIII. WILLIAM KEMBLE, born February 19, 1868. Unmarried and still living (1888).

NOTE.—The three branches representing the descendants of GEORGE JACKSON, NICHOLAS HENRY, and LEMUEL THEODORE ESLING in the sixth, seventh and eight generations, are believed to be entirely Protestant.

The issue of Henry Clay and Sarah Weaver Esling was one son.

I. HENRY CLAY[2], born April 5, 1864. Baptized. Unmarried and still living (1888). Member of American Catholic Historical Society.

SEVENTH GENERATION.

The issue of George Waterman and Mary E. Downing Esling were

I. GEORGE DOWNING, born August 27, 1863. Married June, 1888, Emma Lockhart. Still living (1888).

II. WALTER ATWOOD, born November 5, 1864. Married Anna Schaffer. Still living (1888). Issue. See eighth generation.

III. EDWARD EUGENE, born March 9, 1867. Unmarried and still living (1888).

IV. CATHARINE WATERMAN, born August 27, 1871. Died in infancy.

V. ROBERT BURNS, born June 9, 1873. Unmarried and still living (1888).

VI. CHARLES NICHOL, born April 19, 1876. Died in infancy.

VII. PRESTON JONES, born January 5, 1879. Died in infancy.

VIII. WILLIAM PENN (WILLING, according to Registration record), born August 3, 1869. Still living (1888).

The issue of Robert Burns and Emma H. Ross Esling, married October 28, 1869, were

I. WILLIAM ROSS WALLACE, born September 1, 1870. Still living (1888).

II. OMA KATHARINE, born November 18, 1872. Died August 22, 1874.

III. ROBERT BURNS, born August 18, 1875. Still living (1888).

IV. EMMA GERTRUDE, born November 7, 1877. Still living (1888).

The issue of Thomas Manuel and Clara Myers Esling was

I. HENRY MANUEL, born October 14, 1876. Still living (1888).

The issue of Nicholas B——— and Sarah Miller Esling were

I. LAURA, born ——— ———. Still living (1888).

II. MARY E., born April 8, 1871. Still living (1888).

III. KATHARINE ELIZABETH, born September 6, 1872. Died in infancy.

IV. NICHOLAS, born ——— ———. Died in infancy.

V. EMMA, born ——— ———. Died in infancy.

EIGHTH GENERATION.

The issue of Walter Atwood and Anna Schaffer Esling is

I. WILLIAM, born ——— ———.

II. ——— ——— ——— ——— ——— ———

THE SEHNER FAMILY.

Mrs. Ann Maria Sehner, widow of the late John Sehner, died on the morning of July 26, 1887, at Lancaster. She was born August 12, 1806, the eldest daughter of Adolph Christian Fick, and the last survivor of the family. She was baptized September 8, 1806; confirmed in youth by Rev. Dr. Endress, of Trinity Lutheran church, and united in marriage to John Sehner by Rev. P. Wolle, of the Moravian Church, December 15, 1825.

Her father, Adolph C. Fick, was born at Waren, in the Duchy of Mecklenburg, September 17, 1777, served an apprenticeship in Eppendorf, near the free city of Hamburg, receiving at the end of his term an honorable discharge and a strong letter of recommendation. He came to Philadelphia about the year 1799 and settled in Lancaster, where he soon afterwards married Justina M. Ulmer, daughter of Philip Ulmer and wife, Barbara (born Hamerich), and started his business of a butcher. Leaving his family and business, he marched to Baltimore in the service of his adopted country in the war of 1812–15. Returning after an honorable discharge, he continued his business on East King street, adjoining the residence of the parents of Col. William B. Fordney, opposite the home of Robert Coleman, where he died in 1825. His widow survived him 43 years, dying in 1868, in her 83d year.

Her husband, the late John Sehner, born January 4, 1798, died October 24, 1864, carpenter and builder. Was the oldest son of John (Johannes) Sehner, born October 7, 1765, died July 11, 1814, and wife, Catharine, whose maiden name was Rung, and a grandson of Gottlieb Söhner, who landed in Philadelphia from off the ship Fane, Captain Hyndman, October 17, 1749,* and settled in Lancaster, where he was married by Rev. T. F. Handschuh to Maria Barbara Kline, on Sunday, September 18, 1750, in the old Lutheran Church that stood upon the site now occupied by Trinity Lutheran chapel. Pastor Handschuh's text on that day was Psalm xv.

Catharine Rung, wife of John, 1765–1814, was a daughter of Henrich Rung, who married Ann Maria Nicolai in 1761, and who was a daughter of John Dies Nicolai and wife, Elizabeth.

Mrs. Ann Maria Sehner survived her husband twenty-three years, and after years well spent in relieving the sick and distressed within her reach, died at the advanced age of 80 years, 11 months and 14 days.

Of nine children (eight sons and one daughter), four sons—John F., Henry C., Benjamin F. and Edward A., and one daughter, Justina M., wife of George H. Rothermel, of Philadelphia,—survive her.

---

* See Rupp's Coll. 30,000 Names of Emigrants, page 221.

Her deceased children are Albert F., Adolphus C. and Marcus G.; deceased also left two grandchildren and two great-granddaughters—a third great-granddaughter being born a few months after her decease. Her grandsons are Samuel M. Sener and John J. Rothermel.

Henry C. Sehner, born February 6, 1828, was married on January 2, 1855, to Frances A. Coggsdall, born August 27, 1834, and had children, Samuel M. Sener and Albert F., born April 24, 1858, died September 8, 1861; Samuel M. Sener, born October 5, 1855, married on April 5, 1877, Susie T. Murray, born January 3, 1856, who is a daughter of the late Dennis Murray and wife, the late Margaret Donelly, both of whom were members of the Cathedral parish, Philadelphia. Dennis Murray came to Philadelphia from Donegal, Ireland. The children of Samuel M. Sener are Frances M., born February 10, 1878; Gertrude, born August 24, 1880; Ann Maria, born November 17, 1887. Samuel M. Sener became a convert to the Catholic Church, being baptized at St. Anthony's church, Lancaster, by Rev. A. F. Kaul, on June 25, 1874, and was confirmed at the same church by the late Right Rev. J. F. Shanahan, on June 20, 1875, and is a member of the Lancaster Bar, having studied law under the late Congressman O. J. Dickey, and being admitted to practice on March 10, 1877. Frances A. Sehner, mother of Samuel M. Sener, is also a convert to the Catholic Church, having been baptized at St. Anthony's church by Rev. A. F. Kaul, on August 5, 1878.

Jacob Sener, of Carlisle, who celebrated his ninety-fifth birthday on July 16, 1887, dying August 3, 1887, and who served in the war of 1812-15; and the late Gottlieb Sehner, of Manor township, who was the son of Gottlieb (1751-1799) and Magdalena Neff, daughter of the famous Dr. Neff,* were also grandsons of Gottlieb Söhner, of 1749.

On pages 257, 297, 302, 305, 317, 325, 329 and 341 of Volume I. of the Records of the American Catholic Historical Society the name Sener appears either in the capacity of sponsor or that of a child receiving the sacrament of baptism. The appearance of the name is in the register of old St. Joseph's Church, Philadelphia, beginning in 1760 at page 257. Whether or not this family (Francis and Agatha Sener) were of any kin to the family in Lancaster does not appear, but the probability is that they were, as all of the name in America are, in some remote way, connected with one another. By different members of the family the name has been variously spelled Söhner, Sehner and Sener.

---

* Rupp's History of Lancaster county, page 124.

KELLY—HENDRY.

Torrance Kelly was a native and resident of Silverbridge, County Armagh, Ireland. He was a devoted Irish patriot, and was in league with a party that was formed in France, toward the end of the 18th century, for the restoration of the Stuarts to the throne of England. He took a prominent part in the Rebellion of 1798, and fought at the battle of Vinegar Hill. He married Miss Eleanor Clark, of the same place. This lady was a Protestant, but embraced the Catholic faith on the occasion of her marriage. One of her brothers, when quite young, immigrated to America, and settled in Wheeling (now in Western Virginia). He fought in the war of the Revolution, and reached the rank of lieutenant. Many of the best families of West Virginia and Ohio claim descent from him. His immediate descendants are noted for their strong opposition to Catholicity; but one of them, a graduate of West Point, was converted to the faith, and became a prominent member of the Society of Jesus, Rev. James A. Clarke, S. J.

The only son of Torrance and Eleanor Clark Kelly was John Kelly, who immigrated to America in 1801. He settled in Pittsburgh, Pennsylvania, and was a citizen of that place until his decease in 1860. He was distinguished for his great moral rectitude and fervent piety. His residence, one of the first pretentious dwellings built in Pittsburgh, was occupied by his immediate family for fifty years, and is still standing. He married Miss Elizabeth FitzSimons, a descendant, on her mother's side, of an ancient and respectable Scotch family named Carr, and a devoted Catholic. She was a native of Downpatrick, County Down, Barony of Lecale, Ireland. Her great-uncle, Rev. Richard FitzSimons, D. D., of the same place, enjoyed local distinction for piety and learning. Mrs. Kelly was a woman of fine education, and enjoyed the esteem and friendship of many eminent clergymen connected with the early ecclesiastical history of Western Pennsylvania; among them, Prince Gallitzin.

Issue of John and Elizabeth FitzSimons Kelly:

I. ELEANOR THERESA (the first Catholic child baptized in Pittsburgh), married to Hugh MacShane, a Catholic, and a native of Coleraine, Londonderry, Ireland. No issue. Both deceased.

II. WILLIAM (*vide* Appleton's Encyclopædia, Vol. 3; and Z. F. Smicke's History of Kentucky, third edition, page 505). He married Miss Mildred Kelly, of Eddyville, Kentucky (a Protestant, but who came into the Church before her marriage). This lady claims descent from the earliest settlers of Kentucky, being lineally descended from the first white woman born in that state.

(Philadelphia Press, Feb. 13, 1888.)

"OBITUARY.

"WILLIAM KELLY, INVENTOR OF THE BESSEMER STEEL PROCESS.

"LOUISVILLE, Ky., Feb. 12 [SPECIAL].—William Kelly, inventor of what is known as the 'Bessemer steel process,' died in this city last night at the age of 78 years. He removed from Pittsburgh to Lyon county, Kentucky, when quite young, and established immense iron furnaces and forge works. He became convinced that the cost of making steel could be cheapened considerably ; his idea being that iron could be converted into steel without the use of charcoal, by forcing powerful blasts of atmosphere through molten metal, believing that the oxygen of the air would unite with the carbon in the metal and thus produce combustion, and by eliminating the carbon leave it wrought-iron or steel. His experiments were continued for ten years, during which time his process was used at his works. Some English skilled workmen left his employ, took the secret to England, and Henry Bessemer applied for patents in Great Britain and the United States, but patents were awarded to Kelly in this country on the grounds of priority of invention.

"Mr. Kelly first imported Chinese labor into the United States, the first venture being with ten Chinamen, who were followed by fifty more. These were worked at the iron furnaces. Mr. Kelly was a man of wealth and stood high in the community. At the time of his death he was at the head of the axe manufacturing firm of W. C. Kelly & Co."

Issue of William and Mildred Gracey Kelly :

(A) John Gracey Kelly, now cashier of the Braddock Trust Co., Braddock, Pa. Married to Miss Agnes Kenny, of Braddock, Pa., a descendant on her paternal grandmother's side of several old, respectable Catholic Maryland families.

Issue of John Gracey and Agnes Kelly :

    (a) Kenny Kelly, deceased. (b) Mildred Kelly.

(B) William Cody Kelly, of the axe manufacturing firm of W. C. Kelly & Co., Louisville, Ky.

(C) Zurilda (called Lillie), married to Robert Thompson, an ex-Confederate soldier (Protestant). A descendant of a younger branch of the family of the Duke of Ormond, which settled in Kentucky previously to the Revolution. Issue :
    (c) William Thompson. (d) Mary Agnes Thompson. (e) Sidney Thompson. (f) Eliza Cody Thompson. (g) Mildred Thompson.

(D) James Paul Kelly.

(E) Blanche Kelly.

III. ELIZA, married to Michael Cody, a Catholic, and a native of Carrick-on-Suir, Tipperary, Ireland. Later a much respected merchant of Louisville, Ky. Removed to Philadelphia in 1862. Eminent for piety, integrity and benevolence. Both deceased.

IV. MARY BLANCHE, never married. Deceased.

V. JOHN FITZSIMONS, unmarried.

VI. ANN FRANCES, married to Charles F. Hendry, deceased; a Protestant. A descendant of Joseph Hendry, the last survivor of two ancient and noble English families, who emigrated to Virginia in 1635, bringing a large inherited fortune in gold pieces, which he had packed in kegs. About 1700 one of his descendants was led to settle in Burlington county, New Jersey. Having considerable means, he invested in land until his possessions became very extensive. There was an interesting work preserved in the State Library at Trenton about twenty-five years ago, that gave an account of the Hendry possessions. Both the grandfathers of Charles F. Hendry were officers in the army of the Revolution, and served throughout the entire war. Ezekiel Anderson, great-grandfather of Charles F. Hendry, was engaged, on the side of the Colonies, in the French and Indian wars, and fought with Washington at Braddock's Field. In his extreme old age he was one of the volunteer guides who led the army of Washington to the camp of the British, on the eve of the battle of Trenton. His son, Colonel Joseph Anderson, of the Revolutionary army, was born in New Jersey,* November 5, 1757, and was appointed by Washington to be district judge of the territory south of the Ohio river, in 1791. He was United States Senator from Tennessee from 1797 to 1815, and First Comptroller of the United States Treasury from 1815 to 1836. He died in Washington, D. C., April 17, 1837. One of his sons, General Robert Anderson (of Fort Sumpter fame), was born near Louisville, Kentucky, June 14, 1805. Another son became Governor of Ohio. Charles F. Hendry's father was an eminent physician. The Hendry family intermarried with several of the oldest and wealthiest families in New Jersey; among them the Scudders, Andersons, Reeders, Chambers and Howells.

GENEALOGY.

Ezekiel Anderson married Maria Coombes.

Maria Coombes Anderson married Captain Samuel Hendry.

John Anderson Hendry, M. D., married Abbie Chambers.

Charles F. Hendry married Ann F. Kelly.

* In "Appleton's Encyclopædia of American Biography," the birthplace of Joseph Anderson is given as "near Philadelphia." His early life was passed in New Jersey.

ADDENDUM.

Issue of Charles F. and Ann Frances Hendry:

(F)   Mary Ellen Hendry.

(G)   Elizabeth Carmel Hendry.

(H)   Julia Cody Hendry, married to Bernardo Hoff Knight, a Catholic, youngest son of Dr. Isaac Knight, U. S. A., and Ann Catharine Hoff (converts).   On his father's side this gentleman is a lineal descendant of Giles Knight, who came to this country with William Penn, and was one of the " cave dwellers of the Schuylkill."   The Knights settled later at Byberry, Pennsylvania.   On the maternal side he is descended from the early Swede settlers of Delaware; this particular family having belonged to the higher Swedish nobility.   They espoused the cause of the Colonies at a great loss to themselves, and were particularly enraged at their immediate relatives, the Count Donop and General Knyphausen, for coming to this country in command of mercenaries on the side of Great Britain.   When Donop fell at Red Bank, and was buried there, family tradition has preserved the story of the most prominent member of the family going thither, through many difficulties, to enjoy the satisfaction of venting his rage against the unfortunate officer's memory by dancing on his grave.   The family are also related by marriage to the Counts de Guzman, of which family the ex-Empress Eugenie is a member.   Mr. Knight's maternal great-grandfather was an officer on the " Bonhomme Richard," and was severely wounded during its action with the " Serapis."

Mrs. Ann Catharine Knight was a sister to Rear-Admiral Henry Kuhn Hoff, who married a daughter of Commodore Bainbridge.   His son is Commander Hoff, U. S. N., of Washington, D. C.

Dr. Isaac Knight was in the regular service of the United States during the Mexican war, and a surgeon in the Federal army during the late civil war.   His son, Carlos Knight, M. D., deceased, was a surgeon in the U. S. Navy.

(I)   Edwin Chambers Hendry; deceased.

(J)   Paul Augustine Hendry, a hereditary member of the Cincinnati Society, in the State of New Jersey.

ADDENDUM.

Jacob Reeder married Phœbe Scudder.
Phœbe Reeder married Colonel David Chambers.*

One of Jacob Reeder's brothers, Abner Reeder, was president of the first bank of Trenton. His son Jacob's son, Andrew H. Reeder, became first Governor of Kansas (*vide* "Life of Abraham Lincoln," by Messrs. Nicolay & Hay, part called "The Territorial Experiment"). One of Governor Reeder's sons is Brigadier General Frank Reeder; another, Judge Reeder, of Easton, Pa.

According to a modern historian, the Chambers family were of such importance in New Jersey that from the earliest settlement of the State there has been a locality called by their name. At present this is borne by the town of Chambersburg, near Trenton, which is built on land belonging to Abner Chambers, Esq., of Mt. Ephraim, N. J., the son and heir of Robert Chambers, deceased, the eldest son of Col. David Chambers; and the last to hold the office of magistrate, which had been held in succession by his ancestors from the latter part of the seventeenth century. This land has been in the family one hundred and eighty years.

---

* A son of Colonel Chambers, Abner Chambers, married a niece of Governor Howell, of New Jersey. Their daughter Phœbe (called Fannie) married Francis Way, Esq.

REPORTS.

List of Donors to the Library and Cabinet during the two
years ending July 22d, 1888.

His Eminence, James Cardinal Gibbons, Baltimore.
Most Rev. P. J. Ryan, Archbishop of Philadelphia.
Right Rev. H. P. Northrop, Bishop of Charleston.
Right Rev. Francis Janssens, Bishop of Natchez.
Right Rev. F. S. Chatard, Bishop of Vincennes.
Right Rev. James O'Connor, Bishop of Omaha.
Right Rev. Richard Gilmour, Bishop of Cleveland, Ohio.
Right Rev. Louis DeGoesbriand, Bishop of Burlington, Vermont.
Right Rev. James Zilliox, O. S. B., Abbot.

Right Rev. Mgr. Corcoran, D. D.,	Overbrook, Pa.
Very Rev. M. F. Howley, D. D.,	Newfoundland.
Rev. Thomas C. Middleton, D. D., O. S. A,	Villanova, Pa.
Rev. Ign. F. Horstmann, D. D., Chancellor,	Philadelphia.
Rev. J. H. Defouri,	New Mexico.
Rev. R. S. Dewey, S. J.,	Philadelphia.
Rev. M. J. O'Reilly,	Columbia, Pa.
Rev. William P. Treacy,	New Jersey.
Rev. C. Verwyst,	Wisconsin.
Rev. Thomas C. McMillan, C. S. P.,	New York.
Rev. Jules C. Foin,	Pennsylvania.
Rev. John F. Kempker,	Iowa.
Rev. James O'Reilly,	Pennsylvania.
Rev. John Gmeiner,	Minnesota.
Rev. D. A. Quinn,	Rhode Island.
Rev. G. H. Krake,	Pennsylvania.
Rev. P. R. O'Reilly,	Philadelphia.
Rev. Hugh Lane,	Philadelphia.
Rev. E. F. Prendergast,	Philadelphia.
Rev. E. V. Lebreton,	Texas.
Rev. Joseph A. Wirth, C. SS, R.,	New York.
Rev. Theodore Brüner,	New York.
Rev. Richard F. Hanagan,	Philadelphia.
Rev. J. P. Neck, C. M.,	Missouri.
Rev. George F. Houck,	Ohio.

His Excellency, the Governor of New Jersey, 1887.
His Excellency, the Governor of Ohio, 1888.
His Excellency, the Governor of Alabama.
His Excellency, the Governor of Wisconsin.
His Excellency, the Governor of South Carolina.
His Excellency, the Governor of Maine.

L. P. Sylvain, Librarian of Parliament,	Ottawa, Canada.
Hon. J. B. Blanchet, Provincial Secretary,	Quebec, Canada.
C. A. E. Gagnon,	Quebec, Canada.
Department of the Interior, U. S. A.	Washington.
Department of Crown Lands,	Toronto, Canada.
Bureau of Education, U. S. A.	Washington.
State Library,	Harrisburg, Pa.
Notre Dame University,	Indiana.
C. T. A. U.,	Philadelphia.
College of the Holy Cross,	Massachusetts.
Sisters of St. Joseph,	Chestnut Hill, Phila.
Sister M. Gonzaga, St. Joseph's Orphanage,	Philadelphia.
Discalced Carmelite Fathers,	New Orleans.
St. Xavier's College,	Cincinnati, O.
Laval University,	Quebec, Canada.
C. Y. M. N. U.,	N. Y. & Philad'a.
Ursuline Sisters,	Galveston, Texas.
H. McGrath, Publisher,	Philadelphia.
F. Pustet & Co., Publishers,	New York.
Hoffman Bros., Publishers,	Milwaukee.
B. Herder, Publisher,	St. Louis.
Benziger Bros., Publishers,	New York.
F. Lucas, Publisher,	Baltimore.
F. A. Fasy, Publisher,	Philadelphia.

HISTORICAL, SCIENTIFIC AND OTHER SOCIETIES.
DONATIONS AND EXCHANGES.

Georgia Historical Society,	Savannah, Ga.
Old Colony Historical Society,	New Haven, Conn.
Dedham Historical Society,	Dedham, Mass.
Essex Institute,	Essex, Mass.
Virginia State Historical Society,	Richmond, Va.
Ridgway Library,	Philadelphia, Pa.
Maryland Historical Society,	Baltimore, Md.
Wyoming Historical Society,	Wilkesbarre, Pa.

American Antiquarian Society, ... Worcester, Mass.
Wisconsin State Historical Society, . . . Madison, Wis.
Canadian Institute, ... Toronto, Canada.
Mercantile Library, ... New York City.
Boston Historical Society, ... Massachusetts.
Boston Public Library, ... Massachusetts.
Johns-Hopkins University, ... Baltimore, Md.
Presbyterian Historical Society, ... Philadelphia.
Connecticut Historical Society, ... Hartford, Conn.
Minnesota Historical Society, ... St. Paul, Minn.
Yale College, New Haven, Conn.
New York Genealogical and Biographical Society, New York.
Iowa State Historical Society. Iowa.
Congregational Library, ... Boston.
University of California, ... Berkeley, Cal.
California Historical Society, ... San Francisco.
New Jersey Historical Society, ... New Jersey.
Montana Historical Society, ... Helena, Montana.
Carroll Institute Library, ... Washington, D. C.
Pennsylvania Historical Society, . . . Philadelphia, Pa.
Pennsylvania State Library, ... Harrisburg, Pa.
Buffalo Historical Society, ... Buffalo, N. Y.
Minnesota Historical Society, ... Minnesota.
Oneida Historical Society, ... Utica, N. Y.
Chicago Historical Society, ... Chicago, Ill.

RECEIVED FROM PRIVATE INDIVIDUALS.

David Sullivan, Philadelphia.   Daniel Nolan, Illinois.
Martin I. J. Griffin,   "   Harry Steinmetz, Philadelphia.
Miss Elizabeth Coad,   "   P. O'Keefe,   "
Francis X. Reuss,   "   George B. Heckel, Chicago.
John A. Johann,   "   Mrs. Mary McCarty, Philad'a.
H. F. Lyon,   "   Stanton H. Hackett,   "
Prof. J. F. Edwards, N. D., Ind.   W. Cullen,   "
John Flick, Carrolltown, Pa.   Rev. J. Dunn, Meadville, Pa.
L. F. Flick, M. D., Philadelphia.   Rev. Thomas J. Conaty, Mass.
Thomas R. Scanlon,   "   J. G. Rosengarten,   "
J. Dale Dillon, M. D.,   "   John J. McVey,   "
James Anderson,   "   Geo. S. Hookey, Augusta, Ga.
James Monaghan,   "   W. Cummings,   Philad'a.
J. M. Rinkes, West Va.   Mrs. Anna McIlvain,   "
Miss E. Carmel Hendry, Phila.   George D. Wolff,   "
Miss F. G. Snyder,   "   John Brankin,   "

Geo. Edw. Hegener, Lancaster, Pa. John Cavanagh, Philad'a.

O. B. DeMorat, Philadelphia. S. A. Green, Boston.

C. G. Hookey, " C. H. A. Esling, Philad'a.

Michael A. Durney, M. D., Md. J. J. Maitland, "

Miss M. A. Cavenaugh, Phila. Martha T. Shoemaker, "

Charles Magee, " John Slattery, "

Mrs. Elias C. Hathaway. John W. Jennings, "

James Ford, Illinois. Theodore Donnelly, "

Francis T. Furey, Philadelphia. Wm. R. Williams, "

Jno. H. Campbell, Esq., " J. Percy Keating, "

J. Carroll McCaffrey, Esq., Oregon. M. A. Comber, "

Rich'd H. Clarke, LL. D., N. Y. Mrs. L. Foy, "

M. Ulysses Chevalier, France. D. Lawton, "

James A. McCaffrey, Philad'a. John D. Murray, "

James McLaughlin, " F. McNerhany, Washing'n, D. C.

Alfred D. Wilkinson, " Herman D. Nolan, Philad'a.

C. W. Beresford, Esq., " Miss H. Bradshaw, "

F. J. Maher, Mississippi. Andrew J. Keegan. "

Heirs of Paul Reilly, Philadelphia. John T. Reily, West Va.

Maj. Edm'd Mallet, Wash'n, D.C. A. Fleckenstein, Penn'a.

Miss Mary Halloran, Philad'a. John J. Murphy, Canada.

Mrs. Maria Shea, " James J. Treacy, Philad'a.

Hon. Michael Glennan, Virginia. Hon. A. M. Keily, Cairo, Egypt.

C. B. Magee, Jr., Philad'a. Col. J. Thomas Scharf, Baltimore.

P. A. Nolan, Sec. T. A. B. U. of A., Col. Francis J. Crilly, Philad'a.

Philad'a. William F. Kelly, "

John J. O'Rourke, " H. F. McIntosh, Toronto, Can.

William H. McCauley, " C. A. Hardy, Philad'a.

James C. McCambridge, " Miss. Elizabeth Hogan, "

Thos. H. Byrne, Sec. C. Y. M. N. Andrew J. Keegan, "

U., Philad'a. Wm. J. Campbell, M. D., "

S. Edwin Megargee, Esq., " John J. Wall, "

Paul A. Hendry, " J. J. Cassidy, Toronto, Can.

Thomas C. Willcox, Ivy Mills, Pa. Hon. Sam'l J. Randall, M. C.

Jules Junker, Philadelphia. Atlee Douredoure, Philad'a.

George C. Brotherton, " S. W. Pennypacker, Penn'a.

Miss Eleanor C. Donnelly, " A. McEnroe, Philad'a.

E. J. Mollineaux, " ——— Snyder.

P. S. P. Conner, " H. W. Jackson, Philad'a.

Edward J. Aledo, Esq., "

There have been about 500 donations, exchanges and packages, including purchase, received at the Library, making a total of about 3200 items. There have been purchased about 53 lots. The last of these was the Haviland library, which will probably exceed 2500 items; but on account of absence from the city of the Librarian, these have not yet been entered on the Book List of the Society.

The following periodicals are received and filed regularly at the Library, and we take advantage of this opportunity to publicly thank the publishers for their kindness :

American Catholic Quarterly Review, Hardy & Mahony, Pubs., Philada.
American Catholic Historical Researches, M. I. J. Griffin, Pub.,   "
Catholic Standard, Hardy & Mahoney Publishers, Philadelphia.

Catholic, Pittsburg,	Pittsburg, Pa.
Colorado Catholic,	Denver, Col.
Catholic Sentinel,	Portland, Oregon.
Cincinnati Telegraph,	Cincinnati, Ohio.
Catholic, Kansas,	Leavenworth, Kansas.
Catholic Home Journal,	Chicago, Ills.
C. T. A. News,	Philadelphia.
Emerald Vindicator,	Pittsburgh, Pa.
Home Journal,	Spencer, Mass.
Catholic Youth,	Brooklyn, N. Y.
Catholic News (American),	New York City.
I. C. B. U. Journal,	Philadelphia.
Index,	Scranton, Pa.
Messenger of the Sacred Heart,	Philadelphia.
Pilgrim of Our Lady of Martyrs	"
Young Crusader,	Columbus, Ohio.
Carroll Institute Bulletin,	Baltimore.
The Sodalist,	Cincinnati.
Church News,	Washington, D. C.
Catholic Record,	Scranton, Pa.
Starlight,	Philadelphia.
Tablet,	New York.
Messenger,	Iowa.
Catholic Weekly Review,	Toronto, Canada.

MAGAZINES AND NEWSPAPERS IN THE LIBRARY.

Ave Maria, nearly complete.
American Catholic Quarterly Review, complete.
American Antiquarian, odd numbers.
Advocate (Catholic), Louisville, Ky., Vols. 6, 7, 8, 9, 10, 11.

Brownson's Review, Vols. 1, 2, old series. Vols. 1, 2, 4, new series, Boston. Also odd numbers, New York.

Catholic (Pittsburg), from 1885.

Catholic (Colorado), from 1886.

Catholic Sentinel (Oregon), from 1886.

Catholic Historical Researches (Lambing), complete.

Catholic Historical Researches (Griffin), complete.

Catholic Record (Magazine), Philadelphia, complete, 1871 to 1878, end of its publication.

C. Y. M. N. U. Bulletin for 1886.

Catholic Magazine (Cunningham), Philadelphia, complete in 2 Vols., from 1846 to 1848.

Cincinnati Telegraph, Vols. 1, 2, 3, 5, 6, and file from 1886.

Catholic Miscellany, complete from Vol. 6 to Vol. 28.

Catholic Expositor, Vol. 4.

Catholic Knight, Vols. 1, 2, 3, from 1882 to 1885.

Catholic Standard, Philadelphia, complete from 1871.

Celt (American), New York, from 1850 to 1857, not quite complete.

Churchman. Parts of 1847–48. Nearly complete, 1849 to 1870.

Chambers' Journal, incomplete, 1854.

Catholic Youth, complete.

Catholic Herald, Philadelphia, complete, Vols. 1 to 15.

Catholic Herald, New York, incomplete, Vols. 1, 2, 3.

Catholic Home Magazine, Vol. 3.

Catholic World Magazine, complete, save a few numbers.

College Message (St. Viateur's), from 1887.

Catholic Magazine and Protector, Vol. 1, 1801.

Catholic T. A. News, complete, Vol. 1 and file.

Donahoe's Magazine (Boston), needs but few numbers since 1879.

Diary (Catholic), nearly complete, Vols. 1, 3.

The Sodalist, on file 2 years.

Emerald Vindicator, Pittsburg, filed from 1886.

Emerald, The, parts of odd volumes.

Emerald and Globe, parts of odd volumes.

Expositor (Catholic), Vol. 4, 1803.

Fireside (Catholic), New York, 1883–4–5–6.

Frank Leslie's Illustrated Paper, New York, 1885–6–7–8.

Freeman's Journal, same as in report in Vol. 1.

Geschicht's Freund (Savannah Ga.), German O. S. B., 1883.

Harper's Weekly (New York), 1859.

Holy Family (New Orleans), Vol. 1, 1886.

Home Journal (Spencer, Mass.), from 1886.

Illustrated News (New York), 1853.

I. C. B. U. Journal (Philadelphia), from 1873.

Jesuit, The (Boston), 1829, September, to August, 1831. Bound.

Index (Diocesan), Scranton, Pa., complete file.

Irish Shield and Monthly Milesian (New York), Vol., 1829.

Kaleidoscope Magazine (Philadelphia), 1832.

Messenger of the Sacred Heart (Philadelphia), nearly complete.

Metropolitan Magazine, Vol. 1, new series, 1858; old series, Vol. 1, 1853, 1854, 1857.   Bound.

Mirror, Catholic (Baltimore), 1859-60-61-63-64-65-66, nearly complete.

Messenger (Iowa).   File.

Notre Dame Scholastic, complete, Vols. 1, 3, 4 to 13 and 17; incomplete, vols. 16, 18, 19, 20, 23.

New York Catholic News, complete file.

News (Church), Washington, D. C., file complete.

Pilgrim of Our Lady of Martyrs (Philadelphia), 1885 and file complete.

Pilot (Boston), 1844-45-46-47-48.

Pastor (New York), complete till November, 1886.

Catholic Weekly Review (Toronto, Canada), complete.

Pennsylvania Magazine of History and Biography, complete, Vols. 1 to 8; incomplete, Vols. 9 and 10

Penn Monthly, 1873-74-75-76 incomplete; 1877, complete.

Portfolio (Philadelphia), Vol. 4, 1804.

Record, Catholic (Scranton, Pa.), complete file.

Revue de Montreal, 1877-78-79-80 file.

Sodalist (Cincinnati), 1886.

Starlight (Philadelphia), file.

Tablet (New York), bound, Vol. 1, 1857; 1858-9, 1860-1, 1862-3, 1864-5, 1866, complete; 1867, 1868, 1869, 1870, incomplete. File from 1885.

Truth Teller (New York), bound, 1830, 1831; incomplete, 1829, 1831.

Union Bazaar Journal (Philadelphia).   Issued during La Salle College Fair (complete).

United States Catholic Magazine (Baltimore), bound vols. 2, 3 ,4, 5, 6, from 1843.

Youth's Magazine, Vol. 6 (1885).

I thus place before the public, in brief, the condition of our library during the past two years.   Volume I. of our Records gave a more extended report, covering the years of 1884 and 1885.   It will be seen at a glance that our interests have been increased, and that we have been received by other similar societies who have exchanged with us, and welcomed us into the field of history.   It is to be hoped that among our own people a renewed encouragement may be given us.   Our space is so limited that not more than one-fourth of our books, etc., can find shelving room; an effort is being made to remedy this.   Let us hope to have our membership increased, and a renewed activity on the part of the present membership, so that our next valume may be a monument to the usefulness and success of the AMERICAN CATHOLIC HISTORICAL SOCIETY OF PHILADELPHIA.

FRANCIS X. REUSS,

JULY 30, 1888.   *Librarian.*

RULES AND REGULATIONS

FOR THE

GOVERNMENT OF THE LIBRARY.

It shall be the duty of the Library Committee to superintend and direct the use of the Library and its collections, subject to the approval of the Board of Directors.

The Librarian shall have charge and custody of the books and collections, subject to the direction of the Library Committee.

The Committee on Publication of " Records " shall be permitted to take such books and manuscripts from the Library as they may need in order to perform the duty assigned to them by the Society ; and a record to this effect shall be kept by the Librarian in a book prepared for the purpose. It shall be the duty of the Librarian to require such books and manuscripts to be returned as soon as the purpose for which they were obtained has been satisfied.

AS TO THE USE OF THE LIBRARY:

I. All persons are entitled to enter the rooms in which books and other articles are kept, when attended by an officer of the Society or a member of the Board of Directors ; and keys admitting to the rooms shall be furnished to the Librarian, officers of the Society and members of the Board of Directors, who, when they cease to be officers or members of such Board, shall surrender their keys to the Library Committee.

II. Any person who desires to use books in the Library, may be furnished with volumes for consultation by applying to the Librarian. Books shall not be taken out of the Library except by permission of the Board of Directors, and shall not be kept out for a longer period than one month without renewal of such permission.

III. When any book, map, chart or manuscript is delivered to any one for consultation or reference, the Librarian shall make a memorandum of the title of such article and of the name of the person applying for it, which record shall be kept on file in the Library until the volume is returned to him ; and it shall be his duty also to examine all books and manuscripts immediately after they have been used, to ascertain if they be returned in as good condition as they were in when given out.

IV. It shall be the province of the Board of Directors, and none others, to authorize the loan of the Society's books or articles to be used outside of the Library; and to cause a description of books or articles thus loaned to be kept by the Librarian in a book prepared for the purpose, which entry shall contain a receipt for the same from the borrower, as well as the endorsed approval of a member of the Board, together with the date of the transaction.

V. Very rare and valuable books, &c., as above, shall be consulted only in the Library. On no consideration can such rare books, &c., be loaned for use outside of the Library.

VI. All manuscripts and very rare books belonging to the Society shall be kept under lock and key, and shall be used only in the presence of the Librarian or a member of the Library Committee, except by the Publication Committee, as already noted. In case such manuscripts be required for publication, in whole or in part, the fact that they were obtained from the Society shall be required to be stated in connection with their publication.

VII. Manuscripts of a confidential nature shall be retained in a place of special deposit, and shall be consulted only under such regulations as may be prescribed in each case by the Library Committee.

VIII. All books, tracts, manuscripts, maps, &c., belonging to the Society shall be distinctly its property as apart from such articles that may be entrusted to its keeping as temporary deposits subject to recall by the donors. When any articles of any kind whatsoever are sent to the Library by benefactors without any instruction from the donors, it shall be the duty of the Library Committee to record them as absolute gifts. All books, relics, &c., coming into the possession of the Society shall be marked with the name of the donor or depositor, as the case may be, and recorded accordingly, with the date of presentation.

IX. These rules may be revised only after written application to the Board of Directors, signed by at least three members thereof.

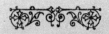

PUBLIC MEETINGS.

SEASON OF 1886–87.

To THE AMERICAN CATHOLIC HISTORICAL SOCIETY OF PHILADELPHIA :

Your Committee on Public Meetings for the season of 1886–87 reports having secured three papers during the season, which were read at two meetings as follows : "Father Rasle and the Abenaquis Mission," by Rev. James J. Bric, S. J , on February 18, 1888 ; "The Early Registers of the Catholic Church in Pennsylvania," by Mr. Philip S. P. Conner, and "Rev. Louis Barth, a Pioneer Missionary in Pennsylvania, and an Administrator of the Diocese of Philadelphia," by Rev. Jules C. Foin, on May 5, 1887.

For the Committee,   C. CARROLL MEYER,
Chairman.

SESSION OF 1887–88.

To THE AMERICAN CATHOLIC HISTORICAL SOCIETY OF PHILADELPHIA :

Your Committee on Public Meetings respectfully report : That, during the past season they have held seven public meetings, at which as many papers upon subjects relating to matters of Catholic history were presented and read. Your Committee take this opportunity of thanking the authors of the several papers read as above, and also of those now in preparation, for the marked courtesy with which they have been treated by all whom they have approached for communications upon subjects relating to Catholicity in America. The following is a list of the papers read, with the names of the authors thereof, viz :

TENTH PUBLIC MEETING—HELD SEPTEMBER 15, 1887.

Celebration of the Centenary of the Constitution of the United States.

1. Oration by Hon. Michael Glennan of Virginia, who being unavoidably detained at home, the oration was delivered by the Very Rev. Ignatius Horstmann, D. D., Chancellor of the Diocese of Philadelphia.

2. An ode entitled "Our Nation's Glory," written especially for this occasion, by Miss Eleanor C. Donnelly, of Philadelphia. Recited by S. Edwin Megargee, Esq , Philadelphia.

3. An historical paper entitled, "Thomas FitzSimons, Pennsylvania's Catholic Signer of the Constitution of the United States, by Martin I. J. Griffin.

Very Rev. Ignatius F. Horstmann, D. D., presiding.

ELEVENTH PUBLIC MEETING—HELD OCTOBER 26, 1887.

Paper by Prof. Michael H. Cross, formerly Organist at the Cathedral of Philadelphia.

Subject: "*The early Music and Choirs of Philadelphia.*"

TWELFTH PUBLIC MEETING—HELD NOVEMBER 29, 1887.

Paper by Rev. John F. Kempker, of the diocese of Dubuque, Iowa.

Subject: "*Catholicity in Lee County, Iowa.*"

THIRTEENTH PUBLIC MEETING—HELD JANUARY 17, 1888.

Paper by Very Rev. C. Jaillet, Vicar-General and Administrator of the Vicariate Apostolic of Brownsville, Texas.

Subject: "*Early Catholicity in Texas.*"

FOURTEENTH PUBLIC MEETING—HELD FEBRUARY 29, 1888.

Paper by H. F. McIntosh, Esq., of Toronto, Canada.

Subject: "*Father Louis della Vagna, Capuchin, Pastor of St. Mary's Church, Toronto, Canada, 1856–57.*"

FIFTEENTH PUBLIC MEETING—HELD THURSDAY, APRIL 5, 1888.

Paper by Major Edmund Mallet, of Washington, D. C.

Subject: "*The Origin of the Flathead Mission of the Rocky Mountains.*"

"*The Origin of the Flathead Mission of Rocky Mountains.*"

" This valuable and instructive paper was specially prepared for the Society by Major Edmund Mallet, LL. B., of Washington, D. C. Major Mallet was the U. S. Special Indian Agent for the District of Puget's Sound, with headquarters at Tulalip, near Portland, Oregon. He was introduced to Archbiship F. N. Blanchet, who authorized him to write the history of his (Archbishop Blanchet's) missionary work, together with his biography. He also presented him with all his collected notes and important documents. With this end in view, Major Mallet has devoted ten years to the collection of a valuable historical library regarding Oregon, and wherever the Archbishop's labors were carried on. Major Mallet intends again to visit Oregon to have original sketches made of historical places to serve in illustrating this valuable book, which will soon be ready for the press. Regarding the paper read before the Society, it is quite original, and will develop many facts in dispute regarding the Flathead early missions."

SIXTEENTH PUBLIC MEETING—HELD MAY 30, 1888.

Paper by Rev. Charles W. Currier, C. SS. R., of Boston, Mass.

Subject: "*The Church of Our Lady of Perpetual Succor, Boston, Mass.*"

Committee:
{ REV. THOMAS C. MIDDLETON, D. D., O. S. A.
ATLEE DOUREDOURE,
EDWARD J. ALEDO,
FRANCIS X. REUSS,
   Chairman.

Alphabetical List of Members.

NAME.	DATE OF ELECTION.
Aledo, Edward J.,	October 30, 1885
Arnù, Pierre M.,	June 29, 1887
Barry, Rev. Thomas J.,	April 6, 1885
Batz, V. G., Right Rev. L.,	August 31, 1887
Bergrath, Rev. M. J.,	May 26, 1887
Brady, James,	September 8, 1886
Bric, S. J., Rev. James J.,	January 14, 1886
Campbell, J. H.,	October 28, 1886
Campbell, M. D., W. J.,	July 22, 1884
Castner, Samuel,	July 29, 1884
Carroll, T. J.,	January 27, 1887
Clarke, LL. D., Richard H.,	January 9, 1885
Colaneri, Rev. A. M.,	February 12, 1885
Conaty, Rev. Thomas J.,	September 8, 1886
Conner, Philip S. P.,	January 9, 1885
Conway, William B.,	September 8, 1886
Corcoran, D. D., Right Rev. James A.,	March 26, 1885
Crosby, George J.,	November 24, 1886
Cross, Michael H.,	September 9, 1886
Dallas, Col. A. J.,	April 27, 1887
Dallet, Ada,	May 30, 1888
Daly, T. M.,	July 29, 1884
Devereux, Peter,	March 9, 1887
Devine, Mrs. Mark,	January 14, 1886
Devine, Mary T.,	January 14, 1886
Douredoure, Atlee,	July 22, 1884
Douredoure, Bernard L.,	July 22, 1884
Elcock, Rev. John J.,	July 22, 1884
Emmet, O. S. A., Rev. John T.,	January 14, 1886
Engel, Joseph M.,	March 10, 1886
English, Edmund,	December 3, 1884
Esling, Charles H. A.,	July 22, 1884
Esling, Henry C.	December 9, 1885
Fahy, Thomas A.,	October 30, 1885
Farrelly, Stephen,	December 3, 1884
Farren, Bernard N.,	May 14, 1885
Fasy, Frank A.,	September 8, 1886
Fitzpatrick, T. J.,	April 28, 1886
Flick, M. D., Lawrence F.,	December 19, 1884

Foy, Frank A.,	December 8, 1886
Furey, Francis T.,	July 22, 1884
Gallagher, Rev. A. J.,	March 26, 1885
Gately, Rev. Michael J.,	April 25, 1888
Glennan, Michael,	September 8, 1886
Gough, Rev. Walter P.,	August 29, 1888
Green, Margaret T.,	December 29, 1886
Green, Thomas H.	November 28, 1888
Griffin, Martin I. J.,	July 22, 1884
Hackett, Stanton H.,	February 24, 1887
Hanagan, Rev. Richard F.,	June 13, 1888
Hardy, Charles A.,	December 19, 1884
Harkins, D. D., Right Rev. M.,	August 31, 1887
Harkins, Rev. P. J.,	October 31, 1888
Harrity, William F.,	September 10, 1884
Harson, M. J.,	May 20, 1886
Haverstick, Horace,	September 14, 1887
Heckel, George B.,	December 9, 1885
Hendry, E. Carmel,	November 2, 1887
Hennessy, Rev. Patrick,	February 29, 1888
Henry, Rev. James,	September 8, 1886
Hiltermann, Rev. Ernest O.,	December 28, 1887
Hookey, Charles G.,	June 3, 1886
Horstmann, D. D., Rev. Ign. F.,	July 22, 1884
Huber, Rev. James A.,	December 29, 1886
Huneker, John F.,	November 2, 1887
Ireland, D. D., Most Rev. John,	September 8, 1886
Jaillet, V. G., Very Rev. C.,	August 31, 1887
Jeggle, O. S. B., Rev. Meinrad,	September 14, 1887
Junker, Jules,	October 30, 1885
Keating, J. Percy,	March 26, 1885
Kehoe, Lawrence,	December 3, 1884
Kelly, Denis B.,	February 1, 1886
Kelly, Rev. Joseph C.,	March 10, 1886
Kempker, Rev. John F.,	January 1, 1886
King, James W.,	January 25, 1888
Krake, Rev. G. H.,	June 8, 1887
Lebreton, Rev. E. V.,	December 8, 1885
Love, M. D., Louis F.,	January 14, 1886
Lyon, Henry F.,	February 1, 1886
Mahony, Daniel H.,	September 10, 1884
Martin, Simon J.,	November 2, 1887
McCabe, Rev. Luke V.,	July 29, 1884
McCaffrey, James A.,	January 14, 1886
McCaffrey, J. Carroll,	July 22, 1884
McCann, M. J.,	September 29, 1886

McCullen, Joseph P.,	December 8, 1886
McDevitt, Rev. Philip R.,	October 31, 1888
McDonald, Rev. O.,	September 8, 1886
McEnroe, Rev. M. C.,	October 30, 1885
McHugh, Rev. John A.,	September 10, 1884
McIntosh, H. F.,	December 14, 1887
McKeone, Charles,	June 8, 1887
McManus, Jr., Frank,	April 28, 1886
McManus, John,	June 8, 1887
McMenamin, John F.,	July 29, 1884
McNulty, Rev. P. F.,	November 24, 1886
McPhilamy, Rev. Hubert P.,	October 31, 1888
McVey, John J.,	September 10, 1884
McWade, Robert M.,	July 22, 1884
Meyer, C. Carroll,	February 1, 1886
Middleton, D. D., O. S. A., Rev. T. C.,	July 22, 1884
Molineaux, E. J.,	February 24, 1887
Morgan, S. J., Rev. John A.,	November 12, 1885
Murphy, Hon. Edward H.,	November 2, 1887
Murphy, Rev. Edward J.,	December 28, 1887
Murphy, M.,	December 19, 1884
Nolan, Philip A.,	July 22, 1884
O'Rourke, John J.,	January 9, 1885
O'Sullivan, D. A.,	November 2, 1887
Penny, Joseph,	October 30, 1885
Power, William J.,	September 10, 1884
Quinn, Patrick,	March 10, 1886
Reily, John T.,	January 27, 1887
Reuss, Francis X.,	July 22, 1884
Ryan, Michael J.,	August 31, 1887
Ryan, D. D., Most Rev. P. J.,	July 22, 1884
Salpointe, D. D., Most Rev. J. B.,	January 25, 1888
Seimetz, Rev. John A.,	September 12, 1888
Sigl, C. SS. R., Rev. Charles,	March 26, 1885
Smith, Walter George,	March 26, 1885
Spellissy, P. Henry,	February 12, 1885
Stang, Rev. William,	December 10, 1884
Sullivan, Jeremiah J.,	November 12, 1885
Thouron, Nicholas,	May 26, 1887
Turner, Rev. James P.,	September 26, 1888
Twibill, Jr., George A.,	May 14, 1885
Walsh, Rev. William,	September 28, 1887
Williams, William R.,	December 19, 1884
Wolff, George D.,	July 22, 1884
Zardetti, D. D., V. G., Very Rev. Otto,	May 26, 1887
Zilliox, O. S. B., Right Rev. James,	January 14, 1886

IN MEMORIAM.

CONSTANT PEQUIGNOT,
DIED JANUARY 29, 1888.

THOMPSON WESTCOTT,
DIED MAY 8, 1888.

[Extract from Minutes of Society's Proceedings.]

"WHEREAS, by the death of Mr. Thompson Westcott the American Catholic Historical Society of Philadelphia has lost one of its most gifted members, the city a distinguished citizen, and the cause of Catholic Church History a learned and unprejudiced writer, therefore be it

"*Resolved* that while we deeply deplore his death, his labors and memory will ever be to us an inspiration in our work ;

"*Resolved* that we hereby express our cordial sympathy with his family in their great loss ;

"*Resolved* that these resolutions be recorded in the minute book of the Society and that we make public recognition of his worth."

ROBERT COULTON DAVIS,
DIED AUGUST 24, 1888.

VERY REV. M. A. WALSH, LL. D., V. G.
DIED NOVEMBER 22, 1888.

[Extract from Minutes.]

"WHEREAS God, in His all-wise Providence, has seen fit to remove from among us His faithful servant, Very Rev. Maurice A. Walsh, LL. D., Vicar-General of the Archdiocese of Philadelphia, whose qualities as a priest and as a man endeared him to the hearts of all, and won for him the grace and benediction of a well-rounded career in God's service, therefore be it

"*Resolved* that, while we deeply deplore the loss that the Church and our Society have sustained, we also take occasion to express our heartiest appreciation of the services he has rendered to religion and to the special part of the Church's work in which we are engaged, in as much as the Church had no more faithful servant nor the Society a more earnest co-operator and liberal patron; and be it

"*Resolved* that, in appreciation of these services, and as a perpetual commemoration of our esteem for him, we publish this minute in the second volume of our ' Records ' and transmit copies to his relatives."

ELLEN EWING SHERMAN,
DIED NOVEMBER 28, 1888.

[Extract from Minutes.]

"WHEREAS, we are called upon to mourn the death of one of our most esteemed members, Mrs. Ellen Ewing Sherman, wife of the illustrious soldier, General W. T. Sherman; therefore be it

"*Resolved*, that we not only acknowledge and admire her loyalty to Church and country as well as her bounteous kindness to the poor and the afflicted, but also express our special appreciation of the aid and encouragement extended by her to this Society; be it

"*Resolved*, that in tendering to her illustrious husband and devoted children our heartfelt condolence, we adopt as a fitting meed of praise to her memory the words of the Wise Man describing the Valiant Woman: ' Let her works praise her in the gates,' (Proverbs xxxi., 31); and be it

"*Resolved*, that a copy of these resolutions be spread upon the minutes of the Society, be printed in the second volume of our " RECORDS," and be forwarded to her bereaved husband."

REQUIESCANT IN PACE.

INDEX.

(391)

M.